PRAISE FOR PRINCE AND THE *PARADE* AND *SIGN O' THE TIMES* ERA STUDIO SESSIONS

★★★★★—*Classic Pop Magazine*

★★★★★ "The second book is just as complex, moving and illuminating and it tells an even more interesting story."—***Rolling Stone*** (Germany)

★★★★★ "Tudahl's access both to the prosaic notations on timesheets and the first-hand accounts of Prince's closest collaborators is as unparalleled as his work is exhaustive."—**Jason Draper**, Record Collector

"Duane Tudahl has accomplished the impossible by capturing lightning in a bottle twice."
—**Funkatopia**

"Book of the year. A Masterpiece."
—**Violet Reality Podcast**

"Astounding. . . To call it a deep dive is a grave injustice."
—*Mix Magazine*

"Essential."
—**Jay Gabler**, Rock And Roll Book Club, *The Current*

"This book is an invaluable piece of reference material which is important not only in the context of Prince's legacy, but also in terms of the history of music as a whole."
—**True Funk Soldier**

"Thank you, Duane, for writing your *Empire Strikes Back!*"
—**Nicky T**, Purple Primetime

"Duane is the one person who has managed to pull all of the threads together and represent Prince's work in the best possible way."
—**Craig Mortimer-Zhika**, Prince Museum

"Duane Tudahl is the leading scholar of Prince's work."
—**Per Nilsen**, Prince biographer and author of *Dance, Music, Sex, Romance* and *The Vault*

ADDITIONAL PRAISE FOR THE
PRINCE STUDIO SESSIONS SERIES

"Loved the first edition of Prince sessions! It tells the truth, nothing but the truth! Thank you, Duane, for your honesty and diligence."
—**Apollonia**, co-star of *Purple Rain*, singer for Apollonia 6

"Duane is the quintessential Prince historian. This book will definitely give you accurate insight into Prince's creative process."
—**Matt "Dr. Fink" Fink**, member of the Revolution, Prince's keyboard player

"The only thing better than reading about Prince's music is listening to it. Duane Tudahl inspires us to do both."
—**Alan Leeds**, tour manager, production manager for Prince

"My brother, Alan Leeds, is known as the 'official' archivist for James Brown, so I know what it takes to assemble an authoritative discography. Duane Tudahl is to the music of Prince what Alan Leeds is to the music of James Brown."
—**Eric Leeds**, member of Madhouse, Prince's sax player

"I don't give a lot of interviews about working for Prince, as most authors I've found are interested in band drama more than the music and how it was created. Duane, on the other hand, is only interested in getting the accurate facts and reporting them."
—**Matt "Atlanta Bliss" Blistan**, trumpet player for Prince

"Duane took me back to a time period before I met Prince and gave me insight to him through the music sessions that helped me understand better the Prince I was so privileged to know."
—**Devin Devasquez**, Playboy model and friend of Prince

"Duane has done a fabulous job at sticking to the facts as they were presented. I highly recommend it and look forward to the next studio session books."
—**Brenda Bennett**, member of Vanity 6 and Apollonia 6

"Duane Tudahl has a potent and powerful mind. His ability to connect person, place, and thing is worthy of a music historian and archivist medal. I'm thrilled he's continuing his work with Prince's music history and keeping it clear and readily available to the next generation of musicians and fans who would benefit from this extraordinary artist, Prince, and how he worked and created. Enjoy!"
—**Susannah Melvoin**, co-lead singer for the Family/Deluxe and Prince's fiancée

"A must-read for anyone interested in understanding the complexities and vicissitudes of Prince's musical journey."
—**Albert Magnoli**, writer and director of *Purple Rain*

"Historians and scholars will have Duane Tudahl to thank for the meticulous effort he has brought to understanding Prince Rogers Nelson through the lens of how he spent his days."
—**Susan Rogers**, Prince's recording engineer

"I have often wondered if the legacy of Prince would remain in good hands. After reading Duane Tudahl's works, I am sure it is."
—**Levi Seacer Jr.**, member of the New Power Generation, Prince's bass player and guitarist

"Simply put, the work Tudahl has done on this book is astounding."
—**Chris Johnson**, host of Purple Knights podcast

"Mr. Tudahl has crafted a masterpiece!"
—**Shawn K. Carter**, host of The Enemy radio show and Public Enemy camp Member

"This book is brilliant!"
—**"St. Paul" Peterson**, co-lead singer for the Family/Deluxe

PRINCE AND THE *PARADE* AND *SIGN O' THE TIMES* ERA STUDIO SESSIONS

1985 AND 1986

PRINCE STUDIO SESSIONS

by Duane Tudahl

The **Prince Studio Sessions** series provides readers with a meticulously re-searched and engaging account of Prince's studio sessions. Each volume is filled with first-hand accounts from the people, musicians, singers, and studio engineers who knew Prince best, weaving an intimate portrait of the beloved musician.

PRINCE AND THE *PARADE* AND *SIGN O' THE TIMES* ERA STUDIO SESSIONS

1985 AND 1986

Duane Tudahl

ROWMAN & LITTLEFIELD
Lanham • Boulder • New York • London

Published by Rowman & Littlefield
An imprint of The Rowman & Littlefield Publishing Group, Inc.
4501 Forbes Boulevard, Suite 200, Lanham, Maryland 20706
www.rowman.com

86-90 Paul Street, London, EC2A 4NE

British Library Cataloguing in Publication Information Available

Library of Congress Cataloging-in-Publication Data

Names: Tudahl, Duane, author.
Title: Prince and the *Parade* and *Sign O' The Times* era studio sessions : 1985 and
    1986 / Duane Tudahl.
Identifiers: LCCN 2020051581 (print) | LCCN 2020051582 (ebook) | ISBN
    9781538144510 (cloth) | ISBN 9781538144527 (ebook)
Subjects: LCSH: Prince—Criticism and interpretation. | Prince—Chronology. | Rock
    music—United States—1981-1990—History and criticism.
Classification: LCC ML420.P974 T825 2021 (print) | LCC ML420.P974 (ebook) |
    DDC 781.66092—dc23
LC record available at https://lccn.loc.gov/2020051581
LC ebook record available at https://lccn.loc.gov/2020051582

ISBN 9781538166345 (pbk. : alk. paper)

∞™ The paper used in this publication meets the minimum requirements of
American National Standard for Information Sciences—Permanence of Paper
for Printed Library Materials, ANSI/NISO Z39.48-1992.

CONTENTS

CONTENTS

FOREWORD

The first time I met Prince was at a party after the Grammys in a restaurant in LA. He was standing alone by a wall, so I went up and introduced myself to him: "Hi, my name's Elton and I'm a huge fan of yours and I just wanted to say. . . ." That was as far as I got—Prince just walked off without a word. As you can imagine, that was quite a deflating experience, but I knew how shy he was—*everyone* knew how shy Prince was—and I loved his music so much that a few years later I tried again. I went backstage when he was playing his residency at the Rio in Las Vegas, and I was doing the same at Caesar's Palace. He'd got the hotel to build him his own nightclub, Club 3121, everything painted purple, and I'd see him driving around town in a Bentley on which the paintwork turned purple when the sun hit it. This time, he asked me to play onstage with him that night. He wanted me to sing The Beatles' "The Long and Winding Road." I told him I didn't know the words. He said that he didn't either, and that he had them written out on the floor of the stage. So I went onstage with him, and we started playing "The Long and Winding Road." It's sounding great. Midway through the song, I looked around. No Prince: he'd just walked off again.

Clearly, my experience wasn't entirely unique: there are plenty of other examples of Prince's improbable behavior in this book. You could see them as being the result of rudeness or nervousness, but I prefer to think that Prince was just off in his own world, one that no one else could really comprehend. He reminded me a lot of my late friend Marc Bolan and not only because Prince was clearly a big fan of Marc's band T. Rex: If you want to know how big a fan, just listen to "Cream," then play T. Rex's "Get It On," or "Bang a Gong" as they called it in America. It was that they were both incredibly charismatic, but somehow otherworldly, as if they'd come from another planet and were just passing through Earth en route to somewhere else. There was something at the center of them you could never fully understand.

This book covers part of Prince's great moment, when he was writing one incredible song after another. Every major artist has one, the period where they're on a roll, where they can't seem to do anything wrong. But Prince's great moment seems slightly inexplicable and unearthly too, even more so when you read about it in the kind of detail contained here: The sheer number of tracks he wrote and recorded, the speed at which he worked, the perfect simplicity of a song like "Kiss" or "Sign O' The Times," the incredible taste and subtlety of his arrangements, the way you watched as his influence spread throughout pop. I used to listen to his albums with my mouth hanging open—how had he done it? How did he make doing it look so easy?

I felt the same way watching him live. I've never seen anyone with that degree of control over his audience, with that ability to manipulate a crowd. He was a very modern artist—he used the latest technology, he did something completely new. But in another way, he seemed strangely old-fashioned. He was part of a tradition, maybe the last in a tradition, of African American artists that could do everything, that were demanding, that put on a show where every aspect was perfect—the playing, the backing vocals, the moves, the clothes—without losing any sense of spontaneity or excitement. You could trace a line back from Prince through James Brown, Little Richard, even to Duke Ellington. I'm not sure that I've seen or heard anyone I could say that about since Prince.

I got to play with him one more time, in London at the O2 during his 21 Nights in London residency. He asked if I'd play "The Long and Winding Road" again, and this time he stayed onstage throughout. It was a real thrill—as exciting as playing with John Lennon, or Bob Dylan, or Ray Charles—but then, watching Prince perform that night from the audience was just as thrilling. It was one of the greatest performances I've ever seen in my life. When he passed away, I said that we all knelt at Prince's feet, and I meant it. I like to think that if you're a real musician you recognize quality when you see it, but you didn't need to be a musician to recognize that in Prince you had quality that was extraordinarily high. You just needed ears and eyes.

—Elton John, January, 2021

PREFACE

What's the use in half a story, half a dream?[1]

—lyrics from "The Ladder"

Everything starts with a need. . . .

In the 1980s, we needed Prince. We didn't realize it, but we did. If you don't think so, imagine the eighties without him. No *Purple Rain*. No *1999*. No Prince sitting naked on the cover of *Lovesexy*. Okay, we didn't *need* that one, but we wanted it. We wanted someone to slap us upside the head with a funky bass line or shock our senses with a song that had NO bass line. We needed that because in many ways, music had gone stale and there was little danger left. We needed someone to threaten the status quo but also to push us to get off our asses and dance. We needed someone to remind us of the power of funk, the unbridled joy of riding a greasy groove, and earning the sweat from dancing all night to a pounding thump you could feel in your core. Prince brought that danger in so many ways.

According to Eric Clapton, "This is someone who is a reincarnation of Little Richard, Jimi Hendrix, and James Brown in one. I thought, that's exactly what the world *needed*."[2] When one of the greatest guitarists of all time explains the *need* for Prince, you take notice.

I started writing the first book in this series because I needed to tell *his* story, but as I wrote it, I realized that it was also the story of the people that Prince handpicked to be near him. These select few were important because they were there at his side when he created some of his most important music. And just like writing a song, writing a book is a lot of work and a thousand obstacles will block it from being finished. Books don't get done until someone feels the *need* to write it. Once I finished the first volume, I realized that, although it was a complete story, *his* story wasn't finished being told—which brings me to this book and the other half of the dream.

Wait a minute, supposedly sequels never lived up to the original. Well, this isn't really a sequel at all. It is the second half of Prince's story while he was working with the Revolution. The first book in this series was about the rise of Prince and the birth of the Revolution and how vital they were to Prince's success and how deeply involved in his work they'd become, but that was only half of the story. The second half explains how he opened himself up to them, showing his truth and vulnerability, which fueled his creativity, energizing him to fashion what many consider to be his most inspired album, *Sign O' The Times*, and it starts with him at the peak of his popularity.

This isn't the story of Prince's impact. We all can see that in ourselves—because you wouldn't be reading this if he didn't influence you in some way—but this book is about *his* contributions to his music and more accurately, what parts of *himself* were exposed because there *is* a lot of Prince in his art. His songs were a combination of diary, observation, and confessional.

Prince wore many masks and didn't reveal himself to his fans. There were glimpses, but he seemed to enjoy the mystery and the playful deception we accepted from him. Not that he was tricking us, but he was using every chance he had to reveal just enough about himself to keep us interested. A clever smile here and a raised eyebrow there said a lot from a man who refused to talk. He was always protective of his story because the missing pieces kept us intrigued; but as enjoyable (or frustrating) as that was, his life took on bigger meaning when we lost him as early as we did. Bruce Springsteen eloquently reflected about Prince's passing and said, "Any death gives you renewed sight. It's a part of what the dead pass on to us. A chance to look at our lives and look at the world again."[3]

Personally, I want to know more about him because it takes his music to a different level and gives us a chance to add to his legacy. I want people to learn *how* he did it, but it is also vital to know *why* because "why" questions are the ones that open doors that reveal the character inside of Prince instead of the character we know as "Prince."

"I think that you can't understand his music unless you understand the man," reveals his former fiancée Susannah Melvoin. "I think that everyone's interpretation is valid of him as the musician, but to really understand the music, is to understand who *he* was. Not many people got that chance."

Although this book has been in the works for years, months were spent working alone in our collective isolation of 2020 due to the pandemic. Not seeing those we care for or having that healing touch from a loved one has forced us to use a part of ourselves that came to Prince naturally because being alone in his recording studio and muting out the world allowed him to give birth to his art and share his intimacy in a way that he often struggled with, according to many in his life. "Isolation for him wasn't a hindrance," explains Susannah. "Isolation was a time for him to communicate what he *needed* to say. So music and isolation were his language."

Today, we need Prince at the exact time we know he isn't available. We need that escape and we need the unity of his fams/fans. We need to wave our arms slowly to the whooo-whooo-ooooo-ooooo of "Purple Rain." We need to stand shoulder-to-shoulder with the others who share this experience, remembering that his music touches every race, gender, sexual identity, and religion. It virtually wipes out what keeps us apart and finds the commonalities that connect us to one another because we are *all* part of one huge family and our family has lost its leader. Because we can't have him, we need those who knew him to remind the world that he was, *and still is*, important.

This book is Prince's story told through the prism of his time in the recording studio and the part of him he wanted us all to know, his music.

I don't want to deify him. In fact, it is even more intriguing when you know his achievements in the framework of his journey. It is infinitely more impressive that a man who has gone on record about feeling **"kicked out"**[4] of his home as a child was able to focus his energy on creating the wealth of music that he did. As a person, he wasn't perfect by any standard. He was a flawed man who recognized that his calling was music, and he labored to become the best musician possible. Yes, his story will contain heartbreak, pain, loss, and failure, but there will also be resurrection, joy, and a legacy of music that continues to inspire millions. Despite all the chaos, *that* is a lesson for everyone.

"There's even more to this genius than you realize," explained his engineer Susan Rogers, "and the true story of who Prince was and what he did during his lifetime is a story that needs to be told and shared and understood."[5]

Listening to a good song is like a journey. Listening to a great song is like a journey with your best friend. I hope that some of these personal recollections by those who were in the room with Prince help create a great journey for you because the music in this book covers not only some of Prince's best work but also some of the best music anywhere; so open your heart and open your mind, and please go find this incredible era of music in your collection and relive it with a great set of headphones. If you don't have this music, buy the albums, CDs, or individual songs and listen as you read this book. Knowing the passion and stories behind this incredible period will make it much more intimate, almost as if he's revealing his life to you through his music. Hopefully, this will give you a new appreciation and perspective as you listen again for the first time with new ears.

My greatest wish is that this book puts you in the room when these sounds were born and lets you feel as if you are sitting next to the maestro, whose rigorous training and skills make it appear as if he is pulling music from the air. And please share this experience with someone from the next generation and watch the echoes of his sounds and the ripples of his influence spread as far as possible. Let them know that once there was a man named Prince, and after he stepped up to the mic, music was never the same.

Prince said, *"Like books, and black lives, albums still matter."*[6]

I hope that books like this help fill a little of that need and remind us all to celebrate and dance. We *need* to dance.

JANUARY 1985

There's not much I want [the public] to know about me, other than the music.[1]

—Prince

Prince knew that expectations were high for his next move.

A new year and a new mountain to conquer. *Purple Rain* had not just happened, it had exploded. Although that seems obvious in retrospect, few knew how big the movie, the album, *and* Prince would become once it was launched. The naïve dream of success from a child who had moved from home to home was not only realized, but it was also achieved, and the days of being underestimated were in the rearview mirror. He had created an industry and with that came responsibilities to those around him.

With his career-defining album, *Purple Rain*, still the number 1 Pop Album on the charts (and would for a total of 24 weeks), and the other three albums he produced, *Ice Cream Castle* by the Time, *The Glamorous Life* by Sheila E., and *Apollonia 6* by Apollonia 6 were at 34, 47, and 134, respectively. The movie had been released on home video (in the United States) on November 16, 1984, and reached number 1 on the *Billboard* Top Videocassette Sales chart and on the *Billboard* Top Videodisks charts and number 2 on the *Billboard* Top Videocassette rentals chart. The press was knocking at his door for interviews, information, and insights, but Prince maintained his distance and his mystery. According to those around him, Prince was physically drained and what should have been the greatest time of his life was keeping him from where he wanted to be—in the studio. He was two months into the middle of the biggest tour of his career, and it was taking its toll on him. "What do you do when you have the number one album, number one single, and number one movie?" questioned Revolution drummer Bobby "Bobby Z" Rivkin. "I mean there's just nowhere to go."[2]

Revolution bassist Mark Brown [aka "BrownMark"] agreed. "What happens is you reach the mountain peak and where do you go from there? And that's what happened to the whole band, the Revolution with Prince. It's like we reached this pinnacle of success where we were to a point where we were saying to ourselves, 'Wow, what do we do now?' And Prince, he was already two albums down the road, and we haven't even finished the *Purple Rain* tour yet."[3]

Prince had many projects planned and being on the road ultimately had to take a backseat to his studio work. According to Prince, **"If you tour too much as an artist, you will burn up all your energy."**[4]

Although few outside of his purple bubble realized it at the time, Prince had already packed his parachute to get out of the *Purple Rain* era and was excited to move on. The music he was playing from *Purple Rain* was relatively new to his fans, but he'd been focusing on these songs for a year and a half, and his reach as an artist had expanded beyond that project. Even though his album was launched slightly more than five months earlier, he'd already completed work on the follow-up, *Around The World In A Day*, and expected it to be released in spring. He was also planning the music for his next project, the second album by percussionist Sheila E., as well as deciding on the direction of his career after *Purple Rain*, but before that, he had a tour to complete.

Music is often recorded in a vacuum with no knowledge of how it will be received by the audience. Every song is a Hail Mary thrown down the field hoping that there is someone who catches what the performer was feeling and runs with it. Studio work can be a solitary experience, especially for Prince, who generally recorded alone, so the road seems like it would be an amazing contrast filled with adulation and glory. When it goes well, it qualifies as a victory lap that allows musicians to connect with their fans, but when certain levels of success are reached, the freedoms experienced before often turn claustrophobic. It is just another week filled with security guards, the low-frequency hum of a limo or van, and a new place to sleep in a city that can't be experienced, dictated by a strict unforgiving clock controlled by someone else. Successful artists at this point in their careers have a choice: Do they stay in the confining prison of their hotel rooms waiting for their 2 hours of loving feedback or find a way to play music without the immediate response from a crowd. Prince decided to take every opportunity to make new music, but it was always limited by a tour schedule that could not be easily altered.

"He was restless and bored by halfway through the tour," revealed his keyboard player Matt "Dr. Fink" Fink.[5]

> Prince sat us all down in the dressing room and said, "Well, I'm taking two years off after this." We all said, "Really, two years?" And he said, "Yep! And you all can do whatever you want, take a break, do solo records, take a vacation, whatever you want to do, and you're still going to be on retainer." We were all excited about that in a way, but I thought to myself, "Wait a minute, we're not going to Europe to do *Purple Rain*, or Japan or Australia?" And he goes, "No." That disappointed me. I thought, "You should be milking the hell out of this. You should be touring the world with this. And stay out for a year and do the US even more" and he just said, "No" because he hated being on the road. Six months was his limit, he burnt out after that! I said, "Take a break for a month, and then we'll go out and do some more" and he just didn't want to do it. I've never understood that to this day why he didn't do that.

"Yeah, I think he got bored, and he would get bored on other tours too," adds fellow Revolution keyboard player Lisa Coleman.

> He would get sick of singing "I Wanna Be Your Lover" and I witnessed him go through cycles of that, like, "I never want to sing that song again," and he just moved really quickly. It's wild because when he did hit that success with *Purple Rain*, he was too bored to do what you needed to do. You need to do the work and sustain it, and stay on the road for a year, because it doesn't just go away, it sort of like bubbles up and down and up and down for like the next year, and artists for the most part, they'll stay out for a year and support that record, and each single as it comes out does its thing, but Prince was like, "I will love you forever!" or would you believe six months? [laughs]

The tour was the biggest of his career, but there were compromises that were out of his control. He'd originally envisioned the Time—his rival band from *Purple Rain*—joining him on the road, but lead singer Morris Day left the group and parted ways with Prince, causing the band to break up. Some of the remaining members had been consolidated into the Family, a new band he was grooming that had a lot of potential, but their album was not complete, and they had never played live, so they didn't qualify as the opening spot. This created an opportunity for Sheila E., whose debut album, *The Glamorous Life*, garnered great reviews, but most people had no idea that he'd written, produced, and oversaw just about everything on her album.

By all accounts, Prince lived to make music, and *new* music was his lifeblood. Touring and playing the same music every night, although financially rewarding, was a repetitive life that he didn't always enjoy. According to band member Lisa, the extreme highs and lows could all happen within the span of a few hours. "I can remember a couple of times standing in the wings waiting to go on and we'd hear the screaming start. And as a band, we'd look at each other contorting from the screaming and plug our ears and wonder, 'What the hell is this?' It was incredible! But then, at the end of the night, we'd be back in the 'quiet zone' and thinking about what was going on in the world. It was a very bizarre life. It was like nothing else."[6]

Regardless of the craziness of the road, there was also a certainty about it. The positive aspect of a regimented schedule that had to be kept was the daily chance to jam with his handpicked team of musicians and the opportunity to create. Prince was surrounded with a road-tested team of people who were all there to accommodate what he wanted. "It circles back to the whole idea of his work ethic," explains Robert "Cubby" Colby, who ran the soundboard during his concerts. "If he was going to work that hard every day, he certainly was going to surround himself with the people that were going to contribute, to work the hardest."

Despite appearances, Prince did things for reasons. And he surrounded himself with those he trusted, and at this moment in his life, the Revolution was his family. "It was the human, normal side of Prince that reached out to create the Revolution," explained Lisa. "Each one of us is an interesting breed of person. There's a naïve quality about us that lent itself to our loyalty to Prince. We were totally dedicated to working as hard as he did. We were like his kids. We could do right, and we could do wrong. We could make him proud or we could make him mad. It was set up for us like that psychologically."[7]

The Revolution was his first band that actually had a name known to the public, but there was likely a reason for that. Until this last album, Prince had a tight band but didn't allow them to maintain full billing with him. It would always be "Prince" at the front, but with the five people who worked with him from *Purple Rain* to *Parade*: "Bobby Z," "Dr. Fink," "BrownMark," Lisa Coleman, and Wendy Melvoin, he acknowledged something in each of them that he felt deserved to be recognized, according to Coleman. "He saw each of us like a band in our own right. Like Mark was the funk band, Matt was the synth band, Wendy's the funky Joni Mitchell, I'm the 'girl' thing. . . . It was like he was in the studio with all his influences, and whether it was a girly song, a ballad, or some hot, funky, rock thing, he could deliver."[8]

"Sonically and visually, I believe Prince knew that we were all aspects of himself," agreed Wendy. "Musically, though, that translated in a singular way when playing together. I might never have been comfortable with wearing lingerie, but I was comfortable being his female counterpart onstage. That was important to him."[9]

"I think [we] were like the cast of the original *Star Wars* with a Han Solo, a Princess Leia, [and] someone had to be a Chewbacca," BrownMark jokingly described the band members to *Wax Poetics* magazine. "He had us blocked and staged in his imagination."[10]

Purple Rain had sold more albums than all of his previous albums combined, and the movie locked in the band's importance to Prince and their relationship with him. So with this new exposure, there were literally millions of new fans around the world, and to the majority of that new audience, it was—and *always* would be—"Prince *AND* the Revolution."

TUESDAY, JANUARY 1, 1985

Venue: Reunion Arena (Dallas, Texas)
Capacity: 18,276 (sold out)

> *Prince was a teacher every day. He would be able to tell if that student was getting the homework from the night before, or the day before, or the show before. He just had his own way of knowing that. Either you knew what to do, or you didn't know what to do. You needed to be ahead of the game.*
>
> —Robert "Cubby" Colby

As soon as Prince and the band finished the final encore, the crew began breaking down the stage and packing it for the next city. In general, Prince wasn't patient, but when it came to the road crew, he was a little more tolerant. Regardless of Prince's demanding work ethic, he understood that there was a machine that worked behind him, and the road team wasn't following Prince; he was often following them after they had worked all night. "He knew what we were up against," says Colby. "He knew what the lighting crew team was up against every day, how difficult it was to load in this mammoth Roy Bennett production and this mammoth sound system and get this all right. And then he'd want to rehearse at 3:00 in the afternoon. We'd have nine trucks to unload. It's only 8:00 in the morning, but we'd make it happen. We'd make it happen to the point where he'd go in and say, 'Cubby, can I play my guitar?' 'Sorry Prince, not ready yet.' The worst thing you could do was say 'Yes' when it was not ready."

"We'd say, 'Prince, we'll take the purple piano to your dressing room, okay?' That was much safer and better. There wasn't anything to it, we had multiples of everything. It wasn't a problem. It was just proactive thinking. He'd walk in the door, he would very seldom go to his own dressing room, he just went to his playground, and that was the stage."

But the stage wasn't the only option he'd have when he felt the need to record. "What we would do is have a mobile truck in some of the biggest cities like Los Angeles, New Orleans, Dallas, and New York," explains his recording engineer Susan Rogers.

> Most of the time, at least during the *Purple Rain* tour he'd come off stage and go over to a recording studio on the road. Prior to that tour, I had a big thick directory of studios around the country, so it was my job to take road cases with tapes in them on the road with us, because we were making Sheila's record and recording for Prince as well. So, I'd have to go into that directory, find local studios, and see the brief little summaries of who's recorded there, maybe what equipment they had. I'd call these folks up and say, "Do you have an opening? Can you take a special client tonight? Can you take Prince tonight?"
>
> Who does that? Who makes a record for another artist while they are on tour? It is just an unimaginable amount of work but that is what he did.

THURSDAY, JANUARY 3, 1985

Venue: The Omni (Atlanta, Georgia)
Capacity: ±15,500 (sold out)

> *We've given away a lot of money. I found out recently that money is sort of like blood. If you hoard it and keep it all tied up amongst yourself, you sooner or later get sick. So, we just try to keep it in circulation.*[11]

—Prince

One of the most overlooked elements of Prince's career was his charity work. For the five shows at the Omni, Prince designated 482 "Purple Circle" seats for $50, and the proceeds helped fund Marva Collins' Westside Preparatory School in Chicago. "Without Prince's money, there would be no institute," explained Marva in 1986. "Multiply the first 200 teachers by 30 students each, and you get 6,000 pupils who Prince has helped us reach so far."[12]

FRIDAY, JANUARY 4, 1985 A.M. (ESTIMATE)

"**Toy Box**" [instrumental] (tracking, overdubs)
Master Sound Studios (Atlanta, Georgia) | after January 3 show
Producer: Prince | Artist: Sheila E. | Engineers: Susan Rogers and David Tickle

> *It was Prince's record once again. He wrote the lyrics, and it was a Prince project. Although I think Sheila may have had the lyrical inspiration this time, particularly on "Toy Box," but definitely this was another Prince record.*[13]
>
> —Susan Rogers

Prince literally couldn't stop working on music. Not just *his* songs but music in general. It was what fed him, even when he was on the road. Just because he'd done a 4-hour soundcheck and a 3-hour show, he would still be ready to create more music according to tour manager Alan Leeds. "He was like a funnel, it was as if somebody was pouring these songs into him and they would just continue to come out the other end like a water spigot that wouldn't turn off, but instead of water it was songs. The machinery of a record company couldn't digest and properly market music as quickly as he wanted. Fundamentally, his problem was simply he was more prolific than the market could bear."[14]

Because of this, Prince poured his music into other projects. During the previous year, he'd recorded and released entire albums for Sheila E., the Time, and Apollonia 6 and had started working on music for the Family and Mazarati as well as full albums of his own. Once *Purple Rain* erupted, those around him shifted. The Time dissolved and Apollonia 6 would appear on stage during the tour as a special guest, but there were no solid plans to record a follow-up album. The Family and Mazarati were still in Minneapolis working on their debut albums, so the only side act on the current tour was Sheila E. Because of her immediate availability and the success of her first album, he decided to focus on music for her as-yet-untitled second album, but working with Prince in the studio was not always a collaboration.

"Of course, Prince did play the instruments on her record, but that had a lot more to do with Prince's personality than it had to do with Sheila's abilities," explains Rogers. "It was faster for him to play the bass, the guitar, or the keyboard, and he wrote the songs. But when she did record on her own, she's incredibly talented. She doesn't have the talent that he does, but then who does? So, just because he played on things, he didn't mean to undercut her talent."[15]

When creating the basic tracks for the song, he set the foundation with his usual mix of live drums, percussion (cabasa, bongos, and claps), and a pattern from the Linn LM-1 drum machine. He also added bass and keyboards, including the Yamaha DX7 to the track. Prince combined that with a guitar section that was adjusted to play at double speed, which sounded similar to one he'd written for Apollonia 6's "Blue Limousine."

At the end of the night, he'd created an instrumental version of the song, and instead of vocals, they recorded a series of moans from several members of Sheila's band to fill in the space.

Status: An instrumental of "Toy Box" (6:20) appears to have been completed on this date. Sheila's vocals would be added, and the track would be edited (5:36) and released on August 26, 1985, as the fourth track on her second album, *Romance 1600.*

Although members of Sheila's band are credited on the song, it is likely that they were just for the vocal moaning and that all of the instruments were recorded by Prince and Sheila.

Because of the speed that Prince was recording on tour, the nonstop pace of their travels and the lack of sleep, proper notations were not always kept, and some of the finer details about the specifics of certain sessions have been lost to time. "I didn't see myself in a historical context, and I really wish I had," recalled Rogers. "I was 26 years old or something like that and too naïve to recognize what a big deal he was and how important he was, so I didn't memorize the details of circumstance. I was focused on the details of my job."[16]

The recording dates listed are as accurate as possible and every effort has been made to share all of the memories of those who were there.

FRIDAY, JANUARY 4, 1985

Venue: The Omni (Atlanta, Georgia)
Capacity: ±15,500 (sold out)

Prince had grown as an artist, and his ego and his entourage had expanded as well. The new success also caused a change in the surroundings and the perks, but sometimes that ended up causing some distance between Prince and the band. "When we were on the *Dirty Mind* tour [in 1980–1981], we were in vans and station wagons, and we were *really* together," reveals Lisa.

> We shared a dressing room. I'd have to get naked in front of five boys, and we just knew each other, and it was a family, and then with each tour it just grew a little bit, and a little bit, and a little bit, and then we got buses and then I was, "Cool man, we got buses!" And then with *Purple Rain*, he had his own bus, and then we would go to the airport and some security people would come take him away and he'd go fly separately, and for him it was great at first. He was like, "Yeah man, I'm the shit. I'm fucking Elvis," and we were like, "Bye, Prince."

"It isolates you," she continues.

> You're untouchable. All of a sudden, you're surrounded with people who want to keep people *away* from you, and like that's the greatest thing in the world. But it's also like the most dangerous thing for your life, and for a guy that was already an injured child, this was terrible for him. He needed exactly the opposite, but for his career, he had to go and be this guy. He was Prince, he was the one, and he knew that there was no way out, he was already headed down this road and maybe that's why he cut the *Purple Rain* tour short.

SATURDAY, JANUARY 5, 1985–SUNDAY, JANUARY 6, 1985 (ESTIMATE)

"Toy Box" (vocals, various overdubs, mix)
"Fish Fries" (tracking, mix)
"Dear Michaelangelo" [instrumental] (tracking, mix)
Master Sound Studios (Atlanta, Georgia) | after January 4 concert
Producer: Prince | Artist: Sheila E. | Engineers: Susan Rogers and David Tickle

That second record was done during the tour. So, wherever we'd stop, if we had four hours, we'd just go into the studio. It was just a matter of, "Let's call ahead of time. We're going to this city, let's see if we can get a studio." So that was a blur, again.[17]

—Sheila E.

Additional recording took place after the Friday night concert and Sheila was brought in to sing on "Toy Box." Despite her success, many people—including Sheila herself—underplayed her vocal abilities. "I must say I'm not a singer," she confessed in 1987. "I'm vastly improved over what I was when I started. But you can't compare me to the great singers. To me, somebody like Patti LaBelle is a singer."[18]

Rogers also recalled how Sheila's voice had matured since recording her debut album with Prince.

Sheila never did get comfortable with the singing. She reached a point where she was able to just go in and do it. She wasn't entirely comfortable, but she hid it well. She never protested, she never dragged her feet when it was time to go up and do vocals. And, by the time that [her second album *Romance 1600*] came along, she did it pretty quickly. It took a while on *The Glamorous Life*, but a tour will do for your voice what no studio time or rehearsal time can do. By the time she came off the road singing every night, she was warmed up. Her voice was in shape, she was able to go in and do the vocal pretty quickly.[19]

Sheila was not only more comfortable with the strength of her voice, she seemed at ease around Prince, and her spirited attitude was reflected in her vocals, which included her shouting and playing around. "Eddie M." Mininfield, who likely added his horn to the song, recalls the energy of that session. "'Toy Box' was fun because Sheila had to act really crazy. I remember we really got into it to get Sheila motivated and they were clownin'. They always had their jokes, so it was a fun atmosphere."

"We were just going for it," Sheila explained in a radio interview with Questlove in 2017. "A lot of times it wasn't planned. We're just playing and whatever ended up happening is what it was."[20]

The lyrics for "Toy Box" reflect that as they bounce back and forth between the playfully innocent and blatant references to sex or a vagina.

Prince would also record a track listed as "Fish Fries," which was a basic repetitive keyboard/bass/drum and percussion groove. It appears that no lyrics were written or recorded for the number, and it was likely just an exercise for Sheila and Prince to play in the studio, something that happened a lot during their time together. "I know I recorded over 100, 200 songs," detailed Sheila about her years of studio work with Prince. "Him and I. Just by ourselves. No one else. That's a lot of good music."[21]

With an entire day off from the tour, Prince likely took advantage of the time to record "Dear Michaelangelo." The basic tracks—which were either recorded during this session or the following week while recording in Houston—started with a blend of drums performed by Prince and included his keyboard work on the Oberheim OB-SX and the Yamaha DX7. His guitar work ended with feedback similar to the previous year's "Computer Blue" as well as on the then unreleased "Rearrange" from December 1981.

The first pass of the track didn't contain saxophone, Sheila's percussion, or vocals.

Status: "Dear Michaelangelo" (5:53) was edited (4:37) for release on Sheila's *Romance 1600* album. Prince's vocal version (5:22) was issued posthumously on the *Originals* collection in 2019. Another edit (4:55) and probably an instrumental version remain unreleased.

The 7-minute instrumental "Fish Fries" remained unreleased during Prince's lifetime.

SUNDAY, JANUARY 6, 1985

Venue: The Omni (Atlanta, Georgia)
Capacity: ±15,500 (sold out)

MONDAY, JANUARY 7, 1985

Venue: The Omni (Atlanta, Georgia)
Capacity: ±15,500 (sold out)

TUESDAY, JANUARY 8, 1985

Venue: The Omni (Atlanta, Georgia)
Capacity: ±15,500 (sold out)

The album version of "Take Me With U" is very poppy, but when we played "Take Me With U" on tour we took it to another place.[22]

—Matt Fink

Prince decided to shoot a promotional video for the next single from *Purple Rain*, "Take Me With U" on this date. As he did with "I Would Die 4 U" and "Baby I'm A Star" the previous November, Prince once again enlisted director Paul Becher and his crew to document the performance. The concert video would promote the single, the album, and the tour.

During this show, Prince sang "Happy Birthday" to Bobby who was celebrating his birthday the following day.

The Atlanta leg of the tour ended well with critics raving about his performance. Bo Emerson wrote in the Atlanta Journal, "Prince dominated the crowd as much with his physical virtuosity as with his compelling Funk-and-Roll."[23] The crew traveled to Houston for the next seven shows, but Prince wasn't ready to leave Georgia, as Susan remembers.

Sometimes after the show, the band and crew would take off and Prince and I would stay with the tapes and whatever musicians he needed in the city where we were. Everyone else would take off and we'd record the whole rest of the night, into the day and we'd leave just in time for him to get on a plane to make it for soundcheck. I'd have to take the next flight because I'd have to pack up all the gear and all the tapes and back things up or make rough mixes and I'd catch the next flight and I'd join them at soundcheck. We'd sleep on the plane or wherever we could. If it was bus distance, he'd get on the bus because it was easier for him to get to the next city, but no one I have ever known has worked that many hours.

WEDNESDAY, JANUARY 9, 1985

"Sister Fate" (tracking, vocals, various overdubs, mix)
"Sister Fate" [instrumental] (probable mix)
Cheshire Studios (Atlanta, Georgia) | after the January 8 concert
Producer: Prince | Artist: Sheila E. | Engineers: David Tickle and Susan Rogers

*Prince really liked Cheshire [Studios] because it works the
same way that Sunset Sound [Studios] works.*

—Susan Rogers

Prince was recording as much as possible, and even when he had the chance to
calm down in between shows he was working. Both Prince and Sheila E. reportedly maintained a small mobile recording system on their buses for any musical
inspirations. No full songs were completed with that set up, so when there was a
longer stay in a city, Prince would settle down in one place for the duration and
create music. It is unclear why Prince left Master Sound Studios and switched
to Cheshire Studios, but it was probably a scheduling conflict. Prince recorded
on a whim, and if one studio wasn't available, he'd want to make sure that there
was backup just in case.

"Cheshire is another studio that we really enjoyed," reflects Susan Rogers,
who was the most important person on the tour when it came to facilitating
Prince's need to make music. "Prince was very particular about his studios.
He didn't want them to be too fancy and sterile and clean because it feels like a
hotel, but then he didn't want them to be too funky and dirty and ratty either,
and when we could find a place that had the right comfort factor where all the
equipment worked, we were happy and we could get work done."

Rogers continues:

> [Cheshire is] private, it's just about the right size, the proportions of it, the wood.
> The fact that the studio owner is not a helicopter owner. He doesn't hover over
> you. When looking for studios, I always had to keep Sunset Sound in mind as the
> target, and you could just tell in an instant if Prince will like this place or Prince
> is going to hate this place based on his love of Sunset. We went there more than
> once passing through the South because it was a studio he liked.

The romance of *being* on the road often led to romance *on* the road, and according to those around him, many felt that Prince had a hard time being monogamous. It is likely that he had dreams of finding that one person to share his life
with, but his actions were not those of a man who put a priority on that. "While
Prince and I were crazy for each other back in the day and worked together
constantly, we were not a constant couple," Sheila explained in her 2014 autobiography. "I tried to ignore the sadness I felt about not being the only woman
in his life, but I learned to deal with it early on."[24]

During the previous year, Prince had been dating Susannah Melvoin, the
twin sister of Revolution guitarist Wendy, but they'd broken up early in the

Purple Rain tour, and he had moved on to others. According to Susannah, that was the way he was, even when they were dating. "I know that he was seeing other people at the time, although it never occurred to me to say, 'Hey, if you're gonna be coming after me, you may want to tell your friends that it's gotta be just you and me.' There's none of that. None. Right over my head. It never even occurred to me to say anything like that. But it caused some ruckus."[25]

"He was dating all of us at one point," bluntly explains Jill Jones, a singer who'd lived with Prince and collaborated with him many times in the studio. "Everybody was really screwed up and twisted. There wasn't much solidarity among us as women because we were girls. I really wish we'd all united at some point and . . . well, he wouldn't have been the player that he was."

The list was extensive and many of the women he dated inspired his art. Every woman brought out a part of him and their influence can be heard in the songs he created. Pillow talk could easily translate into lyrics, so the music that was inspired by his romantic side didn't just hint at how he understood women, it was based on true intimacy—or at least the level of intimacy that Prince understood. "If a woman is aware that this is what's happening, then you don't get your feelings hurt," reveals Jones. "But if you think it's true love, you're going to go down the wrong road."

"He wasn't monogamous," explains Susannah. "There was no 'being good' at it. He wasn't."

Because of Sheila's spot on the tour and their obvious chemistry, rumors were swirling around Prince and Sheila's relationship, and like everything else in his life, that would inspire his music, including songs like "Sister Fate."

> *There's a nasty rumor goin' around.*
> *People think that U, U and I are going down.*[26]
>
> —lyrics to "Sister Fate"

"The story was just things that Prince and I talked about," remembered Sheila. "Our life was pretty bizarre at that time. It was crazy. Some of it was true with what we talked about."[27]

The *Purple Rain* tour began, and so did our romantic relationship. It was as simple and as sudden as that. Thrown into close proximity with the man who'd been wooing me romantically for years, and in the high-octane environment of a world tour with all its attendant madness, my defenses were finally broken. We were working hard and playing hard, throwing ourselves into a nonstop, exhausting, and creative explosion of living, loving, performing, and recording. Plus, we were doing our best to keep our fledgling relationship a secret. There were many levels of secrecy here. We couldn't hide it from those in our inner circle, but like any relationship that begins in the workplace (however untraditional our workplace might have been), we knew it was best to keep things private for professional reasons.[28]

Prince had Sheila working with him on the basic recording of "Sister Fate," enlisting her to add her distinct flavor on conga, timbales, cymbals, and shakers over his Yamaha DX7 riff. Prince would also add claps, bass, LM-1 drums, Hammond organ, and a few other elements to the track along with some guitar work, possibly from Steph Birnbaum. It is also reasonable to assume that Eddie M. recorded his signature sax (and possibly some background vocals) on this date as well.

Sheila's keyboard players Ken Grey and Susie Davis are rumored to be on this track, but Davis disagrees. "No, I'm not playing on that. I'm barely on [*Romance 1600*]. It was a disappointment that Sheila didn't incorporate more of the band into the record, but it was Prince's record."

By the end of the session, Prince's guide vocals were probably still on the song. An instrumental version was also created. Prince traveled to Houston after the session was complete.

Status: The 7-minute version of "Sister Fate" was edited (3:40) and released on *Romance 1600*. He also created an extended version (5:48), edited instrumental version (3:38), and an edited 7-inch single (3:37). The 15-second intro would be recorded and added on a later date, making the album track slightly longer (3:55).

Prince appears to have felt such a strong connection to this track that the songs he wrote for Sheila's projects would be credited as "Sister Fate Music."

Usually, Prince didn't just do one mix of a track as he looked for the sound he wanted. Over time, there would often be close to a dozen different mixes done of a song, some of them slightly different, while others were drastically altered to the point that he re-recorded the number entirely. "A song would be on the multi-track seven or eight minutes long, and then you'd do mixes expressly for the purpose of cutting them into album-length versions, single versions and remixes," details Rogers.

So, there'd be different iterations of a lot of songs. And then other times, maybe the arrangement just wouldn't quite come together. Then you'd redo it. And songs would frustratingly morph sometimes. It would get a little bit scary that you'd print a mix, be happy with it, it'd be a nice piece of work, and then he'd decide that he wanted to rework it and add new parts. And with him, very rarely were there free tracks available, if he had really gotten into it. So sometimes you'd start erasing sources on the multi-track. Rarely, but sometimes he would do that.

What that means is that if Prince erased elements from the original tapes to make room for more instruments or singing, there were completed mixes that contained elements that were no longer on the original source tapes, causing some confusion when comparing recordings.

While on the road, he'd sometimes wait to make the changes back in the Los Angeles studio, remembers Sunset Sound engineer, "Peggy Mac" Leonard [formerly Peggy McCreary] who'd worked with him since 1981. "There were times that he would bring stuff from elsewhere mixed and ready and he would decide to add something to it, and we would remix it [at Sunset Sound]. He might finish something and then revisit it here. He liked our echo chambers and he loved our piano sound and stuff like that, so he would usually do that at some point."

THURSDAY, JANUARY 10, 1985

Venue: The Summit (Houston, Texas)
Capacity: 17,094 (sold out)

At almost every stop on the tour, records were shattered. When tickets for the first three concerts at the Summit went on sale, they all sold out in a single day, the biggest one-day-ticket sales at the time. Three more shows went on sale to accommodate the unprecedented demand.

Tonight was the first of six sold out shows at the Summit.

FRIDAY, JANUARY 11, 1985

Venue: The Summit (Houston, Texas)
Capacity: 17,094 (sold out)

SUNDAY, JANUARY 13, 1985

Venue: The Summit (Houston, Texas)
Capacity: 17,094 (sold out)

MONDAY, JANUARY 14, 1985 (ESTIMATE)

"Dear Michaelangelo" (sax and percussion overdubs, Prince vocals, mix)
The Summit (Houston, Texas–Le Mobile Studios) | 3:00 a.m. after January
   13 show
Producer: Prince | Artist: Sheila E. | Engineer: Susan Rogers

> *Prince recorded that live at 3 a.m. at the arena. He did it*
> *himself. I remember he went and got his hair done at the salon,*
> *then we went back to the arena.*

> —Wally Safford

After tonight's concert, he went through his usual routine of cleaning up, chang-ing his clothes, and recording.

After getting his hair done, Prince returned to the stage of the empty arena and added his vocals to "Dear Michaelangelo." This early version contained only Prince at this point with Sheila adding her vocals and percussion during a future session.

MONDAY, JANUARY 14, 1985

Venue: The Summit (Houston, Texas)
Capacity: 17,094 (attendance unknown)

> *We would videotape every show. Oftentimes, we'd watch it on*
> *the bus afterwards. I think Prince was just always working*
> *and he wanted to perfect himself.*[29]

> —Lisa Coleman

17

With Prince constantly adjusting the show, he would sometimes rely on the works of his protégé acts for source material. Apollonia 6 had recently released "Blue Limousine," and Prince led the Revolution through a rehearsal to get his band familiar with the track. Apollonia, Susan Moonsie, and Brenda Bennett were asked to join the tour to create something new for the show but also to promote their album.

TUESDAY, JANUARY 15, 1985 (ESTIMATE)

Venue: The Summit (Houston, Texas)
Capacity: 17,094 (attendance unknown)

> *[Prince] would consider 1 a.m.—after playing a stadium show—the point at which his day could begin. One of Jimi Hendrix's former girlfriends said Jimi would put on his guitar to walk from the bed to the bathroom. Prince was the same way. Making music was his way of being in the world.*[30]
>
> —Susan Rogers

With an epic tour like this, multiple shows were planned in the same arena, so Prince would set up camp on the stage and record with his traveling mobile unit. Any days that didn't contain a performance would be the perfect place to jam with the Revolution either looking for a new song idea or changing the show, so it wouldn't become too redundant for him. "He doesn't dial it back in rehearsal," remembers Michael Soltys, a guitar technician who witnessed many rehearsals. "He just wails on it like he's doing a live show. We would go into these jam sessions where he'd say, 'Bobby give me a beat,' and then everybody would just start improvising and seriously they could jam for two hours or more, nonstop, just mixing things up. The rehearsals can be grueling, ten hours long, twelve hours long."

On days like this, work could also take place on whatever he was recording. Prince could be social when necessary, but his priority was always on the music, according to Rogers. "The poor kid was so naturally shy; he didn't want to mingle because he didn't have anything to say—he wanted to be on stage playing."[31]

It is likely that Prince continued working on "Sister Fate" on this date, including Sheila's lead and background vocals.

WEDNESDAY, JANUARY 16, 1985 (A.M.)

Venue: Texas Southern University, University Auditorium
Capacity: 1,800

> *Being in Prince's band was like getting in a sports car with a racing driver. Even though you felt a bit scared—why is he going so fast?—he could handle it, and it brought so much joy.*[32]
>
> —Lisa Coleman

Prince wanted to bring that joy to those who couldn't attend the regular shows, so on days like this, he paid the crew and band to perform for those who were often overlooked. At 10:30 in the morning, Prince and the band staged a free matinee for the MD Anderson Cancer Center and invited the children who were suffering from the disease, even pulling up several audience members to dance with Prince during "Baby I'm A Star."

At his core, he wanted to help others and share his music with people who were truly in need. Susan Rogers recalled a multitude of times that he did this over the course of her five years with him.

We'd have a big arena show in the evening and during the day we'd take a small truck and we loaded up with extra equipment and we'd go play for sick children. He would do that on one condition: no press, no publicity. He didn't want the fame from it. He just wanted to play to these kids who couldn't come out to a big arena show and we'd set up the scarves and the flowers and the lights, and we'd do a full set, not just one or two songs for these kids on the condition that it be kept quiet. There are countless examples of who this man was, and because he was so quiet, there were a lot of rumors about him out there. But I'll be damned if I'll let his memory be one of "Oh, he was just some freak." He was no freak. He was unusual, but he was a good man.[33]

WEDNESDAY, JANUARY 16, 1985

Venue: The Summit (Houston, Texas)
Capacity: 17,094 (attendance unknown)

Keeping up with Prince during "Baby I'm A Star" was kind of crazy. It turned into "Simon Says" with the horn punches and the stops on the one, but the energy it created put him in another space, which took the audience and the band to another level.[34]

—"Bobby Z" Rivkin

During the stay in Texas, the three members of Apollonia 6 joined him on stage multiple times.

"I was on the road a lot during the *Purple Rain* tour anyway, because I was out there with Roy," remembers Brenda who was married to LeRoy "Roy" Bennett, the lighting director for the tour. "I was on stage a lot of the nights during the encores. Anytime Susan, I, and Apollonia happened to be there, it was like, 'Okay, you guys are here, you're coming on stage.'" For this performance, Brenda was asked by Prince to join her on stage to sing the first verse of "Blue Limousine," which was played during the "Baby I'm A Star" jam. Prince had been recording with her for several years and was by many accounts fond of her voice. "During the active years I spent working with Prince, he had spoken to me a couple of times about doing a solo album with me," reflected Brenda.

He thought my performances with Vanity 6 and Apollonia 6 were good, but he also realized that the music I was doing at the time wasn't really *me* or the best for my type of voice. He has a good instinct about things like that and asked if I would be interested in doing a solo project with him outside of Apollonia 6. I thanked him and wholeheartedly agreed. But with the success of the *Purple Rain* film and then the tour, Prince's path turned in a different direction.[35]

A Brenda Bennett solo album produced by Prince never materialized.

THURSDAY, JANUARY 17, 1985

Venue: The Summit (Houston, Texas)
Capacity: 17,094 (attendance unknown)

It took a handful of years for us to work up to being that completely fabulous Purple Rain *band, so tight and good. I think we lived up to the flamboyant image because we worked so hard.*[36]

—Lisa Coleman

Despite *Purple Rain* falling out of the number 1 position on the *Billboard* Top 200 album chart for the first time since August of 1984, the final show of his historic six-night stay in Houston ended on a high note. Apollonia 6 once again joined the band for the encore of "Baby I'm A Star," and Prince left the city in awe. The Summit no longer functions as a concert hall, but this historic run for Prince was listed in the top 20 of all-time grosses for the arena.

Prince was a person who unapologetically worked hard, especially when inspired, and a day off between shows was often filled with other work, as Susan Rogers recalled. "We finished the show [at the Summit] and the rest of the band traveled on to Alabama, and Prince and I stayed in town. I was with him at the video studio and we edited the video for 'Take Me With U.'"[37]

Before the editing could begin, Prince decided to spend the rest of the night recording more music for Sheila's album.

FRIDAY, JANUARY 18, 1985 (A.M.)

"Dear Michaelangelo" (overdubs, mix)
"A Love Bizarre" (tracking, mix)
Cheshire Studios (Atlanta, Georgia) | evening into following morning
Producer: Prince | Artist: Sheila E. | Engineer: Susan Rogers

> *I had an incredible time last night. Spent all night in the studio with Prince & Sheila. And Prince had me co-sing this beautiful song with Sheila called "Dear Michaelangelo." I swear it is one of the prettiest pop songs I've ever heard. It moves me.*[38]

—Susie Davis

Prince and Susan Rogers worked on the video for "Take Me With U" and then flew to Atlanta to continue recording on "Dear Michaelangelo" at Cheshire studios during a day off from the tour. "My journal of January 18th says, 'fly to Atlanta for a recording session,'" recalls Sheila's keyboardist Susie Davis who provided background vocals for the track. "He was very specific. I remember him telling me to sing breathier. I thought I was singing breathy and he was like, 'No, sing *breathier*.' So, he's very, very demanding."

He immediately started working on the next track, "A Love Bizarre," with Sheila reportedly providing the drum intro to the song. The rest of the track came together quickly because Prince had fleshed it out with the Revolution during a soundcheck the previous month, adding lyrics and creating the signature riff to the song with them. "I remember working on that," recalls Lisa. "That was just a cool little harmony line that I played."

"If you were playing something new at soundcheck, it was probably going to end up on someone's record," explains Wendy.

Once again, the bulk of the song was a solo performance, according to Davis. "At 2 a.m. he started another song and I watched him create it out of nothing. First the drums, then keys, then bass, guitar, more keys… he just kept adding layer after layer. I was determined to stay awake to witness it as it was amazing watching him work. He created the fattest, funkiest track called 'A Love Bizarre' and at 8 in the morning I got to sing background vocals on it."

Eddie M. was one of several people invited to join them during his time at Cheshire while they were recording "A Love Bizarre."

> I just remember walking in the studio and it just had to be one of the funkiest tracks and I was just happy to be a part of it. The cool thing about it was he wanted the group to chant in the back with the vocals. It was me, Susie Davis, Stef [Burns, aka Steph Birnbaum], and I think Jerome [Benton, formerly of the Time]. It was a group thing and it was really fun. It was really funky, and I was a fan and at that point, I kind of had gotten the whole thing down on how to please him, so I had no fear of it and he just let me have my freedom on that. He played the track and I think we did the vocals first and then the horns. He very rarely told me what to play, unless there was a melody line that he really wanted to hear, but as far as playing because that is what is so cool. Prince was more like 'play the melody' and then he told me where to go and do my thing. That was pretty much it. The long version of it went on forever. Back then you could just stretch, and nobody was tripping.
>
> I think Sheila was definitely there. I think everyone stuck around. I mean he was just burning. Jerome was hanging out with us, and [Prince's] security people. Everybody would come in crashing at different corners of the room and it was like camping. You'd go to work when you were called on. "Don't go to the motel, we may need you."

After recording in Atlanta, Prince traveled to Birmingham, Alabama for the next concert.

Status: Additional work on "A Love Bizarre," including Sheila's percussion, would take place during the tour, and the track was eventually edited (3:46) and released as a single. The full version (12:18) was included on her *Romance 1600* album. The B-side of the single would include "A Love Bizarre (Part II)" (3:48), which was simply another section of the album version. A blend of Parts I and II (7:13) was released as a 12-inch mix and backed with "Save the People," a song that contained no input from Prince.

The single peaked at number 11 on the US *Billboard* Hot 100 Chart, and number 2 on the *Billboard* Black Chart. The highest position for the song was on the *Billboard* Hot Dance/Disco–Club Play chart, where it reached number 1.

The song would be the only track listed as "produced, written, and arranged by Sheila E. and Prince."

SATURDAY, JANUARY 19, 1985

Venue: Jefferson Civic Center Coliseum (Birmingham, Alabama)
Capacity: 17,700 (sold out)

If Prince was unhappy, the tour had the potential to be difficult, and the repetitive grind of the tour was taking its toll on him, remembers Bobby Z. "What he thought of yesterday was already old. It was just the fact that he was trapped in this Broadway play, and couldn't really change it. 'Baby I'm A Star' was when he kinda cut loose, but otherwise he was stuck doing it, couldn't call out different songs. Everything's automated. It would've had to run the way it did. So he became trapped in the 'Kid' character."

"Take Me With U" was performed again, perhaps to help ease the boredom.

A second show in Birmingham the following evening was postponed until early February. Instead, the tour left for Cincinnati directly after the concert.

SUNDAY, JANUARY 20, 1985

"Dear Michaelangelo" (various overdubs, mix)
"A Love Bizarre" (Sheila E. vocal, overdubs)

"**A Love Bizarre**" [12-inch version] (mix)
"**A Love Bizarre**" [instrumental] (mix)
"**Small Grey Monkey**" [early title for "**Merci For The Speed Of A Mad Clown In Summer**"] (tracking, overdubs, mix)
5th Floor Recording Studio, Cincinnati, Ohio | 8 a.m.–afternoon
Producer: Prince | Artist: Sheila E. | Engineers: Susan Rogers and Gary Platt

He had two bodyguards and the tour manager would come up first and check everything out. They looked at the studio, made sure nobody was there, made sure it was cool. Then they brought him in, and he came up the elevator. They were asking people to not look at him or make eye contact. He just came in and said, "Hey you ready? Let's go."

—Gary Platt

Prince was in constant motion, and at any point, he could be inspired to record a new song or add elements to existing unreleased tracks, so the engineers and band members knew that their schedule was at the whim of Prince's creative urges, as Susan Rogers recalled:

On the road we had trunks, labeled "T1," "T2" and "T3," big trunks that carried our tapes. We also had what was called a gig truck, because there were thirteen tractor trailers on the road during the *Purple Rain* tour. There was one small truck that carried a second set of equipment specifically for use in the studio. It carried a second bass, a second LM-1 drum machine, backup guitars, finger cymbals, and anything that he might need in the studio—his microphones, and backups of everything. This little truck would be parked and ready to go so that at the end of the show—if we were in Cincinnati and I had found a studio that day, the studio would be on hold—he would come off stage, and I would have the driver take the second truck to the studio and we'd set the whole equipment up and he'd walk in and then we worked.[39]

Rogers booked the room, likely because of its incredible history of funk music, which included music by the Ohio Players, Bootsy Collins, Faze-O, and Zapp, among others. As soon as it was scheduled, 5th Floor Recording Studio engineer Gary Platt was brought in to make sure everything was working properly.

We got there and it was 3 o'clock in the morning. Prince had played a show, and then waited on his bus outside the studio. He came in probably about 8 o'clock. In the meantime, I thought, "Oh boy we've got a bad cable on this mic, it's crackling." I went over and was changing the mic cable and plugged it in and someone came in, sat down and played the piano, that happens all the time. So, I plugged it in and he just kind of sideways kicked me, I was down on my knees almost and he kicked me, and I fell over. And I said, "It's nice to meet you too," and kind of got a laugh. And he said, "I thought you said it'd be ready." I looked up and it was Prince, and I said, "Well it's ready now." And he was like, "Well all right, let's get going." It was funny.

Susan Rogers recalls similar situations on the road during that period.

I was never unaware of how grateful I was, but that's not to say that it wasn't hard. I had some really difficult moments. I remember we were on the *Purple Rain* tour, and we were at a studio late at night with Sheila there, working on Sheila's record. Prince was in one of his bratty moods, and he was insulting me, he was calling me names. And it was a small, tiny control room. It was hard to get from one end of the room to the other when you had to change tapes to do something like that. And I'm squeezing past him. He called me something along the lines of being fat. I'm not fat. Never been fat, but he called me fat. He was laughing about it, and I remember exchanging looks with Sheila, and Sheila just looked at me like, "I am so sorry, and I would defend you if I could." And I looked back at her like, "I know you would, just let it go." He could be like that, because he had a bee in his bonnet, a burr under his saddle, whatever. Something would be irritating him, and sometimes he needed a target. And on that day, it was me. But there were other days, it was Peggy. You're the target *that* day, and you just have to endure it until the next day comes. Sometimes his mood would change during the day, but sometimes you'd just go the whole session being the target.

"We had tape in the machine, he kind of knew what he wanted to do," remembers Platt.

He gave me a cassette and I put it in the machine, listened to it, and put that on the 24-track and kind of played around with that, then he started making a tune for it. It was a tape of the manual for the Tascam tape machine. He recorded the cassette. And the guy talked like that, "Thank you, and welcome to the Tascam model 5" and the announcer was like, "Now turn the knob to the left and you'll be recording," that kind of thing. I think it was just one of those things he was doing to kind of fool around to get used to the flow. Then he kind of started the tune that he was going to finally wind up putting on.

Sheila joined in this game by reading the manual as well, and her description referenced a recent track as she gave detailed instructions about how to handle her "toy box." This would be blended with the music he was recording. It isn't clear how far they got with the track according to Platt. "He put a beat down, put music in there, I don't know what it sounds like, I wish I did. So many times, I wish I had a camera, but the fact is they're very secretive, very careful. They didn't want anybody around to let them know what they were doing."

It is likely that "Small Grey Monkey" was based on something Sheila had previously written, and it was used as an experimental test to see what the studio could do. "[That song] was something Sheila had done with her band," Susan Rogers explained to *Uptown* magazine. "He just flipped out at how well it was played."[40] Recording would continue on the song later in the week and possibly eventually at Sunset Sound.

Although work may have begun on "Small Grey Monkey," it is probable that most of the time was spent adding Sheila's lead vocals to "A Love Bizarre" and "Dear Michaelangelo." Sheila added percussion, specifically timbales, bongos, and cowbell. A mix for both was done, which included delaying the introduction of drums and percussion and restructuring the sound on "Dear Michaelangelo" to emphasize Sheila's vocals and the choir-like background vocals. Eddie M.'s sax was recorded and blended with the main keyboard lines, and the track was ultimately edited to eliminate the long instrumental section at the end. It is unclear if any other recordings took place during this session.

Before heading to the arena for the soundcheck, Prince made a rough mix of whatever music he was working on, and this became a pattern for him for the entire week. "He was just non-stop. He was pretty manic. I mean he did not sleep at all," explains Platt. "He would come in and do his thing, play at night, come back in late, as soon as he got away, soon as he was done, he'd come back in and keep going. He just went around for days."

Status: There were multiple takes of the song that was listed as "Small Grey Monkey" but would eventually become "Merci For The Speed Of A Mad Clown In Summer" (2:47). It would be released on Sheila E.'s second album, *Romance 1600.* The bass line from "Merci For The Speed Of A Mad Clown In Summer" seems to have inspired the bass line in his 1986 song "2 Nigs United 4 West Compton."

The carnival music at the beginning of the track ("Carnival Midway" from Volume 1 of the *Authentic Sound Effects* library) was also used on Queen's "Brighton Rock" from 1974's *Sheer Heart Attack.*

A 6-minute instrumental version of "A Love Bizarre" was being considered for the B-side of "A Love Bizarre."

MONDAY, JANUARY 21, 1985

Venue: Riverfront Coliseum (Cincinnati, Ohio)
Capacity: 14,869 (sold out)

This was the first of three shows in Cincinnati. After the concert, Prince headed back to the recording studio.

TUESDAY, JANUARY 22, 1985

"Bedtime Story" (tracking, mix)
5th Floor Recording Studio, Cincinnati, Ohio | after January 21 concert
Producer: Prince | Artist: Sheila E. | Engineers: Susan Rogers, David Tickle, and Gary Platt

His voice was so soft-spoken and soothing, it was just so easy to talk to Prince over the phone because he seemed much more relaxed. He said my voice was musical and he liked it because it comforted him and helped him sleep. I guess that's why he wrote "Bedtime Story" for me. Many times, we would talk until the break of dawn. This ritual was becoming addictive and I began to fall in love with talking to Prince on the phone.[41]

—Devin Devasquez

Eddie M. recalls "Bedtime Story" being introduced to the band before it was formally recorded:

He was messing with that song at soundchecks and he stayed up all night after we played one of the nights we were playing in town. He went back to the venue after the gig and he started recording and messing around and the next thing you know, they were waking me up to come into the studio. And that was what was recorded there. I was surprised, and still to this day I am amazed about how much music that man holds, and I just think he's so filled with ideas. I've never been around anyone so filled with music and passion and love. For him, it just seems like it is ongoing, and it is very rare that you hear something that sounds the same. It kept you on your toes.

The daily schedule of a tour as big as the *Purple Rain* tour is oppressive. Every day consisted of a small amount of sleep, followed by a long soundcheck, then dinner, the concert, and then either an afterparty or back in the recording studio, so there was no understanding about what was going on in the world. The tour was a traveling bubble, which limited Prince's access to outside inspiration. He would occasionally go to movies or to a museum with Sheila or some of the members of the Revolution, but to get new unfiltered inspiration, he would periodically reach beyond the bubble. During this time, he was also romancing *Playboy* model Devin Devasquez, who he'd met the previous month in Chicago. She had joined the tour for several shows, wearing some of his clothes and watching him during soundchecks. "I had never seen a soundcheck before and he went and played every instrument on the stage. The bass, the drums, he was totally showing off. He was totally trying to impress me at that time. And I felt like the romance and the way it was going with him, he put a lot of his feelings into the music instead of verbally saying it to a girl."

On many evenings, he would spend hours talking to Devasquez on the phone. "Literally he would ask me questions like, what did you eat today, and do you believe in God? I asked him questions like, 'Why do you write such sexual songs?' And he says, 'I write about life and sex is a part of life.' And he goes, 'Why do you pose nude?' He was telling me about his life, about having this little dog that Wendy and Lisa had given him for Christmas. And he just sounded like a normal person. He was very, very down to earth."

He even asked her if she'd like to sing for a project that he'd develop for her or have a part in his next movie, but she declined all of his professional offers. "That's really the only way you could be close with Prince is if you worked with him because he was a workaholic," explains Devasquez. "Even when I did see him, I was in a beautiful hotel waiting for him to call me on the phone because he was either in the studio or busy and he would call me, but he would be the one controlling when I would see him."

According to her, Prince revealed how he was influenced by their time together on the phone when he wrote "Bedtime Story."

I don't think Prince would write a song for somebody that didn't inspire him in some way. So, it definitely was an inspiration for him to write a song about me and he was the one that pointed it out. It was the busiest time in his life, and it was the busiest time in my life too. He would say, "Devin, you're too much distraction. I have to work. And I'm married to my work." He would say he could only take me in small doses because he wanted to hang out and have fun. But he was working, so that's why he wrote the lyrics. "She was so fine, but her Prince had no time. Stay with me, tell me a bedtime story." And that was always how it was. When we should be sleeping, we were talking on the phone and I was telling him stories and he was telling me stories until he felt like sleeping. He would fall asleep in my arms with us talking in person too. It was always like he had a hard time sleeping and for some reason talking on the phone to me at that time helped him to relax and go to sleep.

Devin continues: "I believe Prince told his autobiography through the music, through the people that he was with that were influencing his life, whether he was dating them, whether he was working with them, he wrote music about the people and the things that were going on in his life at that period in time. He was inspired by everything around him that he would put what he really wanted to say more in the music than he would with words.

During this session, Prince would record the basic tracks including drums, Yamaha DX7 keyboard, bass, piano, and his guide vocals. Eddie M. added his sax as well. It is likely that Wendy and Lisa helped record the track and Steph Birnbaum supposedly played a 12-string guitar as well, but it is unclear if he performed on this date or during a future session. Sheila would likely record her parts the following night.

A rough mix of the song was recorded to cassette at the end of the shift.

Status: "Bedtime Story" (3:37) would undergo additional overdubs and mixing with a newly recorded beginning and would be included on Sheila E.'s *Romance 1600* album, and on August 12, 1985, it was released as the album's second single (3:45). It did not appear on the *Billboard* charts.

Note: It is possible that "Bedtime Story" was recorded on January 23.

TUESDAY, JANUARY 22, 1985

Venue: Riverfront Coliseum (Cincinnati, Ohio)
Capacity: 14,869 (sold out)

Anyone who was around back then knew what was hap-
pening. I was working. When they were sleeping, I was
jamming. When they woke up, I had another groove.[42]

—Prince

Prince didn't set aside much time for sleep as he scheduled a long soundcheck that afternoon with the band running through "Let's Go Crazy," "Computer Blue," "Free," and the "Baby I'm A Star" encore jam, which was rehearsed with Eddie M. and Eric Leeds on horns, adding the horn part from "A Love Bizarre" that Eddie had recorded previously in the month. According to his soundman "Cubby" Colby, these sessions were vital to Prince. "There were many, many mornings where I'd be going to bed at 5 or 6 in the morning and because we were already set up, he wanted to rehearse on those show days at 2 because there was no load-in on multiple show days. We would always be in there at 2 in the afternoon for . . . well, they were never just soundchecks. They were rehearsals or music events or dance, choreography or whatever it would be."

According to Jill Jones, his soundchecks and the extra time Prince spent reshaping the performances over the course of the tour were crucial for him. "I think that kept away the boredom and may have been the discipline that he used in order to even stay out on the road, doing a show over and over and over."

"If Prince was awake, and he was awake for most of the hours of the day back then, he would take business meetings, personal stuff, in the first few hours of the morning. But the rest of the day was devoted to making music," recalled Susan Rogers. "I think the alternative was unthinkable. He was a kid from a poor background in North Minneapolis. He had a very loving heart, but I think Prince was well aware that time matters. He was using this powerful engine, the engine of his creativity, this incredible brain he had coupled with his unparalleled work ethic. All of those things he knew he had early in life, so he was going to use it. He was going to run it as hard as he could until the energy ran out."[43]

WEDNESDAY, JANUARY 23, 1985

"**Small Grey Monkey**" [early title for "**Merci For The Speed Of A Mad Clown In Summer**"] (overdubs, mix)
"**Bedtime Story**" (Sheila vocals, mix)
"**Bedtime Story**" [duet] (mix)
"**Bedtime Story**" [instrumental] (mix)

"Toy Box" (possible new recording, mix)
5th Floor Recording Studio, Cincinnati, Ohio | after January 22 concert
Producer: Prince | Artist: Sheila E. | Engineers: Susan Rogers and Gary Platt

Prince was behind that one ["Small Grey Monkey"/ "Merci For The Speed Of A Mad Clown in Summer"]. That was his keys and Benny [Rietveld] playing bass.

—Eddie M.

It is likely that Prince and Sheila continued working on "Small Grey Monkey," but it appears that much of the time during this session was spent on Sheila's vocals and percussion (including shakers and congas) for "Bedtime Story." An instrumental mix and a version that turned the song into a duet between Prince and Sheila were created, but possibly the most interesting part of the session was Sheila recording a love note that Prince had written to the instrumental version of the "Bedtime Story" that started with the phrase "Sweet and sour dreams, did you say your prayers?" The words were a playful romantic note from the female character to her male lover and sounded very much like conversations Prince and Sheila or Prince and Devin likely had.

"I think Prince liked romancing a girl, and thought, I've got to romance *this* one in the right way," reveals Devin. "I was from the South and I'm very old fashioned. I never called him. He always called me, and I think he liked calling me. He even called me from a pay phone once. I didn't know at first what to really think of him."

Devin was not aware of anyone else he was romancing at the time or that Prince was asking another woman he had been romancing to record the song that her intimate conversations had inspired.

What made it romantic was when I would see him, we would go dancing, we would have fun, and then he would say, "It's time for you to go to your room now." And I would go to my room, which was down the hall from his room, and then he would call me on the phone and talk to me for two hours before I went to sleep. So, it was kind of like, how could I remotely think there was another girl in the picture when you're talking to a guy this much.

Additional work was probably done on "Toy Box," but it is unclear if it is a re-recording with Sheila's band, or if it is a mix of the song she'd recorded with Prince.

Status: The spoken word version of "Bedtime Story," as well as the duet mix remained unreleased during Prince's lifetime.

WEDNESDAY, JANUARY 23, 1985

Venue: The Riverfront Coliseum (Cincinnati, Ohio)
Capacity: 14,869 (sold out)

The reviews were almost universally stellar with the *AvantGuardian* stating that "all the performers gave everything they had," and hoping that the tour would pay another visit soon.[44]

THURSDAY, JANUARY 24, 1985

"Merci For The Speed Of A Mad Clown In Summer" [previously listed as **"Small Grey Monkey"**] (edits, mix)
"Bedtime Story" (various overdubs, mix)
5th Floor Recording Studio, Cincinnati, Ohio | after January 23 concert
Producer: Prince | Artist: Sheila E. | Engineers: Susan Rogers and Gary Platt

> *We'd play the show and when I got out at 1 o'clock in the morning, I'd go out and take a shower and eat and go into the studio around 3 in the morning and we'd work until the next day until about 6 when we had to play again.*[45]
>
> —Sheila E.

Additional overdubbing, mixing, and editing were done on "Small Grey Monkey"/"Merci For The Speed Of A Mad Clown In Summer," and by the end of the session, the song had been reduced to 2 minutes despite the track continuing for another 3 minutes. Sheila's sped-up vocals would be removed in the mix and those areas would eventually be replaced by Eddie M.'s horn. This may have taken place during this session or later at Sunset Sound.

The sound effects at the beginning of the released version of "Merci For The Speed Of A Mad Clown In Summer" were also likely added on a later date at Sunset Sound.

Prince (and possibly Wendy) added some overdubs to "Bedtime Story," and an updated mix was created.

FRIDAY, JANUARY 25, 1985

"Take Me With U" with "Baby I'm A Star" as the B-side is released as the fifth single from *Purple Rain*. It peaked at number 25 on the Pop Chart and number 40 on the Black Chart.

"Take Me With U" wasn't the last song recorded for *Purple Rain*, but it was the final song added to the album and now it would be the album's final single. With the tour scheduled to wrap in April—just in time for the pending release of his follow up album, *Around The World In A Day*—Prince was finishing the sentence and getting ready to start a new conversation.

FRIDAY, JANUARY 25, 1985

Venue: Mid-South Coliseum (Memphis, Tennessee)
Capacity: 11,800 (sold out)

We were the lab animals for sure. We'd be the testing ground for any artists he was working on, and we wouldn't really know it.[46]

—"Bobby Z" Rivkin

During the soundchecks in Memphis, Prince continued teaching the Revolution new music, including the recently recorded "Bedtime Story." Occasionally, he'd play new songs like this during the concerts, likely because it seemed to be important for Prince to continue to update what they played. "The show changed a bit," remembers Dr. Fink. "It was just to change it up for himself, the group and also the audience. He wanted to keep it fresh on the road so he wasn't playing the same thing every night over and over again. He'd get bored, which goes back to probably why he didn't want to keep playing 'Purple Rain' for a year straight and being on a year-long tour all over the world. It just didn't appeal to him obviously, or he would have done it."

SATURDAY, JANUARY 26, 1985

Venue: Mid-South Coliseum (Memphis, Tennessee)
Capacity: 11,800 (sold out)

The following day, Prince, Sheila, their bands, and a select group of others traveled to Los Angeles to perform at the American Music Awards. With an expected audience of millions, this was a chance for Prince to morph from movie star to undeniable rock star in front of the world, so there was likely extra pressure on him to deliver.

MONDAY, JANUARY 28, 1985

American Music Awards
Venue: Shrine Auditorium (Los Angeles, California)

> *For all of us, life is death without adventure. And adventure only comes to those who are willing to take chances. I'd just like to thank, first of all, God. All of the American public. My band, Wendy, Lisa, Matt, Mark and Bobby and all the staff at Warner Brothers, Dick Clark and all of you here tonight. I'm just . . . I don't know . . . I'm very thankful to be here. I'm very thankful for all of you.*[47]

—Prince

Prince was on top of the world. He was nominated in 10 categories and took home three awards, including Favorite Album, for *Purple Rain*, in both the Pop/Rock and Soul/R&B categories, and Favorite Soul/R&B Single for "When Doves Cry." Sheila E. gave an incredible performance of the Prince-penned "The Glamorous Life" and he had initially requested to perform "Paisley Park," which was intended as the lead-off single from his next album, *Around The World In A Day*. It was an example of how Prince had moved on from the *Purple Rain* era, despite the fact that the album and tour were still popular. Abrupt changes in his focus would become a trademark of his career, and his seemingly erratic choices revealed that Prince didn't make *business* decisions, he made *creative* ones. Prince's promotional plan had to be changed when it was discovered that the award show only allowed performances of nominated songs, so they played one of the most emotional versions of "Purple Rain." Even in a room filled with many of the biggest names in entertainment, Prince's performance stood out. By the end of the show, Prince seemed invincible.

But what should have been one of the best nights of his career quickly went south. Most of rock's biggest stars were gathering at A&M Studios to sing on "We Are The World," the US response to "Do They Know It's Christmas." Both tracks were charity projects created to help feed starving people in Africa. "We Are The World" was written by Michael Jackson and Lionel Richie, and Prince was asked by the album's co-producer Quincy Jones to participate, but Prince declined the invitation to the frustration of everyone around him, including his manager Bob Cavallo.

> I said, "Are you going to talk to Quincy? He expects you to go there." He says, "I'm not going. I'll play guitar." So, I call Quincy and he says, "I don't need him to play guitar, we got fucking guitars." So, I say, "Quincy, you know Prince is really sick. He can't go and he'll infect other people." I made all this up right there. So, I go to Prince, "If you're not gonna go tonight you have to go home. You have to hideout; I'm telling everybody you're sick. If they see you out, it's gonna be the headlines tomorrow, 'Rock Royalty Saves Children While Prince Fucking Parties.' You can't do that!" What does he do? He gets in the car and he goes out to party.

"He had us go to Carlos 'n Charlie's and have a fucking party," recalled Wendy. "I remember it perfectly, thinking, 'This is so wrong.' We were embarrassed. Everybody in the band was horrified. And that's where it felt like, there's something shifting here, where he's getting nasty. The entitlement—it was almost like a kid with too much candy."[48]

What Prince needed to do was simply stay out of the spotlight for the rest of the night. Unfortunately, as they were leaving El Privado's (the private bar and disco above Carlos 'n Charlie's), a photographer was attempting to take Prince's photos as he got in his limo.

"The paparazzi goes over to the passenger side back door, opened it up, and shot off like a shutterbug of probably 20 shots," according to one of Prince's bodyguards, Wally Safford. "It was like an automatic bang. Prince said, 'Get the film! Get the film!' So, I went after him. He was running up the street on Sunset along with the other three or four paparazzi. I caught up to him. [The photographer] had a long-lensed camera. He swung it at my face and I ducked. Then I punched him in the eye and knocked him into the bushes as I was trying to grab the film."[49] Shortly afterward, Wally and Sheila's bodyguard Lawrence "Big Larry" Gibson were arrested.

Alan Leeds remembered going to sleep not knowing what had just happened. "At maybe four o'clock, four-thirty, the phone rings and it's (Prince's bodyguard) Chick. 'Hey, buddy, better get back up!' 'What?' 'Well, we were at Carlos 'n Charlie's, and Big Larry, he's in jail, the sheriff's got him.' I've had scandals on tour where musicians got busted and shit happens, but I've never read anything that was on page A1. It was just plain weird."[50]

Prince didn't understand the optics involved and tried to explain it away, but it was no longer effective. **"A lot of times I've been accused of siccing bodyguards on people,"** he rationalized. **"You know what happened in L.A.? My man, the photographer, tried to get in the car! I don't have any problem with somebody I know trying to get in the car with me and my woman in it. But someone like that? Just to get a picture?"**[51]

"So, it's in all the papers, just that exact headline I predicted and that hurt him," concludes Cavallo. "That hurt his image because all the artists who were in awe of him, weren't in awe of him for another 5–6 years. You know what I mean. The tide was turning on him and I blame it all on that night."

The effects were also intimately felt in the Prince camp, when—several weeks later—his lead bodyguard "Big Chick" Huntsberry quit. **"I think that after the L.A. incident, he feared for his job,"** reflected Prince. **"So, if I said something, he'd say, 'What are you jumping on me for? What's wrong? Why all of sudden are you changing?' And I'd say, 'I'm not changing.' Finally, he just said, 'I'm tired. I've had enough.' I said fine, and he went home. I waited a few weeks and called him. I told him that his job was still there and that I was alone. So, he said that he'd see me when I was in New York. He didn't show up."**[52]

TUESDAY, JANUARY 29, 1985

Venue: University of Texas at Austin–Frank Erwin Center (Austin, Texas)
Capacity: 16,112 (sold out)

Prince and the band quickly resumed the tour with two sold out concerts in Austin, Texas, but the press from the previous night's events were starting to spread. "Prince's Bodyguards Arrested in Scuffle With Photographers"[53] and

"Prince and his Bodyguards Hit With $15 Mil. Lawsuit"[54] screamed the head-lines. The news was quickly changing the narrative, and the focus was turning from his music to the wizard behind the curtain.

WEDNESDAY, JANUARY 30, 1985

Venue: University of Texas at Austin–Frank Erwin Center (Austin, Texas)
Capacity: 16,112 (sold out)

WEDNESDAY, JANUARY 30, 1985 (ESTIMATE)

"She's Always in My Hair" (7-inch edit)
Sunset Sound, unknown studio
Producer: Prince (not in attendance) | Artist: Prince | Engineer: "Peggy
  Mac" Leonard (likely)

A quick mix of "She's Always In My Hair" was created for an upcoming release. Prince did not attend the session.

Status: The 7-inch version of "She's Always In My Hair" (3:27) would be re-leased as the B-side for "Paisley Park" (in the United Kingdom) and "Raspberry Beret" (in the rest of the world).

Prince was making it look easy, but underneath the calm, there was a machine that was in place and everything had to go through one man. But unlike most people, it was pushing him even harder, according to Susan Rogers.

> Let's talk about Prince and stress, because this little guy has more output than you've ever seen. Think of Steve Jobs. It's like asking if Steve Jobs was stressed out. Well, yeah, of course. That's how he got his work done. It's that level. The heat in that oven is so hot. It's a very active furnace and what would burn down someone else's house is just the norm for a guy like Prince. So yeah, he was a re-ally taut string. He had to be, because he's making millions, he made a movie, and

at some point, in the tour, he's nominated for an Academy Award. The Grammys. They want him to play at the American Music Awards. Elizabeth Taylor's coming out to see him. There's all this, and the kid is, what, 25 years old? So to say he was stressed wouldn't be an accurate depiction, but to say that his nervous system was operating at a really, almost unimaginable level for most people, a really fast rate of arousal would be very, very true. He didn't relax. He certainly didn't need to. And imagine, stress shuts down the cognitive processes, because you're just so afraid, and you're just protecting yourself. You can't really be very creative when you're stressed. But when your nervous system is operating at this really fast frequency, and you feel good, you can be at your most creative.

FEBRUARY 1985

FRIDAY, FEBRUARY 1, 1985

"4 The Tears In Your Eyes" [version 1] (tracking, overdubs, mix)
Louisiana Superdome (New Orleans, Louisiana-Le Mobile Studios) | sound-
   check
Producer: Prince | Artist: Prince | Engineer: Susan Rogers

Venue: Louisiana Superdome (New Orleans, Louisiana)
Capacity: 60,000 (sold out)

> *I talked to the people who were doing USA For Africa, and*
> *they said it was cool that I gave up a song for the album,*
> *which was the best for both of us, I think. I'm strongest in*
> *a situation where I'm surrounded by people I know. It's*
> *better that I did it that way.*[1]

—Prince

The press may have been turning on Prince, but as a performer he was practically untouchable. He'd sold out the Superdome, a sports stadium that held
60,000 screaming Prince fans. It was the largest venue of his career at that point,
and an accomplishment that would take years for him to duplicate and even
then, he would rarely do it as the main performer. "This was an astonishing

moment for me," Susan Rogers reflected in awe. "I was on the side as the band was taking the stage and was hit by the sound of 60,000 people. I have never heard anything like that before. Prince and the stage looked so small in a place of that size. It was great just to realize what this guy had accomplished. . . . I'm looking at Prince like, 'Wow, you are the guy I go to work for every day.'"[2]

Susan's vantage point was one perspective, but actually being on stage twenty feet from Prince was unlike anything Lisa had ever experienced. "When we played the Superdome, Prince had them turn the house lights on, because he wanted to see the crowd. That was totally insane. And the screaming was so loud, our ears were distorting. It was like the Beatles, because I can't hear anything."[3]

Before the concert, Prince ran the band through a long soundcheck that included "A Love Bizarre," "Erotic City," James Brown's "Bodyheat," Sly and the Family Stone's "You Caught Me Smiling Again," Elvis Presley's "Jailhouse Rock," "Free," "Strange Relationship," "Let's Go Crazy," and introduced a new song to the band that he'd written (and reportedly demoed on the guitar) the previous day in his New Orleans hotel, "4 The Tears In Your Eyes." He taught it to the band one person at a time. With Wendy and then Lisa, who used a harpsichord patch on her Yamaha DX7 keyboard (she even playfully performed the theme from *The Munsters* at one point while they were learning it), and eventually everyone, including Bobby on the Simmons SDS-V electronic drum pads, the song came together fairly quickly. Prince even had them try adding a flute tone to the track. "We had the mobile truck at the soundcheck, and Prince taught '4 The Tears In Your Eyes' to the band," remembers Rogers. "As soon as the show was over, he and I took the tapes and went into the mobile truck and did what we normally would do after a show that we had recorded and listened to those tapes and we put up the tape for '4 The Tears In Your Eyes' and we worked on it all through the night."

At various times during the recordings, the acoustic guitar was not unlike the guitar on Talking Head's version of "Psycho Killer" from their 1984 concert film *Stop Making Sense*. Prince apparently wasn't happy with the way the track sounded after the session with the band and decided to create one that was unfiltered. As he reworked the song, the harpsichord elements would be removed.

Status: "4 The Tears In Your Eyes" (3:25) was re-recorded and released on the *We Are The World* album, on April 12, 1985. It was tracked once more in June with Wendy and Lisa during the creation of the music video. That version was released in 1993 on *The Hits/The B-Sides*.

"4 The Tears In Your Eyes" as recorded with the Revolution remains unreleased.

SATURDAY, FEBRUARY 2, 1985

"4 The Tears In Your Eyes" [version 2] (tracking, overdubs, mix)
Louisiana Superdome (New Orleans, Louisiana-Le Mobile Studios)
Producer: Prince | Artist: Prince | Engineer: Susan Rogers

> *That was a remarkable day. This was after the whole terrible incident of the ["We Are The World"] event.*[4]
>
> —Susan Rogers

On a rare day off from the tour, Prince asked Susan Rogers to join him in the mobile truck so he could continue recording "4 The Tears In Your Eyes" after everyone left. His choice to spend the day focused on the song was likely an indication of how important this composition was for him. "It was funny to go from the night before at the Superdome with 60,000 people and the noise was deafening and the next day," remembers Rogers. "We were there, and it was virtually empty."[5]

He and I did the song alone in the truck. I remember we hadn't eaten all day and at 5 or 6 in the evening he asked if I could find him something to eat. We were in the Superdome; I couldn't just go outside and get him a hamburger. I remember I went upstairs and there were some people cleaning. I told them that Prince was downstairs in the truck recording a song and that he was hungry, and I asked them if there were any sandwiches or anything around. They gave me some salami and cheese, some pickles, some potato chips, some crackers and a can of warm Coca-Cola. That's all there was. So, I took that and went down to him and I thought, "Oh, God." But he was grateful for it. He said, "Oh, thanks. I was so hungry." He sat there and ate this salami and cheese and crackers and drank that warm Coke. He was happy to have it. We finished the song, we mixed it right there in the truck and we put it away. And then later on when I read about how those people had $15,000 worth of food in that ["We Are The World"] session in A&M and it was such a sacrifice, I thought about how, without anybody knowing about it, he and I, on our day off—we hadn't had a day off for a long time—we sat in that truck by ourselves, he drank a warm Coke and ate this. I do want to say that he put in his time for the cause, and I think in a very noble and gracious way, although no one was there to see it. Especially for this guy who was the number one pop star in the world at the time, he could have taken one look at that cheese and cracker plate and said: "Take that damn thing out of here!" But he was so grateful to have it, it was so wonderful. And it was indicative of the kind of guy he ultimately is.[6]

The song was a heartfelt testament to how Prince felt about Jesus and about the sacrifices that his savior had made for him. It is ironic that this understated and introspective song would be recorded on the same date that the crowd's deafening roar filled the packed arena sealing his place in history.

Despite Prince's quiet work on the song, the bad publicity from the incident at Carlos 'n Charlie's was everywhere, and the repercussions from all of this would be felt for a long time. Even *Saturday Night Live* mocked the situation in a March episode by opening with Prince (played by Billy Crystal) doing his own tribute singing "I Am the World," while Mr. T and Hulk Hogan attacked the other celebrities who attempted to perform with him.

In November, seven months after the *We Are The World* album was released, MTV aired an interview with Prince where he tried to explain his position, but by then deep damage had been done. **"I probably just would have clammed up with so many great people in the room. I'm an admirer of all the people who participated in that particular outing. I don't want there to be any hard feelings."[7]**

SUNDAY, FEBRUARY 3, 1985

Venue: Jefferson Civic Center Coliseum (Birmingham, Alabama)
Capacity: 17,700 (±12,000 tickets sold)

> *Our technical crew was as professional and efficient as the performers. Still, every tour has that one "Murphy's Law Day" where everything that can go wrong does go wrong. Ours was a one-off in Birmingham, Alabama.[8]*

—Alan Leeds

For almost every show of the tour, the concert would begin like the movie and the album, with "Let's Go Crazy" and the band's dramatic appearance would be revealed when the curtain vanished on the downbeat of the song, but this time, the curtain got stuck, according to Alan Leeds.

The curtain mechanism stalled about knee high off the stage. The song was nearly over before the crew finished manually (and clumsily) gathering the bulk over the truss above. Little did we know, our night from hell was just beginning. Later in the show, Prince had a quick change after which he re-emerged via a hydraulic lift. First, Prince bumped his head under the stage climbing onto the lift. Then, the song started and once again mechanics failed . . . this time with just the top of his sore cranium protruding into the audience sight lines. It looked like a cantaloupe laying on the stage. Finally, a couple crew guys pushed him the rest of the way up. He was not happy."[9]

"I was doing the 75th *Purple Rain* show, doing the same thing over and over—for the same kids who go to Spice Girls shows," Prince explained to *Icon* magazine, **"and I just lost it. I said: 'I can't do it!' They were putting the guitar on me and it hit me in the eye and cut me and blood started going down my shirt. And I said, 'I have to go onstage,' but I knew I had to get away from all that. I couldn't play the game."**[10]

A storm was brewing that would make travel more difficult. Everyone else had already checked out of the hotel except for Prince who went back to shower and change, potentially stranding the tour in Alabama. "Now, if this was the real world, one would grab Prince and explain the situation," detailed Alan's wife, Gwen Leeds, "but this was the purple world where nothing was real anymore. And this night of all nights, Chick wasn't about to allow anyone to intercept them. We could only assume he would tell Prince about the storm on the way to the hotel. But before their car was out of the arena, Chick was on the radio. 'Tell Alan, Prince says he needs to be at his hotel room before anybody goes anywhere.'"[11]

Time was precious if they wanted to beat the storm because US 78 was rapidly icing up, so Prince needed to change his plans and go straight to the *airport* immediately. It was up to Alan to explain the urgency to Prince, but there was still the issue of the bad show.

I seriously wondered if I still had a job. But I had to act as if I did, because we had a show in Memphis to worry about. The bus felt like a funeral home, everyone knew what I was in for, and I'd like to think some of the techs felt a bit guilty, since I was really taking one for the team. I went to Prince's suite and knocked on the door. He opened it, turned his back and stalked towards a large dining room table pointing for me to sit down. For a few minutes—which seemed like hours—he just glared and said nothing. Finally, he snapped, "What can you tell me so that I know none of this is going to happen again?"

I went through each fuck-up, one by one, offering rather technical explanations of what had gone wrong and what we intended to do to prevent any repeats. He wasn't convinced. And the opening curtain bit had been shaky long before Birmingham. The quiet in the room was stagnant. Then I realized that Prince was still in his stage clothes. He hadn't even showered. So, I gulped and changed the subject. Chick hadn't said a word about the storm, the bus, or the flight—Thanks a bunch, Chick—On top of everything, now I had to explain that Prince's fancy leisurely night on his bus was a wrap or he risked blowing the next show. Somehow, we landed in icy Memphis about four in the morning. Prince was silent the whole way.[12]

"All it meant to me was what I'd known for years; life on the road was always an adventure," continued Leeds. "And since I still had a job, I guess I could finally assume that I had succeeded in making him like having me around. After all, he had fired others for much less."[13]

This show was initially scheduled to take place on January 20, 1985, but it was rescheduled for this matinee performance 14 days later. It is possible that the band version of "4 The Tears In Your Eyes" was recorded during the soundcheck for this show instead of February 1, and that he'd actually recorded a guitar demo for the track on that date.

MONDAY, FEBRUARY 4, 1985

Venue: Mid-South Coliseum (Memphis, Tennessee)
Capacity: 11,800 (sold out)

Prince and the Revolution had now been on the road for three months. It was his most successful tour ever, and despite the grueling nature of the shows, Sheila was enjoying her time in the spotlight as the opening act. "It was a lot of fun. It was just like being with a lot of family and friends. We didn't know how successful it was gonna be. They just kept adding dates every time we went to another city, if we did two or three dates it became a week, so we just stayed out as long as we could."[14]

But Prince was burnt out and had already announced to his band that the tour was going to be cut short and that he'd be releasing *Around The World In A Day*, a new album of freshly recorded material very soon.

A break in the tour had been scheduled, so Prince flew back to Los Angeles. Of course, Prince didn't see it as a chance to rest. He scheduled time at Sunset Sound to continue recording without the interruptions of daily live performances.

TUESDAY, FEBRUARY 5, 1985

"**Romance 1600**" (tracking, vocals, overdubs, mix)
Sunset Sound, Studio 3 | 3 p.m.–2:15 a.m. (booked: lockout)
Producers: Sheila E./Prince (neither is circled) | Artist: Sheila E. | Engineer:
    Prince | Assistant Engineer: "Peggy Mac" Leonard

> *Peggy Mac was a staff engineer at Sunset Sound, and when Prince worked at Sunset, he liked working with Peggy. When I came along, and after I did the tech work at his home, he would bring me out to Sunset as well so that Peggy, Prince, and I could all work together.*[15]

—Susan Rogers

A nine-day break of the tour found Prince in Los Angeles to continue work on Sheila's second album in a familiar and comfortable place. Since 1981, when he worked on his *Controversy* album through *1999* and the sessions for *Purple Rain* and his upcoming *Around The World In A Day* album, Prince considered Sunset Sound his home in Los Angeles and Peggy Mac was his main engineer. "I loved working with her. It was just nice," reflected Rogers. "She was, and is, funny. And she knew things I didn't know. I knew things she didn't know. Prince was such a difficult task master that it was nice to have someone take the slack. We got along well."[16]

"I liked Susan a lot and I was happy that there was somebody to help so that I could actually go to the bathroom if I needed to, or grab something to eat and somebody would take over," laughs Peggy.

To Prince, every album had to have a proper title track. At this point, her album was still being called "Toy Box," but following the tour stop in New Orleans, the tone shifted. After seeing the Mardi Gras masks and a screening of the Miloš Forman film *Amadeus*, the look and style of the album changed, so an appropriate tune was written to reflect that decision. Starting at 3 p.m., Prince created a basic Linn LM-1 pattern and had it filtered through a flanger, giving it a different flavor than the usual drums sounds he'd been using. "When I think of Prince and all the percussion and drums he and I did, it really boggles my mind," reflected his drummer Bobby Z.

> He was a very proficient drummer, especially in the studio. The studio was a blank canvas for Prince, and the drums were no exception. There were no rules for how to record drums, but the beat was always front and center. A lot of the drum tracks were recorded in a very unorthodox way. And of course, the super advantage he had over all of the musicians that played for him was that he heard it all in his head and could play your part. Having said that, he loved to be challenged, but only if your ideas were good![17]

He followed the drums with a keyboard riff similar to one that he'd eventually revisit for his 1991 hit "Diamonds and Pearls." Over the next several hours, Prince wrote the lyrics and recorded his scratch vocals for Sheila to follow. She added her Latin flair to the track with a variety of percussion instruments, likely including a shaker, shekere, bongos, and castanets. Sheila probably recorded her vocals on this date as well.

Later in the session, Prince wanted to add saxophone, so he requested "Eddie M." drop by the studio. "I played after everything was recorded," recalls Mininfield. "He would have me hang out close by so if he'd need me in the next 2–3 hours, he'd call the hotel and have them bring me over."

Once all of the elements were put to tape, the last 2 hours were spent mixing the track and three TDK C-60 cassettes were made of the song.

Status: "Romance 1600" (3:53, 3:57 with extra talking at the end of the song) was released as the title track on Sheila's second album.

WEDNESDAY, FEBRUARY 6, 1985

"**Romance 1600 intro**" (tracking, mix)
Romance 1600 album assembly ["**Romance 1600**," "**Toy Box**," "**Bedtime Story**," "**A Love Bizarre**," "**Sister Fate**," "**Dear Michaelangelo**," and "**Merci For The Speed Of A Mad Clown In Summer**"—the order is unknown]
Sunset Sound, Studio 3 | 2 p.m.–10 a.m. (booked: lockout)
Producer: Prince | Artist: Sheila E. | Engineers: "Peggy Mac" Leonard, David Tickle, and likely Susan Rogers

*I was really surprised at how good it sounded. I didn't listen
to each individual track. I just went ahead with the next track
and listened to them all at once at the end.*[18]

—Sheila E.

Beginning at 2 p.m., Prince and Sheila assembled the seven tracks that had
been recorded specifically for her second album. After 2 hours of structuring
and shuffling the songs, the configuration was decided, but now that the order
was clear, it was also obvious that the album needed a strong intro. With Sheila
on drums and percussion, Eddie M. on sax, and Prince on piano and likely
the Yamaha DX7 (and possibly Benny Rietveld on bass), they spent 4 hours
structuring a high energy instrumental segment that would start the album. After
multiple takes, the track was complete, and it was attached to the beginning of
"Sister Fate."

"With Sheila, the sessions were different. She was more of a colleague,"
explains Peggy Mac. "What I remember is that she would play drums, and they
would have a lot of fun. They worked well together. She had been on the road
with other respected musicians like Santana, and she came from a musical family, so she wasn't green."

Prince and Sheila continued working on the album, including small elements that he felt were missing. When it came to recording the overdubs and
additional elements on this and other projects, Sheila remembered Prince's
unorthodox technique:

> We had 24 tracks, so where it says bass and he's playing bass, he just put another
> sound in the middle of something and I'd have to grab that little sound for one or
> two bars or a phrase and take it and sample that so I can play it on the drums be-
> cause it was on the bass track. But no one would know that because they weren't
> sitting there with him. So, I was punching him in on stuff that he couldn't punch
> himself in as far as playing guitar solos or lines or whatever. If he couldn't do it, I
> was his engineer for a lot of this stuff. So even if a keyboard part says, "keyboard
> left and right," he would just punch in some other weird sound instead of going
> to another track, just punch it in the middle and there was tons of that throughout
> a song. So, when you hear stuff coming in and out it's because he punched it in
> there and it's only going to happen at that place, at that sound and you'll never
> hear it again. He didn't find a space; he'd just punch right in.[19]

As always, Prince was focused on the music and not on anyone else's mood.
Music energized him, but it could also drain those around him, especially if they
weren't involved in the recording, as Eddie M. recalls. "They had me hang out

a while and I started to get very frustrated because I really wanted to go home because everyone else got a break and I was kind of being a little pissed about it. If I'm going to sit here, I need to do something, or you need to send me home. I'll come back. He was like, 'No. Sit down. We'll call you when I need you.' So, I sat there. It was okay. I became Sheila's sideman. They wanted me to be a part of her sound, so therefore there were no breaks."

At the end of this 20-hour session, two C-90 cassettes were made of the album for them to review.

Status: "Romance 1600 intro" (0:15) was attached to the beginning of "Sister Fate" and was the first sequence heard on Sheila's *Romance 1600* album.

THURSDAY, FEBRUARY 7, 1985

"**Toy Box**" (edits)
"**Bedtime Story**" (additional Sheila vocals, mix)
Romance 1600 album assembly
Sunset Sound, Studio 3 | 8:30 p.m.–4:30 a.m. (booked: lockout)
Producers: Sheila E./Prince (neither is circled) | Artist: Sheila E. | Engineers: Prince, "Peggy Mac" Leonard, David Tickle, and Susan Rogers

> *Prince doesn't care about what it sounds like as far as mic'ing things and taking the time to make it sound good. It's what you play from [the heart].*[20]
>
> —Sheila E.

"For sequencing an album, you have to have a lot of extra sources at the ready," Susan Rogers details about the process. "You'd have to have sound effects on vinyl, or sound effect CDs, a little bit later on. You had to be ready to do crossfades, you had to have at least three 1/2-inch stereo machines, because it would've been 1/4 inches in the earlier days. So, you had to have your multi-track ready, and you had to have your 1/2-inch tapes ready and you had to be ready to patch in to do crossfades. And also, to record brand new pieces that might be used to sequence these things together. And he'd say, 'Hey, put up an empty 14-inch reel.'"

Although scheduled to start at 6:30 p.m., Sheila and Prince didn't show up until 2 hours later. Prince decided to start shuffling the order of the compilation as well as tweaking some of the songs, specifically "Toy Box," which was edited down to 5:36. Various crossfades were done once the new order was decided. Additional work may have also been completed on "Bedtime Story."

Susan remembers that Prince would have a cassette of the assembly dubbed so he could "Just drive around and live with it for a little bit." When he'd return to the studio, he'd lock down the order that he wanted. "Sequences would come together, and then often when we were pretty sure it was a good sequence, we'd take it to Bernie Grundman at Grundman Mastering. He'd press sides, just acetates. Then we'd listen to them for the quality of the mastering, but also to just live with them as a sequence. And then sometimes Prince would change his mind."

The session wrapped up at 4:30 in the morning, but apparently Prince still wasn't satisfied with the content and structure for the album.

FRIDAY, FEBRUARY 8, 1985

"**Yellow**" (tracking, overdubs, Sheila's vocal, horns, edit, mix)
Romance 1600 album assembly (Side 1: "**Sister Fate**," "**Dear Michael-angelo**," "**A Love Bizarre**" Side 2: "**Toy Box**," "**Yellow**," "**Romance 1600**," "**Merci For The Speed Of A Mad Clown In Summer**," and "**Bedtime Story**")
"**Paisley Park**" (likely edits for 12-inch)
Sunset Sound, Studio 3 | 2 p.m.–6 a.m. (booked: lockout)
Producer: Prince | Artist: Sheila E. | Engineers: "Peggy Mac" Leonard, David Tickle, and Susan Rogers

I'll tell you one thing about Sheila: She has a tremendous amount of courage and a huge heart. Prince has a great ability to be able to pull the best performances out of people. You never saw somebody who was more devoted or determined to do her best, in every situation.[21]

—Susan Rogers

Although the album had been compiled, Prince apparently felt it was still missing a track, so when he and Sheila regrouped at Sunset Sound at two in the afternoon, they spent the next few hours writing and recording "Yellow." Using lyrics inspired by Sheila (including references to her father's car and her younger sister, Zina), they recorded an upbeat jazzy track. After several rehearsals, they locked down the idea and once the basic tracks—including tom-toms, bongo, Yamaha DX7 synth, bass, and Prince's guide vocal—were recorded, he wanted to include horns and reached out to Eddie M. "I was going to play on 'Yellow,' but they'd flown me back home because they thought they were done," remembers Eddie, "and since I had already flown back they decided to use some guys in LA so I didn't do anything on 'Yellow.'" The horn section (credited as "The Horn E. Players"), which contained a few players who'd worked with Prince in the past on "Our Destiny," included John Liotine, Steve Madaio, Ron Jannelli, Dick Hyde, Robert Martin, and Tim Misica, were gathered, and from 8 p.m. to midnight they recorded their section for the track.

For the next 2 hours, Sheila recorded her lead and Prince added his low background vocals to "Yellow," which was mixed and then placed on the album after "Toy Box" and before "Romance 1600." According to Peggy Mac, assembling an album was a puzzle that Prince enjoyed putting together, especially before the era of CDs, when the releases were on LPs and cassettes, which contained two sides. "He was always thinking about what was gonna be the first cut, what would be the last on that side and stuff like that and that's what you do when you're doing an album. You put a strong first cut, you put a strong last cut, and then you make it work in between. I watched that over and over again."

Because Prince was scheduled to fly to England for the British Phonographic Industry (BPI) Awards, eventually known simply as "The Brits," it was crucial that her album was completed, so the session began earlier than usual and lasted longer than expected with 9 hours of overtime for the engineers.

Two C-60 tapes were made of the compilation and the session ended at 6 a.m.

Status: "Yellow" (2:11) was added to Sheila's *Romance 1600* album. It was never released as a single. It is likely that Prince also worked on the 12-inch remix of "Paisley Park" during this session.

Prince flew to England that weekend. There is an apocryphal tale that Prince met the Bangles' singer Susanna Hoffs on that flight, but that scenario is unlikely because the Bangles were already touring in Europe. They would eventually record "Manic Monday," but it appears that they did not formally meet until later in the year.

MONDAY, FEBRUARY 11, 1985

Prince appeared at the BPI Awards at the Grosvenor House Hotel in London, England. He won two awards, "Best Film Soundtrack" for *Purple Rain* and Prince and the Revolution bested Michael Jackson, Bruce Springsteen, Lionel Richie, and ZZ Top for "Best International Artist." On both occasions when he was announced as the winner, Chick Huntsberry, his imposing 6'6", 320-pound bodyguard, walked in front of him, arrogantly clearing his way to the stage. Prince would later be assailed by the British press for his unnecessarily egotistical behavior.

WEDNESDAY, FEBRUARY 13, 1985

"Feline" (tracking, overdub, mix)
Sunset Sound, Studio 3 | 6:30 p.m.–2:30 a.m. (booked: 2 p.m.–open)
Producers: Sheila E./Prince (neither is circled) | Artist: Prince | Engineer: "Peggy Mac" Leonard

> *We're always working and we're always together. He loves his guitar. He loves his music. His main girlfriend is his music. Musically, Prince is the best. He's a genius. The only other person I felt this way about was when I used to play for my father.*[22]
>
> —Sheila E.

Prince began recording the Family's debut album the previous summer. The collection was assembled, but because of the *Purple Rain* tour, it had been sitting on the shelf waiting for the next phase. Today Prince decided to rework "Feline," one of the tracks that was left on the cutting room floor. Originally, the track was eliminated because singer "St. Paul" Peterson didn't feel comfortable with parts of the rap at the end, so Prince, who had continued jamming to the track with the Revolution during soundchecks, decided to repurpose the song for Sheila E. "There was a reason why I don't think it went on the album," explained Eric Leeds, sax player for the Family. "[Prince] wrote a very, very risqué lyric for it. I mean, you can only imagine what the implications were from the title, 'Feline.' Paul Peterson did the vocals on it, and I believe Paul had some reservations about singing these lyrics."[23]

"I'm glad he didn't put it out because I was living with my mother at the time, and I would have had hell to pay," reflects Paul. "Mom is no longer with us and she could handle it, but not when I was living underneath her roof. That's respect. I don't recall having a direct conversation with Prince about it. Most likely, I told Susannah. Because they were a couple at the time. She probably went to Prince and said, 'Paul's mom is going to have a fit over this,' because my mom said, 'I'm going to spank Prince when I meet him.' That's exactly what she said, 'I'm going to spank him.'"

Although "Feline" was taken back from the Family, this happened with other artists as well for other reasons. "Often he would record a song for someone and then maybe have a problem with that person and pull the song away," according to Rogers. "He just was funny like that. He'd withhold affection and he'd withhold songs. So, it could've been, 'I'll show you, I'll take this away from you and give it to Sheila.'"

Prince (and likely Sheila on drums) jammed for multiple takes on the groove from 6:30 in the evening until taking a break for dinner. When recording resumed, more keyboards, guitar, and several layers of Sheila's background vocals were added to the track, including an ending created from feedback similar to the (then-unreleased) long version of "Computer Blue" or "Rearrange." The song also featured Prince's sped up guitar, similar to the way he did with "Toy Box" as well as some updated lyrics to reflect a female point of view. The horns recorded for the original version were dropped in favor of a heavier guitar part. A mix was dubbed to a single C-60 cassette and the session ended at 2:30 a.m.

The following day after sessions like this were generally odd for engineers like Peggy Mac. "I thought he was coming in, but he'd be gone. [Sunset Sound] would say 'Pack it up,' and usually there would be no notice, so it was like Okay! And I'd pack up everything and gather up all the lyrics and all that kind of stuff that was just around the studio, throw it in the Anvil case and they'd come get it and he'd be off. It was time for him to change scenery."

Status: Multiple versions of "Feline" were reportedly attempted with a variety of mixes, but the song remained unreleased during Prince's lifetime. It is unclear if Sheila ever recorded lead vocals for the track, but it is likely that she did at some point. Eventually elements from the rap were repurposed when she recorded "Holly Rock."

THURSDAY, FEBRUARY 14, 1985

Venue: Tacoma Dome (Tacoma, Washington)
Capacity: 24,450 (sold out)

Prince spent the soundcheck reworking "Baby I'm A Star" probably because of the upcoming performance at the Grammys in less than two weeks. While he was updating the arrangement with the band, he was conscious about the clock because it would be broadcast live so there would be no editing involved. Over the next few weeks, he'd drill it into the band making sure everyone knew their sections.

"He was a stickler with all of that," Wendy explained to Alan Light. "'Don't fuck up your parts.' 'Don't fuck up your choreography,' to the nth degree. That was not fun. Because he really kind of liked to humiliate you in order for you to do better; it was one of his tactics. Instead of encouraging, like, 'You can do it! Come on, girl!' he'd be like, 'You look white and dorky, and what are you doing up here?' And you'd be shamed into doing it right. So, there was a lot of pressure."[24]

FRIDAY, FEBRUARY 15, 1985

Venue: Tacoma Dome (Tacoma, Washington)
Capacity: 24,450 (sold out)

MONDAY, FEBRUARY 18, 1985

Venue: The Forum (Inglewood, California)
Capacity: 16,000 (sold out but exact number is unknown)

This was the first of six sold out shows at the Forum, a feat that had only been accomplished by Led Zeppelin, Rod Stewart, and Neil Diamond. Because of the demand for tickets, Prince also scheduled an additional three shows at the nearby Long Beach Arena for early March.

Although the six nights at the Forum were all sold out, and the audience often drowned out the performance with their enthusiasm, the reviews were positive but with a caveat. Richard Cromelin of the *Los Angeles Times* wrote that the show was as "fascinating as it was indulgent," and that Prince "becomes so self-absorbed in his struggle of spirit versus flesh that he loses sight of such things as joy and spontaneity. But the payoffs are worth the risks and losses."[25]

TUESDAY, FEBRUARY 19, 1985

Venue: The Forum (Inglewood, California)
Capacity: 16,000 (sold out but exact number is unknown)

WEDNESDAY, FEBRUARY 20, 1985

Venue: The Forum (Inglewood, California)
Capacity: 16,000 (sold out but exact number is unknown)

THURSDAY, FEBRUARY 21, 1985

Location: Warner Bros. Records offices (Burbank, California)

Once again, he was faced with, "How do you follow something?" Here was this fabulously, remarkably successful project, Purple Rain. *Anything you do fails in comparison, so what's the age-old answer? Do something opposite. Do something different.*[26]

—Alan Leeds

Prince previewed his next album, *Around The World In A Day*, for Warner Bros. executives at a hastily arranged listening party at the company's main offices in Burbank, California. "Prince had someone call [Warner Bros. executive] Mo Ostin's office at noon, he wanted to come over at 4 o'clock and play the album for key execs and it was up to Mo to put the group of people together for the conference run," recalled Marylou Badeaux, the Research Director for the label's Black Music department. "I must say from a personal standpoint; I had been a little concerned about Prince. I wasn't sure where his head was at. I was a little concerned. Just how he was emotionally."[27]

The conference room was cleared out, the table and most of the chairs were removed, the lighting was muted, and flowers were spread on the floor. Prince's step-brother Duane was leading the security and entered with Prince, Wendy, and Lisa, and they were joined by Joni Mitchell and Prince's father, John L. Nelson. Badeaux continued, "They're all holding flowers. Prince is holding flowers. We're like, Haight-Ashbury. He sits down basically next to me on the floor and Wendy and Lisa are within a couple of feet. He doesn't say a word."[28]

> As the record is going on, and I'm looking around the room, and people are in shock. They're trying to be cool, so they're clapping afterwards. It was funny. What I remember most personally was looking at him, and he was two feet from me and just looking at him and he kinda smiled at me. And I thought to myself. He's okay. All the concerns I had had before, he's okay. He's in a really good place. That was what I sensed—it may or may not have been true—he was just in a good place. He just sat there quietly and kind of watched, and I'm sure he vibed what was going on in there. How he felt about it, I don't know. Right before it was over as is typical with him in that time frame, he got up and left. So, there was no way for anyone to come up and say, "Hey man I loved your new record." Or whatever stuff they would do. He just quietly disappeared.[29]

The executives seemed confused. Coming off the biggest album of the year, they expected it to be similar, but *Around The World In A Day* went in a direction they hadn't anticipated, so all of the plans they had for promotion had to be changed and it was apparent on many of their faces, as Badeaux recalls. "On the part of the Warner people. 'What are we going to do with this? It's interesting, but it isn't commercial.' I remember distinctly that Wendy who came up to me afterwards and said, 'Do you think they liked it?' She was worried. Prince had left by then. I said, 'Wendy, it's a wonderful album.' I knew [the other execs] were waiting for *Purple Rain 2*. I also knew in my heart he wouldn't ever deliver *Purple Rain 2* then or ever. He did it, he'd been there, he moved on. That's the way he operates."[30]

Prince would look at how some people reacted to the album and take a more philosophical view. **"People think, 'Oh, the new album isn't half as powerful as *Purple Rain* or *1999*.' You know how easy it would have been to open**

Around The World In A Day **with the guitar solo that's on the end of 'Let's Go Crazy'? You know how easy it would have been to just put it in a different key? That would have shut everybody up who said the album wasn't half as powerful."**[31]

Eric Leeds remembers Prince's attitude at the time.

> He was very determined that *Around The World In A Day* was gonna be as different from *Purple Rain* as anything could be, which was, some would say, a courageous thing to do, because when you have an album that sells, 13, 14 million copies, a lot of times the artist—not just the record company, but the artist—feels obligated to kind of play it safe. Prince really couldn't do that anyway, I mean, it was a conscious decision. He has stated that he was very determined that *Around The World In A Day* was going to be very different.[32]

"Look, he could have kept making *Purple Rains*," reasoned Matt Fink. "We had, like, forty additional songs from that album alone. He wanted to do *Around The World In A Day* to clear the air, change the dial. I think he thought, 'Oh my God, *Purple Rain* is my *Thriller*. Now what? I'll never top it, so I'll just experiment, change direction, and reinvent the wheel.'"[33]

FRIDAY, FEBRUARY 22, 1985

Venue: The Forum (Inglewood, California)
Capacity: 16,000 (sold out but exact number is unknown)

During the soundcheck, Prince ran the band through "America," and "G-Spot."

SATURDAY, FEBRUARY 23, 1985

Venue: The Forum (Inglewood, California)
Capacity: 16,000 (sold out but exact number is unknown)

Rock royalty showed up tonight for Prince's show when Bruce Springsteen and Madonna joined him for "Baby I'm A Star," the debut of "America," and

"Purple Rain." The respect and admiration from two of the biggest performers of that era reveals how deeply Prince was revered by his peers, despite any
controversies. "I felt a great kinship with Prince. And he was a guy, when I'd go
to see him, I'd say, 'Oh, man, Okay, back to the drawing board,'" Springsteen
would reflect after Prince's passing. "He just took it to another level."[34]

Earlier in tonight's concert, Prince performed the live premiere of "4 The
Tears In Your Eyes" as well as "Raspberry Beret."

SUNDAY, FEBRUARY 24, 1985

Venue: The Forum (Inglewood, California)
Capacity: 16,000 (sold out but exact number is unknown)

During the soundcheck, Prince and the band rehearsed "Let's Work," "Paisley
Park," "Irresistible Bitch," and the unreleased "Temptation," "Chocolate," and
"4 The Tears In Your Eyes." They also ran through Ray Charles' "Drown in
My Own Tears."

"He was tinkering with those songs in rehearsals, and a few of them started
to show up near the end of the tour," says Eric Leeds. "I remember 'America.'
I had already heard the original long version, before there were even any vocals
out on it. We jammed a couple of times on that," recalled Eric. "There were a
lot of things that he would pull out of his little bag at soundcheck that I had no
familiarity with at all!"[35]

MONDAY, FEBRUARY 25, 1985 (A.M.)

Venue: Santa Monica Civic Auditorium (Santa Monica, California)
Capacity: 3,000

> *The students were bussed to the show not knowing whom they*
> *were going to see. Prince did not want publicity for this, so only*
> *a few people knew about it.*[36]
>
> —Ingrid Geyer

After a six-night run at the Forum, Prince quietly scheduled a concert for children with disabilities while in town. An abbreviated matinee performance was arranged at the Santa Monica Civic Auditorium for those who couldn't attend a regular show at the Forum. Prince seemed to understand that he was given a gift, and on occasions like this, he was giving back to the people who deserved some extra love. "Hundreds of children watched the concert from their wheelchairs, and Prince provided signers for the deaf students," remembered Ingrid Geyer, the teacher with the Los Angeles Unified School District who had asked Prince if he was available to do a special show. He agreed and paid for the entire event. "Prince was a loving, generous and gentle man," Geyer continued. "For many of the children, it would be the only live show they would ever see."[37]

The show included a rare performance of "4 The Tears In Your Eyes," and Prince invited Lisa Coleman's brother David who wrote the original version of "Around The World In A Day," to perform with the band. "I played with them at the Santa Monica Civic Center on the *Purple Rain* tour during the afternoon. First, we did a soundcheck and set up the cello and I set up near Bobby and Matt. I set up a riq, which is a tambourine with thick bells on it. I went in and talked to Prince in his dressing room and he asked me what instruments I brought, and he decided to set me up with the cello on stage. I ended up playing percussion for the entire show and it was great being up there. That was the only time I played live with him."

MONDAY, FEBRUARY 25, 1985

"**America**" (edit and mix)
Sunset Sound, Studio 1 (likely) | unknown start time
Producer: Prince | Artist: Prince | Engineer: "Peggy Mac" Leonard

I didn't like him as much when he was the biggest star on the planet. That attitude was now part of his personality after Purple Rain. *And then the bodyguards came, and then the protection. He became less accessible. Less human, in a way. Less a participant, and more of the mega star.*

—"Peggy Mac" Leonard

Sunset Sound was still Prince's home, but like a child going off to college, Prince had noticeably changed after he returned. In the past, it was common for him to show up at any time at the studio and expect people to be ready. Sunset Sound employee Paul Levy remembers Prince's urgency during that period. "Sometimes he could do a show, he would come in around 11 or 12 at night, with his stage clothes on and he went into the studio as fast as he could before he forgot something. That's what the guy was all about. He had so much stuff coming out of his head, he was so afraid of losing a great idea or some tune or something. When he got out of the car, he'd run into the studio because he was still probably pumped up, you know . . . 'I've got some ideas!'"

And Prince's relationship with engineers like Peggy Mac became strained. Being constantly on call and expected to be ready was draining on every level, and rest was a language that he didn't understand. "He told me the only reason he did go home was because he knew I had to sleep. I was like, "Really?," recalled Peggy.[38]

"When you work with people who are that creative, you realize that they're processing, this is what they need, and they need it now. I honored that, as much as I could. I don't want to hear any excuses, just get it done."

On this date, Prince had a rare session in Studio 1 working on an edit and a quick mix for "America," which had debuted during a concert a few nights earlier. The song was being prepped as a potential single from *Around The World In A Day*.

TUESDAY, FEBRUARY 26, 1985

Grammy Award Ceremony
Venue: Shrine Auditorium (Los Angeles, California)

After the end of his run of shows in Los Angeles, Prince was back at the Shrine Auditorium to attend the Grammy Awards where he once again ruled the night, winning "Best Album of Original Score Written for a Motion Picture or Television Special" for *Purple Rain* with Lisa Coleman, Wendy Melvoin, and John L. Nelson; "Best Rock Vocal Performance by a Duo or Group" for "Purple Rain" with the Revolution; and "Best R&B Song" for "I Feel For You" as performed by Chaka Khan. His work was nominated in several other categories including "Best R&B Instrumental Performance" for Sheila E.'s "Shortberry Strawcake" and "Best R&B Song" for her "The Glamorous Life." *Purple Rain* was also nominated for "Album of the Year" but lost out to Lionel Richie's *Can't Slow Down.*

Prince closed the show with an earth-shattering performance of "Baby I'm A Star" that included the audience joining him on stage.

WEDNESDAY, FEBRUARY 27, 1985

Venue: Cow Palace (Daly City, California)
Capacity: 13,083 (sold out)

The first of another run of sold out shows. Tickets for all six Cow Palace concerts were gone within a day. During the soundcheck before the show, Prince ran the band through a number of tracks, including: "Erotic City," "Let's Go Crazy;" "Delirious," and the unreleased "Jerk Out."

Despite the band being on tour for almost four months, Prince was still working on improving the performances. "He was always saying, 'What are you doing with your other hand?' There was a lot of choreography of the back row, for me and Matt and Lisa. Certainly, more than any other backline. And so, we weren't exempt," explained Bobby. "Every move, every bar, every measure had some kind of visual or musical element."[39]

THURSDAY, FEBRUARY 28, 1985

Venue: Cow Palace (Daly City, California)
Capacity: 13,083 (sold out)

During a soundcheck in Daly City, he ran the band through an update of "Do Me, Baby," adding touches that few, except Prince, would notice.

MARCH 1985

FRIDAY, MARCH 1, 1985

Venue: Cow Palace (Daly City, California)
Capacity: 13,083 (sold out)

SATURDAY, MARCH 2, 1985

On his day off from the Cow Palace run of shows, concert promoter Bill Graham threw a party for the Revolution and Prince's crew in his home in San Francisco. It is likely that Prince attended.

SUNDAY, MARCH 3, 1985 (MATINEE PERFORMANCE)

Venue: Cow Palace (Daly City, California)
Capacity: 13,083 (sold out)

Prince began the show with "Controversy," followed by the usual opener "Let's Go Crazy." "Controversy" had been played sporadically as an instrumental part of "Take Me With U," but not performed in its entirety on this tour, but it was a standard soundcheck song for the Revolution, so it was an easy way for Prince to keep the shows unique.

They also played "Raspberry Beret" instead of "Possessed."

MONDAY, MARCH 4, 1985

Venue: Cow Palace (Daly City, California)
Capacity: 13,083 (sold out)

> *I spent five years working for James Brown, who was similarly prolific and self-motivated, but Prince made James Brown seem lazy. It was a freak of nature.*[1]

—Alan Leeds

During the soundcheck Prince had the band run through "17 Days." He apparently enjoyed how it came together, and like the previous evening, "Let's Go Crazy" became the second song in the set on this date after opening it with "17 Days."

TUESDAY, MARCH 5, 1985

Venue: Cow Palace (Daly City, California)
Capacity: 13,083 (sold out)

The soundcheck included Prince playing bass on a few instrumental jams that contained elements of the then-unreleased "Jerk Out" and "Chocolate." Prince also sings a line from Jesse Johnson's recently released "Be Your Man."

The following day, everyone traveled to Las Cruces, New Mexico, for the next shows.

THURSDAY, MARCH 7, 1985

Venue: NMSU Pan Am Center (Las Cruces, New Mexico)
Capacity: 11,500 (±9,100 tickets sold)

FRIDAY, MARCH 8, 1985

Venue: NMSU Pan Am Center (Las Cruces, New Mexico)
Capacity: 11,500 (±10,000 tickets sold)

SUNDAY, MARCH 10, 1985

Venue: Long Beach Arena (Long Beach, California)
Capacity: 13,574 (attendance unknown)

It is a testament to how popular Prince was that he was able to fill another arena in the Los Angeles area for three consecutive nights just two weeks after a sold-out series of six shows. Michael Jackson supposedly snuck in to watch the show. He had seen Prince on his previous tour, and the two of them maintained a mutual respect. Prince had been in the audience for two shows of the Jackson's *Victory Tour* the previous year.

The soundcheck for this concert included Prince teaching the band "Sister Fate," but it is unclear if it was ever actually performed in concert.

MONDAY, MARCH 11, 1985

Venue: Long Beach Arena (Long Beach, California)
Capacity: 13,574 (attendance unknown)

As a musician, he was incomparable and his attitude about
the music was so infectious. He demanded that it be infectious.

—Susie Davis

To help ease his boredom, Prince would grab an instrument and start performing, even during the opening act. "He could play anything," according to Susie
Davis who recalls Prince contributing during Sheila's set, but not letting the
audience in on the secret. "He was doing this thing with us where he would
sit in one of the dressing rooms off to the side and have a guitar and vocal mic,
and he'd play along with us and not be visible to anyone. You could hear him
in your monitors, he'd just play guitar or sing whatever he wanted just for fun.
I think he was using the live shows as a way to just improvise and jam. He was
very playful. He'd just make up whatever he wanted to. I remember sometimes
hearing what he was playing and being like, that's not how we've rehearsed the
song! That happened a bunch of times over the course of the *Purple Rain* tour."

TUESDAY, MARCH 12, 1985

Venue: Long Beach Arena (Long Beach, California)
Capacity: 13,574 (attendance unknown)

THURSDAY, MARCH 14, 1985

"Rough" [also listed as **"Tough,"** **"Too Tough,"** and **"Too Rough"**] (vocal
    overdubs, mix)
"I Don't Wanna Stop" (listen, possible mix)
Sunset Sound, Studio 1 (likely) | unknown start time
Producer: Prince | Artists: The Family/Jill Jones | Engineers: "Peggy Mac"
    Leonard and Susan Rogers

Imagine a guy who has limitless energy, talent, resources,
drive, stamina, vision, recognizes and develops/recruits talent,
and is incredibly successful at it. That was Prince.[2]

—"St. Paul" Peterson

The tour traveled across the country to Nassau, New York, for an East Coast leg of the tour, but Prince stayed behind in Los Angeles to work at Sunset Sound, looking for music for the Family, which was scheduled to be another of his upcoming protégé acts.

Prince enjoyed surrounding himself with people who were committed to him, and it is apparent that loyalty and devotion made him happy. When Morris Day left Prince's first protégé act, the Time collapsed. Instead of abandoning the remaining people, Prince rewarded their loyalty by forming a new group, the Family, moving "St. Paul" Peterson from keyboard player to the band's front man. Jellybean Johnson continued as the drummer, and *Purple Rain* star Jerome Benton, the hype man and Morris's on-stage valet, was placed in the same position in the new group. The first assembly of the Family's debut album had been compiled, but Prince continued to look for "new" tracks in case he felt something worked in context with the other songs.

The two songs that Prince worked on during this session were both 16-track recordings from his home studio sessions dating back to 1980. "Rough" was originally recorded with Prince on vocals, but the song featured Alexander O'Neal's lead vocals, conceivably from when he was being groomed as the front man for the band that became the Time. "I Don't Wanna Stop" was given to Ren Woods who re-recorded the track for her *Azz Izz* album, but after the initial printing, Prince decided to pull the song from her project.

Prince was likely reviewing the tracks for possible inclusion on the upcoming Family album, but he wasn't auditioning the songs for the band. As with almost every project, *he* would be the one who would listen and decide if the song was appropriate. "At the time, you've got to understand, he wasn't asking my opinion," explains Peterson. "I was an employee. That's what it was. It was not a collaborative thing. I totally understand that now."

On this date, Prince may have overdubbed his own lead vocal, likely changing the title of the song from "Too Tough" to "Rough."

Status: The songs were not included on *The Family* album, but Paul and Susannah Melvoin reportedly added their voices to "Rough" (5:35), and the 6-minute "I Don't Wanna Stop" on a later date. Both were also early candidates for Jill Jones's album, but they were removed and remain unreleased.

Note: It is possible that some of this work was done on the previous day.

SUNDAY, MARCH 17, 1985

Venue: Nassau Veterans Memorial Coliseum (Uniondale, New York)
Capacity: 16,700 (sold out)

Tonight was the first of seven shows in New York. Once again, reviews were positive with *Newsday* calling it "exhilarating" and comparing Prince to James Brown, Jackie Wilson, and Jimi Hendrix. The critic also spotlighted Wendy's performance as "muscular, passionate and soaring."[3]

MONDAY, MARCH 18, 1985

Venue: Nassau Veterans Memorial Coliseum (Uniondale, New York)
Capacity: 16,700 (sold out)

You'd finish the "load-in" day, do a show that night, and the next day he'd be thinking, well my gear is already set up at the Nassau Coliseum! I used to often call it the fire drill. If the phone rang before noon, he wanted everybody down at the gig by two. So, he could record, rehearse, lighting cues. Don't forget, he was recording every show on a VHS tape, audio and lighting. He'd go in, house lights would be off, and the band would be on stage and they'd be performing. He'd be out there calling lighting cues, and they'd be touching up lighting stuff. That was the only time to be able to do that. Same thing with the band parts and listening to the mix. Then, when he got tired of doing that, he'd come up on stage and jam, and we'd finish up by five.

—Robert "Cubby" Colby

After the show, Prince and everyone had a day off. It is unclear if any recording took place, although it is possible that additional work was done on "Rough" and "I Don't Wanna Stop" for the Family.

WEDNESDAY, MARCH 20, 1985 (A.M.)

Venue: Lehman College Center for the Performing Arts (New York, New York)
Capacity: 2,300

This is the fifth concert like this on this tour, and quite frankly, they have not been publicized because they are closed affairs. He happens to get gratification out of playing for people who might not ever be able to attend a rock concert.[4]

—Alan Leeds

Four days earlier, the local Board of Education had asked Prince to perform a benefit show for children in need, so Prince and the Revolution, Sheila E., Eric Leeds, and others put on a matinee concert for more than two thousand deaf, blind, and other special needs children at Lehman College's Center for the Performing Arts in the Bronx. They were bussed in from public and private schools as well as various United Cerebral Palsy centers around the city to watch the performance. Two rows of seats were removed to give better access for wheelchairs and multiple children were carried to their seats. As before, sign language interpreters were signing the lyrics from both sides of the stage because Prince wanted to make sure that everyone enjoyed the show, regardless of the person's ability to see or hear him. "I felt the vibrations,"[5] said 20-year-old Christopher Buckland, a deaf student who reportedly enjoyed the show. It was his first rock concert.

"Some of them have never attended anything like it," said the tour's production designer Roy Bennett. "That's why Prince does it."[6]

During the "Baby I'm A Star" encore, Prince hugged many of the children who were brought on stage. "These shows give us energy," explained Doug Henders, who videotaped several concerts on the tour for Prince. "It's the spirit of giving, which is pretty rare."[7]

Prince also paid for a generator to compensate for the auditorium's much weaker electric system and covered the cost for over a dozen extra crew members to help set up the light and sound system. "It was a full arena show in a concert hall," proudly explained Jane Salodof of Lehman College.[8]

"I was never rich, so I have very little regard for money now," reasoned Prince. **"I only have respect for it inasmuch as it can feed somebody. I can give a lot of things away, a lot of presents and money. Money is best spent**

67

on somebody who needs it. That's all I'm going to say. I don't like to make a big deal about the things I do that way."[9]

The concert contained two then-unreleased songs: "4 The Tears In Your Eyes" and an instrumental interpolation of the Family's upcoming song "High Fashion."

WEDNESDAY, MARCH 20, 1985

Venue: Nassau Veterans Memorial Coliseum (Uniondale, New York)
Capacity: 16,700 (sold out)

> *I don't envy anyone's lifestyle. I'm happy with my situation. I would like to be Prince one night . . . but just one night because he's 5 foot 2.*[10]
>
> —Eddie Murphy

Prince opened the show with a rare appearance of "17 Days." Eddie Murphy reportedly joined Prince onstage during the "Baby I'm A Star" encore jam. He was also joined by "St. Paul" Peterson. "Prince used to call for me to come out and hang out on the *Purple Rain* tour," remembers Peterson, "and he would have me sit in on 'Baby I'm A Star,' and take a solo on the end."

FRIDAY, MARCH 22, 1985

Venue: Nassau Veterans Memorial Coliseum (Uniondale, New York)
Capacity: 16,700 (sold out)

SATURDAY, MARCH 23, 1985

Venue: Nassau Veterans Memorial Coliseum (Uniondale, New York)
Capacity: 16,700 (sold out)

*Our soundchecks were three hours of pure hell! You'd get off a
tour bus, and he just wants to jam from 4 p.m. to 7:30, when
the doors open. Sometimes people were coming in and we had to
quit, as the audience were rushing towards the stage.*[11]

—BrownMark

During the soundcheck, Prince and the Revolution jammed on an instrumental
version of "100 MPH," which he'd eventually give to Mazarati.

Prince continued to alter the show. He added "Take Me With U," which
included bits of "All The Critics Love U In New York," "Raspberry Beret,"
"Head," "America," and a few verses of the then-unreleased "Condition Of
The Heart."

SUNDAY, MARCH 24, 1985

Venue: Nassau Veterans Memorial Coliseum (Uniondale, New York)
Capacity: 16,700 (sold out)

Once again, Prince began the show with "17 Days," for at least the third time
he'd done that during the tour.

MONDAY, MARCH 25, 1985

"Jerk Out" (transfer)
song idea (mix)
Sunset Sound, Studio 1 (likely) | afternoon session
Producer: Prince | Artist: Prince | Engineer: unknown

*He knew I was trying to keep [Mazarati] a secret from him,
because I just didn't know how he would respond to it. . . . But
he actually said, "Let me help you with it." So that's where it
came about.*

—BrownMark

With the void generated from the Time breaking up in 1984, Prince had created the Family, but he also expressed interest in a band that BrownMark had previously been secretly working with, Mazarati. "I always wanted to do rock music," discloses Mark, "and Prince didn't really do rock and I really wanted to do a rock band, so I figured since I can't do it, I'll live it through someone else. I pulled a couple of my high school buddies together and rehearsed them at my house for about a year and half. Kept them in secret, didn't tell anybody, and then, we did a show at the Cabooze [in Minneapolis]. We sold out their first gig just by word of mouth. It was pretty amazing, that's when I knew I had something."

Minneapolis isn't like Los Angeles or New York where you can be anonymous, if needed. Many of the local bandmembers in the Twin Cities had shifted between groups over time so there was an incestuous knowledge about the music scene and Prince was someone with his ear to the ground looking for new local talent to potentially hire and shape their careers with his ideas and music. "After the Time self-destructed, he needed someone to take the place of the Time, so I think Mazarati was it," according to Mazarati guitar player Tony Christian. "We played at the [Minnesota Black Music Awards] with the Time in 1984, and I guess we blew the Time away."[12]

The band was quickly signed to his new Paisley Park label and like almost every example involving Prince's side projects, this was based in two things: Prince's overwhelming passion for having an outside venue for his music and Prince's need to control. He had been going through his archives looking for music that would best fit Mazarati and had already discussed songs like "100 MPH" with the band, so while he was in town he had "Jerk Out" pulled for them. "Jerk Out" was an older track—originally recorded on 16-track and intended for the Time—but he apparently felt that it would work for Mazarati as well. Prince and the Revolution had been jamming on the song the previous month in Daly City during the soundchecks before the Cow Palace shows. BrownMark disagreed about the song being a good fit for Mazarati. "We didn't like it. That was one of the ones he just handed down."

On the other hand, Prince also wanted Mazarati to record their album under his watchful eye, which seemed perfect, according to Mark. "It was good because I was still a beginner, I never produced, I never did anything before, so Mazarati was like my first experience with actual production."

"David Z" Rivkin would be brought on to help oversee the upcoming April sessions, but he recognized that Prince would be contributing to their sound and image as well as pushing some of his own tracks on the band. "It was mainly

BrownMark's project, but Prince wanted to make sure there were some hits on there."[13]

While in the studio, Prince also recorded a new song idea, but there are no details about it available.

Status: "Jerk Out" (7:08) would be worked on by Mazarati but not released by them. It was eventually repurposed for the Time and released in 1990 on their *Pandemonium* album. The track would reach number 9 on the *Billboard* Hot 100, number 6 on the *Billboard* Hot Dance Disco, and number 1 on the *Billboard* R&B Singles Chart.

MONDAY, MARCH 25, 1985

57th Academy Awards
Venue: Dorothy Chandler Pavilion, Los Angeles, CA

> *This is very unbelievable. I could never imagine this in my wildest dreams. I would like to thank the Academy. Mr. Albert Magnoli, my managers Steven, Bob and Joe, Bobby, Mark and Matt who couldn't be with us today, and most of all, God.*[14]
>
> —Prince

At the Academy Awards presentation in Los Angeles, Prince won his first and only Oscar for "Best Original Song Score" for *Purple Rain.* In contrast to his passionate performance at the Grammys the previous month, he didn't perform and quietly addressed the crowd after he received the statue. Even the *Hollywood Reporter* noted that the "flamboyant singer made an unusually subdued appearance to accept his prize."[15]

There were many people involved, but Prince was the artist who had created *Purple Rain* and once he won this award there was no denying his genius. He owned the night, but more importantly he earned the respect of his peers and of the general public, so the balance of power with everyone—his record label, his employees, and his management—undeniably shifted toward Prince.

"We knew that we could argue, and we did, and then he would win and that would be that," recognizes his manager Bob Cavallo. "I tell you, as soon as *Purple Rain* was a giant hit, and then he wins a goddamn Oscar, I was no longer a manager. I was an expediter. I was just a guy doing his bidding."

"He was frustrated they were trying to manage him, and he wasn't having it," reveals Susannah. "They were trying to manage him, and you don't manage him. At that point, he was like, 'Nobody should be telling me what I should be doing. They should just be facilitating my needs and my wants.'"

TUESDAY, MARCH 26, 1985

Venue: Hartford Civic Center, (Hartford, Connecticut)
Capacity: ±16,000 (sold out)

"Noon Rendezvous" was played. The show closed with "America" and "When The Saints Go Marching In."

WEDNESDAY, MARCH 27, 1985

Venue: Centrum (Worcester, Massachusetts)
Capacity: 12,073 (sold out)

THURSDAY, MARCH 28, 1985 (A.M.)

Venue: Marriott Inn (Worcester, Massachusetts)
Capacity: (attendance unknown)

After the previous evening's concert, Prince and the band played an hour-long aftershow at the Worcester Marriott Inn, another example of how passionate Prince was about not just creating music, but living it.

THURSDAY, MARCH 28, 1985

Venue: Centrum (Worcester, Massachusetts)
Capacity: 12,073 (sold out)

As Prince prepared for a worldwide live broadcast of his concert coming up in two days, he added a few extra songs into the set, including: "When U Were Mine," "Head," "Still Waiting," "I Wanna Be Your Lover," B. B. King's "I Got Some Help I Don't Need," which has often been referred to as "Blues In G," and "I Feel For You," which had won a Grammy the previous month. He also included "4 The Tears In Your Eyes," once again.

SATURDAY, MARCH 30, 1985

Venue: Carrier Dome (Syracuse, New York)
Capacity: ±40,000 (±35,000 tickets sold)
transmitted live via satellite

> *Nobody lived like him. Nobody had that talent; nobody had that panache. He really was one of a kind. Watch the Syracuse '85 concert video. When you watch him, you realize he's probably the greatest entertainer of all time. Nobody had the songs, the dances, the moves, the look.*[16]
>
> —"Bobby Z" Rivkin

With the tour winding down, and many fans unable to attend the shows, it was decided that a concert video would bring the experience to their homes, and with home video now a rapidly growing market, it made financial sense to do a live worldwide broadcast of the show. It aired live in Europe through the German television show *Rockpalast* on WDR. At this point in his career, Prince had only played three shows in Europe, and with the exception of those who saw the 1981 concerts, this was the first opportunity for his European fans to experience him playing live. Despite it airing in the middle of the night, and transmitting live on the radio in several countries, it attracted a great deal of attention.

Because of the focus this would bring, it appears that Prince wanted everyone who worked with him on hand for the show, so Apollonia, Susan Moonsie and Brenda Bennett were flown in to be part of the encore. "The Syracuse show, we knew it was going to be a different thing," reflects Brenda. "There was definitely a sense of excitement about it, and that this was going to be, not just our usual *Purple Rain* show. It was going to be the *Purple Rain* show. He wasn't nervous, but at the same time he was anxious."

"It was incredible," reminisces Apollonia. "I look back and think we were just these bunch of young kids, having a wonderful time and the world was embracing us. And I kept thinking, 'Man, we really worked hard for this. We really worked hard!'"

Status: This show was slightly reedited and first released on two video cassettes under the name of "Double Live" before being rereleased as *Prince and the Revolution: Live* as a single video cassette as well as a laserdisc. The video was nominated for a Grammy Award in the "Best Music Video, Long Form" category. It did not win.

It would be rereleased as a bonus DVD on the posthumous *Purple Rain* Deluxe collection in 2017.

APRIL 1985

No one was really thinking about a sequel for Purple Rain. *I discussed it with [Prince's manager] Bob Cavallo, but Prince was off already on another album and another movie,* Under The Cherry Moon

—Albert Magnoli

Prince was moving away from every aspect of *Purple Rain*, and the idea of a sequel was likely too close to what he'd already done. Eric Leeds recalls what he was like as an artist and the range of opportunities Prince had created. "Once he got *Purple Rain* behind him, then I think he kind of felt that the handcuffs had been taken off of him. So for the next several years, and particularly right after that, I think he was really open to just say, 'Okay, let me see, where can I go!'"

According to those around him, he felt that he'd mastered the process of making a successful movie and was looking to replicate that experience—film a movie, time in the studio recording for himself and for others, and then tour, but this time he wanted to go in a different direction than *Purple Rain*. "All any of us knew, myself included, was that he wanted to make another movie," remembered Susannah Melvoin during this era. "On what? We don't know yet. And he just started recording songs. And then it started to sort of reveal itself."[1]

Instead of a movie with songs being performed by his band, the music would help set the scene and inspire the mood. Becky Johnston would be hired to develop the screenplay for his second movie, a 1940s' style comedy that would be called *Under The Cherry Moon*.

Convincing Cavallo, Ruffalo, & Fargnoli that this was the right project was important, remembers Susannah. "He was asking management to find the money to support this idea, and they were saying, 'How are we going to pay for this?' And Prince would say, 'I don't know, find it.'"

To make the public aware that Prince was formally ending his current tour and moving on from *Purple Rain*, he had his manager, Steve Fargnoli, release a statement to the press: "Prince is withdrawing from the live performance scene for an indefinite period of time. Prince's concert April 7 at Miami's Orange Bowl will be his last performance for an indeterminate number of years. I asked Prince what he planned to do? He told me, 'I'm going to look for the ladder.' I asked him what that meant. All he said was, 'Sometimes it snows in April.'"

There was speculation that the announcement was done to try and sell out the show in Miami, which holds up to 80,000 people, depending on how the show is staged.

Prince would eventually sell more than 53,000 tickets for the show—an amazing number, but far short of capacity and one of the few concerts on the tour that wasn't sold out.

MONDAY, APRIL 1, 1985

Venue: Market Square Arena (Indianapolis, Indiana)
Capacity: 16,089 (sold out)

The soundcheck for this performance included Prince and the band jamming on several of the songs he'd recorded for the Family.

WEDNESDAY, APRIL 3, 1985

Venue: Leon County Civic Center (Tallahassee, Florida)
Capacity: 12,541 (sold out)

THURSDAY, APRIL 4, 1985

Venue: Lakeland Civic Center (Lakeland, Florida)
Capacity: 9,376 (sold out)

FRIDAY, APRIL 5, 1985

Venue: Lakeland Civic Center (Lakeland, Florida)
Capacity: 9,376 (sold out)

SUNDAY, APRIL 7, 1985

Venue: Orange Bowl (Miami, Florida)
Capacity: 75,500 (53,083 attended)

> *I don't think you can go through anything together like the*
> Purple Rain *tour or that movie without feeling like you're in*
> *some kind of special club. The five of us are battle-tested Prince*
> *warriors.*[2]

—"Bobby Z" Rivkin

Prince traditionally ended his tours somewhere between March and early May, so scheduling the last performance for April 7 at Miami's Orange Bowl (or "Purple Bowl" as printed on the tickets) was not surprising. What was unexpected was that the tour was concluding on Easter Sunday, which upset some of the religious leaders in Florida who protested the event and wanted the concert rescheduled or called off completely. "City officials refused their petition to cancel our permits, so they were limited to picketing outside the stadium," Alan Leeds explained. "Nobody paid them any attention, nothing was about to break our purple Easter egg!"[3]

Prince and the band ignored the threats from the protesters and jammed for the tour's final soundcheck, running through known songs like "Erotic City," "Something In The Water (Does Not Compute)," "17 Days," James

Brown's "Bodyheat," B.B. King's "I Got Some Help I Don't Need" (referred to as "Blues in G"), and by then-unreleased numbers "Strange Relationship," "The Ladder," and "High Fashion." There were several loose jams as well as the soundcheck staple "Controversy," which was blended with the as-yet-unreleased track "Mutiny."

Prince started the show wishing everyone a happy Easter and followed it with "**My name is Prince, and I've come to play with you**" one last time. He'd started the first show in Detroit almost exactly 5 months earlier with practically the same introduction, but during that time, the set list evolved to reflect more of his newer music. The concert was preceded by the as-yet-unreleased "4 The Tears In Your Eyes" played on the PA and "Temptation," which was introduced as being "from the new album *Around The World In A Day*." But it wasn't just the tour that had changed; so had Prince's focus. This show was an ending, and a new beginning into uncharted fame with a blank sheet of paper to fill.

The Orange Bowl was the first outdoor venue of this tour, so everyone was on edge because of the rain that had been drenching the area, and the grey overcast sky that threatened to cause further problems, as Alan Leeds recalled.

> The clouds quickly gave way to a gorgeous evening, but the damp grounds threw us an unexpected curveball. Around the middle of the show production manager Tom Marzullo excitedly grabbed me and said, "We gotta cut the encore short tonight. He can't stay out there much longer." I assumed Tom was worried about a possible curfew violation, so I cut him short and snapped, "I don't care what it costs. Let him play all night!" Then he pointed to the legs of the stage, braced by a labyrinth of steel. The wet, soft ground was slowly swallowing up the sinking stage like it was quicksand. Worse yet, one side of the huge stage was sinking faster than the other so things were getting a bit uneven on deck. We nervously finished the show. But, in the end, it can be said that the seemingly never-ending *Purple Rain* tour was relegated to unceremoniously sinking away.[4]

After the show, Prince wanted a clean break from *Purple Rain*, including his look, and he suggested to Sheila that they both cut their hair. She left him to have hers trimmed and returned to compare styles. "I went to his room, and when he opened the door, I saw he cut only a little bit of his hair, and I chopped my hair off to my neck."[5]

"The hairstyles always tipped us off," reflected BrownMark. "When the hairstyles changed, you knew something was coming. And then the clothes changed."[6]

The end of the tour likely brought some relief to Prince according to Eric Leeds. "Prince had a bad day every day of that tour because he was scared shit-less because all of a sudden, everything he had ever hoped and dreamed for, had just happened. And there was a big part of Prince that could never get past, 'Is this all there is?' And the other thing was, he said, 'Now what?'"

The tour was over, and everything associated with *Purple Rain* was being dismantled and banished to the past. With the new album coming out, Prince could have taken time off the road for a short period and blended the *Purple Rain* tour into an *Around The World In A Day* world tour, which would have helped sell the record and maintained his presence in the market, but Prince decided that he'd finished everything involving *Purple Rain*. "I don't think he ever liked to look back," explains Lisa. "Whether that was the wounded child or whatever it was, he was going to say, 'Fuck you,' to the past, as everything was only yet to come."

He was finished with *Purple Rain*, but before he'd even released the follow-up album, he leapfrogged over it and was already making plans for his next project. Prince still maintained that there would be a two-year hiatus, but the break was away from live performances, not making music, as Matt Fink recalls. "He didn't fulfill his promise of taking the two-year break, and he called us up and said, 'Well, I need you in the studio,' and he started working on the *Parade* album."

Prince wasn't the only one drained from his time away from home. Sheila—who had been in months of rehearsals and on the road before the *Purple Rain* tour started in November of 1984—had worked hard as his opening act, and during their travels they'd recorded her second album.

Unfortunately for Sheila, she didn't get the opportunity to enjoy the financial gains from her 100+ shows. "I'd been working flat out for well over a year on the biggest tour in the world. So, it came as the most dreadful, terrible shock when Prince's account managers told me that I was a million dollars in debt."[7]

"It turns out that every time people told me, 'Sure, we'll fix that for you,' my account had been charged. I'd been so naïve. I thought all the expenses for costumes and hair, equipment and staff would be covered by Prince and his team as part of the tour—as they had been on my previous tours with Lionel and Marvin. I had no idea I was expected to pay for it all myself."[8]

Despite, or maybe because of, sharing managers with Prince, Sheila had assumed that she, like Prince, would also reap in the windfall from the tour and that their managers would make sure her tour expenses were covered. "I felt like such a fool. I spent years paying back what I owed. This meant that, whether

I wanted to or not, I'd have to carry on working at that level and that pace for some time to come. Creatively and personally, that was a bitter pill to swallow."[9]

Prince's organization had previously negotiated the same financial control over Morris Day when he was touring with the Time, and his debt after the tour added to the resentment that destroyed his band. Sheila was someone who was as motivated as Prince, but this situation could potentially put their relationship to the test.

When it came to finances, members of the Revolution were also confused about how he showed his appreciation financially, recalls Lisa. "We had just gone through the whole thing with the *Purple Rain* tour, and we could tell, 'Okay this is making bazillions of dollars,' and at the end of the tour he gave us a bonus check, and it was for $10,000. We didn't know what to say. We were just gobsmacked. He made a big deal about it and presented us with the checks and everything. 'What do you think?' Like, 'Thanks.'"

BrownMark felt a similar frustration at the end of the tour. "He looked at me and said, 'You will never work another day in your life after this tour.' He said that to my face." But when he was given an amount similar to Wendy and Lisa, his pain came to the surface. "Everybody was unhappy; everybody was in such shock after that bonus. It was the beginning of the end, because it was an insult. We felt cheated. That's when I made my move."

Over the next few weeks, BrownMark would weigh the options of continuing to work for Prince.

THURSDAY, APRIL 11, 1985

Prince was always about what was happening now, but just as important was what was happening next. Next tour, next song, next project, next look. It kept him vital and kept others from catching up to him. A trip to Brazil was planned with Prince, Jerome Benton, Steve Fargnoli, Alan Leeds, and several of Prince's bodyguards to relax with a stay at the *Cesar Park Hotel on Copacabana Beach*, but even before the trip, Jerome recalled that Prince was already busy planning the next year and he explained it to him as the tour wound down. "We're going to do this movie. I'm writing this movie," Prince told Benton. "This is what we need to do. We're going to travel. We're going to Rio de Janeiro. We're going to go there and spend about seven days there.' 'Oh, really? What do I need?' 'A passport, that's all you need'"[10]

On the first day of the vacation, practically everyone in the group wanted to relax on the beach and when Prince finally decided to join them, he was wearing silk pajamas and high heel boots, as Alan Leeds recalled. "We ignored the pj's and said, 'Prince, you can't go down there in boots. You'll twist an ankle in the sand.' Rande [Rande Laiderman, Prince's chef] then pulled out sandals and various beachwear she had bought him for the occasion. He looked at it and turned up his nose. 'I'm supposed to look like this?' Rather than try to convince him he'd be okay on a beach in shorts, T-shirt and sandals, I chose another approach. 'You don't want to be recognized and spoil the chance at some fun, so for once dress to blend in with us regular folk.' He reluctantly bought it. Trunks and t-shirt went on under his clothes, all except the sandals.

According to Alan Leeds, Prince was completely out of his element.

So, we went trudging through the lobby and across the street where he dejectedly swapped his boots for flip flops before stepping in the sand. We had picked up a bunch of body boards and Jerome and Wally were already off eagerly riding waves. After about fifteen minutes of sitting around ("Do I need sunscreen on all my exposed areas?"), Prince finally asked about the water. Would the salt hurt his eyes? Were the waves safe? Suddenly I got it. He had never been to a beach . . . at least not an ocean! He had reverted to a little boy, intimidated by nature's vastness (not to mention petrified at the prospect of being viewed as an ill at ease novice). I didn't say a word, just led the way. I grabbed a board and dove headfirst into the robust waves. He hesitated . . . went in gingerly. Then the man took over from the boy and he got bolder. Long and short of it is that it turned out he was a decent swimmer and he had a ball. At the end of the day, he was the last one out of the water.

The next morning, he knocked on my door surprisingly early and asked what we had planned. I told him we could spend the morning back at the beach and then do some sight-seeing. He curtly said, "We did that already. Can we get a flight back home?"[11]

His friend, "David Z" Rivkin, remembers Prince's rapid turnaround. "He'd said he was going to Rio and like three or four days later I'm standing in the club in downtown Minneapolis and all of a sudden he's standing right there, and I went, 'I thought you went to Rio?' And he says, 'I got bored.' In three days? What do you mean you got bored? I laughed my ass off like crazy."

FRIDAY, APRIL 12, 1985

USA For Africa's *We Are The World* album, which included Prince's "4 The Tears In Your Eyes," was released, and the album quickly reached the top of the *Billboard* chart.

～

Back home from Rio, Prince once again reached out to Susannah Melvoin. Their relationship had stopped during the *Purple Rain* tour, but she was still working for him. "I'd been in Minneapolis rehearsing with the Family and he and I weren't speaking." Eventually, she and Prince reconnected, and they became an item again.

The dynamics of Prince dating Wendy's twin were always going to be potentially problematic, and Wendy recognized this even before the start of *Purple Rain*. "I knew that he was romancing her. I took him outside at Sunset Sound and I said, 'I just want you to understand something. We're twins and if you get involved with one, you get involved with the other so please don't hurt us. It would really be bad. I'm always going to choose her. Always.'"

Prince had been maintaining a relationship with Devin Devasquez through the last several months of the tour, but he eventually broke it off with her when she called his home. "He said, 'Devin, I'm sorry I can't see you anymore because I live with someone,'" recalls Devasquez. "And I went, 'What?' It was kind of a shock. I didn't really know there was another one in the picture because he called me so much. So I said, 'Okay, I understand.' And I hung up, very confused because I had such a beautiful relationship with him."

Devasquez would remain close to him, escorting Prince's father to concerts and the premiere of *Under The Cherry Moon*. Prince had her sign with Cavallo, Ruffalo, & Fargnoli to help her with her career, which also kept her close to him.

MONDAY, APRIL 15, 1985

"**Feel U Up**" (mix)
"**Feel U Up**" [instrumental] (mix)
"**Tick, Tick, Bang**" (mix)
Sunset Sound, Studio 3 | unknown time (booked: lockout)
Producer: Prince | Artist: Prince | Engineers: "Peggy Mac" Leonard and
    Coke Johnson

[Prince] was pulled in a million directions. He didn't stop recording, and he had so many different projects. He was consumed with being a superstar.[12]

—"Bobby Z" Rivkin

Prince returned to Los Angeles and immediately went back to work on his first session after the tour, creating new mixes on two songs from his vault. "He knew how he wanted it to sound," recalls Sunset Sound staff engineer Coke Johnson. "If he brought a tape in, I'd spend about an hour, hour and a half listening to it, hooking up compressors, EQing it, getting a good quality mix for what we had on tape. Then, he would come in and listen."

Johnson remembers Prince's increased air of confidence as he arrived. "When he came walking into the studio, there was definitely a swagger. He had a tan trench coat and his Ray-Bans on. He was looking above me as he was walking in, but he wouldn't make eye contact. He held his chin up, held his head high and walked right past, kind of strutting. You know how his walk is. He just kind of strutted right past everybody and went into the studio."

On this day, he was likely auditioning the songs for a future project, but also auditioning Coke Johnson as his engineer. Mixes for the unreleased 1981 tracks "Tick, Tick, Bang" and "Feel U Up" (as well as an instrumental version of "Feel U Up") were created.

"He would do instrumental versions of a song for a number of reasons," explains Susan Rogers. "He might be contemplating having someone else do the lead vocal on it. A song may be for the Family or maybe it'll be for Jill [Jones] or something like that. Also, the instrumental mixes were necessary if you're going to do a dance mix, if you're going to do a 12-inch. Occasionally, I know a label would ask you for those instrumental mixes, so you just get in the habit of doing them."

Apparently, the session was considered a success and Coke was brought aboard to work with Prince on a regular basis.

Status: The early version of "Feel U Up" (6:35) remained in the vault until it was issued posthumously (in a blended form with "Irresistible Bitch" that was created by Prince) in 2019 on the *1999* Super Deluxe Edition. Prince eventually re-recorded "Feel U Up" in 1986. "Tick, Tick, Bang" (3:08) would also be re-recorded and included on the *Graffiti Bridge* soundtrack in 1990.

TUESDAY, APRIL 16, 1985

"Lemon Cake" [jam that featured elements from **"New Position"**] (tracking, overdubs)
untitled instrumental (tracking, mix)
"Life Can Be So Nice" (tracking, mix)
The Family album (mix with Clare Fischer orchestra)
Sunset Sound, Studio 3 | unknown time (booked: lockout)
Producer: Prince | Artist: Prince | Engineers: "Peggy Mac" Leonard, Coke Johnson, and Susan Rogers

> *I was told to pack for LA. I said, "How long do you think I will be gone?" They said, "Oh, three weeks." I packed for three weeks and I was out there for six months. He was very excited to start the* Parade *album. He had his techs, he had everybody he needed, he had Peggy, he had me. We were all ready to go.*[13]

—Susan Rogers

The period of rest was over and the two-year period of renewal that Prince had told everyone to expect was gone. As soon as he grew bored, he changed his mind, and everyone was expected to turn on a dime. "In hindsight," Bobby Z reflected, "it was fatigue talking."[14]

Once again Prince came home to Sunset Sound, and his favorite room, Studio 3, to work on some of the songs he had been piecing together during the tour. "It was a big enough room that we could have everything set up all at once," Rogers explained. "The piano could always be mic'd, the B-3 organ could be mic'd and ready and go, drum kit could be set up and ready to go, and he would have his keyboard, bass, and guitars with him in the control room."[15]

In the studio, an engineer spends more time alone with an artist than almost anyone, especially with a performer like Prince who has the ability to record everything on his own. Someone like Peggy Leonard, who had a history of months of nonstop grueling 18-hour days, had noticed subtle changes in Prince after the tour. "I could tell his passion was waning. I felt like maybe he had caught up to the rest of us and gotten tired. People change, they mature, I thought he was maturing, and I just thought maybe he was growing up a little bit and settling down with the rest of us a little. He was changing, he was growing."

"That was the most meaningful era, his most significant songwriting. He had a different command of himself. He was turning into more of a man," agreed Wendy.[16]

The session started off with Prince warming back up with Wendy on guitar, Lisa on the Yamaha DX7, and Sheila E. on drums. Prince played guitar and sang, but the jam was reportedly more of an exercise in fun instead of a true song, including Prince talking to others in the room. "I do remember that. I think he might have yelled my name out in 'Lemon Cake,'" laughs Johnson. The music was rumored to contain elements of "New Position," a track he'd record during the next week.

The title that he gave to the jam was likely based on a variety of different elements. Prince had a serious sweet tooth and enjoyed lemon cake, specifically if it was made by his lighting director Roy Bennett. "All the lemon cake thing was based on our connection and love and respect for each other," reflects Bennett. "It was like everything we shared together. The more I think about my life with Prince and what he had with others, I realize he and I had a very distinct relationship. Beyond the band and girlfriends. We were a team."

He also enjoyed the lemon cake from Greenblatt's Deli on Sunset (not far from Sunset Sound) or made by Sheila E. as she explained to *Billboard* magazine in 2020. "One day I mentioned to him that I make a good chocolate and lemon cake. His response was, 'Oh, I didn't know you cooked.' I said, 'Of course I do. The next day I baked a lemon cake. It was love at first sight and one of his favorite things that we would share in the studio."[17]

The busy session continued with Prince working on another brief instrumental and then shifting his focus when the elements from Clare Fischer's orchestration of *The Family* album were delivered to the studio.

When the updated mixes were eventually played for members of the Family, it was obvious that this took their music in a new direction, recalls singer Paul Peterson.

> It spoke right to my heart because I grew up playing Be-bop, but all those superimposed harmonies over the one chord wonder were way beyond anything Bach would necessarily allow. And I was blown away, especially how they mixed it. Because they ripped a bunch of stuff out to feature that. Instead of hiding it because it didn't necessarily always jive with stuff that was going on, they took that off and featured it, which was brilliant. Whether that was Prince, or David Z, I'm not sure because I wasn't there when they were mixing it, but David's brilliant.

With the session likely continuing into the next morning, Prince aggressively pushed for more from everyone around him, according to Susan Rogers. "We worked incredibly long hours on [*Parade*] and we had a great time. I remember one marathon session when we went twenty-four hours and early the next morning, at about nine o'clock in the morning we were ready to go home and then he said: 'Fresh tape!' So, we put up a fresh tape."[18] The song was "Life Can Be So Nice," which included input from Sheila, Lisa, and Wendy.

"'Life Can Be So Nice' was a thing we did together at Sunset Sound," recalls Wendy. "I remember the drum that was Lisa and him with these weird little ideas and then we needed to get some flavor with the acoustic and I was like, 'Why don't we try a Brazilian rhythm there with an acoustic guitar?' And so that laid sort of like a weird foundation and then started, I put a bassline on it. . . . I don't know if he kept it, he might've redone it, but I remember playing the bass and guitars."

Status: Sheila E. released a song called "Lemon Cake" in April of 2020, but it has nothing in common with the "Lemon Cake" jam, which remains on the shelf. "Life Can Be So Nice" (3:12) would be embellished in future sessions. A slightly edited version (3:14) would be included on Prince's 1986 album, *Parade.*

Clare Fischer would add an arrangement to "Life Can Be So Nice" on July 3, 1985. Fischer continued his arrangement beyond the track that had been provided, giving Prince the option to extend the duration of the track or continue to use the abrupt ending.

The Family's self-titled album was released on August 12, 1985, in the United Kingdom, and a week later in the United States.

WEDNESDAY, APRIL 17, 1985

"Christopher Tracy's Parade" [listed as **"Wendy's Parade"**] (tracking, over-dubs, mix)
"New Position" [not listed] (tracking, overdubs, mix)
"I Wonder U" [not listed] (tracking, overdubs, mix)
"Under The Cherry Moon" (tracking, overdubs, mix)
Sunset Sound, Studio 3 | 4 p.m.–1:30 a.m. (booked: lockout)
Producer: Prince | Artist: Prince | Engineers: "Peggy Mac" Leonard and Susan Rogers

We had completely settled in with everything during that time. It was great music and it just went so smoothly. That was one of those incredible times when he would sometimes just say, "Don't stop the tape," and he would just start playing.

—"Peggy Mac" Leonard

After a few days, Prince was once again back in the studio state of mind, and Peggy Mac and Susan Rogers were prepared to record his next song and follow his new focus, the soundtrack album to his next movie. "That album was one instance where he did have a vision in mind and we knew this album was starting," Rogers recalled. "And in my experience with him, that was the only one where, okay, we're making an album now. He had just come back from Rio, [and] he came home very inspired."[19]

Susan remembered that there was a difference in the way Prince recorded the songs on this date. Instead of laying down a drum track for an individual song and then overdubbing it until the number was complete, as he'd always done, he made an odd request when he arrived at 4 p.m.:

> He said, "Put up a roll of tape. I'm gonna start playing drums, and when I stop, don't stop the tape. Just keep going, just let it roll." We didn't know what he was gonna do. He sat down behind the drum set and taped his lyrics up on a music stand in front of him, we pressed "record" on the tape machine, and he played the entire drum track to "Christopher Tracy's Parade." Then he played the drum track to "New Position," then he played the drum track to "I Wonder U." Then he played the drum track to "Under The Cherry Moon." Four drum tracks in a row, all first takes. When one would stop, he'd wait a few seconds and then start the other one. And then the tape ran out. Then he came back in and he said, "Alright, here we go! Where is my bass?"
>
> Over the next several hours he added bass, keyboards and other musical elements and then his vocals, bringing each song to life. Blending new songs with pieces of tracks he'd been crafting; he created a beautiful suite of music. What had started in his head was now taking shape with each of the tracks getting a distinct personality and sound even though he'd visualized this entire 4 song, 10-minute sequence all in one piece.[20]

"Susan and I both were just amazed at that," explains Peggy, "for the tempo of one song to melt into the next one, with the space in between, it was perfect. I remember Susan and I sitting in the car listening to the mixes going, 'Oh my God, that's incredible.' We thought this was gonna be some kind of magical album."

"Eventually we did have to cut the tape and we did have to treat them as individual songs," reflected Rogers. "It was really exciting, but it was the only time he ever did that."[21]

Prince was dabbling in some of the sounds of those who came before him ("Under The Cherry Moon" appears to be slightly influenced by Sly and the Family Stone's "Just Like A Baby" from 1971), but still paving new experimental ground with what he could squeeze out of the Fairlight CMI keyboard for this. Prince asked "Cubby" Colby about the keyboard and the story is a prime example of how those around him worked hard to make Prince's work as smooth as possible. "I didn't know what a Fairlight was, somebody else told me what it was. 'My God, it's a $70,000 keyboard!' Well, he wants one, so okay, I found one."

The session ended at 1:30 a.m. and a quick mix was completed, although it is likely that "I Wonder U" and "Under The Cherry Moon" may not have contained lyrics at this point. It appears that no cassettes were made.

The first track was originally called "Wendy's Parade" despite the fact that she was likely not in the studio during the basic tracking of this song. When Wendy heard it, she was pleasantly surprised. "I thought, 'Oh, he's just kind of trying to highlight me right now. It's cute. Okay! Let's go with this.'"

"He was delighted with Wendy and her performance and what she added to his band," observed Susan. "He couldn't have been happier. He was bringing her further and further up the pedestal to join him, to stand beside him."[22]

Status: "Wendy's Parade" (2:10) would be released as "Christopher Tracy's Parade" (2:10) on *Parade.* "New Position" (2:20), which borrowed the title, but nothing else, from a song recorded by Prince for Vanity 6 in 1982, "I Wonder U" (1:37), and "Under The Cherry Moon" (2:57) would also wind up on the album, the latter being the title of Prince's second movie.

Note: According to Todd Herreman, who was Prince's Fairlight keyboard technician during this era, "The Fairlight IIx that Prince bought—that version retailed for $36k US. It was the Series III (the late 1986 to early 1990's) that was a new-from-the-ground-up beast that was up to 16 audio channels, with up to 100k sample rate, that went for $70-100k depending on the configuration."

THURSDAY, APRIL 18, 1985

"**Christopher Tracy's Parade**" [listed as "**Wendy's Parade**"] (overdubs)
"**New Position**" [not listed] (overdubs)
"**I Wonder U**" [not listed] (overdubs, including vocals)
"**Under The Cherry Moon**" [not listed] (overdubs, including vocals)
Sunset Sound, Studio 3 | 5 p.m.–11 p.m. (booked: lockout)
Producer: Prince | Artist: Prince | Engineers: "Peggy Mac" Leonard and Susan Rogers

That was the first time that he was wearing big necklaces and I can hear when he's playing the drums on "Under The Cherry Moon." I can hear his necklace rattling. He was experimenting with a new haircut at that time too. His hair was very straight cut, like kind of a page boy and he had a Chinese looking suit. He was changing his look once again.[23]

—Susan Rogers

When Prince was creating a new album, he'd often change his look, but that was generally accompanied by a change in his sound. For this new project, he was also changing his own rules about his vocals. During this session he brought in Wendy and Lisa, as he often did, but for the first time he blended his own vocals completely with Wendy's. He was obviously enamored with her sound and eventually eliminated his own voice from the final released version of "I Wonder U," so it featured Wendy's lead vocals exclusively. He'd used the voices of his protégés in the past for their own releases, but "I Wonder U" was the first time he was doing it for one of his own songs, and it was a great example of how much he was trusting Wendy and Lisa and how he was expanding his range. "We were young and came up as one," Wendy explained to *Wax Poetics* magazine. "It's intangible, really, oblique in its way, but we just worked together, lived together, were together."[24]

"[Wendy] was the perfect complement to him," revealed Lisa. "She had what Prince had, but with a little different version, so it was almost like me on piano. We shared a lot in common, but then there was a lot that was different that we could teach each other. And that's what we did. The three of us hung out all of the time. It was music, music, music."[25]

Even during his life outside the studio, music was at the front of his mind and simple conversations could influence a song, and his understanding of how music works could create something unexpected. "He could take one of those songs, and turn that shit into a hit. Here's an example. In Rio de Janeiro, someone gave him a note and it was talking about how much she admired him and it was written in broken English," recalled Jerome Benton. "I remember her standing there and her broken English saying, 'I wonder, I wonder.' The lyrics in the song are exactly what the letter said. 'I wonder you, you're on my mind, for all times.' It's crazy."[26]

During this session, Wendy and Lisa helped Prince with the overdubs to these tracks, adding background vocals, Yamaha DX7 and Fairlight keyboards, piano, synth flute, and finger cymbals on top of the various sound effects Prince was cleverly placing on his newest songs.

"They brought new chords to him that he would not have thought of," according to Susan Rogers. "They enriched his music deeply and not to mention these beautiful, funny women were just so great to be around. They are two of the most extraordinary people and two of the greatest musicians I have ever heard in my life."[27]

When Prince was excited about something he'd created, he had a child-like joy sharing his music with everyone, especially Wendy and Lisa. "We would do that for each other and there was nobody better than he was at playing you something," remembers Lisa. "He would do this in the control room if he'd play you back a song and play it really loud and then he'd know where to bring down the fader for a second and say something funky, and then put it right back up again and he'd be laughing. He was just really good at that. He liked playing you something."

While Prince's bond with Wendy, Lisa, and Susan Rogers was growing, Prince's relationship with his long-time engineer "Peggy Mac" Leonard was struggling. The unrelenting pace since 1981 and the long hours had taken their toll on her physically and emotionally. "By the time of *Under The Cherry Moon*, I was checked out and I was letting Susan take over, because I was so done. With the intensity of the work and the intensity of the man, it was *too* intense. And I was tired of always trying to read him and not being able to relax even a little bit."

"I love Peggy! She's straight up," explains Jill Jones. "She always was, and she always will be, clearly, because she would snap at him too, like, 'I'm tired!' I'd come in and I'd see Peggy trying to rest in the side room. The TV would be on, and he was doing his vocals alone in the studio. I'd be like, 'He's still in there?' She'd nod and say, 'mm-hmm.' I was like, 'I'm sorry.'"

Peggy would continue working with Prince for the next several months, but the engineering reigns were shifting to Susan Rogers.

THURSDAY, APRIL 18, 1985

"**Jerk Out**" (vocal overdubs)
Sunset Sound, Studio 2 | 2 p.m.–12:30 a.m. (booked: lockout)
Producer: Prince | Artist: Mazarati (but Prince was listed) | Engineers: "David Z" Rivkin and Coke Johnson

*"Jerk Out" was the first song we did, I don't know why it didn't
make it [on the album], but it's just not us.*[28]

—Tony Christian

At the same time that Prince was working on his new album in Studio 3, there
was an album being made for Mazarati in Studio 2 using songs that were being conceived by the band and by Prince's bassist Mark Brown (aka "Brown-
Mark"), as well as tracks that Prince had written and previously recorded. "He
was running back and forth, just like he wanted Paisley Park eventually to be
like. Some people doing this over here and someone else doing this over there,
it's what he always wanted," recalled David Z.[29]

David Z who was not only a Minneapolis recording engineer of note (he engineered "Funkytown" by Lipps Inc.), but he was also the brother of Prince's
drummer "Bobby Z" Rivkin. "Prince called me one day and said, 'Can you
come out to LA for the weekend? I got some stuff for you to do.'"[30] David Z
packed very little and flew to Los Angeles. "When I got there, I went in and saw
Prince in Studio 3, and he told me I would be working in Studio 2 to produce
a new group he had signed [to his Paisley Park label] called Mazarati. Then he
says, 'You'll probably be here about a month.' So, I went out and bought more
clothes."[31]

Although Mazarati was officially recording in Studio 2 and Prince was set up
in Studio 3, there was a very blurred line with Prince overseeing both sessions,
which bothered Peggy. "I felt like our sessions were kind of splintered in that
way, because it kind of lost its momentum. When it got to be like this with the
two studios, it was 'hurry up and wait' and I hate hurry up and wait."

From 2 p.m. to 7 p.m. and then for another 4 and a half hours after their dinner break, David Z worked with Terry Casey and the band members to get the
lead and background vocals (which were blended with Prince's voice), crafting
everything to match the vibe of the band, but more importantly, how Prince
wanted them to be branded. "The concept was cool, basically radical punky
black guys with ripped jeans, doing rock music," explained David Z. "That was
a great concept like a Living Colour kinda thing, way before its time."

The vocal work mirrored what Prince had originally recorded so strictly that
it includes a reference to his former girlfriend and protégée Vanity, who'd left
the Prince camp in 1983.

A quick mix was completed, and the session was over by 1 a.m. A single
C-60 was used for the output.

FRIDAY, APRIL 19, 1985

"**Christopher Tracy's Parade**" [listed as "**Wendy's Parade**"] (overdubs, mix)
"**New Position**" [not listed] (overdubs, mix)
"**I Wonder U**" [not listed] (overdubs, mix)
"**Under The Cherry Moon**" (overdubs, mix)
"**Evolsidog**" [instrumental, listed as "**Untitled track**"] (tracking, overdubs, mix)
"**Others Here With Us**" (tracking, mix)
"**Tibet**" (tracking, mix)
Sunset Sound, Studio 3 | 2 p.m.–2:30 a.m. (booked: lockout)
Producer: Prince | Artist: Prince | Engineer: "Peggy Mac" Leonard |
   Assistant Engineer: Susan Rogers

Prince got a FAIRLIGHT! This was the coolest sampler key-board monster ever! We loved it and it inspired a lot of unique ideas. The type of songs that used sound effects and flutes and orchestral samples, etc. It was a brand-new box of crayons in a preschool with no grown-ups around to tell us not to color on the walls.[32]

—Lisa Coleman

The sheer number of songs Prince could create during a single recording session was staggering. Bands like the Beatles were able to record an album in a few days, at least early in their career, but that was generally based on having rehearsed or performed the tracks until the band was a tight unit. Prince, on the other hand, would often record multiple new songs during a single session. One of the secrets of Prince's prolific legacy was that he was always looking to expand his sound, so he would audition new equipment or new pedals for his guitar. Sometimes he'd try them out and if they were too complicated or didn't feel right, he'd send it back. "**[The instrument I choose] depends on the song, it depends on the color,**" according to Prince. "**They all sound differently. It's very strange, I try to stay original in my work and a lot of sounds have been used now, and I'm looking for new instruments and new sounds and new rhythms.**"[33]

   The basic work during this session involved additional overdubs for the tracks he'd recorded two days earlier. After midnight (or some other time on April 20), Prince continued experimenting with the Fairlight and began recording "Others Here With Us" which was, according to Peggy, "A very strange song." Indeed, the track was one of the more bizarre numbers he'd ever attempted. Using a thick drum beat for a foundation, Prince went wild with the Fairlight sampler, which was still a relatively new toy for him, including many of the samples such as: "Humans2," "Screams5," and "Laf3" for the laughter and "oohs." Near the end of the song, he also used a sample called "Tibet." The result was a haunting, eerie, and layered track, far removed from the upbeat songs that had been so popular on his last album.

When it came to writing the lyrics to his songs, Prince wasn't concerned where he wrote them, remembered Peggy.

> It's funny. He often wrote lyrics on anything that was in the room, including track sheets and napkins. I brought in a legal pad, and he would use that sometimes. But when he was in a rush to get his ideas out, he didn't care what he scribbled on. What's amazing to me is Prince wrote some of the most incredible music I'd ever heard, and the lyrics would be born on an envelope or whatever was handy. But it wasn't the paper; it was the words and music together that always revealed a part of him.[34]

Apparently intrigued with the "Tibet" sample, Prince reportedly built a track around it—with another keyboard patch, and called it—appropriately— "Tibet," but it was supposedly more of an audio experiment instead of an actual song. It is likely that Prince also worked on "Evolsidog"—the title being a backwards spelling of "God is Love." At the end of this session, it was probably still an instrumental based on a steel drum groove he'd played on the Fairlight, similar to the one he'd used on "New Position." The inspiration for the steel drum sound can be traced to a gift from his former girlfriend, Vanity 6/Apollonia 6 member Susan Moonsie. "I went to Trinidad to Carnival because that's where I'm originally from and when I came back I brought him a present, which was a steel drum made by one of the more famous people in Trinidad. I gave it to Prince and he opened this thing up and just started playing it just like that! And I'm like, 'Are you kidding me? You know how to play this thing?' And he looked at me like, you know, 'Duh.' I said, 'I didn't know. I thought you'd have fun just trying to figure it out, but you already know how to play it? Oh, okay, fine. It's *you*.'"

"He was always looking for that next thing to make his music better or make it different and make it *his* thing," continues Moonsie, "and he loved it."

All of the songs were given quick mixes and the session was over at 2:30 in the morning.

Status: The instrumental from this session would eventually evolve into "Evol-sidog." That song and "Others Here With Us" (2:40) were offered as possible songs for Prince's abandoned *Crystal Ball II* project in 2000. Both tracks and the experimental "Tibet" remained unreleased during his lifetime.

In 1986, "Others Here With Us" was considered for use in *The Dawn* film project.

Clare Fischer oversaw the orchestral recording for "Others Here With Us," "I Wonder U," and "Under The Cherry Moon" on June 24, 1985.

On a side note, the Bangles were recording "I Got Nothing" in Sunset Sound's Studio 1 on this date. Prince had no involvement with that track, but within the next few weeks, he'd offer songs to the group for their next album, which would change the course of their career.

Also, "Tibet" and "Others Here With Us" may have been recorded during the session on April 20, if they weren't tracked after midnight on April 19.

FRIDAY, APRIL 19, 1985

> "Jerk Out" (overdubs)
> "100 MPH" (vocal overdubs with David Z)
> Sunset Sound, Studio 2 | 1 p.m.–11 p.m. (booked: lockout)
> Producer: Prince | Artist: Mazarati (listed as Prince) | Engineer: "David Z"
>   Rivkin | Assistant Engineer: Coke Johnson

> *Between the studios was a basketball court. If you leave the doors open while you're playing basketball you could hear what was going on in both studios. He could be working in Studio 3, just walk back to the lounge and stick his head outside and listen to what we were doing over there and make suggestions.*
>
> —Coke Johnson

From 1 p.m. to 5 p.m. Terry Casey recorded vocals to "100 MPH" with David Z overseeing the session. After dinner, additional vocal work was likely done on "Jerk Out." The emphasis on Prince's music would open up the door for the band, but it was moving in a different direction than BrownMark had envisioned. "We were trying to be a rock band. We wanted to do some Aerosmith, we wanted to do some serious rock. We understood that being black that was a bridge that would be hard to cross coming out, so that's why we kinda went with some more rhythmic music and slowly, but surely, the plan was to go more for mainstream rock, that's what it was, Mazarati was a more mainstream rock band."

At the end of the shift, two TDK C-60 tapes were created.

SATURDAY, APRIL 20, 1985

"Old Friends 4 Sale" (tracking, overdubs, mix)
"Life Can Be So Nice" (possible overdubs, mix)
"Cloreen Bacon Skin" (mix)
Sunset Sound, Studio 3 | 12:30 p.m.–8 p.m. (booked: lockout)
Producer: Prince | Artist: Prince and the Revolution | Engineers: "Peggy Mac" Leonard and Susan Rogers

> *This was a very somber, sad day in the studio. It was very personal.*
>
> —"Peggy Mac" Leonard

It is almost impossible to understand this stage of Prince's career without a look at his troubled youth, which many claim shaped his life and relationships. His mother and father separated when Prince was young and he stayed at his mother's home for a period. **"I was at home living with my mother and my sister, and [my father] had just gone and left his piano. He didn't allow anybody to play it when he was there because we would just bang on it. So once he left, then I started doing it because nobody else would."**[35]

Music became his focus and despite showing a dedication to the craft, Prince felt that his mother and stepfather discouraged it. **"I don't think they wanted me to be a musician. But I think it was mainly because of my father, who disliked the idea that he was a musician, and it really broke up their life."**[36] After a series of disagreements, he wasn't able to stay with his mother and had similar results with his aunt and father. **"I was very bitter when I was young. I was insecure and I'd attack anybody. I couldn't keep a girlfriend for two weeks. We'd argue about anything."**[37]

After a severe fight with his father, Prince phoned him and "**begged him to take me back after he kicked me out. He said 'no,' so I called my sister and asked her to ask him. So she did, and afterward told me that all I had to do was call him back, tell him I was sorry, and he'd take me back. So I did, and he still said 'no.' I sat crying at that phone booth for two hours. That's the last time I cried.**"[38]

With no place to go, he ultimately moved in with his friend and future band mate André Anderson (later "André Cymone"). "**André Cymone's house was the last stop after going from my dad's to my aunt's, to different homes and going through just a bunch of junk. And once I got there, I had realized that I was going to have to play according to the program and do exactly what was expected of me.**"[39]

"**When I was sixteen, I was completely broke and needed to get a job,**" he detailed to Arsenio Hall. "**So, I got the Yellow Pages out, and I couldn't find one thing that I wanted to do. So, I decided I was going to push as hard as I could to be a musician, and win at it.**"[40]

"I think music saved him," explained Peggy. "He taught himself to play all these different instruments and music was aching to get out of him for all those years, because it just never stopped."[41]

Prince pushed hard to be the best at everything he did and according to his manager Bob Cavallo, Prince was certain that he'd achieve that. "Of all the talents he had, and they were huge, the one that blew me away the most was his confidence."[42] But underneath that flawless exterior was a man who rehearsed harder than anyone, recorded longer than anyone, and did the work necessary to appear perfect.

"I think growing up like that makes you insecure. He knew, deep down inside, even though nobody wanted him, he knew who he was. But, that's gotta scar you when your mom and your dad kicks you out," reasons Peggy, noting that even in the studio, away from his fans, the image that Prince wanted the world to see was that he was infallible. "I never even saw him trip. He never made a mistake."

Although Prince played it cool for the public, there were a few who were close enough to Prince to know a side of him that was hidden from the world.

At the time, one of the most recognizable of these for Prince was his lead bodyguard, "Big Chick" Huntsberry. Not only was he now a star from his role in *Purple Rain*, but he was also an intimidating presence next to him during the recent award shows. He'd treated Huntsberry's family like his own, giving them birthday presents and enjoying dinner at their home. "He loved mom's spaghetti and meatballs and the chocolate chip cake was a big one," Big Chick's daughter, Rebecca, told *People* magazine in 2016. "He'd call and say, 'Linda can you make me a chocolate chip cake?' And she would say, 'Well sure, honey.'"[43]

When Big Chick quit working as his bodyguard, it was devastating for Prince. Even more damaging was the recent news that he'd sold his story to the *National Enquirer*, supposedly to get money for a cocaine habit as Huntsberry later detailed.

> I was on drugs, bad, but Prince never touched them. He was clean. I couldn't take the pressure. If I wouldn't have been on drugs, I would never have left him. I really had a love for Prince. Not queer or anything, but a son love. It really hurt me when we split up. I started thinking things that were probably not happening. I started thinking he was doing me wrong, which he wasn't. Prince begged me to come back. He called me from New York and said he needed me. I wanted to go back and help him so bad, but because of drugs I didn't. As long as I was doing them, I couldn't even think.[44]

The news of this intimate violation shook Prince to his core and inspired him to write "Old Friends 4 Sale," one of the most personal tracks of his career to date detailing the people who he felt hurt him, as Peggy recalls. "The 'two friends of mine that got stuck in the snow' probably means Jimmy Jam and Terry Lewis because of when they missed the concert [in 1983] because of a snowstorm and were fired by Prince, and the drug references in the song are probably referring to other people that he worked with that had habits like that."

Prince's heartfelt writing exposed his pain about having his trust betrayed for money with lyrics like:

> *The sun set in my mind this evening, 4 someone who said they would die 4 me ... they sold some old pictures and all my little memories. Chump change is 2 unravel the mystery . . .*[45]

"I got to see a vulnerable side that most people don't see," explains Peggy about studio work on days like today. "Everyone on the outside saw a performer. I always just saw this guy, from a very early age. I saw vulnerability, and I saw a talent, and I saw a genius that I could appreciate."

Prince may not have allowed himself to seem vulnerable in life, but in his lyrics, he often expressed a longing that revealed a side he cautiously had hidden from everyone, according to Lisa.

> He sang the part of the lonely person a lot, like "When You Were Mine" or "The Beautiful Ones." Even though he's got the prowess of a "love god," an incredible

kind of fantasy person, at the same time he was a very vulnerable person. Those big brown eyes would kill you. But he struggled with his success. I think it was hard for him to decide when he could just be Prince, the guy, and when he had to become Prince, the superstar. He gave himself so thoroughly to it.[46]

"He wanted to meet people's expectations, but you can't do that with a lot of words," explains Lisa. "The best way to do that is to let them fill in the blanks. So, say as little as possible and then you're off the hook, and then they call you mysterious. Fringe benefits! So he just kind of cashed in on that, I'm scared shitless. He was like a deer in the headlights if anybody talked to him, but that was the real truth."

Prince began building the somber "Old Friends 4 Sale" without the help of any other musicians. "This was all him in the studio," remembers Peggy. "You can tell it was his drumming. It's just his style."

Susan Rogers felt that Prince "was becoming a much better drummer. Working with Sheila influenced him a lot. He felt a lot more confident and became a pretty good drummer. He still liked using the LM-1, but he wanted some other options."[47]

The track ended up being fairly minimal, with the day's mix featuring only drums, bass, and the Fairlight synth. No guitars and nothing flashy, which allows his lead and background vocals to be more penetrating, driving home his pain to the listener. Prince likely also recorded a few overdubs on "Life Can Be So Nice" and shuffled elements from the original, longer jam.

After the quick mixes of the two tracks (and possibly "Cloreen Bacon Skin"), the songs were recorded on four C-60 tapes and the session in this studio was over at 8 p.m., which was earlier than usual for Prince. He then went directly into Studio 2 to record with Mazarati, which was typical of how hard he worked and how much he demanded of others.

Status: The version of "Old Friends 4 Sale" (3:29) from this session remains unreleased, although the vocals were ultimately rewritten and re-recorded, reflecting a different perspective by Prince with some distance from the actual events. The updated track was released in 1999 on *The Vault . . . Old Friends 4 Sale*, an album that Prince would dismiss as a **"contractual obligation"**[48] to Warner Bros. as opposed to one with an artist vision.

Clare Fischer recorded additional orchestration for the track on July 3, 1985.

SATURDAY, APRIL 20, 1985

"Jerk Out" (vocal overdubs with David Z)
"100 MPH" (vocal overdubs with David Z)
"Suzy" [BrownMark demo listed as **"Suzi"**] (tracking, mix)
Sunset Sound, Studio 2 | 1 p.m.–5:30 a.m. (booked: lockout)
Producer: Prince | Artist: Mazarati (listed as Prince) | Engineer: "David Z"
   Rivkin | Assistant Engineer: Coke Johnson

> *[Prince] had a couple of songs he wrote—"100 MPH" and*
> *"Jerk Out"—that he wanted them to do. We just put their*
> *voices on them.*[49]
>
> —"David Z" Rivkin

Prince reportedly joined the session after he finished in Studio 3. Vocal overdubs on "Jerk Out" and "100 MPH" were recorded from 9 p.m. to 2 a.m., but it is unclear how long he stayed for the process. Prince's involvement in "Suzy" is not known.

SUNDAY, APRIL 21, 1985

"Sometimes It Snows In April" (tracking and overdubs)
Parade album [first assembly]
Sunset Sound, Studio 3 | 3 p.m.–10 p.m. (booked: lockout)
Producer: Prince | Artist: Prince | Engineers: "Peggy Mac" Leonard and
   Susan Rogers | Assistant Engineer: Coke Johnson

> *["Sometimes It Snows In April"] was written on the spot and*
> *recorded in a couple of hours. A beautiful moment, hanging out*
> *for a while, recording at Sunset Sound.*[50]
>
> —Wendy Melvoin

Occasionally there is a song that is the perfect reflection of the era in which it was recorded, while other songs gain poignancy over time. Tracks like "When Doves Cry" have the ability to take the listener back to the first time it was played on the radio. To many, it returns them to the summer of 1984 and the feeling of discovery and anticipation of Prince's career: a young talented artist on top of the world with so much potential. On the other hand, songs like "Sometimes It Snows In April" don't find their place in history until forced there by circumstance. This track always held a special place for many fans, but the loss of Prince exactly 31 years after this session added an emotional weight to the track that no one could have predicted, with lines like "Those kind of cars don't pass you every day"[51] making it difficult to hear without reliving the incredible loss. Time allowed the song to mature and reveal a deeper meaning, providing a sonic link back to a younger Prince in the studio, safely exploring his heart with Wendy and Lisa.

"It was a quiet night, and I remember playing the chords," Lisa detailed in 2017, "and when I played those, Prince would always laugh and offer to pay me more money. He'd pretend to reach into his pocket and bring out some dollars. I remember hitting notes, and he turned around and gave me the money sign. That always meant he liked it. And it's just so bizarre to me what that song means to us now. It was April 21 when we wrote it, he died on the same date, and we were writing about a pretend death for a movie [soundtrack]. I'm still processing that whole thing."[52]

"That's the thing about our relationship that I think we helped him explore more is that when we were together, his ballads changed," reflected Wendy.

> By the time *Around The World In A Day* came up through *Sign O' The Times,* I can only speak to my era, his ballads became really beautiful and really more personal. "Sometimes It Snows In April" is a perfect example of that. By the time the three of us were in our room doing that and he started singing those lyrics over these chords we were doing, I could see in him that it allowed him to feel even bigger feelings that weren't overly sexualized or angry or just bratty, which he's the master at. He could explore that side that is brokenhearted in a way that doesn't have a pretense or fakery to it.[53]

Although most of the song was written in the studio, its origin dates back to a number Prince had written before he signed with Warner Bros. The title and chorus remained the same, but the bulk of the song was newly created so it fit into the movie, as Wendy recalls. "He had this song idea, but he looked at me and Lisa and was like, 'Whatcha got? What can you do on it? Let's do something. Just the three of us.' And so, we came up with the riff and started playing it. It came very fast."

With Lisa isolated in the studio playing piano and Prince and Wendy sitting in front of the console, Prince ran them through the number quickly and started recording almost immediately, while they were still working on the details of the song. "As a matter of fact," reveals Wendy, "it came so fast that I was like, 'Prince, I don't like my vocal on that. Can I do it again?' He goes, 'No, it's fine.' And my singing was out of tune."

> Prince had a funny sense of harmonics. On "Sometimes It Snows In April" when we do the change—"Sometimes I wish that life was never ending"—we found the chord, but he couldn't quite find the melody to match. He liked when things sounded ugly. He responded to it because of his ear. He could attach to something that was like, dissonant. But dissonant for me, in all the like, yucky ways. I like things when they rub, but he liked things that were mistakes. It sounds like a mistake and he's like "They're not a mistake if you do it twice."

"'Sometimes It Snows In April' was really the pinnacle of our relationship together [with Prince]," observed Lisa. "The three of us had kind of a love affair. And when we wrote that song, it was just the three of us sitting together in a room. I really loved it, and I had hoped we would follow that trail further. Like make a whole record like that or something. But that didn't happen."[54]

"He opted out," added Wendy.[55]

At some point late in this session, Prince quickly assembled the first pass for his (probably as-yet-untitled) *Parade* album, which included: "Wendy's Parade," "New Position," "I Wonder U," "Under The Cherry Moon," "Others Here With Us," "Sometimes It Snows In April," "Old Friends 4 Sale," and "Life Can Be So Nice." The fact that in less than a week, Prince recorded and assembled a complete album worth of music is astounding. This was likely not an official album compilation but more accurately an assembly of songs so he could hear how they sounded in context. The actual first compilation of the album would take place in early May. Of the songs in the collection, six ended up on the final version of the album, and "Old Friends 4 Sale" was eventually reworked with new lyrics and released. The remaining track, "Others Here With Us," remains unreleased.

Many of the songs were adjusted on the way to the album release with overdubs and orchestral elements, but today's session contained the heart of Prince's work on the album, and it never changed, reflects Peggy Mac. "The only song that was mine that remained unchanged from the original sessions was 'Sometimes It Snows In April,' and the rest were changed."

By 10 p.m., the 7-hour session was over.

Status: "Sometimes It Snows In April" (6:50) was released on *Parade* in March 1986. Clare Fischer recorded the orchestration on July 27, 1985, but his arrangement did not appear on the soundtrack, although 2 minutes and 20 seconds can be heard near the end of *Under The Cherry Moon.*

On March 29, 2004, during his Musicology *tour, Prince played "Sometimes It Snows In April" and dedicated it to Lisa's brother, David, who'd recently passed away.*

MONDAY, APRIL 22, 1985

Around The World In A Day *is a funky album.*[56]

—Prince

Around The World In A Day is released.

You only get to make a first impression once. The majority of Prince fans were new Prince fans and many of them only recognized songs from *Purple Rain* and perhaps *1999*. Where he led them and what he revealed indicated that he was less concerned with making new fans and more committed to showcasing his artistry and seeing if he could bring some of them along.

Alan Leeds explained Prince's mindset at that time. "'Get another record out, show another side, while I've got all those people paying attention to me. The press is following me around when I go to the hairstylist, I can't go across the street without a mob scene.' Like, it was unbelievable, that tour! And it was just part of him that said, 'While I have this enormous impact on people, I should kind of try to do something weird with it. And let's see how far I can go.'"[57]

"This was the record that would really show whether or not he was going to be a legacy artist," observed Matt Fink. "The sales weren't huge compared to *Purple Rain*, but he was regrouping to establish his legacy, as not just a guy who made hit records, but an artist who would be around for decades."[58]

"I thought *Around The World In A Day* was Prince scratching an itch," declared his manager, Bob Cavallo. "It was wonderful, but it hurt *Purple Rain*. It was too soon for the marketplace."[59]

To make the challenge even more daunting, Prince initially decided not to release any singles from the album, so that the project was heard as one statement instead of as a series of singles.

In many ways, *Around The World In A Day* was Prince's final album that expressed his youthful innocence. The bulk of the album was completed before the *Purple Rain* tour, with several of the songs recorded even before the tidal wave of *Purple Rain* washed over everything, and the naïve charm is obvious once it is recognized that the album was completed before the *Purple Rain* tour jaded him.

The first words from Prince are an invitation to join him on a journey. "Open your heart, open your mind. A train is leaving all day."[60] And with that, you are instructed how to behave, and he soon adds "laughter is all you pay."[61] The album runs the spectrum of emotions from the giddy playfulness of "Tambourine" to the anthemic "America" and concludes with his redemption seeking conversation with God in "Temptation." At the core of the album is a man who is expressing confidence in his talent, and looking for salvation. He is admitting that he may not have all the answers, but he is on the path to find them, and he offers a psychedelic roadmap to get there. As he said in "Paisley Park," "admission is easy, just say you believe."[62] "He's telling you what to do and what to think," recognizes Wendy, "but he's lonely."

The music on the album has its roots in pop, but the underlying theme is one of a happiness that is removed from others. Prince's world seemed filled with joy, regret, fresh love, and conflicts, both internal and external, but the album's lyrics projected hints of his growing isolation, with five of the nine tracks containing words like "loneliness," "alone," and "lonely."

Prince detailed his difficulty with relationships in a *Rolling Stone* interview with Neal Karlen in 1985.

> **Sometimes everybody in the band comes over, and we have very long talks. They're few and far between, and I do a lot of the talking. Whenever we're done, one of them will come up to me and say, "Take care of yourself. You know I really love you." I think they love me so much, and I love them so much, that if they came over all the time, I wouldn't be able to be to them what I am, and they wouldn't be able to do for me, what they do. I think we all need our individual spaces, and when we come together with what we've concocted in our heads, it's cool.**[63]

It is easy to feel his honest pain on songs like "Condition Of The Heart," when he recognizes that, **"Sometimes money buys you everything, and nothing."**[64] "'Condition Of The Heart' is a work of genius," explained Susan Rogers.

> [It] is Prince doing something he did very rarely. He's telling us how he feels. And because he did it so rarely, I think audiences probably didn't even recognize it

when they heard it. He was lonely. Because he did what he needed to do in order to protect himself, to be a star. You must cut off a part of your psyche to keep it alive, so that you can continue to create. And after *Purple Rain*, I think he was well aware he'd be famous from then on. And life would never be normal. So, the people who wanted him—whether it's a dame in Paris or a woman in London, or just whatever—the people who wanted him, the people who wanted to be near him, the people who spoke to him, from this point on, he would never know what they wanted. And he would always have to be skeptical. And life is changing, and he'd always be a boss and he'd always have employees. And the kid that he'd known was gone. The Kid, in the movie *Purple Rain*. The kid he'd known as himself was gone.[65]

Lisa still marvels at Prince's musical growth. "He wrote things like 'Raspberry Beret' where it's so like a story, and so clever. It's almost Beatle-esque or something. 'My boss was Mr. McGee. . . .' And he didn't like the Beatles, so he came by it honestly."

"'Raspberry Beret' was a brilliant story," agrees Wendy. "His lyric writing on *Around The World In A Day* had surpassed everything he had done up to that point."

The album seemed inclusive with many more people than usual credited as contributing to his vision. Even seemingly random sounds in the songs can be traced back to those around him. "I have a song called 'Holy Man' and he took that cough in the beginning and put it on 'Raspberry Beret.' It was a real cough. That was on the demo, and he loved it," remembers Bobby Z. "So he took my cough."

The artwork was baffling to some of those it depicted, including Jill Jones who felt confused why she was apparently represented as a crying older woman. "What he showcased me as, was kind of a wake-up call to be looking at the old woman who was crying and in the green dress. I was offended. I was like, 'Are you kidding me?' And he said, 'It's because I'm gonna know you forever and we're best friends' and I was like, 'But I'm in tears and this is how you see the future' and I thought oh no, that was horrible. The haircut is mine, everything. And he told the painters to paint it, so once you see that, the big question was always . . . why?'"

Although Jones had attended a lot of the *Purple Rain* shows, she and Prince had grown apart, but Jill remembers that it changed when she was in the hospital. "I had a surgery and it was after the tour, and he sent me a whole load of kids' toys. I was like, 'everybody else sent a ton of flowers, why do I have candy necklaces?' He was a kid on a certain level. It was crazy. He has to be charming, and his charm has always won me over."

His undeniably charismatic appeal was still working with many, but not all, of the critics. *Rolling Stone* magazine proclaimed that "Prince has grown up," and that the release was the "Prince album you can bring home to your parents." The *New York Times* drew favorable comparisons with the Beatles' "Sgt. Pepper" and "Their Satanic Majesties Request" by the Rolling Stones, and proclaimed that it was "an instrumental and stylistic tour de force, Prince's finest hour—for now."[66]

But the tide had slightly turned, and some critics were looking for a crack in his royal armor, hoping to get ahead of a growing backlash, like the review in *New Musical Express*, which stated that the album sounded like "Prince's musical fusions smack . . . of a dead-end desperation," and pondering "Has the purple one reached his ceiling?"[67]

Prince was philosophical about those who wanted to pop his bubble. "**Not long ago I talked to George Clinton, a man who knows and has done so much for funk. George told me how much he liked *Around The World In A Day*. You know how much more his words mean than those from some mamma-jamma wearing glasses and an alligator shirt behind a typewriter?**"[68]

"**In people's minds, it all boils down to 'Is Prince getting too big for his breeches?' I wish people would understand that I always thought I was bad. I wouldn't have got into the business if I didn't think I was bad.**"[69]

Once again Prince was choosing to maintain his image and the price of always being the character "Prince" and not his true self was using up valuable time and energy that he likely needed to recharge his batteries. Being in character all the time and being in control in every situation caused walls to go up in ways he didn't imagine, according to people like Susan Rogers who spent the bulk of her time with the most honest representation of him, which was while he was recording his music. "My personal theory is that Prince was his most true self in the studio. So, there's the Prince we saw on stage. There's the man we saw taking interviews, which everyone knows by now, he was uncomfortable with. There was the man that people knew as a business partner. There were his friends. He was the band leader that his bandmates knew. And he was of course the lover, the intimate partner of his girlfriends. But when he was in the studio, he didn't really have to answer to anybody, because there was no producer there. All he needed was an engineer to keep the ball rolling, and he could work by himself."[70]

MONDAY, APRIL 22, 1985

"**Christopher Tracy's Parade**" [listed as "**Wendy's Parade**"] (vocal over-
   dubs, mix)
"**I Wonder U**" (vocal overdubs, mix)
"**Life Can Be So Nice**" (vocal overdubs, mix)
"**Life Can Be So Nice**" [instrumental] (mix)
Sunset Sound, Studio 3 | 2 p.m.–2 a.m. (booked: lockout)
Producer: Prince | Artist: Prince | Engineers: "Peggy Mac" Leonard and
   Susan Rogers

> *Everything and everyone around him inspired him—he was
> always listening for something that stirred his soul—so we all
> felt a part of his art in some way. But he was always the one in
> charge and he made sure you knew that!*[71]
>
> —"Peggy Mac" Leonard

Today's session consisted of vocal overdubs for some of his recent recordings. Wendy and Lisa were brought in to add their voices to "Wendy's Parade," "I Wonder U," and possibly a few other tracks from the last few days. They would change as the project took shape, so what they were recording today, may not have made it into the final mix, remembers Wendy. "The lyrics were all coming and being kind of tweaked as his script was being done. So by the time those four songs were started, when we went in to do our part, there was no, 'This is going to be for scene two and scene six and he'll be playing at us with Kristin Scott Thomas.' None of that."

After 9 and a half hours of vocal overdubs, the tracks were given a rough mix. An instrumental version of "Life Can Be So Nice" was also supposedly created on this date.

TUESDAY, APRIL 23, 1985

"**Christopher Tracy's Parade**" [listed as "**Wendy's Parade**"] (overdubs)
"**Evolsidog**" (overdubs, mix)
"**New Position**" (overdubs)
Sunset Sound, Studio 3 | 10:30 a.m.–8 p.m. (booked: lockout)
Producer: Prince | Artist: Prince | Engineers: "Peggy Mac" Leonard and
   Susan Rogers

People think of music in terms of a simple four count. But between one, two, three, four—for Prince it was a whole world. Trigonometry and calculus were all things that were happening between the notes and during the bar. It was a full event, every note.[72]

—"Bobby Z" Rivkin

Additional work was done on "Wendy's Parade," "Evolsidog," and "New Position" during this session, but it is likely that Prince left Wendy and Lisa in charge and did not attend. During the overdubs for "Evolsidog," it is probable that they helped the (still instrumental) song take shape. The track itself is a playful, reggae type of groove on steel drums that contains a backwards guitar and drums, Yamaha DX7 keyboard elements, and tambourine.

Additional work was done on "New Position" and "Wendy's Parade" as well.

Status: A nearly 8-minute version of "Evolsidog" was edited down to 3 minutes, but neither were released during Prince's lifetime. Wendy and Lisa would eventually add strings to another edit of the song (2:45) on July 2, 1985. That also remains unreleased.

WEDNESDAY, APRIL 24, 1985

"Christopher Tracy's Parade" [listed as **"Wendy's Parade"**] (overdubs, mix)
"Under The Cherry Moon" (overdubs, mix)
"Holly Rock" (tracking, overdubs, mix)
Sunset Sound, Studio 3 | 11 a.m.–4:30 a.m. (booked: lockout)
Producer: Prince | Artists: Prince and Sheila E. | Engineers: "Peggy Mac" Leonard and Susan Rogers | Assistant Engineer: Mike Kloster

I think he liked performing with somebody as opposed to just by himself because a lot of times, you feed off another musician so I think there were times that he liked that and other times he liked the solitude of just being alone and being in there creating.

—"Peggy Mac" Leonard

With the success of the *Purple Rain* tour, Sheila E. was now in the limelight, and she was hired to act in *Krush Groove*, a film directed by Michael Schultz, based on the early days of Def Jam Recordings and then up-and-coming record producer Russell Simmons. Sheila plays a fictionalized version of herself as the female love interest for the main character. "'Holly Rock' came about for the *Krush Groove* soundtrack and she needed a track," recalls her sax player "Eddie M." Mininfield, "and that was kind of an overnight track."

Prince and Sheila worked on the song together, with Sheila playing drums and Prince covering bass and guitars. Prince recorded the guide vocals while playing a cymbal to keep the beat, and eventually Sheila replaced his voice with hers, mimicking almost all of his playful, almost over-the-top lead. The track was likely inspired by the Flintstones television show, which changed the name of "Hollywood" to "Hollyrock"—the prehistoric home of Stoney Curtis and Cary Granite—although there is also an obvious influence from the "Rock, rock, planet rock" chorus on 1982's "Planet Rock" by Afrika Bambaataa & The Soul Sonic Force.

After the basic jam was recorded, they overdubbed bongos, timbales, keyboards, and a few other elements. Prince's sped up guitar serves as a musical call back to "Toy Box" and "Feline." Although Sheila's lead vocals had likely not been recorded, it is probable that some of the background vocals were tracked during this session.

Earlier in the session, 8 and a half hours were spent recording a variety of overdubs, including horns with John Liotine, Steven Medaio, and Carlton Smith on "Wendy's Parade," and adding mandolin and strings with Novi Novog, Suzie Katayama, David Coleman, Richard Feves, and Annette C. Atkinson on "Under The Cherry Moon." These overdubs were likely overseen by Lisa and Wendy.

Status: "Holly Rock" (6:35) was released as a 12-inch extended version and edited (3:58) for release as the 7-inch single. A different edit (4:56) was included on the *Krush Groove* soundtrack, which was released on September 3, 1985. The song did not have any chart impact in the United States, but was a moderate hit in Europe, hitting number 8 in the Netherlands.

Prince's original version of the track was included on the posthumous *Originals* album in 2019. The lyric about being "badder than a wicked witch" came from "Feline," and would later show up on "Dead On It." The horn overdubs from this session on "Wendy's Parade" appear to have been omitted and replaced by Clare Fischer's arrangement when the song was ultimately released as "Christopher Tracy's Parade." The strings on "Under The Cherry Moon" were also not included in the final mix, although the mandolin was kept.

THURSDAY, APRIL 25, 1985

"Holly Rock" (overdub, mix, edit, copy)
"America" [12-inch single version] (mix)
Sunset Sound, Studio 3 | 2 p.m.–12 a.m. (booked: lockout)
Producer: Prince | Artist: Sheila E. | Engineer: "Peggy Mac" Leonard

> *We would always do these songs with Prince singing lead vo-*
> *cals and then it would be sent to another artist and they would*
> *mimic his lead vocal with the timing and the inflections and*
> *things like that.*[73]
>
> —Susan Rogers

After beginning this session creating a mix for the 12-inch of "America," Prince shifted his focus back to finishing yesterday's song, "Holly Rock." At 6 p.m., additional work took place with Eddie M. playing sax and Sheila recording her vocals, including a mention of her "toy box" in the lyrics. It is unclear if that was still the title of her album by this point, but regardless, it was a reference they seemed to enjoy repeating. Although Sheila's guitarist, Stef Burns [Steph Birnbaum], is mentioned by name, it is unclear if he participated on the song. Prince had also added the sound of a kiss smack on the track, which may have influenced the next track he'd record.

Six C-60 tapes were made of the mixes from this session, and by midnight it was over.

SATURDAY, APRIL 27, 1985

"Kiss" [listed as **"Your Eyes"**] (tracking and overdubs)
Sunset Sound, Studio 2 | 2 p.m.–4 a.m. (booked: lockout)
Producer: Prince | Artist: Prince | Engineer: "David Z" Rivkin | Assistant
   Engineer: Coke Johnson

> *"When Doves Cry" and "Kiss"—you go to a higher plane*
> *[of creativity] with that. They don't sound like anything*
> *else. They aren't conscious efforts; you just have to get them*

out. They're gifts. Terence Trent D'arby asked me where "Kiss" came from, and I have no idea. Nothing in it makes sense. Nothing! The hi-hat doesn't make sense.[74]

—Prince

Prince continued to oversee the work in Studio 2 and Studio 3, bouncing back and forth when necessary. "We were in the studios next to each other, checking each other's progress," recalled engineer Susan Rogers. "And at some point, they said that they needed a song. Prince stopped what he was doing, I remember this very clearly, he had a little boom box, a little pale green one which he had to record ideas on, and he took it and an acoustic guitar to the next room, put it down, put in a cassette and pressed record. On the acoustic guitar he then played 'Kiss.' It took a few minutes to get the lyrics and he then took out the cassette and said: 'Here, finish this off.'"[75]

"Prince gave us this straight version with just one verse, an acoustic guitar and voice, no rhythm," explained David Z. "The song sounded like a folk song that Stephen Stills might have done. I didn't quite know what to do with it and neither did the group."[76]

"Nobody liked the song," recalled Mazarati member Tony Christian. "It sounded like a country version of something else."[77]

"I didn't like it," agrees BrownMark, "because it wasn't what I wanted for Mazarati. I wanted a rock band. He saw something different than I did."

In 2003, BrownMark expanded on how he felt on this evening. "It sounded like a banjo and he was just singing these words. I couldn't stand the song. There is no way in the world that we are putting this on this record. It was just too different; it doesn't even match what they are. And he said, 'Make it fit them.' We went into the studio and we put the feel on it."[78]

The full story of how the song came together will never be known. David Z and BrownMark disagree about some of the details regarding how they breathed life into the track, but the one item that is consistent in every version is that everyone in the room felt the basic demo that Prince presented to the band needed a lot of work. "We were trying to build a song out of nothing, piece by piece. It was just a collection of ideas built around the idea of a song that wasn't finished yet. We didn't know where it was going," remembered David Z.[79]

"We went into the studio and came up with a funky beat for it. I said, 'I'm going to do this my way," details BrownMark. "I'm going to make it a Mazarati song' and put a funky beat on it and put a funky bass line on it. Actually, the bass that is in the remix. That was the feel of the original bass line."

According to engineer Coke Johnson, the track's signature groove came from how they created the drum track. "We started fiddling around with it. We used the same changes, but instead of using that acoustic guitar, we ended up gating that guitar and the hi-hat. That is the weird sound you're hearing. It's playing the same rhythm the hi-hat's doing, but it's doing the changes the acoustic guitar did. That is one of the biggest hooks with it. David thought of the idea, and I hooked up the gate. He was flipping the switch to throw the delay in and out, and actually created that sound for 'Kiss'."

"It created a pretty cool rhythm that was constantly changing in tone and complexity but was still steady," detailed David Z. "Then I played some guitar chords and gated them through a Kepex unit and used that to trigger various combinations of the hi-hat tracks. That gave us the basic rhythm groove for the song."[80]

The song was structured, but Prince had only provided the first verse. "We were working on it and he was next door in the next studio. I just said, 'We need a second verse,' and he's so quick, he just jotted it down and handed it to me and we did it. When he got inspired, it was instant. It was like a faucet he couldn't turn off."

With the groove in place and the entire song written, Terry Casey added his lead vocals that were boosted by the catchy background vocals of Tony Christian (born Bruce DeShazer) and Marvin "Marv" Gunn. "Bruce and Marvin are great singers," continued David Z, "so they did some gospel harmonies in the background. Basically, that is what it was; there is nothing else on there. There's drums, the acoustic guitar rhythm, the piano part and the background vocals."[81] At this point, it also contained BrownMark's bass.

According to David Z, the track wasn't quite working. "We were getting a little frustrated, and we were exhausted."[82] Unable to resolve it at that moment, two cassettes were created of a rough mix of the track and everyone left shortly after 4 a.m.

SUNDAY, APRIL 28, 1985

"Kiss" [listed as "Your Kiss"] (Prince vocal and guitar overdubs, mix)
"Kiss" [Dance Mix] (probable overdubs, edits, mix)
"All My Dreams" (tracking, mix)
"Evolsidog" (vocal and other overdubs, mix)
"Evolsidog" [instrumental] (probable mix)
Sunset Sound, Studio 3 | 12:00 noon–9:15 a.m. (booked: lockout)
Producer: Prince | Artist: Prince | Engineers: "Peggy Mac" Leonard and Susan Rogers

*I remember him walking across the courtyard saying, "That's
a really good one!" And then the next thing I knew, he took it.
[laughs]*

—"Peggy Mac" Leonard

Coke Johnson remembers what happened when Prince arrived early for today's
session and asked to hear "Kiss." "We played it for Prince, who went ballistic,
went out to the basketball court playing it loud on the ghetto blaster. He pretty
much said: 'This is too good for Mazarati.' It pissed us off as we had been up
all night working on it."

Prince took the tape back into Studio 3 and began making his own changes.
He quickly eliminated BrownMark's bass ("It fills up the bottom so much you
really don't miss the bass part, especially if you only use it on the first downbeat," explained David Z)[83] and added the James Brown "Papa's Got A Brand
New Bag" style E9sus4 guitar chord as well as his vocals, which he recorded an
octave higher than Terry's. David Z asked him what was going on and Prince
confirmed his earlier position on the song. "He said to me, 'This is too good for
you guys. I'm taking it back.'"[84]

"The final result of the song was not what he had expected," Tony details how
Prince approached them. "He said: 'I liked the cut you did last night; I want to
use it.' Of course, you guys will get paid for it.' We said: 'Sure!' Because we were
flattered that Prince would even put something that we did on his record."[85]

"All the vocal work was done. All the music was laid in already," explains
BrownMark. "The only thing that Prince put in was the little [makes guitar
sound like the beginning of each stanza of 'Kiss']. He put that in. He put his signature on it, which really changed the song dramatically, with his high pitched
voice it really added a whole different feel to this thing because Mazarati, they
didn't sing it high like Prince, they sang it in more of their natural voices, and
so it was a little different, but the background everything is all the same when
we did it."

"We were playing ping-pong [at Sunset Sound] and 'Hey! That's the song
we did last night, but Prince's voice was on it. He's quick!' It took Prince less
than an hour to put the guitar and his vocals on the song," remembered Tony
Christian. "I was credited on background vocals, and I got a gold record and
everything, but I guess I was really naïve and new to the business. In this business you can easily get screwed out of a couple of millions."[86]

"He didn't ask anybody," according to David Z. "Of course, to him it was
his song. He promised all kinds of stuff to us to make this thing happen, but in
a way, he didn't consider anyone's reactions. But on the other hand, he did it

and it was fine, probably better than if Mazarati had done it. I prefer his version, the cool guitar part and all, he definitely put his thing on it, no question about that. It wasn't like—'Hey that was our hit!' It wasn't that kinda thing. Maybe [Mazarati] felt that way, I was the producer so what did I care? Maybe we would have had a big hit with it, maybe not. It was so drastically different from Prince's version and his delivery was great."[87]

"Kiss" straddled the line between innovative and familiar. The track itself is a simple groove that is masked with undeniably clever studio tricks that stood out even more once the bass was removed. Additional elements like the piano were influenced by Bo Diddley's "Say Man" and the background vocals were lifted from Brenda Lee's "Sweet Nothin's." The lyrics borrowed elements such as the "you don't have to be rich" section from "You Got To Be A Man" by Frank Williams and the Rocketeers, and the chorus of "I just want your extra time and your kiss" was likely influenced by Joni Mitchell singing "I need your confidence baby, and the gift of your extra time" on "Jericho" from her 1977 *Don Juan's Reckless Daughter* LP. All of this was blended with a light seasoning of James Brown to make something so unique that Prince almost had no choice but to take it back. He was a man who was always looking for a new sound, and it was provided for him.

In the end, the basic song was written by Prince, but without David Z, Coke Johnson, and BrownMark, the track probably wouldn't have gone to number 1 on the charts. It would be one of the only times that he shared "co-producer" credit with anyone on a "Prince" song, which reflects how much he respected the work done without his input. Despite the new sound created by this mix, BrownMark was unhappy with some of Prince's decisions, including removing the bass from the track. He'd done this in 1984 on "When Doves Cry," but that was no longer the exception. "Taking the bass out of music . . . that was the beginning of it. He started eliminating bass from the music. I don't know if maybe he sensed that I was doing things on the side. I don't know, but I think he was preparing himself for my departure."

"That's where a lot of the tensions started between me and him," admitted BrownMark. "From that point forward, our relationship started to disintegrate."[88]

BrownMark dedicated himself to making Mazarati the best band possible, but he felt that the way he'd been handled after the *Purple Rain* tour left him feeling undervalued, both financially and as a performer. For now, BrownMark decided to continue working for Prince, but he would eventually renegotiate a private deal as a freelance band member. It would increase his salary, but he would no longer be a full member of the group. "What I learned was that this isn't about the Revolution. That's just a name. This is about Prince looking out for Prince and that's when I realize that his management didn't care at all about us. We were hired help."

Prince appears to have started working on the dance mix for "Kiss" using some of the same elements from the original tracks. He also continued overdubbing the recently recorded "Evolsidog" and began the basic work on "All My Dreams." Both were ambitiously different and stand out from the pop sound of his latest hits. Once again, technology was helping Prince find a new direction, as Lisa recalled. "The Fairlight was just inspiration for a writer like Prince, and for all of us. There were flute sounds, wind sounds, voice samples, hand clap sounds. We would just build these songs around it."[89]

"Evolsidog" was likely finished by the end of the session, but "All My Dreams" existed as an instrumental. Rough mixes were completed, and the tracks were dubbed to three C-60 cassettes. The shift ended at 9:15 the following morning, once more wearing down the engineers by requiring them to stay an extra 13 hours after their shift was scheduled to wrap.

Status: The instrumental version of "All My Dreams" (6:54) remains unreleased. Vocals and a new intro were added over the next few days. The song was considered for use on *Parade*, and in many of his never fully realized projects like *Dream Factory*, *The Dawn*, and *Roadhouse Garden*. Prince also reused the slowed-down speech from "All My Dreams" at the end of his 1998 release, "Acknowledge Me." The song was eventually included on the Super Deluxe Edition of *Sign O' The Times* in 2020.

It is possible that the extended version of "Kiss" was also started on this day, but that is unverified.

MONDAY, APRIL 29, 1985

"**All My Dreams**" [listed as "**In My Dreams**"] (overdubs, likely including vocals)
Sunset Sound, Studio 3 | 7:30 p.m.–5:30 a.m. (booked: lockout)
Producer: Prince | Artist: Prince | Engineer: "Peggy Mac" Leonard

Captain Crunch. That was one of his favorite cereals.

—Wally Safford

"All My Dreams," was a track that was reminiscent of another artist from that period, according to Wendy. "It reminded me of classic Kid Creole and The Coconuts. Prince had this cool sort of personality when he was singing it. One track he sang through a megaphone and the other track was a clean track and he mixed the two."[90]

Prince was so playful with the sound of his voice that he slowed it down, which inspired Wendy, Susannah, and Lisa's chant about a "double speed playhouse."

According to Lisa, Prince was specific about what he wanted for their vocals. "Prince would tell us when we would be doing background vocals, 'Sing like you are Betty Davis.'* If we weren't in the studio, we would watch old black and white films from that whole 'Puttin' On The Ritz' era."[91]

They also added a section that they quietly paraphrase parts of "Morning Verse for Grades 5-8" by Rudolf Steiner—a composition that reflects on the wonders of Earth and the universe.

> We all, meaning me, Wendy and Susannah, went to Highland Hall Waldorf School. It was a Rudolf Steiner school, and every morning we would have to start the day with this morning verse. We're a bunch of kids saying this, so it was just interesting. They had you look at the world and consider the sun and the stars and the beasts and the plants and just take everything in and then start your day. Prince just thought that was kooky and amazing, which it is. It's both kooky and amazing because it is pretty amazing to give kids that message and to start each day with that. So we said that verse in the background. We were kids in a candy store, so you know how much he loved just saying things and then flipping it backwards or putting little messages in songs. When we came with that, he was just floored. He loved it. He was like, "What else you got?"

"We just had that kind of relationship, I guess," reflects Lisa. "We were young and in love and it was cool. You just get excited about little things. Luckily some of those little things were kind of interesting, like the morning prayer. Some of them were just silly, but when you're young and excited, it's like, 'You like Chinese food? I like Chinese food! Let's put that in a song!'"

The track also features live drums layered with the new Fairlight keyboard.

---

*It is unclear if Prince was referring to singer Betty Davis (wife of Miles Davis), or Bette Davis (classic era film actress and singer). The printed interview spells the singer as "Betty," but the context of the sentence implies black and white film star Bette Davis. When asked about this quote, Lisa Coleman responds equally perplexed. "I remember when he said that to me and I bet he meant Betty Davis, but I took it to mean Bette Davis!!! And I figured, what's the difference?! They'd both sing in raspy and compelling tones! So…. It was ME either misunderstanding him, or he knew me too well and suggested Bette Davis to me because I would 'get' that."

MONDAY, APRIL 29, 1985

"Fear The Shadow" [early title for **"Strawberry Lover"**] (overdubs, mix)
Sunset Sound, Studio 2 | 3 p.m.–11:30 p.m. (booked: lockout)
Producer: Prince | Artist: Mazarati (listed as Prince) | Engineer: "David Z"
  Rivkin | Assistant Engineer: Coke Johnson

> *I had done that song in my studio, back at home, and that was
> what I wanted Mazarati to be real hard rock. "Strawberry
> Lover" did have a different title to it and Prince said, "Why
> don't we try it?" because he was all into the passion fruit. He
> was in his fruit stage.*
>
> —BrownMark

Prince continued to walk across the basketball court in between the studios to
check in with how Mazarati was doing. While Prince wasn't as heavy handed as
he was with the Time and the Family, he did like to drop by to add his touch,
remembers BrownMark. "He used to ask me what could he help me with, and
I said, 'Man, I think it would be cool if you just played on some of the stuff,'
'cause Prince was huge and I was just trying to get Mazarati out there and what
exposure that would be, Prince playing on their stuff, so that's kind of how that
came about."

"He was being our director of that project," continues BrownMark, "so he
went through my songs that I had written for them and he kinda picked through
them and asked me if I needed help on certain things. On songs he thought were
weaker he would step in and try to help me beef it up a little bit."

Once Mazarati recorded "Fear The Shadow," ("The Shadow" was Brown-
Mark's nickname from the early days of working with Mazarati), Prince explained that he liked the music, but wanted to change it to "Strawberry Lover"
and add his own flavor to the lyrics according to BrownMark.

> He started talking about strawberries and said, "Let me help you write this song"
> and "Let's change it up a little bit." As a beginning songwriter, my lyrics tended
> to be very abstract and very deep, meaning nobody could understand them but
> myself, because I wasn't sure how to express myself in words, through a song,
> which is typical of a beginning writer. So, he saw that and that's where he offered
> his help.

It is not a stretch to imagine that Prince was inspired by his own lyrics on "A Love Bizarre," which contained a reference to his lover's "strawberry mind." He may have also been influenced by the Brothers Johnson song, "Strawberry Letter 23," and possibly even "Strawberry Fields" by the Beatles. "This is the Beatles movement," explained BrownMark about the music from this period. "From *Purple Rain* into *Around The World*. . . . We were entering this Beatles phase. *Sgt Pepper*. The clothing changed, the sound, everything. Totally."[92]

"Prince writes so fast," remembered Tony Christian. "He's in, out, gone for 10 minutes, and the paper is full of lyrics. Wow!"[93]

Three C-60 cassettes were made of the track.

Status: "Strawberry Lover" (5:30) would be released on Mazarati's debut album.

TUESDAY, APRIL 30, 1985

"**Strawberry Lover**" [formerly "**Fear The Shadow**"] (vocal overdubs)
"**She's Just That Kind Of Lady**" [listed as "**She's That Lady**"] (vocal and
  guitar overdubs)
Sunset Sound, Studio 2 | 1 p.m.–3:15 a.m. (booked: lockout)
Producer: Prince | Artist: Mazarati (listed as Prince) | Engineer: "David Z"
  Rivkin | Assistant Engineer: Coke Johnson

> *He basically gave me the lyrics and kind of showed me how it should be sung.*
>
> —BrownMark

When Prince returned to Studio 2, he recorded his new lyrics for "Strawberry Lover." It is likely that the rest of the band's vocals were added after that, with lead singer Sir Terry Casey mirroring Prince's guide vocals.

Work was also done on "She's Just That Kind Of Lady," but it is unclear if Prince participated in that track.

A single C-60 cassette was made of the song, likely for Prince, and the session was over at 3:15 a.m.

Status: "She's Just That Kind Of Lady" (4:31) was released on Mazarati's eponymous album in March 1986.

TUESDAY, APRIL 30, 1985

"All My Dreams" (vocal overdubs, mix)
Sunset Sound, Studio 3 | 4 p.m.–2 a.m. (booked: lockout)
Producer: Prince | Artist: Prince | Engineers: "Peggy Mac" Leonard and
Susan Rogers

> *He was totally the captain of the ship, he's the one who decided
> what sounds he wanted. My job was to realize those sounds, to
> give him the sound he wanted and needed.*[94]
>
> —Susan Rogers

Prince arrived late to this session, likely because he was in Studio 2 adding his vocals to "Strawberry Lover" and working with Mazarati. Peggy quickly prepped for Prince to add his vocals to "All My Dreams."

A mix was created of the song, but additional work would continue on the track the following day.

MAY 1985

"**Velvet Kitty Cat**" (tracking and overdubs, mix)
"**New Position**" (likely mix)
"**All My Dreams**" (crossfades and mix)
"**Under The Cherry Moon**" (mix with new oboe)
"**Under The Cherry Moon**" [instrumental] (mix)
Parade album compilation [contains "**Wendy's Parade**," "**New Position**,"
    "**I Wonder U**," "**Under The Cherry Moon**," "**Others Here With Us**,"
    "**Life Can Be So Nice**," "**Velvet Kitty Cat**," "**Sometimes It Snows In
    April**," "**Kiss**," "**Old Friends 4 Sale**," "**All My Dreams**"]
Sunset Sound, Studio 3 | 1 p.m.–6:30 a.m. (booked: lockout)
Producer: Prince | Artist: Prince | Engineers: "Peggy Mac" Leonard and
    Susan Rogers

> *He recorded so fast; I mean we recorded an album in three
> weeks. Where's the fun? He just took six months of potential
> work and finished it in three weeks, so of course he wanted to
> keep going so songs were always being pulled off and re-edited.*[1]
>
> —Susan Rogers

May started off with Prince updating the mixes for several of his recently recorded songs, including "New Position," "Under The Cherry Moon," and "All
My Dreams" and sequencing them into the first real version of his new (as-yet-

untitled) album. He spent 9 hours working on the new mixes, which included additional instrumental overdubs and crossfades to help the tracks flow together on the new collection. "Those first five songs including 'Life Can Be So Nice' were the beginning and the nucleus of the record," recalled Susan Rogers. "We did go back later to Minnesota and we did add 'Mountains' and 'Girls & Boys,' but the nucleus of that album remained those first songs and then skipping over to 'Life Can Be So Nice' and 'Sometimes It Snows In April.'"[2]

After midnight, Prince also revisited an early track and updated it with the band. "Velvet Kitty Cat" had been originally recorded in 1983, but it lacked energy, so they rehearsed it and recorded a much more aggressive rockabilly version of the song using music based on Jerry Lee Lewis' version of "Whole Lotta Shakin' Goin' On." Multiple takes were done of the band rehearsing the track, and the final version was added to this compilation. Peggy recalls how important it was when Prince worked on a second take. "Sometimes he'd do the whole song and then he'd do another take. He'd say, 'Let's do one more' and it's like 'Okay, thank God! I'll do this real quick.' I would literally hold my breath waiting for him to say can we do another one."

> Here's the thing. If you're rushing through it, you'd EQ real fast, you'd patch everything, you'd push the phase button on the one that was supposed to be pushed and then throw the faders up and you better not touch it until it was at the end. You'd see that the snare was too loud or not loud enough or the toms needed to be up or something like that. Then you'd want to change it. Sometimes I would just kind of slowly scoot up the fader, but he could hear it. And he'd say, "Don't touch anything." Technically as an engineer, it was horrible for me, because you didn't have time to do anything. You didn't have time to tweak or perfect anything. He was always like "Don't blow the groove."

"Why did he do a second take?" reflects Peggy. "Maybe he would just do it because he would want it to see if anything would be different. If there was something better or maybe he just did it because he didn't wanna stop playing. Who knew why?"

The lineup for the first assembly of this album included:

"Wendy's Parade"	"Life Can Be So Nice"
"New Position"	"Velvet Kitty Cat"
"I Wonder U"	"Sometimes It Snows In April"
"Under The Cherry Moon"	"Kiss"
"Others Here With Us"	"Old Friends 4 Sale"
	"All My Dreams"

This was a rough assembly, but much of this album would remain in the final collection. Eventually Prince decided that this lineup of songs didn't convey what he had in mind for the upcoming film, so this early compilation was scrapped. The tracks that Prince used relied on the input of Wendy and Lisa, and his music was reflecting this change. "This was obviously a transitional phase, whereas his music expanded," explained his tour manager Alan Leeds, "so did the scope of the instrumentation of the band. So, I think the use of Wendy and Lisa was just the beginning of that."[3]

With the tracks being sent out of house to be embellished by Clare Fischer, an alternate title was given to the project. "The code name was 'The Marx Brothers,'" according to Fischer's engineer Arne Frager. "Nobody in the Prince organization wanted anyone to know what we were working on. We weren't allowed to mention Prince's name either, so we called it 'the Marx Brothers.'"

The session ended at 6:30 the following morning after the mixes and two C-90 cassettes were made of the collection. The engineers clocked 10 hours of overtime, but Prince continued to work everyone hard.

Status: "Velvet Kitty Cat" (2:42) has not been released. This is different than the version included on the *Purple Rain* Deluxe set in 2017.

This early compilation of *Parade* also remains unreleased.

THURSDAY, MAY 2, 1985

"Velvet Kitty Cat" (overdubs, mix)
"Too Rough" (likely mix)
Sunset Sound, Studio 3 | 4 p.m.–4 a.m. (booked: lockout)
Producer: Prince | Artist: Prince | Engineer: "Peggy Mac" Leonard

[The Revolution] really got to be a brain that knew when he would just yell out horns, Matt and I would look at each other and go, "Okay, horns!" We kinda know what he means. And so yeah, we were almost like puppets. "Puppet, make me a toy. Make little toys really fast." [laughs][4]

—Lisa Coleman

Prince continued working on the newly recorded update of "Velvet Kitty Cat" from the previous day's effort. He also pulled "Too Rough" out of the vault once again for another quick mix. That track was offered to Mother's Finest singer Joyce Kennedy, but she declined it. "I don't think it's some of his best work," Kennedy told *Rock & Soul* magazine. "It's weird. The hook and the vocal lead are good, but the rest of the song, I don't know, it's really strange. I've lived with it for a while, but I wasn't totally sure it was right, even if it was Prince." Prince was at the top of his popularity and at that moment, everything he touched was turning gold. Kennedy recognized that as she continued her thoughts. "Politically, I want to do it. It's a Prince song, and it'll make people go to the album and find all the wonderful stuff on it. But maybe it's not worth being cloned into that bag of females doing Prince tunes."[5]

It is unclear if Kennedy ever recorded "Too Rough." Prince would quickly rebound, and he was about to match the perfect band with a song he'd originally recorded the previous year for Apollonia 6.

Status: The 6-minute version of "Too Rough" would be considered for Jill Jones' album, but it didn't make the cut and remains unreleased.

FRIDAY, MAY 3, 1985

"**Jealous Girl**" (possible mix)
"**Manic Monday**" (possible mix)
"**America**" (possible edits)
"**All Day, All Night**" (possible overdubs, mix)
"**Can't Stop This Feeling I Got**" (possible mix)
"**Don't Let Him Fool Ya**" (mix)
Sunset Sound, Studio 3 | 12:00 noon–3:15 a.m. (booked: lockout)
Producer: Prince | Artist: Prince | Engineers: "Peggy Mac" Leonard and
    Susan Rogers

> *He had the strongest work ethic of any musician I've ever known. And I've known a lot 'cause I've been in this business since 1978, so that's almost 40 years now.*[6]
>
> —Susan Rogers

To understand Prince, it is important to recognize *who* he surrounded himself with during this period. The Revolution was vital to his sound when he wanted to explore and work in a band setting, but the core of those around him were female, including his engineers Peggy Leonard and Susan Rogers, and he gave all of them a vast amount of responsibility and power, at least within the limits that he permitted *anyone* to have control. "He needed to be the alpha male to get done what he needed to get done; he couldn't spend any mental energy battling with people for dominance or position," recalled Rogers. "If you wanted your own way of doing things, you shouldn't be working for Prince—and women are, it's safe to say, more inclined to let a man lead. He also liked outsiders and liked feeling like one himself. There weren't many female technicians, so I was a rare bird and he liked the rare birds."[7]

"I think he gave women a chance," adds Peggy. "You had to empower yourself in that position. It's like with Wendy, he kept saying, 'Learn to solo, learn to solo.' He put pressure on you. He just opened the door, he just gave that space to you and you better do with it what you want, what you could, or you would be gone."

His days in the studio weren't always centered around making *new* music. Sometimes entire days would be spent working on music that had already been recorded for various reasons. One of those reasons was when he decided he wanted to work with another artist.

The Bangles were a band of four women based out of Los Angeles who'd released their debut album, *All Over The Place*, the previous May. "Prince and I both watched the ["Hero Takes A Fall"] video," recalls Apollonia. "[Susanna Hoffs] was wearing a maid outfit and he went wild over her!"

"Prince saw our video "Hero Takes A Fall,'" explained Hoffs, "and actually Apollonia said, 'You've got to get their record,' so he got the record and he loved it."[8]

"I am a huge Bangles fan," remembered Apollonia. "We chilled before Prince met the group. It was partly my love for the Beatles and these were all girls in the band. Playing hard! Just doing the work!"[9]

The idea of the Bangles recording the track that Kotero and Prince had penned intrigued him.

"Prince really liked our first album," explained the band's guitarist Vicki Peterson. "He liked the song 'Hero Takes a Fall,' which is a great compliment, because we liked his music. He contacted us, and said, 'I've got a couple of songs for you. I'd like to know if you're interested,' and of course we were."[10]

"We were working with Peggy and David Leonard, a husband-and-wife engineer team who had done a lot of stuff with Prince," remembered Hoffs. "Somehow word got to me to go to Sunset Sound and pick up the cassette from Prince. It was the old days of cassettes. I didn't actually see Prince that day, because . . . I don't know, either he wasn't there, or he just wasn't coming out of the studio or something."[11]

The tape included "Manic Monday" (likely containing vocals by Apollonia 6) and a 1981 version of "Jealous Girl" (containing Prince's vocal), and when she played the first track, Susanna immediately liked it. "It was cool. The title was really great. It just reminded me of 'Manic Depression,' the Hendrix song, and had kind of a psychedelic thing. And then it had these great harmonies, and there were a lot of things about it where I just thought, 'This is a really good fit for the Bangles.' So, I'm grateful to him for giving us that song, because it ended up being our first radio hit."[12]

Prince suggested to the group that they simply add their voices to what he'd already recorded, but they respectfully declined, according to Hoffs. "I think when he first heard that we weren't going to, he was a little surprised, but I think in the end he liked it more because he admired the fact that we just did it our own way and changed it."[13]

"Prince had to actually approve every note that was on that song," recalled Peggy who engineered both the original session with Prince and the session with the Bangles. "I don't think he had given a song like that to anybody that he wasn't working with. The Bangles had David Kahne working on it and Prince wasn't in the studio when they were cutting it. That was kind of his baby and I think David Kahne made that song really poppy. When you listen to actually what [Prince and I] cut, it was a great song, but David Kahne made it sparkle. He really did."

Vicki Peterson referred to it as "a 'Banglefication' of a Prince arrangement."[14] Before the song was released, she remembered that Prince visited the band while they were working on the arrangement for their tour.

I have a memory of him coming to a rehearsal and I was very nervous when he walked in. It was just the four of us. We didn't have our keyboard player who sort of does that harpsichord figure. He wasn't there that day because we were just sort of working up the songs for a tour and it was very rough and was very much the guitar version. And we played the song for him one time through, and I remember being really apologetic like, "Well, we don't have the keyboards" and he goes "You don't need the keyboards." And then he goes, "It's gonna go." And then he walked out, and we're like, what does that mean "It's gonna go?" What did he mean? Who says these words and then leaves?[15]

Later in today's session, Prince also updated his vocals for "All Day, All Night," a song that had been recorded live the previous summer. Additionally, he took two tracks from 1982 out of the vault, "Can't Stop This Feeling I Got" and "Don't Let Him Fool Ya," to mix. "America," which had been edited a few weeks earlier, was edited once again for an upcoming single release, but it is unlikely that this version was ever officially issued.

The session ended just after 3 in the morning when four TDK C-60 cassette copies were created.

Status: Although "Can't Stop This Feeling I Got" (2:36) and "Don't Let Him Fool Ya" (4:31) were previously recorded, they were mixed on this date. Both tracks were released posthumously on the *1999* Super Deluxe Edition in 2019. He re-recorded "Can't Stop This Feeling I Got" for 1990's *Graffiti Bridge* album.

"All Day, All Night" (5:35) was eventually released on Jill Jones' debut album. The version with Prince's vocals remains unreleased.

"Manic Monday" (3:03) would be featured on The Bangles *Different Light* album, released on January 2, 1986, as its lead single. The song peaked at number 2 on the *Billboard* Hot 100 the week of April 19, with Prince's "Kiss" holding the number 1 position. Prince's own version of "Manic Monday" (2:51) was released on *Originals* in June 2019.

This version of "Jealous Girl" remains unreleased.

SATURDAY, MAY 4, 1985

Unknown tracks [possibly **"Manic Monday"** and **"Jealous Girl"**] (listening session)
Sunset Sound, Studio 3 | 3:00 p.m.–4:00 p.m. (booked: lockout)
Producer: Prince | Artist: Prince | Engineer: "Peggy Mac" Leonard

He was so prolific. Who knows how much stuff he wrote that nobody's ever heard. These were huge hits back in the eighties and it only took him 15 minutes to write these things.

—Paul Levy

It is possible that "Manic Monday" and "Jealous Girl" were reviewed by Prince on this date before they were given to the Bangles.

SUNDAY, MAY 5, 1985–MONDAY, MAY 6, 1985

"Weekend" (mix)
"100 MPH" (mix)
Sunset Sound, Studio 2 | 2:30 p.m.–12:45 a.m. (booked: lockout)
Sunset Sound, Studio 2 | 1:30 p.m.–6:00 a.m. (booked: lockout)
Producer: Prince | Artist: Mazarati (listed as Prince) | Engineer: "David Z"
    Rivkin | Assistant Engineer: Coke Johnson

> *There was no sleep because there was so much going on. It's*
> *like being at a casino and the machines are paying out and you*
> *don't even realize it's daytime outside.*
>
> —Tony Christian

On occasion, BrownMark expressed that he wasn't always happy with Prince's participation on the album, but that sentiment wasn't always held by the band members, according to guitarist Tony Christian. "We had some discussion of what the band thought about being taken over by Prince. I'm sure he had more songs, but he didn't force anything on us, and BrownMark didn't try to pursue him one way or the other. We were very happy to have a Prince song on the album, because he was hot, and we were definitely playing on his fame."[16]

"[Prince is] a producer who gets results, who's put this town on the map, not just in this country, but all over the world," agreed Sir Terry Casey. "He cracks the whip, sure he does, but this talk that he's an asshole and all that, why anyone who heads a big organization like his, works the same way. It's great to get the whip cracked by somebody like Prince who is so professional."[17]

To have Prince's songs on an album gave it instant credibility. "100 MPH" would be Mazarati's biggest hit when it was released as a single.

MONDAY, MAY 6, 1985

Parade album (playback and copy)
"**Jerk Out**" (overdubs, mix)
"**100 MPH**" (overdubs, mix)
"**Jealous Girl**" (likely transfer to new reel)
"**Manic Monday**" (likely transfer to new reel)
Sunset Sound, Studio 3 | 3:00 p.m.–6:00 a.m. (booked: lockout)
Producer:· Prince | Artists: Prince and Mazarati | Engineer: "Peggy Mac"
  Leonard

> *Recording* Parade *was the best period for me. Everything about*
> Parade *worked out so well—it was a great blend of funky, . . .*
> *without being psychedelic; it didn't fit into a genre.*[18]
>
> —Wendy Melvoin

With a few days since he'd put together the as-yet-untitled *Parade* album, Prince listened to it again in the studio and probably spent some time adjusting the order and mixes. It is also likely that he was preparing to send the tapes to Clare Fischer to add his orchestral arrangement to the tracks. Prince was happy with the way Fischer added his touches to *The Family* album and he wanted his influence on this project as well.

According to Fischer, "Prince doesn't write or read music, so he sends us cassette tapes and my son [Brent] has a brilliant pair of ears, so I have him transcribe them."

"It was a top-secret project and the tape that he sent us was the tape with the whole album on it," according to Brent Fischer. "So I started transcribing those Prince songs one-by-one and giving him the kind of detail that he had been missing from his rough sketches, writing out the entire bass line, the drum fills, all the vocal parts, including background vocal parts. Everything he needed to wrap the music in a velvet cloth of a Clare Fischer arrangement."[19]

Once the tape was received by the Fischers, they worked frantically to have it completed and rehearsed within the next few days.

During this session, Prince also brought Mazarati's "Jerk Out" and "100 MPH" back into the studio after David Z mixed them. It was common for Prince to add his own flavor over someone else's sound. "I've never seen anyone grab your instrument and show you how to do something. He had the ability to play everything, and if he wanted to tweak something, or whatever he wanted to do, he could come right over and he could show you what he's hearing,"[20] BrownMark explained. "'Here, let me have that bass,' and he would show me. He was a phenomenal musician. I don't think since Mozart there's ever gonna be anybody else. Not in our generation."[21]

Prince supposedly added a few musical overdubs to "Jerk Out" and "100 MPH" and mixed them down once again. It appears that "Jealous Girl" and likely "Manic Monday" were placed on new tapes during this session, probably to be able to give them to the Bangles if they chose to use either or both songs as their master.

Two C-90 tapes were made at the end of the session.

TUESDAY, MAY 7, 1985

American gossip magazine *The National Enquirer* published an exposé about Prince titled "The Real Prince—He's Trapped in a Bizarre Secret World of Terror." The information was gathered from an interview with Prince's body-guard "Big Chick" Huntsberry. Chick's view of Prince was based on a perspective few were granted, so his thoughts were revealing, and in retrospect often correct. When he said that, "Prince loves music. His only interests in life are himself and music—that's it." It is hard to deny that there is some truth there. That was probably one of the most painful experiences for Prince, having some-one as close as Chick was to him, quoted saying "Prince is certainly the weirdest guy I've ever met, and it's not put on for publicity—he really is weird!"[22]

Prince would downplay how much it hurt him later that year in a *Rolling Stone* interview. "**I never believe anything in the *Enquirer*. I remember read-ing stories when I was ten years old, saying, 'I was fucked by a flying saucer, and here's my baby to prove it.' I think they just took everything he said and blew it up. It makes for a better story. They're just doing their thing. Right on for them. The only thing that bothers me is when my fans think I live in a prison. This is not a prison.**"[23]

Chick passed away in April 1990 at the age of 49. Before he passed, Hunt-sberry had stopped using cocaine and had become a minister. Although he and Prince never worked together again, Prince showed his love for Chick by performing a benefit show for his family on April 30, 1990, at a club near Min-neapolis in Golden Valley called Rupert's.

Prince would eventually update the lyrics to "Old Friends 4 Sale," hiding the pain he'd felt from Chick's betrayal. The new lyrics were not as personal and eliminated any references to Huntsberry and to being vulnerable.

This was the official date on the cover of the magazine, but it was probably on the newsstands earlier, and Prince had likely heard that this was going to be released even before that.

TUESDAY, MAY 7, 1985

"Jerk Out" (review and possible mix)
"100 MPH" (review and possible mix)
"Weekend" [early title for "I Guess It's All Over"] (review, copy)
Sunset Sound, Studio 3 | 3:00 p.m.–6:30 p.m. (booked: lockout)
Producer: Prince | Artist: Mazarati (listed as Prince) | Engineer: Prince |
    Assistant Engineer: "Peggy Mac" Leonard

> *By the time I pick up an instrument—be it the keyboard, the guitar, the bass, whatever—I've already heard the whole song in my head. All I'm doing at that point is committing it to music. If you trust that there's a God and let Him do his thing through you, the songs come.*[24]
>
> —Prince

Prince was constantly formulating new tunes in his head for his own records, and he maintained a strong influence over the music he created for his protégé acts and in all tasks in the studio, remembers Peggy. "My job was to stay out of his way. And in some way help him achieve his vision, but it's not like he talked to me, this song's going this way and what do you think? It wasn't like that. You just kind of had to interpret what he was doing."

Prince reviewed the last few sessions that David Z had been overseeing with Mazarati, including a new song, "Weekend." Although he liked the basic groove for "Weekend," he wanted to change the lyrics, so he rewrote the song giving it a new title, "I Guess It's All Over."

It appears that Prince did a rough assembly of the album and gave that to David Z to finesse. Five C-60 tapes were made of the collection and Prince cut the session short after 3 hours.

TUESDAY, MAY 7, 1985

"**I Guess It's All Over**" [new title for **"Weekend"**] (mix)
Mazarati album (edits and crossfades)
Sunset Sound, Studio 2 | 3:00 p.m.–1:30 a.m. (booked: lockout)
Producer: Prince | Artist: Mazarati (listed as Prince) | Engineer: "David Z"
    Rivkin | Assistant Engineer: Coke Johnson

> *[The Mazarati LP] started out as a producer project with
> just me trying to find a unique, different sound and image for
> them. Prince came in at the end of the project along with David
> Rivkin to put on the finishing touches. He also did the solo on
> "I Guess It's All Over."*[25]
>
> —BrownMark

The new lyrics to "I Guess It's All Over" were recorded and Prince added a
12-string guitar solo to the track. The rest of the session consisted of David Z
working on some additional edits and crossfades while he compiled the album.
The song "Jerk Out" was left off the collection when it didn't fit the band's new
direction, according to engineer Coke Johnson. "'Jerk Out' was just a slamming
dance groove. This was supposed to be more glam rock, harder edged, not so
disco, funk oriented. It didn't fit the concept."
Three C-90 cassettes were made of the newest version of the album.

WEDNESDAY, MAY 8, 1985

"**100 MPH**" (mix, crossfade, and edit)
"**Strawberry Lover**" (edits, vocal overdubs, and mix)
Sunset Sound, Studio 3 | 4:00 p.m.–9:00 a.m. (booked: lockout)
Producer: Prince | Artist: Mazarati (listed as Prince) | Engineer: Prince |
    Assistant Engineers: "Peggy Mac" Leonard and Coke Johnson

> *It was Mark Brown's project. Prince traditionally doesn't take
> a lot of interest in male groups. When it comes to hands-on
> interest, it ain't going to be the guys that get it!*[26]
>
> —Alan Leeds

Despite Prince's work with the Time, Prince was overwhelmingly drawn to working with female artists. Groups like Vanity 6, Apollonia 6, the Bangles, Sheila E., Sheena Easton, and others all benefited from his ability to write music from a female perspective. He seemed to thrive in situations that included female energy, so his insistence on overseeing Mazarati felt slightly out of place. Although his complete list of reasons for it will never be known, it is important that the band be put in historical context. Mazarati would be the first band signed to Paisley Park Records, even though their debut album wasn't the first released on the label. At this moment, he was overseeing two bands to replace the Time, and it was likely important for Prince to prove to others that the Time was great *because* of him. The idea of having his new protégé bands not stack up against Morris Day and Jesse Johnson might potentially bother him, so he maintained as much control as possible.

When Prince heard the Mazarati album, he decided to take the tapes into Studio 3 and create his own mixes on songs like "100 MPH" so they'd reflect how he envisioned the band. It is likely that Prince also worked on the cross-fades and mixes for several of the tracks and perhaps even adjusted the order of the songs, which was appreciated, according to BrownMark. "He was just trying to help us out. I mean nobody's feelings were being hurt. He was just trying to come up with a record that would get them on the map."

"Prince came in with total confidence and authority over everybody within his realm," explains Coke Johnson. "He rarely questioned his decisions. It was like he had God-given answers from his heart and from his gut about what he wanted to do and how it should sound, and all that stuff. His name was Prince, but he was the king of his domain."

THURSDAY, MAY 9, 1985

"**100 MPH**" (edits, vocal overdubs, and more edits)
"**Strawberry Lover**" (edits, vocal overdubs, and more edits)
Sunset Sound, Studio 3 | 4:00 p.m.–4:45 a.m. (booked: lockout)
Producer: Prince | Artist: Mazarati (listed as Prince) | Engineer: Prince |
  Assistant Engineers: "Peggy Mac" Leonard and Coke Johnson (Peggy
  Mac left at 10:30 p.m.)

He'd change his mind at 3 o'clock in the morning and want to do something different. Yeah, he did that a lot.

—"David Z" Rivkin

Prince continued to work on tweaks to the remaining tracks for the Mazarati album, including some additional vocals by Sir Terry Casey on "Strawberry Lover." He was making adjustments to the songs during the entire night, fixing what he felt needed work and smoothing over sections that sounded clunky to his ear.

Two C-90 cassettes were made of the session, but when he listened to it, Prince must have felt that it wasn't ready yet because a few hours later, he'd be back in the studio working on the Mazarati album once again.

FRIDAY, MAY 10, 1985

"**Strawberry Lover**" (edits, vocal overdubs, and mix)
"**I Guess It's All Over**" (mix)
"**My Man**" (tracking, mix)
Sunset Sound, Studio 3 | 6:00 p.m.–7:00 a.m. (booked: lockout)
Producer: Prince | Artists: Mazarati and Jill Jones (listed as Prince) |
    Engineer: Prince | Assistant Engineers: Coke Johnson and Susan Rogers

> *Prince doesn't do anything else but work in the studio. If he's not in the studio he's either on tour or rehearsing with the band. He never takes a vacation and in the little time off he does have he goes back in the studio again. He sometimes doesn't come out for days, that's just the way he is, a very driven man.*[27]
>
> —Jill Jones

Prince went back into the studio to make the final tweaks on the Mazarati tracks, spending about 8 and a half hours working with Coke and Susan on the over-dubs and crossfades between the songs for the final compilation of their album, plus additional mixing on "I Guess It's All Over," and adding Jill Jones on background vocals for "Strawberry Lover." Although it had been a while since he'd worked with Jones, he apparently wanted her voice on the track, so he asked her to swing by the studio, as she recalls. "During the *Purple Rain* tour, we weren't speaking, actually. We had had a falling out and we were not talking, but I did go on the tour just to visit everybody else, and I wouldn't talk to him. And then at the end of it, we got back together after the final show in Miami."

At 2:30 he began working on a new track called "My Man," supposedly based on a rough demo he recorded on his acoustic guitar. "That one I actually really, really liked," recalls Jones. "Prince wrote that, of course. I had gotten into Elvis for some reason. Prince and I watched [Elvis's '68 Comeback Special] together. It was pretty phenomenal just to watch Elvis in his prime. He looked the best. 'My Man' came off of watching that inspiration." It wasn't just the music that inspired them. Even Elvis's name in lights ended up having an influence on how her logo was designed according to Jones. "Ideally, we had wanted to show the words 'Jill Jones,' behind me like how Elvis had the letters of his name behind him. And since then everybody's done it. Even Beyoncé's done it."

For the song, Prince recorded a combination of Fairlight, Yamaha DX7, bass guitar, and acoustic and electric guitar over a blend of snare and a Linn LM-1 drum track.

The 13-hour session ended at 7 in the morning when two C-90 cassettes were created of the day's recordings.

Status: "My Man" (3:15) would eventually contain Jones's vocals when it was released on her debut album in 1987. Clare Fischer oversaw the orchestral recording for "My Man" on June 24, 1985.

SUNDAY, MAY 12, 1985

"My Man" (overdubs)
"Our Destiny" (overdubs)
Sunset Sound, Studio 3 | 2:30 p.m.–8:00 p.m. (booked: lockout)
Producer: Prince | Artist: Jill Jones (listed as Prince) | Engineer: Prince |
    Assistant Engineer: "Peggy Mac" Leonard

> *He really kind of let me do what I wanted to, and I could mimic him to the letter with the screams if he wanted that in a song. I had that down.*
>
> —Jill Jones

Prince continued recording overdubs for "My Man" and 1984's "Our Destiny," which already contained Jill Jones's vocals. Often Prince would have David Z record her vocals, but it is possible that Jones was brought in on this date for vocals on "My Man." "I think Prince was just torn. Is she going to be rock and roll? But then sometimes he would have me exaggerate the vocals so much, whereas David Z might want to calm them down more because Prince was so exaggerated that it wasn't really timely for what was happening on the radio."

There were days he'd come in with no agenda as if he was looking for something to do, as Peggy recounts. "On days like this, sometimes he'd walk in with stuff written down. Sometimes he'd just walk in to see what inspired him. Sometimes he'd noodle around then leave. You could just tell. He would come in, and he would be very energetic and ready to go. And then, sometimes he'd come in very contemplative. He'd just sit and play the piano. And you're always ready for anything. Then after four or five hours, he would leave. Sometimes, it seemed to me like he'd just come in to play around in the studio. He just came in to escape the world."

The music created today was output to five C-60 cassettes at the end of this short session.

MONDAY, MAY 13, 1985

The Family album compiled
"Paisley Park" (tape copy)
Sunset Sound, Studio 3 | 2:30 p.m.–5:30 p.m. (booked: lockout)
Producer: Prince | Artist: Prince (listed but it was the Family) | Engineer:
"Peggy Mac" Leonard

> *I love Paul and Susannah and everything and their vocals on* [*The Family* album] *really certainly set it apart from what it is. But I heard all of that music when I was putting my parts on* [the record] *with Prince's vocals on it, so it could've been a great Prince album.*[28]
>
> —Eric Leeds

Peggy spent 3 hours assembling the Family's self titled album (including Clare Fischer's score) and running off a copy of "Paisley Park" from Prince's *Around The World In A Day* album. The tape would be sent to Warner Bros. to create the single. The session ended with her making 13 cassettes (12 C-90 and 1 C-60) of the Family compilation, likely for the band as well as Warner Bros.

Prince often left projects incomplete or never fully realized, and those ended up being stored away in his vault. With the odds of this album being released growing, members of the band recognized that their rehearsals may pay off if everything lines up, but until it is physically for sale, there was doubt, according to sax player Eric Leeds. "Here is this guy who already has a reputation of thinking whatever he does on Monday may have little to nothing to do with what he wants to do on Tuesday. So, I had no expectations that this album would ever come out, because a year is a long time for somebody like him to get involved with something else, then completely lose interest."

Prince continued working on the project, although it is unclear if he attended this session.

During the time that *The Family* album was being compiled in Los Angeles, the actual band was in Minneapolis, preparing for the release and rehearsing in Prince's new warehouse located at 6953 Washington Avenue S. in Edina. "It was myself, Susannah Melvoin, Jellybean Johnson, [formerly] of the Time, on drums, Jerome Benton, from the Time, and "St. Paul" Peterson," detailed sax player Eric Leeds. "The five of us were going to be the actual group. We were the ones who were gonna be signed."[29]

As they rehearsed for their eventual live show, the core band was expanded, and Prince was looking for a guitarist, remembered Levi Seacer Jr. "Sheila said to him, 'Oh, I know somebody in the Bay Area.' They flew me out to Minneapolis, but I didn't meet Prince at first. I was just in that circle. I auditioned for the Family's band and actually got the gig. I had the gig for two days, and then something came up and Prince sent a message saying, 'Oh, man. I really liked you, but I had to do some other things with that. Man, you're hot. It's cool. I'm going to keep you in mind.'"[30] Levi was later recruited for Prince's *Sign O' The Times* band, and he remained with him for years.

Miko Weaver, who was in Sheila's band, was hired on guitar, Bill Carrothers and (Wendy and Susannah's brother) Jonathan Melvoin on keyboards, and multiple bass players were considered before deciding on Allen Flowers. Wally Safford and Greg Brooks also joined Jerome on stage during the concert.

Prince was hoping to recreate Clare Fischer's work from the album, so Lisa's brother David was also asked to join. "When they put on a live act, someone called me and said, 'Come on out to Minneapolis and we'll put together a string section.' Jonathan [Melvoin] was also involved. We'd do two keyboard players, Novi [Novog] on viola, myself on cello and we'd audition a violinist. As we got it together and the day came that Prince just decided not to go with the strings.

He just said it wasn't appropriate for their first shows. I played bass with them for a short time, but it wasn't appropriate. For bass, I kind of play a little reggae or some kind of eclectic bass and they needed someone that was a little more flashy, more like Stanley Clark, so I went back to LA."

"We recorded almost every one of the Family rehearsals out at the warehouse," remembers Peterson. "We rehearsed there, and Sheila was rehearsing at the same time. We'd video tape all of our rehearsals. We used to send little competition videos back and forth to Sheila. Make fun of her and call her out, because we were coming up at the same time. She had a hot band and we had a hot band."

"**There is a real heavy competition thing that's good and healthy**," agreed Prince. "**We're like four little gangs. My band, Sheila E., the Family, and Mazarati. There used to be Vanity 6 and the Time, and it was the same thing.**"[31]

Eric Leeds explained what was expected of all of Prince's protégé bands. "The plan was that there was going to be a tour in the fall of '85. It was going to be Sheila and her band as the headliner, the Family, and Mazarati."

Prince had also commissioned a script tentatively called "Desire," that would be a battle between the Family and Mazarati. The idea was to create another *Purple Rain* type film, but it never made it past the script stage. "A lot of times we'd be driving over to see his management, and he'd have all these ideas about that," recalls Susannah Melvoin. "I'm familiar with that. It was talked about. I think he was having someone else write it. I never saw him write one word on it."

"Prince had ideas for Sheila E. around that time, and then Sheila would come by the Warehouse," remembered Susan Rogers. "And there were ideas for the Family as well. So, there were recordings taking place at that warehouse, in that space. It also included Jill Jones, and other artists. So, it was like a parade of artists coming in and out. It felt like a factory for music."[32]

Prince was also rehearsing with the Revolution during this period.

TUESDAY, MAY 14, 1985

Parade album compiled
Sunset Sound, Studio 3 | 2:00 p.m.–4:00 p.m. (booked: lockout)
Producer: Prince | Artist: Prince | Engineer: "Peggy Mac" Leonard

> *When you're gonna put an album together, there's gonna be a look that accompanies that album. Think of black and white for the* Parade *album or think of black and white for the* Dirty Mind *record. You're touring that album. So, you're really selective about what that album contains. So, you've got thirty-five minutes to say something that needs to hold you for the next year. That's it. Prince said this himself in interviews, the album matters. Not the single. The album. And anything that doesn't make the album, goes into the vault, or is a B-side.*[33]

—Susan Rogers

The aesthetics of Prince's album art and personal style are something that deserves an entire book dedicated to them. Sometimes they could be complex, and sometimes it was just heading in an entirely different direction, as Lisa explains. "He could just flip things and that would work, like the difference between *Around The World In A Day* and *Parade*. One is in color and one is in black and white. It's like really obvious, he would just flip things and say, 'Now if I do that, that'll work!'"

Peggy dubbed the May 1 *Parade* album assembly to three C-90 tapes, and the brief session was over. This was likely done without Prince present.

WEDNESDAY, MAY 15, 1985

> **We're not too much into singles. It's about the book, you know?**[34]

—Prince

"Raspberry Beret," (backed with "She's Always In My Hair") was released in the United States, and it would become Prince's seventh Top 10 hit but topped out at number 3 on the Black chart and number 2 on the Pop Chart (behind Duran Duran's "A View To A Kill," which was benefiting from the additional promotion as the title track from that summer's James Bond movie). Prince continued to focus on the album as a whole, but Warner Bros. wanted to release this as a single to capitalize on it getting radio airplay.

"Once again, Prince was so far outside the box and wouldn't listen to the 'big execs' as to their reasons for a single," explains Marylou Badeaux of Warner Bros. "It was only after we continued talking to his management that a single was finally given an okay. The album wasn't being received well from radio. They were looking for *Purple Rain 2* as well. I always felt he saw this as a deeply personal album—just my viewpoint—and as a 'complete work of art,' so why a single?"

"I wanted this album to be listened to, judged, critiqued as a whole," disclosed Prince. **"It's hard to take a trip and go around the block and stop when the trip is 400 miles. Dig?"**[35]

While the decision is seen as pioneering by some, it is seen by others as misreading his audience and not grasping the record company's role in the success of his music, explained Susan Rogers. "That may or may not have been a mistake, that was pretty risky. There's no doubt the record companies and program directors across the country had a lot to do with *Purple Rain* being successful. I mean it was marketed well; it wasn't just his talent that got it over. There's a lot of other people behind the scene. I think that Prince just didn't understand the input of many other people when he chose to just release that record as a whole."

"[Prince] had no time for people who could not share his vision," adds Badeaux, "whatever that might be in the moment."

WEDNESDAY, MAY 15, 1985

"The Dance Electric" (listen and mix)
Sunset Sound, Studio 3 | 12:00 noon–2:00 a.m. (booked: lockout)
Producer: Prince | Artist: Prince | Engineer: "Peggy Mac" Leonard

> *I was in the studio and he called me up and said, "Listen man, I got this song that I think we should really hook up and we should do this." And he played it to me over the phone and I said, "Yeah, that sounds like something that's right up my street." So, we hooked up.*[36]
>
> —André Cymone

Today's session was divided into two sections, listening to the track from noon to 2:30 in the afternoon and then mixing the track from 9 p.m. to 2 in the morning. "He'd keep me waiting a lot and he would come in with an attitude because he kept me waiting so long," explains Peggy. "There were times that he kept me waiting for 8 hours. I used to knit a lot of sweaters!"

It appears that during the break in the session, André Cymone was at Ocean Way Studios recording his vocals for the track. "André had reappeared in his life right around that time and whenever people did reappear the first thing he would do is go in and cut a track," reflected Susan Rogers. "It could have been recorded with him in mind. I know that he spent a long time on it and was very proud of it."[37]

Cymone and Prince at their core were brothers and their history dates back to living together in Cymone's basement. "He'd come to live with our family, and eventually my mother 'adopted' him," recalled Cymone. "We were able to rehearse in the basement. I was like, 'We are going to be the biggest band. I'm saying, the Jackson 5 ain't got shit on us.' All I ever did was practice. We engaged in 'battle of the bands' [contests] and won almost all of them."[38]

Two teenagers with musical talent and a dream. Because of their living situation, there would be disagreements, but there was always a mutual honesty and respect between them, and when Prince signed with Warner Bros., Cymone played bass in Prince's band and stayed with him for his first three albums. After he and Prince parted, they both followed different musical paths. "I was flailing away doing my new-wave thing and wasn't really having much success," revealed Cymone, "and Prince was having all kinds of success; everything he touched was working out in his favor. His record company backed him and understood his vision. Me, on the other hand, I had a record company that didn't know what I was trying to do. It was a totally different situation."[39]

Prince told his version of reconnecting with Cymone during an interview he did with MTV. "**I saw him in a discotheque one night and grabbed him by his shirt and said, 'Come on, I got this hit. You know I got this hit, don't you? The Dance Electric'?**"[40]

"First of all, he didn't grab me by the lapels," corrects Cymone. "One thing that Prince knows about me is, because he probably knows me better than a lot of people, you just don't grab me by the lapels, and you don't grab my guitar out of my hand and start playing. Things like that are just not a reality. It definitely wasn't at a club or anything like that. He reached out and said, 'Listen, I got this song.'"

Once the connection was reestablished, Prince brought the master tape of "The Dance Electric" to Ocean Way Studios in Hollywood. "We sat down, listened to it and hung out, and he kind of gave me the whole run down on it where he was coming from with the track, and so he actually left it there and just said, 'Do what you feel. Do what you do.'"[41]

"To tell you the truth, even though there were other issues surrounding it, I think it was a beautiful thing because we got a chance to actually work together and we hadn't done that in a long, long, long time."

"I think he honestly wanted to help me," reflected Cymone, "but on his terms."[42]

Once the tape arrived back at Sunset Sound, Peggy spent the rest of the session working on a mix.

Status: "The Dance Electric" (5:44) would be released on André Cymone's album *A.C.* on August 16, 1985, and before that, on a single in July 1985.

Prince's own version was posthumously released on *Purple Rain* Deluxe in July 2017.

FRIDAY, MAY 17, 1985

"The Dance Electric" (mix)
Sunset Sound, Studio 3 | 7:30 p.m.–2:30 a.m. (booked: lockout)
Producer: Prince | Artist: Prince | Engineer: "Peggy Mac" Leonard

> *It wasn't like that song was a dog—that was a funky ass song. Hell yeah, that's a funky ass song.*[43]
>
> —André Cymone

Peggy did some additional mixing of "The Dance Electric" and by the end of the session, she'd created a version for Prince.

Note: The following day, Prince flew back to Minneapolis. It is possible that another mixing session took place on Monday, May 20, 1985, at Sunset Sound without Prince, with Peggy Mac overseeing it.

MONDAY, MAY 20, 1985

The 5th Minnesota Music Awards
Venue: Carlton Celebrity Room (Bloomington, Minnesota)

Although Prince was in town for part of the week, he had traveled to Boston to attend a benefit show that included a performance by Sheila E., so he was unable to participate in the 5th Minnesota Music Awards. In every category that he was nominated, he dominated.

- Major Label 45/12-inch record ("When Doves Cry")
- Major Label Release (*Purple Rain*)
- Band of The Year (Prince and the Revolution)
- Artist of the Year
- Musician of the Year
- Male Vocalist
- Record Producer (Prince—*Purple Rain*)
- Recording Engineer (David Rivkin—Prince—*Purple Rain*)
- Songwriter (Prince—"When Doves Cry")

He even tied on an award based on technical achievement for Digital Processing with 3M. It was truly his night, and the hometown crowd was giving him his due. Mazarati was nominated as "Best Funk/Dance Group," but the band lost to another local band, Westside.

BrownMark, Bobby Z, and Matt Fink attended and gathered most of his awards, while his sister Tyka accepted the "Musician of the Year" award in his absence.

FRIDAY, MAY 24, 1985

"Paisley Park" was released as the first single from *Around The World In A Day* in the United Kingdom, backed by "She's Always In My Hair." It would eventually reach number 18 on the UK Singles Chart.

Status: In addition to the initial United Kingdom release, "Paisley Park" was also the first single in other European countries and Australia, with "Raspberry Beret" being issued as the second single. The 12-inch single of "Paisley Park" includes a remix version of the song.

Prince had been in Minneapolis, but because of a power outage, he flew to Los Angeles to continue recording.

FRIDAY, MAY 24, 1985–SATURDAY, MAY 25, 1985

"**Hello**" (tracking and overdub, mix)
"**Pop Life**" (edits)
"**Raspberry Beret**" (12-inch mix and edits)
Sunset Sound, Studio 3 | 9:00 p.m.–3:30 p.m. (booked: lockout)
Producer: Prince | Artist: Prince | Engineers: "Peggy Mac" Leonard, David
    Leonard, and Susan Rogers

> *I just wrote a song called "Hello" which is going to be on
> the flip side of "Pop Life." It says at the end, "Life is cruel
> enough without cruel words." I get a lot of cruel words. A
> lot of people do.*[44]
>
> —Prince

Prince cultivated an image that nothing could hurt him, but the truth is that
the opinions of others did matter to him. As an artist, he could control what
he recorded, but he couldn't control how people reacted to his music or his
decisions. He'd been on an amazing ride of popularity, but the same critics who
were praising him seemed to be critical of his newest work as well as his personal
life. Still reeling from the incident in February in front of Carlos 'n Charlie's
during the "We Are The World" recording, he decided to respond with the
language he spoke best, his music. Susan Rogers recalled that session:

> He was also smart enough at this point to know that there was really nothing he
> could do about it. He couldn't hold a press conference or anything. Once the cat
> was out of the bag, there wasn't really anything he could do except to record his
> song and give his version of it. He could have gotten on his high horse and writ-
> ten a whole album around it; you know: "I was misunderstood!" But he didn't.
> I think once he wrote the song and recorded it, he put the whole thing behind
> him.[45]

"**As far as the incident concerning the photographer goes, it's on the flip
side of 'Pop Life.'**" Prince explained in an interview for *Rolling Stone* magazine. "**The main thing it says is that we're against hungry children, and our
record stands tall. There is just as much hunger back here at home, and
we'll do everything we can, but y'all got to understand that a flower that has
water will grow and the man misunderstood will go.**"[46]

Prince created the track quickly using the Fairlight, Oberheim OB-Xs, and the Yamaha DX7 keyboards and some guitar on top. "Oberheims were a huge part of our sound, and the presets were so great and big and fat!" explained Lisa. "Prince was incredibly bold in the way he would just use a preset and then brighten the fuck out of it! He would turn the filter way up so the sound would cut through the mix."[47]

Jill Jones was recruited to add her vocals. "I had to sing that part and whatever else. I only remember being alone singing my part. I really didn't like that song that much."

He added a number of instruments, including the "Tibet" patch from the Fairlight, which is the same sample he'd used on "Tibet" and "Others Here With Us," the previous month. Once Prince was finished with "Hello," it was obvious that it wouldn't work in the design of his *Parade* project, both in theme and the yearlong delay of the release. Prince seemed more interested in getting his statement out to the public as quickly as possible. "I think that he intended it always as a B-side," explained Susan Rogers. "I got the feeling that he didn't really want to interrupt his major work. It was just something that happened, he just wanted to get it out of him. It was his way of answering his critics."[48]

Jill felt he had crossed the line with the incident at Carlos 'n Charlie's. "That was not cool. I think that was the moment that he messed up. And I remember one of my aunts was kind of laughing, going, 'That boy going to learn, one way or the other.' It's like they got him in check. No amount of writing lame songs like "Hello" was going to fix it."

The session continued well into the afternoon of the following day ending at 3:30, with additional time spent editing "Pop Life" and the 12-inch of "Raspberry Beret." Four C-60 cassettes were created from these songs.

"He wasn't tolerant of human weakness," Peggy details. "You can't even be tired. You couldn't even fucking yawn. Of course, you'd yawn. Sometimes he could tell I was exhausted, that's when he'd say, 'Get in there and watch Dallas or something!' And it's not like you could sleep. 'Peggy!' he would get on the intercom if he couldn't find me because obviously, I wasn't in the lounge where I could hear it. I could hear that yelling my name everywhere. It was hell when you were going to the bathroom. That'll seize you right up. [laughs]"

Status: The 4-and-a-half-minute take of "Hello" would be edited (3:23) and released on July 10, 1985, as the B-side for "Pop Life." The "Hello (Fresh Dance Mix)" (6:38) was the result of a future edit as well, and issued as the B-side for both "Pop Life (Fresh Dance Mix)" and "Pop Life (Extended Version)" (9:07).

SUNDAY, MAY 26, 1985

"Hello" (edits)
"Stella & Charles" (tracking and overdub)
"Come Elektra Tuesday" (tracking and overdub, mix)
"Heaven" (tracking, overdubs, mix)
"Electric Intercourse" (mix)
Sunset Sound, Studio 3 | 7:00 p.m.–12:00 noon (booked: lockout)
Producer: Prince | Artists: Prince (and likely Jill Jones) | Engineers: "Peggy
  Mac" Leonard and Susan Rogers

> *The main thing with Prince was efficiency. He needed the
> world to stay out of his way, and he needed engineers to serve
> as facilitators of his vision and his art.*[49]
>
> —Susan Rogers

"Speed was important. He would rather have fast than flawless," remembers Peggy. "And that was actually so different from what was going on in that era. A lot of people would take days to get a drum sound before they would even start tracking. There was an urgency that he had to get that stuff out. It couldn't wait. Maybe he thought it would go away."

Prince had the ability to just focus on his work in a way that few other musicians could do, and that dedication fueled his prolific reputation. He did isolate himself in the studio and simply create without needing others to alter his vision. With the number of songs being recorded, there were always going to be great ones, ones that were put away to potentially be revisited, and barely fleshed-out ideas that were never touched again. "He would sometimes record two or three songs in a day, but he wouldn't always finish each song. He'd sometimes get the ideas down," notes Peggy. He would be working and simply say, "fresh tape" and the session would go in a different direction. "Usually that would happen when the song was going stale. When he lost the inspiration for that song. Because you could tell when things were kind of musically petering out. And so, then he would take a break and he would go out and start playing and you'd think 'Okay. Any time now, any moment now.' And then you could hear a riff coming together and sure enough, then it was like the adrenaline rush. Flipping it over and getting it all ready."

During this session he continued working on the extended version of "Hello," and by the end of the shift, he had completed the mix. Although he'd later go back and make changes to both the 7-inch and 12-inch versions, it seems that Prince was eager to share his response with the public, once again allowing the music to make the statement for him, pushing back at the recent criticism in the press. "If you're on top and you're eccentric, they've got a gun for you," offered his lighting director Roy Bennett. "It just happens. The media is vicious. If there's something that they don't understand, they're going to be hurtful, and it did hurt, I'm sure."[50]

Possibly as a follow-up about redemption, Prince recorded "Heaven," which contains the lyrics: "All the people [that] we are bad to, means another loss. Soon our hearts are heavy 'til no man could bear the cross."[51] Prince was quietly autobiographical on "Heaven," referencing his own deep pain, his distinct view of the world and his philosophy about how we treat others. Prince would eventually revisit elements of this the following summer when he recorded "The Cross."

A track called "Stella & Charles" was started but not completed. The song was likely originally planned for Jill Jones, who thinks she knows the source of the title. "Charles is his cousin's name, but Stella? We did watch *A Streetcar Named Desire* with Marlon Brando. He would watch that movie a lot." Unfortunately, the story of Stella and Charles was never told because the song didn't make it to the lyric stage, so according to Peggy, it was probably considered a work in progress jam and put away for another date. "For me, it shifted from jam to a song when a lyric came on, but you just never knew, because of all the decisions going on in his head. It wasn't like we'd have a little chat, brush each other's hair, and talk about what his plans were. He just told you what was gonna happen." There is no evidence of "Stella & Charles" being worked on again.

"Come Elektra Tuesday" is a catchy song about missing his partner and the anticipation of waiting until the weekend to make love again. Once again drawing on his lexicon of film history, he compared his lover to 1920s movie star Jean Harlow in her prime. Prince had previously mentioned Greta Garbo in Vanity 6's "3 × 2 = 6," and Clara Bow (who coincidentally starred in 1929's "The Saturday Night Kid" with Harlow) in "Condition of the Heart," so he was obviously a fan of movies from that era. It was likely that he had been reflecting on this period because of how he was presenting the Family's two singers, Susannah Melvoin and Paul Peterson, as glamorous stars from that generation.

Prince often used a standard method of getting the sound of the drums on tracks like this, remembers Coke Johnson. "We had a little device called a 'clap trap.' It was an 8-inch by 12-inch little piece of electronic gear. You could send a snare into it, and it would trigger the clap on the output, and then you could adjust the pitch, the length and how raggedy the clap was. Or you could just play it manually with the trigger button, so he could just sit there and drop that in instead of the snare which gives it a more human feel."

A quick mix of "Electric Intercourse" was also completed, but it is unclear if it was the studio version or the live take he'd done on August 3, 1983, at First Avenue. This 17-hour session wrapped up at noon.

Status: It is interesting to note that of the five songs from today's session, only one, "Hello," was released by Prince as the B-side. "Stella & Charles," "Come Elektra Tuesday" (4:21), "Heaven" (8:03), and the studio version of "Electric Intercourse" (4:57) remained unreleased during his lifetime. "Heaven" was strongly considered for Prince's next film, *The Dawn*, but when that project was canceled, it went back into the vault. "Electric Intercourse" would eventually be included in the posthumous *Purple Rain* Deluxe CD set in 2017.

Prince revisited the Elektra/Electra concept multiple times in his career. Besides "Come Elektra Tuesday," it was the name of a character in "The Ladder," and a name he suggested to Jill Jones and then gave to his protégé Carmen Electra.

MONDAY, MAY 27, 1985

"Polka-Dotted Tiger" (likely tracking, mix)
"Zebra With The Blonde Hair" (likely tracking, mix)
"Married Man" (likely tracking, Prince vocal, mix)
"Killin' At The Soda Shop" (likely tracking, mix)
Sunset Sound, Studio 3 | unknown start time
Producer: Prince | Artist: Jill Jones | Engineers: "Peggy Mac" Leonard and Susan Rogers

He's always looking for a new challenge. There are very few artists willing to take creative risks the way Prince does. Some records that he has made, Around The World In A Day, *for instance, get crushed by the critics. But that does not bother him at all. He makes these albums to challenge himself.*[52]

—Jill Jones

Jill's history with Prince went back to the *Dirty Mind* tour, and she'd recorded with him sporadically over the last several years on songs like "Mia Bocca" and "G-Spot," so the idea of her own project had been discussed but rarely went any further than the occasional song, according to Jones. "Prince dangled the album idea in front of me for a while. It came up in the beginning and then it turned out that I had to work with [Vanity 6] and sing back up for them behind the curtain and I did some things for the Time. He did utilize me, and I was happy to do it but then, when I got to Minneapolis, I was a little bit miserable because this was not the same person that I really knew and there were a lot of head games in the midst of it and it wasn't really cool."

With this new batch of songs, it appeared that Jones's solo album was becoming a reality but with the project, there was a change in Prince's relationship with her once again.

> All of a sudden it became very convoluted. If there's an argument, it's like, "Well, are we dating now? Oh, now we're not, because now I'm working. Oh, okay." Totally blurred lines. And he liked blurring lines. Because emotionally, he could deal with your emotions, and angst or whatever, about wanting to be a performer, a musician. He could deal with all of that. But what he couldn't deal with is if you were actually having an issue with him about his character, his personality, his morals, which it came down to the personal relationship. He would blur those lines.

Just hours after his previous session, Prince was back at Sunset Sound and recorded another four tracks for Jones's proposed solo project. At this point there was only a rough idea of where to go with the album. Prince wanted to put an identity on every artist he produced and if today's songs were any indication, he wanted her to be quirky and odd.

"'Killin' At The Soda Shop,' that kind of stuff, he knew I liked the weirder of any of his songs. The weirder the better, the ones that had no structure or rhyme or reason."

"Polka-Dotted Tiger" and "Zebra With The Blonde Hair" are also both whimsical, playful songs that were done quickly in the studio, largely made up of sounds Prince discovered while playing with the Fairlight and Yamaha DX7 synths. "Zebra With The Blonde Hair" is an instrumental with a title likely inspired by the mention of a "young zebra" in "Polka-Dotted Tiger." The lyrics in "Polka-Dotted Tiger" appear to be ad-libbed as they sound like Jones's train of thought with little regard for rhyme. It is likely that what she is singing is a reaction to the avant-garde bed of music that Prince had created for the song.

"Married Man" is a guitar-based rocker about infidelity and how being intimate with a married man is only for a married woman. "He was in tune with what he was trying to push on me, and I love that song, by the way. I love the really grungy guitar. I love that song, but he didn't want that one to get finished. I was just like, who's he going to give it to? But he wouldn't revisit it, and he would not send it to David Z. No, that became a song that was not going to go anywhere."

Music was often Prince's main form of communication, and because of that, he was specific about what he recorded and how he was influenced by the energy of those around him. Although it might not be from this session, Jones tells a story about how specific he could be about influences that took him out of his zone. "I think that's how he actually speaks to a person, if he's really vibing. A friend was telling me, they were in a session with him once and he couldn't get this one part right, and he just turned around and said, 'You in the striped shirt, go home and change that shirt. That shirt is killing my vibe.' [laughs]"

Status: "Killin' At The Soda Shop," "Zebra With The Blonde Hair," "Polka-Dotted Tiger," and "Married Man" all remained unreleased during Prince's lifetime.

It appears that Clare Fischer wrote and recorded an orchestral arrangement for "Killin' At The Soda Shop" at some point. Elements from that arrangement would later be repurposed as the intro to the title track for his 1990 *Graffiti Bridge* album.

TUESDAY, MAY 28, 1985

"Polka-Dotted Tiger" (overdubs, mix)
"Drawers" [re-titled **"Little Rock"**] (tracking, mix)
Sunset Sound, Studio 3 | 9:00 p.m.–5:00 a.m. (booked: lockout)
Producer: Prince | Artists: Prince/Jill Jones | Engineer: "Peggy Mac" Leonard

I have always taken my time to try out new things or other arrangements, as a process to discover who I was as an artist and what I actually wanted.[53]

—Jill Jones

Although the session was planned for 4:30 p.m., Prince arrived 4 and a half hours later and began working on an instrumental track listed as "Drawers." The rest of the studio time was spent working on overdubs and a rough mix for "Polka-Dotted Tiger." It is likely that Jones's vocals were recorded at this time as well, and Prince always tried to keep it an intimate environment when doing vocals, according to Peggy. "When Jill came down, I usually left the room, because he would record her, so I wasn't usually in there."

After 3 hours of additional overdubs, Prince requested two C-60 cassettes of the day's work. The session ended at 5 in the morning.

Status: "Drawers" was likely reworked by Eric Leeds for his *Times Squared* album and retitled "Little Rock."

WEDNESDAY, MAY 29, 1985

> "**Living Doll**" [listed as "**Song #1**"] (tracking)
> "**Married Man**" [listed as "**Song #2**"] (mix, possible Jill's vocals)
> "**Zebra With The Blonde Hair**" [listed as "**Song #3**"] (mix)
> "**Killin' At The Soda Shop**" [listed as "**Song #4**"] (Prince vocals, possibly Jill's vocals, mix)
> Sunset Sound, Studio 3 | 5:00 p.m.–1:00 a.m. (booked: lockout)
> Producer: Prince | Artist: Jill Jones (listed as Prince) | Engineer: "Peggy Mac" Leonard

> *Most people will plan an album, get together with a producer, do pre-production and work out arrangements, book studio time, and go in and make a record. But Prince wasn't like that. He didn't work like that. Prince recorded constantly. So, things that were coming into fruition may or may not be part of a record.*[54]
>
> —Susan Rogers

Prince was quickly collecting a variety of songs to offer to Jones for her album, so he asked her to the studio to play several for her, including the instrumental "Zebra With The Blonde Hair" and "Married Man." "We had a really cool vibe on it because I remember how it sort of picks up, and our vocals were really close on it. It just had a really good vibe. When I came to sing it, and that was just the coolest lyrics, it'd be like, 'Nobody wants a married man.' I think I was just like, yeah, nobody," laughed Jill. "Even I don't!"

Prince spent part of the session recording Jones's vocals for "Married Man," but it is unlikely any lyrics were added to "Zebra With The Blonde Hair."

"Killin' At The Soda Shop" was probably inspired by the raw guitar work on "Married Man," and Prince recorded it in a similar way with the guitar and the Fairlight synth blended with an aggressive beat. Like all of the tracks he was giving to Jones, Prince recorded them with his own scratch vocals as a reference when he'd play it for Jill. "I loved that song. I wanted to do it, and was excited," exclaims Jones. "He and I had so much fun recording that one. It was very punky and over the top and it had a lot of guitars. There was a part where he just kind of went crazy in the studio, and he was like, 'Do you want to do it' and I was like, 'I would *love* to do this song' because it was kind of edgy. And it was very Elvis like, and he loved the Elvis thing if I pulled that off. It was just great working with him on that because he had a really sheer enjoyment in the studio. He really actually connects better when you're working with him musically."

David Z remembered some of the details about "Living Doll," and why he felt it was a comfortable fit. "It's kind of a Barbie doll song, one of those sex songs. She was set up to be a cutesy, sort of a sex object and that fit the bill."[55]

If Jill recorded her vocals on this day, she also added multiple layers of background vocals as well. "I think your main job as a background singer is to blend," reflects Jones. "I think he recognized our tones were really close, and where he could go sometimes and I couldn't, or vice versa. He utilized that. It was cool for me. I love that we were able to do that. Teena Marie trained me as a backing vocalist."

The session ended at 1 a.m. It is unclear why Prince didn't make a copy of this session on cassette.

THURSDAY, MAY 30, 1985

"**Drawers Burnin'**" [listed as "**Song #1**"] (tracking, overdub, and mix)
"**For Love**" [listed as "**4 Love (Tie U With A Chain)**"] (tracking, overdub, and mix)
Sunset Sound, Studio 3 | 4:00 p.m.–5:00 a.m. (booked: lockout)
Producer: Prince | Artists: Prince and Jill Jones | Engineers: "Peggy Mac" Leonard, Susan Rogers, and Coke Johnson

We were at Sunset Sound and we were discussing what we were going to be doing in the ["The Screams of Passion"] video and Prince came in and said, "While you're here, let's cut this now."[56]

—Eric Leeds

As a band, the Family's "The Screams of Passion" music video was being planned and Prince asked the band to drop by the studio to discuss how to prepare. "We were going to start rehearsing for the video and shoot it in a few days," according to Eric Leeds. "Jerome, Jellybean, Paul, Susannah and myself found us in Sunset Sound Studios to do a little impromptu session that later became the song 'For Love' which ended up on Jill Jones's album."[57]

As a band, the Family hadn't participated on the music for their album, but some members were present during those sessions in the summer of 1984.

"I was there when we cut the drums on *The Family* album, but he wouldn't let me do it," laments Jellybean. "He had me play electronic handclaps along with him on the drums. We were there for a lot of that shit."

"We were hanging out at Sunset Sound, he was cutting this song for Jill, and he realized 'Damn, Bean hasn't played in the studio with me,'" continues Jellybean, "so he made me go in and play the drums for 'For Love.'"

"He had me play on the Jill Jones record at Sunset Sound," remembers Paul Peterson. "He asked if I could play bass on that. He knew I could play because he'd seen me playing keyboards."

Although Paul grew up in a household filled with musicians, he credits a lot of his skill on the bass to Prince. "Prince is probably one of the most underrated bass players there is. He is so greasy. I picked up so much in my short amount of time when I was there because he'd play bass with a pick. That's where I picked that up and that's what I've known for years, is that kind of rhythmic, sloppy, funky, not necessarily playing notes but kind of ghost notes and that kind of thing. He was the instigator of all that."[58]

The jam that led to the recording took place between 4 p.m. and 11 that night with Eric on sax, Jellybean Johnson on drums, Paul on bass, and Prince on guitar. The song was centered around an iconic sax riff that can be traced back to the March 10, 1985 soundcheck before the Long Beach, California, concert, although it is unclear if that was the first time it was introduced to Prince by Eric. Over the following six hours and the subsequent days, Eric added some additional sax parts and Prince would overdub additional guitar, OB-8 synth bass, organ, tambourine, and vocals, but with Eric, Jellybean, and

Paul playing on the song (and Susannah in attendance), it was as close to the Family playing together on a released track during that period even if it ended up on Jill Jones's album. "It was off the chain," reflects Jellybean. "Prince could have put it on there as the Family. He could have literally done that."

During the song, Jill did her impressions of several of Prince's protégées, including Susannah, followed by the band saying, "Goodnight Susannah," then continuing with more over the top impressions of Sheila E., Teena Marie, Sheena Easton, and Vanity. "He was having fun in the studio, and probably in between a take we were talking about something and I came in and just started," remembers Jones. "In between takes you could be laughing your ass off. I definitely knew how to throw some shade when I wanted to, but in a fun way, because Teena definitely had distinct ways of singing."

Earlier in the session, Prince and others set the mischievous tone when he worked on a playfully vulgar blues jam, he referred to as "Drawers Burnin'" which was a one-chord R&B vamp (with a chorus that sounds similar to Fleetwood Mac's 1975 song "World Turning") that contained seemingly ad-libbed sections about Prince's relationship with the press from earlier in the spring. Prince plays the part of an angry old blues artist when he sings, "Asshole tried to take my picture, I kicked him in the neck."[59] Despite the humorous tone of the jam, it is obvious that the incident at Carlos 'n Charlie's was still very much on his mind.

After 13 hours, six C-60 cassettes were made of the session, and it ended at 5 a.m.

Status: "For Love" would be edited (4:28) and included on Jill's self-titled album in 1987. The 3-minute jam referred to as "Drawers Burnin'" remained unreleased during Prince's lifetime.

FRIDAY, MAY 31, 1985

> "**For Love**" [listed as "**4 Love**"] (overdub and mix/edit)
> "**Paisley Park**" [12-inch version] (likely mix)
> Sunset Sound, Studio 3 | 12:00 noon–2:30 a.m. (booked: lockout)
> Producer: Prince | Artists: Prince and Jill Jones | Engineer: "Peggy Mac" Leonard

I really enjoyed it when it was just the two of us. Because he usually didn't have a bad attitude with just me. It was around other people that he would do that. With us, it was just like two people working together. He didn't have to have an attitude. Don't get me wrong, he always *had an attitude, but he wasn't necessarily really super mean.*

—"Peggy Mac" Leonard

Whatever Prince wanted to do in the studio, got done. The schedule was exclusively his, and there wasn't anyone looking over his shoulder or keeping him on time. Even in his quiet moments, he was searching for a song in the studio, and he did it without regard for anyone else's schedule. He'd sit at the piano for hours just waiting for the song to form in his head, giving Peggy an intimate piano recital that could last for hours. "Piano was different, because piano would flow with him. I absolutely loved it and it would make my heart melt to watch him play. He was amazing."

"Sometimes he'd stop playing the piano, come back in, we'd work on the song that we had already been working on. It wasn't like he'd say, 'I need to take a break, I'm gonna go play the piano for a while.' You didn't get that."

Prince recorded a few overdubs on "For Love," and then sat at the piano for a few hours casting his net and hoping to find something that motivated him, but apparently nothing intrigued him, so he left the studio for 6 and a half hours. "I think that's why he would leave all of a sudden," explains Peggy. "It was like, 'Okay, I'm not inspired anymore, I'm done.' And he would go on to another experience to find some inspiration." When he returned, he spent the next 3 hours overdubbing and mixing "For Love" and the 12-inch version of "Paisley Park."

It is unlikely that this specific mix of "Paisley Park" was ever released.

JUNE 1985

SATURDAY, JUNE 1, 1985

Around The World In A Day reaches number 1 on the *Billboard* album chart, bumping USA For Africa's *We Are The World* from the top spot. It remained there for only three weeks, a drastic change from the six months *Purple Rain* had spent in that position. Compared to the steamroller of *Purple Rain*, any album would be considered a letdown, but *Around The World In A Day* was certified multiplatinum slightly more than two months after the release, indicating 2 million copies shipped in the United States, which was only a fraction of *Purple Rain*, and pointing out that Prince had a deeply loyal fanbase who weren't going to be leaving the party after *Purple Rain*. **"The same 3 million that bought *1999* bought *Around The World In A Day*,"** observed Prince. **"It's important to me that those people believe in what we're trying to say as opposed to just digging it because it's a hit."**[1]

In retrospect, Alan Leeds feels that the album was a victim of proximity to *Purple Rain* and stands on its own. "I think it was a good record that was very well crafted and contains some excellent songwriting. And was actually a lot more successful than we tend to give it credit for. Granted, some of that was automatic because of *Purple Rain* and the popularity he was enjoying, you could make the argument people were going to buy any record he put out, but they played it too, it was good."[2]

Warner Bros. was concerned about sales. Prince kept an eye on sales as well but seemed more focused on following his heart and having something important to say. **"You do it because it's right to do at that time. You don't do it because you can sell a million."**[3]

But not everyone in the band was happy with the direction and their involvement. "Obviously the *Purple Rain* album was the most successful and we got the most creative input on the record as far as some co-writes and playing on the album," explained Matt Fink. "*Around The World In A Day*—I really didn't participate in very much. That one was another one of Prince going in and doing what he wanted to do away from the band, except for maybe a little bit of input from Wendy and Lisa on that record."[4]

The summer of 1985 would be even harder for members of the Revolution as Prince unapologetically focused on projects that didn't directly involve them, including his next movie.

SUNDAY, JUNE 2, 1985

Unnamed New Song (tracking and probable overdubs)
"Living Doll" (possible overdubs and mix)
"For Love" [listed as **"4 Love"**] (possible overdubs and mix)
Sunset Sound, Studio 3 | 3:30 p.m.–unknown (booked: lockout)
Producer: Prince | Artists: Prince and Jill Jones | Engineer: "Peggy Mac"
    Leonard

> *Until one actually sits down and talks to me, they can't really know me.*[5]
>
> —Prince

"No one really knows Prince," agreed Jill Jones. "People think they do, but none of us does."[6] By most accounts, Prince had a volatile relationship with Jones. "To be really honest, I think 'For Love' might be the most honest part of our relationship," reveals Jill. They had lived together, and she knew him intimately, so they understood how to push each other's buttons, but at the same time they also respected each other enough to express themselves artistically. The studio seemed to be their sanctuary according to Jones. "I can't recall any fighting when recording, so I think that we got along the best [in the studio]."

Prince was preparing for a week of shooting videos, so it is likely that the new song he recorded today was an unnamed instrumental. Prince left after only 2 hours, but reportedly returned 6 hours later at 11:30 p.m. wanting to record for the rest of the night. "I think that was when he was clubbing or he had a meeting," recalls Peggy Mac. "He never told me what he was doing, just . . . 'I'll be back at 8:00.' I was like, 'Okay.' Sometimes he didn't make it back. That's the hardest thing, just sitting there waiting and then trying to get your energy up to get going once he got there." It is likely that Prince worked on additional over-dubs for some of the tracks he'd recently recorded for Jones.

During late night sessions like this, he'd reach out to people he needed in the studio, but Prince's schedule often conflicted with the sleep of those around him. "I got such a phobia when the phone would ring past three in the morning," remembered Wendy. "I'd be like, 'Oh my God, I don't wanna answer it' because it meant you'd have to be on a plane in three hours. Or he'd call you and say, 'What are you doing?' 'I'm sleeping.' 'Well I'm cutting [music], you're missing.'"[7]

Prince didn't seem to comprehend the difference between someone not *wanting* to do something and not being physically able to do it because of exhaustion, and he got confused when others couldn't keep his schedule because he seemed to feel that they weren't interested in participating, according to Jones. "He would get so hurt when you finally were like, 'No. I'm not doing X, Y, and Z.' And he almost looked at you like he didn't understand. He didn't have this cognitive skill of understanding another person's boundaries, and instead of confronting you, he'd just cut it short and move on. He wasn't interested. So, that's why I've often thought, hmm . . . must've been something else going on with that."

After this session, Prince put Jill Jones's album to the side until late July.

Eventually, Prince and Jill recorded a follow up track to "For Love." "Prince was like, 'Well, we did a 'For Love.' We should do a '4 Lust,'" she remembers. "We were really getting along, really, really, really great, and unfortunately for us, once we started focusing back on the music stuff, then you couldn't be together anymore. Then you couldn't just hang out. That was the drawback."

Prince's behavior during this week changed slightly as he had been spending more time outside the studio with Jones. "Working together put a little damper on it. We were really getting along. He was having fun. He was actually going out of the house, doing things. It was really chill. Not everything had anything to do with music. Going to movies again, doing stuff that had been done earlier, like in '82 and '83, and then one day I was with his dad, just sitting in the house and his dad said, I was like 'Delilah,' and I was like, 'Delilah? Like in the Bible?'"

"And he goes, 'Yes, because he doesn't want to work.'" Although Prince took a brief respite on recording during part of June, he quickly reverted back to his old habits and his regular schedule in the studio.

It is unclear when "4 Lust" was recorded, although it was likely during this period. It remains unreleased.

MONDAY, JUNE 3, 1985

Copies of songs (copy various tracks)
Sunset Sound, Studio 3 | 2:00 p.m.–7:30 p.m. (booked: lockout)
Producer: Prince | Artists: various | Engineer: Susan Rogers

> *I'm under the assumption that things you want in your life you should give away. If you want more money, give it away. If you want more love, give it away. If you want more music, do the same so. . . . I used to give a lot of songs away. I think that is why I'm so blessed with so much music throughout my career.*[8]
>
> —Prince

Prince reached out to Karen Krattinger, an employee who helped coordinate many of his events, to schedule a birthday party for later in the week in Minneapolis. He asked that it have a masquerade theme and it was to celebrate his birthday as well as to draw attention to *Around The World In A Day*. Creating something like this with no notice was expected of his employees and the ones who stayed were the ones who recognized that Prince didn't like being refused. In Prince's world, "no" was not an option, so everyone understood that they worked hard on every part of his career, but he worked hard as well and led by example.

"We generally delivered," reflects Peggy, "and if you didn't, you were out, so you just made it happen the best way you could. He didn't want explanations. Just do it. Just make it happen. We spoiled him. We never said no, and that's what you did, you facilitated his creative flow."

Prince requested that Susan Rogers gather a collection of recently recorded (and still unreleased) songs he had written for others. When he did this, it was either for copyright purposes or to assemble a variety of his tracks for a party tape and with his birthday falling later in the week, it was probably for the latter. The entire tracklist is unclear, but it likely included songs for Mazarati ("Suzy," "100 MPH"), the Family ("Nothing Compares 2 U," "River Run Dry," and "The Screams of Passion"), and Sheila E. ("Holly Rock," "Sister Fate") among them.

It is unlikely that Prince attended this short session because he was working on the video for the Family's upcoming release "The Screams Of Passion."

MONDAY, JUNE 3, 1985

[Prince] was there for part of the video, but he wasn't really there (all the time). He wasn't the little guy dictator in the background saying, "No, they can't do this, or this is how it should be." It wasn't like that.[9]

—Susannah Melvoin

The Family recorded their only music video for "The Screams Of Passion" at SIR Studios. By this time, the band had gelled, and they worked well together, remembered Susannah. "We had been in rehearsals for such a long time [preparing] to go on the road. We were rehearsing for a year [so] doing the music video was just part of the rehearsal thing, [because] we were in work mode. I saw it only as a job, but not a job where I said, 'Oh, this is a pain in the ass to do and I wish I was home by 5 p.m.' It was sort of a package deal in terms of how I felt about it. It was just part of the plan."[10]

"We'd already done photo shoots for the album cover," explained Eric Leeds. "We were all ready to do the first video, which was another interesting thing—my debut as a bass player!"[11]

> After Prince kind of gave us an idea of what he was looking for the concept of the video, which Jerome did the choreography for, I kind of had a question for [Prince] afterwards. I said, "Well, boss, exactly what the hell do I do here, because there's no horn in this song, and that kind of leaves me out in the cold, doesn't it?" I don't even know at that point if he'd even thought about it yet specifically, because he kind of hesitated for a minute and looked and just kind of said, "Oh, well, you'll play bass guitar." And I said, "I'll WHAT?" I mean, I was just like "Okay, this is different!" So, I laughed and said, "Well, in for a dime, in for a dollar!" So, I rehearsed doing the choreography with the five of us, for about

two or three days, having never in my life even held a bass guitar. Luckily, it was a song that the bass part was just a recurring rhythm, so Paul put my fingers in the right spot, so at least I was moving my fingers in the right fret, and I had a lot of friends of mine when they saw that video, and saw the bass they said, "What's up with the bass guitar?" So, anyway, that was part of the trip of being part of the Prince thing.[12]

TUESDAY, JUNE 4, 1985–THURSDAY, JUNE 6, 1985

I'm always partial to [the video for] "Raspberry Beret," because it's kind of a step away from who we are. There's a cartoon about us in there. It's just really clever. It's fun and the finished product, I think, was really playful, and pretty cool.[13]

—"Bobby Z" Rivkin

Prince had scheduled several days to record videos for future releases. Now that "Raspberry Beret" was a single, a video was designed, and a director was hired. "For 'Raspberry Beret,' we filmed a whole video, then Prince got a Japanese animator to do a completely different video and we mashed the two up," recalled producer Simon Field. "He would mess with directors. He would give them the impression that they'd be in charge of the video, then halfway through he'd go, 'Thank you,' take what he liked, and edit it himself."[14]

"The whole concept of that video was to bring the album cover to life," explained Wendy.

So, if you look at the album cover and the animated drawings on it, you'll be able to pick out everybody represented in the video as well. I have a couple of strong memories of it. One is I was very upset that I had to play that acoustic guitar in it, because it was huge. And, I'm a fairly aesthetic person and I like my guitars to kind of match the size of me. So, this thing was more like playing a guitarron, like a mariachi band. And Prince, he loved that it was so huge on me. "I love that you're so little and that you're taking control of something so big." I didn't like the guitar. The other memory I have is that Pat Smear from Nirvana was one of the extras in it.[15]

"That's when Pat had dreadlocks all the way down to his butt," related Dave Grohl, Smear's band member from Nirvana and Foo Fighters. "He loves Prince, so he put together a white ensemble and goes down to the auditions, at a rehearsal space in Los Angeles. He gets there, and everyone has to do a synchronized dance. Pat can't dance. So, he got cut. They sent him home. He starts walking down the hallway and hears, 'Hey you!' He turns around and there's a big bodyguard standing next to Prince. And Prince whispers in the bodyguard's ear. The bodyguard says, 'You can stay. He likes your hair.' They wanted his hair in the video!"[16]

Wendy continues: "Novi and Suzie Katayama, and [Lisa's brother] David are playing the string instruments. It was the first video we did where there were extras around too, so that was weird. It was the first scripted video we had done and not a performance video. So, it was interesting. It took much longer than we thought it would take. I could tell Prince was slightly annoyed by how long it took. He was just not a very patient guy."[17]

Before "Raspberry Beret," Prince had Lisa and Wendy join him in the studio for an intimate performance of "4 The Tears In Your Eyes." "We did the video at SIR on Sunset in one day and it was done live," remembered Susan Rogers.

> He didn't want to use playback; he didn't want to use the album version of it. He wanted to use the live video version which is ultimately so beautiful. He needed to get really psyched up to do that, I think, with proper emotion. That day there were a few crew members which he hated to have around, but he had to, because it was a video production and these people were necessary, and he went off in a dark corner by himself to just sort of meditate on it, before going back and singing it and I think the version they did is beautiful.[18]

The final version of the video featured Prince, Lisa, and Wendy playing the song, and for this shoot, Prince was the one playing the huge 12-string acoustic guitar. There were no distracting special effects, which allowed their deep friendship and affection to come through. It still remains one of the most private and personal videos that he ever released.

It is possible that a Sheila E. video was also done this week, but this has not been confirmed.

WEDNESDAY, JUNE 5, 1985 (ESTIMATE)

"**Raspberry Beret**" [video mix] (mix)
"**4 The Tears In Your Eyes**" [multiple takes] (tracking mix)
SIR Mobile Studio (likely) | unknown (booked: lockout)
Producer: Prince | Artists: Prince and the Revolution | Engineer: Susan Rogers

Susan Rogers was tasked with creating a proper audio mix for the two videos. After the videos were shot, Prince flew back to Minneapolis for his birthday gathering.

FRIDAY, JUNE 7, 1985

Venue: Prom Ballroom (Saint Paul, Minnesota)
Attendance: approximately 250

Prince's 27th birthday was celebrated with a masquerade party and a live concert at the St. Paul Prom Ballroom. The celebration was also intended to recognize his latest album, *Around The World In A Day*, but his performance reflected none of its contents. Instead, he and the Revolution ran through several as-yet-unreleased tracks including "A Love Bizarre," "Mutiny," "Sometimes It Snows In April," "Drawers Burnin'," and a jam on "Holly Rock" as well as "Irresistible Bitch" (including James Brown's "Bodyheat"), "Possessed," and "The Bird."

The following day, Prince flew back to Los Angeles.

TUESDAY, JUNE 11, 1985

"**Hello**" (edits, copies)
"**The Screams Of Passion**" [12-inch version] (edits, crossfades, mix, copy)
Sunset Sound, Studio 3 | 2:00 p.m.–12:30 a.m. (booked: 2 p.m.–open)
Producer: Prince | Artists: Prince/The Family (not listed) | Engineers: "Peggy Mac" Leonard and Susan Rogers | Assistant Engineer: Mike Kloster

> *My first impression of ["The Screams of Passion"] was: he put some thought into the lyrics. He was being poetic. He was using metaphor. So, I felt that he was rising to an occasion that was demanding that he be more thoughtful and musical, like it was bringing something out in him that he was capable of doing, like a deeper more thoughtful use of metaphor and poetry and melody. So, I was like, "Wow, this is great."*
>
> —Susannah Melvoin

After the brief detour on songs for Jill Jones and various music videos, Prince did some additional work on "Hello," which was a release of his own, and "The Screams of Passion," which was slated to be the first single for the Family. Since the Family had just shot their video the previous week, it was important for Prince to wrap up the 12-inch version of the track so it could be released in July. It is likely that work had already been done on the track, but some additional edits and crossfades were needed for the extended version, which prominently featured Clare Fischer's arrangement.

"'The Screams of Passion' was the perfect marriage of sophisticated funk and orchestration," remembers Jellybean Johnson. "It caught me totally off guard how the strings meshed in with that funky ass groove. It was just a sensual ass song man, just a sexy motherfucking song. I'll never forget, I was damn near in tears."

Prince also brought "Hello" back out and spent 6 hours overdubbing extra guitars and vocals, and editing both the single version and the extended version. This 7-inch release is one of the rare songs by Prince that contained sections that weren't on the 12-inch mix.

Once a single C-46 cassette was made of the "Hello" edit and eight C-90 cassettes were created for the extended "The Screams of Passion," the session wrapped up at 12:30 a.m. It appears that Prince did not do any recording in the studio until after he returned from a trip to France that was scheduled for the following week.

Status: The extended mix of "The Screams Of Passion" (6:45) was issued on July 17, 1985. It went to number 63 on the Hot 100 Chart and number 9 on the Black Singles Chart.

WEDNESDAY, JUNE 12, 1985

"Sister Fate" [12-inch version] (Sheila edits and crossfades)
Sunset Sound, Studio 3 | 2:00 p.m.–12:30 a.m. (booked: 7 p.m.–open)
Producer: Sheila E. (listed) | Artist: Sheila E. | Engineer: "Peggy Mac" Leonard

Looking back, it feels like he was racing the clock to musically say as much as he could as quickly as possible—the idea of taking a break was alien to him.[19]

—"Peggy Mac" Leonard

Seven hours were spent creating the remix of "Sister Fate," which includes an instrumental chorus at the start followed by a sax solo by "Eddie M." Mininfield, as well as multiple other "new" elements.

Two C-60 cassettes were created of today's mix.

Status: The extended version of "Sister Fate" (5:46) was released that summer and didn't chart.

THURSDAY, JUNE 13, 1985 (ESTIMATE)

"Under The Cherry Moon" (overdubs, mix)
The Complex Studios (Los Angeles, California)
Producers: Wendy and Lisa | Artist: Prince | Engineer: David Tickle

> *Wendy and Lisa are in a rare category in that they are more than mere accompanists. They can take a song that someone else has written and I wouldn't say that they'd rewrite it, because they wouldn't be so presumptuous, but they can truly interpret a song, understanding the ground that it was written on.*

—Susan Rogers

With the amount of recording Prince was doing and the plans he was lining up for his second film, there was no way he could do everything himself. He began relying on several people, including Clare Fischer for the orchestral parts he couldn't do, David Z for the vocal recording that he couldn't cover, and Wendy and Lisa to fill in the elements that he couldn't hear. "[Prince] always trusted them musically," confirmed Susan Rogers.

There was no doubt. He respected Lisa Coleman's talent incredibly, and Wendy's. But now he was getting a closer friendship with them. They were more comfortable with being around the studio and he was more comfortable with giving them a tape and saying: "Put whatever you want on it and give it back to me." He was realizing that their sound, which was very much different from his, could complement his in a way that was not compromising. No competition, and it also was in a direction that he wanted to go. I think if they had brought their sound to him earlier, it might not have been appropriate, whereas now on *Parade* it expressed what he wanted to express. So, he was willing to incorporate it.[20]

"Lisa's a very unorthodox musician," explained BrownMark. "I've never heard anyone voice piano like her. That's what Prince loved about her. And if he felt he could learn from you, he wanted you."[21]

"You could see that it just worked," Jill Jones explained what she observed about Prince's relationship with Wendy. "His behavior onstage lightened up a lot more—the nuances, the eye contact, the interaction between those two specifically. There was something a little more human and charming and cute, because Wendy used to dote on him all the time and tell him how cute he was, and maybe it was because there was finally a girl around who didn't want to, like, shag him. Somebody saying wonderful, feminine, nurturing things, but there's no payoff like, 'What can I get from this sexually?'"[22]

Offstage he trusted them enough to have them work on his music independently, so they set up shop at The Complex Studios in Los Angeles to embellish a number of his songs, and to bring him ideas. "I think Sunset Sound was booked," explains Wendy. "He was very busy, and it felt more like out of necessity that we were engaged in that role at that point, but he felt safest with it. Maybe it was a quality control thing, cause we had good quality control."

During this session, Lisa and Wendy added a variety of overdubs to "Under The Cherry Moon," possibly even creating a longer version of the track. Prince did not attend or participate.

Status: The updated version of "Under The Cherry Moon" doesn't appear to have been used in the film and remains unreleased.

The recording dates from The Complex Studios have not been verified, and many of these dates are estimates.

SATURDAY, JUNE 15, 1985 (ESTIMATE)

"Strange Relationship" (overdubs, mix)
"The Dawn" (overdubs, mix)
The Complex Studios (Los Angeles, California)
Producers: Wendy and Lisa | Artist: Prince | Engineer: David Tickle

There was tons of stuff that he was just doing on his own, I mean, he was just living in the studio. And there was a lot of other stuff that Wendy and Lisa were working with him on, too. A lot of which didn't see the light of day. It was absolutely ridiculous.[23]

—Eric Leeds

"Lisa and Wendy are writers themselves and they write well, and they had a sensitivity to Prince as a writer that is hard to find," explains Susan Rogers. "They are in a small group of musicians who usually end up being studio musicians because they are so good at taking what someone else wrote, receiving it, understanding it, putting their own unique spin on it, yet remaining true to the original sense of the song."

Today they were adding overdubs to "Strange Relationship" and "The Dawn," two songs that he'd been crafting for more than a year, although "Strange Relationship" dates back over 2 years earlier, as Prince recorded it during the *1999* tour. Wendy recalled that they "got a master tape [of "Strange Relationship"] that had Prince's vocals, piano and drums. He said, 'Take it and finish it.' So, Lisa and I went back to Los Angeles and created the other parts to it."[24]

"We also played the congas on it and put it through the old school publison," continues Wendy. The publison is a piece of studio equipment that can shift the pitch of a sound. Prince would use that a great deal on his recordings in 1986, especially on his work as "Camille." They would also add horns and strings (from the Fairlight) on "The Dawn."

In many ways, Prince had made them an extension of himself, and this partnership put some strain on the band. "We worked with him more than anyone else," remembered Lisa. "For a while we were just about the only people he worked with. We were Prince's embellishers. We embellished his musical vision."[25]

Status: Additional mixing for "Strange Relationship" (6:25) would take place the following week, and it would eventually be edited (4:01) and remixed, losing almost everything that Wendy and Lisa added to the track, for release on Prince's *Sign O' The Times* album. The version that was approved by Prince from the upcoming sessions was included on the *Sign O' The Times* Super Deluxe Edition in 2020.

"The Dawn" (14:51) remains unreleased, although Prince performed the number in Melbourne, Australia, during his 2016 Piano & A Microphone tour, seemingly in connection with the passing of Denise Matthews (aka Vanity) the day before. He subsequently started performing it during other Piano & A Microphone Tour shows as well.

MONDAY, JUNE 17, 1985 (ESTIMATE)

"Strange Relationship" (overdubs and mix)
The Complex Studios (Los Angeles, California)
Producers: Wendy and Lisa | Artist: Prince | Engineer: David Tickle

> *We'd be here in LA and he'd send us tapes with a piano and vocal, just an idea, and then we'd produce it. We would do all the instruments and background vocals.*[26]
>
> —Lisa Coleman

Additional recording was done on "Strange Relationship." Wendy and Lisa would work on the track over multiple days, during that time they'd overdub congas, finger cymbals, tambourine, and Fairlight and Oberheim keyboards. It appears that they also recorded a guitar through the keyboard, treating it as an effects pedal in an effort to bring new sounds to him. They also blended their background vocals with Prince's, making the sound thicker.

Prince did not attend this session.

TUESDAY, JUNE 18, 1985 (ESTIMATE)

"Teacher, Teacher" (overdubs, mix)
The Complex Studios (Los Angeles, California)
Producers: Wendy and Lisa | Artist: Prince | Engineer: David Tickle

> *We were in studios all over the world, writing and finishing tracks that were all incredibly diverse and odd.*[27]
>
> —Wendy Melvoin

"Teacher, Teacher" was originally recorded on a 16-track tape in 1982. The song was a completely solo number that contained Prince clapping; playing guitar, bass, and drums; and singing all of the vocals.

"It was a sketch and he had a vocal and maybe a guitar, and probably a drum machine or something keeping a beat," remembers Lisa. "We just played everything, and all the vocals, and there were several songs like that that he would just send to us."

Wendy and Lisa added additional vocal harmonies, electric and acoustic guitar, Linn LM-1 drums, claps, new organ, synth strings, bass, finger cymbals (which had been introduced to Prince by Lisa's brother David), and a layer of a calliope over a new intro of harpsichord all blended together to add a resounding density to the track.

Status: Prince's original take of "Teacher, Teacher" (3:36) was included on the early configurations of *Dream Factory* but not placed on *Crystal Ball* or *Sign O' The Times*. The early version was posthumously released on the *1999* Super Deluxe Edition in 2019, and the updated version from this session (3:08) found a home on the *Sign O' The Times* Super Deluxe Edition in 2020.

TUESDAY, JUNE 18, 1985

Prince, his manager Steve Fargnoli, and a few others flew to France to prepare for *Under The Cherry Moon*. While staying at the Nova Park Hotel off the Champs-Élysées in Paris, they met with potential cast members and scouted locations. "That was a very friendly and kind warm place," remembered Jerome Benton. "We were riding around on scooters. Prince was riding around on a scooter, Wally, Gilbert, and we're all going down these little cobblestone roads because it was amazing. It was a journey that was unbelievable."[28]

As always, Prince worked on multiple songs for the upcoming soundtrack, allowing the culture of the area to influence his sound. Many of these inspired tracks would be revisited by Prince after he returned home.

WEDNESDAY, JUNE 19, 1985

The 12-inch of "Raspberry Beret," titled "New Mix" (also known as "Extended Remix" in some countries), was released. It was backed with an extended version of "She's Always In My Hair."

THURSDAY, JUNE 20, 1985

"Sister Fate" [remix] (edits, mix)
Sunset Sound, Studio 3 | 8:00 p.m.–1:30 a.m. (booked: 8 p.m.–open)
Producer: (none listed) | Artist: Sheila E. | Engineer: David Leonard (cred-
ited as "Davey Crockett") | Assistant Engineer: Mike Kloster

> *Sheila was a veteran musician and I think he liked that. He*
> *liked the collaboration with her because she had good ideas and*
> *he liked the way she played drums and stuff like that, and I saw*
> *him not directing her as much as other people, letting her have*
> *some say in the music.*
>
> —"Peggy Mac" Leonard

As he was doing with Wendy and Lisa, Prince was also trusting Sheila E. to add her own flavor to his music, while remaining faithful to what he wanted, which was a luxury he gave to only a select few. On this date, Sheila was working on a remix of "Sister Fate," and she appears to have been in a playful mood. On the work order, she called herself "little snot" and the engineer David Leonard was listed as "Davey Crockett." She'd also write many of her credits in reverse without the use of a mirror. "That was typical Sheila E. work because she's got this unique talent to be able to write backwards without thinking about it," recalls engineer Mike Kloster. "It's kind of a very unique talent. She's even got personalized drumsticks with her name signed backwards."

After 4 hours of editing, two C-60 cassettes were made of what they accomplished. Prince was out of the country, so his participation would come from his review of the cassette which was sent via FedEx.

FRIDAY, JUNE 21, 1985

"Strange Relationship" (overdubs, mix)
"Teacher, Teacher" (multiple mixes)
The Complex Studios (Los Angeles, California)
Producers: Wendy and Lisa | Artist: Prince | Engineer: David Tickle

If he saw something was working or something inspired him—whether it was a person or something somebody wore or something somebody played—he would follow that trail, and then things would follow really quickly. Nothing was ever really gradual, even though we would sometimes work on things for a really long time.[29]

—Lisa Coleman

Additional overdubs and mixing took place on "Strange Relationship" and "Teacher, Teacher." The session likely went past midnight, so work on "Teacher, Teacher" may have gone into the next day.

SATURDAY, JUNE 22, 1985

"Pop Life" [Sheila's remix] (overdubs, edits)
Sunset Sound, Studio 3 | 12:30 p.m.–2:30 a.m.
Producer: (Susan Hale spelled backward) | Artist: Sheila E. (listed as "Bugger Buttface" spelled backward) | Engineer: David Leonard listed as "Davey Crockett" (spelled backward) | Assistant Engineer: Mike Kloster (listed as "Mikey Baby" spelled backward)

[Prince] said, "I just need you to mix that song. Mix it and get it done," and so I did.[30]

—Sheila E.

Starting at 12:30 in the afternoon, Sheila begins working on a remix of "Pop Life."

"We were working with tape," recalled Sheila, "so we're cutting up tape and cutting up the pieces and taping them to the wall and we would tape it back together and that's how I edited the song. It was interesting because when it goes 'pop-pop-pop' you know things like that. That's cut tape. You take a razor blade and you just start cutting all the pieces and putting it back together. It's so much easier now, but it's more fun doing it the other way."[31]

Normally while Prince was away, he'd have a cassette created for his review, but it was apparent the remix of "Pop Life" was incomplete, so no cassettes were created of the session.

Status: Sheila's remix of "Pop Life" (6:16), titled "Fresh Dance Mix," was released on the 12-inch of "Pop Life" on July 31, 1985 in the United States.

SUNDAY, JUNE 23, 1985

"Pop Life" [Sheila's remix] (overdubs, edits))
"Life Can Be So Nice" (likely vocal overdubs, mix)
Sunset Sound, Studio 3 | 11:00 a.m.–9:30 p.m.
Producer: Sheila E. (listed as "Vanity" spelled backward) | Artist: Sheila
   E. (listed as "Chiquita Banana" spelled backward) | Engineer: David
   Leonard (listed as "Davey Crockett" and "Frito Bandito" spelled back-
   ward) | Assistant Engineer: Mike Kloster (listed as "Nestle Crunch White
   Chocolate" spelled backward)

*I had heard all kinds of things throughout the years about
what working with him was like, but he's the sweetest, nicest
guy you'd ever want to meet. He makes you feel you can do anything. There are no rules, no limits. He sets you on a pedestal
and says, "You can do it."*[32]

—Sheila E.

More work was done by Sheila on the remix for "Pop Life," including the addition of her chanting elements of the French traditional song, "Frère Jacques."
"Pop Life" was finished and mixed down to a half-inch tape.

With Prince still away in France, Sheila's growing confidence in her abilities
in the studio continued to be expressed on the daily work order. Besides writing
the names—and nicknames—backward, (Sheila signed it as "Ananab Atiuqihc"
which is "Chiquita Banana" backward), she also wrote: *"Suzzana's English muf-
fin head. Plys the big nose off her big head and her big lip from when I hit her! Ha
Ha!!!"* which was also written backward.

A mix of "Life Can Be So Nice," which included cowbells that were likely
overdubbed during this session, was also likely created. Normally Wendy and
Lisa would have output this from their sessions at The Complex Studios, but
they were out of town attending the Bobby Poe's 14th Annual Radio/Records
Seminar & Awards Banquet in Atlanta and accepting an award for Prince who
was still in France, so that track was output from here on this date.

Three C-60 cassettes were made of their work.

TUESDAY, JUNE 25, 1985

"My Sex" (overdubs, possible mix)
"Too Rough" (likely overdubs, mix)
The Complex Studios (Los Angeles, California)
Producers: Wendy and Lisa | Artist: Prince | Engineer: David Tickle

> *It seems like it was going well because he kept sending more songs and we were working nonstop so we just assumed he was digging it.*
>
> —Lisa Coleman

With Wendy and Lisa back in Los Angeles, work continued at The Complex Studios. Among the tasks supposedly done today was updating "My Sex," a song Prince had previously recorded, possibly as early as 1983 during the *1999* tour. In addition, "Too Rough" (now likely called "Rough") was reportedly worked on as well, although no details are available.

Status: "My Sex" was intended for Jill Jones, potentially as the title track for her album, but it was ultimately removed from the collection and remained unreleased during Prince's lifetime.

WEDNESDAY, JUNE 26, 1985

"Teacher, Teacher" (overdubs and mix)
"Yah, You Know" (overdubs and mix)
The Complex Studios (Los Angeles, California)
Producers: Wendy and Lisa | Artist: Prince | Engineer: David Tickle

> *I wonder why he rejected ["Yah, You Know"] and didn't give it to someone else. It's not a bad little hook. Someone could have done something with it.*
>
> —Susan Rogers

Wendy and Lisa also worked on a track that Prince had originally recorded on June 5, 1982, called "Yah, You Know," a song that makes light of the Scandinavian accents of many of the locals in Minnesota and that area of the country (as heard in the movie *Fargo*). For so many musicians, a song like "Yah, You Know" might have been a major success on the pop charts, but Prince treated it as a throwaway track, possibly because it features a recurring riff that sounds like a variation of "Dirty Water," originally released in 1966 by the Standells.

The original 16-track song had been recorded in Prince's home studio (listed as "Starr Studios" on the tape box, as if it had been overseen by his fictional producer, Jamie Starr), as a solo performance by Prince who sang lead and two background tracks and played synths over a Linn LM-1 drum pattern. The song contains a quick musical reference to *The Andy Griffith Show* when he sings about watching television like a fool. During this session, Wendy and Lisa added background vocals and a few other elements to the track.

Status: The original version of "Yah, You Know" (3:11) would be posthumously released on the *1999* Super Deluxe Edition in October 2019. The updated version remains in the vault.

THURSDAY, JUNE 27, 1985

"Carousel" (tracking and overdubs)
The Complex Studios (Los Angeles, California)
Producers: Wendy and Lisa | Artist: Prince | Engineer: David Tickle

A lot of the songs were test studies, to hear how something sounds.[33]

—Lisa Coleman

In addition to embellishing Prince's music, Wendy and Lisa were also creating their own music to submit to Prince. During today's session, they composed an instrumental they called "Carousel." "Wendy and I wrote that at the Complex, but just the music. And then Prince heard it and loved it."

Their version of the song contains what sounds like a calliope as well as sound effects of children on a merry-go-round, similar to those used on Prince's unreleased instrumental version of "Paisley Park" from 1984. All of these blended together to create a jubilant wall of sound that places the listener on a carousel.

Status: Prince enjoyed the 5-minute "Carousel" and would eventually add lyrics and retitle it "Power Fantastic" when it was re-recorded in March 1986. "Power Fantastic" was released on Prince's 1993 *The Hits/The B-Sides* collection, but all versions of "Carousel" remained unreleased during Prince's lifetime.

Prince returned home from Paris with a number of newly inspired song ideas. "The man would come from the airport to the studio," details Rogers. "You'd get a call that said he's on his way. Robbie Paster would take his luggage to his house and Prince would just come straight to the studio or warehouse. He worked pretty damn constantly. That was who he was. And you could imagine that feverish brain on an airplane. He's going to be thinking of songs."

He was obviously inspired by his time in France as the next batch of songs he recorded were published as "Parisongs," a nod to his time in the city of lights.

FRIDAY, JUNE 28, 1985 (ESTIMATE)

"Jealous Girl" (rehearsal)
Washington Avenue Warehouse (Edina, Minnesota)

Now that Prince was back in Minneapolis, it appears that the entire Revolution gathered at the warehouse, where he spent the day teaching them "Jealous Girl." It is unknown why as the song was never released or played live by Prince. It is possible that the song was on his mind as he'd recently offered it to the Bangles, although they chose not to record it.

With Prince's decision not to tour behind *Around The World In A Day*, he needed to promote it somehow, so he elected to allow *Rolling Stone* to interview him for a cover article. Neal Karlen flew to Minneapolis and spent several days (including a birthday party for Prince's father), speaking to Prince for his first major interview in years. Considering his shyness and lack of interest in opening up with reporters, Prince was uncharacteristically content with the results, according to Susannah Melvoin. "He came back and he said, 'That's the best interview I've ever done!'"

JULY 1985

"Strange Relationship" (edit, mix)
The Complex Studios (Los Angeles, California)
Producers: Wendy and Lisa | Artist: Prince | Engineer: David Tickle

> *He could do everything himself. He created the Revolution*
> *when he didn't have to, but we were playing the music. And*
> *he loved it. He was on the high wire and we were down here,*
> *pushing the air up, keeping him up there. It was good for him*
> *because he was such a singular, perfect Prince.*[1]
>
> —Lisa Coleman

While working on "Strange Relationship," Wendy and Lisa added sitar to the track, giving it an exotic feel, likely inspired by Lisa's brother David's interest in the sounds from other parts of the world, but the actual instrument wasn't used on the track. "The sitar sound came from a sample from the Fairlight," reveals Wendy.[2]

"I think he was really pleased with it," she continues. "I don't remember specifically because we had to send it back to him, so I wasn't there for his initial hearing it vibe." Prince seemed so intrigued with the sitar that he'd add it to multiple tracks from this era, including "Adore," "Big Tall Wall," "The Cross," "Crucial," and "Mountains."

TUESDAY, JULY 2, 1985

"Yah, You Know" (horns, mix)
"Evolsidog" (strings, mix)
The Complex Studios (Los Angeles, California)
Producers: Wendy and Lisa | Artist: Prince | Engineer: David Tickle

> *We really fooled around with a lot of tape manipulation and*
> *playing with vari-speed and flipping things backwards and*
> *then adding the strings. It was just really different because you*
> *wouldn't listen to that kind of groove and think, "Yeah, we need*
> *strings," but it was an opportunity to try something different.*
>
> —Lisa Coleman

Clare Fischer arranged many of Prince's recent songs with an orchestra, but Prince had originally asked Lisa and Wendy to add strings on songs from the *Purple Rain* era, and they would continue that on occasion. "We started doing that before the Clare Fischer phase," explains Lisa. "So we started dabbling in it, because Prince was saying, 'Try strings on this,' or, 'Try some orchestral horns and stuff.' We started first with our little group, and it was usually [Lisa's brother] David, Suzie [Katayama], and Novi [Novog]. Then we brought Sid [Page] in. Sid was great to work with because he had worked with Sly Stone and all that. It was really fun meeting him and having his abilities and his sensibilities. He kind of helped, knowing how to voice things."

Two tracks were given to them for this session, "Yah, You Know" and "Evolsidog." From 11 a.m. to 2 p.m., John J. Liotine, Steven P. Madaio, and Carleton Smith were recruited to add their horns to "Yah, You Know" and from 5 p.m. to 11:30 p.m., Suzie Katayama, Novi Novog, and Sid Page were brought in to record a string arrangement for "Evolsidog."

"I never worried like, 'Oh no, we're going to go too far.' I kind of liked it when I felt like we're going too far or it's too weird because it would poke [Prince] and he'd either hate it and erase it," remembers Lisa, "or he'd be really inspired and say, 'Yeah, keep going.'"

FRIDAY, JULY 5, 1985–MONDAY, JULY 8, 1985

I don't think that Susan Rogers slept more than a couple of hours a night for many years because I don't think she even felt comfortable handing it off to another engineer because she was like, "I want to do this with you and I want to make it right, Prince, and I'm here for you, whatever you need and let's keep going," and that was one of the reasons why he trusted her.

—Susannah Melvoin

The Flying Cloud Drive warehouse was no longer available, so a new warehouse was procured on Washington Avenue in May, initially leased for a limited period. Prince, the Family, and Sheila E. all used this space for rehearsals, but the lease on it ran out. So a new location was found not far away, but according to Susan Rogers the move was complicated because Prince decided to change his equipment as well.

Prince was tired of using the API console, so he ordered a brand new Soundcraft [TS24] console, an updated version. On this Friday the crew and I were told to move everything into this new warehouse. The console arrived on Friday afternoon. We got it out of the crate, got it all set up and there was no paperwork with this brand new console. This was Friday night and now the factory was closed, so I had to trace down every single wire to the pinouts at the back of the console and I was there all Friday night. About six o'clock in the morning Prince came down with Sheila and I was there by myself, still wiring. Although he would never go so far as to be complimentary, he did say to Sheila: "See Susan is the only one who knows what I'm about." And that was his way of saying "thanks," as close as he'd ever get. Of course, I was gonna do it for him. By noon the next day I finished wiring up the console, so I stayed there, and then he came down Saturday night around six o'clock and set up with the band. They started rehearsing and he said: "I hate this place! Get me out of here!" We had to get him back to the old warehouse on Washington [Avenue], and now I had to rip out the whole thing, take out all these connectors and then repack everything.

It's now Sunday, and we are setting everything back up. At some point on Monday morning, this is now the fourth day, he came in and said: "Great! Let's record."[3]

"That was fairly typical working with Prince," reflected Rogers. "Where he said: 'Move this mountain!' And you moved the mountain. Whether you had to do it with only a toy shovel or whatever, you just got it done. It was amazing the things that he would call upon us to do."[4]

MONDAY, JULY 8, 1985

"**Girls & Boys**" (tracking, overdubs, mix)
"♥ **or $**" [aka "**Love Or Money**"] (tracking, overdubs, mix)
"**Alexa De Paris**" (tracking, overdubs, mix)
Washington Avenue Warehouse (Edina, Minnesota)
Producer: Prince | Artist: Prince | Engineers: Susan Rogers and David Tickle

I've seen him write on all instruments. I think it starts some-
times in his head with the lyrics. A new keyboard instrument or
a new kind of guitar, like in "Girls & Boys," that synth guitar
that whines like a duck. That inspired him to do that. Instru-
ments could be inspiring for him, and I think being in the stu-
dio and new boards and new gear just keeps it fresh for him.[5]

—"Bobby Z" Rivkin

The Family and Sheila E. had been rehearsing at the warehouse, but now that recording equipment was set up for Prince, he wanted, or more accurately *needed*,
to record. It didn't matter that Susan had been up for days, he had music in him
that he *had* to get out, so he called Wendy, Lisa, Matt, Mark, and Bobby to meet
him at the warehouse.

"'Girls & Boys' and 'Love or Money' . . . that was the band," explains Wendy.

I remember hours of rehearsal with those songs at the warehouse. There was an
energy in the room just because the grooves were so good, especially with "Girls
& Boys." It's centered around that synth guitar. [Roland G-707 guitar synth]
That was so hard to play. And so heavy. I remember Bobby on those synth drum
pads [Simmons drum pads with the SDS-V module] having to learn that and
I remember Prince running up to the riser back and forth to show Bobby that
groove and then playing it for hours, getting into the zone. It's like a long-distance
runner. You know how they hit their high. There's no difference. When the gears
have finally locked and there's like an ineffable quality to every musician listening.
It's all about listening and the skill of listening and finding all the little holes to
link your chain. And once it happens, that's why that band was so good for that
amount of time.

During sessions like this, Wendy recalls that everyone had their part of the
sound.

Bobby was a genius at just meat and potatoes and his foot, just a solid foot. Huge kick sound. He was great at that. Then you knew Matt, you were going to get some great fucking lines and he knew Lisa was going to blanket it with a wave. And you knew Mark was just going to rumble fatter than anybody could, almost inaudibly, inaudible notes, and then you knew I was going to play weird chords and rhythm. It's centered around that synth guitar. So, everyone knew their ingredient. That's the celery, that's the chili pepper. There's the pepper and garlic salt. Prince knew it all. He was a Black Hat Chef.

Even as Prince was singing a song about romance, his inner thoughts reveal that he continued to associate romance with being abandoned, when he sings "I can take a breakup if you say that you care."[6] Prince often revealed his romantic Achilles' heel in his work and sometimes disliked being so exposed, according to many around him, reveals his lighting tech Roy Bennett. "That was pretty much his life and his heart. I think he might have regretted that he did that, because he's very vulnerable. He and I always had that same mindset: 'Never give yourself away.' The audience always wants what they can't have—once they get it, they're bored."

On a historical note, "Girls & Boys," "Love Or Money," and "Alexa De Paris" were likely the first Prince tracks from the batch he'd listed as "Parisongs," one of many umbrellas, such as Ecnirp Music, Girlsongs, and Controversy Music, in which he copyrighted his songs. While he had referenced Paris and France in many songs including "Condition Of The Heart," "The Belle Of St. Mark," and even very early in his career with "It's Gonna Be Lonely," this is the first batch that seemed to be directly influenced by his time in the city of love. He would release songs from the Family as "Parisongs," but they were actually recorded the previous summer. On "Girls & Boys," Prince sang "I love you baby, I love you so much. Maybe we can stay in touch,"[7] which perhaps reveals what his inspiration may have been when in France. "I often wondered if there was a girl that inspired him," speculates Lisa. "I know how new love inspires new and fresh ideas. Even though he was in relationships during this time, I know that he had little flings. Sometimes I would just get a feeling. Like a little flurry of songs would come up and I'd say, 'there must be a girl that got him reeling.' These songs end up being more fluttery and excited. 'Girls & Boys' and certain songs like that, they had this energy level to them that was like a buzz. 'Oh, what's going on Prince?'"

Since April, he had been rekindling his relationship with Susannah Melvoin and because they were working on getting close once again, he included her in his music. She shared lead vocals for the Family, and they were also rehearsing at the warehouse, so she was close by and when he wanted her voice on tracks like the ones recorded on this date, she was available.

Prince had an idea for adding a female French voice to the track, so he reached out to Marie France, the head of his wardrobe department on tour. "He called her in the middle of the night to come down," recalled Rogers. "She was a middle-aged woman who really didn't have a clue of what he wanted, and her voice was kind of monotone, but it was just what he wanted."

"So, I go to the studio," recalled France, "and Prince gives me a sheet of paper with a written paragraph and says, 'Can you translate it?' [laughs] I translated a bit literally, but I thought it was beautiful as well as poetic even though it isn't fluent French. And that's when he tells me, 'Well there's a mic over there, and you're going to say the text.' I was really very surprised because I wasn't expecting that at all."[8]

Everyone seemed pleased with her performance. "Wendy and Lisa, who were there applauded, and they told me, 'Thank you very much.' And I was thinking, on a second take I will feel much more at ease, and it will be much better, but there was only one take."[9]

It appears that she likely helped him phonetically say, *"Vous êtes très belle"* ("You're very beautiful") and he placed this in the song. Because her performance was outside the range of her usual duties, she was told that she would be paid the studio musician union fee. "Prince, from what his manager told me, insisted that I receive a big check. It was a way to thank me. And in exchange, I signed to renounce my rights on the recording. But it was a big check, which enabled me to buy a Mercedes."[10]

"Love or Money" was also fleshed out as a jam during this session.

While in France, Prince had found inspiration for a third track from this session, but it was not a romantic muse. Instead, he found it in a way that appealed to his artistry. Steve Fargnoli's niece, Alexa Fioroni was only 15 years old, but she'd already been a professional dancer for several years and had been training in classical ballet at the Paris Opera Ballet School. When Prince heard of this young prodigy, he asked if he could see her dance, so she attended a private party at a nightclub in Paris. "I know it was past my bedtime, it was 11, midnight, and I'm dancing," recalls Fioroni. "I only saw him for a moment sitting in one of those little lounge couches with his scarf, and I recall that I wanted to have him come dance on the dance floor. I tried to wave him to get to dance with me, and he just kind of shook his head, looked at me, 'No.' I shrugged my shoulders, and went back dancing."

Alexa and her mother left the party and didn't see Prince again for months. When he returned to work on the film, she found out how she'd been his momentary muse. "My uncle told me that Prince composed an instrumental for me. I was in disbelief. I listened to it, and I'm like, 'Oh yeah, I could see why he would think that. That was my personality.' I was not as aware of the privilege, and how large and inspiring that was. It's a beautiful piece. He was an extremely generous spirit."

The song was "Alexa De Paris." She would be featured as a young dancer in the video for "Girls & Boys," and played a minor part in *Under The Cherry Moon*. "I am in the movie in the section where Prince is playing in the piano bar by himself, and there's a little dancer. In that scene there's a silhouette of a little person twirling. That's me in the background in a little skirt, kind of like one of those little dolls in a jewelry box for little girls. That's who I am," details Fioroni. "I'm in the credits as 'The Dancer.'"

Prince oversaw "Alexa De Paris," but the recording also included Lisa, Wendy, Matt, and possibly Mark as well as Wendy's brother Jonathan on finger cymbals.

Status: "Girls & Boys" (5:36) would be edited (3:27) and released as a single on August 1, 1986, backed by "Under The Cherry Moon." The album version was released on the 12-inch single with the extended version of "Erotic City" on the B-side.

"Love Or Money" (3:57) was considered for the *Parade* album, but released as a B-side of "Kiss" on February 5, 1986. An extended version (6:50) was released on the 12-inch for "Kiss." The song was officially listed as the stylized "♥ or $," but will be referred to as "Love Or Money" in the text.

"Alexa De Paris" (3:20) would be released on May 7, 1986, as the B-side for the single for "Mountains." An extended version (4:54) was included on the "Mountains" 12-inch. Orchestral elements were recorded by Clare Fischer on August 21, 1985, and used in the released film. Prince may have written lyrics for "Alexa De Paris," but they were likely never recorded.

Note: Much of the recording for this session probably took place on July 9 after midnight.

TUESDAY, JULY 9, 1985

"**Girls & Boys**" (horn overdubs, mix)
"**Love or Money**" (horn overdubs, mix)
"**Love or Money**" [instrumental] (mix)
Washington Avenue Warehouse (Edina, Minnesota)
Producer: Prince | Artist: Prince | Engineers: Susan Rogers and David Tickle

*This was a big warehouse. The Family would rehearse during
the day, and the Revolution would do some rehearsals in the
evening, on the same basic set. We were also doing recording
right then, too.*[11]

—Eric Leeds

"I remember the afternoon that I did my parts for "Girls & Boys" and "Love or
Money," and I was literally sitting on one of the band risers, coming up with the
parts," recalled Eric Leeds.[12]

I had the tracks being blasted back at me through the entire PA system and I
was recording literally with no headphones, no isolation, nothing. I did my parts
for "Girls & Boys" and "Love or Money" and there were people running about,
because rehearsal had just broken up. We had a pool table and a ping pong table
in the corner, and Prince was playing pool while I was sitting recording, and he
was yelling at me when I would come up with a part that he liked, "Yeah, I like
that, keep that" while we were recording. And poor Susan Rogers was going
crazy trying to keep all this isolation, and there was none. It was just completely
spontaneous, and it was a ball! This is how to make music! So literally those horn
parts and solos on those were completely mine. In fact, on "Love or Money" he
went back and took my horn solo and then overdubbed some accompanying
orchestrations to it.[13]

"There's a lot of music that has horns on it," points out Leeds, who recalls
that this was the first time he played baritone sax for Prince. "The horn arrangements are very nice to listen to. But if they weren't there, you really wouldn't
miss them. And I try to go beyond that. And on songs like 'Girls & Boys,' I
think I've achieved that. Because when a lot of people think of 'Girls & Boys,'
they think of that baritone line. Without that, it's not the same song. 'Love or
Money': the same thing."[14]

Eric doubled up some of the sax and added flute to "Love Or Money." A quick mix of the two tracks was completed, including an instrumental of "Love Or Money," and the session was over for the night.

WEDNESDAY, JULY 10, 1985

"Pop Life" (with "Hello" as the B-side) was released as the second US single from *Around The World In A Day*. It reached number 8 on the Black Chart and number 7 on the Pop Chart.

WEDNESDAY, JULY 10, 1985

"Happy Birthday, Mr. Christian" (transfer)
Sunset Sound, Studio 2 | 7:45 p.m.–8:00 p.m. (booked: 5 p.m.–6 p.m.)
Producer: (none listed) | Artist: Apollonia 6 | Engineer: Mike Kloster

The song "Happy Birthday, Mr. Christian" is about the story of a schoolteacher that I had. He was super cute, and all the girls used to flirt with him. And he would sit all the pretty girls in the front of the class and young girls forget to sit with their legs crossed and all that. I used to always look and go, "These big dummies. Look what he's doing, he's checking out our legs." [laughs] And I told Prince about that.

—Apollonia

Prince was not in Los Angeles during this session, so it is likely that he requested a transfer of this song for the Apollonia 6 video project that was being created to promote their album. Apollonia remembers how he brought it to them. "Prince said, 'We're gonna make a video,' and we first thought it was gonna be for 'Sex Shooter.' And he says, 'No, we'll probably do like a whole bunch of videos.' We were like, 'Okay.' And then, we talked about attaching it and making it all one story, like a mini-movie."

The collection included all six of the tracks from their 1984 album and featured Brenda Bennett, Susan Moonsie, and Apollonia as well as Ricky Nelson, Edy Williams, and Buck Henry.

WEDNESDAY, JULY 10, 1985

"**Neon Telephone**" [instrumental] (tracking, overdubs, mix)
"**God Is Everywhere**" (tracking, overdubs, mix)
Washington Avenue Warehouse (Edina, Minnesota)
Producer: Prince | Artist: Prince and the Revolution | Engineers: Susan
    Rogers and David Tickle

*When I talk about God, I don't mean some dude in a cape
and a beard coming down to Earth. To me, he's in everything if you look at it that way.* [15]

—Prince

Using Sheila, Wendy, Lisa, Susannah, and possibly Matt Fink, Prince put together a gospel sounding track called "God Is Everywhere," a song that detailed
his religious views. Lisa reveals that Prince was always seeking out a higher
power and how he filtered it into his philosophy. "He read magazines like crazy,
and he always wanted to be up on everything, fashion and everything, but he
also read a lot of self-help books, he read religion, he read things about the mind
and he was really interested in how humans function, but at the same time, he
did like self-editing of what he read, he took from it whatever he wanted and left
the rest."

   "**I'm studying religion and philosophy,**" Prince explained in 1997, "**that's
what I want my music to reflect. It's hard to put that in a pop song.**"[16]

   Prince would occasionally dip into gospel-sounding music, but in the overall span of his career it was just another place that he could spend some time
mastering before he moved on. "What genre didn't he have a knack for, is the
question you gotta ask," explains Bobby Z. "At any given moment, there can be
a blues jam or rockabilly jam, a fusion jam. On any given day, the music was all
over the place."

   Prince also worked on a playful song he'd written called "Neon Telephone,"
backed by the Revolution, with Bobby on tambourine. The track is another
song about a long-distance relationship, a theme he'd visited in "Bedtime Story,"
"17 Days," "I Love You (A Million Miles)," and "How Come U Don't Call Me
Anymore."

   The title was likely inspired by a telephone that he owned that would become
a prop for the Mary Sharon character in *Under The Cherry Moon* as Susan Rog-

ers recalls. "I remember the telephone that he had. It was one of those clear bodied ones where you could see the wires and the different colored components inside it. When I think of the song, I think of that telephone in his home office in the house on Kiowa Trail. 'Neon Telephone' was just one of those many things that we just churned out one after another. But what a hook, what a hook!"

It is likely that "Neon Telephone" contained no lyrics by the end of this session, so an instrumental version was committed to a cassette so Prince could flesh out the lyrics.

Status: "Neon Telephone" (3:41 with the drum count in) was not released by Prince but would be given to Paisley Park Records artist Three O' Clock for their album, *Vermillion* in 1988. "God Is Everywhere" was considered for use in Prince's upcoming movie project *The Dawn*. The track would be revisited in September, but it remained unreleased during Prince's lifetime.

THURSDAY, JULY 11, 1985

Venue: 7th Street Entry
Capacity: (attendance unknown)

> *Once Prince and I started working together and recording songs, we started going to First Ave to just play the songs to see what the fans would think.*[17]
>
> —Sheila E.

As he often was with new music, Prince wanted to quickly get a reaction from others about his recently recorded songs, so he invited Sheila E. to join him on the small stage at the 7th Street Entry, which is the club connected to First Avenue, for a quick two-song jam. Borrowing the instruments from the band Ring Theatre, who were headlining that evening, Prince played bass and sang lead on "Girls & Boys" and "Holly Rock," as Sheila got behind their drums and sang backup on the second song.

THURSDAY, JULY 11, 1985

"Venus De Milo" (tracking, mix)
"God Is Everywhere" (overdubs, mix)
"Neon Telephone" (vocals likely, mix)
Washington Avenue Warehouse (Edina, Minnesota)
Producer: Prince | Artist: Prince and the Revolution | Engineers: Susan
    Rogers and David Tickle

> *We just kept creating and creating as we would come into the*
> *room and if he had an idea, we'd just kind of run through it*
> *and then just play it.*[18]
>
> —Sheila E.

After returning home from their showcase at 7th Street Entry, Prince and Sheila
went back to the warehouse to record a number which had been an instrumental
track Prince had written several years earlier, "Venus De Milo," which was probably briefly revisited (and likely retitled) while in France.

During this period, Sheila's drums and percussion remained set up in the
warehouse, both for rehearsals and for recording with Prince. It was an era of
constant recording and he was pushing the envelope with the sounds he was
hearing, and when he had something in his head, he was generally in a rush to
get it to tape. For "Venus De Milo," he asked Sheila to play drums as he accompanied her on piano. "When we played it, it was so different for me musically, so
different from most anything we had done together," reflected Sheila E. in 2019.
"And I just thought . . . you're just incredible. This is such an amazing, beautiful,
heartfelt song. I love that song."[19]

The title of the song may have been a tribute to Miles Davis. A track named
"Venus De Milo" (written by saxophonist Gerry Mulligan) appeared on his
1957 album *Birth Of The Cool*. The two compositions have nothing in common except for the title. The statue of Venus De Milo was the muse for Prince's
character in *Under The Cherry Moon*, and he'd use images of the ancient Greek
statue in the artwork for the album and the single of "Kiss." Prince was a fan of
Davis and his 1985 album *You're Under Arrest* can be seen in Prince's/Christo-
pher's bedroom in *Under The Cherry Moon*.

Before the night was over, Prince would mix "Venus De Milo," as well as
"God Is Everywhere," and yesterday's "Neon Telephone," which now contained his vocals. The new mix probably contained the sound effect of the

phone ringing and the background vocals by Wendy and Lisa (and likely Susannah) that were probably recorded during this session.

Status: There were apparently two versions of "Venus De Milo" (1:55 and 5:22), but only the shorter one was included on the *Parade* album. Clare Fischer added his touches on August 13, 1985, and elements of it were used in the *Under The Cherry Moon* movie, but the longer version remained unreleased during Prince's lifetime.

Note: "Venus De Milo" may have been tracked on the evening of July 10, or after midnight during the morning of July 11. Also, Sheila E. has stated publicly that "Venus De Milo" was recorded at Sunset Sound. Although there is some evidence that it was tracked at Prince's Washington Avenue warehouse, it is vital to acknowledge her recollections as she was involved in the session, so her thoughts on this session are historically important. It is likely that Wendy and Lisa were also in the studio during this session, but it is unclear if they participated, although Susan Rogers sheds some light on the origins of the track and who was involved. "'Venus De Milo' was done at the warehouse on Washington Avenue. Sheila was around, she played the drums, he played the piano and then he did everything else. Nobody else was involved."

FRIDAY, JULY 12, 1985

"Happy Birthday, Mr. Christian" (transfer)
Sunset Sound, Studio 1 | 4:15 p.m.–8:00 p.m. (booked: 1 p.m.–4 p.m.)
Producer: (none listed) | Artist: Apollonia 6 | Engineer: Paul Levy

> *I was definitely into the whole idea of doing this mini movie, an LP version of a video. An LP video that was taking the songs and creating this whole story around them and all this other stuff.*
>
> —Brenda Bennett

Paul Levy engineered this short edit of "Happy Birthday, Mr. Christian," once again probably for use in the Apollonia 6 video collection. Prince did not attend this session.

Once the shoot was complete, the video collection was given a rough edit, which included an instrumental version of a song that had been removed from their album. "I love that you can hear our song Prince and I co-wrote together 'Manic Monday' in the video," recalls Apollonia. "We had so much fun filming together. So many great memories."

Despite the efforts of everyone involved, the project was shut down before it was completed, as Apollonia reflects. "Prince obviously didn't like it. I don't know if it was the production value or he just didn't like the way it turned out after all. He didn't want to put any more money into it to edit."

"That never got done because Prince took one look at it and literally tossed it in the waste basket and said, 'This is a piece of shit,' got up and walked out," reveals Brenda Bennett. "That's why it never got finished."

"We all came to the conclusion that he was tired of it," continues Apollonia. "'*Purple Rain* got the Oscar, and I'm moving on.' Reinvent, chameleon, reinvent. Like David Bowie, reinvent something new. New protégés, new collaborators, new music, new looks. And in the process of that, he really wounded a lot of us."

Tragically, Ricky Nelson, who starred in the video as the late "Mr. Christian," passed away six months later in an airplane crash.

Apollonia remembers:

Fast-forwarding to 2014, June 28, when we're celebrating [*Purple Rain's*] 30th anniversary at Paisley Park, just he and I and 3rdEyeGirl, we talked about it. And he says, "We could release the video." And I was like, "What video?" And he says, "The video," he goes, "of you guys." And I was like, "Oh, the long-form video." I go, "Can I help edit?" He goes, "Why don't you just edit it yourself?" I said, "No, I'm not an editor. I would like to supervise and give my ideas, and we could have Susan and Brenda involved, it would be beautiful." And he says, "All right." He said we could release it with some new music, and then re-release the old stuff with the video and then go out and maybe tour!

Although Apollonia, Brenda, and Susan appeared together on stage at First Avenue during a 2016 Revolution reunion after Prince passed away, a full Apollonia 6 tour has not materialized.

SATURDAY, JULY 13, 1985

Prince's video of "4 The Tears In Your Eyes" aired during the Live Aid concert. An estimated 1.9 billion people from 150 nations watched the event during the worldwide broadcast. Prince had recently finished his massive *Purple Rain* tour and declined to perform, but what could have kept him away from such an event with such an awe-inspiring global audience? "A lot of reasons," explains Lisa. "He didn't particularly like those things. He didn't like not having control over the environment, the daylight . . . I don't know."

SATURDAY, JULY 13, 1985

> "Neon Telephone" (mix)
> "Girls & Boys" (mix)
> "Love Or Money" (mix)
> Washington Avenue Warehouse (Edina, Minnesota)
> Producer: Prince | Artist: Prince and the Revolution | Engineer: David Tickle
>   (likely)

> *"Love or Money" was one of my favorites, along with "Girls & Boys."*[20]
>
> —Eric Leeds

While Live Aid was being broadcast, Prince and his engineer created new mixes for "Neon Telephone," "Love Or Money," and "Girls & Boys." During Prince's mixes, he wouldn't just work with the elements that existed, he'd often adjust the song completely. Because he had mastered almost every instrument he needed (the main exceptions being brass and woodwinds), he was free to replace any of the instruments and even the vocals on a whim. When he traveled, he reportedly used a Sennheiser MD431, a mic he maintained for live events, but in the studio, he had another mic he requested. "He used two mics, one for lower and one for upper parts of the scale. The upper end at Sunset Sound and at home what he liked was the very valuable, very rare Neumann U47," explains Susan Rogers. "When he finds something he likes, he continues to use it. And he used that for the vocals on 'Girls & Boys.'"[21]

SUNDAY, JULY 14, 1985

"Do U Lie?" (tracking, mix)
Washington Avenue Warehouse (Edina, Minnesota)
Producer: Prince | Artist: Prince | Engineers: Susan Rogers and David Tickle

On "Do U Lie?," Prince was the one that came up with those odd little progressions. It was a definite, gifted intuition on how to get what he wanted.[22]

—Wendy Melvoin

The core of Prince's music was often the drums and percussion. During his jams in the past with Sheila, Morris Day, or Bobby Z, he'd often find the basics for a song and he'd build on that groove, hiding the complexity of his beats. "His rhythms aren't obviously unique until you write them down. He liked to put cymbals on the three, fills going into the one, fills on the two—a lot of stuff on the two," detailed Bobby. "He recorded many of the tracks with drums first."[23]

Over the course of his career, Prince almost always had a tight relationship with his drummers, and he had a history of inviting Morris Day or Sheila to jam with him as he looked for a groove that could grow into a song. His closeness to Wendy and Lisa extended to their families, including Wendy and Susannah's brother Jonathan. "He was looking for a jazz drummer. I think that he might have been germinating the idea of Madhouse," recalled Susan Rogers. "He needed another drummer to be the basis of that *new* band and Jonathan was brought around. He was toying with the idea of having another band to be his foil, his competition and he was gonna need the right musicians, so I think that is one of the reasons why he starts accumulating other musicians."[24]

Prince also enlisted Mark, Matt, Wendy, and Lisa to work on "Do U Lie?", a track Prince had likely originally demoed during his time in France. "Jonathan's playing the drums on that, and it was lovely," reflects Wendy. "He was incredibly musical and he knew he had a great ear and was really subtle. Prince didn't really give them much direction because they knew Jonathan was a great jazz drummer. So he just kind of went for it. It just worked."

Sandra Francisco, credited as "little gypsy girl," recorded the spoken word section (which translates as, "Children who lie don't go to heaven"). It is unclear when her part was taped.

Status: "Do U Lie?" (2:39) was released on Prince's *Parade* album.

WEDNESDAY, JULY 17, 1985 (ESTIMATE)

> **"Neon Telephone"** (mix)
> **"Do U Lie?"** (mix)
> Washington Avenue Warehouse (Edina, Minnesota)
> Producer: Prince | Artist: Prince and the Revolution | Engineers: David
> Tickle and Susan Rogers

The only reason why [he had us mixing], was that he was so busy, and he trusted us to do it.

—Wendy Melvoin

It appears that Prince was traveling during this week, so at some point he left Wendy, Lisa, and Susan to oversee a variety of mixes. Prince pushed everyone around him hard and demanded an extreme level of dedication and focus, which meant very little down time for those around him. Working with him directly was often stressful, so during the times that he was away, the days were a little more casual.

"I was remembering how stilted our behaviors could be in his presence because he was so controlling," according to Susan Rogers. "It was like training for the Olympics or something, when you're there with your coach, that pressure is forcing you to perform. But were we that much different? No, we may have moved a little bit slower, but we might have laughed more."

It is not that there wasn't humor while working with Prince, there was, but the mood was always dictated by him. "He always came off to the media as being mysterious and quiet and shy," recalled Fink, "but with us in the band, we all yucked it up pretty hard."[25]

"Prince used to refer to a certain walk he'd call it the 'George Jefferson pimp walk,' from *The Jeffersons* TV show," remembers Wendy. "I remember specific times, for his own giggles, he'd actually have the band do that 'George Jefferson pimp walk,' so he could laugh at us because we were so bad at it. Especially Matt, because Matt would get the biggest laughs. But because of those experiences, and him referring to that particular walk, we knew that when he'd come into rehearsals with that walk, that the day wasn't going to go well."

Lisa explains:

The thing about him was when he was there, he could be Mr. Mood swings, you know? We had different names for him, like "Steve." Steve was the cool guy who you could hang out with and he wore gym socks and played basketball, and he was a nice guy. Then there was "Marilyn," and Marilyn was like, she's so needy and you can't do anything that's sexier, you know what I mean? He would talk softly, and it was just like walking on eggshells. And then there was "George Jefferson," who was just, "Yeah, big up." He would be fun to work with; we'd usually do something really funky like a "Cloreen Bacon Skin" kind of track with George Jefferson. So that was the thing, if he was in the studio it was just, you'd have to be aware of which person was going to show up. So, when he wasn't there it was just more free, and you could just have fun.

Prince's humor stretched across to his protégé artists, including Sheila's band, remembers Susie Davis. "We sent them 'The Paisley Family,' which was the song that was sung to the tune of The Addams Family, which had lyrics like, 'Nobody comes to see 'em, they won't get their per diem.' And then we got this videotape back a few days later from Prince."

The video was called "Karl's Cousin" and Prince led members of the Revolution and the Family as they mocked Sheila's drummer, Karl Perazzo and keyboardist Davis to the tune of the Family's "High Fashion." "This video was specifically just to dog us," laughs Davis. "In this videotape Susannah Melvoin is wearing a DX7 around her neck and she's stomping out of time to the music the entire time, because she's parroting me and it's so funny. Prince is having so much fun doing it."

THURSDAY, JULY 18, 1985 (ESTIMATE)

"**Neon Telephone**" (mix)
"**Love Or Money**" [instrumental] (mix)
Washington Avenue Warehouse (Edina, Minnesota)
Producer: Prince | Artist: Prince and the Revolution | Engineers: David Tickle and Susan Rogers

["Love Or Money" was] *written 4 the character of Mary Sharon.*[26]

—Prince

As he did with "Love Or Money," "Neon Telephone" was also written for Mary Sharon, the female lead in *Under The Cherry Moon*, but it would ultimately not fit in the context of the movie or soundtrack album.

During this session, Wendy and Lisa updated the mix of "Neon Telephone." After midnight, they also produced a mostly instrumental mix of "Love Or Money." The only vocal parts remaining were the "love or money" chants in the chorus. A mix like this was generally created for some type of situation in which the lead vocals could be performed at a later date to the preexisting track.

It is unclear if any additional songs were worked on during this session.

FRIDAY, JULY 19, 1985

The Family's first single, "The Screams Of Passion," is released, a month before the album. The single reached number 63 on the US *Billboard* Hot 100 Chart, number 9 on the *Billboard* Black Chart, and number 10 in the *Billboard* Hot Dance/Disco-Club Play chart.

SUNDAY, JULY 21, 1985 (ESTIMATE)

"Carousel" (mix)
"Girl O' My Dreams" (mix)
Washington Avenue Warehouse (Edina, Minnesota)
Producers: Wendy and Lisa (likely) | Artist: Prince and the Revolution | Engineers: Susan Rogers and David Tickle

> *There was a promise and a potential to everything, so we'd record something—back then it was always making a cassette—so you'd have these cassettes and it would burn a hole in your pocket. You just couldn't wait to play the cassette for him.*
>
> —Lisa Coleman

Prince had tasked Wendy, Lisa, and Susan Rogers to do a variety of mixes of items from the vault. On this date, "Girl O' My Dreams," a track originally recorded in 1982, was taken off the shelf and a mix was created for Prince to hear, as well as an update of "Carousel." It is unclear if Lisa and Wendy recorded anything new on these mixes.

MONDAY, JULY 22, 1985 (ESTIMATE)

"**Girl**" (overdub and mix)
Washington Avenue Warehouse (Edina, Minnesota)
Producer: Prince | Artist: Prince and the Revolution | Engineers: Susan
  Rogers and David Tickle

> *He sometimes would phone me and give me a list of tapes and*
> *say: "Pull these out and give me rough mixes of them so I can*
> *listen to them." "Girl" was one of those.*[27]
>
> —Susan Rogers

Prince was writing constantly so he didn't go back into his vaults often, but sometimes something would trigger his memory about a track, and he'd seek it out to listen to it with fresh ears. As he had been working on songs with titles like "Girls & Boys," it is possible that triggered him to relisten to an unreleased song he'd recorded a few years earlier for Vanity 6 called "Boy." "The basic track was old, he recorded that a long time ago," remembered Susan Rogers. "So I pulled it out and did a rough mix. It was never properly mixed. I spent merely 30 minutes on it at the most. He was very happy with it and just made it a B-side."[28]

Prince had last worked on the song in the fall of 1984 while they were getting ready for the *Purple Rain* tour, but the song dates back to 1983 or earlier. When he took it out of the vault in 1984, he changed the original perspective of the song from female to male by hiding Vanity's voice, leaving only his scratch vocals, and adding "Girl" to replace any reference to "Boy" in the chorus, creating a new track. Some additional mixing was done during this session and the song was completed quickly.

It is possible that Prince did not attend this session and that it was overseen by Wendy, Lisa, and Susan Rogers.

Status: On October 2, 1985, "Girl" (3:47) was included as the B-side for "America." The Vanity 6 version of "Boy" remained unreleased during his lifetime.

TUESDAY, JULY 23, 1985

"Call Of The Wild" (tracking, overdubs)
Washington Avenue Warehouse (Edina, Minnesota)
Producer: Prince | Artist: Prince and the Revolution | Engineer: Susan
    Rogers (assumed)

In his mind he was always creating for huge audiences and
playing to the world.[29]

—Lisa Coleman

Once Prince returned to Minneapolis, he was probably eager to get back into the studio. Instead of continuing to create pop songs, he decided to try something different. Susannah Melvoin had been suggesting Led Zeppelin to him, and they had been in the news because the band just had an historic reunion 10 days earlier at Live Aid. It appears that Prince's reaction to this was "Call Of The Wild," a heavy bass, guitar, and drum arena rocker, the type he hadn't written for a while. When Prince recorded songs like this, he was very specific about his drums. "He liked very clean and punchy drum sounds—a lot of attack," according to Susan Rogers. "We'd take a kick drum and pull all the mid-range out of it, very similar to a heavy-metal kick drum. He liked a very prominent hi-hat and claps to be low-pitched, fat and sustained. He wanted the rhythm guitar to be clean and direct, using really thick 11-gauge strings. It was really hard for me to unlearn Prince—everything I did after that reflected his ear, for better or worse."[30]

The song expressed Prince's observations about how others view their sexual behavior and their devotion to God, by calling out a message to his fans to be strong and celebrate that they are free. He criticizes the "9-to-5 people" about their lack of understanding of his philosophy on sex, freedom, and love. "He struggled with being ethical, with being graceful on a human level. He dealt with a pure unconscious mind that was unfiltered to get his needs met creatively," reveals Susannah. "Get his sexual id created, fulfilled. . . . All of it belongs in the same area of creation for him. Even religion. His creations, sex, religion, all of it comes from his inner world, his inner mind, and that's the guy I know. That's the guy that he *knew* I knew."

Prince put the song on the shelf until autumn, when he updated the mix.

Status: "Call Of The Wild" (5:05) remained unreleased during Prince's lifetime, but elements of the song were repurposed for the unreleased "We Got The Power," when it was recorded in October 1988.

THURSDAY, JULY 25, 1985

"(U Got The) Good Drawers" (tracking, overdubs)
"Under The Cherry Moon" (orchestra mix)
"Life Can Be So Nice" (orchestra mix)
"Life Can Be So Nice" [extended mix] (possible tracking, overdubs, mix)
Washington Avenue Warehouse (Edina, Minnesota) | evening into the next
    day
Producer: Prince | Artist: Prince | Engineer: Susan Rogers

Prince's approach to playing jazz was a little different from
his approach to playing anything else. At times, he had a great
sense of spontaneity, particularly in jam sessions and also
often in our club "aftershows." But once he started to formalize
something, I often felt that his determination to control every-
thing worked against it being allowed to find its own way in a
more orthodox jazz sense.[31]

—Eric Leeds

During these free-form sessions Prince would call out a new key and tempo and
everyone in the room would keep up. He'd often experiment, but even in these
jams that expanded his musical language, he relied on what he knew and grew
from that base of knowledge. Susan Rogers recalled how Prince explained his
musical roots.

Prince used to talk about "the street you live on." By that he meant the music that
is your home base, the music that feels the most right to you. It's a voice that when
you hear it you just know these are my people. This just feels right. I think Prince
was on to something when he said, "Home base. It's the street where you live."
Now, that said, he believed that we can visit other neighborhoods and we can love
other music that's not our home base. Whether it's salsa or jazz or it's folk rock
or just whatever. You can visit other streets, but there's something you're always
going to love best about your home base.[32]

There were several untitled instrumental jams, but one got a little more attention when Prince ad-libbed a few lyrics on a loose groove he referred to as
"(U Got The) Good Drawers" (or "Good Drawers"). The players included Eric
Leeds on sax, Susannah on keyboards, and Prince. What was unique about this
session was that he was playing without his usual drummers and was trying H.B.

Bennett on the skins. "H.B. was the complete antithesis of the kind of drummer that I thought Prince would have dug because Prince was a drum machine guy and Sheila and people like that are on top of the beat players," details Leeds. "Where H.B. was much more way back behind the beat. Now his timing was impeccable, and he'd swung his ass off, but he had a fat sounding snare drum that was just a little bit behind the beat that I thought was going to not be where Prince lived. When we did that 'Good Drawers' jam that night, Prince came to me afterwards and said, 'Where'd this guy come from?' 'Well, he's my best friend. We played in bands for years, he's my closest thing to a brother that I have, other than Alan.'"

"H.B. is a drummer *and* a musician and he basically says, 'I'm the drummer. I control things here.' He'd say, 'You may be the captain, but I'm the navigator. I'm the one that gets us from point A to point B. You tell me where you want to go. I'm the one who gets us there.' And all of a sudden here's a guy who was basically taking the reins and Prince was like, 'Holy shit.'"

Prince and Susan Rogers would also work on the Clare Fischer orchestration mixes for "Under The Cherry Moon" and "Life Can Be So Nice." It is possible that a longer version of "Life Can Be So Nice" was created during this session as well.

Status: "(U Got The) Good Drawers" (or "Good Drawers") and the other jams recorded on this date remained unreleased during Prince's lifetime, although it is likely that some of these elements turned up later in work by Eric and some of the later Madhouse songs.

MONDAY, JULY 29, 1985

Prince's *Purple Rain* concert from Syracuse, New York, performed on March 30, 1985, was released on VHS and Betamax. It reached number 2 on both the Top Videocassette Sales and the Music Videocassette chart in the United States by late August. It was certified Gold and Platinum by the Recording Industry Association of America (RIAA) on August 6, 1985.

WEDNESDAY, JULY 31, 1985

The 12-inch single of "Pop Life" (also known as "Fresh Dance Mix") is released with "Hello" on the B-side.

WEDNESDAY, JULY 31, 1985

Studio Jam with Eric Leeds and H.B. Bennett
"Old Friends 4 Sale" (mix with orchestra)
"Old Friends 4 Sale" [instrumental] (possible mix)
"Sometimes It Snows In April" (mix with orchestra)
Washington Avenue Warehouse (Edina, Minnesota)
Producer: Prince | Artist: Prince | Engineer: Susan Rogers

Once again, Prince gathered Eric, Susannah, and H.B. Bennett on drums and spent several hours playing around with a variety of familiar grooves including: "Bedtime Story," "Hello," and 1983's "My Summertime Thing," looking for something new. It was common for Prince to use a riff from one track and morph it into another song, leaving the old elements behind and creating an all new number by the end of the session. It is also likely that he used sessions like this to flesh out some of the songs he'd written in Paris, including "An Honest Man" and "God Is Everywhere."

In addition to the jams, Prince created a mix that blended "Old Friends 4 Sale" with the early July orchestration. He also listened to, and possibly created a mix of, "Sometimes It Snows In April" using Fischer's work from four days earlier, but decided to feature his original stripped-down version instead.

Status: In August 1999, Prince released "Old Friends 4 Sale" with rewritten lyrics and updated vocals as the eighth track on *The Vault: Old Friends 4 Sale.* Today's mix of "Old Friends 4 Sale" (3:28) that contains his original lyrics was not released by Prince.

The following summer, Prince once again reached out to H.B. and hired him to be the drummer for Madhouse on the Sign O' The Times *tour as Eric Leeds recalls. "H.B. was my closest dearest friend and was one of the greatest musicians and drummers I ever played with, but he should not have been the Madhouse drummer. Unfortunately, Prince didn't decide that until after he had hired him and then two days later fired him. It's just like, 'Motherfucker!' I said, 'First of all, this is your band. You have the right to make the decision. And I'm not even going to say that it isn't necessarily the right decision, but why in the fuck did you hire him to begin with?' And after that, I said, 'That's the last time I'm ever going to introduce a friend of mine.'"*

AUGUST 1985

THURSDAY, AUGUST 1, 1985

"Splash" (tracking, mix)
Washington Avenue Warehouse (Edina, Minnesota)
Producer: Prince | Artist: Prince and the Revolution | Engineer: Susan
Rogers

> *As he's playing these instruments, and he's playing every in-*
> *strument one at a time, I'm simultaneously mixing it. And*
> *getting sounds, and dialing things in, and as the song is taking*
> *shape, the mix is taking shape. So, by the time we've finished*
> *the final overdub, we're ready to really just tweak the mix a*
> *little bit. And then you print it and you're done. And then what*
> *we spent a lot of time doing, is doing alternate mixes.*[1]

—Susan Rogers

Despite having an archive of hundreds of unreleased songs, Prince continued to
write and record new music at an almost inhuman pace. **"To stop recording,
to put a cap on your work and then put a boundary on it, it actually for me
is to put a boundary on your gift that comes from God and I can't do that.
I write so much because I know it is therapy for me or evolving your spirit
actually, every time you go back into the well and examine it. So, the more**

I write, the more stuff I'd put out, the quicker I get to my destination. [My music is a soundtrack] to my psyche."[2]

But to keep up that momentum, Susan Rogers recalls how Prince would find inspiration in any place he could. "I had kind of a tote bag with me at the house and it had a copy of Goethe's *Faust* in it and some wintergreen Tic Tacs or gum. It had the word 'wintergreen' on it, while he was writing a song 'Splash.' And then in the lyric is 'cherry blue wintergreen, fireworks and rain in every scene.' And I remember thinking 'Damn him, that was him rooting through my bag!'"

"That's such a Prince thing to do," observes Wendy. "He was so into that. Like, 'What do you got in there? What do you got in there?'"

"We would say, 'Why are you doing a Wrigley spearmint gum commercial?' Or something," adds Lisa. "We would make fun of him and sing it in girly voices and he'd just say, 'shut up, sing it right.'"

Prince recorded the basic tracks by himself in the studio and created a mix at the end of the session but decided to revisit it multiple times, including having Wendy, Lisa, and Clare Fischer add their respective flairs to the song.

It appears that Prince flew out of Minneapolis after this session, possibly to New York.

Status: "Splash" (4:00) was issued in 2001 through his online NPG Music Club. It was also slated for *Roadhouse Garden*, a Prince and the Revolution album that Prince considered releasing in 1999. The project was ultimately abandoned.

SATURDAY, AUGUST 3, 1985–SUNDAY, AUGUST 4, 1985

"**Empty Room**" (tracking, mix)
Washington Avenue Warehouse (Edina, Minnesota) | evening into next day
Producer: Prince | Artist: Prince and the Revolution | Engineer: Susan
Rogers

It was insane. It was Bobby and Vicki's wedding [celebration], and he made everybody go back to the studio to record this song.
—Susannah Melvoin

It was a busy weekend for celebrating with those closest to Prince. A surprise party was planned for Susan Rogers' birthday and a gathering was also arranged to celebrate the recent wedding of Bobby Z and his bride, Vicki. "I got married, but I had a party three months later," remembered Bobby Z. "Then the night before my huge party, I had a party in my mother's party room at her apartment complex that Prince came to. He was having some sort of fight with Susannah, and at the end of this party he asked if we could rehearse. He said, we could bring the party over there, and we recorded 'Empty Room.' That, I think, was about Susannah."[3]

To understand the context of this, the scene needs to be set with the fact that Prince and Susannah were struggling. He was constantly busy, and his attention was often divided between his music, and his work. Their fights were getting more frequent and the reality of them continuing as a couple was shaky. Bobby's history with Prince was extensive, and in many ways, he was one of his closest friends and confidants, and he recognized that Bobby had found a perfect partner in Vicki. "Prince loved Vicki. Vicki is like the *Revolution*'s wife," explained Susannah. "She was the non-musician wife of one of his band members that he actually really, really liked, and she is an extraordinary human being."

Prince wasn't someone who scheduled many non-music-related events, although he made time for the intimate celebration of their commitment, but the day started with a reminder of Susannah's presence. "He woke up that morning and he saw this hair in his bathroom, and he taped it to the mirror," explains Melvoin who also attended the event.

> After Bobby and Vicki had done their vows and everybody was in the room and Prince is behind, in back of everybody. He's just standing there, looking at the whole thing, wide-eyed, doey-eyed. And looking at me and seeing me and seeing me talking to all my friends, Bobby, Vicki, Matt, his family, my family. He knew how entwined I was with all of it. This wasn't like, "I'm leaving some anonymous person." He realized that this is *my* Susannah. This is the person I really care about. I love her. He may have had that moment with everybody who was so loving each other on that day. It may have been that moment where he was like, what did I do?

"And it's when he went to the studio, and he called Bobby and everybody else in the band and said, 'Come and record,' and they did 'Empty Room.' It was totally not a surprise coming from him. It was always 'Prince first,' always. No one was like, 'Goddamn him, we're not going. I'm putting my foot down.' It was like, 'Okay, let's just get this over with.'"

"He fought with [Susannah] the day of our wedding party, and he wanted to be with family. We were his family," reasons Vicki. "I feel like we were his family and he wanted to bring us back [to the studio], and he didn't want the day to end. That's what I felt."

"Vicki said the right answer," affirms Bobby Z. "She's like, 'Sure, we'll come out.' And most people were shocked. And then he said, 'Well, you can bring the party out there,' so it was fun."

"He just wanted to take the party to his place," observes Lisa. "That totally makes sense. If he didn't like something, he would leave. If he did like something, he would leave and take you with him."

Wendy went with the band to the studio but was frustrated at his power play. "He pulled us away from the fucking party, and we had to record the song, and it's like, 'Oh, you fucking baby. Can we now just go to the party and celebrate? No, you want to go, and get it out of your system, and sing about your breakup. Come on. It was just stupid."

"And then we did this really sad song. It was pretty," reflects Bobby. "Vicki and I were the last ones there in the control room, she fell asleep and he said, 'You guys have a big day tomorrow, you gotta get her out of here.' But she was a trooper in the end. And I thought it was an incredible song. And I thought we played really well, I thought it was a good take. Sad song, but happy night. It was so emotional"

The song, a slow, heartfelt ballad, was written directly for Susannah, detailing his pain about losing his connection with her, and even referenced the strand of her hair he'd found that morning. The lyrics reveal that he was heartbroken about her leaving him, but not acknowledging any issues that he may have brought to the breakup.

"He recorded that song and played it for me the next day and left," remembered Susannah. "He was having a hard time, and I could hear he was troubled in the song and he was sad, and I was sad."[4]

Status: This version of "Empty Room" (3:21) was never released by Prince. A promotional video was produced and, although technically unreleased, it was played on the screens during the "Ultimate Live Experience Tour" in March 1995. "Empty Room" was re-recorded on March 18, 1992, at Paisley Park, and a later version (from 2002) was released on *C-Note* in 2004.

This weekend was not just a party for Bobby and Vicki, it was also Susan Rogers' birthday. "I still have the birthday card that Prince gave me. Karen Krattinger told me that they passed it around, the employees signed it and they gave it to Prince to sign it. First, he just signed it and gave it back to Karen and then he said, 'No wait.' And he took it back and he wrote, 'Your patience and loyalty outshines the sun.' That was so sweet."

"If you were waiting on compliments, don't hold your breath because you will be waiting a long time. Even if he did, he didn't give you a direct compliment, but he'd do something nice and that was his way of saying 'thank you.'"

TUESDAY, AUGUST 6, 1985 (ESTIMATE)

"My Sex" (Jill Jones vocal overdubs)
Electric Lady Studios, New York, Studio A
Producer: "David Z" Rivkin | Artist: Jill Jones | Engineer: "David Z" Rivkin

> *That was recorded a long time before and we ended up doing something with it in Minneapolis. I don't think he really committed to it; I just think I wanted that song more than he was willing to give it to me.*
>
> —Jill Jones

Jill Jones had recently moved to New York, but she wasn't very far away from her Minneapolis roots, in fact Jill was roommates with actress Vivica Fox and another friend in an apartment that was paid for by Prince. "He got engaged to Susannah the same week I got a $14,000 a month apartment here in New York," recalls Jones. "He always had irons in the fire. Always had things going on. It was bizarre because I was like his child, so it was very weird and shifted into a weird situation. No different than having a pet."

"We had a real strain because of that, because suddenly I was pushed into this position of being now secretive," reflected Jones in 2017. "Before we were private, but then to be pushed into being secretive, that actually bothered me."[5]

Jill's uncomfortable relationship with Prince would also affect the speed and dedication he would have on her album, which would end up dragging on for years. It would also influence how she dealt with Prince, which ended up putting some distance between them.

Prince had spent part of the summer looking for a sound for Jones, and he kept making attempts at a variety of options hoping to stumble on to the right direction, so he reached into his back catalog for a song he'd worked on a few years earlier called "My Sex," which sounded like a combination of Devo and Vanity 6. He did some additional work on it and then played it for Jill to get her opinion, but it appears that he had already made up his mind by the time he played it for her. "It was going to be on my record, but he didn't want to release it," remembers Jones. "The lyrics said, 'I don't want to know your name, all I want to do is introduce my sex to yours . . . ' or something like that. I actually think I told him *he* should do it. But then after a while he started thinking that that kind of stuff was beneath him."

It is likely that Prince did not attend this session, so David Z oversaw the recording of Jill's vocals during her stay in New York and booked time at Electric Lady Studios for a large batch of songs recorded for Jill.

Status: Although the 4-and-a-half-minute "My Sex" was considered for Jill Jones's 1987 album, it remained unreleased during Prince's lifetime.

WEDNESDAY, AUGUST 7, 1985

"Under The Cherry Moon" (mix with orchestra)
Washington Avenue Warehouse (Edina, Minnesota)
Producer: Prince | Artist: Prince and the Revolution | Engineer: Susan Rogers

> *One of the good features was that he allowed me freedom and space to make value judgments. Most people want to tell you exactly what they want for an arrangement but then again, they are not the writers, so there is always a superimposition of their limited scope on what they conceive. A writer has to fight to get what he does. The worst person in conjunction with this is the producer who thinks that he has a special orientation toward what it should be. That's like comparing apples and bananas. I think that I was accepted by Prince because of the fact that my writing was of a professional level through years of experience.[6]*
>
> —Clare Fischer

Prince spent several hours creating a mix of "Under The Cherry Moon" that combined the studio track with Clare Fischer's orchestra, but it was not included on the album. An instrumental with Fischer orchestration that lasted 1 and a half minutes was used in the film.

SATURDAY, AUGUST 10, 1985

"Sexual Suicide" (tracking, horns, mix)
Washington Avenue Warehouse (Edina, Minnesota)
Producer: Prince | Artist: Prince and the Revolution | Engineer: Susan Rogers

> *"Sexual Suicide" has this horn section that's nothing but baritone saxes; it sounds like a truck coming at you.*[7]
>
> —Prince

The journey from concept to completion is unique to each composition. The seed of the song may exist as a joke or an idea and be blown up into a full song, but the final result sometimes has little bearing on the original thought. "Sexual Suicide" is one of those songs that began as a simple piano demo, but the song Prince could hear in his head was much heavier. By the time Prince had finished recording the basic tracks, it was still fairly sparse and needed horns, so once again, he called in Eric Leeds.

"It was one of the first times where he asked me to just come in on my own. He wasn't there. And it was late at night. In fact, it was at the warehouse in Edina, and it was just Susan and myself. I came in and I hadn't written anything, because I hadn't heard the song. Just came in and did an extemporaneous thing on it."

Leeds recorded his sax lines and Susan mixed the track so Prince could listen to the results. Prince apparently enjoyed some of the elements of the track but wanted to make some changes.

Status: "Sexual Suicide" (3:39) was released on the *Crystal Ball* album in 1998. The version from this date was not released during Prince's lifetime.

SUNDAY, AUGUST 11, 1985

"**Sexual Suicide**" (horn overdubs, mix)
"**Unknown track**" (horn overdubs, mix)
Washington Avenue Warehouse (Edina, Minnesota)
Producer: Prince | Artist: Prince and the Revolution | Engineer: Susan
  Rogers

> *August 10, 1985 is when I did "Sexual Suicide." Actually, I did*
> *the first version on August 10, and then re-did it on August 11.*[8]
>
> —Eric Leeds

Prince was not entirely satisfied with the results of "Sexual Suicide," so he had Susan reach out to Eric asking him to come back in to help find a better way. "There were parts of it that he really liked, and he wanted the rest of it to kind of be like this one part that I did," recalled Leeds. "So, I said okay, that's cool."[9]

> For whatever reason, I came up with some little device where I stacked the horns, and I had like five or six horns stacked and I was using some non-chordal tones in there, that had no relationship to the chord structure, or the key signature of the song at all. I was trying to give it more of a vocal quality, so that you heard the horns, not so much as a melody, but almost as if it was talking. I think a saxophone—particularly a tenor almost more than any of the wind instruments—is the one that is closest to a human voice. Susan put a harmonizer on the baritone, to really whack it out. So that's what I did. And then I put on another little thing . . . it was wall to wall stuff. He just got thrilled with it. He thought it was the greatest thing in the world he'd ever heard. Of course, the song didn't come out until like 10 years later!

Leeds would use the harmonic device that he used in this song on some of his later work, including the title track to his *Times Squared* album in 1991. Eric also added sax to another unknown track during this session.

TUESDAY, AUGUST 13, 1985

The Family played their first and only concert at First Avenue in Minneapolis.

> *We only got to play one show at First Avenue and that was*
> *a pretty famous show. Janet Jackson was there. Obviously,*

Prince was there, and it was an incredible experience. In those days we were dressing up in smoking jackets and silk pajamas, and that was kind of the persona of the band. It was very high class, as they say.[10]

—"St. Paul" Peterson

When Prince was putting together a band, he worked it from every angle and expected everyone to perform as hard and as passionately as he would, and pushing someone out of their comfort zone was something he did on a regular basis. "Prince puts you in situations that you don't think you're ready for," explained "St. Paul" Peterson. "He saw something in me that I didn't see in myself. He obviously thought I was ready to front the band with a little guidance from him or shall we say, a *lot* of guidance from him, but I was scared to death."[11]

The Family was being groomed to replace Prince's biggest protégé project, the Time, so there was a lot at stake. Prince had overseen all of the music and had heavily promoted them, which resulted in multiple best-selling albums and critical reviews and created stars out of most of the members. When Morris Day left and the Time self-destructed, Prince had the opportunity to show that their success was based on *his* work, so he poured himself into this new band. The bottom line is that Prince would not allow a band that was under his authority, especially one that was intended to prove a point, to perform until they were ready. After months of preparation and the US album release one week away (it had been released in the United Kingdom the previous day), Prince apparently recognized that the band was tight enough to perform in public, so he made a call to First Avenue and booked the night for their debut. "We rehearsed for months," explained St. Paul. "Getting ready, making sure that the choreography was right. Prince was really involved with that, with the show, and Jerome would help with the steps, just trying to get the whole branding of that band happening. Prince would call these shows at First Avenue and people would just show up and the place was packed."[12]

Peterson was fronting a band in public knowing that he could no longer enjoy the anonymity that came from being the keyboard player when he played with the Time, and like anyone who was that age with a great responsibility, his mind was racing. "Am I going to make Prince proud and the rest of my band members proud? Am I going to make my family proud? Am I going to screw up? All the same nerves you get whenever I still go on stage. Am I prepared? Do I have this stuff cold? How do I sound? Am I going to overplay? All this inner dialogue that you have as a musician, as an artist, and you'd get out and you go on autopilot and then when it's done, it's like, did that really just happen?"[13]

"Before we went out on stage, we were at his house," recalls Susannah. "I'll never forget this, he said, 'You give it everything you've got, because that's the only way you're going to show anybody what your worth is.' I remember that. I remember that he definitely wanted you to connect to that part of you that was very uncomfortable."

> He came to me right before the show with a stuffed animal, this large stuffed animal. He said, "I want you to take this stuffed animal on stage and I want you to roll around on the ground and kind of rough it up. Just get really into it. I want you to just get on the ground and we just maul it," or whatever. I started to cry. I was like, "I can't do that. It's hard enough for me already to get up there and scream. And it's the first show and you want me to do what?' Anyway, I did my version of it. I ended up placating him in some way. I had this stuffed animal up there and I did something. I don't remember what it was. When I got off stage, he gave me the biggest hug and he said, "You did it."

Peterson had a similar experience after the show. "Prince grabbed me and hugged me, and told me what a great job I did. I was a 20-year-old kid, getting that endorsement of the biggest pop star at that time. That's one of the things I do remember."

Prince was cautious about giving the band too much space to reveal their characters as he was likely still hurting from allowing the Time to become a group that could be praised outside of the glow of Prince. "He was determined not to make that mistake with us," reveals Eric Leeds.

> The crazy thing is that he created that character for Morris. Prince could be Morris, better than Morris could be Morris. But when you got guys like Jimmy, and Terry, and Jesse [Johnson] that were Prince's peers. He grew up with them. And although he's the one that made it to a degree, they weren't going to let him ever forget. "No, wait a minute, dude. We all grew up together. And yeah, this is your house and everything, but guess what? We're still us. And we still have our own thing." And he realized that. That he could only go so far with that group, without it busting apart.

An intense schedule of rehearsals and the expectation of a major release within a week had turned Paul, Susannah, Jerome Benton, Jellybean Johnson, and Eric Leeds into a true family. Each of them were looking forward to an exciting future, recognizing that all of the work that had gone into the band was now finally paying off. "I'm sure that [Prince] wanted to take us on the road at some point, but he had other stuff going on," remembered Paul. "He shipped me out to acting, singing, and dancing lessons in LA while he was making *Cherry Moon*."[14]

"We could do no wrong," reflected St. Paul. "It's too bad we never got to tour."

After the concert, Prince flew to New York, and according to Susannah, he quickly reached out to her.

> Two days later I got a call, "Can you please come to New York?" I get to New York, and we're there for a day and he says, "I just want to go out and have a day with you. Let's go shopping." I'm like, "Okay, let's go shopping." And we get into the limo and he says to the guy, "Are there any jewelry stores close by?" The guy says, "Yeah, as a matter of fact, just up the street is Van Cleef & Arpels." So, we get there and there's this extraordinarily beautiful ring. And I was like, "Wow, that's beautiful." And he goes, "We'll take it." And that's it. We'll take it. And we walk out and it's on my finger.[15]

THURSDAY, AUGUST 15, 1985

"A Love Bizarre" [Dance Mix, listed as **"Love Bazaar"**] (edit and mix)
Sunset Sound, Studio 1 | 12:30 p.m.–5:45 p.m. (booked: 12 p.m.–8 p.m.)
Producer: Sheila E. | Artist: Sheila E. | Engineers: David Leonard and "Peggy Mac" Leonard | Assistant Engineer: David Glover

> *We just worked because we loved being in the studio, so half the time we'd go until we couldn't go anymore—there was no separation for when one project started, and one ended because we were just mixing everything and we kept putting out product.*[16]
>
> —Sheila E.

While Prince was away, Sheila oversaw the mixing and editing for the "Dance Mix" of "A Love Bizarre."

A cassette was made from the session and sent to Prince.

Status: No "Dance Mix" for "A Love Bizarre" has surfaced, but the 12-inch version is the same as the album version (12:18), however in Europe there was a different 12-inch (7:13) called "A Love Bizarre" (pts. I & II) and a medley of "The Glamorous Life," "Sister Fate," and "A Love Bizarre" (7:04).

The following day, André Cymone's version of "The Dance Electric" is released on his third album, *A.C.* When the single was issued, it reached number 10 on the Black Chart but did not enter the Pop Chart.

FRIDAY, AUGUST 16, 1985

> *We're flying to Paris, and we're there in Paris for a couple of days, and that's when he says, "I want you to be my wife."*[17]
>
> —Susannah Melvoin

Prince and Susannah leave for France. At the time, she was being considered as the female lead for *Under The Cherry Moon,* but Prince had other plans. "I was asleep. He came in and woke me up and said 'I have something to tell you. Come sit up here. Sit, sit.' He was pacing. I said, 'Are you okay?' He was like, 'I have something to tell you.' Literally the blood was rushing out of my head. I thought something terrible was happening. Then he got very close, and he took my hand, and he said, 'I don't want you to be in this film. I want you to be my wife.'"

According to Susannah, as soon as she accepted, she was immediately treated differently by those around Prince. "I remember Jerome saying, 'Well, you're the one! He's going to keep you hidden for a while.' Jerome was really instrumental in helping me understand how much Prince loved me. He would always tell me, 'There's nobody he loves more than you. You've just got to know that.' Because I wouldn't understand why. Why am I not on set all the time? There's my sister and everybody's there, and why am I being sort of kept away? He'd say, 'He just can't stand losing you.'"[18]

Casting for the movie was an immediate concern. Apollonia's part in *Purple Rain* was such a star-making role and *Under The Cherry Moon* demanded that the new female lead would also have to be able to shine next to Prince. Little-known English actress Kristin Scott Thomas, who would later receive critical acclaim for her work in *The Horse Whisperer* and *Gosford Park* as well as Golden Globe, Oscar, Screen Actors Guild, and BAFTA nominations for her work in *The English Patient*, was asked to read for the part. "It was extraordinary when I got the call to come and do this audition for that. I mean I'd been listening to 'Raspberry Beret' nonstop on my Walkman and I'm just obsessed with Prince."[19] Scott read for a smaller role, but once Prince watched her audition video, he seemed intrigued. "What happened was, I was invited to dinner by Prince and his associates and it was then that they said, 'Would you like to audition for the lead?' And I said, 'Yes, please.'"[20] Another audition followed, and everyone felt she was right for the role. "I got the part. Why? I have no idea, but I did, and it was the most extraordinary experience."[21]

MONDAY, AUGUST 19, 1985 (ESTIMATE)

"Venus De Milo" [short version] (overdubs and mix)
"Venus De Milo" [long version] (overdubs and mix)
"Splash" (mix multiple versions)
The Complex Studios (Los Angeles, California)
Producers: Prince, Wendy, and Lisa | Artist: Prince | Engineer: David Tickle | Second Engineer: Sharon Rice

He had most of "Splash" done. It was one of the things he left me and Lisa alone to do all these vocals on, and we were like, "Let's fucking blow his mind. We're going to put our recorders on it."

—Wendy Melvoin

"Prince was great at being able to be his own band, and change styles, and do all that," acknowledges Wendy. "But you do get to a point, sometimes, where it's like, 'I'm repeating myself.' So, then you look for other things to come in and give a different flavor."

Wendy and Lisa were asked to fill in the sounds for "Splash," so they decided to pour everything into helping him fulfill his vision, including sound effects, more Fairlight keyboards, percussion, and their signature background vocal layers. They also reached back into their bag of instruments from their childhood, adding the sounds of their wooden recorders. "We all went to a

Waldorf school—Lisa, and me, and Susannah, and Jonathan, and David—and they teach you how to play recorders. So, we played recorders on 'Splash,' all those little lines in between, on the verses, and he just loved all that out of the box stuff. He loved us giving him more tools. He loved it and we loved doing it."

"Yeah," agrees Lisa. "It was like finding a room in your house that you didn't know was there."

Additional work was also done on the longer and shorter versions of "Venus De Milo." Prince did not attend this session.

MONDAY, AUGUST 19, 1985

Release of the Family's self-titled album on Paisley Park Records.

> *[Paisley Park Records] had always been a dream of his. If he had a chance to go out and do his own thing, why wouldn't he do it?*[22]
>
> —Jerome Benton

Around The World In A Day was his first release on Paisley Park Records, but the debut album by the Family was a new venture for Prince. It was the first release by a protégé band for this label. "I think it's a great record, man," reflected St. Paul. "The thing I can't get over is that he picked me and I'm forever grateful for that. It changed the course of my career forever."[23]

"He was brilliant," adds Peterson. "I didn't realize how brilliant of a marketer he was as well."

> He knew exactly what it should look like, sound like, be presented as, how the concert should be presented, how the character should act, interact, what they should say, how they should say it. How they should walk, how they should talk. Crazy. The music was incredibly funky, but the Clare Fischer element put on top of the one chord wonders—that's what I call those one chord wonders because they're just funky, and that's what they're supposed to be—when you superimpose all this incredible harmony over the top that makes it that much more sophisticated. Sure, that's where Prince went, and we got to go Valentino & Hugh Hefner with this because it's so highbrow now with the strings. Truly, for me that's what separates it.

Prince decided that *The Family* album would not be a direct copy of the Time. The addition of Eric Leeds' and Clare Fischer's work gave the collection a lush feel that was different from anything else he'd released. The sonic wall actually foreshadowed the orchestral blend on his *Parade* album, as well as the funky jazz he'd ride on Madhouse *8*.

Reviews of the music in this collection were fairly positive. *Rolling Stone* hailed the album as "easily 1985's best dance record,"[24] and Prince's hometown paper declared it "easily the most impressive Royal Court debut since the Time's."[25] The *Santa Cruz Sentinel* called "Yes" a "criminally funky piece of freshness. This is not a song that talks about it—it does it."[26]

Prince had set out to create something timeless and it exceeded expectations. If he was looking to replace the Time, he'd found a way to do it without having to compete on their playing field, and the future of the band looked bright and promising. Despite not enjoying every song on the album, Eric Leeds looks back at it fondly. "If I had not had any involvement with Prince whatsoever, I probably would have liked *The Family* album, more so than maybe anything else that he had been doing at that time. There was more stuff on that album that would have been more where I'm at musically."

THURSDAY, AUGUST 22, 1985 (ESTIMATE)

"Splash" (rough mix)
"Venus De Milo" [short version] (mix)
"Venus De Milo" [long version] (mix)
"Do U Lie?" (orchestra mix)
"Alexa De Paris" (orchestra mix)
The Complex Studios (Los Angeles, California)
Producers: Prince, Wendy, and Lisa | Artist: Prince | Engineer: David Tickle
| Assistant Engineer: Sharon Rice

The tapes from the previous date's session with Clare Fischer were brought to Wendy and Lisa at The Complex Studios and a portion of the day was spent blending "Alexa De Paris" and "Do U Lie?" with Fischer's respective orchestral scores. An updated mix of "Splash" and both versions of "Venus De Milo" also took place on this date. A tape was likely sent to Prince for review.

MONDAY, AUGUST 26, 1985

Sheila E.'s second album, *Romance 1600*, is released on Paisley Park Records. Two weeks and two releases on Prince's new "Paisley Park" record label.

> *They thought the whole thing about the first album was to sell*
> *sex, which was how it was presented. But for the second album,*
> *I cut my hair and wore a long-sleeved blouse and long pants,*
> *because I wanted to be seen as a strong musician. But no one*
> *got it.*[27]
>
> —Sheila E.

Reviews of *Romance 1600* included *The Citizen* in Ottawa who praised Sheila E. as the "most promising Prince spinoff,"[28] but many of the reviews were largely lukewarm, if not entirely critical. *People*[29] magazine praised "Merci For The Speed Of A Mad Clown In Summer," but only for the title and because the song was an instrumental. The lyrics of other tracks ranged from "foolishness" to "cornball," saving their rare praise for Prince's "mean bass" and Eddie M.'s sax, ending the harsh review with "the LP's final score is *Romance 1600*, Music 0."

Rolling Stone[30] gave the album 2 out of 5 stars and also praised Eddie M.'s work, notably his sax solo on "Dear Michaelangelo," which they called "a piece of genuine inspiration." Unfortunately, they reported that the only standout track was "A Love Bizarre," and even that song had major flaws.

It is likely that some of the reviews were a reaction to Prince's involvement and the backlash that was gathering steam. Although it wouldn't have the same success as her debut album, several stand out tracks including "Sister Fate," "Bedtime Story," and "A Love Bizarre" helped the album reach number 12 in the *Billboard* Soul LP's chart. It peaked at number 50 on the *Billboard* Pop Album Chart.

Despite the layers of secrecy in place to keep the general public from understanding how deeply Prince was involved with the music of his protégés, both Sheila E.'s album and the recent release from the Family were insightfully summed up by critic Evelyn Erskine who felt that "each seems to be playing out a part of Prince's personality through separate well-staged dramas."[31]

SEPTEMBER 1985

THURSDAY, SEPTEMBER 5, 1985

"Alexa De Paris" (orchestra mix)
"Venus De Milo" [long version] (orchestra mix)
"Venus De Milo" [short version] (orchestra mix)
"Do U Lie?" (orchestra mix)
"Splash" (rough mix)
Sunset Sound, Studio 3 | 10:30 a.m.–5:15 p.m. (booked: 12 noon–open)
Producer: Prince | Artist: Prince | Engineer: "Peggy Mac" Leonard |
    Assistant Engineer: Mike Kloster

I don't think I really have a favorite [Prince song to play live],
*but if I had to choose one it would be "Alexa De Paris." It's such
a musical piece that captures the creative personalities of the
Revolution when we were with Prince.*[1]

—BrownMark

Prince, Susannah, and Susan Rogers were all in France by this date, and while they were gone, work on Prince's music was still being completed at Sunset Sound by Peggy Leonard. Wendy and Lisa had worked on the orchestral mixes in August, and today from 10:30 a.m. to 5 p.m. additional mixes were created, blending Clare Fischer's orchestra with both versions of "Venus De Milo," as well as "Do U Lie?," and "Alexa De Paris."

"['Alexa De Paris'] is just an awesome piece of musical art. Phenomenal, the musical approach to it." reflected BrownMark. "You get deep inside the minds of the Revolution and where our heads were at that time and see how deep Prince can go with his musical ability."[2]

At the end of the session two C-60 cassettes were made, one of them likely went to Prince in France.

FRIDAY, SEPTEMBER 6, 1985

"Go" (tracking, mix)
Pumacrest Mobile Recording Unit (from Advision Studios), in Nice, France
Producer: Prince | Artist: Prince | Engineer: Susan Rogers

> *I'd rather you just walk out the door and go. I don't want to feel the pain.*[3]
>
> —lyrics to "Go"

Prince was days away from the start of filming *Under The Cherry Moon*, and under a great deal of pressure, which would occasionally surface as a fight to blow off steam with someone close to him. Susannah often took the brunt of the arguments simply because she was staying with him, and on this occasion, it was unclear how they'd recover. "That tussle they were going through was really ridiculous. Really, really tough," remembers Susan Rogers. "It was terrible to see Susannah go through it. And I knew Prince was hurting too."

Like many artists, pain is the first ingredient for their art, and Prince's frustration inspired him to seclude himself for a few hours to record "Go," a composition written from the viewpoint of a man whose heart was broken by his lover's infidelity, but the depressing topic was wrapped in an infectious pop song. Prince once again used his music as his diary, giving a glimpse into his heart and struggles. Even Susannah, who made up with Prince afterward, recognized the power of the song. "Love it. It's one of his great melodies, and a beautiful song."

"Prince was out of the country because he sent us a cassette and we drove from LA to Minneapolis listening to that cassette over and over," remembers Lisa. "My sister came with us and she had a newborn baby and that was in the fall because her baby was only like two months old. The baby loved that song. Every time we put that song on, she would stop crying."

What many of his compositions, including this one, reveal was that when Prince's relationships suffered, he generally felt that it wasn't because of his *own* actions; he blamed the damage almost exclusively on his partner and would disagree wholeheartedly to express that he was not at fault no matter what the cause. He was revealing his vulnerability and despite all of his romantic songs, his instinct for control wouldn't allow him to be exposed and weak for too long, according to Susannah.

> He's the contrarian of all contrarians and it has to do with his prowess, his musical prowess, his ego, his creative part and if you're also emotionally attached to it, he's even more vulnerable. "Don't expect me to be anything like you or anyone else. I am always different and always will be. You cannot count on me to be anything other than contrary, so you just can't figure me out." It was unbelievably frustrating. There was so much of it that would be like "Can you just fucking stop it?" He was always the guy who would do it first and then he'd disappear and then you couldn't get your hands on him. He'd be slippery. He'd be gone out of your sight. You couldn't go like "You fucker, how could you do that?" He'd be gone.

"He was that way with everybody," continues Susannah. "[He'd be thinking] 'No one is going to get me. I'll get you first.' We used to say that he kicked you in the ass when your back was turned. Laughing."

It was a trait that would eventually damage and even destroy many of his professional and personal relationships and change the course of his career more than once.

Status: "Go" (4:48) remained unreleased during Prince's life.

SATURDAY, SEPTEMBER 7, 1985

"A Love Bizarre" (edit, crossfades, and mix)
Sunset Sound, Studio 3 | 9:00 p.m.–11:45 a.m. (booked: 6 p.m.–open)
Producer: Sheila E. | Artist: Sheila E. | Engineer: "Peggy Mac" Leonard |
    Assistant Engineer: Mike Kloster

An edit of Sheila's "A Love Bizarre" was done during this brief session. It is likely because of changes Prince recommended based on the previous remix. A single C-60 cassette was created and shipped to him in France.

SATURDAY, SEPTEMBER 7, 1985

Becky Johnston's third and final draft of *Under The Cherry Moon* is completed. The movie was scheduled to start shooting in slightly more than a week, so preproduction was in full gear and Mary Lambert was working hard to accommodate Prince's vision.

MONDAY, SEPTEMBER 9, 1985

"The Screams Of Passion" (insert edits)
Sunset Sound, Studio 3 | 7:00 p.m.–8:30 p.m. (booked: 7 p.m.–open)
Producer: Prince | Artist: The Family | Engineer: "Peggy Mac" Leonard | Assistant Engineer: Mike Kloster

Peggy Mac oversees a brief edit for the Family's "The Screams Of Passion." At the end of the session, a single C-60 tape is made for Prince.

THURSDAY, SEPTEMBER 12, 1985

Rolling Stone magazine's interview with Prince is published. The well-received and candid cover story gave Prince the opportunity to speak on many topics including: religion, fame, his music, his band, Chick and the *National Enquirer* story, and the event with a photographer earlier in the year.

MONDAY, SEPTEMBER 16, 1985

Shooting of *Under The Cherry Moon* begins in Nice, France.

> *I think that Prince was so accustomed to making music on his own, because he could be the engineer, the producer, the writer, the keyboard player, and the guitar player. He could do it all himself without ever really having to communicate to anybody. And he's a genius at doing that. Movie making is a whole different medium.*[4]
>
> —Jimmy Jam

Mary Lambert had directed many of Madonna's early videos, so she was well-known and respected in the music community. Lambert reportedly met Prince when she was hired to direct Sheila E.'s "The Glamorous Life" video, so she was familiar with how Prince treated most directors. "He basically directed his own videos," revealed Lisa, who witnessed this behavior on multiple projects. "He would get help from people on the technical side, but he didn't let anyone else have creative control."[5] Lambert had been brought back to direct *Under The Cherry Moon*, but with all things involving Prince, he ended up wanting to control every part of the production and decided that he was best suited to take her job. "Mary Lambert was a really, really cool director, a really cool lady," recalled Prince's costar Jerome Benton, "but I guess her creativity just didn't match up at the time with Prince."[6]

> The difference I see is that she had to *learn* us. She couldn't learn what Prince knew about us just in a couple of weeks or even a month or even in a shoot. She's an amazing director. She didn't hit the notes that apparently needed to be hit. And what happens with Prince's band when you can't solo, you're out. No, he didn't come with the credentials of knowing which camera lens to use, but he knew *our* comedy, so there were some flaws in some of his directing, but he was brave enough to take hold of it and get it done and nobody would direct me.[7]

Lambert issued a statement: "I'm leaving under totally amicable circumstances. It's just become quite apparent that Prince has such a strong vision of what this movie should be, a vision that extends to so many areas of the film, that it makes no sense for me to stand between him and the film anymore. So, I'm going off to work on my own feature and letting him finish his."[8] Soon award-winning actor, Terence Stamp (*Superman I* and *II*) would back out of the project due to "scheduling conflicts." He was replaced by Steven Berkoff (*Rambo*, the James Bond film *Octopussy*, and *Beverly Hills Cop*).

"As I recall, Madonna was supposed to be in *Under The Cherry Moon*," remembers Rebecca Ross, one of the editors on the movie. "It's a little known fact that he wanted her. I don't know how far the conversations went, but I know that he wanted her to do it. And I know that that was the connection with Mary Lambert. Can you imagine Madonna and Terence Stamp? It would have been a totally different movie."

Despite the stories about how he ran the set, his female lead, Kristin Scott Thomas, enjoyed her time with Prince. "He wasn't difficult to work with. I don't think anyone thought that. I don't know where these rumors come from. Everybody loved working with him. We just had a really good time making this movie."[9]

Prince's managers wanted another movie. *Under The Cherry Moon* was not what they imagined so they fought him on it, but by this time Prince had enough clout to make all of the decisions, according to his manager Bob Cavallo. "He believed that he should make the movie in black and white. I said, 'Why the fuck are we making this picture in the south of France? All of this is gonna cost a fortune.' He says, 'I want the people in my community to see the south of France.' I understood that. I said, 'Then we have to shoot it in color! I mean what is the south of France without color?' He was picturing it based on the films he had seen. I said, 'Is this a thing about racism where the father shoots you and you die for the love of his daughter? Why are you dying at the end? And why are we having this reactionary ending where some white guy kills you?' He says, 'I think my audience will just be blown away by it.' He saw himself almost operatically."

With Prince demanding control of every aspect of the movie, he seemed less interested in trusting those around him, and more interested in making a pure statement and not filtering the movie through someone else's vision. As he often did, if there was someone who had a skill he hadn't mastered, he relied on bringing in an expert, so he hired renowned cinematographer Michael Ballhaus (*Goodfellas, Bram Stoker's Dracula,* and *The Age of Innocence*) to design the look, but ultimately it was Prince's project and any success or failure would be seen as his responsibility.

TUESDAY, SEPTEMBER 17, 1985 (ESTIMATE)

"**Go**" (edit, mix)
"**Girl**" [extended version] (output to tape likely)
"**Girl**" [7-inch version] (output to tape likely)
Ocean Way Studios, Hollywood, California
Producers: Prince, Wendy, and Lisa | Artist: Prince and the Revolution | Engineer: David Tickle

While Prince was in France, he continued to rely on those he trusted to help keep him on schedule. Wendy and Lisa spent time at Ocean Way Studios in California overseeing an edit of "Go" and preparing a copy of "Girl" to be used as the B-side for the upcoming single release of "America."

During the time Susannah was home in Minneapolis, she met with an interior architect to help design Prince's newly purchased house on Galpin Blvd.

in Chanhassen, about four miles north of Kiowa Trail where Prince lived at the time. Now that they were engaged, it would be their home, and Prince trusted her to design a nest for him to create and live out his dreams.

WEDNESDAY, SEPTEMBER 25, 1985

"You're My Love" (rough mix)
"Call Of The Wild" (rough mix)
"Sexual Suicide" (mix)
"Alexa De Paris" (mix)
"Love or Money" (mix)
"Moonbeam Levels" (mix)
"Empty Room" (mix)
"Splash" (mix)
"Hello" [extended mix] (mix)
Sunset Sound, Studio 3 | 10:00 p.m.–7:00 a.m. (booked: 10 p.m.–open)
Producer: Prince | Artist: Prince | Engineer: Susan Rogers | Assistant
    Engineer: Coke Johnson

He would ask for stuff to be mixed and sent to him.

—Susan Rogers

Over her 5 years employed by Prince, Susan Rogers traveled around the world recording his music. Recently she'd been in France working on *Under The Cherry Moon*, and she also apparently spent a brief period back at Sunset Sound providing him with the tracks he would potentially need for upcoming projects. The session began surprisingly late, so from 10 in the evening to 7 the following morning, Rogers worked on mixes for the movie ("Alexa De Paris," "Love Or Money," "Sexual Suicide," and "Moonbeam Levels"), for upcoming releases ("Hello–extended mix"), and probably others ("Splash," "Empty Room," "Call Of The Wild," and "You're My Love") just to hear and then assign them to a project.

Two C-60 cassettes were created for Prince.

Status: Of these 9 songs, 6 were not released on any of Prince's current projects.

Note: This is the first work order that was filed under "Paisley Park" records. "Cherry Moon Productions" was crossed out, and Warner Bros. was no longer listed as the client. Cavallo, Ruffalo, & Fargnoli were representing this specific session. It would shift back to Warner Bros. after this session.

THURSDAY, SEPTEMBER 26, 1985

"**Sexual Suicide**" (rough mix)
"**God Is Everywhere**" (rough mix)
Sunset Sound, Studio 3 | 1:30 p.m.–9:00 p.m. (booked: 1 p.m.–open)
Producer: Prince | Artist: Prince | Engineers: Susan Rogers and "Peggy
   Mac" Leonard | Assistant Engineer: Paul Levy

He sang about really personal things and took a lot of chances with how he looked, what he was saying and how he performed. He was really courageous. Think about things we hold very close. Our personal identities, our religious and sexual and racial identities. He was putting it all out there in a big, strong way, like whoever you are, whatever you are, it's all good. He made risk-taking cool and made your dark side something to be proud of. People really connected to all of that.[10]

—Lisa Coleman

Prince's persona often expressed two seemingly inconsistent sides of himself, the sacred and the sexual, both of which held an important part in his personality and his image. Rarely does an artist find a way to be seen as both a hedonist and holy, yet when doing songs like "Sexual Suicide" and "God Is Everywhere," Prince announced both of them loudly as if there wasn't a contradiction, and to him, there likely wasn't.

"He was okay if you didn't respect him, but he really needed to be understood. That mattered a lot to him. And he would open up with people who understood him. I know when we were in the studio, there'd be times it was just the two of us, he'd get bored and he'd just start to talk and he'd just talk about whatever was on his mind. And it could be women, it could be music, it could be his band. It could be other artists and he'd just talk," according to Susan Rogers. "We had one-on-one conversations that were back and forth a little bit, but I was really very cautious about crossing a line and getting too close to him."[11]

Peggy Mac agrees that there were times that she didn't allow herself to be vulnerable with him, because it would often backfire. "It was one of these things where you went into this understanding that you better be in a calm state because you *had* to be. You couldn't be up, 'cause he'd squash you down. You couldn't be sad either. You just had to be kind of neutral. I kept my face neutral; I kept my actions neutral; I would go and kick the wall when I left the studio if he frustrated me, but you just didn't give him anything to feed on. I didn't wanna give him any ammunition to use against me."

One C-60 and one C-90 were created from this session for Prince.

Note: While Peggy and Susan worked at Sunset Sound on some of the songs for Under The Cherry Moon, *David Tickle spent several days at a local studio in Minneapolis, also working on mixes of other tracks, probably including: "Do U Lie?" "Kiss," "Love Or Money," "Sometimes It Snows In April," and a copy of "Alexa De Paris," which it appears was simultaneously being mixed in Los Angeles.*

FRIDAY, SEPTEMBER 27, 1985

All Titles for Paisley Park Album assembled
(**"Alexa De Paris," "Venus De Milo," "Do You Lie?," "Sexual Suicide,"
"God Is Everywhere," "You're My Love," "Call Of The Wild"**)
Sunset Sound, Studio 3 | 12:00 noon–7:30 p.m. (booked: 1 p.m.–open)
Producer: Prince | Artist: Prince | Engineers: Susan Rogers or "Peggy Mac"
Leonard

Prince requested a series of songs to be compiled. Although this was listed as being "for Paisley Park album," it was probably not considered a true compilation for the *Parade* album, but instead it was more likely for Prince to listen and review for consideration for the movie.

One TDK C-90 cassette was dubbed and sent to him.

SUNDAY, SEPTEMBER 29, 1985

"The Screams Of Passion" (edit)
Sunset Sound, Studio 1 | 6:00 p.m.–8:15 p.m. (booked: 6:00 p.m.–open)
Producer: Prince | Artist: The Family | Engineer: "Peggy Mac" Leonard |
 Assistant Engineer: Mike Kloster

> *You've got to remember [that] Prince was only one person with*
> *great ideas. So, he can only implement ideas as he could, one*
> *at a time or maybe two at a time. But something's going to lose*
> *attention. Something's going to lose the element of having the*
> *important stuff done when it needs to be done. A lot of Prince's*
> *projects ended up that way. Still it didn't take away from his*
> *greatness though. Even Prince on a half-ass idea is better than*
> *most.*[12]

—Jerome Benton

This drastically abbreviated session consisted of Peggy overseeing an edit of
"The Screams Of Passion." The track had already been out, so this was possibly created for a promo or radio version. The song had just entered the *Billboard* Top 100 where it peaked at number 63, before falling off the charts after
six weeks, which was frustrating Paul Peterson. "The single was out and there
was no promotion, nothing. We didn't have any idea what was going on. It was
just so unorganized."[13]

Despite the long ramp up time and the incredible music that was created
for the project, there were no firm deals in place for the band members so they
were working on a handshake and a promise, but at the time some of them
could barely pay their bills. "It wasn't easy," recalls Peterson. "I was living at
my mother's house!"

"We didn't sign the contract that was put in front of us, because it needed to
be restructured," explained Jerome. "And I remember a conversation of 'Let's
wait till I get back from doing *Under The Cherry Moon* to do this stuff.'"[14]

"[The reaction to the Family concert was] a sign of things to come. However, I never knew *what* was to come. I was never let in on the plan. I was told
enough. I was a paid employee. Again, I wasn't that tight with him," reveals
Peterson. "Prince went off and started his movie. He moved me to LA, and I
started singing, acting, and dancing lessons. He never told me what he had me

doing that stuff for. Ever. A smart person would go, 'He's grooming you for a movie, Paul.' But he never came out and said that."

A single C-60 cassette was made of the day's work and because Peterson was now in Los Angeles, he either picked up the cassette at Sunset Sound or was there for the session. Prince was still in France and couldn't attend, so the work order was signed by St. Paul.

MONDAY, SEPTEMBER 30, 1985

"Holly Rock" by Sheila E. was released on the soundtrack of *Krush Groove*, which peaked at number 79 on the *Billboard* Top Pop Albums Chart and number 14 on the *Billboard* Top Black Albums Chart. The song had been released as a single earlier in the year.

OCTOBER 1985

October was a busy month for Prince, but not in the studio. Because he was directing as well as the lead actor, he had a full plate, and he was also overseeing the scoring, rewriting the movie, and in many ways, he was co-producing the film as well. Any of these are a full-time job, but doing them *all* is practically unprecedented, especially for a man who was making his directorial debut after acting in only one movie. And yet, Prince still insisted on having a piano in his hotel room in case inspiration struck him—and it always did.

The stakes for Prince could not have been higher. A hit would solidify his status in Hollywood and a flop could derail his movie career completely. If he felt the pressure, he wasn't showing it. "He was in a great mood as far as I could see," remembers his editor Rebecca Ross. "He'd never had any failures at that point, so he was pretty high on everything that was going on in his life, and he had carte blanche, so it was fun."

WEDNESDAY, OCTOBER 2, 1985

"America," the third single from *Around The World In A Day*, is released in the United States (backed by "Girl"). The track reached number 46 on the Pop Chart and number 35 on the Black Chart.

SUNDAY, OCTOBER 27, 1985

> *The band came over to do some photographs* [some of which are featured on the *Parade* LP -ed.] *and we just wanted to play really bad. I just kind of missed America. It wasn't planned, but we did it. Strangely enough, we hadn't played in a long time and we had a lot of pent-up energy and we may have gone overboard. Maybe I'm getting younger or wilder. I have a strange feeling that the next time we tour it's going to be pretty ridiculous as far as the hotness goes. We have a lot of energy.*[1]

> —Prince

Because the schedule for *Under The Cherry Moon* was tight, Prince took advantage of a day off from filming to sit down for an interview for MTV. Prince had a reputation for enjoying controversial issues and shocking critics with his ribald comments and performances, but this was a structured monologue disguised as a series of questions and answers. Instead of allowing a journalist to interrogate him, the carefully crafted interview was based on questions reportedly supplied by the network in advance, but conducted by his manager, Steven Fargnoli. Prince's responses appeared designed to explain some of the issues that had come up over the last year including: his religious views, his musical influences, if he'd sold out to his black audience, his father, working with André Cymone, the information that his bodyguard had revealed about him, the incidents that occurred after the American Music Awards, and the backlash that he was facing.

Prince also shot a video for "America" in the open air Théâtre de Verdure in Nice. Dressed in the same coat he'd worn in the "4 The Tears In Your Eyes" video as well as the concert video with Sheila E., Prince and the Revolution performed a near hour-long concert that also included "Paisley Park," "Delirious," "Little Red Corvette," and "Purple Rain." "They set up a huge, massive circus tent that fit about 1,500 people, but there was no real ventilation going on in there," detailed Wendy. "All I can remember is it was so hot in that tent and we're moving around so much that by the end of the filming of it, Prince and I walked off stage and they had to have oxygen tanks for the two of us because we were about ready to pass out."[2]

In typical Prince fashion, even though he was shooting a video to promote the song, he updated the track when performing it live, as Eric Leeds remembered. "At that point he wanted to use me and Eddie M. on ['America'], so we were in the rehearsals for that the night before and there was going to be solo spots and some of the little horn riffs that he came up for us to do and then said, 'Okay, Eric's going to solo here, Eddie's going to solo here.' But in the middle of it, I told Prince, 'I've got an idea for a more extended horn line that might work at certain parts of the song.' And I played it for him, and he said, 'Yeah, that's cool. So, teach it to Eddie,' which I did, and that's kind of the crazy horn line that's played over and over again and in between the solos."[3] The song also contained elements from Miles Davis's "Spanish Key" that can be heard at 1:40 in the "America" video. The original lick can be found from 11:47 onward in "Spanish Key," from *Bitches Brew* (1971).

After the concert, Prince asked the band to stay in France during the production as Matt Fink remembers. "He had us fly out to Nice for ten days and he kept us out there for four weeks. He wanted us to hang out with him and just watch him film. So, we went down to the set a lot. It was great, a free ticket to come to Nice and hang out. But at the same time, it was like, where is my creativity? I'm just sitting here watching some guy do his thing, and I am not getting involved. It's just wasting my time. That is why I felt underutilized. Put me in the movie! [laughs]. Give me a part, make me an extra or something . . . why are you keeping us here so long?"

There was no way that the Family could do any promotional appearances with Susannah Melvoin and Jerome Benton in France, and with Prince paying for Paul Peterson to relocate to Los Angeles for dancing and acting lessons, so everything about the band stalled, including the contract negotiations Paul was having with Prince. "When I went to Prince and said, 'These things in this contract aren't right,' he said, 'Go talk to my manager,' and I respected that. So, when I went to talk to his managers they said, 'We're not changing a damn thing in here.' That's when I went, 'Oh, well, what are my options?' Nobody in their right mind would seek to get out of something with a guy who's on top of the world."

"We had been rehearsing now for months with a thirteen-piece band and played one show on the first album, that's it, one show," recalled the band's drummer Jellybean Johnson.

> And it was tight as hell, had it all down and shit, and then [Prince] up and leaves. "Screams Of Passion" is out and he has Paul out in LA with no deal, we had no signed contracts, it was just a handshake. And he's got Paul taking all these acting, dancing, and singing classes trying to get the white boy out of him. And in

the meantime, every major record label is seeing this motherfucker and knowing how big Prince was at the time, anything that was associated with him, somebody wanted a piece of, so all these record companies were saying, "Oh, you're not signed to him? What do you want?" And Paul being a young, eighteen, nineteen, twenty years old, shit, I can't blame him.[4]

"And next thing I know through a great friend, he's being offered a record deal and then there became a bidding war with a couple of labels," added Jerome. "Of course, if a deal ain't right, you don't sign it. But one of those deals came to a head and what do we do? I don't tell somebody not to do something because of the money. Paul had his needs. He was receiving only a certain amount of money."[5]

St. Paul felt trapped, and when he was offered a much larger contract to write and produce his own music, he began to feel that he was ready for the change, and the decision to break away from Prince was rapidly becoming a reality.

The things that got me to that point—number one was pay, right? That was number one. Number two, I had been groomed my entire life to write my own music, to play my own music, to produce my own music. I think it was more around the time when the offers came in saying we want you to do this. I was like, well, naturally, of course, I can do this. Of course, I can leave the most successful rock star and do this on my own. I can write it. I can write those songs better than him. Cocky, ego, indestructible, but that's why you're 20 when you have those thoughts. [laughs]

When he saw the amount being offered, it made the decision even easier. "I was like, there's three more zeros after that paycheck. Three! So anyway, it was significant." But there was a conversation that was necessary with Prince before Peterson could leave the safety of the nest and that happened faster than expected.

"Prince found out what I was doing, and he called me on the phone. It was scary. Frightening, and I was shaking. Makes me a little weirded out even thinking about it. How do you tell somebody who's invested a lot of money into you . . . 'I don't care, bye-bye?' But that's exactly what I did. Because I had no contract. They weren't negotiating with me." The discussion became heated with Peterson holding his ground about the lack of care they'd been given. "I said, 'If you're gonna be in charge of this band, you can't do four million other things at the same time.' He said, 'Yes I can! I did it with the Time, didn't I? I did it with Sheila E. I did it with Vanity 6.'"[6]

Prince eventually turned it all back on St. Paul. "He said 'What do you need? A house?' I said. 'Well, yeah.' He said, 'Well, you've got to *work*.' I was like 'What do you think I've been doing?'"

"So that was my conversation with him and then I did call and talk with [Jellybean] and Jerome, and I can't remember if Eric was on the line or not. And telling them what was going on. And they said, 'Well, you've got to do what you got to do. Go get that money.'" According to Paul, everyone in the band could relate. "They were in the same boat with the contract negotiations. They weren't happy that I was leaving by any means. I remember [Jellybean] saying, 'Baby bro, you gotta do what you want to do. We'll be alright.'"[7]

Susannah remembers how she was confronted about it. "Prince came to me, and he said, 'How do you feel about that? I said, 'How do *you* feel about that?' He said, 'Are you mad at him?' I said, 'Not really.' I didn't want to say to Prince, 'Well not really, I mean he was offered a shit ton of money. He's got a family, whatever.'"

Despite the damage caused by the breakup of this carefully crafted group, Susannah thinks that Prince had other reasons that he was relieved it ended. "He didn't want me to go anywhere. He didn't want me to be famous. He wanted me to be *his*. If I were famous, I would be adored by others, and he didn't want me to be adored by anybody but him. So, I was *his* and *his* to adore, *his* to have. And I had to just buck up."

"The relationship that he had with Susannah at the time was already getting in the way of anything that might have happened with the Family," agrees Eric Leeds. "I don't know if Susannah would have been long for the band, because what if the band had started to really become successful? Prince was not going to have his girlfriend being up on stage, in that role, because that's *his* girlfriend. Now he was going to get jealous of her, in that situation."

"I know Prince wasn't exactly pleased with me leaving," realized Paul. "He did threaten a huge lawsuit, and that was nerve-wracking for a 20-year-old. As far as how it affected the others, I think they fared just fine. They all either went on to play with Prince or in [Jellybean's] case, produce great records with Jam and Lewis."[8]

"It's a heartbreaker, but at the same time, Paul got an offer to do a record and make hundreds of thousands of dollars when we were only making $140 a week," reflects Susannah. "He just went, I'm out, and he left."

"Our first reaction was, okay, we didn't see this coming, and obviously that's the end of this project," reflected Eric.

So, whatever this *was* going to be, it's not gonna be. Jerome was already in Nice because he was the co-star with Prince in *Under The Cherry Moon*, so Jerome's relationship with Prince was certainly going to be there. I really never had a discussion with Susannah or Jellybean for a while after that. My initial reaction was, "Okay, this is a drag because this was a really cool album and we were kind of looking forward to the possibility of going on tour and seeing what was going to happen with this," but since I had already been doing these things with Prince and his music, Alan immediately told me, "I wouldn't be too concerned, because I have a feeling that Prince is gonna immediately just put you in his band." And that's pretty much what happened. So, I was very, very, very fortunate to have been in that situation, and it was very shortly after that, of course, that Prince decided to not only just add me but to expand.[9]

"Almost overnight, the [Revolution] went from 5 members to 11. And first thing, he came to me and said, 'I want to add a trumpet. Do you know someone?' I said, 'Absolutely. Matt Blistan'"[10] Blistan was contacted and would audition for the band at the end of November while recording "Mountains" with Prince. He'd quickly be nicknamed "Atlanta Bliss" by Prince.

It would take a few weeks before every detail was decided, but once it was, it changed the course and the mood of next summer's tour.

NOVEMBER 1985

October had been filled with chaos. The Family was crumbling and could not proceed without "St. Paul" Peterson, so all of the months of recording and planning that Prince had put into the band was collapsing around him. If he had started the Family to show how he could create another band as powerful as the Time, the outcome was disappointing. He was successful in designing a groundbreaking new group, but—just like the Time—they self-destructed. Writing and producing his protégé groups was second nature for him, but keeping the bands together was turning out to be much harder than expected. There was still the option of continuing without Paul by boosting Susannah up to the lead singer.

"He asked me if I wanted to do that," remembers Susannah, "and I said 'no,' because I think I felt he didn't want me to say 'Yes,' and so I did what was right for us. It was some of the most fruitful periods of time working with him closely, and loving him. So, for me, it was like I really did think we were onto something else already." Talk of her fronting the band went no further than the initial discussions.

Prince's *Parade* album was also in flux with "Old Friends 4 Sale" and "All My Dreams" removed from the sequence around this time.

Throughout the confusion, Prince continued working on his film and had Wendy and Lisa record elements for the movie score, with Susan Rogers engineering the sessions. He also sent them to London to oversee editing the video for "America."

TUESDAY, NOVEMBER 5, 1985 (ESTIMATE)

"An Honest Man" [piano bar, scene 12] (multiple versions, probably from the set)
"Venus De Milo" [Piano bar scene] (tracking, multiple versions)
Under The Cherry Moon **score** (playback, or mix)
Pumacrest Mobile Recording Unit (from Advision Studios), in Nice, France
Producer: Prince | Artist: Prince | Engineer: Susan Rogers

> *We spent a lot of time in the South of France, and a lot of
> the recording was done on a truck and taken to a studio and
> blended and then sent back to Minneapolis.*[1]
>
> —Lisa Coleman

"Prince had so much money that he could afford to hire a truck from England to come to the South of France with a crew of three," recalls Susan. "The three guys from the Advision truck were Larry, Barry, and Gary. Larry was the driver. Barry was the assistant engineer and Gary was the tech. Those guys were great. And we would park the truck on set."

While Prince was shooting, he was shifting his time from inside the recording studio to being on the movie set, so he'd create music with Wendy and Lisa, but he'd also rely on them (as well as Susan) to help score and make musical changes to the songs that existed, remembered Rogers.

> When we were in France doing the *Cherry Moon* movie, I was there with him the whole time. For the first time I didn't have too much to do. We had a mobile truck there in case he wanted to record. He had Wendy and Lisa come out and from there, to keep us busy, sent us to England for three weeks. He got us a little apartment and a chauffeured car, and three weeks of time at Advision Studios. Great studio. He just said: "Go, write, come up with something and then come back to France."[2]

By November 9, the crowd that Prince had flown to France began to disperse. BrownMark flew back to the states, and the following day Prince left for London with Wendy, Lisa, and Susan Rogers to do more editing on the "America" video and to spend some time recording at Advision Studio.

SATURDAY, NOVEMBER 9, 1985–SUNDAY, NOVEMBER 10, 1985 (ESTIMATE)

"I Wonder U" (mix)
"Soul Sister" [variation of "New Position"] (mix)
"New Position" (guitar overdubs and mix)
"Christopher Tracy's Parade" [possibly still named "Wendy's Parade"] (mix)
Advision Studios (London, England)
Producers: Wendy and Lisa | Artist: Prince and the Revolution | Engineer: Susan Rogers

During the filming of Under The Cherry Moon, *there was some down-time when we didn't have to be on the set. Wendy, Lisa and I were in England and Prince joined us for a couple of days at Advision Studios.*[3]

—Susan Rogers

Once they arrived in London, Rogers recalls how she felt about the studio. "I liked that room. It was tiny, but it was a legendary studio. We didn't spend much time there, but we were working on the first few songs on the *Parade* album. I remember working on 'New Position.'"

For this weekend, Prince was traveling with Susan Rogers, Wendy, and Lisa and contributed to the first batch of mixes, which involved work on several of the tracks from the first day of recording his *Parade* album in mid-April, including "I Wonder U," "Christopher Tracy's Parade," and "New Position."

"We did another version of 'New Position' with additional lyrics and we played around with it," remembered Rogers. "I don't remember it being specifically slower, but it was a different version."[4]

The additions to "New Position" likely included a section that had Prince, Wendy, and Lisa chanting "Big ol' soul sister." This had been used by the Revolution during rehearsals and live concerts from previous years and can be heard on his June 7, 1984 birthday show, during "Possessed," during the recent performance of "America" in Nice (which was being edited into a music video during this same week), as well as on the *Purple Rain* tour, and it would continue during the *Parade* tour. Although it is unclear exactly when this part of the song was recorded, Wendy recalls how it came about. "Prince came up with 'Big ol' soul sister.' And he said, 'Do it. Do it. Just sing it. I think it was just a kind of a refrain. It's great! I loved it.'"

This session lasted into the following day. It is likely that Prince had to get back to Nice to continue working on the film.

Status: The "Soul Sister" (2:19, 2:24) variation of "New Position," was not included on the *Parade* album. A version with horns was added, but that may be the orchestra from Clare Fischer. All studio recordings of "Soul Sister" remained unreleased during Prince's lifetime.

THURSDAY, NOVEMBER 14, 1985–FRIDAY, NOVEMBER 15, 1985 (ESTIMATE)

"**Mountains**" [instrumental demo] (tracking)
"**It's For You**" [piano piece by Lisa] (tracking)
"**Sometimes It Snows In April**" (mix with strings)
"**Life Can Be So Nice**" (mix)
"**Do U Lie?**" (mix)
"**Kiss**" (mix)
"**Love Or Money**" (mix)
"**Sometimes It Snows In April**" (mix)
Advision Studios (London, England)
Producers: Wendy and Lisa | Artist: Prince and the Revolution | Engineer: Susan Rogers

> *Wendy and Lisa wrote and recorded a few pieces of music and one of the standout tracks from that was "Mountains."*
>
> —Susan Rogers

Prince was keeping Wendy and Lisa busy in the studio remixing multiple tracks for *Under The Cherry Moon*, including "Sometimes It Snows In April," "Life Can Be So Nice," "Do U Lie?," "Kiss," and "Love Or Money." Some of this work involved creating a blend of the studio tracks and Clare Fischer's orchestral elements, which were likely being considered for the score at this point.

In addition to updating the mixes of the older tracks, they were working on new songs to present to Prince, including "Mountains," which actually dates back years earlier, remembers Lisa. "'Mountains' was a song that I wrote when I was 13 or something, and just played on the piano all the time. And so, we messed around with it, and arranged it."

According to Susan Rogers, it wasn't just "Mountains" that was being created during their time in London. "We also did a couple of other tracks; one was a song that Lisa called 'It's For You.' At Advision Studios they had a 9-foot Bösendorfer piano, perfect for Lisa. She played this incredibly beautiful instrumental piece, at the end of it we could hear the phone ring in the next room, and we could hear Lisa say: 'It's for you.' And that's what we always called that song."[5]

At the end of the shift, cassettes were made of all of the tracks for Prince to review. Susan recalls how he reacted to the tape of "Mountains." "When we came back to France, Wendy played Prince the cassette and Prince was very, very excited about it. He added a horn arrangement and when we got back to the United States we recorded it."

"When he heard it, he was like, 'What's that?' 'Oh, this old thing?'" laughs Lisa. "He was like, 'Yeah that.' And then he took it away and wrote lyrics. I remember being on a plane, and I don't remember where we were going, but we were on a plane and then he came up and handed me his notebook and he had written the lyrics, I just remember seeing '17 mountains,' and I was like, 'What's that? That sounds cool!' And the song was born."

Status: The instrumental demo for "Mountains" was re-recorded by Prince and the Revolution at the end of November. Prince was inspired to create a melody for the song and write some of his more cryptic lyrics for the track. There is no additional information about "It's For You," and it is unclear if it was ever recorded by Prince.

FRIDAY, NOVEMBER 15, 1985

MTV Presents Prince aired on the music network. The interview was well-received by the audience and this combined with his *Rolling Stone* interview gave the most insights into Prince in years. After it aired, he maintained his rule about privacy and only conducted a handful of interviews during the rest of the 1980s.

MONDAY, NOVEMBER 18, 1985 (ESTIMATE)

"Sexual Suicide" (possibly Wendy's vocals, mix)
"Christopher Tracy's Parade" (mix)
"New Position" (mix)
"I Wonder U" (mix)
"Under The Cherry Moon" (mix)
"Girls & Boys" (mix)
Pumacrest Mobile Recording Unit (from Advision Studios), in Nice, France
Producers: Wendy and Lisa | Artist: Prince and the Revolution | Engineer: Susan Rogers

[Having the mobile truck on set] was especially fun because I wasn't chained to Prince's hip. He was really busy on the movie set, so I had more free time than I normally would have, and he had to go to bed early because he had to be up early. But when he did go out in the evening, oh, that meant that I was free to go out in the evening too.

—Susan Rogers

Susan explains the process of recording music during this period. "Many of these scenes were shot in the South of France. In France, of course, you take these two-hour lunches. Prince didn't need two hours for lunch, he didn't need a nap. So, I'd be there in that truck and in that two-hour lunch break, he'd come into the truck and we'd work on 'Sexual Suicide,' we'd work on 'Splash' and some really fun titles. Then he'd have to go back to the set, but I could stay with Eric and do horn parts and things in the truck. For example, we'd do mix pieces. We just had so much fun."

Prince played "Sexual Suicide" for Wendy and asked for her help on the track. "I love 'Sexual Suicide.' It's one of my all-time favorites. I did not play on that, but he asked me to go in and double his vocal and he had me sing it in a mobile truck."

Although it is unclear if Wendy's vocals were recorded on this date and in this particular mobile truck, he was insistent that she add her voice during one of the sessions. "I remember singing it and being like, 'Oh, this is something.' I was like, 'That's incredible. You've got to put that one out.' And he was like, 'No. No. No. No. No. No.' I don't know why he didn't release that. He just didn't think it was right, I guess. I don't know. Too funky? Sometimes I thought he held back things that were so funky. Sometimes he felt that way. I'm like, 'Why isn't that out there?' 'Dream Factory' was another one."

This batch of songs were also being considered for the *Parade* project and *Under The Cherry Moon*, so they were being given a new mix. Additional overdubs were likely part of this session as well.

THURSDAY, NOVEMBER 21, 1985

Today was the end of principal photography for *Under The Cherry Moon* and a wrap party was held at Le Grand Escurial in Nice, France.

FRIDAY, NOVEMBER 22, 1985

Music videos for "Love Or Money," "Kiss," and "Girls & Boys" were scheduled to be shot at the Studio de la Victorine in Nice, France. "Love Or Money" was to include the full band playing the song with a checkered black and white background, with Prince performing on the dance riser similar to what he'd used on the American Music Awards. "Kiss" would comprise footage of Dr. Fink and BrownMark by a pool, Bobby Z in bed, and Lisa standing by the shore with a cape blowing in the wind, and an additional part that looked like she was an element of a painting. Wendy would be seen in a bubble bath, as well as playing guitar while Prince sang. Both tracks were to be filmed in black and white, but only "Girls & Boys" was actually shot. Photographs of some of these situations were taken by Jeff Katz and can be found in the artwork for *Parade*.

All of the effort appears to have been put into the video for "Girls & Boys." Because of the breakup of the Family, what would have normally been an event with the Revolution had expanded to include Eric Leeds, Miko Weaver, Jerome Benton, Wally Safford, and Greg Brooks. Susannah Melvoin was also in the video.

With the initial filming finished, just about everyone was scheduled to fly home to Minneapolis in the next day or two, so Prince invited them to dinner after the video shoot.

TUESDAY, NOVEMBER 26, 1985

Prince and Jerome Benton returned to Minneapolis and Prince had his first opportunity to see his new home on Galpin Blvd. The rest of Thanksgiving week was spent moving all of Prince's belongings to the new home that he would be sharing with Susannah. "It was like his dream," she recalls how Prince reacted. "[He was saying] I have my studio now in my house. I used to have one in my old house. Now I've got a really nice one. I've got the studio at Sunset Sound here. Same guys who designed it, same board, everything was the same. I've got my girl and I've got this big beautiful house, with all that beautiful land. It was extraordinary how big that house was and how much land he had. He'd look out in his backyard and we'd be like, 'Wow, look what we have! It's incredible!' Then he could go downstairs and create."

Because his studio wasn't functioning yet, and was not until early the next year, he would continue to record at the warehouse.

Eric Leeds recalls his part in these Minneapolis sessions:

It's Friday, November 29th and Alan [Leeds] calls, and he says, "He wants everybody up in Minneapolis tomorrow. Prince all of a sudden got excited about it and he wants to start to do something with the expanded band with Miko on guitar now." And that's when he said to me, he wants a trumpet player. He said, "Call Blistan." So, I called Matt and I said, "Matt, I got some good news and I got some bad news. The good news is you might have a gig. So, the bad news is, the audition is in Minneapolis tomorrow morning." And he said, "Oh shit." So, we flew up the next morning and we got in there that day, that Saturday morning, went right into the warehouse and we jammed.

SATURDAY, NOVEMBER 30, 1985

> **"Mountains"** (tracking and overdubs)
> **"Dream Factory"** (tracking, overdubs and mix)
> **"An Honest Man"** (likely tracking, edit, and mix)
> **"Touch Me/Hold Me"** (likely overdubs and mix)
> Washington Avenue Warehouse (Edina, Minnesota)
> Producer: Prince | Artist: Prince and the Revolution | Engineer: Susan Rogers

> *I remember around that time that Prince was a little disappointed. What surprised him was that Paul left to go up to Hollywood to pursue a career. Prince had paid for him to take singing and acting lessons so that Paul could be singing and acting for him and Paul had the idea in mind of acting and singing for himself. So, Prince was disappointed, and "Dream Factory" came about.[6]*

> —Susan Rogers

The reality is that Prince occasionally carried grudges. Paul Peterson leaving the Family was still on his mind, and when Prince wasn't in control of a situation, he often did what he could to regain that control, which now included folding in members of the Family into a recording session like this, explains Wendy. "Paul had left, and we were doing those songs. I think [Prince] felt a sense of having to save the ship from going down. I think he was working overtime and his impatience level was at 100. So, you could tell the mood he was in. Bobby used to say it all the time, you could tell what mood he was in depending on the hairdo. And if he was wearing this do-rag like this, walking into rehearsal, don't talk to him. So, you could tell. So, there was a lot of having to read the room."

As he'd done when creating the song "Mutiny" for the Family to reflect how he felt about the Time breaking up, he wrote a song that would express his frustrations. "It was one of those that was done very quickly," remembered Susan. "Sometimes he would get an idea and he'd do a song and say: 'Let's get the band together, it will sound like this and look like this and it's gonna be this' . . . and then it faded pretty fast."[7]

The band was assembled and "Dream Factory" was rehearsed. Using the fictionalized place he'd introduced in Sheila E.'s track "Holly Rock," Prince shaped his lyrics to reflect the damage that is caused by putting your faith in a "Dream Factory" instead of sticking with Prince. He would exaggerate that the track was **"4 a turncoat, who after a quick brush with success, lost themselves in a haze of wine, women and pills . . . or so the fiction goes? This person is not Prince"**[8] as he explained in the song: **"Listen 2 the story of a man I am not."**[9]

The song contained references to how he felt that Peterson had abandoned those around him (**"Don't forget your friends. They're all u got."**[10]) and the pain he'd caused them. Prince even recorded a chant as a direct diss to Paul: "St. Paul, punk of the month" that was eventually edited out, but Prince would revisit the line during his performances in 1986.

"It really, really freaked Prince hard. I don't think he'd been that fucked by somebody. Maybe ever, other than Vanity. I had never seen it," reveals Wendy. "[Those lyrics] were childish, and he turned it into a shtick."

"He could be bratty," explains Susan Rogers.

Bratty at best and cruel at worst. Here I am equivocating, but I want to say, to understand where brattiness or even cruelty came from in him, just like in most people, you have to consider what's the burr under their saddle? What's the thing that's hurting them? And it's natural for 3-year olds as well as 93-year olds to strike out when something's hurting them, lash out. It's not necessarily the thing that's causing the hurt. I don't know how in the hell—without using drugs, without running around, throwing televisions outside of hotel windows or destroying bathrooms or whatever the other rock star behavior—I don't know how Prince handled the pressure to be a young man, a multimillionaire. To be surrounded by all these people, but everyone you're surrounded by gets a paycheck from you. All the people you call friends get a paycheck from you. How do you handle that pressure? And I can't imagine that any one of us, the best of us, wouldn't turn into a brat. And I think most of us would become at times a little cruel, I bet we all would. I say this, but I consider it pretty damn normal. And when viewed through the lens of the pressures he must have been under at age 24, 25, 26, I'm surprised that that's as bad as he got.

"He was trying to deal with personalities," adds Lisa. "That was kind of new to him. Before that was the Time and Vanity 6, he was really on top of those things. He was in control of them more and then the Time kind of grew legs, and then they became their own thing. But with the Family and because he was with Susannah, and then Paul Peterson being another leading man and ultimately saying, 'See ya later,' it really flipped him out. He didn't quite know what to do with that. He was hurt a long time."

"Prince was broken," reveals Wendy. "Deeply powerful and broken. He just was."

Lisa adds, "When you look around at the people he had around him, he had a lot of really nice people, that really had a lot of love. I think he appreciated that every once in a while and we knew that and we could forgive his tantrums and the way that he acted out in immature ways was part of his charm. But it was frustrating at the same time. But then he'd turn and write a song for you that was really a nice song. Or he'd buy you a present or he'd act like Steve the funny guy and you just kind of get over it."

There was anger about Paul Peterson leaving, but Prince channeled that resentment into a story of right and wrong and how Hollywood was a place where you made deals bargaining away your soul, and he created a song that was hopefully a warning to others. "At least in Prince's camp you're somewhat protected, you're under an umbrella of a guy who has morals," reflected Rogers. "In Hollywood, the way Prince saw it, you're on your own and Hollywood is far more decadent than anything he'd ever be in his way of thinking."[11]

"Dream Factory" may have come together quickly, but it was an important song that would inspire his next album. Normally that would be enough for one session, but this one also featured Prince and the band recording "Mountains," originally an untitled instrumental recorded by Wendy and Lisa at Advision studios in London from earlier in the month. He changed some of the sounds to make it his.

Prince's lyrics start out with "**Once upon a time in a land called 'Fantasy'**," which is similar to how he began "The Ladder" on his last album ("**Once upon a time in the land called Sinaplenty**"),[12] but what follows was likely influenced, at least partially, by his interest in the Bible and how Jesus explained that the power of faith could move mountains. Prince changed the power of *faith* to *love*, but the ideas are similar.

> **It's only mountains, and the sea.**
> **Love will conquer if you just believe.**
>
> —lyrics to "Mountains"[13]

> *Truly I tell you, if you have faith and do not doubt . . . you can*
> *say to this mountain, 'Go, throw yourself into the sea,' and it*
> *will be done.*
>
> —Matthew 21:21[14]

"'Mountains' was a live recording with the entire band, plus Eric Leeds and Atlanta Bliss," recalled Bobby Z. "That was recorded as a big production. Very rare, everybody playing at once."[15]

"'Mountains' my first introduction to not only working with Prince, but being creative with him in a recording situation," Matt Blistan recalled. "That was something that sort of sticks out in my mind as another milestone."[16]

"I remember after we did the recording session that day," reflected Eric. "Prince looked at Matt and said, 'You have the gig. Let your hair grow.'"[17]

Bassist BrownMark explained what recording songs with the band involved. "It was just like performing. We would rehearse for a performance, and they would just have the tapes rolling and Prince just edits." Despite the upbeat song being performed, the Revolution was already starting to splinter from within, at least according to BrownMark. "My heart wasn't there; it was time to move on."

At that time, BrownMark felt that he was being marginalized as a bass player when Prince removed the bass from the album version of "Kiss" and "When Doves Cry," and a series of conflicts between them only added to his feelings of confusion. "I don't know why he was treating me like that. Jealousy? What did he have to be jealous of? But it was some kind of insecurity. I quit. He begged me to stay. So, I said, 'You're treating me like a hired bass player? Then I want a contract.' And that's what I became."[18] "I told Mark he was making a mistake, that he should stay," revealed Bobby Z. "But he didn't listen. . . . Then I guess, the unravelling began."[19]

Status: Although it may have originally been recorded for consideration for a potential continuation of the Family, this 4-minute version of "Dream Factory" was edited (2:38) and repurposed as the title track for his unreleased *Dream*

Factory album and eventually released on Prince's *Crystal Ball* CD in 1998 (3:07).

"Mountains" (3:57) would be released on the soundtrack to *Under The Cherry Moon*. The music would be used under the credits in the movie and the song was released as the album's second single on May 7, 1986. It would peak at number 23 in the *Billboard* Hot 100 and number 15 on Hot Black Singles. The 5-minute instrumental version originally recorded by Wendy and Lisa was not placed on any Prince album during his lifetime.

It is possible that "An Honest Man" was recorded on this date with Prince, both as an intimate track with Prince playing piano and singing and also a longer variation with him reportedly leading the full band, while providing a guide vocal and instructions about what he wanted the band to play, but it was likely tracked during the session that started on November 29, or possibly at some-time in early December. It appears that it was actually rehearsed and put to tape in the early morning hours of November 30.

Eric remembers, "While we're doing it, Prince said, 'You want to put an ar-rangement on this?' And this was some silly ass song and Prince was in a playful mood that day. So, I actually told him, 'Prince . . . maybe this is a song *you* need to do the arrangement on.' And Prince laughed and then looked at me and he said, 'You don't want to touch this one?' And I looked and said, 'Not with a 10-foot pole.' So, whatever it was, I think was *his* arrangement on it."

"There is a version that exists of 'An Honest Man' with horns," remembered Susan Rogers. "In fact: for 'An Honest Man,' there's a master and then there is a piece called 'horn pieces.' So, I know it was done with horns at some point."[20]

Some additional overdubs and a mix for Sheila's "Touch Me/Hold Me" may have also taken place during this session.

Status: The 5-minute "An Honest Man" remains unreleased, but he'd drasti-cally rework the song the following week, at which time the horn arrangement was likely recorded.

DECEMBER 1985

"Mountains" (possible overdubs and mix)
"Dream Factory" (possible overdubs, mix)
Washington Avenue Warehouse (Edina, Minnesota)
Producer: Prince | Artist: Prince and the Revolution | Engineer: Susan
   Rogers

> *The most distinctive thing about Prince's sound and about his
> band and his music really was his use of keyboards, I think,
> more than anything else. So now, obviously, he's bringing in
> instruments that for the first five, six years of his music he had
> never used before, so, by definition, that certainly was going to
> be something very different for the Prince fans. It's like, what
> the hell are these guys playing and what are they doing?*[1]

> —Eric Leeds

It is likely that Prince continued working on "Mountains," although it is unknown what he overdubbed to the song and Wendy may have contributed some
additional bass to the track during this session. It was obvious that Prince was
not only looking for a new sound, but he was also embracing a more mature
musical view and allowing those around him to influence his direction. With

the Family at an end, Prince was taking advantage of the musical language he'd been exploring while recording their album.

Eric Leeds recalls how the session wrapped up. "A huge snowstorm hit that day and we had to bail out of there because we were going to get snowed in. So, we all left the warehouse about four or five that afternoon and it snowed like about twelve inches at night. And then Matt and I were able to fly out and that was the end of that. Then he basically said, 'Okay, we're done until January.'"

TUESDAY, DECEMBER 3, 1985

A movie is a little bit more complex, but to me it's just a larger version of an album. There are scenes and there are songs, and they all go together to make this painting, and . . . I'm the painter. Y'all is the paintees.[2]

—Prince

Prince had been overseeing the editing while shooting in France, and when the team traveled back to the United States, Prince visited San Francisco hoping to continue editing *Under The Cherry Moon*. While in the Bay Area, he considered working at Fantasy Studios (likely recommended by Sheila as she'd recorded there). "It was a film facility as well," explains studio engineer Michael Rosen. "They did *One Flew Over the Cuckoo's Nest*, and *Amadeus*, so he booked the film facility to edit *Under the Cherry Moon*, and before they had even started, he came looking around the studios and he told the studio manager that he would book them, but he wanted to book *all* four studios and send everybody home because he didn't want anybody around while he was working. And if I remember correctly, his people even specified what kind of plants he liked in the building and stuff like that and they did everything he wanted and then at the last minute he said, 'Yeah, I think I'll do it someplace else.'"

"He actually showed up there, but it might've been just for one or two days. Maybe they didn't realize he showed up, but he did show up," maintains editor Rebecca Ross. "Sheila E. even came with him and that was the first time I met her. We basically just got it all set up and had a couple of days with a video editor. Just started and then we moved everything to Bel Air. It was a huge house and we had the whole editing room set up in the breakfast room and adjoining work out room that overlooked the tennis court."

Privacy would be preserved, and Prince had once again found a way to work from home.

WEDNESDAY, DECEMBER 4, 1985

"Holly Rock" [7-inch] (edit, safety copy)
Sunset Sound, Studio 3 | 1:00 p.m.–1:30 p.m. (booked: 12:30 p.m.–open)
Producer: Sheila E. | Artist: Sheila E. | Engineer: Mike Kloster

He loved driving around town, blaring music in the car. He'd
play the Cocteau Twins, Miles Davis, Jimi Hendrix, Nino
Rota, Roxy Music's Avalon *album. He once made me a mix-*
tape with nothing but Miles Davis songs on it.[3]

—Jill Jones

This brief session was scheduled to make a 7-inch single edit for release and a safety copy for "Holly Rock."

Prince often requested cassette tapes of his music so he could play them in the car to hear how they sounded away from the expensive speakers of the recording studio. Prince was still in San Francisco and did not attend this session.

Prince's range of influences was growing. His father was a jazz musician, so he had a base of knowledge about jazz, and Prince surrounded himself with people who were able to expand his musical lexicon. "[Wendy, Lisa and Eric Leeds] made it their own project of turning Prince on to different kinds of music," related Alan Leeds. "Eric would give him jazz records and turned Prince on to *Sketches of Spain* and *Kind of Blue* and other stuff. Gradually the three of them had an impact on Prince and he felt that he needed to know this music and figure out what he liked and didn't like. He had a very genuine interest in expanding his musical curiosity. Young black guys were attracted to Miles because of his politics—he was an icon."[4]

I think as Prince learned more about Miles, he started to see some of himself in Miles. He was fascinated with Miles and used to ask Eric about stories about Miles and he'd share recordings with him. He'd show him video recordings and Prince would be fascinated and say, 'Look at the way Miles is standing.'—he was just studying his moves or his posture. There was a real fascination with the iconic aspect of Miles.[5]

Eric also had an interest in getting Prince and Miles together. "Whenever I would find an article or something, where Miles would make reference, or make a compliment about Prince, I always made sure to let Prince know. Because I was really hoping that maybe one day, they would hook up."

THURSDAY, DECEMBER 5, 1985

Prince arrived back in Los Angeles to continue editing his movie. Alan Leeds recalled that while they were at LAX, Prince had a chance encounter with Miles Davis.

> We got off the plane and were walking to baggage and towards where Prince's driver was waiting. And as we were walking through baggage claim I spotted Miles Davis and I poked Prince in the ribs and pointed. I introduced myself and it ended up with Prince getting into Miles's car, which was parked a little in front of his. I didn't get in with him and they sat and chatted for twenty minutes or so and swapped phone numbers. Prior to this, Miles had signed with Warner Bros and I'm sure there had been some conversation with Warner executives about the possibility of him doing something with Miles. We knew Miles had aspirations beyond the jazz category, and so it was a no-brainer to think "We've got Miles and Prince under one roof, let's get them together." It just made perfect sense.[6]

Note: It is possible that this meeting took place on December 7.

FRIDAY, DECEMBER 6, 1985 (ESTIMATE)

"High Fashion," the second and final single from the Family is released. Although it spent 12 weeks on the *Billboard* Black Singles Chart, and peaked at number 34, it went largely unnoticed due to lack of interest from Prince, frustrating the band and engineer David Z.

> I think *The Family* album was a great experiment. And it was unfortunate, because the second single, which was "High Fashion," had a great 12-inch version of it. "The Screams Of Passion" and then "High Fashion"—I thought it was gonna be like a one-two punch. But then Prince backed out, and I remember I said on the phone, "At least wait until the second single is released and then quit." But no, it didn't work like that. He yanked it and then there was no promo, no money.[7]

The 12-inch mix of "High Fashion" (7:07) remained unreleased during Prince's lifetime.

SUNDAY, DECEMBER 8, 1985 (ESTIMATE)

"Eternity" (tracking, overdubs, mix)
"Eternity" [instrumental] (mix)
Sunset Sound, Studio 3
Producer: Prince | Artist: Prince | Engineer: Coke Johnson

> *We would work fast and quietly, without speaking. He would*
> *first record the drums from top to bottom, listening to nothing,*
> *just with the song in his head. Next thing, he'd play the bass*
> *part, the keyboard part, the rhythm guitar. Then his vocals,*
> *alone in the control room.*[8]

—Susan Rogers

For the first time since the summer, Prince returned to Sunset Sound, and once again began working exclusively in Studio 3. "Most of the stuff I did was in 3," recalls his engineer Coke Johnson. "Studio 2 had the bigger recording space, but 3 was where Prince would set up because he would have them move a king-size bed out into the recording space. Some of his crew would come in there and decorate the whole studio with candles and purple sashes hanging around and scarves. The temperature had to be right. The lighting had to be right. It had to be just the ultimate cool recording space."

"Candles and drapes, tapestries. He'd just vibe it up, because studios can be pretty dry when you first walk in and put on the bright lights. So it was important," explained Lisa. "He put a bed in there or something. There'd always be a place to lie down and either just write or hang out. There was always a vibe to his music that there was something going on behind it. It wasn't just the song. It was three-dimensional and there was like, 'What is he doing in there?' It was like you could imagine him doing things while he's singing. There was just a feeling and an air that there was something going on. And usually because there was."[9]

Prince spent the shift working on a sparse keyboard heavy track called "Eternity." "He was singing with his falsetto-type thing because he was fishing it for a girl to sing," according to Coke. "He was up the octave."

When the mix was completed, the falsetto take of his voice was hidden in the mix.

The song would be offered to Sheena Easton, who had a top 10 hit with Prince's "Sugar Walls" the previous year from her *A Private Heaven* album. Her current work was being produced by David Leonard, who was married to engineer Peggy Leonard. He'd also engineered multiple songs for Prince. "I chose David to produce this because I wanted a new approach, really fresh and different. I didn't want to go to a producer who's already evolved a very definite style. When you have material from a genius like Prince, his material is different to begin with. He writes material such that it would be a shame and a crime to have it treated in a stock manner. So, I think it deserved the time and attention and the care and the effort to take the risks we did," said Sheena Easton.[10]

The track would be a basic song using drums and a [Ensoniq] Mirage keyboard, guitar and a few vocal tracks. When it was released by Sheena, Prince was credited as "Rocker Happyfeller" on keyboards and "Freddie 'The Phantom'" on guitar.

Status: "Eternity" (4:16) was first included on Sheena Easton's 1987 album, *No Sound But A Heart*. In June 1987, it was released as a single (3:50), which failed to chart.

Two 12-inch mixes, "Eternity" (Dub) (6:18) and "Eternity" (Shep Pettibone Mix) (6:25), were also released.

Note: "Eternity" may have been recorded after midnight on this date or on December 14.

MONDAY, DECEMBER 9, 1985 (ESTIMATE)

"She Pony" (tracking, overdubs mix)
Sunset Sound, Studio 3 | (booked: lockout)
Producer: Prince | Artist: Prince | Engineer: Coke Johnson

He is a cutie. We used to call him a "little pony." He was so cutie.[11]

—Wendy Melvoin

Over his career, Prince referenced a "pony" or "horses" in at least a dozen songs including "Horny Pony," "Alphabet St.," "Le Grind," "The Future," "Raspberry Beret," "Letitgo," "The Latest Fashion," and "Little Red Corvette." For "She Pony," Prince was alone in the studio jamming.

Status: The instrumental "She Pony" remained unreleased during Prince's lifetime. Sheila E. may have done some additional recording on this track at some point.

Note: "She Pony" may have been recorded as late as February 1986, but any specific date is speculation. It is likely that he wrote lyrics for the song at some point.

WEDNESDAY, DECEMBER 11, 1985 (ESTIMATE)

"Dream Factory" (edits, mix)
"Mountains" (possible edit, mix)
"Rough" (Jill vocals, mix)
"My Man" (possible Jill vocals, mix)
Sunset Sound, Studio 3 (likely) | (booked: lockout)
Producer: Prince | Artists: Prince (and Jill Jones) | Engineers: "Peggy Mac" Leonard, Coke Johnson, and Susan Rogers

I was always willing to try something. I'd never, never at the beginning would go, "No," but in the middle of some recordings I would even go, "This is not working." The interesting thing is our battlefields were so rarely on studio ground or about studio stuff. The other stuff was just outside of it.

—Jill Jones

Editing work took place on "Dream Factory," possibly eliminating a third verse. The elements that were discarded included a chant about "Everybody will have short hair, next year," which would be resurrected in the extended version of "Kiss" and "St. Paul, punk of the month" which would soon reappear in Prince's live shows. Prince held on to his frustrations (including his current grievance with Paul Peterson) and in most situations, if you crossed him, he kept that door closed. "You didn't, *NOT* get along with Prince, if you wanted to be there," explains Peggy Mac. "You didn't push back."

Jill Jones was tasked with recording her vocals for "Rough" and "My Man" during this time, if not during this session, sometime during this week. St. Paul and Susannah had added their vocals to "Rough," but with the demise of the Family, any tracks slated for them were considered for others. There was some audio leakage between the tracks on "Rough," but Prince decided to allow it. "It was fun when I did it. I recorded it with Prince. I remember because he would be the only one who would allow that leakage to happen. David Z would've made us sit up there all night trying to fix it. 'You done, David?' He would have been like, 'That's really bothering me.' [laughs]"

Additional editing, and possibly some overdubbing was likely done on "Mountains" during this session.

FRIDAY, DECEMBER 13, 1985 (ESTIMATE)

"**With You**" (tape copy for Clare Fischer)
Sunset Sound, Studio 3 (likely) | (booked: lockout)
Producer: Prince | Artist: Prince (for Jill Jones) | Engineers: "Peggy Mac" Leonard, Coke Johnson, and Susan Rogers

A copy of "With You" was created and given to Clare Fischer for his orchestral embellishments. It is unlikely that Prince attended this brief session.

MONDAY, DECEMBER 16, 1985

Parade album compilation
"**Anotherloverholenyohead**" [listed as "**Hole In Your Head**"] (tracking, overdubs, mix)
"**Christopher Tracy's Parade**" (mix)
"**Christopher Tracy's Parade**" (strings only mix)
"**New Position**" (mix)
"**New Position**" (strings only mix, and crossfades to "**I Wonder U**")
"**I Wonder U**" (mix)
"**I Wonder U**" (strings only mix)
"**Under The Cherry Moon**" (mix)
"**Under The Cherry Moon**" (strings only mix)
"**Girls & Boys**" (mix)
"**Life Can Be So Nice**" (mix)
"**Life Can Be So Nice**" (strings only mix)

"Venus De Milo" (strings only mix)
"Venus De Milo" [long version] (strings only mix)
"Venus De Milo" [album version] (mix)
"Mountains" (mix)
"Do U Lie?" (strings mix)
"Kiss" (mix)
"Sometimes It Snows In April" (strings mix)
"Alexa De Paris" (mix)
"Love Or Money" (mix)
"Soul Sister" (mix)
"Soul Sister" [instrumental] (likely mix)
Sunset Sound, Studio 3 | 12:30 p.m.–7:30 a.m. (booked: lockout)
Producer: Prince | Artist: Prince | Engineers: Coke Johnson and Susan
　　Rogers

During that time, '82–85, I think that he was a master pop
piano player, and a master gospel piano player and when
those two worked together in tandem, he came up with amaz-
ing songs. And the kind of progressions he came up with, which
delivered songs like "Anotherloverholenyohead." Those big
chords—they're untouchable.[12]

—Lisa Coleman

By this point, Prince had decided what would likely be on the soundtrack
album, so he had to mold the list of songs to fit into the movie and this meant
creating the film score, at least the early version of it, so it could be used as the
movie was being edited. Because of this, today's session began with 4 hours
of the engineers creating quick mixes and safety copies of practically all of the
songs being considered for the movie's soundtrack. Safety copies are created so
that if there is a mistake made on the edits, the original tape isn't accidentally
destroyed. If the edits or mixes don't work out, Prince would still have the
pristine version from the original session. Once the safety copies were done, the
tracks were edited and mixed. "I do remember one specific day or two where
we remixed instrumental versions of all the stuff that was current at that time,"
recalls Johnson.

The biggest change in many of the numbers was creating an orchestral mix
that included only strings, likely for the film.

At this point, it seems that "Christopher Tracy's Parade" was still being generally referred to as "Wendy's Parade" on the studio documents, but that changed at some point during this period. Wendy was disappointed with the decision, but ultimately agreed with the outcome. "When he changed it to 'Christopher Tracy's Parade,' I was like, 'Oh, damn. Too bad.' But he probably felt it was better in the spirit of the movie." Regardless of the eventual change in title, the phrase "Little Girl Wendy's Parade" remained in the song "Kiss."

The album was mostly complete, but Prince must have felt that it was missing the iconic song to provide deeper insights into the characters, like "When Doves Cry" had done in *Purple Rain*. In his first movie, the songs helped propel the story and revealed hidden understandings about the character's emotional state, generally, but not always, in a subtle fashion. For *Under The Cherry Moon*, most of the music was not meant to be a "live" performance, so it would require the score, and just as importantly the linking song, to carry the weight of advancing the plot for the movie.

Prince spent the next 11 hours recording a new song called "Anotherloverholenyohead," which was tentatively titled "Hole In Yo' Head." The full title was likely inspired by Sly Stone's funky song titles ("Thank You Falettinme Be Mice Elf Agin") and the way Sheila spoke and wrote when she was in a playful mood. Prince recorded the track alone in the studio, although he'd recruit Susannah to add her voice to the chorus in a future session. "It's just stacks of Prince's vocals," explained Bobby Z. "That trick that he uses on 'D.M.S.R.,' where you just stack them and create like a real loud, crowd-sounding thing."[13]

Even years later, Susan Rogers looks back in frustration about the "stupid [Roland G-707] guitar synth thing, which didn't track very well."

> Meaning, it was hard to reproduce. It didn't track the notes that you played. So, as [Prince] would be playing the part, what he would physically play wouldn't necessarily correspond to the notes that you would hear, the pitches that you would hear, or the durations that you'd hear. That's what I mean when I say it didn't track well. It was a pain in the ass, that piece of crap. He normally wouldn't put up with that for so much as a moment. But the tone of it was so cool, and the mistakes of it were just sort of personable in a way. Because it had its own unique voice, he hung in there with it to be able to get that song realized.

With the addition of "Anotherloverholenyohead," Prince was able to lock down what he felt should be on the album and the first post filming album configuration was created, recalled Rogers.

> I have a memory of at some point putting "Moonbeam Levels" on *Purple Rain*. And then taking it off. Because we put "Moonbeam Levels" on a couple of times.

We put it on *Around The World In A Day*. And to the best of my recollection we even tried it on the *Parade* album. But it was never quite right, and that was always disappointing to me, because I love that song so much.[14]

Susan Rogers related:

One of the most important lessons Prince taught me is that when you make an album, it needs to feature a kernel, and that core of that record is going to be, in his case, it would be your six best songs. For most mere mortals, it might be only three. For him, it would be, let's say, six or eight songs, that this is the heart of the record. More likely six. Other songs are chosen to complement that seed, which is why so much good stuff ended up in the vault. Because it didn't make the best kernel. A song like "Splash," or something like that just didn't complement the other messages or perhaps was redundant with the other messages on the record. So "Anotherloverholenyohead" and "New Position," these songs are expressing a little bit of strife in the relationship. Even "Kiss" is Prince pushing back against, "Don't presume to think you know what I need. *This* is what I need."

The final 2 hours of the session were spent doing additional mixing on "Anotherloverholenyohead" and the running order of the album. The session ended at 7:30 in the morning, and just before everyone left, Prince had everything dubbed to two C-90 cassettes.

Status: The 6-minute "Anotherloverholenyohead" was edited to 4:01 for the *Parade* album and 3:23 for release as a single.

"Anotherloverholenyohead" would be added to the album soon after this session. Despite a wide selection of tracks that he'd record over the next month, the songs on the album and their order did not change after this assembly.

TUESDAY, DECEMBER 17, 1985

"**An Honest Man**" [version 2] (tracking, overdubs, mix)
"**Kiss**" (mix)
"**Sometimes It Snows In April**" (mix)
"**Anotherloverholenyohead**" [listed as "**Another Lover**"] (vocal overdubs, mix)
"**I Wonder U**" [instrumental] (mix)
"**I Wonder U**" (mix)
Sunset Sound, Studio 3 | 6:30 p.m.–4:15 a.m. (booked: lockout)
Producer: Prince | Artist: Prince | Engineers: Susan Rogers and Coke Johnson

I've always been honest in my music.[15]

—Prince

Prince decided to retrack "An Honest Man" and started the session working on the song, which went back to the spirit of the earliest version and featured Prince once again sitting at the piano without any backing band supporting him. The same lyrics were used on all variations of the track, but this piano version would also feature several sound effects including an ocean and a playground (similar to the instrumental of "Paisley Park" from 1984) and multiple layers of his vocals. When the track was mixed, the piano was removed and the sound effects were almost imperceptible.

Susannah was asked to add her harmonizing background vocals for yesterday's "Anotherloverholenyohead." "He loved that song. He let me do it by myself and left and came back and that was done." When Prince returned and listened to what they'd accomplished, he seemed happy. "He had a huge smile on his face."

The rest of the session was spent working on additional mixes for several songs that were being used in the movie, including "Kiss," "Sometimes It Snows In April," "Anotherloverholenyohead," and "I Wonder U." At least one of these tracks, "I Wonder U," was mixed as an instrumental and all of these updated versions (with the exception of "An Honest Man" and the instrumental version of "I Wonder U") were blended into the soundtrack during 5 hours of edits and crossfades.

At 4:15 in the morning, Prince wrapped up the session after placing all of the tracks on a C-90 cassette.

Status: Prince released "An Honest Man" (1:13) in 1998 on his *Crystal Ball* set. For the released mix, the song would feature a strings arrangement that would be recorded by Clare Fischer on January 10, 1986.

Note: It is possible that Prince recorded an updated version of "An Honest Man" earlier in the week.

WEDNESDAY, DECEMBER 18, 1985

"**Love On A Blue Train**" [faster version] (likely tracking, overdubs, mix)
"**Love On A Blue Train**" (tracking, overdubs, mix)
Sunset Sound, Studio 3 | (booked: lockout)
Producer: Prince | Artist: Sheila E. | Engineers: Susan Rogers, Coke Johnson, and "David Z" Rivkin

He was really happy with ["Love On A Blue Train"], we spent a lot of time on that.[16]

—Susan Rogers

The credits on some of Prince's side projects didn't always reflect who was actually involved, according to Susan Rogers.

> On the third album, Sheila had more control over that than she had before, and I was not properly credited on that. I did a lot of engineering [on it]. I introduced basic tracks for the whole thing of "Love On A Blue Train," for "Koo Koo" the basic track, "Pride And The Passion," "One Day"—those songs were things that I did and engineered. I think because I was Prince's engineer, Sheila was trying to downplay Prince's involvement, therefore my involvement. And I think that's why my name was left off the engineering credit. She immediately apologized for it and said she was gonna have it corrected with the next pass. To me it didn't matter because I knew. She wanted to look, I think, a little bit more autonomous in the making of that record, so it was important that my name was left off for that reason.[17]

Prince had overseen the two albums he'd recorded with Sheila E. and now that he was back in Los Angeles he apparently thought that they should record some new tracks for her next release, so he created "Love On A Blue Train." Starting with the drums as always, Prince added bass, and the [Ensoniq] Mirage keyboard to the track, along with Sheila flavoring it with percussion. At an early point in the session, the song was supposedly a much faster groove than the version that was released. He'd eventually alter the arrangement and discard the faster direction he'd originally proposed. Prince spent the entire session recording the track with members of Sheila's band.

During this period, Susannah would have usually joined him in the studio, but she flew back up to Minneapolis to work with Karen Krattinger on the home that she and Prince would share.

A tent-revival Gospel-style intro to her album may have been attempted during this session as well, using members of Sheila E.'s band, but even if it was recorded during this session, it was not included in the final release.

The song contains a classic funk reference to the Gap Band's 1979 hit "I Don't Believe You Want To Get Up And Dance (Oops!)" [aka "Oops Upside Your Head"] with the chant "Jerome! Upside yo' head," which had also been used during the Family's concert earlier in the year.

Status: "Love On A Blue Train" (7:41) was released on a Japanese 4-track maxi-single 12-inch and CD. It was edited (5:29) for her third album and reduced even further (4:02) for the "Single Edit" release. The faster run-through version remained unreleased during Prince's lifetime.

FRIDAY, DECEMBER 20, 1985 (ESTIMATE)

"My Man" (mix)
"Rough" [listed as "Too Rough"] (mix)
Sunset Sound, Studio 3 | (booked: lockout)
Producer: Prince | Artist: Jill Jones or Sheila E. | Engineers: Susan Rogers
    and Coke Johnson

> *That record, to me, was as if he gave me the best, most diverse*
> *variety filled banquet of songs and I could carry them all off.*[18]
>
> —Jill Jones

Additional mixes for "My Man" and "Too Rough" were done during this period. It is likely that they were planned for Jill Jones's album.

SUNDAY, DECEMBER 22, 1985

"Love On A Blue Train" (listed as "Blue Train") (rough mix)
"Sexual Suicide" (mix)
"Sexual Suicide" [instrumental] (likely mix)
"With You" (mix with orchestra)
"Rough" [listed as "Too Rough"] (likely mix)
Sunset Sound, Studio 3 | 1:00 p.m.–7:00 a.m. (booked: lockout)
Producer: Prince | Artists: Prince, Sheila E., and Jill Jones | Engineers: Susan
    Rogers and Coke Johnson

> *Prince was Prince. The clothes that you see him in, all the pic-*
> *tures you see of him, that was his daily wear. He never showed*
> *up wearing blue jeans or a t-shirt or tennis shoes or anything.*
> *Every day, that's who Prince was.*
>
> —Coke Johnson

Prince was rarely out of character. And a major trait of his was his reputation for high expectations for himself, as well as those around him, even on the weekend before Christmas, reflects Lisa. "I remember when we were really deep into it, nothing else mattered. Weekdays and weekends didn't exist anymore. It was all the same day. Holidays, it was kind of, 'Okay we have to stop for a minute.' It was kind of inconvenient. It didn't match what we were doing."

"What were really the constant themes for me were gratitude, appreciation, and a strong determination to do everything humanly possible to facilitate his work," explained Susan Rogers.

> It mattered a great deal to me that I stayed up longer than him, because he would go to bed, and I'd be in the studio pulling patch cords, putting all the wires away, and making copies of things. I would routinely get fewer hours of sleep than he did, because I had to be the last one out and the first one back in the studio. I tried really, really hard to be what he needed. I wanted to serve this man that I admired and who I knew was a genius and did great work. All that mattered to me back then was to get these records made.[19]

On the final day in the studio before the holidays, he spent the bulk of the session creating additional mixes for "Rough," "With You," "Love On A Blue Train," a song called "Love" (which might have been an abbreviation for "Love On A Blue Train" or "Anotherloverholenyohead"), and multiple mixes of "Sexual Suicide," including at least one instrumental version.

After a 15-hour marathon in the studio, Prince requested that three C-60 tapes be made of the day's work. When that was finished, his tapes were packed up to be shipped to Minneapolis. It was unclear how long he'd be away from Los Angeles, but while he was gone, he wanted his tapes if inspiration struck. "We'd take what we absolutely needed, what I thought we were going to be continuing to work on," explains Rogers. "A lot of things stayed at Sunset in their tape vault, and then I had to keep track of all this stuff, because he might ask, at any time, day or night, where is such-and-such tape."

Prince left for Minneapolis. As usual, holidays were often an obstacle when it came to making music. Although he may not want to take the day off, those around him preferred to spend time with their friends or family, or even just time away from Prince recovering from their hectic work schedule. But to Prince, it was another day he could be making music.

When on tour, he would offer to fly in a family member for his crew, but they'd still be on call for whatever was needed. When it came to his studio time, he would do as much as he could alone, explains Susannah. "When you talk about compassion, he didn't know how to be there for other people. Those kinds of holidays are about being there for somebody or allowing somebody to be in your space. It gets quiet, it gets introspective and it gets familial. It gets vulnerable, super vulnerable. That was a time that he recoiled from because he had the hardest time being *that* guy. So, he spent a lot of Christmases alone, working. It was a compulsion to stay away from the feelings, to stay away from being vulnerable."

Prince's most direct form of socializing was creating and sharing his music, often hiding his deeper personal feelings from those he saw practically every day. "He's a very complex personality and he's very complex artistically," Rogers offers up insightfully. "I was around him all the time, but I can't say that I knew him that well, because my function wasn't to know him on a personal level."

Beyond his music which bonded him to others, he could be socially awkward according to many of the people he allowed in his circle. "The only way he could communicate with people was by playing an instrument, or by being with other musicians and communicating with music," recalled Wendy. "Frankly, outside of that it was difficult."[20]

"It was hard for him," Bob Merlis, the vice president of publicity at Warner Bros. recalled. "I remember him once telling me 'I speak in musical terms. I could have a great conversation with Miles Davis.'"[21]

The day after Christmas, Prince flew back to Los Angeles, and he requested that Susan Rogers return to California as well, as she recalls. "I remember getting a call from Alan Leeds. It was around Christmas time, because I had a Christmas tree up in my condo and Leeds says, 'Pack your bags, and go on to Los Angeles.' And I said, 'How long should I pack for?' Which is an obvious question and Alan said, 'Two weeks.' So, I stuffed a big suitcase with two weeks' worth of winter clothes and I went out to Los Angeles. I came home months later. I came home in a very different season to a brown stick in the middle of the living room and a pile of desiccated pine needles on the floor."

THURSDAY, DECEMBER 26, 1985

"A Couple Miles" (tracking, overdubs, mix)
"Can I Play With U?" [listed as "Can I Play With You"] (tracking, overdubs, mix)
Sunset Sound, Studio 3 | 2:00 p.m.–2:30 a.m. (booked: open)
Producer: Prince | Artist: Prince | Engineers: Susan Rogers and Coke Johnson

Miles Davis I learned a lot from. I learned a lot about space from Miles. Space is a sound too, and it can be used very inventively.[22]

—Prince

Prince was inspired after his personal introduction to Miles Davis earlier in the month, according to Alan Leeds. "Once Prince has got a passion for something, he jumps right on it."[23]

The session started at 2 in the afternoon with Prince working on an instrumental that he'd list as "A Couple Miles" by laying down both Simmons SDS-V synth drums, as well as a layer of live drums, including hi-hat and cymbals, then adding piano and Oberheim OB-X synths.

Once he was done with the first track at 8 p.m., he switched to "Can I Play With U?," a second jam, using a similar recording sequence. After 5 more hours of recording with the same basic set of instruments (including some guitar work as well), he spent the next 2 and a half hours writing lyrics and adding his vocals to the track, creating a rough mix of the song as it progressed.

Prince reached out to Eric Leeds, who was on vacation with his family in Florida, about working on these tracks. "I was aware that Miles was a fan of Prince's. And I mentioned once to Prince, just off-handed in the middle of rehearsal one day, that I had read a recent interview with Miles, and he said something very, very complimentary about Prince. And Prince just said, 'Eric, that's what makes it worthwhile, when someone like that will say something.' And that's about all it was. So anyway, when I heard later that Prince was actually interested in maybe doing something with Miles, well, I was going to make damn well sure that I was involved with this."[24]

Status: "Can I Play With U?" (6:35) and "A Couple Miles" (4:30) remained unreleased during Prince's life. "Can I Play With U?" (with Miles Davis on trumpet) was included in the posthumous *Sign O' The Times* Super Deluxe Edition in 2020.

FRIDAY, DECEMBER 27, 1985

"Can I Play With U?" (horn overdubs)
"A Couple Miles" (possible sax overdubs)
Sunset Sound, Studio 3 | 7:00 p.m.–12:30 a.m. (booked: open)
Producer: Prince | Artist: Prince | Engineer: Coke Johnson | Assistant Engineer: Alexander Waverly

I was a little pissed because I wanted to spend the whole of the holiday with my parents and Alan said, "He's only going to need you for like a couple of days and then you can fly back to Florida"—I ended up being there for about three weeks! We were in the studio almost every day.[25]

—Eric Leeds

Prince had planned to start the session at 4 in the afternoon, but Eric was delayed getting into town because he had to fly from Miami to Atlanta to pick up his horns and then turn around and immediately fly out to Los Angeles. "By the time I got to LA, I was fried, and I knew I was probably going to be in the studio all night. I had a quick nap and then went to the studio. So, the first thing that happens when I get there is that he has this track up and he said, 'I've been talking to Miles.' I said, 'Really?!' and he said, 'Yeah and I've got a track here that I want to send to him. Here it is, I'm going out to have dinner—do whatever you want with it.' I said, 'Okay.'"

"There was another song that we did after 'Can I Play With U?' called 'A Couple Miles,' it was a really nice song," remembered Eric. "I don't recall Prince ever saying it was something he was going to give to Miles or wanted Miles to hear, but he was just in a Miles Davis frame of mind and it was like a tribute to him. It's a little dated now because of the sound of the drum machine, but the song was a much hipper song than "Can I Play With U?" It had a hipper melody and had a nice little bridge that allowed me to do some interesting orchestrations with a multi-sax horn section."[26]

Leeds recorded tenor and baritone sax on both "Can I Play With U?" and "A Couple Miles." "Miles was living in Malibu at the time, and Prince was telling me, 'As soon as we do the song, we're going to go over to Miles' place, over to his home, and give it to him.' I said, 'You're damn right we are!' Now, that never happened. Prince actually had a couple of phone conversations with Miles about it. And then the tape was sent to Miles."

A C-60 tape was dubbed of "Can I Play With U?". The song's title can be seen as not only a flirty comment to a woman, but also a clever invitation from Prince to Miles to join him in creating music.

The relationship Prince would have with Miles would be one of respect, and yet some distance because Prince's control in the studio was absolute. Every band he had produced and every project he'd overseen was basically an extension of himself, and this was the first time he was venturing into much deeper waters. "First of all, you're dealing with two people who are control freaks," according to Alan Leeds. "And if Miles is a control freak, multiply that by five when you come to Prince! As enamored as he was with Miles, it was never to the extent that he wanted to sacrifice his control."

"I loved Miles, because he was more of a music fan than most people would expect," Prince explained to *Code* magazine. **"Miles loved good musicians and cool people, but he was also the type of guy to invite Mick Jagger to his house and make him sit outside. He was the type of guy who would tell you to meet him in the dressing room, then be sitting there butt naked. But I loved him."**[27]

SATURDAY, DECEMBER 28, 1985

This session was collectively called **"Paisley Jam"** and included:
"Madrid" (tracking, mix)
"Slaughterhouse" (tracking, mix)
"Breathless" (tracking, mix)
"Just Can't Stop" (tracking, mix)
"Run Amok" (tracking, mix)
"12 Keys" [early version of **"The Question of U"**] (tracking, mix)
"High Colonic" (tracking, mix)
"Mobile" (tracking, mix)
Sunset Sound, Studio 3 | 6:00 p.m.–11:30 p.m. (booked: lockout)
Producer: Prince | Artists: Prince/The Flesh | Engineer: Coke Johnson |
 Assistant Engineer: Alexander Waverly (likely)

> *Miles was influential in convincing Prince [to] feel more confi-*
> *dent in doing that thing you do when you're playing jazz, which*
> *is to stretch the scales, invert the chords, harmonically stretch*
> *something, screw with the rhythms and the polyrhythms. Miles*
> *gave him the confidence to do that because it really validated*
> *Prince. And then he got involved in working with Eric Leeds,*
> *and he was really instrumental in helping him mold a certain*
> *jazz philosophy, and Prince was learning quickly. I suppose*
> *you could say he was a quick learner.*[28]

> —Wendy Melvoin

Likely inspired by Miles, Prince gathered several musicians in his circle to spend an evening with him in the studio to see what transpired. Prince seemed to want a true flow of music, so he invited Eric Leeds and Sheila into the studio and asked her guitarist Levi Seacer Jr., to join them on bass. The session was scheduled for 3 in the afternoon, but in true jazz fashion, the recording didn't start until 6 p.m. Eric and Prince had worked together the previous year on several sax-based instrumentals for the Family, but those were just two musicians trading ideas. "This was the first project that we ever referred to as 'the Flesh,'" remembered Leeds, "a name that would come up again several times later, but we called it this just for our own working title, just so we could distinguish this group of material from anything else."[29]

Leeds continued:

> We went in and played nonstop all night, filling up I don't know how many tapes, all instrumental jams. And I gave titles to the songs, things like "Slaughterhouse," "Run Amok," "Mobile," "Madrid," all these things. A song that I called "Twelve Keys," which was actually the song "The Question of U," which he recorded his version of it years later. We did a whole bunch of stuff during all those jam sessions.[30]

The Flesh project would expand over the course of the next month, exciting Prince momentarily, but like many of his projects, it would take a backseat to other ideas. "It's some amazing music," recalled Leeds. "Very unstructured, because they were just jams, which doesn't necessarily lend itself to a project."[31]

The range of Prince's talent constantly impressed and confused those around him. Levi had participated in a few sessions with Sheila the previous summer, so they were on each other's radar. "When I first heard [Prince], there was nothing but hayfields, snow, and cows out there. I didn't know how he was coming up with all that funk from a place where there was five months of winter and thirty degrees below zero. How was that happening? What were his influences? Did he go to church? Where was it coming from? That's what was trippin' me out about Prince."[32]

Four hours were spent on the songs and then another 90 minutes listening to the mixes. In a change of his usual method, Prince recorded the entire session to half-inch tapes, which are normally used for mixes, but Prince seemed to be eager to catch the energy of the jam as it went down without any additional studio tricks. Eric recalled how this idea was presented in the studio. "Prince was laughing and saying, 'My accountant's telling me I spend too much money in the studio. So, we're not going to spend money on a 24-track. We're gonna go live to a 2-track.'"[33]

"I don't know anything about what we were going to do," remembers Seacer. "Prince was like, 'Hey man, we're going to roll the tape and see what comes out, and he just kept rolling. We had tapes, like six, seven feet high. Three, four rows of tape. Just cut, cut, cut. I just know that we did a lot of material."

"We were recording to half-inch tape," confirms Coke Johnson. "There were two reasons for that. One was because it was a lot cheaper than rolling two-inch tape for a couple of hours. Another is that if it was recorded directly to half-inch, then, while we were listening back to it, I would edit those songs. Physically cut the half-inch tape, and cut section to that section, to this section, all at Prince's directive, changing the arrangement to where it was hipper."

The entire session was such a loose jam that even basic rules of recording were not always followed, remembers Eric. "'Slaughterhouse' was in two parts, I believe because the master tape ran out and there was an overlap for a second reel to start recording. We never assembled the two parts."

The edited "Paisley Jam" was recorded to a single C-90 cassette.

Eric felt that the Flesh sessions were, "One of the most incredible things that we ever did."[34]

Status: "Slaughterhouse" (8:07 and 1:47), "U Just Can't Stop" (6:00), "Run Amok" (8:00), "Mobile" (6:17), "Madrid" (9:15), an edit of "Madrid" (6:32), "Breathless," (6:53), "High Colonic" [sometimes listed as "High Calonic"] (9:45), and "12 Keys" (6:28) all remain un-released, although "Madrid" (including some elements from "High Colonic") later evolved into "Andorra" on Eric Leeds' *Times Squared* album.

This sequence may not reflect the actual recording order from this date.

SUNDAY, DECEMBER 29, 1985

This session was collectively called "**Paisley Jam**" and included:
"**Madrid**" (horn overdubs, mix)
"**Slaughterhouse**" (horn overdubs, mix)
"**Breathless**" (horn overdubs, mix)
"**Just Can't Stop**" (horn overdubs, mix)
"**Run Amok**" (horn overdubs, mix)
"**12 Keys**" [early version of "**The Question of U**"] (horn overdubs, mix)
"**High Colonic**" (horn overdubs, mix)
"**Mobile**" (horn overdubs, mix)
Sunset Sound, Studio 3 | 1:00 p.m.–11:30 p.m. (booked: lockout)
Producer: Prince | Artists: Prince/The Flesh | Engineer: Coke Johnson |
    Assistant Engineer: Alexander Waverly (likely)

*The next night I came in and I was there on my own. He just
gave me the studio and said, "Put overdubs on them." So I just
messed around with them and just put a whole lot of flute and
saxophone overdubs and made some sections work on some of
the other things.*

—Eric Leeds

After 2 hours of rough mixes, Eric recorded his overdubs until 11:30 that evening. Four TDK C-90 tapes were created of the session, one of them likely for Prince as he wasn't in the studio for most of this date.

MONDAY, DECEMBER 30, 1985

"**A Couple Miles**" (horn overdub, mix)
"**Jams**"—title for multiple tracks, including:
"**Villanova Junction**" [also known as "**Voodoo Who**"] (tracking, sax overdubs, rough mix)
"**Give Me Yo' Most Strongest Whiskey**" [also known as "**Finest Whiskey**"] (tracking, sax overdubs, rough mix)
"**Love 2 U**" [also known as "**Damn**"] (tracking, mix)
"**U Gotta Shake Something**" [listed as "**Shake Something**"] (tracking, overdubs, mix)
Sunset Sound, Studio 3 | 1:00 p.m.–5:00 a.m. (booked: lockout)
Producer: Prince | Artists: Prince/The Flesh | Engineers: Susan Rogers and Coke Johnson

I know that we did a lot of material man, but the one I remember the most is "U Gotta Shake Something."

—Levi Seacer Jr.

Like the previous day, this session began with 8 hours of Eric overdubbing several of the tracks they'd previously recorded, as well as "A Couple Miles." "We actually did some more jams on the 30th," remembers Eric. "Sheila and Levi came in later that day and we did some other jams that I called 'Voodoo Who,' 'Most Strongest Whiskey,' and 'U Gotta Shake Something,' and that was Sheila, Prince and Levi, and myself."

Prince's musical vocabulary was growing. The exponential gains since *Purple Rain* were stunning, drifting away from pure pop to include almost any genre he was inspired to explore, so when Sheila and Levi arrived at the studio, Prince wanted to run through even more jams with them. The most structured track was "U Gotta Shake Something," a long, fully formed, but slightly repetitive jam that was recorded to sound like it was from an actual concert. "We overdubbed crowd noise to mimic a live recording," explains Leeds, "and I added the "radio" announcement at the top of the song. This was the first reference [in the music] to the name 'Flesh.'"

"They would just turn the tape on and play," observed Eric's brother, Alan Leeds. "It was really quite improvisational. Out of that came some riffs. Somebody would come up with a lead line or a melody, and Prince would say, 'That's good, keep playing that,' and they'd improvise on it."[35]

"We were just having fun for like 12 minutes," remembers Levi. "Man, it was cool."

> He can write ten songs in a day. He starts by jamming on stuff. And then he's like, "Okay let's go somewhere else with it." And I'll record a different bass line. And we even made. . . . I mean they're not really mistakes, because I dropped out. Because I was giving it like 16 bars of space. And he's like, "Levi, why you stop? Keep going." It's a lot of things like that. "You're not sexy!" When he says, "You're not sexy," it's like, "No, I don't like that. Come back in! Stay right there." It was fun, man.

Seacer continues:

> When we used to work in the studio, I used to look in his eyes and you could tell when it was done and when it wasn't. When it wasn't, he would look up in the sky. It was almost like he was talking to a spirit, "It ain't there, we have to keep going." And until he actually took his eyes from the sky and looked straight across, that's when I knew it was done. Then it was time to mix that. It was hard, man, because the ideas he was doing getting up to the final ones were cool, but all of that kind of stuff went in the vault. I don't know of any artist on the planet who even has that kind of body of work. Because they'd have to write it, sing it, and play it. He did a lot of his own recording, too, like an engineer. They'd have to be able to do all of those things to even have a third of that kind of catalog. It's crazy, man. Then, they'd have to be prolific on top of that. It's one thing to be like, "I worked really, really hard." But you could be working hard on some stuff that ain't happening. Here was a guy who could deliver, and he had a work ethic like that. That was rare.[36]

"Voodoo Who" was a cover of "Villanova Junction" by Jimi Hendrix. Prince also included some lyrics from Sade's 1985 song, "Is It A Crime." "['Voodoo Who'] was just a real loose jam with Prince on guitar and piano, Sheila on drums, Levi on bass and myself," remembers Eric. "Just the four of us."

"Give Me Yo' Most Strongest Whiskey" is also a cover, originally recorded by Denise LaSalle for her album *Love Talkin'*. It was written by George Jackson and Denise LaSalle and she'd released it as a single earlier in the year.

The band also worked on a song called "Damn," which also has Prince in a playfully instructive mood, telling Levi when to play the bass, letting Eric know what instruments he should be using for overdubs and referring to the band as "James Black and the Whites," a variation of the New York band "James White and the Blacks." Several musical elements from "Damn," as well as the "James Black/White" reference—repeated as "Jimmy" instead of "James"—would find their way into "U Gotta Shake Something."

After 5 and a half hours of recording, the last 2 and a half hours were spent on a few overdubs and mixing the day's tracks. Four TDK C-60 cassettes were created of the music from this session.

Status: "U Gotta Shake Something" (15:20), "Villanova Junction" (5:31), "Give Me Yo' Most Strongest Whiskey" (1:14), and the 7-minute jam called "Love 2 U" (also referred to as "Damn") all remained unreleased during Prince's lifetime.

TUESDAY, DECEMBER 31, 1985

Prince attended a Patti LaBelle performance at the Universal Amphitheatre in Los Angeles. He reportedly flew back to Minneapolis after the concert.

JANUARY 1986

1986 appeared to be another amazing year for Prince. A new movie, a new album, and a tour to promote the film. As much as he was pushing himself professionally, he was doing the same with his personal life. He was maturing as an artist and building a home with the woman he loved. He was entering the year filled with promise, and as an engaged man, there was the opportunity for him to express that in his music. Everything was already planned. All that was required was for the plan to be executed.

The year started off with some confusion, as Eric Leeds remembers.

> We had been doing things for about a week and a half, and then all of a sudden I didn't get a call from Prince for a day. And I'm at the hotel in LA and I called the studio and I said, "Where's Prince?" And they said, "Well, he went home." So I called Prince—back in those days, we all had Prince's phone number—and I said, "Where are you?" He said he went home. And he said, "Well, where are you at?" "I'm still in LA," he didn't cut me loose. "Can I leave?" And he said, "Oh shit, you're still there? Stay there. I'll come back tomorrow." I said, "Oh fuck."

THURSDAY, JANUARY 2, 1986

"All Day, All Night" (vocals, mix)
"Kiss" [12 inch version] (mix)
Sunset Sound, Studio 3 | 5:30 p.m.–12:30 a.m. (booked: lockout)
Producer: Prince | Artist: Prince | Engineer: Coke Johnson

*It is important that you believe in yourself. I do musically.
I go into the studio and I believe in what I'm doing, and
the people around me believe in what they're doing. It's a
group effort. And it's very fulfilling.*[1]

—Prince

The first session of the new year found Prince working on a song from two years earlier, "All Day, All Night." The track had been recorded when Prince and the Revolution debuted it during his birthday show at First Avenue on June 7, 1984, but he spent some time making adjustments to the song.

At this point in Prince's "record/release/tour" schedule, he would often concentrate intensely about what songs best told the story he wanted to present. Usually the prospect of a deadline helped him make his decisions, and part of that involved going through the music recorded during that era and deciding if it worked for the theme of the album, remembers Eric. "When the release date of his next album would start to approach, he would start to focus, and you knew he might be looking at anything that he had been recording in the last six months, the last year, nine months or whatever. And only then he might start to get an idea of what he wanted the next album to be about."

An extended version of "Kiss" was started, but it is unclear how far they got on the track. Two C-90 cassettes were created at the end of the evening.

Status: "All Day, All Night" (5:41) would eventually find a home on Jill Jones's album in 1987. Prince's version remained unreleased during his lifetime.

On October 11, 2009, for his two performances in Paris, France, Prince named the concerts after this song, with the 5 p.m. show listed as "All Day" and the 10 p.m. show as "All Night." He also performed the track and used chants from the song multiple times during the concerts and others that followed over the next week.

The Bangles' *Different Light* album was also released on January 2. It contained the Prince-penned "Manic Monday."

FRIDAY, JANUARY 3, 1986

"Love And Sex" [version 2, sometimes listed as **"Love & Sex"**] (tracking, mix)
Sunset Sound, Studio 3 | 7:00 p.m.–3:30 a.m. (booked: lockout)
Producer: Prince | Artist: Prince | Engineer: Coke Johnson

I try not to repeat myself. It's the hardest thing in the world to do. There are only so many notes one human being can master.[2]

—Prince

After years of recording music, it was inevitable that he'd repeat himself, even if it was just reusing the same title as a song he'd recorded two years earlier. "Love And Sex," which has nothing in common musically and lyrically with his original 1984 recording, began as many of his songs did, with Prince laying down the basic groove on his drum kit, which he covered with several [Ensoniq] Mirage tracks, using presets "Rock Guitar 5ths" and "Nylon Strings," as well as guitar and bass, which were both likely played from the control room and recorded in the big room of the studio through his amplifier. The lyrics were written from a female perspective ("Look at you, out of control with a crazy girl"[3]), and some of the musical elements from the song were likely influenced by Sheila, specifically his use of agogô bells, a Latin instrument similar to a cow bell. After 7 hours of recording and overdubs, an additional hour was spent creating the proper aural mood. The way the song was recorded and mixed actually gives the listener the feeling of being on the Ferris wheel referenced in the lyrics.

Prince's philosophy on both "love" and "sex" can be better understood from an interview he had done in 1981. **"More than my songs have to do with sex, they have to do with one human's love for another . . . the need for love, the need for sexuality, basic freedom, equality. I'm afraid these things don't necessarily come out. I think my problem is that my attitude is so sexual that it overshadows anything else."**[4]

It is possible that "Love And Sex" was written and tracked at some point during the previous week, but it appears that the majority of the song was recorded on this date.

271

Status: "Love And Sex" (4:11) was re-recorded for Sheila E. This version with Prince singing on the track remained unreleased during his lifetime, but was included on 2020's *Sign O' The Times* Super Deluxe Edition. Sheila's updated "Love And Sex" remains unreleased.

SATURDAY, JANUARY 4, 1986

"**Tricky**" [working title] (tracking, mix)
Sunset Sound, Studio 3 | 2:30 p.m.–3:00 p.m. (booked: lockout)
Producer: Prince | Artist: Prince | Engineer: Coke Johnson

> *"Tricky" referred to something that was done for the* Under the Cherry Moon *soundtrack. Because Tricky was Jerome's character in the movie. I was hanging around some of those days and I have a feeling that maybe I was involved.*[5]

—Eric Leeds

This was early in postproduction for *Under The Cherry Moon*, but it is likely that Prince quickly recorded some piano segments that he played directly to tape as part of the score for the movie as a placeholder for the editors. Susan Rogers recalls the setup that he would use during this period. "He had an edited version of the movie on video tape, on VHS and we set up at Sunset Sound with three speakers—left, center and right—and a video monitor, black and white of course, in front of him and all his instruments around him, especially the Fairlight and he would watch the movie and we'd have tape rolling, and he would write. And he'd just score as it was going on."[6]

It is likely that Prince was inspired by the way Miles Davis had created the score for Louis Malle's influential 1958 film *Ascenseur pour l'échafaud* (also released as *Lift To The Scaffold* in the United Kingdom and *Frantic* in the United States). For that project, Davis didn't rely on a predetermined series of written pieces. Instead, he gave his jazz quintet a few basic harmonic ideas and then simply watched the film and added his own musical interpretations of the emotions of the scene. The results were critically acclaimed and the US release of *Jazz Track*, which contained an entire side of that score, was nominated for a Grammy in 1960.

Status: The music recorded during this very brief session was likely used in an early cut of *Under The Cherry Moon*. He would continue scoring the movie over the next several months in a similar fashion.

SUNDAY, JANUARY 5, 1986

This session was collectively called **"Everybody's Jams"** and included:
"Groove In C Minor" (tracking)
"Slow Groove In G Major" (tracking)
"Slow Groove In G Flat Minor" (tracking)
"For Love" [listed as **"Groove On '4 Love' In B Flat"** and **"Groove On '4 Love' In G Flat Minor"**] (tracking)
"Junk Music" [including **"Up From Below"** and **"Y'all Want Some More?"**] (tracking)
Sunset Sound, Studio 3 | 8:00 p.m.–3:30 a.m. (booked: lockout)
Producer: Prince | Artists: Prince/The Flesh | Engineer: Coke Johnson | Assistant Engineer: Mike Kloster

We recorded a lot in '86, that was probably the most prolific . . . at least the most amount of time that I was in the studio with him. I started out in January of '86 spending six weeks with him in Sunset Sound in LA. We were in the studio doing all kinds of things, most of which never saw the light of day. A lot of which were instrumental jam sessions.[7]

—Eric Leeds

Prince loved to play. There really is no other way to explain it. Whether it was 4-hour soundchecks, all-day rehearsals, or just gathering fellow musicians to jam, making music was when he was most comfortable. "It gave him life, just like people need air and food, he needed music," explains his drummer Bobby Z. "He was a different species, literally a different species. Music for him was not the way any mortal that we know thinks about it."

Prince continued to experiment with this jazz/rock blend and decided to extend and expand the Flesh sessions, adding Wendy, her brother Jonathan Melvoin, and Lisa to the sessions. "I never knew that it was a project specifically because Wendy and I were in the studio all the time and playing and some of it was jamming and some of it was getting down to work and doing chores and background vocals and things like that," remembers Lisa. "It wasn't till years later that I realized, 'What? It was called what?' I didn't even know."

At approximately 9:45 p.m., Prince placed everyone in the main room of Studio 3 and arranged it so they could add to the creation of the music, details Eric.

> Prince would have a talkback mic that was fit into all of our headphones. So he would be giving us direction to that, and occasionally you can hear some of these directions that went to tape, but most of the time we would just hear him in our headphones. Like on "Junk Music," he sat behind the drums and he just said, "Okay, we're in this key." And then he just hit it, and boom, we're into it. That was all and he didn't give us any direction on that. Any form that any of it had was basically just constructed by, I think, me and Wendy and Lisa as we were going along. And it was one of the few times where Prince was actually listening to what else was going along and actually reacting to it as a drummer.

The group came up with multiple free-form songs as a unit and also revisited a song Prince and Leeds recorded months earlier for Jill Jones, "4 Love," turning it into an instrumental jam, as Eric recalls. "We just fell into that. We were just grooving on whatever it was and then he just started playing on guitar, I don't even know if anyone else knew what it was, but I did."

Leeds continues:

> The complete "Junk Music" was 67 minutes 37 seconds and was recorded "live" to 2-track on five reels. Each reel probably had 15 minutes. Coke Johnson was keeping two machines going and alternating fresh reels of tape that overlapped as we were recording. On "Groove In C Minor," the personnel was Sheila on drums, Prince on bass, Wendy on guitar, Lisa on piano, myself, and Jonathan Melvoin on congas. For "Slow Groove in G Major" Prince moved to guitar, and Wendy moved to bass—actually switched instruments on the fly about 45 seconds into it. All else the same. "Slow Groove in G flat minor," "Groove on '4 Love' in B flat" and "Groove on '4 Love' in G minor" all had the same personnel.

Eric recalled the experience of some of the sessions like "Everybody's Jam." "Some of the more interesting and more enjoyable music from my point of view was when Sheila, Prince, Wendy and Lisa and I would just go into the studio and just jam. It may not have the harmonic sophistication of a straight-up jazz band, but the ethic was very similar. That's the closest we got to the jazz concept."[8] In fact, the music inspired many of Prince's future projects, including Madhouse, *Sign O' The Times*, and *Lovesexy*.

Susan Rogers noted how Prince's wide musical knowledge was reflected on the songs he performed with the Flesh.

You can hear it in his fingers. You can hear him walk toward jazz in some of his gestures. You can hear him walk toward the blues in some of his gestures. So you can tell that this kid listened to a lot of jazz. And he listened to a lot of rock. What I love listening to is how his fingers can never stay on those strings. He can never commit to blues. He can never commit to jazz. And what he comes back to consistently is pop. That's who he is. And that's Prince's genius. Prince was a pop hook writer, a melody writer, with a genius for rhythm. And that's so rare.

Wendy and Lisa took something different from the Flesh sessions. "They weren't even sessions," reflects Lisa. "I didn't think they were sessions. They were jams."

Wendy concurs, "I think he was doing a lot of grooming with Eric. That was the era where I felt like, 'Oh, people are going to get replaced.' This is when things started smelling weird to me."

"I hate to say it, but whenever anybody else was playing with us, it just always smelled like an audition," admits Lisa. "It did have that feeling like there was something else. It was like, 'What are these, tryouts?' Everyone's pulling out their best gym tumbles."

Within a year, Wendy, Lisa, and almost the entire Revolution would be gone, and Prince would invite Levi Seacer Jr, Eric Leeds, and Sheila E. to join his band.

Status: The session included: "4 Love" (27:44 combined), "Groove In C Minor" (8:02), "Slow Groove In G Minor" (9:55), "Slow Groove In G Flat Minor" (13:02), "Junk Music" (1:03:17), and an edit of "Junk Music" (19:44). "Up From Below" (5:07) and "Y'all Want Some More?" (1:33) were part of the full "Junk Music." All of these tracks remained unreleased during Prince's lifetime, although parts of "Junk Music" briefly appeared in *Under The Cherry Moon.*

MONDAY, JANUARY 6, 1986

Parade album compiled (includes: **"Christopher Tracy's Parade," "New Position," "I Wonder U," "Under The Cherry Moon," "Girls & Boys," "Life Can Be So Nice," "Venus De Milo," "Mountains," "Do U Lie?," "Kiss," "Anotherloverholenyohead,"** and **"Sometimes It Snows In April"**)
Sunset Sound, Studio 3 | (booked: lockout)
Producer: Prince | Artist: Prince | Engineers: Coke Johnson and Susan Rogers

Once again, Prince put together the *Parade* album for review. Additional time was probably spent on crossfades and minor edits to create a flow that was logical for the film and both aesthetically and artistically pleasing.

TUESDAY, JANUARY 7, 1986

"Can I Play With U?" (safety copy made, probable mix)
"Evolsidog" (mix and overdubs)
"Evolsidog" [instrumental] (mix)
"Mia Bocca" (mix and overdubs)
"Rough" [listed as **"Too Rough"**] (mix and overdubs)
Sunset Sound, Studio 1 | 3:00 p.m.–4:00 p.m.
Sunset Sound, Studio 3 | 10:30 a.m.–3:00 a.m.
Producer: Prince | Artist: Prince | Engineers: Stephen Shelton (Studio 1),
   Coke Johnson (Studio 3)

> *There were plans of making a movie, called "The Dawn." It was gonna be a black* West Side Story, *a musical, starring Mazarati and The Family, rival bands fighting it out or whatever. This was almost the same time as* Under The Cherry Moon. *I don't think Prince would have been in the movie, just directing it. There was a song called "Evolsidog" they were going to use. It sounded something like "Free."* [9]
>
> —Tony Christian

Even before Prince finished *Under The Cherry Moon*, he was imagining his next movie, tentatively called "The Dawn." A treatment for the film (or possibly Broadway play) was being prepared that would be a battle between Mazarati and the Family, but with the Family no longer a band there was confusion about what to do.

Mazarati was still a card Prince had up his sleeve that would be played in the next two months, so he seemed to be ready to add them to a production to promote their music in the same way he had done with the Time. Now that feature films were a successful option, it seemed that movies would be a wise way to get attention for his protégé projects.

With this in mind, he apparently worked on music that he was considering for his film projects. The instrumental of "Mia Bocca" (credited as "Mia Boca") was in the *Under The Cherry Moon* movie, but it is unclear if "Evolsidog" made it into any cuts. The instrumentals were also created as he was likely planning to have Jill or Sheila record them for their projects.

This extended session started at 10:30 in the morning and lasted until after midnight with Prince mixing and overdubbing "Mia Bocca" and "Evolsidog" until 8 a.m. After a 2-hour break, Eric was brought in. "I think 'Too Rough' was the only one that I played on. It was a pretty convoluted horn arrangement that I did on it and that was going to take a while. So he left, and then came back when it was done. I figured out over a long period of time, if he was just leaving some stuff for me to do on my own, it was stuff that wasn't that important."

While Prince was out, he requested a safety copy made of "Can I Play With U?" in Studio 1, likely so he could edit the track.

The final hour was spent creating rough mixes of the tracks, including the instrumental versions, and dubbing them to two TDK C-60 tapes and one C-90 before the session ended at 3 p.m. Along the way, Prince would often make multiple copies of mixes to test them out. Any song could have a variety of mixes that featured different instruments or moods. "What you have to understand is that the transition from a recording state to a mix state had to be instantaneous," recalls Sunset Sound engineer Stephen Shelton, who'd worked with Prince multiple times.

> Whether it meant he would allow time if we were running a lot of live instruments in the studio, we'd often make mixes for cassette off of the monitor board which is not the same capability of reverb and effects and some of the controls as you would when it is switched over into a mixing mode. And it always had a multitrack machine and two track machines ready to record because in the middle of a mixing session he might decide to do a different vocal or a different instrument overdub and you had to switch to be able to do that.

Because of this, Prince likely has many different mixed versions of his songs, each with unique vocals and instrumentation.

WEDNESDAY, JANUARY 8, 1986

"**Everybody's Jam**" [listed as "**Everybodies Jam**] (mix and overdubs)
"**Rough**" [listed as "**Too Rough**"] (mix and overdubs)
"**A Couple Miles**" (probable mix)
Sunset Sound, Studio 3 | 3:30 p.m.–2:30 a.m. (booked: lockout)
Producer: Prince | Artist: Prince | Engineer: Coke Johnson

"A Couple Miles" he left for me. He just said, "Here is the track, double the melody and whatever else you want to do with it, do it. I'm going to dinner, I'll come back later."

—Eric Leeds

Prince had a new weapon in his arsenal, and he appeared to want to push the limits on what Eric could do with his own music as well as with the Flesh sessions. "Prince threw the whole thing in my lap and said, 'Why don't you take all of the stuff that we did with Wendy and Lisa and make me an album.'"

"The fact that here we are in Sunset Sound Studios and he's giving me the opportunity to have a major world class facility at my beck and call to be able to just spend a couple of nights and screw around with this music was a wonderful compliment and opportunity for him to give to me just to mess around because he was interested."

The first 6 hours were spent mixing and possibly overdubbing "Rough" and "A Couple Miles" (which was being considered for the Flesh project) with Prince, but once he left, Eric and Coke Johnson sat down to create a project from the random recordings, as Leeds recalls.

What I like about those sessions is that it was probably my favorite playing of anything that I've done on any of the stuff I ever did with Prince. Not just because they were instrumental jams and this is what I do, you know? Wendy and Lisa, they have a harmonic vocabulary that was so much more sophisticated than Prince's and anyone else. So that's what I related to. So I actually had something to play off of that was much more interesting for me as a player. Because even though we were basically just jamming, they were taking things in different keys and all different voicings and Lisa has a harmonic sense that's really, really cool. So she could really give me some really hip shit to play off of. That's why I enjoy playing with them.

Three C-60 cassettes were created, one of which Prince would review to see how the project was progressing.

THURSDAY, JANUARY 9, 1986

"**Junk Music**" (edits)
"**Up From Below**" (edits)
Multiple cues for **Under The Cherry Moon** **score** (tracking, mix)
Sunset Sound, Studio 3 | 7:00 p.m.–11:00 p.m. (booked: lockout)
Producer: Prince | Artist: Prince | Engineer: Coke Johnson

Prince, either uses or doesn't use what I have. When he gets it, I understand he listens to the strings separately, he'll listen to the brass separately and the woodwinds separately and then he'll put it all together and listen to it. So when we got to his movie, Cherry Moon, *most of the music that was what you might refer to as an 'underscore' was the backgrounds that I had written for certain songs of his, that he took the voices and his part out. Now I would have preferred to write the individual sections, but on the other hand, it worked out just fine.*

—Clare Fischer

Prince bookended this session with a total of 13 and a half hours working on the score for *Under The Cherry Moon*, which included locating items in his archive that he felt could be placed in many of the scenes—some of which included various Clare Fischer orchestral work, including string selections from "I Wonder U," "Life Can Be So Nice," and the title track. He also recorded new music when needed. Most of this new material was created using the Yamaha DX7 as well as Eric on flute and sax. In between those tasks, he and Leeds spent 4 hours reviewing some of the new music they'd recorded as the Flesh. "Junk Music" and another track or two were edited for the potential Flesh album, and possibly as elements for the score.

Although Prince had won the Academy Award the previous year for "Original Song Score" for *Purple Rain*, the reality was that he wasn't experienced at actually creating a score, which requires a musician to think in terms of the emotions of a scene and find a way to express that musically. "He didn't understand story arc that way, and that's why he wouldn't be a good composer for other people's stories," offers Wendy who didn't directly work on the *Under The Cherry Moon* score with Prince. "We were good for *him*. We composed *his* story and that's what we did for him."

"Wendy is a fabulous musician," explains Eric. "She's got Emmy Awards in film and TV work, which is a musical discipline that is completely separate from anything that she would ever have to deal with Prince. Prince's way of doing soundtrack music was just to rummage through his vault, and try to pick out something. . . . 'Oh, maybe that'll work.' I was in the studio for him, like off and on for like a week. And we'd come in and just do little dibs and dabs of stuff, and God knows what. I do remember he used a little bit of that same 'Junk Music.'"

One C-90 cassette was made at the end of the shift.

FRIDAY, JANUARY 10, 1986

"**Madrid**" [part of "**Paisley Jam**"] (mix and edits)
"**Y'all Want Some More?**" (probable mix, edit)
Multiple cues for *Under The Cherry Moon* **score** (tracking, mix)
Sunset Sound, Studio 3 | 8:00 p.m.–5:00 a.m.
Producer: Prince | Artist: Prince | Engineer: Coke Johnson

> *There were a couple of times where he said to me "Grab your*
> *horn and run in really quick and play this scale" and that*
> *would take five or ten seconds. Something that he might have or*
> *might have not ended up on the movie soundtrack."*[10]
>
> —Eric Leeds

As the editor sent Prince edited sequences, Prince continued to score them by himself with the help of Eric on sax or flute. Once the day's process was finished, he asked Eric to continue working on *The Flesh* album. Additional editing was being done on "Madrid" and "Y'all Want Some More?" by Eric and Coke.

While Prince was indulging this experiment, he apparently wasn't taking it completely seriously, remembers Leeds.

> He actually called me at the studio one night and he said, "I'm going over to Tramps, come on over and meet me." And I said, "Prince, I'm working." And he said, "No, you can do it tomorrow. I need somebody to hang with me tonight." And I said, "Prince I'm having fun doing this." He gave me the fricking studio. So this is where I want to be, and Prince said, "Oh, man come on, you'll do it tomorrow." I said, "No Prince. Sorry. I'm here tonight. You go have a good time." He said, "Fuck you." [laughs] That's what it was like.

SATURDAY, JANUARY 11, 1986

"**Mobile**" (mix and edits)
"**Kiss**" [12-inch version] (edits, mix)
Sunset Sound, Studio 3 | 12:00 noon–4:30 a.m. (booked: lockout)
Producer: Prince | Artist: Prince | Engineer: Coke Johnson

For the extended mixes, we would either cut it down from the long track to a releasable single, three to four minute song, or we would take that three to four minute song and mix out different sections to make it a 10 minute extended version for discos.

—Coke Johnson

Eric and Coke continued to work on the Flesh project, focusing on "Mobile" for the first four hours. The track was mixed, and then their attention shifted to creating the 12-inch version of "Kiss." It is unclear how much progress was done on the longer version of the track because Prince was working on other business outside of the studio during this period.

After 6 and a half hours of editing, overdubbing, and mixing, the evening's music was dubbed to two C-60 and two C-90 cassettes. Once that was complete, the 16-hour session was over.

SUNDAY, JANUARY 12, 1986

"**Neon Telephone**" (new mix)
"**Splash**" (new mix)
"**Teacher, Teacher**" (new mix)
"**An Honest Man**" [instrumental] (mix for movie)
"**Venus De Milo**" [orchestra only] (mix for movie)
"**Venus De Milo**" [piano mix for movie]
"**Everything But You**" (review, possible overdubs, mix)
"**Last Heart**" [listed as "**Baby, My Heart**"] (probable tracking and vocals, mix)
"**Last Heart**" [instrumental] (mix)
"**Conversation Piece**" (tracking, overdubs, mix)
Sunset Sound, Studio 3 | 3:30 p.m.–10:00 a.m. (booked: lockout)
Producer: Prince | Artist: Prince | Engineers: Coke Johnson and Susan Rogers

"Conversation Piece" probably alluded to the fact that it was just Prince and myself. If I remember correctly, what I did on the horns was pretty spur of the moment off the top of my head.[11]

—Eric Leeds

For the first 2 hours of the sessions, Prince continued to mix multiple tracks that likely included "Neon Telephone," "Splash," "Teacher, Teacher," "Venus De Milo," and "An Honest Man" for consideration in the movie. Many of these either contained Clare Fischer's orchestra or were mixed as an instrumental.

At 5:30 p.m., Prince switched from mixing to tracking one of three new songs: "Last Heart," "Conversation Piece," and a song written by Wendy and Lisa called "Everything But You." It appears that "Everything But You" was reviewed by Prince first. It is unclear how much work was done on the track, but it is unlikely that Prince added his lead vocals.

He followed it up with "Last Heart," a song that blends his own potential weakness with his threat of violence against his lover, a theme he'd hinted about in multiple songs over the course of his career, including: "I Would Die 4 U," "Sarah," "If I Was Your Girlfriend," and the unreleased 1982 version of "Extralovable."

Peggy Leonard recalls how she felt engineering sessions and songs like this.

Was he easy to work with? No. Was he amazing to work with? Yes. He was a musical genius. He was fascinating to watch, but he was scary as a human being because you never knew who you were going to get. I never expected him to be nice. I don't think he was ever *nice* to me. I think he was as nice as he was to anybody, except for somebody that he was sleeping with, which we weren't, ever. I thought he was probably the most physically perfect, attractive person I had ever met. But the thought of being vulnerable with him just made me hyperventilate, because sometimes he was mean. I didn't want him to know that much about me. I didn't want to give him any ammo.

"There were many moments where it was not tender; it was like, overcooked. 'Stick in a fork in it, it's done!' [laughs] But for the most part, really authentic." recalled Susannah.

When he was with me, and Wendy and Lisa—I use the word tender, I don't want to say vulnerable, because he wasn't—but he was relaxed in a way that seemed more familial. I just sensed that when he was with Wendy and Lisa and I, there was no awkwardness. There was no dead air. There was no self-consciousness. There was nothing self-conscious about it. So he presented himself much more tender than I think most people have ever known him to be. He was a layered and complicated man.[12]

The track featured Prince on his usual line up of instruments: drums, bass, guitar, and the Yamaha DX7 synth, and Eric Leeds on sax. Once his sax overdubs were completed, he and Prince worked on a funky track called "Conversation Piece," as Leeds detailed. "That was a pretty crazy instrumental that we did that I think was going to be part of this movie musical that he was going to do. It was one of his brainstorms at that time. He had a whole idea for doing like a Broadway kind of musical and I think that was going to be part of it."[13]

"I think I'm just doubling a synth line that was on ["Conversation Piece"]," continues Eric. "A couple of little synth hits and then there was a solo spot in it. I'm not even listening to the song half the time because Prince doesn't pay me to *like* his music, he's paying me to *play* it."

From 5 a.m. to 8 a.m., it appears that all additional vocals were recorded for the earlier tracks, including multiple versions of Susannah's and Prince's blended background for "Last Heart."

Two hours of additional mixing followed, and after Prince had the work dubbed to a pair of TDK C-60 tapes, the session ended at 10 a.m.

Status: "Last Heart" (3:02) was released on *Crystal Ball* in 1998. "Conversation Piece" (7:41) would eventually be edited down (3:16), but all versions remained unreleased during Prince's lifetime. "Everything But You" would be included on Wendy and Lisa's eponymous debut album, released on August 25, 1987.

Note: It is possible that "Last Heart" was originally recorded on an earlier date, but this is unverified.

MONDAY, JANUARY 13, 1986

"Splash" (mix and edits)
"Neon Telephone" (mix)
"Neon Telephone" [instrumental] (mix)
Sunset Sound, Studio 3 | 7:00 p.m.–6:30 a.m. (booked: lockout)
Producer: Prince | Artist: Prince | Engineers: Coke Johnson and Susan Rogers

Prince would come in in a good mood, a bad mood, or a neutral mood. But he'd basically get right to work and be quiet, for the most part. It was boom, boom, boom, boom, boom, boom. It was the genius in his laboratory. It was the artist in his studio, creating. He needed silence. He needed concentration. He needed the world to be nonexistent. He needed the phone to not ring. He needed people not coming in and out. He needed to create. He needed his engineer to be quiet, unobtrusive, and to have an extraordinary level of stamina. To be relentlessly self-sacrificing. It doesn't matter if I'm hot, cold, tired, thirsty. It doesn't matter. It doesn't matter if I'm sick, well, having a birthday or an anniversary, or if I've got a family at home who's ill. That didn't matter. So those of us who could be that for him, could allow him to just be the working man that he was. That's what it was like for him. He was somewhat extraordinary in that regard.[14]

—Susan Rogers

"Neon Telephone" and "Splash" were mixed, both likely considered for placement in *Under The Cherry Moon*. The 11-and-a-half-hour session probably included other songs, but no documentation could be located.

Two C-60 tapes were made of the mixes and the session ended at 6:30 a.m.

TUESDAY, JANUARY 14, 1986

"**Kiss**" [extended version] (mix)
"**Go**" (overdubs, possibly Wendy and Lisa vocal overdubs, mix)
"**Go**" [instrumental] (mix)
"**Neon Telephone**" (mix)
"**Neon Telephone**" [instrumental] (mix)
"**Eternity**" (mix)
"**Eternity**" [instrumental] (mix)
"**Sexual Suicide**" (mix)
"**Sexual Suicide**" [instrumental] (mix)
"**Alexa De Paris**" (mix)
"**Love or Money**" (mix)
"**Old Friends 4 Sale**" [orchestra mix] (mix)
"**Splash**" (mix)
"**Last Heart**" (mix)
Sunset Sound, Studio 3 | 11:30 a.m.–1:30 a.m. (booked: lockout)
Producer: Prince | Artist: Prince | Engineers: Susan Rogers and Coke Johnson

There's some quintessential thing about ["Go"], the tempo for one thing is so confident and it's so bad ass, but if you listen to it and just think of how confident that tempo is. It was a great collaboration and we did all these really cool vocals together. It was a time when Prince and Wendy and myself were really prolific and there was an ease about this song.[15]

—Lisa Coleman

Five hours after the previous session, Prince was back with another full plate of work. At least 10 tracks were mixed or overdubbed during this shift, including (but not limited to): "Go," "Neon Telephone," "Eternity," "Sexual Suicide," "Alexa De Paris," "Love or Money," "Old Friends 4 Sale," "Splash," "Last Heart," as well as the extended version of "Kiss." Instrumental versions were created from at least three of the tracks ("Go," "Eternity," and "Sexual Suicide") and Clare Fischer's orchestration was likely blended with at least one track, "Old Friends 4 Sale."

After a 2-hour break at 4 p.m., Wendy and Lisa added their vocals and a few overdubs to "Go," a track from September. It is possible that Wendy and Lisa also did some work on the long version of "Kiss."

At the end of the session, Prince didn't have Sunset Sound supply any cassettes for dubbing, so it appears Prince added these tracks to a tape that he may have already had from a previous session.

WEDNESDAY, JANUARY 15, 1986

"**Kiss**" [extended version] (overdubs, crossfades, and edits)
"**Y'all Want Some More?**" (edits and mix)
"**Anotherloverholenyohead**" (copy for Clare Fischer)
"**Love Or Money**" (copy for Clare Fischer)
Sunset Sound, Studio 3 | 2:00 p.m.–9:30 a.m. (booked: lockout)
Producer: Prince | Artist: Prince (listed as "Marx Bros.") | Engineers: Coke Johnson and Susan Rogers

Prince was happy with some of the stuff we produced [for the Flesh project], *and there was a sense that something might come out of it that was worthy of release. But it was a very loose idea.*[16]

—Eric Leeds

Eric was still working on a possible Flesh album with the jazz jams recorded recently. During the session, Prince worked on the mix and edited "Y'all Want Some More?," a short driving drum, guitar, and piano heavy song. "'Y'all Want Some More?' was actually just a little tag of something," explains Leeds. "I just lifted about a couple of minutes of it that I put in the sequence."

Work continued on the extended version of "Kiss," probably including a playful argument between Prince and Jill Jones as an older married couple. "Sophie and Saul. Why were we playing a Jewish couple?," laughs Jones. "We goofed around. We always had impressions. When I think about it now, what a sweet relationship, because you don't often have that simpatico with somebody. It was like you're best buddies. I'm so happy when I hear these things because I go, 'Wow, I was so super freaking comfortable with this person.'"

Before the session was complete, copies of "Anotherloverholenyohead" and "Love Or Money" were likely made for Clare Fischer and his orchestral embellishments.

As everything was wrapping up, two C-60 cassettes were made of the work completed and the session ended at 9:30 a.m.

THURSDAY, JANUARY 16, 1986

"Kiss" [extended version] (crossfades and edits)
"Love or Money" [7-inch single] (mix)
Sunset Sound, Studio 3 | 2:00 p.m.–9:30 p.m. (booked: lockout)
Producer: Prince | Artist: Prince | Engineers: Coke Johnson and Susan Rogers

> We didn't know the half of it. We just had our heads down, working. It would be sometimes after the fact that we would find out. Wow, that was that big? That went to number one? Oh, my God! It's still surreal.[17]
>
> —Lisa Coleman

With the *Parade* album scheduled for release at the end of March, today's session featured 7 and a half hours of editing and mixing for the extended version of "Kiss"—which was slated as the first single from the album—and the 7-inch release for "Love Or Money," which would be on the flip side of the "Kiss" single.

FRIDAY, JANUARY 17, 1986

"Kiss" [extended version] (edits and cassette copies)
Parade album assembly (sent to be mastered)
Sunset Sound, Studio 3 | 11:00 a.m.–6:00 p.m. (booked: lockout)
Producer: Prince | Artist: Prince | Engineer: Coke Johnson

> *At this point [Prince] was well aware there's no question about his importance as an artist. I think the tensions that were happening in his life, including personal tensions as well as business tensions, would bubble under the surface of the* Parade *record and ultimately feed the next album, which was* Sign O' The Times.*[18]*

—Susan Rogers

Additional edits for the extended version of "Kiss" were performed during this session, which seems to be dragging on by this point. "The thing that could have made 'Kiss' take so long was because he wasn't there the whole time," explains Johnson. "And so, if he shows up at 11:00 in the morning and we start working on it, and then, he takes a break for three hours, I have to leave that mix up right where it was for when he comes back. Because we didn't have the automation you do today. So, I would want everything to be just like he left it, so we could continue working on it when he came back."

The *Parade* album was assembled and sent to Bernie Grundman for mastering. Once the album was complete, it was important to view it in the context of what it was: a soundtrack album that embellished the movie. *Purple Rain* was tightly crafted from the eye of writer/director Albert Magnoli to accentuate the emotional story being told in the film. Both *Purple Rain*, the movie, and *Purple Rain*, the album, worked flawlessly together and separately. *Parade*, despite containing several timeless songs, has trouble supporting the plot of the movie. "It is intended to accompany a story, this story that runs through the movie," explained Susan Rogers. "But it's not as tight with that story as the *Purple Rain* album was to the *Purple Rain* movie."[19]

"At this point," continued Rogers, "I think Prince was trying to position himself as an artist who would appeal to both North American and European audiences, who liked both soul R&B music, as well as pop music. It was becoming quite clear at this point that he was first and foremost a pop artist."[20]

At the end of this abbreviated session, six cassettes (two C-60 tapes and four C-90 tapes) were dubbed of the day's assembly. The lineup for the final album was likely the same as what was compiled during this session.

Prince was probably absent for most of this session as there was a 4-and-a-half-hour break during this 7-hour session. He was likely meeting with some of the members on the team who were designing the cover as he approved the exterior layout for the *Parade* album on this date. Those behind the artwork included Jeff Katz (photography), Laura LiPuma and Jeffrey Kent Ayeroff (art direction), or Ann Field (collage).

SATURDAY, JANUARY 18, 1986

"**Kiss**" [extended version] (edits, mix)
"**Junk Music**" (mix)
Sunset Sound, Studio 3 | 9:00 p.m.–2:00 a.m. (booked: lockout)
Producer: Prince | Artist: Prince | Engineer: Coke Johnson

Work would continue on "Kiss" and the Flesh project. It is unclear if Prince attended this session.

SUNDAY, JANUARY 19, 1986

"**Kiss**" [extended version] (edits, overdubs, and mix)
"**All Day, All Night**" (edits, overdubs, and mix)
"**All Day, All Night**" [instrumental mix] (probable mix)
"**Roadhouse Garden**" (possible overdubs, mix)
"**Mountains**" [long version] (listen)
Sunset Sound, Studio 3 | 11:00 a.m.–4:30 a.m. (booked: lockout)
Producer: Prince | Artist: Prince | Engineers: Susan Rogers and Coke Johnson

Those were some crazy times, but Prince was always a purist. You couldn't get caught with cocaine and pot or anything around him or you were off the tour or off the gig. He was all about his health. He would drink that Évian water and he

would eat some Doritos, the Famous Amos cookies and we'd
have all that stuff stocked in there. Then, he'd go to a fancy
restaurant and eat healthy food. But then he always had a
Universal Gym set up in one of the ISO [isolation] booths.

—Coke Johnson

Prince liked his junk food, but worked hard to hide it. "He ate like a little kid at the time when I was with him," recalled Susan Rogers. "He had a sweet tooth. He lived on Doritos and cake."[21]

"Back then, there were sugar cubes. Those little half-inch squares," remembers Coke Johnson. "And he would have his coffee with, if he said, 'One sugar,' he just wanted a cup of coffee. But if he said, 'Two sugars,' you knew you were in for it. You're going to be there for hours. Because he was such a purist, sugar would give him an energy buzz off that, and the caffeine."

The day started early with Prince requesting a tape copy of something he'd recorded previously—possibly from yesterday's session—so from 11 a.m., Johnson was back in the studio and spent 2 hours dubbing cassettes for him, which was something that happened periodically, according to Johnson. "A lot of the time, that was because he didn't have a copy of it anymore. A lot of cassettes get lost or get stolen. This was back before we had CDs. He would remember a song but then he would want to hear it so that he could hear parts he wanted to add or take away or redo in his head." It is likely that one of the songs that was dubbed to cassette was a long version of "Mountains," for consideration as an upcoming release. Once the dubbing was complete, Prince arrived ready to work.

Studio 3 was its own self-contained world, and once Prince discovered it, he set up camp there. Susan Rogers remembers how well that studio fit Prince's needs. "It's a perfectly designed studio for music making. So when you walk in that main entrance and you don't see daylight, you don't know if it's day or night."

You are in your own space where your needs can be met. You've got your own bathroom, you've got your own lounge, you've got your own refrigerator. And you've got this space for recording that is not too big and not too small. And the best thing about it, like any great studio should be, it is not too sterile, and it is not too funky. You feel like you're in a musical womb where music can grow and be incubated. In my opinion, it's certainly my favorite studio in the world. I compare them all to Sunset.

From 1:30 in the afternoon until 9 p.m., Prince continued editing the extended version of "Kiss," although it is likely that he also created the single edit of the track for release. He also worked on a mix of "An Honest Man" that would be used in the movie.

After 9 p.m., Prince decided to take "Roadhouse Garden"—which was originally recorded in 1984—off the shelf for some editing and overdubbing. A stripped down version of "All Day, All Night" was created, probably for consideration for Jill Jones. Finally, the extended version of "Mountains" was reviewed, but it is unclear if Prince added anything to the track on this date.

During the final 2 and a half hours of mixing, four C-90 cassettes were made of the day's work and the session ended at 4:30 in the morning.

Status: The single for "Kiss" (3:46) has a slightly alternate ending from the album version (3:38) with 8 seconds of funky guitar in a fade out.

It is likely that Prince was unavailable during the next week because he appears to not have attended any recording sessions until January 28 or 29. In his absence, Eric Leeds continued working in the studio on the Flesh project.

MONDAY, JANUARY 20, 1986

> **"Mobile"** (edit, mix)
> **"Kiss"** [extended version] (edit, mix)
> Sunset Sound, Studio 3 | 4:00 p.m.–12:00 midnight (booked: lockout)
> Producer: Prince | Artist: Prince | Engineer: Coke Johnson

> *The Flesh stuff was really hot, and I think the Madhouse idea grew out of that.*[22]
>
> —Alan Leeds

Prince was unable to attend the session, so Eric and Coke continued working on elements for *The Flesh* album, with edits on "Mobile" and likely other tracks that were being considered. The extended version of "Kiss" was also given 3 hours of editing. By midnight, everything had been mixed and a single C-60 cassette was created for Prince.

TUESDAY, JANUARY 21, 1986

"Kiss" [extended version] (edit, mix)
"Mobile" (edit, mix)
"Groove" [likely **"Paisley Jam"**] (edit, mix)
Sunset Sound, Studio 3 | 5:00 p.m.–7:00 a.m. (booked: lockout)
Producer: Prince | Artist: Prince | Engineer: Coke Johnson

Work continued on the "Kiss" 12-inch, as well as "Mobile" and part of the "Paisley Jam." A single C-60 cassette was created to give to Prince because he appears to have not attended this 14-hour session.

WEDNESDAY, JANUARY 22, 1986

The Flesh album assembled
"Conversation Piece" (edit, mix)
"Kiss" [extended version] (likely review)
"Love Or Money" (edit, mix)
Sunset Sound, Studio 3 | 4:00 p.m.–2:00 a.m. (booked: lockout)
Producer: Prince | Artist: Prince | Engineer: Coke Johnson

> *I had a ball working on that stuff. I gave him a sequenced album that was going to be called "The Flesh." Now I know it was not going to be released. It was just for us, but I think he was just curious at that point, to just see what I'd end up doing with it.*[23]
>
> —Eric Leeds

With the release of "Kiss" approaching, Prince had decided on "Love Or Money" as the B-side and had an additional mix done of it for review. The track was recorded the previous summer and had been sitting on the shelf waiting for a home. "'Love or Money' was never meant to be included on the album," explains Eric. "It was only meant to be a B-side."[24]

During this session, Eric likely edited "Conversation Piece" from 7:41 to 3:16, before completing his assembly of *The Flesh* album and four C-60 cassettes, including one for Prince, were created.

According to Eric, the lineup for this collection included:

Side A:
"Junk Music" (20:25)

Side B:
"U Gotta Shake Something" (15:23)
"Up From Below" (4:57)
"Conversation Piece" (3:16)
"Y'all Want Some More?" (1:36)

Eric explains:

Since I was sequencing for vinyl, side A would have been an edit of "Junk Music." I'm pretty sure that side B led off with "U Gotta Shake Something." The second track on side B would have been "Up From Below," which was actually part of the unedited "Junk Music"—there were several tempo shifts thru the full jam—so I isolated it, did a quick fade in and presented it as a stand-alone piece. Track three [was] "Conversation Piece." I'm not sure it really fit with everything else, so if I were doing it today, I probably wouldn't have included it. The last track on side B was definitely "Y'all Want Some More?," which was also a segment lifted from the full "Junk Music" jam, and served as a reprise of the opening theme of "Junk Music." Now if I were sequencing for a CD, I would start with "Shake Something," *then* go to "Junk Music," "Up From Below," and finish with "Y'all Want Some More?"

In the end, it would eventually be another Prince idea that he had to get out of his head and on to tape. An experiment that would be used to expand his palette, but not one that went any further than 30 seconds of "Junk Music" in *Under The Cherry Moon* in the scene where Christopher Tracy races against Mary Sharon on the horse racetrack.

MONDAY, JANUARY 27, 1986

Prince attended the American Music Awards in Los Angeles, where he presented the award for "Favorite Single" in the pop-rock category to Huey Lewis and the News for "Power Of Love."

The event was much more subdued than the previous year when Prince shined brightly. This year Prince was nominated in three categories and lost all of them. The biggest event of the night for him was premiering his new look for this era.

MONDAY, JANUARY 27, 1986

"**All Titles**" listed (likely including "**Venus De Milo**" [long version], "**Alexa De Paris**," "**Life Can Be So Nice**," "**Christopher Tracy's Parade**," "**New Position**," "**I Wonder U**," "**Under The Cherry Moon**," "**Sometimes It Snows In April**," and "**Do U Lie?**")
Sunset Sound, Studio 3 | (booked: lockout)
Producer: Prince | Artist: Prince | Engineer: Susan Rogers

He probably might've been using his music to inspire the movie, rather than having the movie itself inspire his music. He was aware that he was lost at sea with Under The Cherry Moon. *And sometimes his mood could be just so damn dark. He knew he was in trouble.*

—Susan Rogers

It appears that Prince did not attend this session, but he instructed Susan Rogers to put together a variety of "orchestra only" mixes for the tracks that he apparently hoped to place in the movie. The list of songs included "Venus De Milo," "Alexa De Paris," "Life Can Be So Nice," "Christopher Tracy's Parade," "New Position," "I Wonder U," "Under The Cherry Moon," "Sometimes It Snows In April," "Do U Lie?", and likely a few other songs.

TUESDAY, JANUARY 28, 1986

"**Mia Bocca**" (mixed, compiled with edits and crossfades for Jill Jones's album)
"**G-Spot**" (mixed, compiled with edits and crossfades for Jill Jones's album)
"**Baby, You're A Trip**" [listed as "**Baby U're A Trip**"] (mixed, compiled with edits and crossfades for Jill Jones's album)
Multiple cues for *Under The Cherry Moon* score (tracking, mix)
Sunset Sound, Studio 3 | 7:00 p.m.–4:30 a.m. (booked: lockout)
Producer: Prince | Artist: Jill Jones | Engineer: Coke Johnson

It took us a long time to actually commit to working on an album because I'd been working on everybody else's albums for years and I think at some point, because I could stay in so many different styles, it was very difficult to figure out who I was.[25]

—Jill Jones

Since 1982, Prince had been dangling the carrot of an album in front of Jill Jones, and for the most part it kept being delayed. For the first time in months, Prince began working on her album again in earnest, and much older tracks like "Mia Bocca," "G-Spot," and "Baby, You're A Trip" were all updated, potentially for her collection. "Baby, You're A Trip" dated back to July 8, 1982, and even contained the phrase "something in the water does not compute," which referenced a track with the same title that was recorded earlier in the spring.

Because the song had been recorded in 1982 during a period of time that Jones was getting to know him, it resonated with her on a deeper level than expected.

> Prince was writing from the point of view of someone who was star struck. To be honest, I kept thinking, "Is he writing this from *my* point of view? Is *this* how he thinks I see him?" It was mind-blowing thinking somebody could know me so well. What girl ever wants a guy to know she loves him that much? It was a little like being completely naked.
>
> I loved it when Prince did more gospel-type songs. When he kept things simple or when he'd rage in the vocal room all by himself, screaming these emotional thoughts, that was pure conviction. So when I heard "Baby, You're A Trip," I thought it was beautiful.[26]

Prince had recorded a vocally challenging, gospel like coda to the song that would eventually be revisited by Jones, then reworked and also blended with Clare Fischer's orchestral elements from "Mia Bocca" and placed at the start of her album, by David Z Rivkin, cleverly bookending her album. When Jones heard the vocal gymnastics that Prince had recorded, she took it as a challenge. "I was like, I can do it and it was David Z who wanted that at the beginning [of the album]. Prince wouldn't have put it there. David Z had me nail it almost note for note. It was like a feather in his cap because this could be a really great record. We really had something there, and Prince should have kept going, but the problem is that he was being pulled in so many different directions."

"Jill was awesome," remembers Coke. "She was one of the purple elite back then. I don't know what their personal relationship was, but she was very talented, very excited to be there at the studio. We all loved Prince, but I think she loved Prince more than *I* loved him. [laughs]. He was actually spending time on their relationship and helping her move her career down the road."

"G-Spot" was also taken off the shelf and given a new mix and edited for crossfading and fitting on Jones's album. "'G-Spot' has a funny life because he started it in Kiowa Trail," recalls Jill. "He played the initial lines of the saxophone and I've always personally liked that part. I was walking to the laundry room. I could see because he had those glass sliding doors downstairs [imitates Prince on the sax playing two notes over and over]. That's a memory that will never leave, and I don't even know how to explain it. He sat there all day. His house was not soundproof. You're upstairs, trying to watch television and . . . [imitates Prince's two notes on the sax again]. Wow. That's a guy that's dedicated! Funniest image ever!"

At this stage her album was tentatively going to include:

Intro/"Mia Bocca" (7:40)
"G-Spot" (4:30)
"With You" (4:15)
"Too Rough" (6:10)

"Boom, Boom (Can't U Feel The Beat of My Heart)" (6:09)
"My Man" (4:20)
"4 Love" (8:40)
"Baby, You're A Trip" (6:00)

There were many tracks that were likely considered, including "Miss Understood," "Polka-Dotted Tiger," "Zebra With The Blonde Hair," "Killin' At The Soda Shop," "Married Man," and "Living Doll," and were not included in this compilation.

Although Prince had finally kept his promise to compile Jones's album, this collection would once again be placed back on the shelf. "It got pushed off and yet he was using me on everybody's stuff, but I think there was a thing of thinking that I would leave," reflects Jill. "He just wanted the ultimate control."

Before the session ended at 4:30 in the morning, Prince continued working on scoring more of his movie, including a scene that had him speaking to a statue of Venus de Milo ("Venus, listen. Today is a wonderful day. I think I might be leaving the business soon."). The exchange likely influenced a song he'd be recording this week.

Two C-60 tapes were created of today's collection.

Status: This sequence was eventually dismissed, and new compilations would be created in February and November. Several of these tracks, including "Too

Rough" and "Boom, Boom (Can't U Feel The Beat Of My Heart)," would be considered for Jill Jones's second album, but that album and these tracks would remain unreleased during Prince's lifetime.

This session may have been slightly delayed because it was a national day of mourning when the *Challenger* Space Shuttle broke apart 73 seconds into its flight earlier in the day. All seven crew members, including five NASA astronauts, one payload specialist, and a civilian schoolteacher, were killed instantly. Prince was inspired to write about this tragedy a few months later on "Sign O' The Times."

WEDNESDAY, JANUARY 29, 1986

"**With You**" (mix, overdubs, edit, and copy)
Sunset Sound, Studio 3 | 6:00 p.m.–11:00 p.m. (booked: lockout)
Producer: Prince | Artist: Prince | Engineer: Coke Johnson

A brief session that had Prince adding guitar and piano overdubs to "With You" was the final work done on Jill Jones's album for several weeks. A quick mix and likely an edit were completed during the last 30 minutes before it was output to two C-60 tapes. The session ended after that.

THURSDAY, JANUARY 30, 1986

"**Wonderful Day**" (tracking, mix)
"**Wonderful Day**" [instrumental] (mix)
"**Under The Cherry Moon**" [instrumental version, no orchestra mix] (likely mix)
"**Old Friends 4 Sale**" [strings only] (likely mix)
Parade album commercial (review and sampling of songs for ad)
Sunset Sound, Studio 3 | 6:00 p.m.–2:30 a.m. (booked: lockout)
Producer: Prince | Artist: Prince and the Revolution | Engineers: Coke Johnson and Susan Rogers

*The songs came so fast and furious. ["Wonderful Day"] was
one that we didn't spend much time on. I don't remember much
about it. It was one of those that he spat out in probably less
than a day, laid it down very fast.*[27]

—Susan Rogers

Prince continued working on music, not only for *Parade*, but for future projects
of his own and his protégés, likely for the simple reason that he just liked to
record and couldn't stop. **"I want the biggest shelf in the record store—the
most titles,"** proclaimed Prince. **"I know they're not all going to sell, but I
know somebody's going to buy at least one of each."**[28]
Starting at 6 p.m., Prince went back to the idea that was planted two days
earlier when scoring the Venus De Milo scene. Inspired by that, he recorded
"Wonderful Day" until midnight, laying down synth drums, bass, guitar, piano,
and a keyboard part that sounded like a calliope. His addition of a real hi-hat
cymbal gave the song a more human feeling.
Understanding why Prince recorded certain songs can be difficult, but Susan
Rogers explained why she felt he created this track. "As I can recall, 'Wonderful
Day' was one of those songs almost like 'Christopher Tracy's Parade' on the *Parade* album, where it serves the function of getting the album started. It served a
musical function, because you needed something upbeat here, and it also served
a storytelling function. 'Wonderful Day' is something he did very quickly and
for all I know, may have intended to replace later on with another upbeat song
once he had a little bit more time to find the right thing."[29]
At midnight, Prince created multiple mixes of the song (one of them without
any vocals, and two before Wendy would add her vocals the following day) and
probably also worked on an instrumental mix of "Under The Cherry Moon"
and a "strings only" mix of "Old Friends 4 Sale," both of which were created
and considered for the movie. The last 90 minutes in the studio were spent
gathering samples of various songs from *Parade* for a radio spot to advertise
the album. It is unclear if he was present during this part or if he simply asked
his engineer to find the samples for him. Wendy and Lisa would be tasked with
recording the minute-long narration for the commercial at some point before the
ad was completed in late April.
The session ended at 2:30 a.m.

Status: Work on "Wonderful Day" (3:48) would continue the following day.
It was used during the scene that contains Prince and Jerome's Butterscotch/

Chocolate scene in *Under The Cherry Moon*. The full version remained un-released during Prince's lifetime, but was included on the *Sign O' The Time*s Super Deluxe Edition in 2020. An extended mix containing Wendy and Lisa (7:34) was also included on that collection.

FRIDAY, JANUARY 31, 1986

> "**Wonderful Day**" [listed as "**It's A Wonderful Day**"] (overdubs, Wendy and Lisa vocals, mix, copies)
> "**Wonderful Day** [instrumental] (likely mix)
> "**Wonderful Day** [extended mix] (edit, mix)
> Sunset Sound, Studio 3 | 11:00 a.m.–10:00 p.m. (booked: lockout)
> Producer: Prince | Artist: Prince | Engineer: Coke Johnson

> *As Prince and the Revolution, there's probably four albums in the vault from that era. But we worked on other peoples' stuff, especially Lisa and I worked on a lot of the other offshoots of the band and other people he was working with. I think there's probably four in there. I hope that they get to be heard.*[30]
>
> —Wendy Melvoin

Today's session started only a few hours after the previous session ended. In the past, he'd just burn out many of his engineers, but his current Sunset Sound staff engineer, Coke Johnson, had a different philosophy about their time in the studio and the demands Prince would place on everyone around him. "Prince would overwork just about anybody," recalls Johnson. "His work ethic was so strong that Peggy didn't want to spend two full nights in the studio. That might have been where he was because I would just go in there and crash on the couch and wake up and get a hamburger the next morning and be good to go for another 10 or 12 hours. There was nothing more important in my life than working in the studio and recording Prince. That was priority one."

When the session started at 11 a.m., Wendy and Lisa joined Prince to work on "Wonderful Day" and helped contribute 8 hours of additional overdubs, including at least 2 hours of vocals, before the song was mixed. "We helped him with 'Wonderful Day.' We didn't write it, but we helped him. I think he liked my voice," recalls Wendy. "He came to us with this seed, and he said, 'What are you going to do to this?' And so we helped him kind of plant his seeds, if you can think of that in terms of music. That's what we kind of offered him."

Once that was finished and a safety copy of the mix was created, four C-60 cassettes were dubbed and the session ended at 10 p.m., which was early for Prince. He and Wendy and Lisa were flying back to Minneapolis to begin rehearsals with the Revolution, but first Prince would attend a performance by Mazarati the following evening.

FEBRUARY 1986

SATURDAY, FEBRUARY 1, 1986

Venue: Roy Wilkins Auditorium (Saint Paul, Minnesota)
Capacity: 5,000 (attendance unknown)
Guest Appearance: Mazarati

Prince and BrownMark joined Mazarati onstage for 15 minutes at the Winter Carnival's Funfair for a performance of "America."

MONDAY, FEBRUARY 3, 1986

Washington Avenue Warehouse (Edina, Minnesota) | 12 noon

Me and Blistan flew to Minneapolis from Atlanta on February 2, went to the warehouse that night to set up our gear and the next day rehearsals started. That was with the new expanded Revolution. With Blistan, myself, Miko Weaver, Jerome, Wally Safford, and Greg Brooks.[1]

—Eric Leeds

At the beginning of January, a memo was distributed to the band members to announce that rehearsals for "The New Revolution" with an expanded lineup were slated to begin at the Washington Avenue warehouse in Edina. Because of the breakup of the Family, Prince added Jerome Benton, Miko Weaver, and Eric Leeds to the Revolution. Susannah Melvoin was not officially part of the band, although she would sing during several of the shows that year.

He'd also include his bodyguards Wally Safford and Greg Brooks—both of whom were part of the "Baby I'm A Star" finale during the *Purple Rain* tour as dancers and Matt Blistan, aka "Atlanta Bliss" on trumpet. "Trumpet is not an easy instrument," explained Bliss. "And to play the instrument in front of Prince, 14 hours a day, that was definitely a challenge. Prince kicked me in the ass and I enjoyed it."[2]

Not everyone was happy with the tour being planned as a bigger funk review type show with an expanded band (and likely that it was being referred to as the "New Revolution") as tour manager Alan Leeds recalled.

> I think there were some members of the original Revolution who felt that that unit hadn't said everything it wanted to say, and saw it as, "We're the group that made it, and anybody else is an invader of our turf" kind of thing. Not really with malice, not with bitterness, not with resentment of the people, because quite frankly, most of the new members were welcomed with open arms, once it became apparent with Prince's vision. Because, I mean let's face it, Jerome and Eric, I mean, they were already friendly with these guys. There were already friendships. So it wasn't of a personal nature, it was just that for a couple of these kids, all of a sudden their whole dream existence had been re-invented behind their backs, so to speak.[3]

"He never announced shit to us," declares Wendy. "It was at rehearsal and they were behind me and I kept going, 'Well, when are they going to get out of my space?' They're right behind me next to my amp and I'm like, 'What is happening here?' But we were like, 'All right, well let's just see where this goes.'"

"The boss brought us in. It was the boss's idea. It was the boss's journey and how could the boss be wrong when the fans love it?" as Jerome explained in 2017 to De Angela Duff on her *Behind The Film* podcast. "I was there to help have fun and I did my job and I loved doing my job. It didn't matter what anybody else thought. I was working with my friend or let's say my boss, my mentor, my friend."[4]

Alan expanded on Prince's reasoning for the bigger show. "His music was growing. And the irony is that Lisa had so much to do with him opening up to new music. But so did Eric and so did Sheila in their own ways. They brought him to things that he hadn't heard before. His pallet had grown so tremendously that five pieces weren't going to handle it. And here comes Eric and he says, 'Get a trumpet player so we can do parts.' And now it becomes the 'counter revolution.'"[5]

> It had nothing to do with the quality of musicianship, or their personalities or anything. It was just time for a change, and he wanted some new blood, and a bigger group, and an opportunity to explore different kinds of music.[6]

For a short period, Prince was looking at how he could creatively double the size of the Revolution. Susan Rogers remembers:

> This was a time when he was experimenting with the structure of the band, he wanted Sheila in there in some capacity. Of course he wasn't ready to lose Bobby Z, but he was trying to figure out how he could incorporate Sheila and her band into his own band. Prince's mother is a twin, and he kind of had this twin concept going on. He was looking for a manner of getting Susannah in the band who is Wendy's twin and having Miko Weaver be in the band, to have sort of two of everything. Atlanta Bliss was around, now he had two horn players, and he was trying to figure out how he could have a whole band made of twins. And he was thinking of dressing Lisa and Matt Fink alike, you know. He was thinking of this whole twin concept. They rehearsed it a few times, but it didn't work out.[7]

Rehearsals were slated to officially begin at noon, but it was understood that everyone arrived earlier so they weren't docked. The January memo was clear about that and listed that a "$250.00 late fine will be enforced" and that there would be "no exceptions." "We were always at rehearsals," remembered Lisa.

> We just went every day at 10 o'clock in the morning, and it was usually from then until 7 p.m. as a schedule, and we'd usually play late into the night, ordering hamburgers or whatever. It was like a normal job. We'd get set up in the morning and Prince would come in a little later than us and you never knew what kind of mood he would be in. We'd wait as he walked up to the mic and either he'd say something like, being normal: "Okay, let's start at the top of the show," or he'd say—and this was the most annoying thing—when he'd say: "Big up." It was like: "Uh oh, he's in a bad mood."[8]

As he did with his concerts, practically all his rehearsals were videotaped, not for posterity, but for something more immediate, recalled Bobby Z. "Documenting what we did was commonplace, and he used it as a tool to improve. We would watch videos as part of our rehearsals, and it caused a dramatic improvement. When you see yourself look stupid, you fix yourself a lot better. All he had to do was show it to you."[9]

Prince had given the band a sheet with approximately two dozen songs to learn, including "Whole Lotta Shakin' Goin' On," which was written by Dave "Curlee" Williams and James Faye "Roy" Hall, but made popular by Jerry Lee Lewis, and two songs by Joni Mitchell ("A Case Of You" and "Blue Motel Room"—which was one of several songs rehearsed but never performed on the tour) and this list was daunting to some of the band members, including Eric Leeds.

> I remember that the original set list that we got for what would have been the *Parade* tour—which never really was a tour, it was just a bunch of running gigs—it must have been about 25 or 30 songs, including a lot of older stuff. And some things that we never even really got around to doing. And for some of those older songs like "I Wanna Be Your Lover," "Soft and Wet," and some of those things? That was the first time that I ever listened to those songs, and probably the last time I ever listened to them. On any given day, for the first couple of weeks, we'd be working on maybe just a handful of songs every day. And then finally, until we got a show together, that we could start to work on it. It was coming in and then running the show down, once or twice a day or something. We might run the show down, and then we'd just jam for the rest of the day.

WEDNESDAY, FEBRUARY 5, 1986

"Kiss" backed by "Love Or Money" was released as the leadoff single from *Parade*, but there was opposition from Warner Bros. "He gave it to them and they hated it," recalled David Z. "They said, 'We can't put this out. There's no bass, sounds like a demo.' Prince must have had enough power to say, 'You're not getting another song, that's the one we're going to put out.'"

Despite the pushback, "Kiss" reached number one (his first since "Let's Go Crazy") where it stayed for two weeks as well as the top position on the Hot R&B Singles Chart (known then as the "Hot Black Singles Chart"), remaining there for four weeks. "You could really see the resistance of the corporate power of a major record label to something that was so different from what they were expecting," according to David Z. "That record was up against the paranoia of radio and the power of corporate record labels. That time, the record and the artist won."[10]

Note: Eric Leeds's work was a vital part of The Family *album, but "Love or Money" (or "♥ or $," which was the proper name) was the first release by Prince to feature him.*

SUNDAY, FEBRUARY 9, 1986

"Duet With Dad" [working title, also listed as **"Sunday Afternoon"**] (overdubs, mix, copies)
Sunset Sound, Studio 3 | 2:30 p.m.–4:30 p.m. (booked: not listed)
Producer: Prince | Artist: Prince | Engineer: Coke Johnson

*The lyrics [my father and I] write are similar, the same
thing. Our personalities are a lot alike, but his music is
like nothing I've ever heard before. It's more complex. A
lot of beautiful melodies are hidden beneath the complexity. That's why we work so well together. My melodies are
a little different from the way he does them. I'm a little
stricter with melody.*[11]

—Prince

For two years, Prince's father, John L. Nelson, had been back in his life. After a
long period of distance, they found communication with each other on a musical level and apparently inspired each other. "Prince's music started to change
when John L. came into the fold," observed Jill Jones. "Prince's dad could play
the most intricate chord structures, and Prince started working on his chops
more. It was nice to see them together. Prince was very generous with his father,
offering him support and pushing his dad to do new music. At the same time,
John L.'s presence pushed Prince as well: he practiced more and started including beautiful orchestrations and Clare Fischer strings."[12]

Despite the newly established connection they'd shared, Prince's relationship with his father was always complicated. There was love, but at the same
time, there was a strained history that was still healing. **"It's really hard for
my father to show emotion,"** Prince explained to Neal Karlen in 1985. **"He
never says, 'I love you,' and when we hug or something, we bang our heads
together like in some Charlie Chaplin movie. But a while ago, he was telling
me how I always had to be careful. My father told me, 'If anything happens
to you, I'm gone.' All I thought at first was that it was a real nice thing to say.
But then I thought about it for a while and realized something. That was my
father's way of saying 'I love you.'"**

Many people try to relate John L. Nelson with the Kid's father in *Purple
Rain*, but he wasn't entirely based on Prince's dad. There were elements of him

in there, but the role was embellished for dramatic effect. **"We used parts of my past and present to make the story pop more**," according to Prince **"but it was a story. My dad wouldn't have nothing to do with guns. He never swore, still doesn't, and never drinks**."

"He had a lot of reverence for his father," reflected Wendy. Lisa detailed how Prince would react when his father would visit the warehouse. "If his dad came to a rehearsal, we'd have to not cuss, and some of the songs we weren't even allowed to sing. We would accidentally be like, [sings] 'Oh, motherfucker—' and then, 'Oops!' 'Remember . . . we're not singing in this run-through because Dad's here.'"[13]

Prince's memories of his father could be seen by some as abusive, but there were times that he found humor in their history during sessions like this one according to Todd Herreman, who would soon become his Fairlight tech.

> We were all having a conversation in the studio and Prince just stopped talking mid-sentence and we're like waiting and waiting for the rest of the sentence to come out and then he just started laughing. And it's like, "What's so funny?" And he said it reminded him of something that happened when he was a kid and he was in the car with his dad. So he tells the story of when he was younger and his dad is driving and Prince is sitting in the passenger seat and his dad is talking and his dad stops mid-sentence and Prince is like waiting for the rest of the sentence and waiting, waiting so finally Prince says, "Are you going to finish the sentence, dad?" Or something like that and his dad smacks him and says, "Shut up, boy, can't you see I'm talking?" And Prince remembered that in the control room when he stopped mid-sentence, and he just cracked up. That was just one of those funny moments.

Although it may be easy to describe his relationship with his father as "rough," Prince saw it differently. **"I wouldn't call it 'rough.' He was a very strict disciplinarian, but all fathers were. I learned the difference between right and wrong, so I don't consider it so rough**."[14]

This brief 2-hour session involved Prince and his father playing together, John L. on piano and Prince switching between guitar and bass. "They were just jamming," remembers Coke Johnson. "It wasn't anything that got released, or anything like that."

A single C-60 cassette was made of the session.

Status: The multiple tracks known as "Duet With Dad," which has also been listed as "Sunday Afternoon," remained unreleased during Prince's lifetime. The songs were named as such because they were recorded on a Sunday afternoon and are likely unrelated to "Sunday Afternoon," a track Prince wrote for Candy Dulfer.

MONDAY, FEBRUARY 10, 1986

"**Kiss**" (overdubs, vocals, mix, copies)
Multiple cues for **Under The Cherry Moon score** (tracking) likely including: "**Christopher Tracy at Piano**," "**A Little Possessive**," and "**Mary On Drums**"
Sunset Sound, Studio 3 (likely) | (booked: lockout)
Producer: Prince | Artist: Prince | Engineer: Coke Johnson

> *When we weren't touring, everything consisted of pretty much what was happening in the studio, because that's the only place he was.*

> —Susan Rogers

Work continued on the movie score with several cues composed or performed, including the drums for Mary Sharon's drum solo at her party, the piano elements from "An Honest Man" at the beginning of the movie, and "A Little Possessive," which was a variation on "Do U Lie?" played during the scene when Isaac leaves a message on Mrs. Wellington's answering machine.

Additional work was also done on "Kiss" with Mazarati's Tony Christian and Marvin Gunn brought in to add additional background vocals.

TUESDAY, FEBRUARY 11, 1986–WEDNESDAY, FEBRUARY 12, 1986

Rehearsal for "**Kiss**" video shoot
Laird International Studios (The Culver Studios)

> *When Prince's manager called and asked me to direct "Kiss," the first thing out of my mouth was, "I'd like to speak to Prince first, and I'm not doing it unless I can bring in my own hair, makeup, models and choreographer." A few minutes later,*

*Prince called me. He was charming. The conversation was
brief and there was a lot of giggling on his end.*[15]

—Rebecca Blake

The work on these days were largely spent lighting and rehearsing for the video,
which was designed based on conversations between Blake and Prince.

I was on a heavy vampire kick—I was into Anne Rice very early—so that's where
the black veil on the dancer's head comes from. Prince was brilliant in terms of
dance and choreography. You could show him something and three seconds
later he could do it perfectly. He came to the set with buttons all over his pants.
I said, "What's with the buttons?" He said, "Should have told me you don't like
buttons." He's funnier than people know. I'd put him next to a six-foot-tall model
and he would give me an expression like, "Are you kidding? Where's my apple
box?"[16]

THURSDAY, FEBRUARY 13, 1986

Laird International Studios (The Culver Studios)

*The day we did the "Kiss" video I remember very well; it was
one of the few times the two of us got to spend totally alone.*[17]

—Wendy Melvoin

It appears that Prince had been under a lot of stress during the spring, working
on *Under The Cherry Moon* and having a break from that brought out his more
intimate side with Wendy, the only member of the Revolution involved. "He
was the one who decided at the last minute to use Wendy Melvoin in the video,"
recalled Rebecca Blake. "They had great chemistry, and they were funny together. Her facial expressions in that video were perfect."[18]

"We spent the week just preparing for the video and then we did the video,"
reflects Wendy. "What I remember is that it was very calm. It was just very calm,
and we were really playful with each other, so there wasn't a lot of pressure.
That video shoot didn't have a lot of pressure, and most of them did, and that
one just didn't."[19]

Sheila and her band were in Los Angeles to record a segment for a Valentine's Day taping of *The Tonight Show with Johnny Carson*, where they played a medley of "A Love Bizarre" and "Merci For The Speed Of A Mad Clown In Summer." During the second part of the song, Sheila sat behind the drums, a move that made her more of a band member instead of the person in the spotlight, a position that brought a lot of additional scrutiny. Times like this likely influenced her feelings about needing a change. "I wanted to get away from the pressure of being a solo artist," admitted Sheila when reflecting on where she was during this period. "It was important for me to get back to playing the drums because I was just tired of having a band and being the one out front all the time. I wasn't thinking that the move was going to affect my career."[20]

Prince continued working on the "Kiss" video during this week. He also approved the interior artwork for the *Parade* album on this date. After the video was finished shooting, Wendy flew back to Minneapolis where rehearsals continued. When Prince wasn't available because he was out of town, she would generally be in charge of rehearsing the band. He would get tapes of the progress and make changes remotely if needed, as Lisa recalls.

> Sometimes he'd have to leave for a week or two and we'd keep on rehearsing. We felt like we wanted to really kick some ass and we were like, "We're going to show him," and we'd video the rehearsals and he would think it was funny sometimes. I don't remember what song, but we were rehearsing something and kicked the shit out of the song, and then we got to the end of it, and Wendy was like, "That really sucked you guys. Let's try it again." Prince loved imitating her, sounding like a little kid. "That was horrible. Take it from the top, one more time."
>
> [Prince] was like, "You guys are harder on yourselves than I am," because we *were* kind of hard on ourselves. Especially the vocals.

Prince playfully acted this out on stage during the May 23, 1986 show in San Francisco when he said, "You guys sound like shit!" in between "A Love Bizarre" and "Kiss."

MONDAY, FEBRUARY 17, 1986

"G-Spot" (overdubs and mix)
"Euphoria Highway" [version 1] (tracking, mix)
Sunset Sound, Studio 3 | 11:00 a.m.–2:30 a.m. (booked: lockout)
Producer: Prince | Artist: Jill Jones (Prince crossed out) | Engineer: Coke
   Johnson

> *Prince sometimes used a live drummer. He sometimes played*
> *drums himself, but principally in the years when I was with*
> *him from* Purple Rain *through* Sign O' The Times *he pre-*
> *ferred that LM-1.*[21]
>
> —Susan Rogers

It had been months since Prince worked on "G-Spot," and he brought it out to overdub his guitar and add a new snare to the percussion but not enough to recreate the feeling of sex as he'd done on other tracks. In fact, with the exception of the lyrics that detail a woman's body, how to please her, and her position during sex, the song maintains a deep chill that turns sex into something almost clinical. "G-Spot" uses the drum machine, which robotically removes any passion from the track, explained Jill Jones. "It takes all the sensuality away from it."[22]

His work on "G-Spot" wrapped up at 5 p.m. and after dinner Prince started a new song. Beginning, as usual, with a Linn LM-1 groove, he then spent 9 hours adding bass, several layers of synth, including the [Oberheim] OB-8, congas, and multiple sound effects to a new song, "Euphoria Highway."

The lyrics for the song reflected his thoughts in some ways, as he mentions Bobby—although it was not specifically his drummer Bobby Z—but more of a fictionalized version that fit in the story he was telling. In the past, Prince mentioned Bobby's name on tracks like "Mountains" and "Others Here With Us," but on the lyrics to "Euphoria Highway" referenced his drummer Bobby *and* his new wife Vicki. "I think it was modeled on them because he used their names," speculates Jill Jones. She felt that because Bobby had written "River Run Dry" for the Family, "Prince was starting to see him in a different light musically."

The song is written from a scorned and lonely observer of a "love worth dying for" between fictional high school sweethearts. He was the quarterback who occasionally lost the games and she was his partner who maintained her affection for him despite the final score. The singer is also taken by her but recognizes that there was no way he could compete with their pure affection.

"The first verse will break your heart," reveals Bobby. "And that quarterback doesn't win all the time. You know, I'm just a drummer, but I got a love that he would die for, and that's what he wanted, it's what he loved about us."

"He did look up to our relationship," reflects Vicki. "You could see it in his eyes and he accepted me right away."

"Timing is everything in life and I met her at a moment . . . I didn't worry about what my parents thought of her, I was more worried about what *he* thought," explains Bobby. "[Prince and Vicki's] relationship was unique, and they had a relationship that lasted his entire life. He loved her like family."

His gift of a song to them carried more weight than just a seemingly coincidental use of their names in a song. It would often reveal where his thoughts and heart were at that moment, and those around him realized that when he'd pull the curtain back. To be mentioned, especially as an example of a beautiful love, was his way of letting someone know their value. "That's the way he communicated," reveals Wendy.

He ended the shift by recording the two tracks from today's session on a pair of C-60 cassettes.

Status: Prince would re-record the track for Jill Jones. Prince's 5-minute "Euphoria Highway" remained unreleased during his lifetime.

TUESDAY, FEBRUARY 18, 1986

"**Euphoria Highway**" [version 2] (tracking, vocal and instrumental overdubs)
Sunset Sound, Studio 3 | 3:30 p.m.–12:30 a.m. (booked: lockout)
Producer: Prince | Artist: Jill Jones (Prince crossed out) | Engineers: "David Z" Rivkin and Coke Johnson

Prince sometimes gave me a track and then we'd put [Jill's] voice on it.[23]

—"David Z" Rivkin

It is likely that he asked Jill Jones to replace his vocals in the original version, but when they didn't match the tone, Prince apparently reworked the track to fit Jill instead of him making the artist wrap around the song.

Prince would occasionally create a demo for a track, but usually his first full version was good enough to eventually become his final version. For "Euphoria Highway," he started from scratch and recreated the entire song to reflect Jill's energy and voice. Keeping the lyrics, but updating all of the music, he changed the mood giving it a more reflective tone. He asked her to add her voice to the reimagined "Euphoria Highway," and as he'd done with Jones and other protégé acts like the Family, he employed David Z to oversee this 9-hour session.

The updated version contains a much more defined pop feel, but it changes gears and for the final 2 minutes becomes a moody synth-based instrumental. "I only know that the bootleg that everybody has, is just the last part where it goes into the jam section," according to Jill.

Two C-60 cassettes were made for Prince at the end of the session.

WEDNESDAY, FEBRUARY 19, 1986

"**Euphoria Highway**" (vocal overdubs, mix)
Sunset Sound, Studio 3 | 2:30 p.m.–7:30 p.m. (booked: lockout)
Producer: Prince | Artist: Jill Jones (Prince crossed out) | Engineers: "David
   Z" Rivkin and Coke Johnson

> *Creating music is really like giving birth. Music is like the universe: The sounds are like the planets, the air and the light fitting together.*[24]
>
> —Prince

It is unlikely that Prince attended this brief session, so after 5 hours of David Z overseeing Jill Jones's singing, a single C-60 cassette was created of the rough mix with her vocals for Prince to review.

THURSDAY, FEBRUARY 20, 1986

"Euphoria Highway" (various overdubs, mix)
"Euphoria Highway" [instrumental] (mix)
Jill Jones album assembled
Sunset Sound, Studio 3 | 1:00 p.m.–5:00 a.m. (booked: lockout)
Producers: Prince ("David Z" Rivkin also listed) | Artist: Jill Jones | Engineer:
    Coke Johnson

> *Fargnoli, Cavallo and Ruffalo always wanted a record. They*
> *wanted something. But I also think that when we started hang-*
> *ing out, or going out again, Prince couldn't relax into a rela-*
> *tionship and just be like, "You do your thing, I'll do mine." He*
> *had to start trying to put you to work, or find something to keep*
> *a level of normal separation, or to get distance again, because*
> *emotionally he would be responsible. He was less responsible for*
> *your emotions if he was more responsible for your record. That*
> *was easier to handle.*

—Jill Jones

Prince spent the first 4 hours continuing to overdub additional musical elements to "Euphoria Highway," before assembling Jill Jones's album. During
the first assembly of the evening, he updated the mixes on several of the tracks
and worked to blend them together when needed. At this point, the lineup
likely included: "Intro"/"Mia Bocca," "G-Spot," "With You," "Boom, Boom
(Can't You Feel The Beat Of My Heart)," "Rough," "Baby, You're A Trip," "4
Love," "My Man," and "Euphoria Highway."

After 3 hours of compiling the album, Prince left the studio, probably to
listen to the songs in his car. When he returned to the studio at midnight, they
worked on *another* assembly and five C-60 cassettes were created of the latest
attempt. The 16-hour session ended at 5 in the morning.

It is possible that Prince also created an instrumental version of "Euphoria High-
way" at some point, if not today, then during this week.

FRIDAY, FEBRUARY 21, 1986

"Rough" [listed as **"Too Rough"**] (remix)
Jill Jones album assembled
Sunset Sound, Studio 3 | 4:00 p.m.–12:30 a.m. (booked: lockout)
Producers: Prince ("David Z" Rivkin also listed) | Artist: Jill Jones |
    Engineer: Coke Johnson

> *We put the album together and then after the fact Prince went*
> *"This song needs this; this song needs that" and we went and*
> *remixed and re-recorded over some of the stuff.*[25]
>
> —"David Z" Rivkin

Once again, Prince had more ideas about Jill Jones's album, and spent almost an entire session reworking "Rough" and likely a few other songs. As always, changes like these were to be expected, even after everyone seemed happy with the results, according to David Z. "Prince decided it needed more work or songs. We don't go, 'What?' We go, 'Yes, Okay!'"[26]

"There you are, cutting up your mixes, so if he changes the sequence at any time, you have to have those original pieces that can all be put back together," remembers Susan Rogers. "Because if you've done this beautiful crossfade between song A and song B and later on he decides, 'No, I don't like that order, you've got to redo it. His artistry was always on display, but I hadn't worked with anyone before or since who put the same amount of dedication and care into sequencing an album. He really wanted people to experience side A and side B in order, and in the days of vinyl, he had a 35-minute story in mind."

Three C-60 cassettes were made of today's session.

SATURDAY, FEBRUARY 22, 1986

"Mia Bocca" (remix)
Jill Jones album assembled
"Venus De Milo" (possible mix)
"Love Or Money" (possible mix)
Sunset Sound, Studio 3 | 2:30 p.m.–2:00 a.m. (booked: lockout)
Producers: Prince ("David Z" Rivkin also listed) | Artist: Jill Jones | Engineer:
    Coke Johnson

*I thought it was a really cool album. Stuff like "Mia Bocca," I
thought was really different.*[27]

—"David Z" Rivkin

From 2:30 in the afternoon until 4, Jill Jones's album was reshuffled, but when
Prince heard "Mia Bocca" in context of the assembly, there was apparently
something that he wanted to improve, so he spent 2 hours overdubbing on the
track before adding it back into the assembly.

The next 8 hours were spent compiling Jill's album once more. "All Day,
All Night" may have been added to the assembly, but it is unclear what songs
were eliminated or if the order of the tracks was shuffled. The rest of the session
was spent creating a unique mix of a track or two (likely "Love or Money" and
"Venus De Milo") for *Under The Cherry Moon*. Two C-60 and two C-90 cassettes were created of the day's work and the session ended at 2 in the morning.

THURSDAY, FEBRUARY 27, 1986

"For Love" [previously listed as "**4 Love**"] (overdub and mix)
Sunset Sound, Studio 3 | 11:00 p.m.–7:00 a.m. (booked: lockout)
Producer: Prince | Artist: Jill Jones | Engineer: Coke Johnson

*Mixing with Prince was awesome. He knew how he wanted it
to sound.*

—Coke Johnson

Generally Prince mixed a track at the end of the night and listened to a cassette
of the song in his car. If he wasn't happy with the mix, he'd get rid of the tape
by throwing it into his back seat or—according to legend—out the window of
his car. He'd often work on a new mix the following day, but on occasion Prince
would let something sit for months and then get the tape out of storage, listen
again, and decide to update it as needed.

For this session, Prince asked to begin at 6:30 p.m. but he didn't arrive until
11, which gave Johnson several hours to get the room ready for the mix. Once
Prince reviewed "For Love," he decided to overdub elements of the song and
create a new mix. Eight hours were spent tweaking the song and at the end of
the session, two C-60 cassettes were made, but once again Prince would be

unhappy with the results and would decide to continue working on it when he returned to Sunset Sound a few hours later.

FRIDAY, FEBRUARY 28, 1986

"For Love" [listed as **"4 Love"**] (mix)
"Living Doll" (edits and mix)
Sunset Sound, Studio 3 | 5:00 p.m.–11:30 p.m. (booked: lockout)
Producer: Prince | Artist: Jill Jones (Prince crossed out) | Engineer: Coke Johnson

> *He had a weird thing. It was always power struggles and con-trol to see if you would do what he said. And soon, I just stopped answering. In those late hours, those morning hours, because it was just too much. I couldn't do it. It was one great way to get him off the track, but he actually did not like that. He liked people kissing his ass. He likes it. And if you don't kiss it enough the way he wants it, you're not around.*
>
> —Jill Jones

When Prince worked on an album, the tone was often discovered as the project materialized, but with Jill Jones's album Prince seemed to be struggling and was going back several months and adding "Living Doll," a track he'd recorded the previous spring.

"The only thing I didn't like was *being* a living doll," declared Jones. "I tried to not take all those things and make them literal translations of myself, because they were songs that objectified certain things. It was the deeper songs, like 'Violet Blue' and other things, that I thought had more meat to them." "Living Doll" was added, but within a few months, world events would make Prince reevaluate the use of the song on her album.

Work continued on "Living Doll" and "For Love," but by the end of this ab-breviated shift, no decisions had been made about their use on the album. Two C-60 cassettes were created of the songs, and the following day, Prince would bring both songs back into the studio for additional attention.

The album bounced around creatively, but David Z and Jill had a lot of latitude when it came to their sound, according to Jones. "I think Prince also trusted me to go my way, because once Miles Davis actually gave it the stamp of approval. We played it for him, and it kind of was finished once Miles heard it, technically. Prince told me 'Miles loves you. He just loves you.'"

SUNSET SOUND

6650 SUNSET BLVD. • HOLLYWOOD, CALIF. 90028 • (213) 469-11{

J. NO.		SESSION DATE	ATTENTION:		W.O.
LA18731		12-26-85	Roz Schrank		
STUDIO USED	ARTIST		CLIENT:		
3	PRINCE		WARENR BROS. RECORDS		
PRODUCER	ENGINEER				
PRINCE	Susan Rogers/Coke J.				
TIME BOOKED	ASSISTANT ENGINEER				
	Coke Johnson				

DESCRIPTION OF WORK

TITLES: "A Couple Miles" "Can I Play With You"

STUDIO TIME:

	FROM	TO	HRS.	@
Tracking ①	FROM 2ºº pm	TO 8ºº pm	HRS. 6.0	@
Tracking ②	FROM 8ºº	TO 1ºº am	HRS. 5.0	@
Vocal ods	FROM 1ºº am	TO 2ºº am	HRS. 1.0	@
Ruffs	FROM 2ºº am	TO 2³º am	HRS. 0.5	@ 1.00
	FROM	TO	HRS.	@
	FROM	TO	HRS.	@
	FROM	TO	HRS.	@
	FROM	TO	HRS.	@
	FROM	TO	HRS.	@
	FROM	TO	HRS.	@
	FROM	TO	HRS.	@

OUTBOARD EQUIPMENT:			MATERIALS:	
	@	$		@
Ratta AMS Rev	@ 125	$ 125		@
Ratta Quantec	@ 150	$ 150	1) 2" 456	@ 175
Fairlight	@	$		@
SIR Dx7	@	$		@
SIR OBX-A	@	$		@
SIR Strat	@	$		@

ADDITIONAL INFORMATION	SUNSET PERSONNEL		
FROM _____ TO _____	Engineering Services	12.5 hrs @	30 —
EXPLANATION:	Assistant Engineer Overtime	____ hrs @	
	Maintenance Services	____ hrs @	
		____ hrs @	
			AMOUNT
			SALES TAX
	Food		OTHER
			OTHER
ORIGINAL WORK ORDER			TOTAL
	CLIENT SIGNATURE	Prince	
	all services are subjec		

Prince recorded "Can I Play With U?" and "A Couple Miles" at Sunset Sound to submit to Miles Davis, but he only added his trumpet to "Can I Play With U?". This session was soon followed by a jazz project Prince called The Flesh.
Courtesy of Sunset Sound

SUNSET SOUND

6650 SUNSET BLVD. • HOLLYWOOD, CALIF. 90028 • (213) 469-1186

P.O. NO. *LA 19510*		SESSION DATE 4/22/86	ATTENTION:	W.O. NO.
STUDIO USED III	ARTIST *Prince*		CLIENT: *WB. Re*	
PRODUCER *Prince*	ENGINEER *C Johnson*			
TIME BOOKED	ASSISTANT ENGINEER			

DESCRIPTION OF WORK

TITLES: "Mountains" "LP Comp."

STUDIO TIME:

	FROM		TO		HRS.		@	$
Edits & Playback	FROM 2⁰⁰		TO 7⁰⁰		HRS. 5.0		@ 125—	$
+ Copies	FROM		TO		HRS.		@	$
	FROM		TO		HRS.		@	$
	FROM		TO		HRS.		@	$
	FROM		TO		HRS.		@	$
	FROM		TO		HRS.		@	$
	FROM		TO		HRS.		@	$
	FROM		TO		HRS.		@	$
	FROM		TO		HRS.		@	$
	FROM		TO		HRS.		@	$

OUTBOARD EQUIPMENT:			MATERIALS:		
AMS Rev	@	$		@	$
Quantec	@	$		@	$
	@	$		@	$
	@	$		@	$
	@	$		@	$
	@	$		@	$

ADDITIONAL INFORMATION	SUNSET PERSONNEL		
FROM _____ TO _____	Engineering Services	5 hrs @ 30—	$
EXPLANATION:	Assistant Engineer Overtime	___ hrs @ ___	$
	Maintenance Services	___ hrs @ ___	$
		___ hrs @ ___	$
		AMOUNT	$
		SALES TAX	$
		OTHER	$
		OTHER	$
		TOTAL	$

ORIGINAL WORK ORDER

CLIENT SIGNATURE _____

all services are subject to the

Prince worked on the 12-inch remix for "Mountains" and assembled a version of his *Dream Factory* project on this date. Three of the songs on this unreleased compilation were included on his next album, *Sign O' The Times. Courtesy of Sunset Sound*

NO.	SESSION DATE	ATTENTION:	W.O. NC
LA20060	7-17-86	EMY	2277

STUDIO USED	ARTIST	CLIENT:
3	PRINCE	WARNER RECORDS

PRODUCER	ENGINEER	
PRINCE	COKE JOHNSON	
TIME BOOKED	ASSISTANT ENGINEER	
LOCKOUT	-----	

DESCRIPTION OF WORK

TITLES: Joy in Repetition

STUDIO TIME:

	FROM	TO	HRS.	@	$
Set up	FROM 3⁰⁰ p	TO 3³⁰ p	HRS.	1-a3 @	$
Tracking	FROM 3³⁰ p	TO 5⁰⁰ p	1.5 HRS.	1-b3 @	$
O.D's	FROM 5⁰⁰ p	TO 12ᵐ	7 HRS.	1-c3 @	$
Vocals	FROM 12⁰⁰ m	TO 4⁰⁰ a	4 HRS.	1-c3 @	$
Mixing	FROM 4⁰⁰ a	TO 5⁰⁰ a	1 HRS.	1-d3 @	$
Copies	FROM 5⁰⁰ a	TO 5³⁰ a	.5 HRS.	1-j3 @ (125)	$
	FROM	TO	HRS.	@	$
	FROM	TO	HRS.	@	$
	FROM	TO	HRS.	@	$
	FROM	TO	HRS.	@	$

OUTBOARD EQUIPMENT:			MATERIALS:		
	@	$		@	$
Ratta AMS Rev	@	$	1- Scotch 250 2"	@ 3-A2	$
Ratta Quantec	@ 4-2A	$	2- Scotch ½	@ 3-B2	$
Tutti's Lim Drum	@ 4-2I	$	2- TDK C-60's	@ 3-D1	$
	@	$		@	$
	@	$		@	$
	@	$		@	$

ADDITIONAL INFORMATION	SUNSET PERSONNEL		
FROM _____ TO _____	Engineering Services 14 hrs @ 2-E3		$
EXPLANATION:	Assistant Engineer Overtime ___ hrs @ _____		$
	Maintenance Services ___ hrs @ _____		$
	___ hrs @ _____		$
		AMOUNT	$
		SALES TAX	$
	4-C	OTHER	$
		OTHER	$
		TOTAL	$

ORIGINAL
WORK ORDER

CLIENT SIGNATURE _____

all services are subject to the

Prince recorded "Joy In Repetition" on July 17, 1986. The track would not be released until 1990 on *Graffiti Bridge*, a testament to some of the treasures he had in his vault. *Courtesy of Sunset Sound*

SUNSET SOUND

6650 SUNSET BLVD. • HOLLYWOOD, CALIF. 90028 • (213) 469-1186

J. NO. LA-20616	SESSION DATE 10/18/86	ATTENTION: Roz Schrank	W.O. NO.
STUDIO USED 3	ARTIST PRINCE	CLIENT: WB Records	
PRODUCER PRINCE	ENGINEER Rogers/Johnson		
TIME BOOKED Lockout	ASSISTANT ENGINEER ---------		

DESCRIPTION OF WORK

TITLES: House Quake

STUDIO TIME:

	FROM	TO	HRS.	@	$
Setup	FROM 9³⁰ A	TO 10³⁰	HRS. 1-23	@	$
Trackin	FROM 10³⁰	TO 5³⁰	HRS. 1-63	@	$
Edits	FROM 5³⁰	TO 9³⁰	HRS. 1-23	@	$
Mixing	FROM 9³⁰	TO 1³⁰ A	HRS. 1-d3	@	$
	FROM	TO	HRS.	@	$
	FROM	TO	HRS.	@	$
	FROM	TO	HRS.	@	$
	FROM	TO	HRS.	@	$
	FROM	TO	HRS.	@	$
	FROM	TO	HRS.	@	$

OUTBOARD EQUIPMENT:

	@	$
	@	$
	@	$
	@	$
	@	$
	@	$
	@	$

MATERIALS:

	@		$
2 - Scotch 2"	@ 3-A2	$
3 - Scotch ½	@ 3-B2	$
10 film	@ 3-F1	$
1 - C-60	@ 3-D1	$
	@	$
	@	$

ADDITIONAL INFORMATION

FROM _____ TO _____

EXPLANATION:

SUNSET PERSONNEL

Engineering Services	15 hrs @ 2-E3	$
Assistant Engineer Overtime	_____ hrs @ _____	$
Maintenance Services	_____ hrs @ _____	$
	_____ hrs @ _____	$

	AMOUNT	$
	SALES TAX	$
4-C	OTHER	$
	OTHER	$
	TOTAL	$

ORIGINAL
WORK ORDER

CLIENT SIGNATURE _____ Prince

all services are subject to tl

Prince officially announced that he was disbanding the Revolution, and the following morning he started recording the party anthem, "Housequake." "I could tell there was something wrong," reflected engineer Susan Rogers. "He was off—he was different, there was a silent wall that was basically saying, 'Don't even ask.'" *Courtesy of Sunset Sound*

August 14, 1986. The final show of a sold out 3 night stay at Wembley Arena in London, England. Over his career, Prince would perform at Wembley 35 times. *Photo by Michael Putland*

August 14, 1986. Wembley Arena. **"If you tour too much as an artist**," Prince explained, **"you will burn up all your energy**." *Photo by Michael Putland*

August 14, 1986. Wembley Arena. "Prince felt that the production of the *Purple Rain* tour was regimented," explained tour manager Alan Leeds. "*Parade* was going to be his anti-tour. Normal clothes, i.e. straight hair and a suit, stripped down, no props, real back-to-basics, old-fashioned funk-rock'n'roll tour." *Photo by Michael Putland*

On August, 14, 1986, Sting and Ron Wood (in stripes behind Prince) joined Prince and the Revolution on stage for a version of the Rolling Stones' "Miss You." "When he went to invite these artists on the stage," reflected bandmember BrownMark, "We're sitting back like, 'Whoa! That's Ron Wood. That's Sting!' He invited them all up and we would just be blown away, but for him it was nothing. It was nothing." *Photo by Michael Putland*

August 14, 1986. Wembley Arena. "Musically, it was magical. We were playing better than ever, going to places we'd never visited," reflected Revolution guitarist Wendy Melvoin about the *Parade* tour. *Photo by Michael Putland*

Inside studio 3 at Sunset Sound in Los Angeles, home of the Flesh sessions which featured Prince, Wendy, Lisa, Sheila E., Jonathan Melvoin, Levi Seacer Jr., and Eric Leeds. It is also where he recorded most of the *Parade* album. *Photo by Duane Tudahl*

"[Prince] was recording the *Dream Factory* record, and he asked me to paint the album cover," recalls Susannah Melvoin, "and I have it still to this day." At the time this was requested, it is likely that the *Dream Factory* project was going to be released under the name "The Flesh." *Courtesy of Susannah Melvoin*

Set list for Prince's March 3, 1986 performance. This was his first full concert since the *Purple Rain* tour, the debut of the expanded Revolution, and a peek at the music from his *Parade* album. "It was a challenge to keep up with him," according to new band member Matt Blistan. "He always called things. We had everything from hand signals to verbal cues and you're always on top of your toes. That particular concert was more or less another rehearsal." *Courtesy of Scott Bogen, special thanks to Chrissie Dunlap*

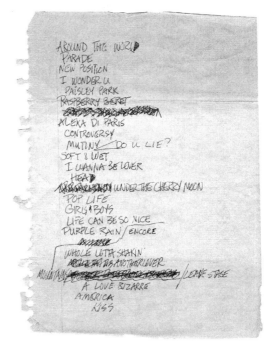

MARCH 1986

"Can I Play With U?" (overdubs, edits, and mix)
"For Love" (listed as **"4 Love"**) (mix, edits)
"Living Doll" (mix, edits)
Jill Jones album compiled
Sunset Sound, Studio 3 | 12:00 noon–1:00 a.m. (booked: lockout)
Producer: Prince | Artist: Jill Jones (Prince crossed out) | Engineer: Coke
   Johnson

> *I remember Prince's reaction when he got the tape* [of "Can I
> Play With U?"] *back—he wasn't enthralled with it. That wasn't
> a reflection of Miles's playing, but more about the composition
> and the significance of the quality of the track in itself.*[1]
>
> —Alan Leeds

Miles Davis recorded his trumpet on Prince's "Can I Play With U?", and
returned it for input, but Prince seemed underwhelmed, not by Davis's performance, but second guessing the original track and about its inclusion in Davis's
next album, *Tutu*. "Prince came to me and Matt Blistan and asked our opinion
of it," says Eric Leeds. "If Prince was going to ask me that, it meant he wasn't
100 percent sure it was great. I said, 'If you're going to do something with Miles,
this shouldn't be it.' And he agreed."[2]

"Prince was really influential to us during that Warner Bros. period. Miles really dug what he was doing at that time So they handed ['Can I Play With U?'] to me and had me mix it to work into the *Tutu* album,"[3] explained Davis's producer, Marcus Miller. "Prince was singing, killing it too, but there wasn't an actual part for Miles. I tried to open some space on it for Miles . . . and we recorded his horn [in February 1986]. Prince heard it again, what we did, and even he realized that it didn't sound as if it belonged on *Tutu*, and maybe we shouldn't use it."[4]

Prince's insecurity about "Can I Play With U?" revealed a vulnerability that he rarely displayed. "It was the first time that I saw Prince swallow the criticism and just go in and see what he could do," recognizes Susannah Melvoin.

Prince updated "Can I Play With U?" during this session, adding overdubs, new lyrics, and a variety of other elements, but despite the effort, Prince decided against allowing the song to be released by Davis.

Work was also wrapped on this phase of Jill Jones's album with a few final edits on "Living Doll" and "For Love," and a quick mix before creating her latest compilation. Five C-60 and two C-90 cassettes were dubbed, and the session wrapped at 1 a.m. It is unclear what songs were on this collection, but the album at this point was erratic and lacked focus.

"There was too much going on for him," discloses Wendy. "I think he was scattered. I think there was just too much happening at once and Lisa and I used to talk about it all the time You're just putting too much out. You're releasing too much. Got too many bands. You've got your hands in too much."

Because of his schedule, it was inevitable that Jill Jones's album was getting pushed aside. Prince was in the middle of editing *Under The Cherry Moon* and after this shift he flew home to continue rehearsing with the band, which was about to debut his new tour in two days.

Status: Today's mix of "Can I Play With U?" (6:34) remained unreleased during Prince's lifetime, but was included on the *Sign O' The Times* Super Deluxe Edition in 2020.

"There's an awful lot of confusion about the collaborations with Prince and Miles Davis, but 'Can I Play With U?' is the only song which Prince ever gave to Miles to put trumpet on, other than the song 'Sticky Wicked,' which was for Chaka Khan and would come out on her *CK* album in 1988. But this was the only song of Prince's, other than that one that Miles ever put his trumpet on."[5]

Miles Davis would perform with Prince at Paisley Park in 1987, but unfortunately, further collaborations between Prince and Davis never materialized, as Eric Leeds explains:

> After all of this, in 1990, or '91, Miles was really adamant about wanting Prince to produce him. And Prince would not. And Prince came to me and said, "Miles is bugging me to produce him." And I looked at Prince, I said, "Dude, what the hell is wrong with you?" And Prince told me, "Eric, I can't go in the studio and tell Miles what to do." And I said, "Why not? You do it with everyone else. It's not about you telling Miles what to do. He's looking for you to provide a musical environment, where he's going to do what he does." "But he wants something different." "That's the whole point! As a composer, as a conceptualist, he wants you to get in the studio, to provide him with an atmosphere that's going to be different." Prince would not do it. So what did Prince do? He asked me, "I need you to do some tracks for Miles." And I said, "Prince, Miles isn't asking me to do tracks for him." And he said, "Well, I want you to." So I went in and did two tracks for Miles.

Miles had reportedly expressed interest in Prince's "Nothing Compares 2 U" so an updated version, and Eric Leeds's song, "Frame Of Mind," were tracked and mixed on January 22, 1991, but they were never released with Davis playing on them.

MONDAY, MARCH 3, 1986

Venue: First Avenue (Minneapolis, Minnesota)
Capacity: 1,600 (1,414 tickets sold + guestlist, sold out)

> *Prince, being such a strong frontman, he could have a lot of strange characters surrounding him and still be the center of everything.*[6]
>
> —Lisa Coleman

This performance would be his first full concert at First Avenue since before the *Purple Rain* tour and expectations were high. It was a new expanded band, and he was launching a new album soon, so there was a lot riding on this show. It is surprising that they hadn't rehearsed more, and that little planning was done for the show. He'd scheduled the performance earlier in the day by having his assistant Karen Krattinger reach out to book the venue for the evening. Even Prince mentioned his lack of prep from the stage at the start of the show when he explained, **"We've only been rehearsing about a week, so we are a little rusty."**[7]

"It was a challenge to keep up with him," according to new band member Matt "Atlanta Bliss" Blistan. "He always called things. We had everything from hand signals to verbal cues and you're always on top of your toes. That particular concert was more or less another rehearsal."[8]

"[Prince] pushed himself constantly, so he would push everybody else," explained his lighting director Roy Bennett. "But he also could see in you your capabilities. He pushed you knowing that you were giving all that you could. And I'm always so grateful for that."[9]

The concert ended up being a mixture of brilliant, awkward, and beautiful with the debut of nine of the twelve album cuts, an upcoming B-side ("Alexa De Paris"), a cover ("Whole Lotta Shakin' Goin' On"), five numbers from *Around The World In A Day* ("Raspberry Beret," "Pop Life," "America," "Paisley Park," and the album's title track), as well as a few songs he'd written for others ("A Love Bizarre" and "Mutiny"), blended with a handful of older tracks. The most noticeable curiosity in the set list was the inclusion of "Purple Rain," which was the only song performed from that movie's soundtrack. The lineup was a serious indication that Prince had moved on from the *Purple Rain* era and wanted to shine a bright spotlight on where he was now.

The show was so loose that the band started "Alexa De Paris" prematurely, with Prince saying: "Chill. You forgot one," then guiding the group to perform "Raspberry Beret," followed by a proper "Alexa De Paris."

Prince used the show as a way of throwing shade at "St. Paul" Peterson for leaving the Family the previous fall. During "Mutiny"—which was originally written as a slight at Morris Day for leaving the Time—Prince added a line from "Dream Factory" and featured the "St. Paul, punk of the month" chant that was edited from the song. "I was there and he knew I was there," remembered Peterson. "I knew he was going to do some sort of public retaliation, so it didn't surprise me at all. So I had fun with it, and had tee shirts made up. I thought it was funny."[10]

Paul wasn't the only one to feel Prince's indignation. Multiple verbal shots were fired at Jimmy Jam, and during "Head" Prince mocked Morris Day's "Oak Tree" by threatening to chop it down and make a wooden leg out of it, followed by a playfully snide performance of the "wooden leg" dance. Morris Day and Paul Peterson would continue to be targets of mockery during upcoming shows.

What is ironic is that Prince was considered to be one of the most dynamic performers in musical history, but he also reportedly hid a fear of performing. "He has stage fright," explains his guitar technician Michael Soltys. "That's why he likes so much light in his face. He doesn't want to see the crowd. And he's really great to be with in a small group of people that he knows well."

"He was always nervous before a show until he got on stage and the lights came up," confirmed current band member, Wally Safford. "He would drink hot tea to settle his stomach before every concert."[11]

Prince seemed to address this during the final encore of the night before "Kiss." **"I just wanted to say something . . . in all seriousness, and in all honesty. . . . Sometimes when you stand up here, you know when I'm here, and, I get real jittery 'cause of this** [motions to crowd], **and it just feels really nice. That's all I can say. See, what it is, love will make you shake, you know what I'm saying? In all forms of the word."**[12]

He also hinted to the crowd about Paisley Park Studios which was still under construction. **"Listen, I've just got a few more things I gotta do, and then when I do 'em, I'm going to come back here and I'm going to build a big clubhouse so we can all hang out like this every day. I'm going to do it, or I'm going to die trying."**[13]

TUESDAY, MARCH 4, 1986

Mazarati's self-titled debut album was released on Paisley Park Records. Although Prince worked on several of the tracks, it was his song "100 MPH"—which was released as the third single from the album—that got the most attention. Unfortunately, the album stalled at number 133 on the *Billboard* Pop Chart and 49 on the Black Chart. Mazarati was BrownMark's project and he explains why he felt the album didn't connect. "Paisley Park was a new label, and it just didn't have the staff. Prince has a terrible habit of running a one-man show, and it is very hard for him, which I understand totally. It was hard to delegate, and so it was a back and forth thing with us, my management and WB to try to get things to happen."

WEDNESDAY, MARCH 5, 1986

The 12-inch version of "Kiss," backed by "Love Or Money," was released.

THURSDAY, MARCH 6, 1986

Venue: Universal Amphitheatre (Universal City, California)
Capacity: 6,189 (likely sold out)

Sheila E. was on tour promoting her second album and Prince joined her onstage at the Universal Amphitheatre to perform on "Head," a cover of Janet Jackson's "What Have You Done For Me Lately?," "Holly Rock," "Kiss," and a duet with Sheila on "A Love Bizarre."

After the show, Prince met up with former Miss America Vanessa Williams who was going to sign with Capitol Records to record an album to be produced by George Clinton. Alan Leeds recalls the conversations that inspired this meeting. "George was looking for material, and wanted to know if Prince would be interested in submitting some material to produce Vanessa Williams on. I went to Prince and he gave us a couple of unreleased Jill Jones songs, 'Eternity' and 'Euphoria Highway.' They were backstage and I think that's when I gave them the tape. The long and short of it is, she never signed with Capitol, he never produced her, that whole thing just kind of went away."[14]

FRIDAY, MARCH 7, 1986

Venue: Universal Amphitheatre (Universal City, California)
Capacity: 6,189 (likely sold out)

Prince joined Sheila E. onstage once more, this time performing on "Head," "Kiss," and "A Love Bizarre."

SATURDAY, MARCH 8, 1986

Venue: Warfield Theatre (San Francisco, California)
Capacity: 2,185 (sold out)

Prince and the Revolution joined Sheila E. onstage during the first of two sold out shows at the Warfield Theatre, in San Francisco, performing on "A Love

Bizarre" (with included parts of "All Day, All Night," the "wooden leg" dance mocking Morris Day's "Oak Tree," the "St. Paul, punk of the month" chant from "Dream Factory"), and "Kiss." The show was videotaped and his duet with Sheila on "A Love Bizarre" would be edited down and released on her home video, *Romance 1600 Live*. The show was directed by Daniel Kleinman, who would also direct the upcoming concert in Detroit, and oversee the principal photography for the *Sign O' The Times* movie in 1987.

The following day members of the band traveled back to Minneapolis, likely for additional rehearsals, and Prince flew to Los Angeles to record new music and continue overseeing the editing of *Under The Cherry Moon*.

MONDAY, MARCH 10, 1986 (ESTIMATE)

"Visions" (tracking)
Various other piano tracks
Galpin Blvd. home studio (Chanhassen, Minnesota)
Producer: Lisa Coleman | Artist: Lisa Coleman | Engineer: Susan Rogers

> *Prince had been thinking of doing piano interludes on a record. He had just got a new grand piano in his house. I played ["Visions"] once and that's what that is. I haven't played it since. We were just testing out the set up.*[15]

—Lisa Coleman

No matter how talented Prince was, there were people who he depended on to bring him something that he might not otherwise hear. Whether it was to inspire him or to fill in the spaces that he couldn't, he surrounded himself with people like Lisa who he could rely on to surprise him, explains Peggy Leonard. "I think Lisa complemented him. If he was stuck on something, she could pick up the riff and do it, and I know that he treated her differently. He respected her. It was more of an equality with her."

"Working with Prince was so exciting because he did everything himself," reflected Lisa. "He had a studio in his basement and he even had me recording him on the drums or punching him in to play a guitar part and it just became like a Crayon in his box. It was something that you can just grab and use it the way you wanted to use. It was fantastic and he even let me use the studio by myself once I learned all this, how it was all hooked up and he would just leave me in there, like, 'Go ahead and fool around.' He'd go take a nap or something. Yes, he took naps."[16]

For this session, Prince asked Lisa and Susan Rogers to record some music on his new piano. "We were just testing out the gear. Susan recorded it and mic'd the piano," recalled Lisa. "Prince wasn't there. He just asked us to do something. He said, 'Make them two and half minute pieces.' So I recorded a few and that's what 'Visions' is."[17]

Status: "Visions" (2:12) was scheduled to be on the *Dream Factory* album, but after that album was cancelled and repurposed, it was never issued by Prince. In 1990, Wendy and Lisa included this composition (now renamed "Minneapolis #1") as the first track on a limited edition bonus CD included with their third album, *Eroica*, along with three other piano instrumentals, possibly recorded at the same time, titled "Minneapolis #2," "Eric's Ghost," and "C-Ya." It was released on the *Sign O' The Times* Super Deluxe Edition in 2020.

The date on this recording is unclear, and it is possible to have been tracked any time in March or April 1986 but is likely around this date as they were setting up the piano in Prince's home while the band was rehearsing without Prince.

TUESDAY, MARCH 11, 1986

"Twosday" (tracking, overdubs, mix)
"Fun Love" (tracking, overdubs, mix)
"Fun Love" [instrumental] (probable mix)
Sunset Sound, Studio 3 | 12:00 noon–11:30 p.m. (booked: lockout)
Producer: Prince | Artist: Prince | Engineer: Coke Johnson

Music is music, ultimately. If it makes you feel good, cool.[18]

—Prince

Prince's mind was still very much on *Under The Cherry Moon,* so most of the music he was recording during this time was written for the film. For 10 hours, Prince worked on two new songs: "Fun Love," a playful song that contains a mention of Mary Sharon, the lead character in the movie, and "Twosday," reportedly an instrumental that had likely gotten its title from the current day of the week.

326

For the final 90 minutes of the session, mixes of the songs, and probably an instrumental version of "Fun Love," were created and recorded to cassette. Five C-60 and two C-90 tapes were used, so it is also likely that Prince had Johnson make copies of an assembly of a larger collection as well, perhaps Jill Jones's album, but it is unknown what those extra cassettes contained.

Prince continued to check in on the editing of his movie, but he also had obligations in Minneapolis, so he flew home to rehearse with the band and record on the new console Susan Rogers was installing in his Galpin Blvd. home studio.

Status: "Fun Love" and "Twosday" would both be revisited later in the month. They remained unreleased during Prince's lifetime.

THURSDAY, MARCH 13, 1986

"The Ballad Of Dorothy Parker" (tracking, overdubs, mix)
Galpin Blvd. home studio (Chanhassen, Minnesota)
Producer: Prince | Artist: Prince | Engineer: Susan Rogers

There are no accidents, and if there are, it's up to us to look at them as something else.[19]

—Prince

After months of preparation, Prince's new home studio was ready to go, and according to Susan Rogers, Prince was excited and couldn't wait to take it for a test drive. "God, he was happy when that studio came online. He had waited so long for that console, and the house was nice, so we got a lot of work done there. The console was the same as the one he loved at Sunset Sound. That he could make recordings that were near that same quality at home meant a great deal to him."

Now that a state of the art studio was 20 feet from his room, he could literally roll out of bed, plug in and record his dreams, and that is exactly what he did. As he had done in the past with tracks like "Manic Monday," Prince composed a song in his sleep, and once again it was about a working woman, but on this number, she was a waitress who enticed him to join her in the bathtub. As soon as he woke up, Prince wanted to get the music to tape immediately, so he quickly scratched out the lyrics to "The Ballad Of Dorothy Parker." Susan Rogers recalled Prince's methods on days like this.

If he came in with lyrics written, like he did with "Dorothy Parker," or with a song that he was going to play acoustic drums on, he would take the lyrics and he'd either tape them to a tom, if he wasn't going to play a tom; or I'd tape them to a mic stand in front of the kit. He would wear headphones and with no click, reading the lyrics, he would play the entire drum part from top to bottom with the fills and the breaks and everything, just mentally singing the song in his head. He'd lay down this acoustic drum track, come into the control room, lay down the bass and then everything else, and then eventually sing it. He would have, not full arrangements in his head, but he'd have basic arrangements in his head as he was making the track. He knew what he wanted it to sound like.[20]

"The fellow who designed this console, whose name was Frank DeMedio, came in from Los Angeles," Rogers adds. "He was hooking it all up and Prince couldn't take it anymore. He says, 'Just send him home. I just got to work.' We put Frank on a plane and we sent him home, and Prince came downstairs and said the magic words: 'Fresh tape.' I put up fresh tape, and we started recording the song."[21]

I hadn't finished testing the audio wiring or anything; in other words I had just soldered the last connection. As always, he's playing every instrument and I'm just panicking on the inside because something doesn't sound right—it's really dull, there's no high end and I can't wait for this song to be finished because I've got to check it out and see what's going on. Of course the song is coming out really well and the whole time I'm thinking, "I wish he would just stop," but that's not going to happen. The whole time he hasn't even said anything, hadn't even commented on it and I know he hears it, but he's really happy because he likes this song. At the very end, he gave me my final instructions and he said, "There's something about this console that doesn't sound like the one at Sunset Sound, it's really dull," and then he goes upstairs and goes to bed. I'm thinking, "Hell yeah it's dull, there's no high end at all!" But he conceived of the song in a dream so he didn't mind that at all because it gave it this dreamy-like quality.[22]

Rogers was able to ascertain the problem. "I got the voltmeter and saw that one half of the power supply's rails were down. Instead of bipolar [+/–] 15 volts, we just had 15 volts. We had half the headroom, and half the frequency response."[23]

According to Rogers this was an illustration about how it was the sculptor and not his expensive chisel that was responsible for the art. "He was a perfect example of an artist who didn't need to rely on any special kind of tool, any special conditions, any special kind of situations; he didn't believe in any voodoo or magic associated with the work. If you've got the goods you can show up at any studio with any console with any microphone and you can record under any circumstances if you're the real deal and that's how he was. He wasn't going to let a little thing like no high end stop him from making music."[24]

Like "Norwegian Wood (This Bird Has Flown)" by the Beatles, "The Ballad Of Dorothy Parker" chronicles a man who is having an affair. The lyrics are a playfully inventive way of hiding how far that the liaison went, and like the Beatles' track, it involves a bathtub.

"He's a clever lyricist, not a great writer of lyrics," continues Rogers, "and I wonder how he thinks of lyrics. Sometimes it is pure narrative. During 'Dorothy Parker,' he is telling a story, and there is an end. Other times he is just expressing an emotional desire or feeling and it is as simple as that."

"'Dorothy Parker' *is* storytelling, and he refers to Joni Mitchell and it's just really an incredible song that takes you places," reflected Bobby Z. "It's just brilliant songwriting. I've always liked it. When he respected someone, he wore it on his sleeve and he touted their music and loved their songs. Joni was obviously one of those people early on, and Carlos Santana early on, were some real heroes of his."[25]

"He loved her because what Joni gave to him was an open heart. So listening to her music brought his defenses down," related Wendy. "It's 100 percent true. He was not intimidated by her. He was *moved* by her."

"'The Ballad Of Dorothy Parker' is an homage to the music he loved," agreed Rogers. "He loved Kate Bush and Joni Mitchell. Prince had a strong feminine sensibility and those writers are sophisticated in a different way. He valued jazz chords and very poetic lyrics. Wendy and Lisa were fans of Joni Mitchell, but Prince was a huge fan."[26]

"**I love all Joni's music,**" Prince told the *Rocky Mountain News*. He also explained that he plays her songs, "**just to keep her name out there. Joni's music should be taught in school, if just from a literature standpoint.**"[27]

Prince was intimately familiar with Mitchell's music, but Susannah recalls how Dorothy Parker recently showed up on his radar. "He ended up knowing who Dorothy Parker was because of the amount of black and white films that we would watch when we were together. It wasn't until I turned him on to *The Philadelphia Story*, George Cukor films, and then we had a couple of encyclopedias and I think it was during this time I had one of old Hollywood, Dorothy Parker was in that."

"Even though Susannah wasn't a player, her involvement with Prince at that time, was equally as important as anything else, just because of the different background in music that they had," confirms Eric Leeds. "Coincidentally, it just really worked with where he was at, at the time."

Once again, Prince's story, his life and the world around him helped him give birth to his art. "He was so good at turning life into music," observed Rogers. "He made music out of the life he was living."[28]

Status: "The Ballad Of Dorothy Parker" (4:07) was released in 1987 on *Sign O' The Times*. Prince asked Clare Fischer to add an orchestra to a 5-minute plus version of the track but decided he preferred the shorter stripped down song and the Prince/Fischer "Dorothy Parker" remained unreleased during his lifetime.

FRIDAY, MARCH 14, 1986

"**Witness 4 The Prosecution**" (tracking, overdubs, and mix)
"**Movie Star**" (probable tracking, overdubs, and mix)
Galpin Blvd. home studio (Chanhassen, Minnesota)
Producer: Prince | Artist: Prince | Engineer: Susan Rogers

Imagine Morris Day doin' ["Movie Star"]*! That's who it was written 4—The Time.*[29]

—Prince

Prince would keep various people in his orbit just because he enjoyed their company. Maybe they reminded him of a certain time in his life, maybe they brought something special to him as a musician, or maybe he just enjoyed their company and their effect on his mood. Jerome Benton was one of those people who Prince seemed to enjoy having around. After the Time broke up, he was added to the *Purple Rain* tour and included in the Family. Once the Family collapsed, Prince invited him to join the upcoming tour as a dancer, but most importantly, he crafted *Under The Cherry Moon* to feature him. "Jerome was just a sweetheart of a person," according to Peggy Mac. "He was like Switzerland. He was always happy. He was always just one of those guys who was always a good guy, and he was funny and he never pulled an attitude. He always made people laugh and he didn't give Prince any ego trip. He did whatever Prince wanted and he was happy to do it."

"Jerome made him laugh all the time and he needed to laugh," remembers Susannah. "That relationship in *Under The Cherry Moon* was a lot like what they were in life."

"Prince enjoyed going out for 20 minutes to see what the vibe was," recalled Benton. "He got what he needed to get from 20 minutes of hanging out. I remember when we started meshing our relationship. We'd be in rehearsal and he'd be saying, 'We're gonna go out tonight.' I said, 'Okay, cool. Where are we going?' 'I'll come by and pick you up.'. . . and I'm waiting. Ten o'clock. I'm like, 'Okay, he should be here in a minute. Eleven o'clock. Okay. Where is he? Where is he at? Twelve o'clock . . .'"[30]

> He pulls up, now we're 35, 40 minutes from the club downtown. We pull up, double park in the no parking zone. Get out of the car. Of course, the bouncer opens the door and we walk right in. Get a quick drink, stand around for a minute. Feel the vibe. Prince was seeing what people loved, what turned people on. Honing all that stuff into a cache of what it was going to take to be successful. We jumped back in the car, we'd go to Perkins or we go to Rudolph's. We'd sit in the corner and he's vibing on what people experienced that night. And then we jumped back in the car and we rolled back through downtown looking at all the crowd clearing out from the clubs and we rode back either to the studio or he'll drop me off at the home. The next morning. He'd call me. "I want you to come by and listen to the song I did." So he was in his element of nurturing what he needed, to continue writing.[31]

During this session, Prince was seemingly inspired by a night similar to this when he wrote and recorded "Movie Star," a song that he indicated (in the liner notes of the 1998 *Crystal Ball* release) was created for the Time. On the recording, Prince talks about getting some "serious drawers" and even uses the Morris/old man voice when he says "mo' drawers." Although the Time had broken up two years earlier and showed no signs of reuniting, they were Prince's first real protégé band and his outlet for his funk and rock recordings. "Morris, especially Jerome. They meant a lot to him," confirms Susan Rogers.

> I think it was hard losing Morris, but I kind of thought that "Movie Star" was about his *own* longings. So many of his own longings he didn't want other people to know about, he didn't want people to associate with Prince, like that pimp persona that Morris exemplified. That was Prince. It sprang from Prince's mind, but he didn't want people to know that that was Prince, so he had this alter ego.

So, when he says, "I wrote 'Movie Star' for the Time," in some way, I'm guessing he might be protecting himself. He doesn't want you to know that's him.

Prince was seemingly inspiring himself because the phrase "makes you feel like a movie star" was in "Raspberry Beret." "Movie Star" also contained the expression "can I play with you," which is either a total coincidence, or an indication that Prince was thinking about the track he'd submitted to Miles Davis.

"Witness 4 The Prosecution"—the title reportedly based on the 1957 Billy Wilder movie starring Tyrone Power and Marlene Dietrich—was a song about a man's denial that he's done anything to hurt the object of his lifelong, obsessive love. The song starts off with a looped sample from the Fairlight that is shattered by the crisp sting of acoustic drums, thumb-plucked bass, and guitar.

Horns and background vocals would be added to the tracks a month later.

"Witness 4 The Prosecution" and "Movie Star" were mixed at the end of the evening.

Status: "Movie Star" (4:25) was included on Prince's *Crystal Ball* album in 1998. Although it was intended for the Time, it is unlikely that Morris Day added his vocals to the track. Miles Davis would perform "Movie Star" during his 1987 and 1988 tours.

The first version of "Witness 4 The Prosecution" (4:00) was never released by Prince but was issued as the first single for the posthumous *Sign O' The Time*s Super Deluxe Edition in 2020.

The theme of love being played out in a courtroom would be revisited on Prince's 1995 release, "Eye Hate U."

SATURDAY, MARCH 15, 1986

"**Movie Star**" (overdubs, mix)
"**The Ballad Of Dorothy Parker**" (overdubs, mix)
"**Witness 4 The Prosecution**" (overdubs, mix)
"**A Place In Heaven**" (tracking, overdubs, and mix)
"**Strange Relationship**" (possible overdubs, mix)
Galpin Blvd. home studio (Chanhassen, Minnesota)
Producer: Prince | Artist: Prince | Engineer: Susan Rogers

Prince was in a recording studio pretty much every day, because first of all, he could be, because he had his own studio by then, but the other thing was he didn't have anything else in his life that he had enough interest to do. So even on days when he might not have anything specific in his mind going on? He was still going to go in the studio, because "Well, what the hell else am I going to do today?"

—Eric Leeds

Unlike most recording studios, which are windowless vaults that mask the passing of time, Prince's new home studio allowed the sun to decorate the room with a warm, colorful light. "At the Galpin house, we had these beautiful stained-glass windows," reflects Susannah. "There were three panels and if you're facing the porch, behind you there was a silver light that would come up. The east morning sun would bring out the beauty. And then there was the drum room and in some of the tracking rooms, there were windows."

One of the by-products of the almost "church-like" atmosphere was "A Place In Heaven," which was tracked either late the previous day, or during this session. The song was another solo effort with Prince adding several Fairlight elements (bells, tympani, and harpsichord), piano, and a guide vocal for Lisa. "'A Place In Heaven' was a song that he intended for Lisa Coleman to sing," remembered Susan Rogers. "I had the impression that it was for a movie of some kind. Having Lisa sing that song could have been something for the female lead in this future movie that he had in his head. I don't know, but he just did a guide vocal on it."[32]

He would work on updating "Movie Star," which likely included recording the background vocals with Susannah and revisiting the mix. Several other recent tracks, including "The Ballad Of Dorothy Parker," and "Witness 4 The Prosecution" were given new mixes and "Strange Relationship," which he continued to take out of the vault and tweak, this time with edits and a new mix. "With 'Strange Relationship,' it was so good that every version worked," Rogers remembered fondly. "There were so many different permutations of that song, and I don't think I ever heard it sound bad. And I think it's another one of those things that was just really fun to take it out and play with it."

Prince enjoyed creating, but he also seemed to get pleasure from sharing songs with those in his inner circle, almost as if he was exposing an extension of himself to those he trusted. "There was a moment when we were all in the room and Prince pressed play and just said, 'Do you like it?'" Lisa recalled when she and Wendy heard "Witness 4 The Prosecution" for the first time. "That was good stuff."[33]

While traveling the following month, Prince would leave "Witness" and several of the other songs for Wendy, Lisa, Susannah, Eric, Atlanta Bliss, and Susan Rogers to add their colors to his paintings.

WEDNESDAY, MARCH 19, 1986

> **"And How"** (tracking, overdubs, mix)
> **"Power Fantastic"** (tracking, mix)
> **"Power Fantastic"** [instrumental] (probable mix)
> Galpin Blvd. home studio (Chanhassen, Minnesota)
> Producer: Prince | Artist: Prince and the Revolution | Engineer: Susan Rogers

I'm really proud of ["Power Fantastic"]. And I thought it was a beautiful collaboration between the three of us.[34]

—Lisa Coleman

Rehearsals for the upcoming tour were in full swing and the band was connected on a deeper level once again after some time apart. Prince was not only preparing the Revolution for a potential tour, he was actively recording at his home studio, but so far he was working mostly as a solo artist, and not as the leader of the band. "It was really a special day, because it was not often that he would have the Revolution come to his private space at the house," reflected Wendy. "Back in the day he would, but once things got really big with him, his home didn't really end up being the hangout zone like it used to. It was much quieter back in those times. So to all be together in his space was a special moment and not common. Kind of a rare moment."[35]

"There was a basement studio that had a large control room and a medium-sized isolation booth right next to it," remembers Susan Rogers. "The piano was upstairs and it was used for smaller projects. We tried to fit the whole band in there once, but it wasn't big enough for a band."[36]

The composition that Prince wanted to record with the band at his new home studio was "Power Fantastic," which was based on the instrumental recorded by Lisa and Wendy called "Carousel." "'Power Fantastic' was a song that the three of us wrote together, Wendy, Prince and myself," according to Lisa, "and the melody that he put on it was so beautiful."

"I didn't expect that he would write anything to it," she continues, "but then when he was like, 'Yeah, I wrote lyrics to it.' I was kind of amazed because I thought stylistically it was a little off. It's kind of jazzy or . . . I don't know what it is! I didn't think it was really a *Prince* song, but then when he added what he added and the way we did it, it fit right in, and I was like, 'Yeah, that *is* a Prince song.'"[37]

"The music was written by Lisa and Wendy," recalled Eric, "but was mistakenly attributed to Prince on the [Prince's *The Hits/The B-Sides*] album. It was a mistake because Prince knew that it was Wendy and Lisa's. Although I think Prince wrote the lyrics for the song, the music and the arrangement was basically Wendy and Lisa's and we rehearsed the song in the warehouse that afternoon."[38]

"After rehearsing he asked if it was possible to do the whole band at the house and I said: 'Well, I think so, I think we have everything we need,'" says Rogers. "We set up the band with Bobby downstairs on the drums, Lisa upstairs on the piano. We had horns on it and Prince was singing his vocal in the control room."[39] Eric, Matt Blistan, and Wendy would also record their respective sax, trumpet, and guitar parts from different sections of the house.

Considering that Prince had spent a great deal of time working with Sheila on the Flesh sessions earlier in the year, Bobby Z recalled that he enjoyed being an active part of the recording. "My involvement with *Parade* was meant to be isolated, because I wasn't really involved with the record and the film that much. But, the [upcoming] *Hit-and-Run* tour was something where I kind of came back into the fold. I really started recording with the band again and everything. I knew that, if this was going to be my last hurrah and if he still wanted me to do the tour, he still wanted me to be in the band, that it was kind of a vote of confidence still. And I was at my best, and totally kicked butt."[40]

Because the arrangement had been rehearsed in the afternoon, the recording went smoothly, especially considering that not everyone could see each other. Prince communicated over the headphones instructing them to spend the first minute warming up, ad-libbing to a peak and then to quietly resolve that brief section once they heard him whisper "shhh." "This whole song is pretty incredible, especially with the beginning like that," remembers Atlanta Bliss. "That's the noise of the world. It's just crazy and crazy and crazy and then all of a sudden it just focuses down. You turn out the lights, turn up the sound and we're really focused. It's everyone that's listening in the one spot. That's what music is about."[41]

"The song was recorded as I remember in one take," remembered Leeds, "and Prince did a scratch vocal, which he then replaced with his final vocal."[42]

The headphone communication helped bring everyone together, despite being scattered around his house, according to Lisa. "That's a great little peek into what we did, that's how we worked. He would be in our headphones and talk us through it. We needed the unifying voice in the headphones saying, 'Okay now do this,' because we couldn't see each other. So it was really odd."

Rogers recalled how the underequipped new studio provided her a unique vantage point for the recording. "The band was all set up in various parts of the house and Prince was going to be in the control room, singing, but there were no headphones for me."[43]

> I had to be in the control room with him and also have the speakers off because we didn't want leakage, so that meant he had to sing in the control room with me hearing no music, only his voice. And we set up the vocal mic in the furthest corner of the control room. He had his headphones on and he sang the song from top to bottom and all I heard was his voice. And it was just heart wrenching and beautiful. This was a magical moment.[44]

Witnessing such an unguarded, and almost intimate, display of his talent was different than anything Rogers had experienced before with Prince. "You'd spend hours watching him sing at rehearsal, but rehearsal has a different kind of performance aspect to it than singing for a record. Singing for a record is singing for a smaller delivery system, the size of the canvas is so much smaller. It's like the difference between watching someone paint a small portrait on a postcard versus painting a mural. So really seeing those performance gestures up close and personal. What a moment!"

Rogers wasn't the only one who felt they'd done something incredible. "It was just one of the most stunning songs we ever did,' explained Leeds. "It shows a sophistication of material, and Prince's vocal on it was just absolutely just spellbinding. That was literally one of the times that we just came out of the studio and we just all had goosebumps. We all really felt that we had just been part of something real, real, special."[45]

"And once and for all, let me reiterate, that it's always been assumed that it was Miles Davis that played the muted trumpet on 'Power Fantastic.' Nope, it never was, it was Atlanta Bliss!"[46]

Prince would record some additional overdubs (including his vocals) and an instrumental version of the track was also mixed.

The band was also enlisted to record the upbeat "And How," which showcased the trumpet and sax of Atlanta Bliss and Eric Leeds, and the voices of

Lisa and Wendy on top of Bobby's drumming. The use of a steel drum gives the song a slightly tropical vibe. This relatively fast recording would be revisited the next day.

Status: Despite the feeling of accomplishment and growth within the group, Prince decided to put the recording of the instrumental warm-up and "Power Fantastic" (6:10) on the shelf until 1993, when a version without the intro (4:45) was released on Prince's *The Hits/The B-Sides* 3 CD set. The first run through of the song would be released as "Power Fantastic (Live In Studio)" (6:22 with an extra 55 seconds of Prince's instructions to the musicians) on the *Sign O' The Times* Super Deluxe Edition in 2020.

The 2-minute "And How" was not released before Prince's passing. The track was expanded (4:13) by David Z and Levi Seacer Jr. and recorded by Jevetta Steele and was released in 1991 on the French version of her first solo album, *Here It Is.*

According to Lisa, Joni Mitchell misheard the lyrics for "Power Fantastic." "One of the funny memories I have of that is that after we recorded it with the band, we were back here in LA and me, Wendy, and Prince, went to Joni's house, and Prince played it for her, and she loved it. She got the lyrics wrong, but it's actually a better lyric. 'Power fantastic, isn't your life elastic,' and that's not the words, it's, 'Power fantastic, is in your life at last.' But 'Isn't your life elastic . . .' 'That's such a great line!' And we were like, 'Oh no, that's not what it is!'"

Despite the comical misinterpretation, the lyrics remained as written.

THURSDAY, MARCH 20, 1986

"And That Says What?" (tracking, mix)
"And How" (overdubs, mix)
Galpin Blvd. home studio (Chanhassen, Minnesota)
Producer: Prince | Artist: Prince | Engineer: Susan Rogers

He was really comfortable with having the band over at the house, because he could have what he'd always wanted: people around him. They used to go upstairs and watch TV or sit in the kitchen which they did for hours and tell jokes. It was nice for him to be able to incorporate his friends and his social life into his home.[47]

—Susan Rogers

For Prince, he wanted to have multiple places to record because once he had the music in his head, it was vital to transfer it to tape where it could live without the risk of it fading away, and almost every session had that urgency. "He would just go in, record and then it would be mixed," according to Susannah. "There was no stopping. He wouldn't stop until it was done. Each song had to be completed. Complete. And it would be a 24-hour period, sometimes 36, but he would never sleep. It would get done."[48]

For today's session, he'd gathered many of the people from the current live lineup to record a new instrumental. Prince was expanding his sound, although the roots of this composition can be traced back to the opening piece of music on Sheila E.'s *Romance 1600* album. Using almost the same lineup as the previous day: Lisa on piano, Matt Fink on keys, Bliss and Leeds on horns, and Wendy on bass, they created a fast paced song that lasted less than 2 minutes. Atlanta Bliss explained the way Prince would write during sessions like this: "Prince works with his musicians and a lot of the time he was singing a line to us and we were playing and he would say: 'Well, no okay, now let's try it like this.' He would feed from our personal playing and develop it from that. When he is writing a song he is developing in our sense also, that's the way that Duke Ellington wrote too. He wrote for his orchestra."[49]

The song's title comes from a comment Prince made once the band finished a take.

In addition to recording "And That Says What?", it is likely that Prince had Miko Weaver, Wally Safford, Jerome Benton, and Greg Brooks add background vocals to "And How" on this date. Once the session was over, Prince left for Los Angeles.

Status: "And That Says What?" (1:45) remained unreleased during his lifetime but was included on the *Sign O' The Times* Super Deluxe Edition in 2020.

Prince left for Los Angeles after the March 20 session. At some point in March, Wendy, Lisa, and Susannah worked on a new track, "Honeymoon Express." "Wendy and I wrote it months before the release of the Wendy & Lisa debut record," recalled Susannah. "In fact, this was a track that neither Wendy, Lisa or myself would have known that in only a few months down the road would find its way onto the first Wendy & Lisa record."[50]

Although he reportedly enjoyed "Honeymoon Express," Prince decided not to release the song.

SATURDAY, MARCH 22, 1986

"**A Love Bizarre**" [live] (overdubs, mix)
Sunset Sound, Studio 3 | 11:00 a.m.–11:30 p.m. (booked: lockout)
Producer: Prince | Artist: Sheila E. (Prince scratched out) | Engineer: Coke Johnson

> *He had a live recording and we brought the 24 track tapes back to Sunset to fix them up.*
>
> —Coke Johnson

Prince spent the session overdubbing and adjusting the audio mix for his live duet with Sheila on "A Love Bizarre," which had been recorded at her recent concert at San Francisco's Warfield Theatre. The new mix would be featured in her upcoming *Romance 1600 Live* video.

SUNDAY, MARCH 23, 1986

"**Boy's Club**" (tracking, mix)
Sunset Sound, Studio 3 | 12:00 noon–6:00 a.m. (booked: lockout)
Producer: Prince | Artist: Sheila E. (Prince scratched out) | Engineer: Coke Johnson

[Prince] was conscious of that fact, that he had to downplay his involvement, but that didn't mean that he wasn't gonna be involved. He chose to not be involved to a certain extent on [Sheila E.'s] third album.[51]

—Susan Rogers

Prince had trained himself to record quickly, so he was able to accomplish a great deal in one session. "He was an established songwriter," explained Susan Rogers. "He could sit down with a notebook and a pen and like an experienced writer immediately call upon inspiration. There was no delay in getting it from his head to the page to the tape, whereas other artists had to go through a growing process of learning to be writers. He couldn't sit around and wait for someone to develop their style as a writer. It would have taken way too much time. It was faster and better and made more sense for him to do it."[52]

It is not entirely clear if Prince wrote "Boy's Club" with others, but he spent 17 hours in the studio recording the track with Sheila and members of her band, including her brother Peter Michael Escovedo as well as her sister Zina, both on congas. The song starts with a machine gun style drum intro, similar to the one recorded earlier in the month on "The Ballad Of Dorothy Parker." The bass, guitar, piano, and a Yamaha DX7 synth all blend with a wide array of percussion including shakers, bongos, agogô bells, Sheila's timbales, and cymbals to make a light dance song about going to a club. Crowd noises, possibly from, or at least inspired by the previous day's session, were also subtly added to the track. Prince's voice can also be heard during the last few seconds of the song.

The final hour was spent creating a mix, and dubbing the song to three C-60 cassettes.

Status: A 5-minute version of "Boy's Club" was edited (3:56) and released on Sheila E.'s self-titled third album in February 1987.

TUESDAY, MARCH 25, 1986

"**Love And Sex**" [version 2A] (tracking, overdubs, mix)
"**Fun Love**" (mix and copy)
"**Twosday**" (mix and copy)
Sunset Sound, Studio 3 | 10:00 a.m.–7:00 a.m. (booked: lockout)
Producer: Prince | Artists: Sheila E. and Prince (not listed) | Engineer: Coke Johnson

Question: *Do you exhaust people?*
Prince: [laughs] *"Yes I do."*[53]

"I'd worked with people before who'd had unreasonable requests," recalled Peggy Mac when thinking back on his aggressive schedule. "Prince's never were. He lived on coffee—that's all he ever lived on that I saw. He didn't want to eat, because that slowed him down. Once those ideas were flowing, Prince tried to fulfill them as best he could, and that's how I helped. That was my life."[54]

"With him, [a session] was typically anywhere between 16 and 24 [hours]," remembered Susan Rogers. "16 would be a fairly short session, but we frequently did 24 hours. That was fairly common. That was how long it took, because he never wanted to come back to a song. If he started it, he wanted to do all the overdubs and mixing it as we went, and then print it, and then it would be done, and then we'd sleep for a few hours and then start another song."[55]

Prince had ended the previous shift at 6 in the morning and returned to Sunset Sound 4 hours later. He'd requested the 2-inch master tape of "Love And Sex"—from the January session—to review, but decided to completely re-record the song. Keeping the direction of the original track, live drums were used again, but now they were covered with a Hammond B-3 organ, piano, and bass, with Prince likely adding his vocals to the track. 3 hours were also spent with Matt Blistan and Eric Leeds adding horns.

Additional mixes and overdubs were probably done on "Fun Love" and "Twosday" as well. Two C-60 cassettes were created of the updated mixes and the 20-hour plus session was over at 7:30 a.m.

WEDNESDAY, MARCH 26, 1986

"**Love And Sex**" (overdubs, mix)
"**A Love Bizarre**" [from live concert video] (crossed out)
Sunset Sound, Studio 3 | 4:00 p.m.–4:30 a.m. (booked: lockout)
Producer: Prince | Artist: Sheila E. (Prince listed) | Engineer: Coke Johnson

He really believed that every single song that he wrote was a hit
when it wasn't. But he believed that so he just kept writing so
it didn't stop him to go, "Well, this is not a great song." Some
of them weren't all great. I know some people are not going to

be happy with me saying it, but it's the truth. They weren't all great.[56]

—Sheila E.

Although Prince originally planned this session for himself, it ended up being focused on music for Sheila E. It is unclear if Prince was in the studio for the entire session, which involved Sheila replacing Prince's vocals with her own for the updated version of "Love And Sex." Once her voice was tracked, she added a few additional overdubs, including her congas and additional percussion. Prince and Sheila's band member Stef Burns added guitar to the track ("I learned a lot from Prince about funk guitar."[57]) and the song was mixed until 3 in the morning.

Follow-up work on the live version of "A Love Bizarre" was slated for the evening, but it is unclear if Sheila E.'s edited concert video was simply screened or if there was any audio mixing involved. Regardless, the video was scheduled to be released in June 1986, so it was vital that it was completed as quickly as possible.

The session ended at 4:30 in the morning with two C-60 cassettes dubbed with the work they'd completed.

Status: Sheila E.'s re-recording of "Love And Sex" (4:16) was considered for, but ultimately not included on, her third solo album. Her version of the song was not released during Prince's lifetime.

At some point during this week, Prince flew back to Minneapolis to work with the expanded Revolution for the upcoming shows, specifically a concert being scheduled for the following week in Boston. Because the rehearsals had been continuing in his absence, the band was tight, but on Monday *Parade* was scheduled for release which was the next stage of the launch of *Under The Cherry Moon*. Prince had a lot on the line.

FRIDAY, MARCH 28, 1986

"**Mountains**" [7-inch and 12-inch] (edits)
"**Wonderful Ass**" (edits for consideration as a B-side)
Sunset Sound, Studio 3 | 10:00 a.m.–12:00 midnight (booked: lockout)
Producer: Prince | Artist: Prince | Engineer: Coke Johnson

He really did something interesting with ["Mountains"]. *He took the song and extended it and got into something else that was cool. He had that one all worked out. By the time Blistan and I came in to put the horns on, that was done.*

—Eric Leeds

Work continued on the edits and remix of "Mountains." After a 7-hour pause in the session, "Wonderful Ass," a track that he'd been tweaking for several years, was brought out for edits as it was in consideration as a B-side.

MONDAY, MARCH 31, 1986

Parade *was a disaster. Apart from* "Kiss," *there's nothing on it I'm particularly proud of. The temptation is to go right back into the studio and make a killer album, but I think half the problem with* Parade *was that I recorded it too soon after* Around The World In A Day *and I just didn't have enough good material ready. I'm not going to make that mistake again.*[58]

—Prince

Parade is released.

Pop music had caught up to Prince, or more accurately caught up to where Prince *was*. Groups like Ready for the World mimicked his brand with sound-alike songs such as "Oh Sheila," but by the time they released their album in fall of 1985, Prince had moved on, so once again Prince took an unexpected turn with his music, adding Clare Fischer's touches on many of the tracks, which took his sound in a completely different direction than his previous release. Despite the potentially dubious and out of character quote credited to Prince about his disappointment, the album is considered a critical success, although there were many who were confused by his new direction, according to Lisa. "It was another very experimental kind of record for us. I remember we had just gotten the Fairlight, and it was like a new toy. It inspired us, and we wrote a lot of new and different-sounding things. Because we were also really high on the popularity of *Purple Rain*, we had all of this momentum, so as musicians we were really bold and brave. I think other musicians can feel that when they listen. There's an irreverence to it, and it's all over the place. It's the kind of stuff that record companies hate, but musicians love."[59]

"To me that album spoke individually to Prince's musical abilities," agreed Wendy. "It didn't sound like anybody else—it was just Prince doing something different. Musically, it reflected him the best."[60]

Despite having some issues with Prince, BrownMark recognized how well everyone in the band was working together. "It was the most musical album we'd done. The Revolution was at its peak, and there was nothing holding us back, he gave us full freedom. We'd jam, and he'd be running around, screaming 'Record that! Run the tape!' Then he'd take that junk home and have it all polished up the next day. Like, 'Wow, dude—do you sleep?'"[61]

Eric Leeds reflected that, "Along with *The Family* album, which I consider a Prince album, there was never anything approaching a perfect Prince album for me, because Prince is too eclectic for my tastes. *Parade* had probably the greatest ratio of songs that really did something for me. I don't really know if Prince was disappointed with *Parade*. If he was disappointed, it was maybe by the fact that it didn't sound more reckless than it did."[62]

"That was a great album and I was really proud of the work I did on that," says Peggy, "but the version I worked on never came out. I was really happy with the music that we recorded for *Under The Cherry Moon*, but not the actual record. That wasn't it. The only song that was mine that stayed unchanged from the original sessions was 'Sometimes It Snows In April,' and the rest was changed. You can hear the drums that I mic'd on 'Under The Cherry Moon,' but everything else is just gone. I think he got so lost on this album. The sound just got washed out."

The reviews were mixed but mostly positive, especially in Europe where *Parade* was announced as the best album of 1986 by two prominent English music publications, the *New Musical Express* and *The Face*, with "Kiss" getting declared the best single by many music critics. In the United States, the album was praised by multiple publications including the *Detroit Free Press*, which stated that the album was: "a confirmation of Prince's place as a superior melodist, arranger and player as well as a celebration of his creativity."[63]

The *New York Times* rated the album as "very good," and highlighted "Girls & Boys" and "Anotherloverholenyohead" as standout tracks. Their review noted the tide that had turned on him over the last year by pointing out that Parade was: "an attempt to recoup ground lost by the negative publicity surrounding Prince personally."[64]

Despite the mostly positive reviews, this was his first album since 1982 that failed to land the top spot in the United States, peaking at number 3 on the *Billboard* Top Pop Albums and number 2 on the *Billboard* Top Black Albums.

For Susan Rogers, her frustration lay not in the music, but in the way the album sounded.

> I love the record. I love "Anotherloverholenyohead," "Girls & Boys," "Under The Cherry Moon." I think "Kiss" is a great song. I wish *Parade* was sonically a little bit more even, because it was done half at the warehouse on the Soundcraft which still couldn't begin to compete with the sonic clarity of Sunset Sound. There's a disparity there. It would have been I think probably a better record if they'd done it all at Sunset Sound. Also because he kept adding songs too, I think it's not as clear and not as concise of a theme package as some of the other albums.[65]
>
> He said sonic clarity wasn't important, he would always say that it didn't matter, that he'd go for the excitement, but it became increasingly important, I thought, as he became more and more popular. You have an obligation to deliver a record that's sonically competitive. After selling a million albums of *Purple Rain* I think we're a little obligated to step up our quality a little bit and speaking personally I kind of wish we had. On *Parade*, I can hear that damned Soundcraft and I'm sorry that we used the Soundcraft to record "Mountains" and record "Girls & Boys." I wish the sound was a little better. I think when you are on top I guess you can pretty much get away with everything, but when I listen to *Parade* now I'm embarrassed at some of the things that we did which I just wish sounded better, but at that time he didn't complain.[66]

"Oh my God. I was like, *this* is the record. This is such a great record," Susannah thoughtfully recalled. "Wendy and Lisa were so vital to his creativity, and that he allowed them to have such a huge influence. I felt that he was being fully realized as an artist, during this particular period. And I felt that *Parade* was a great record. Regardless of if it was for *Under The Cherry Moon* or not. I loved every track that came out of it."

"It's not the ultimate Prince record," argued Rogers. "It's a great record. It's not as important, I think, as the record that followed it."[67]

APRIL 1986

"I don't think he was unhappy with the [*Parade*] record," according to Susan Rogers, "but he was unhappy with a lot of other things."[1]

> He was not happy with that movie. He was not happy with his life at that time. He had made serious judgment errors making a movie, he was aware of that. I do not believe in my heart of hearts that he was disappointed in the [*Parade*] album. I know he was disappointed in the movie. Susannah even related a story to me. I came to the house one morning and she said: "Oh, we had a terrible night last night. He was lying on the floor, just lying face down on the floor saying: 'I hate this movie. I hate this movie. I hate this movie.'" He was really miserable. And he knew it just wasn't happening. Also there were tensions in his relationship with her. He had gone further than he had gone with anybody else, she was wearing his ring and I think . . . while he loved her, he didn't want to lose her, he didn't think he could carry out this commitment. They were fighting a lot, and it was sort of over nothing and he was trying to get the record done.[2]

The month of April would include a number of changes in his relationship with Susannah, and as usual, it would be reflected in his music.

> *He always had an idea of building a place where he or his band could go to create. It was his dream and he stayed with his dream.*[3]

—Jerome Benton

Prince was under a great deal of stress and had entered a series of projects that all had the potential to destroy the momentum he'd gained over the last few years. One of the biggest was a $10 million gamble: construction on his Paisley Park studio complex had begun. Bret Thoeny of Boto Design was the architect for the facility. It was built by Bossardt-Christenson, a local construction company. The 65,000-square-foot complex would house three recording studios and an area that could be used for live events, rehearsals, or locations for films. "Prince's vision at the time was the studios and soundstage, to do his own movies and his own writing," details Susannah. "A rehearsal space where he'd have his offices, have a record company. He just wanted an all-inclusive experience for him. I was there when we bought the land. It was empty. Nothing. We were living in the Galpin house while that was being built."

Chanhassen is 20 minutes away from downtown Minneapolis. Prince's home and rehearsal space was relatively close, but the entire area was largely open fields. Jerome Benton explained Prince's logic behind the location. "He had control, with it being right where it needed to be, right there in the country on the outskirts of Minneapolis. No reason for you to be peeking over his wall if you didn't live there!"[4]

The facility would be a place for work but also act as a home for him. In essence, he would eventually turn the studio in his home to a home in his studio. "A portion of it was like a stay-over where if he was in the studio late, which he always was, he could just crash for a few hours and get back in the studio," according to Thoeny.[5]

The facility wouldn't officially open up until September 11, 1987, but by that point, he had been recording and rehearsing at Paisley Park for several months. Until it was complete, he sometimes referred to his warehouse as "Paisley Park."

TUESDAY, APRIL 1, 1986

"**Mountains**" (horns for 12-inch version, mix)
Washington Avenue Warehouse (Edina, Minnesota)
Producer: Prince | Artist: Prince | Engineers: "David Z" Rivkin and Susan
    Rogers | Assistant Engineer: Todd Herreman

My first session with him blew my freaking mind. I get called at five or six in the morning and it's Susan and she said that Prince wants to record. So this is like being thrown into the deep end, I mean it was my first week there, I had no idea what I was in for and I really didn't know Prince as a musician at that point and I really had no idea what this man was capable of. And he was making the extended mix of "Mountains," for the 12-inch. And I just sat there the whole time with my mouth open and my jaw hitting the floor. I can't believe I'm seeing him do this.

—Todd Herreman

Prince had been using the Fairlight keyboard but sometimes struggled with how to stretch its potential and decided to bring in an expert to help, according to Todd Herreman. "I got a call from Alan Leeds saying, 'We got this Fairlight from you guys, but Prince needs somebody to run it, could you recommend a programmer' and I just said, 'Well, that would be me.' So they flew me up for an interview and I got the gig. And so I basically became a programmer for Prince, but the foot in the door was because I knew how to run the Fairlight."

Although it is unclear of the date for Herreman's first session, it happened around this period at the warehouse when he arrived to watch Prince working on an update of the extended version.

He started by just playing drums for probably five or six minutes and the whole thing is going on in his head. I'm thinking of the movie *Amadeus* when Mozart has the whole symphony in his head and Prince is—maybe that's a bit of a stretch but, Prince is playing drums and I remember him saying, "Are we ready? Roll tape." Because he's ready to go and Susan's trying to dial in a level for one of the tom mics and Prince is just like "Go, go, go." And so, he cut drums and then he's like, "Give me the bass." So I hand him the bass, he says, "Hand me the guitar," so I give him the guitar. And he's laying down guitar shit that was just like—and I'm a John Scofield fan and he's doing these licks that remind me of John Scofield and I'm like, this guy can play like that? It blew my mind and it was really a cool 12-inch. So that was my first session, and I remember going, "Oh my God, what did I just witness?" That happened over and over.

During the session, Matt Blistan and Eric Leeds were brought in to add their horns to the mix. "The horn parts on the album version are pretty sparse," remembered Leeds. "There's a couple of lines, but we did a 12-inch version of that which is my favorite 12-inch that Prince ever did. I think it's a great performance, just the whole idea of the 12-inch. I guess the horn parts in themselves don't really stand out as being anything special, but it was just cool."[6]

Status: The full 11-minute version of "Mountains" would be edited down (9:54) for release.

WEDNESDAY, APRIL 2, 1986

> **"Wonderful Day"** (possible mix for movie)
> **"Do U Lie?"** (possible mix for movie)
> **"Anotherloverholenyohead"** [extended mix] (possible mix)
> Washington Avenue Warehouse (Edina, Minnesota)
> Producer: Prince | Artist: Prince | Engineer: Susan Rogers

> *Every day was thrilling. And I was aware that I was a piece
> in a machine that was operating at an extraordinarily high
> level. So I imagine [its like] a gear in a Ferrari or Maserati.
> You're not necessarily aware of the part you're playing, but you
> know that the whole itself is exceptional. So you just keep up the
> momentum so that all of you can move forward without any
> kinks in the machinery.*[7]

> —Susan Rogers

Prince worked on mixes for "It's A Wonderful Day," "Anotherloverholenyohead," and "Do U Lie?" during this session which went past midnight. An attempt at creating an extended version of "Anotherloverholenyohead" was made, but it would be set aside after this session and revisited during the spring, after the song had been worked out for the live shows.

Once the session wrapped, Prince immediately left town for another one-off performance, this time at the Metro in Boston. So far, the pattern for these "preview" shows mirrored what he'd scheduled for the *Purple Rain* tour 2 years earlier.

Status: The extended version of "Anotherloverholenyohead" that was worked on during this session remains unreleased.

THURSDAY, APRIL 3, 1986

Venue: Metro (Boston, Massachusetts)
Capacity: 1,250 (sold out)

> *I always felt that he was better live than he was on an album. It was more refined. There was a lot more power to it. There was a lot more emotion to it, and it got deeper because he had time to digest what it was.*[8]

—Roy Bennett

In the month since the First Avenue concert, the show had already started morphing. Songs like "Paisley Park" were dropped, and others like "The Dance Electric" and "Love or Money" were added. "(How Much Is) That Doggie In The Window?" followed by a medley that included an instrumental version of "Lady Cab Driver." "Automatic," and "D.M.S.R." was also included and several tracks were shuffled to a different part of the setlist. Prince seemed to be looking for the best lineup of songs, but it was the lineup *of the new band* that was causing frustration for some, recalls Wendy. "The Revolution at the time wondered why he was putting so many people on stage with us. And we're like, 'Why does he need more? What's going on here? Is there a boredom setting in with him? Does he just need more stimulation on stage to play off of?' And that's when things started getting kind of kooky during the *Parade* tour. Plus, he had this crazy relationship with my sister and that ended up spilling really bad stuff onto me and it was awful."

Prince was also trying to put up a wall between the Melvoin twins, keeping them apart as much as possible, which was causing extreme pain for them as Wendy reflects on that period. "It was afterwards that everything started going downhill."

Prince was also transitioning from *Purple Rain* guitar hero to the front man who focused on singing and dancing, giving Wendy a chance to shine on lead guitar with only minor exceptions, as Lisa recalls. "When you think about it, he could play everything on his record, but then he went on tour, he put this band together where eventually he didn't even have to pick up a guitar."

Prince would occasionally play a solo on "Head" and on "America," but Wendy was sharing the spotlight with him as the Keith Richards to his Mick Jagger.

The following day, Prince flew back to Minneapolis to prepare for a trip to France. It is unclear if Prince recorded while he was home.

SUNDAY, APRIL 6, 1986

"Mountains" (copy, edits, 7-inch single, 12-inch comps) 11:59
"Alexa De Paris" (edits for consideration as B-side)
"Alexa De Paris" [7-inch single version] (edit)
Sunset Sound, Studio 1 | 5:00 p.m.–12:00 midnight (booked: lockout)
Producer: Prince | Artist: Prince | Engineers: Coke Johnson and Susan
  Rogers

> *The 12-inch to "Mountains" is a masterpiece.*
>
> —Wendy Melvoin

Seven hours of edits for the release of "Alexa De Paris" and "Mountains" took place in a rare session in Studio 1. If Prince was in attendance, he bounced in and out of the session. Despite being so busy, he obviously knew he had something powerful with "Mountains." Lisa recognizes the pattern to Prince's method. "I think that the really great songs, he spent more time on."

Because the original song and the extended version were recorded at two different times, not all of the elements blended together. In fact, the extended portion was a slightly different speed than the first few minutes, so Prince reached back into his bag of editing tricks and added the sound of an explosion to help the transition. It was something he'd done in the past, remembers his previous guitarist Dez Dickerson. "One of the things he also told me one time was—this was back before Pro Tools and all that stuff—every once in a while, you'd get a take, and the energy and the feel of it was so good that even though there might've been a mistake technically, you wanted to use it. So he said, 'When there's something in the track that you want to keep, but there's something in the track that you don't want in there, put an explosion over it.' That was it. So now you know studio secrets with Prince. Put an explosion over the mistakes."[9]

Elements like Prince's shouting "Hey you, get out on this dance floor" at the beginning of the track were created for a specific reason, remembers Coke Johnson. "I think that was added in as an overdub specifically for the clubs. A lot of times, the club mixes would be remixed from the album mix because he wanted it more slamming. On the album, for airplay, with the 33 RPM records back then, that's why we would always do a test pressing, and bring it back, and make sure we had enough low end on it. Then for the club mix, he wanted to have an over-the-top low end. Something that would not be good for radio, but it would be slamming in the clubs. He would want to also add in stuff that was specific to a club scene. 'Get out on this dance floor and dance!'"

Status: The extended mix of "Mountains" clocks in at 9:56 but was listed as 10:03 on the US promo and US 12-inch disc labels, probably due to the variation in speed of the extended section.

MONDAY, APRIL 7, 1986

Prince travels back to France to film some additional scenes for *Under The Cherry Moon.* The Revolution joined him to shoot the music video for "Mountains."

WEDNESDAY, APRIL 9, 1986

The music video for "Mountains" was filmed at Studio de la Victorine, Nice, France. Over the next several days, additional scenes were filmed for the movie and multiple photo shoots took place around the city.

While Prince and the Revolution were busy in France, Coke Johnson, Susan Rogers, and David Z were preparing all of the songs and cues for the final mix of the movie.

SATURDAY, APRIL 12, 1986

Prince stayed in France while the Revolution returned to the United States.

MONDAY, APRIL 14, 1986

Tensions around the world were heightened when the United States bombed Libya in retaliation for a recent terrorist act in a West Berlin discotheque. Prince abruptly returned home to Minneapolis, but he made a stop in New York to speak with Jill Jones. "I don't know why he stopped there specifically, but he had a car pick me up from my house to pick him up at the airport. There was a newspaper, and Prince showed it to me. And he was like, 'You know what this means?' We had been watching the old Nostradamus movie [*The Man Who Saw Tomorrow*, released in 1981] and that movie actually was a big, crazy thing. It says some king from the Middle East is supposed to survive something and then bomb New York. Now, I don't know if he would be crazy enough to land the plane to come just to show me that newspaper thing. I think it could be possible, because that's just how he was, because he didn't stay in town."

Before he left, Prince also spoke with Jill about her album and they decided to remove certain songs like "Living Doll" and a few other more lightweight numbers. "It was a rainy day, and we just drove around talking about my record. 'Living Doll' was fun, but we took them all off after freaking Libya."

TUESDAY, APRIL 15, 1986

"**The Ballad Of Dorothy Parker**" (various overdubs including horns, mix)
"**Witness 4 The Prosecution**" (various overdubs including horns, mix)
"**Movie Star**" (various overdubs including horns, mix)
Galpin Blvd. home studio (Chanhassen, Minnesota)
Producer: Prince (although he did not attend) | Artist: Prince | Engineer: Susan Rogers

> One remarkable thing about Prince is that he's probably one of the most eclectic artists in all of pop music. The songs that I find myself going back to more often are what Alan and I refer to as his "boutique songs." The greatest example to me is "The Ballad Of Dorothy Parker."[10]
>
> —Eric Leeds

Prince often relied on a small circle of people around him to add their flourish on many of his tracks, and because he couldn't attend this session, he asked for help on several unfinished tracks from the previous month, as Wendy recalls. "Before we went on the *Parade* tour, Lisa and I were doing a lot of work on [what would become] *Sign O' the Times* and we were doing so much recording. We were being left alone with his masters and working with Susan."

Susannah was also asked to join the session, as were Eric Leeds and Matt "Atlanta Bliss" Blistan. "Prince was going to stay over to do some more things in Nice on the film and the rest of us went home after the video shoot," adds Leeds. "But when we left, that's when he told me he wanted me to do the horns on these three songs. I think he told Wendy, 'Be in the studio with him and make sure Eric doesn't get too carried away.'"

On "Witness 4 The Prosecution," Prince had recorded drums, bass, guitar, and vocals and asked for it to be fleshed out, as Susan recalled. "Lisa put a great [Hammond] B3 organ part on it and Wendy, Lisa and Susannah sang the background and then we added some percussion too and we finished off the song and had a great time doing it."[11]

"I do remember being in the room singing those background vocals and getting up really high, trying to work that vibrato," laughed Lisa.[12] Four thick tracks of their background vocals and percussion—including tambourine, and Wendy adding additional bass—helped give the song its sonic depth.

Eric got into the spirit and added an interpolation of the Perry Mason theme to the song. "That to me was a slam dunk. I mean, it was 'Witness 4 The Prosecution.' I said, 'Yeah, I *had* to use that.' To me that was the most obvious thing to do."

According to Eric, there were several ways that a session with Prince would play out. "There were certain days, or certain songs, where he knew exactly what he wanted already. So we were just coming in, and basically, he said, 'This is what I need.' And it was back then, 'Okay, fine. We're done. We're out of there.' But a lot of other times, he might have said, 'I've got something for the verse. I just need to put something on the chorus.' So there were no rules. There was no specific process."

> There were other times when he wouldn't even be there. We would just get called in, and Susan would be there. She'd have some notes and said, "He just needs you to come up with something at two minutes into the song. Eric, he wants you to put a little eight-bar solo, after the second chorus," or whatever. And that's it. So then it was basically up to us. I did a horn arrangement for "The Ballad Of Dorothy Parker" that he asked me to do. Now obviously, he never used it, and I was really, really surprised that he even asked me to do that, because I always thought the song was just perfect the way it was. But I was intrigued, so I did. He was giving me the opportunity to go into a studio and play with his music, however I wanted. He was either going to use it or he wasn't. But it was like, "This is what I like to do." And I was getting paid to do that.

Although his sax would not be in the final mix of "Dorothy Parker," Eric recognized what was happening with Prince and how bonded he felt with this new direction. "I think that after the *Purple Rain* phenomenon he felt a lot freer, very unencumbered to just kind of dive in and do all of these different things that he now felt he could do, and kind of testing himself to see how far he could go, and he had all of these different people that he could do different things with. I think it was probably his biggest period of growth."[13]

On "Movie Star," Prince allowed Leeds to add his own flair, but he had also recorded several synth track sections that he wanted Eric to use as a guide track, which was something he did on occasion. Once again, the horns would not make it to Prince's final mix.

"I think what I can say with any kind of conviction is that we did have really decent quality control," explains Wendy. "We had really good taste and I think he knew that. Me, Lisa, Susannah, Roy Bennett, and Eric Leeds. I think he relied on those people for more than just music, but also a sense of aesthetic in his world. And that aesthetic was super high quality."

Status: This session's slightly extended mix of "The Ballad Of Dorothy Parker" (4:56) featuring Eric Leeds on sax was released in 2020 on the *Sign O' The Times* Super Deluxe Edition.

THURSDAY, APRIL 17, 1986–FRIDAY, APRIL 18, 1986

"Crystal Ball" (tracking, mix)
"Colors" [Wendy instrumental] (tracking, mix)
"Visions" [Lisa instrumental] (mix)
"Strange Relationship" (possible mix)
"Teacher, Teacher" (possible mix)
"Dream Factory" (possible edit, mix)
"Wonderful Day" (mix)
"The Ballad Of Dorothy Parker" (mix)
"Sexual Suicide" (mix)
Dream Factory album (edits, mixes, crossfades)
Galpin Blvd. home studio (Chanhassen, Minnesota)
Producer: Prince | Artist: Prince | Engineer: Susan Rogers | Assistant Engineer: Todd Herreman

> *The song "Crystal Ball" was written in a deepbluefunk depression as Prince pondered his future in a music business that had become more business than music. His only solace during that time was his continuing search 4 a soul mate.*[14]
>
> —*Crystal Ball* CD booklet

The events that influenced Prince's music could range from the subtle sound of an accidental beat or the most recent world event. It is likely that Prince's inspiration for "Crystal Ball" was at least partially influenced by the recent bombing in Libya and the threats for retaliation around the world.

> *As bombs explode around us and hate advances on the right. The only thing that matters, baby, is the love that we make 2night.*[15]

Once again, Prince reached inward and combated the violence in the news, turning it into something more intimate and personal. Susannah remembers Prince's mood when she picked him up. "I got him at the airport and he was so happy and so relieved to see me bring him home to *our* house. I say *our* house because it was at the time. When he came home, that particular time, and we recorded 'Crystal Ball,' I hadn't experienced him like that. Whatever happened when he was in Europe, when Libya was bombed, he came home, and he was like, 'You're here. That's what matters.' I think when he felt that relief and he knew I was there, he got his creative spark to record 'Crystal Ball.' This was our moment. This was our life together."

Prince sang about soldiers drawing swords of sorrow while his "baby draws pictures of sex all over the walls in graphic detail" letting the listener in on what was happening with Susannah in his home while he was working on his music. "He sings at one point 'My baby draws pictures of sex.' When he'd go into the studio I was painting the mural in our pool room, so he was singing about what he knew during that period of time. During that time I was doing a lot of painting and drawing and he was recording the *Dream Factory* record."

"He was prudishly conservative in many ways," according to Susan Rogers. "He was a funny guy because he had these open attitudes about sex, but from an artist's perspective, he inherited his father's wariness of temptations of the flesh. And that's why—around Prince's house—you wouldn't see *Playboy* magazine or porn or any of that stuff."

Prince spent hours recording the basic tracks: guitar, bass, and live drums. Susannah lent the song additional personality with her backing vocals, which were joined by Prince. "To be on a microphone with him inches away, singing—it was so beautiful," said Susannah. "I remember, a few times, him reaching over and stroking my face."[16]

One of the most interesting elements that were added on a future date (likely in June) were multiple layers of a recorder, a woodwind musical instrument that was often used to teach beginning music students. "Wendy and I were like, 'Can we put some recorder on it?' We had them out" remembers Susannah, "because we were moving around some things and he said, 'Put it on.'"

Prince spent a long time working on the track, eventually he'd record several instrumental overdubs, and everything he could to bring this epic production to life, including a variety of sound effects ranging from water and sirens to bombs exploding, pelicans, cats, and traffic. Xylophones, choirs, and horns were likely recorded using either the Fairlight or the Mirage synth.

Herreman recalls Prince's sense of humor about the track.

He was tweaking a drum sound off the Linn and I think Susan was probably cue-ing so you're just hearing "dun, dun dun," and this is going on for minutes and he just started laughing and we're looking at him like, what's so funny? He said, "Okay, I'm actually going to put this on the record, I'm going to put a kick drum for two minutes only on the left hand side so everybody that's listening to it for the first time is going to be running around and checking to see if their speakers are connected."

The spring had been fruitful and Prince was starting to gather songs for his next project, *Dream Factory*, based around a track from the previous November. Among the dozens of songs he'd recently recorded, he found a handful that could work and set about reviewing them to see how they worked as a collection. During this session, mixes took place for "Wonderful Day," "The Ballad Of Dorothy Parker," "Strange Relationship," "Sexual Suicide," "Teacher, Teacher," Lisa's instrumental "Visions," and the album's title track, which may have also been edited on this date. At this point, *Dream Factory* was going to be another Revolution project.

Wendy recalls how busy it was during this period. "It was like the North Pole. This little factory was like toys being made, but they were dreams! Songs, chapters, books. But I guess you could say it was like the equivalent of the Brill Building in New York or Motown's building here—it was like where things were happening. *Dream Factory* came from a really productive time where there was a lot going on at once, and Prince wasn't one to be flat-footed. He'd always put some other kind of metaphor to describe something, so I think 'dream' worked perfect with his lexicon of parables—his life of parables."[17]

Like he'd done with Lisa, Prince recruited Wendy to record an instrumental they'd call "Colors." He'd never shared the spotlight in such a blatant way, so by including individual showcase songs from Wendy and Lisa on the album, he seemingly allowed everyone to understand how he felt about their contributions. Prince left her alone with Susan Rogers as he'd done with Lisa on "Visions." "He wanted interludes for the record. No guidance, just do something and I did it so quickly," explains Wendy. "I was still such a young player, but you could tell I was harmonically sophisticated. I don't know why I chose something so esoteric, but I did. Maybe because I knew it would make for a good interlude. That was my inspiration, and he was proud."

"Colors," as well as some other musical interludes likely recorded during this session were used to link several of his songs. The track was placed at the end of "Starfish And Coffee" on some configurations of *Dream Factory* and would eventually segue into (the as-yet-unrecorded update of) "I Could Never Take The Place Of Your Man" but would be removed before the collection morphed into *Crystal Ball* in fall 1986.

Status: A 12-minute version of "Crystal Ball" would be edited down multiple times, and a 7-inch version was prepared for release (3:30) but was withdrawn when the *Crystal Ball* project was reorganized into *Sign O' The Times*. Clare Fischer would add a variety of instruments to the track on August 4, 1986. The song was released on the *Crystal Ball* 4-CD set in 1998, and on that collection, the drum intro is no longer just on the left but on both left and right.

If it wasn't edited on an earlier date, "Dream Factory" was likely reduced from 4:22 to 3:06 during this session, removing multiple sections including the "St. Paul, punk of the month" chant. The minute-long "Colors" was placed between "Starfish and Coffee" and "In A Large Room With No Light" on the June 3, 1986 configuration of *Dream Factory*. When the final assembly was created in July 1986, "In A Large Room With No Light" was removed and the segue was added to the beginning of "I Could Never Take The Place Of Your Man." When the album evolved into *Crystal Ball* and then *Sign O' The Times*, "Colors" was removed.

The 7-inch edit of "Crystal Ball" and "Colors," were included on the *Sign O' The Times* Super Deluxe Edition in 2020.

According to Morris Hayes, who played keyboards for Prince from 1992 to 2012, Prince remained proud of "Crystal Ball" years later.

> He had one of the engineers go down and get this song, "Crystal Ball," out of the vault. And he brought it in and he just put it up and he played it. And this song, over a period of time, just starts to develop with all of these different things coming in. And I'm sitting there and it's starting to evolve and things are coming in, and Clare Fischer string arrangements and all of this stuff.

"Dude, this is cool. Who's playing drums on this?" He said, "I am." I said, "Okay, that's cool." And then the bass comes and it's got this crazy bass. I said, "Who's playing bass?" He said, "I am. I'm playing bass." And so I'm like, "Okay who's playing keyboard?" He said, "I am." I said, "So wait a minute. You're playing everything on this record right now." Because it's just going, and it's changing tempos, it's moving around. And I'm like, "How are you doing this? You have to play the whole song, because you can't play guitar and bass and keys all at the same"—he says, "I see it done in my head. All of the song is done in my head, so all I'm doing is executing, so I know all the parts I'm going to play before I play it. So he's playing the drums, knowing what's going to happen. He plays the bass and puts that down like it's going to—and I'm like "Are you kidding me?"[18]

FRIDAY, APRIL 18, 1986

"**Big Tall Wall**" (tracking, mix)
Dream Factory album (edits, mixes, crossfades)
Galpin Blvd. home studio (Chanhassen, Minnesota)
Producer: Prince | Artist: Prince | Engineer: Susan Rogers

> *[Prince] finally purchased a condominium for Susannah and persuaded her to go and live in this condominium. It didn't last very long, just for a couple of months. At that time he wrote a song called "Big Tall Wall."*[19]
>
> —Susan Rogers

To spend time with Prince, there was always one unwritten but understood rule: You were there as long as he wanted you there, and the circumstances could change quickly. "There was a lot of time with him, and he could be really private, even in the same space as you," revealed Susannah. "You had to be involved in his work ethic. He spent so much time alone, he was so private, but at the same time he would demand that you become part of that privacy—but you're not allowed to be the expresser; he is. So if there's anything to be said about the work, or about that space in time, it was on *his* terms. And I think everybody respected that. But we got to see that all kind of play itself out. Sometimes it ran really smoothly, and sometimes it had a lot of bumps."[20]

With all of the pressure Prince was under, something had to give, and one part of his life that he could control was his living situation with Susannah. They were engaged, and he didn't want to break it off, but he knew he needed a change, according to Melvoin.

> One morning we woke up, and he said, "You're gonna get your own place. [Prince's bodyguard] Gilbert Davison's going to take you to a place that's in town, and it's nice. You're gonna have your own place." I basically collapsed in bed and I was just like, "Oh my God, now what? I've done everything. I've said 'Yes' to you. I told you I was going to marry you. We've made a life here. You told me to renounce my life with my family? And now you're gonna go tell me I have to get a place? And I did dutifully what I was told. But I was still around the house every day."

Using guitars, bass, drums, and the Mirage synth, Prince recorded "Big Tall Wall" on his own. The lyrics reveal Prince's contradicting views about their relationship, exposing how he likely viewed creating a place for Susannah to be away from him but, at the same time, recognizing that he was turning it into a prison that made it impossible for her to leave him. The song's lyrics even reference the apartment in Lake Calhoun that literally had round walls. "I'm gonna build a big tall wall. Stone circle so you can't get out. . . . True love is what it's all about."[21]

"If you really love someone, you don't move them out," reasons Susan Rogers. "This wasn't going to continue, and this wasn't even a wife. This was a fiancée. It's like I suppose what happens when you fall in love with a friend, when you recognize, 'Oh my God, if we lose this relationship, we're going to lose the friendship too.' And man, he cherished that friendship, that meant so much to him. You could see how the two of them were together. They were so close."

"'Big Tall Wall.' That's the bird in a gilded cage stuff," explains Susannah.

Wendy saw how charismatic Prince could be, but with her sister involved with him, everything hit closer to home for her and caused problems that followed them on stage and into the studio. "He was able to get a lot of good people to love him. A lot of good, decent people were around him to love him like on the recording of *Parade*, there was a lot of love happening there. Once he started really getting into it with Susannah, that's when it all started going to shit. And I think he made a mistake thinking he could get away with these shenanigans with Susannah when he had me and Lisa in the room."

The rest of the session was spent mixing "Big Tall Wall" and creating segues for "Visions," "Dream Factory," "Wonderful Day," and "The Ballad Of Dorothy Parker," so they could be included in the assembly of the *Dream Factory* album that he was creating.

Status: This version of "Big Tall Wall" (6:00) would be added to the unreleased *Dream Factory* album. He would update the track from scratch later in the year. Both versions remained in the vault during his lifetime but were included on the *Sign O' The Times* Super Deluxe Edition in 2020.

SATURDAY, APRIL 19, 1986 (ESTIMATE)

"Starfish And Coffee" (tracking, mix)
Galpin Blvd. home studio (Chanhassen, Minnesota) | started late in day, continued into April 20
Producer: Prince | Artist: Prince | Engineer: Susan Rogers

> *We'd drive everywhere for any reason, all of the time, from getting vanilla milkshakes to going to Minnehaha Falls, going to the lake, sitting at the lake, listening to music, and we would talk about our history and I would tell him about this one girl, Cynthia Rose.*[22]
>
> —Susannah Melvoin

Prince was always looking for a new phrase or angle on a familiar theme that he could process and turn into music. When he found something so unique that he could write a song around a fully realized story, he took advantage of having a new universe to play with and filled it with sounds that helped create an experience. "Starfish And Coffee" gave Prince the opportunity to record something playful and quirky.

I had told Prince this story many, many times about this little girl that Wendy and I went to school with. Her name was Cynthia Rose. And off and on throughout my knowing Prince he would say, "Please tell me about Cynthia." Cynthia was an autistic girl, on the spectrum. I adored her. I watched out for her. I thought that she was so trippy and interesting and kooky, and so lovable. And she would do these certain quirky little things, and so I would tell Prince these stories about her and what she would do and how she would behave. And this was off and on throughout our relationship until '86.

[Susan Rogers and I] were at the kitchen table and he came upstairs, and he said, "Can you write down the story of Cynthia Rose again? Just tell me everything." So I did.[23]

"The story of Cynthia, and who she was, and how she came to be, and how I knew her, and her favorite number was 20, and who the kids in the class were, and what she had for breakfast and what was in, you know, and she would draw happy faces. . . . You know, who Cynthia was."

"Cynthia would say, 'Guess what I had for breakfast this morning?' I'd say, 'What did you have Cynthia?' And she'd say, 'I had starfish and pee pee!' I'd be like, 'Starfish and pee pee? Wow!' And it was always starfish and pee pee. She was [an] extraordinary little girl."

"Prince just loved that story," added Rogers, "and with Susannah, he wrote lyrics about it."[24] Once they worked on the lyrics together, Prince and Rogers went into the studio and used a variety of studio tricks to create Cynthia's playful view of life. "Prince was trying to get the listener to imagine a different world. So we recorded the drum machine, flipped the tape upside down and then overdubbed on top of the backwards drum, which was very fun."

Prince added piano, guitar, bass, and tambourine and a variety of other odd sounds including harp from the Fairlight and Mirage synths, which worked together to create a dreamy atmosphere unlike anything he'd ever recorded. But as he was tracking his vocals, he had a question for Susannah because she brought him the idea and wrote it with him.

"[He] comes back up and says, 'Um, Starfish and Pee pee, that's gotta go.' He goes, 'Do you mind if it's coffee, cause I don't think I can sing pee pee,' I was like, 'It's all good, go ahead, you do what you got to do,' and it was so sweet, it was like, of course you're not going to sing pee pee, so he goes down in the studio, and like six, seven hours later, Susan came to get me and brought me back downstairs and he was standing at the console exhausted, that sweet little smile on his face, and he goes, 'Here it is.' And he just pressed play, and 'Starfish And Coffee' was there."[25]

Prince's handwritten lyrics revealed that he crossed out "pee pee" and wrote "coffee" in red marker.[26] Prince would have Susannah add a few layers of background vocals, and today's work on the track was complete.

Status: "Starfish And Coffee" (2:46) would be released on *Sign O' The Times* in 1987.

SUNDAY, APRIL 20, 1986

"**Witness 4 The Prosecution**" (mix)
"**Movie Star**" (mix)
"**A Place In Heaven**" (overdubs, Lisa lead vocals, mix)
"**Nevaeh Ni Ecalp A**" (tracking, edits, mix)
Galpin Blvd. home studio (Chanhassen, Minnesota)
Producer: Prince | Artist: Prince | Engineer: Susan Rogers (assumed)

> *[Prince and I] challenged each other. We used humor and then*
> *we had like a kind of a sparring kind of a brother-sister kind*
> *of competition, but in the friendliest way. We would try to bust*
> *each other just while we were playing. Like, "Check this out!"*
> *"Oh yeah? Well check this out!" And it was just really healthy*
> *and young.*[27]

—Lisa Coleman

Prince had originally recorded a scratch vocal for "A Place In Heaven" in March, but it is unlikely a track that he expected to release as his own. Susan Rogers remembered: "Prince wanted Lisa to come down and sing the lead. Lisa was willing to do it, but was very tentative about it. She is a good background singer and she was just not comfortable with singing lead. He went away, just took his car and went off for the day and Lisa came down and just she and I worked on it. It came out beautiful, she has got a lovely voice."[28]

Lisa relates:

Prince said, "You sing this one," because he was exploring us more and he liked my voice, but he got mad at me because the line, "Three-year-olds in control," [going up at the end] and he wanted me to go, "Three-year-olds in control." [going lower at end] I went up because it sounds terrible when I go down. And he was like, "But that was the cuteness of it." It wasn't girl-ish. And here comes a little sexism because he thought it needed to be small, like a girl. It really pissed me off, because not only did I sing on it, but we added some strings, and some bell parts or something. To me, I thought it sounded great. We kind of had a little bit of a fight about it and he took all the parts off that I did. He kept my vocal, and he said, "I wish you would've gone down on that line." Sorry!

Wendy also added her vocals to "A Place In Heaven" and once it was completed, work on "Nevaeh Ni Ecalp A," which was the version of "A Place In

Heaven" that blended the song with both backward and forward elements, took place. The composition adjusted the direction of various parts of the song, most notably their vocals, giving the song a confusing, but angelic, energy.

During this session, "Witness 4 The Prosecution" and "Movie Star" were also updated while waiting for him to return. "The task was to push the ball down the field and get this record made," explains Rogers. "So if he's not in the room and I've finished the overdubs, of course I'm going to work on a mix. Adjust the level controllers and the EQ and reverbs and make it sound good."

In addition to the regular recording, a long comical conversation by the girls was ad-libbed directly to tape. "That was me," laughs Wendy. "Susannah and Lisa and I used to talk to him like a Valley girl. He just laughed. He loved it when you talked like you were from the Valley. It amused him and we liked to amuse him. We liked to keep him happy."

Cassettes were made for Prince's approval.

Status: Lisa's version of "A Place In Heaven" (2:46) was not released by Prince but was included on the unreleased *Dream Factory* album and was officially released on the *Sign O' The Times* Super Deluxe Edition in 2020. It is 10 seconds shorter than Prince's vocal version, the difference being the Prince version had a longer intro.

"Nevaeh Ni Ecalp A" (2:33) would be included on the second configuration of *Dream Factory* in June. A 51-second segue containing a bit of "Nevaeh Ni Ecalp A," a Valley Girl talk skit, a sample of "Witness," and Prince introducing "Dream Factory" was added as an unnamed segue before "Dream Factory" with the second or third configuration of the album.

Wendy, Lisa, and Prince were featured on the cover of the current issue of *Rolling Stone* magazine with a banner that read "Wendy and Lisa, Prince's Women." Their story and their commitment to him was one of the main themes of the article. Both Lisa and Wendy spoke boldly to Neal Karlen about their connection and their mutual love for Prince. "We don't want to leave and start our own thing," Lisa commented softly, "because this *is* our own thing—I don't feel like we're just hired musicians taking orders. He's always asking for our ideas."[29]

"I'm not nervous," said Wendy, "and I don't even want to guess what's going to happen. All I know is that this band is going to be together a long, long time."[30]

MONDAY, APRIL 21, 1986 (ESTIMATE)

"**Starfish And Coffee**" [instrumental] (mix)
"**Starfish And Coffee**" (mix)
"**Colors**" (mix)
Dream Factory album (edits, mixes, crossfades)
Galpin Blvd. home studio (Chanhassen, Minnesota)
Producer: Prince | Artist: Prince | Engineer: Susan Rogers

All of my songs are an extension of me, and any one song couldn't have been written without the other. And just like children, I wouldn't place any above the other.[31]

—Prince

"When I talk about Prince being tender," explains Susannah, "I think he recognizes that tender part in people. It was an openness that made him so tender. And I think he recognized that in Cynthia and so that's the part of him that felt so compelled to write the story."[32]

Prince had struck a nerve with "Starfish and Coffee." The storytelling in the song was as authentic as some of his best work and conjured up truth in the same way as "The Ballad Of Dorothy Parker," and he realized that it deserved a place on his upcoming *Dream Factory* album. During today's session, he worked on an additional mix of the track.

Earlier in the session, Prince and Susan had done mixes on Wendy's "Colors" and a few other segues as he continued to compile the *Dream Factory* album.

TUESDAY, APRIL 22, 1986

"**Mountains**" (playback for single release)
Dream Factory album assembled
Sunset Sound, Studio 3 | 2:00 p.m.–7:00 p.m. (booked: open)
Producer: Prince | Artist: Prince | Engineer: Coke Johnson ("David Z" was
   scratched out)

*Prince would put lists together. He was a list maker and I had
a feeling that he was trying things out. He definitely had a
storyboard in his head that nobody was privy to. You'd only see
one chapter at a time.*

—Lisa Coleman

Prince finally assembled all of the recent tracks he'd been gathering into the
Dream Factory collection. This is the track listing:

Side One:
  "Visions"
  "Dream Factory"
  "Wonderful Day"
  "The Ballad Of Dorothy Parker"
  "Big Tall Wall"
  "And That Says What?"

Side Two:
  "Strange Relationship"
  "Teacher, Teacher"
  "Starfish And Coffee"
  "A Place In Heaven"
  "Sexual Suicide"

"A lot of times it was just him putting it in order to have something to look at
and then to consider," explains Eric Leeds. "He really liked to visualize things
before he could start to make decisions on what he was really going to finalize."

Once Prince would assemble the cuts, he'd listen to it in his car, sometimes
looking for the opinion of others, as Alan Leeds recalled.

Prince would casually ask people, be it me, a girlfriend, be it [his manager, Ste-
ven] Fargnoli, be it a bodyguard, depending on where he was, what his mood
was, "What do you think of this?" He just loved playing music for people, and
he would have their undivided attention. You would get in his car, he would ride
around, maybe go to a Dairy Queen and get ice cream or a shake or something
to sip on, sit in the car and listen to the proposed sequence of his next album,
whatever that was. Then he would ask opinions, as to the flow and so on. It was
only in an advisory capacity. You'd tell him what you think and he dropped you
back off. Nine out of ten times it was gonna change 50 times, despite anything
you said, so it was kind of an exercise. It was him surveying the people whose
opinions mattered somewhat, and I'm sure I was hardly the only one.[33]

This short 5-hour session also included Prince reviewing "Mountains" before it was being sent off to Bernie Grundman for mastering. When he left, he
gave the studio time to Sheila who was working on "Soul Salsa," and "Hon E
Man" (listed as "Honey Man") for her third album. He did not return to Sunset
Sound until later in the week.

FRIDAY, APRIL 25, 1986

"Hon E Man" [listed as **"Hon E. Man"**] (mix)
"Fun Love" (mix with Clare Fischer's orchestral parts)
"Fun Love" [instrumental] (Prince guitar overdubs, mix over orchestral parts)
Radio ad for *Parade* [with Wendy and Lisa] (overdubs, edit, mix)
Sunset Sound, Studio 3 | 9:00 a.m.–12:30 a.m. (booked: open)
Producers: Prince, Sheila E. and "David Z" Rivkin | Artists: Prince and Sheila E. | Engineer: Coke Johnson | Assistant Engineer: Paul Levy

> *If you couldn't do something as fast as Prince said it, you'd*
> *have to just move on. He would just be on to the next thing. As*
> *fast as the sentence would come out, you had to have it done.*
>
> —Paul Levy

Sheila had been working on several tracks for her third album, including "Soul Salsa" and "Hon E Man." Prince may have given them a listen during this session and possibly decided to mix "Hon E Man" to give it the vibe he felt it may have been missing.

A new mix of "Fun Love" was fashioned with Prince recording additional guitar and blending it with the orchestra work recently recorded by Clare Fischer. An updated instrumental track was also created using all of these elements.

Finally, the radio spot for the *Parade* album that had been worked on in late January was created. Wendy and Lisa added their voices and it was edited and mixed during this session.

Two C-60 cassettes were dubbed of everything from this session.

SUNDAY, APRIL 27, 1986

"Mountains" [12-inch version] (mix)
Multiple cues for ***Under The Cherry Moon* score** (tracking, mix)
Sunset Sound, Studio 3 | 11:30 a.m.–3:30 a.m. (booked: noon–open)
Producer: Prince | Artist: Prince (although Sheila is listed) | Engineer: Coke Johnson

Another mix of the extended version of "Mountains" was mixed, and multiple cues were done for the movie, likely including: "Christopher Submerges" [copyrighted as "Chris Submerges"] (bathtub scene), the strings from "An Honest Man," "Bela Lugosi" (listed as "Bella Le Go See") (Katy confronts Christopher and Tricky about the rent), and the title track on piano which was used as the intro to the movie.

The name "Bella Le Go See" was likely influenced by song titles such as Sly and the Family Stone's "Thank You (Falettinme Be Mice Elf Agin)." Three C-60 tapes were made of these tracks.

MAY 1986

Prince was going through a period of renewal and change. His latest album, *Parade,* was recently released to good reviews and the first single, "Kiss" was number 1 on the *Billboard* Hot 100 charts. At number 2 was the Bangles' "Manic Monday," which was also written by Prince, so his professional life was going well. The second single, "Mountains," was about to be released, and the world was waiting for the follow-up to *Purple Rain, Under The Cherry Moon.* Not one to ever rest on his laurels, Prince had already begun creating his next project. The previous weeks had him holed up in Minneapolis, where he was recording a great deal and changing his relationship with Susannah Melvoin. She had recently moved out of his home in Minneapolis and he decided to fly to Los Angeles and bury himself in his recording.

Like Prince had done with Mazarati the previous year, he was dividing his time overseeing two sessions conducted in two different studios, but unlike the earlier sessions in April 1985, which were both taking place at Sunset Sound, Prince was spending more time working on his own music at Sunset Sound, while Sheila was less than a mile away at Capitol Studios.

THURSDAY, MAY 1, 1986 (ESTIMATE)

"**Alexa De Paris**" [12-inch version] (mix)
Multiple cues for *Under The Cherry Moon* score
Sunset Sound, Studio 3 (likely) | booked: noon–open
Producer: Prince | Artist: Prince | Engineer: Coke Johnson (assumed)

"Alexa De Paris" will take you there. It's one of those songs where you're in your car driving through the country, turn that up and have a nice night tune to add to your playlist.[1]

—BrownMark

As usual, Prince increased the potential value of a single release by including a non-LP B-side. "Alexa De Paris," an instrumental that was not included on *Parade*, was given a second life as the flip side of "Mountains." A piano only version can also be heard twice in *Under The Cherry Moon*, during the scene in which Tricky dances with Mary Sharon ("Mary And Tricky Dance") as well as in a scene where Prince plays piano ("Christopher And Couples").

A few other cues were tracked during this session.

SATURDAY, MAY 3, 1986

"Various Jams" (tracking, mix)
"Get On Up" (tracking, mix)
Sunset Sound, Studio 3 | 4:00 p.m.–1:00 a.m. (booked: noon–open)
Producer: Prince | Artist: Prince (recording as the Flesh) | Engineer: Coke Johnson

Prince was doing a lot at that time, and he'd have a couple of studios running at the same time. He'd ask if anyone had a song, or if they wanted to collaborate on an idea, and we were all going back and forth.[2]

—Sheila E.

Coke Johnson arrived at the studio at 11:30 in the morning and began setting up for a band recording, but it wasn't until 4 that people started showing up. Johnson recalls:

He'd come in, nice and fresh and I'd be sitting there waiting. We had all his gear ready, so the drums were set up out in the big room on a riser. He had different stations. So there were guitar stations, the bass, the keyboards, all that stuff so no matter where he went in the recording space, it was already set up, routed through the mixer, assigned to tracks. So, if he went to the Linn drum and played, it would go through to [track] one through eight on the multitrack. I'd just mute the drums, but if he played the real drums, those would record on these tracks too.

Sheila and Levi Seacer Jr. had been at Capitol working on a track called "Split Personality," and now they had to split their time between the two studios. When they arrived, Prince, Wendy, Lisa, Atlanta Bliss, and Eric Leeds were working on a jam. During these group sessions, Prince would often be inspired. Sometimes he would hear something amazing and that could dictate the entire direction of the session. Over the course of the 8-hour funk workout, Prince decided to leave the jam and record the classic "Get On Up" by the Esquires (from their 1967 release on Bunky Records). "That was an anomaly because that was a cover song," recognizes Leeds. "I used to like that song when it was new in 1967. I was like, 'Where did you pull this one out of?'"

"Prince wished he would have written it," explains Susannah. "I think on some level he was just like, 'I want to experience what it's like to play this song that I've loved so much.' He was happy. He could access those feelings. Like if he wasn't in a happy place, he wasn't going to do those songs. Those are songs during a time when he was happy. He was connected to that. It would be always connected to an inner experience."

Prince had everyone contributing to the song using guitars, bass, live drums, cowbell, trumpet, and sax. "I don't know who came up with the horn parts," reflects Eric. "Probably him on that one. And then, a couple of days later we came back in and did some more stuff on it."

Prince had them record the Hammond B-3 keyboard through a Leslie cabinet, in which a rotating drum adjusts the sound as an instrument is played.

Susan Rogers explains: "What's cool about it is that the high frequencies at the top of the cabinet can get this really cool effect because it is on a motor and it spins. It's a sound that was kind of popular in the psychedelic era, in the sixties." It can be found on tracks by the Beatles (guitar on "Lucy In The Sky With Diamonds," "You Never Give Me Your Money"), Pink Floyd ("Echoes"), Cream ("Badge"), and the Beach Boys on their *Pet Sounds* album.

"It's somewhat similar to flanging, although technically it's different," continues Rogers, "but it's similar in the sense that it's kind of a psychedelic effect a little bit from the 60s. It was always fun to do. He had his complement of stuff that he liked."

Status: "Get On Up" (4:30) would not be released during Prince's lifetime. The track was re-recorded as "Everybody Get On Up" (4:02) for Carmen Electra's self-titled 1993 album.

SUNDAY, MAY 4, 1986

"**In A Large Room With No Light**" [listed as "**N.A. Large Room**"] (tracking, overdubs, and rough mixes)
"**Get On Up**" (overdubs, mix)
"**Blackberry Jam**" [jam session] (tracking)
Sunset Sound, Studio 3 | 3:00 p.m.–12:00 noon (booked: noon–open)
Producer: Prince | Artist: Prince and the Revolution | Engineers: "David Z" Rivkin and Coke Johnson

> *Prince was obviously growing and reaching out in different directions as a writer and performer, and he was beginning to enjoy the rapport of playing with other musicians, those of his choice . . . granted, it was a select few, but whereas before it was almost a labor for him to play with other musicians in the studio, now he was beginning to appreciate the uniqueness that each personality brought to the studio.*[3]
>
> —Alan Leeds

The spring had been filled with inspiration, and with it, Prince was moving further away from *Purple Rain* and everything about that period. He'd switched from purple to all colors to black and white, from the core Revolution to a band that was twice the original size and from arena rock to boutique jazz, changing the direction of his music seemingly with no regrets. He advanced the ball down the field in a way that left so much behind, sometimes before others were ready, but Prince ran on his own inner clock. However, to create this new direction, he opened himself up to new influences. Eric Leeds, Atlanta Bliss, and Sheila were all guiding him in a direction that was taking him away from the safety of the Revolution. "I guess when you're with a band for so long which he was with the Revolution, he just wanted to try something else," reflected Atlanta Bliss. "That's his nature. He wants to move on, try new sounds, try new people, and see how he can further develop his musical creativity."[4]

Sheila E.'s new sax player at that time ("Eddie M." Mininfield had left Sheila's band at that point), Norbert Stachel, remembers how Sheila left her session at Capitol Studios, bringing him and Levi Seacer, Jr. to today's session.

I already knew what he could do, because that wasn't the first day that I had interacted with him. I was aware of his music, and I was very intimidated by his music, and once I had met him I was extremely intimidated by his personality. I didn't understand him. I sort of felt weird about how he talked to people and treated people, because he acted like he was so much above everybody, in a way. I didn't feel a connected warmth with him. I was just in awe of his musical skill, but I was sort of uncomfortable about him, to be honest.

We talked a few times, but I never really got to know him. He had his guard up. I'm sure there are people who really got to know him and befriended him, and they would get to know the real Prince, not the mask of Prince.

From 3 in the afternoon until midnight, they played. No actual songs, just several hours of grooves listed as "Blackberry Jam." "It was this marathon session, and basically we were just jamming," as Stachel discloses. "Somebody would come up with a drumbeat, then someone else would come out with a bass line and people would just fall in with their instruments, with ideas. When you put a whole bunch of people together, everyone's contributing their part of it, and that's what we did. Yeah, it doesn't mean that you're going to keep everything you record, but you get a lot of ideas without breaking the inertia."

Although Prince had a solid band behind him, in many ways he was a solo artist and could enter a room alone and come out with something brilliant. But during the times that he allowed other musicians to work with him, the merging of their DNA could produce something amazing. During this session, the group jam switched to tracking songs, and the results stunned those in the room.

"'In A Large Room With No Light' happens to be one of my favorite songs that Prince ever did," reports Eric Leeds. "Maybe because it was Wendy and Lisa's song. I love their music, plus it was just cool and it went into a different time signature at the end and Sheila played her ass off on it."

"The horns were myself, Matt Blistan, and Norbert Stachel. He was there for that session, playing alto sax. [The song was] like—Prince does 5th Dimension. It was an absolutely wonderful performance live, and unlike anything Prince has ever done. It was another one of those cases where I really felt that we were part of something special on that one."[5]

"It's one of my all-time favorite songs ever," declares Wendy. "It's a great song."

"I like things that aren't cookie-cutter songs," agrees Stachel. "I appreciate things that have a little more integrity to them."

"The song has this great horn hook for one thing," observes Susan Rogers.

For another thing, it was one of his more poetic titles and catch phrases. I mean, "Did you ever feel your life was like looking for a penny in a large room with no light?" It's one of those songs where Prince is really trying to tell us something. There aren't that many songs where Prince was expressing straight up frustration, because he usually didn't do that, but in this song he is. He's saying, I'm frustrated. Things aren't working out. I think that song is gold and if you're a Prince fan, listen carefully to that song. He's expressing dissatisfaction. A lot of things that express dissatisfaction ended up in the vault because he didn't want people to think of him in a negative light. He did not want people to know that he got cold or that he was sick or that he was in pain and he rarely would confess that he was hurting.

Prince must have recognized the power of the track as well, as he stayed with the song, expanding and embellishing it, chipping away at the block of marble to reveal his sculpture. "He'd run through it for hours. For hours!" remembers Rogers. "Just to get the feel of where he wanted it."

After several attempts, he apparently felt that they'd realized the track's potential, and he went to work fixing the elements that needed replacing. "What Prince did was record a scratch vocal while we were doing the track, then he would overdub a keepable vocal later," remembers Leeds. "And of course there were a lot of background vocals on it that included Wendy, Lisa and Sheila."

Prince spent 7 hours adding his vocals as well as recording the multiple layers of background vocals with many of the players, including Levi, Sheila, Wendy, and Lisa. A few additional instruments were overdubbed, including: agogô bells, congas, and the Linn LM-1.

At some point during the session, Prince used the musicians around him to add something new to the score for *Under The Cherry Moon* as Stachel explains. "The part I was involved with there wasn't any scoring, really. Eric might've written an arrangement, he and I played soprano and I remember hearing it in the movie, the one little scene that I played soprano sax on. But I didn't know that that was going to be part of the movie at the time that we recorded it, it was part of that marathon session."

Overdubs were also done on "Get On Up." The final 5 hours were spent mixing all of the tracks recorded during this session.

Status: "In A Large Room With No Light" (3:26) [also referred to as "Life Is Like Looking For A Penny In A Large Room With No Light"] was part of a longer jam but eventually edited (3:14) and part of an assembly of *Dream Factory*. It was removed before the next configuration and remained in the vault until it was included on the *Sign O' The Times* Super Deluxe Edition in 2020.

According to Prince, the song was considered for his unreleased *Roadhouse Garden* album that had been scheduled for 1999.[6] Prince also re-recorded the song in July 2009 and that updated version was made available via audio stream on July 15, 2009.

MONDAY, MAY 5, 1986

"In A Large Room With No Light" (vocal overdubs, mix)
"Get On Up" (horn overdubs, mix)
Sunset Sound, Studio 3 | 12:00 noon–1:30 a.m. (booked: noon–open)
Producer: Prince | Artists: Prince and the Flesh | Engineers: Coke Johnson and Susan Rogers

> *I didn't see him sitting and writing "to do" lists. He was incredibly spontaneous. Once he had any idea of a song, it didn't stop until it was done.*[7]
>
> —Susannah Melvoin

Yesterday's session blended into today's without a break. Some of the band left, but Prince stayed with his engineer and continued to work on mixes and cassette copies for the first 2 and a half hours, but eventually Coke Johnson, who'd been in the studio with Prince for more than 24 hours straight, left the session and after a short break, Susan Rogers took over. "He would work you into the ground. And so I could work with Prince and [Susan] could tag team him. A lot of times either she or I would be sleeping. There was a break room right across the hall with a couple nice couches and so we could take little catnaps in there."[8]

Very few people were able to keep up with Prince and when he was focused, music poured out of him. "Music came so naturally to him," explains Stachel. "One example was when Sheila picked me and Levi up and we came to the studio, walked in, and Prince is doing an overdub session."

When we walked into the room he was telling a story and joking with Susan. And at first I didn't even realize he was actually doing something. The keyboards were set up, and he was standing with his back to the keyboards telling a story, and he was doing something with his hands behind his back. And we were hearing the music go by, and he says, "Okay, take it one more time from the top, open up a new track." And then he's telling us a story and telling some jokes and just talking randomly, not in rhythm, but he's doing something with his hands, and then I kind of peek around and I see that he's playing the keyboard while he's telling this story, playing the keyboards behind his back. I was speechless. What is this super, meta-human, superhuman trick?

"I also saw him doing that on the Linn, and he was joking around, telling stories, and he's laying the rhythm tracks down without having to focus at all on what he was doing. He was doing it like he was eating a sandwich while telling a story as if he has three brains. I couldn't believe it."

The session consisted of Prince's continued vocal overdubs for "Get On Up" and horn overdubs (with Atlanta Bliss, Eric Leeds, and Stachel), crossfades, and edits for "A Large Room With No Light." One C-90 and two TDK C-60 cassettes were made, and the 34 hour session ended at 1:30 in the morning.

TUESDAY, MAY 6, 1986

"**In A Large Room With No Light**" (mix)
"**Get On Up**" (mix)
Multiple cues for **Under The Cherry Moon** score including "**Isaac Gets Screamed On**," (listed as "**Under The Cherry Moon Theme**"), and "**Mr. Sharon Arrives At Airport**" (tracking, mix)
The Flesh album (sequencing, segues recorded and mixed)
"**Blueberry Jam**" [jam session] (tracking)
Sunset Sound, Studio 3 | 3:30 p.m.–3:30 a.m. (booked: lockout)
Producer: Prince | Artist: Prince | Engineers: Coke Johnson and Susan Rogers

Prince recognized that we're not making records here. We're playing for ideas. He was searching for a new avenue of expression. He said he would have liked to have been a jazz musician. Sometimes when Matt Fink started just playing around at rehearsal and just tearing up the keyboards, Prince would say, "Man, I wish I could play like that." Then he'd say, "If I could play like that, I wouldn't even be talking to y'all right now. You wouldn't even be able to talk to me." And he'd start talking about what an elite jazz musician he would be. So I think meeting Miles, and Prince having a jazz musician for a

*father, and wanting to explore that aspect of his musicality, I
think that's what those sessions were all about.*

—Susan Rogers

The first 6 hours of this date were spent sequencing a project. Although he'd
recently created a version of his *Dream Factory* album, it is more likely that he
was busy with additional work for *The Flesh* album, including crossfades and
segues for the sequence of songs. Additional mixes of "In A Large Room With
No Light" and "Get On Up" were completed. The former would be included
on an upcoming configuration of *Dream Factory*, but "Get On Up" doesn't appear to have ever been officially attached to a project.

Over at Capitol Studios, Sheila and Levi were finishing a song they'd written
about the state of the planet called "The World Is High." Despite having additional work to be done on the score for *Under The Cherry Moon*, Prince wanted
to jam in the studio, and he once again invited Sheila, Levi and Norbert to join
Eric, Atlanta Bliss, and Prince's childhood best friend and former bandmate
André Cymone—who was going to contribute bass—on a free-form jazz jam that
Prince would call "Blueberry Jam."

André remembers, "When we jammed, 90% of the time I was playing bass,
because he was a guitar player and I was a bass player, and he was really good
obviously at what he did, and I was very good at what I did."

Coke Johnson engineered many sessions like this day's "Blueberry Jam."

> A lot of those extended jams where he would just invite players down and de-
> pending on who it was he would have Matt and Eric over in an isolation booth.
> Sometimes they would just have to wait around for 15 minutes until the groove
> got to where they could put some forms in it because it was mainly Prince who
> started on guitar and sometimes it would get going and then he'd just set his
> guitar down because the bass and the keys and everything's playing and he'd go
> over and start playing the real drums. None of the jams really happened with the
> Linn Drum machine. All the jam sessions were pretty much where they just were
> having fun.

The multi-hour session filled over nine tapes. It is unclear if Prince was looking for a sound or just wanted to jam to relax. "I think the beauty of jamming is
if you're jamming with people that are actually creative, because different people
have different levels of creativity, it's actually a beautiful thing because people
often have something that they will bring to a jam," continues Cymone. "When
you start a beat or a bass line or a guitar line, it's basically writing a song. I think

some people, not everybody, but some people look at it that way and it's almost like mining for gold. It's like you have this jam session and you go back later and you go, 'Okay, is there anything in here that's useful?'"

Prince also tracked two cues for *Under The Cherry Moon*, "Isaac Gets Screamed On" (a short variation on the melody of *Under The Cherry Moon* heard after Mary fights with her father), and "Mr. Sharon Arrives At Airport" (the scene where Isaac Sharon arrives at the airport too late because Christopher just took Mary away) with essentially the same musicians but with Wendy on guitar instead of Levi.

The session ended at 3:30 in the morning and was given to the film editors to be placed in the latest cut of the movie.

Status: "Isaac Gets Screamed On" (8 seconds long) and "Mr. Sharon Arrives At Airport" (39 seconds long) were edited into the film.

WEDNESDAY, MAY 7, 1986

The Flesh album compiled [listed as **"All New Titles"**]
"In A Large Room With No Light" (likely mix)
"Get On Up" (mix)
"Blueberry Jam" session [listed as **"Jams"**] (review and edits)
Sunset Sound, Studio 3 | 12:00 noon–11:00 p.m. (booked: lockout)
Producer: Prince | Artist: Prince | Engineers: Susan Rogers and Coke Johnson

Remember that this was the period where he's searching for his next artistic identity. He can't be himself. He can't do Purple Rain *again. He had those three Purple albums in a row,* Controversy, 1999, *and* Purple Rain. *Following that and* Around the World In A Day, *which was just . . . "Now let me think what to do next," because* Around the World In A Day *was done mostly before we even finished* Purple Rain. *From the* Parade *time going forward, he's in a period of reinvention. What will be my next thing? What will be my next look? My next sound? My next world view? It made perfect sense to bring in other players.*

—Susan Rogers

More time was spent working on updating *The Flesh* album, combining yester-day's jamming with what was already assembled earlier in the winter.

The final 5 hours were spent working on crossfades and edits to the music, seemingly to create a jazz project that Prince could release.

WEDNESDAY, MAY 7, 1986

The second single from *Parade*, "Mountains" with "Alexa De Paris" as the B-side was released and topped out at number 15 on the Black Chart and number 23 on the Pop Chart, much lower than "Kiss," which was number 1, and below almost anything he'd released since *Purple Rain*. Only "Take Me With U" and "America" charted lower at number 25 and number 46, respectively, on the Pop Charts.

FRIDAY, MAY 9, 1986

"Paradise Gardens" (mix and overdubs)
"The World Is High" (mix)
Sheila E.'s third album compiled
Sunset Sound, Studio 3 | 2:30 p.m.–5:30 a.m. (booked: open)
Producer: Prince | Artist: Sheila E. (Prince crossed out) | Engineer: Coke
    Johnson

Sunset Sound . . . we lived there. We lived at the studio.[9]

—Sheila E.

Sheila also spent a great deal of time in the studio, both with Prince and record-ing on her own. For this session, it is unlikely that Prince attended, so she and Coke Johnson spent 6 hours overdubbing and mixing "Paradise Gardens," a slow paced song—similar to Prince's "Eternity"—that seems to compare two young lovers to Adam and Eve, and the paradise that was lost when they gave in to their passion. The song was written by Constance Guzman and Sheila E., and appears to have no input from Prince. An updated mix was also done on "The World Is High." Afterward Sheila and Coke began the first assembly of her third album. Because Prince was the Executive Producer of her album, he had a say in how it was assembled and likely left instructions about how he wanted it to be compiled. The remaining 9 hours were spent building the album and blending the tracks with edits and overdubs.

The exact line-up for this assembly of Sheila's third album is not known, but it likely contained the following tracks:

"Love On A Blue Train"   "Boy's Club"
"Wednesday Like A River"   "Hon E Man"
"Hold Me"   "Paradise Gardens"
"The World Is High"   "Love And Sex"

Five of these compositions would remain on the released album, but all of the tracks would be given additional attention before they were officially released in February 1987. Prince and Sheila would record further songs for the collection over the next several months.

At the end of the shift, "Paradise Gardens" and "The World Is High," were dubbed to two C-60 tapes, and her album was recorded on two C-90 cassettes, likely one for Sheila and one for Prince.

Status: "Paradise Gardens" (3:59) would be released as the B-side for Sheila E.'s "Koo Koo" the following year. An extended version of the track (6:20) would be released with the "Koo Koo" 12-inch.

SATURDAY, MAY 10, 1986

"**If I Could Get Your Attention**" (tracking, mix)
"**If I Could Get Your Attention**" [instrumental] (probable mix)
"**Frustration**" [instrumental] (tracking, mix)
Sunset Sound, Studio 3 | 3:30 p.m.–8:00 p.m. (booked: open)
Producer: Prince (listed as Percy Bagonia) | Artist: Prince | Engineers: Susan
    Rogers and Coke Johnson

He always created a skeleton, and he added what he liked, dif-
ferent voices, and so on. He did not need anyone. If he needed
someone else he could manage with his alter-egos. It was fasci-
nating. I had the same vocal register as him and I could also

*do the high notes that he could not reach, so he could also call
me for that. We recorded . . . "If I Could Get Your Attention"
and other titles, but that did not correspond to me vocally. A
little too cheerful, while I have a pretty dark temperament. I
can be playful in the chorus, but not when I'm the lead singer
on a piece.*[10]

—Jill Jones

When Prince was in a playful mood, it would be found in his music, but also in
his doodles and his creative license with names. For this track, he referred to
himself as "Percy Bagonia," a pseudonym he'd used since his second album. It
can be found on his handwritten lyrics for "I Feel For You," which was written in the late 1970s,[11] and as recently as the lyrics for "Go" in 1985.[12] "Percy
Bagonia sounds like a made-up thing," remembers Jill Jones. "Percy Bagonia,
or Percy, because it would always be like this kind of African American old-ass
name. You know, something really that nobody would be. That's how you
could almost tell it was a pseudonym for anything, or a nickname, because really it would be a name nobody was using. Percy! Not to take away from all the
Percys out there."

Prince created "If I Could Get Your Attention" as he often did by starting
with the live drums and building the layers on top, this time strongly featuring
the Fairlight. He added his own scratch vocal to the track, but it was likely not
considered for a "Prince" release and was always going to be offered to other
singers, including Jill and Taja Sevelle, who both sang lead, as well as background vocals on this over time.

During this brief session, a short instrumental named "Frustration" was also
tracked. No additional details are available about the song.

Two C-60 cassettes were created, and the abbreviated session ended at 8:00
p.m.

Status: "If I Could Get Your Attention" (2:47) was released on Taja Sevelle's
eponymous debut album in September 1987. It did not chart in the United
States, but peaked at number 48 in the United Kingdom in early 1988. In 1993,
Mayte recorded a demo of the track, but it was not released on her CD.

Prince released a re-recorded version (now titled "If Eye Could Get Ur Attention") on November 9, 2015, via TIDAL.

The 2-minute "Frustration" remains unreleased.

SUNDAY, MAY 11, 1986

"Boy U Bad" (tracking, mix)
"It" (tracking, mix)
"It" [instrumental] (guitar overdub, mix)
Sunset Sound, Studio 3 | 5:30 p.m.–8:30 a.m. (booked: open)
Producer: Prince | Artist: Prince | Engineers: Coke Johnson and Susan
   Rogers | Assistant Engineer: Todd Herreman

> *We were in our twenties and we were closely knit because so
> few of us were doing so much work. All of us who worked for
> Prince, were on this tour of duty, so we were a tribe. One time
> we were at rehearsal and a group of us were talking. Prince
> walked in unexpectedly, and it turns out that what we were
> talking about was some member of the crew that was sort of
> misbehaving, and one of our crew members was just in the
> middle of saying that this so-and-so was an asshole and Prince
> walked in and he says, "Who's an asshole?" And we all stopped
> because we didn't want to rat someone out and Prince said,
> "Let's get this straight. There's only one asshole around here
> and that's me."*[13]

—Susan Rogers

Prince was the head of the organization, but for many under him, there was a unity that went beyond simply being coworkers. There was, and still to this day is, a familial bond that only people who worked for him understand. "Most families are more democratic." explained Rogers. "In amongst ourselves, without Prince in the mix, there was a beautiful system that shared responsibilities and shared talents and strengths, but we all looked to Prince as the hub of this wheel to provide our direction. We were kind of like a family with one very strong and very obvious leader."[14]

Despite having a team, Prince worked well when he was alone. "Isolation for him wasn't a hindrance," explains Susannah. "Isolation was a time for him to communicate. So being alone in a room and writing was his most natural place to communicate what he needed to say to any particular person or an entire fanbase or to the public at large."

Prince appears to have worked alone in the studio on this day and recorded two new tracks during this session. The first was "It," a drum heavy song that found Prince singing about sex was recorded quickly, using several layers of the Fairlight, guitar and, for possibly the first time, a drum track from the Fairlight. He also recorded his vocals through a distorted voice box.

When Prince played "It" for Wendy, she recognized the power of his vocals. "I wept. There were certain tracks of his that had that power and beautiful melody, that had more like a desperation to his voice, that I responded to. I could feel his voice right at that frequency where he's just about to crack and go to falsetto but not quite. And it's just that desperate vocal range that, when he sang it and pushed hard, it was heartbreaking to me. And from that vocal range, that frequency, he could also scream. And I would cry. I would cry when I'd hear it."

He followed that with "Boy U Bad," a guitar heavy instrumental blues jam that sounds as if it might have been recorded with members of the Revolution but was likely another solo track.

The 15-hour session continued into the following morning and at the end of the shift, the two songs were mixed. "It" underwent the biggest change during this session because Prince didn't include his distorted vocals and some of the guitar and synth tracks in the mix, creating a much simpler version of the song. They were both placed on two C-90 cassettes, along with various instrumental mixes of "It," which likely contained some of the elements (guitar and some keyboard) that were eliminated earlier.

Status: "It" (5:25) was edited down (5:10) and released on Prince's *Sign O' The Times* album in 1987. Any instrumentals that Prince created from "It" remained unreleased during his lifetime.

"Boy U Bad" also remained unreleased during Prince's lifetime. Some of the structure of the song would find its way into "U Got The Look" in December.

WEDNESDAY, MAY 14, 1986

Venue: Warfield Theatre (San Francisco, California)
Capacity: 2,175 (attendance unknown)

Prince joined The Bangles at the Warfield Theatre in San Francisco, playing guitar and singing along to "Manic Monday" and "Whole Lotta Shakin' Goin' On," a song he had been performing with the Revolution during the recent series of shows. Unfortunately, not everyone was as familiar with the classic Jerry Lee Lewis track. "We pretended to know how that song went," recalled bassist Michael Steele. "We had no idea how to play it."[15]

THURSDAY, MAY 15, 1986

Untitled track (tracking, mix)
Sunset Sound, Studio 3 | 2:00 a.m.–4:00 a.m. (booked: open)
Producer: Prince | Artist: Prince | Engineer: Susan Rogers

> *People are blown away that he has so much in the vault, but not all of it's great.*
>
> —Wendy Melvoin

On many occasions Prince would just jam in the studio looking for a song, casting a wide net unsure what he would catch. "I think he just loved being in the studio making music," reflects Peggy Leonard. "I think he just loved making music, and having state of the art equipment. I don't think he thought of being in the studio as his *job*. At the end of a record, most musicians drag themselves in, it's like, 'Okay let's go.' He was never like that. When he got like that he left, went home. With him, there was never a deadline. If it didn't move him, he was gone. He would just leave. It wasn't like a producer was bugging him to finish a song or anything."

Wendy recalls how Prince viewed the difference between a full song and an experimental jam. "He wanted to finish everything. He wasn't one of those guys that during the first verse went 'This isn't going to work.' He finished the idea, but he knew when there wasn't a song there, and he knew when the jam wasn't good enough."

It seems that Prince left for France after this 2-hour session, and he returned home within a few days.

Status: It is unknown if the track from today's session was ever released in any form.

MONDAY, MAY 19, 1986 (ESTIMATE)

"Get On Up" (mix)
Washington Avenue Warehouse (Edina, Minnesota)
Producer: Prince | Artist: Prince | Engineer: Susan Rogers

Todd Herreman recalls what it was like in Minneapolis while Prince was traveling and the Revolution was rehearsing.

> He was actually going back and forth to Nice, working on the movie *Under the Cherry Moon* at the time, so a lot of times he wasn't actually at rehearsals but he would have the band rehearsing in the warehouse from 10 to 6. They would actually video tape the rehearsals and they would FedEx the videotape and he'd watch them and send back changes. This guy was the hardest working guy I know. And then he would make, sometimes announced, sometimes unannounced, visits back from Nice to check up on the band. Even when he wasn't always there, if people showed up late to rehearsals, they got docked. He was on top of it. I mean he was really on top of it.

Prince probably wanted time with the band because the following day they were scheduled to perform at the Sixth Annual Minneapolis Music Awards.

A brief mix of "Get On Up" was done on this date, and a cassette was made of the session. It is unclear if Prince oversaw the session or if Susan Rogers was using his suggestions to update the track.

TUESDAY, MAY 20, 1986

Sixth Annual Minnesota Music Awards
Venue: Carlton Celebrity Room (Bloomington, Minnesota)
Capacity: 2,150 (attendance unknown)

*On behalf of Prince and the Revolution, we're working really
hard and it's paying off. Thank you.*[16]

—Wendy Melvoin

Prince had missed the awards show the previous year and wasn't able to accept
the multiple awards he'd won, so for this year's event, he made up for it with
a 40-minute show closer that included: "Raspberry Beret," "Girls & Boys,"
"Life Can Be So Nice," "Controversy" (including "All Day, All Night" chants),
"Mutiny" (including chants from "Holly Rock" and part of the chorus from
"Dream Factory"), "Kiss," and "Love Or Money." Interestingly, Prince played
nothing from *Purple Rain*.

Prince would also take home the award for "Best Original Funk Music" for
"Raspberry Beret," "Best Film/Video Score" for *Parade*, and "Best Cover/
Artwork for Album" for *Around The World In A Day*.

The following day, Prince flew back to Los Angeles.

WEDNESDAY, MAY 21, 1986

The 12-inch single of "Mountains" backed by "Alexa De Paris" is released.

FRIDAY, MAY 23, 1986

Venue: Warfield Theatre (San Francisco, California)
Capacity: 2,175 (sold out)

> *There was a lot of confusion between Prince and his managers
> as to what the right path was, in terms of should he or should
> he not tour. And the cast and the opinions seemed to change on
> a daily basis. I know at varying points Prince wanted a tour
> and he didn't want a tour.*[17]

—Alan Leeds

The *Hit-and-Run* tour that Prince was planning was not a full tour in the strict-
est sense. He'd done a few preview shows, just as he'd done for the *Purple Rain*
tour, but with only a handful of concerts over the course of the next 10 weeks,

it was hard to call it a full tour. Nonetheless, he made his way across the country with what seemed like minimal preparation or fanfare, giving the fans little notice before the concert dates, preferring to announce them only a few days before the actual shows. Prince was playing at the Warfield Theatre for the third time this year having guested with Sheila E. in March and with the Bangles the previous week, so he was familiar with the venue. The set and staging was radically different from the *Purple Rain* tour, as he'd expanded the band to include twice as many people than before.

The band was still called "the Revolution," but some of the members of the group didn't feel that it fit anymore. "The name didn't quite have the same meaning to him anymore since he had expanded the band," explained Eric. "So I just kind of termed it 'The Counter-Revolution'."[18]

Unlike the claustrophobic structure of the *Purple Rain* tour, this was tight but allowed room for exploring and spontaneity on stage. "From my standpoint, the *Parade* gigs were just us going out and playing some music. And that's what I enjoyed about it," continues Eric.

> Prince didn't take it as seriously. He looked at it, said, "Okay, this is the year I'm just going to go out and have some fun. I proved what I can do with *Purple Rain* and now I'm just going to go out and be an R&B act." It didn't mean that he didn't take the music seriously, but he looked like he was having fun and a smile on his face was much more genuine than I recall in any of the other tours. Prince was playful. That's why the *Parade* gigs were the most enjoyable for me of what I did in those years, because that was the loosest show that we did. We did an arrangement of "A Love Bizarre," and we did "Mutiny" in that show, and would do either one of them. He would decide on the gig which one he felt like doing that night. So he would lean over to Wendy, to let her know, and Wendy would count it off. If Wendy counted it off "one, two, one, two, three, four," we knew it was "Mutiny." If she counted off "A, B, A, B, C, D," we knew it was "A Love Bizarre."

Even André Cymone joined the band on stage for a song. "He called me up and we did 'The Dance Electric.' It was just spur of the moment, right there and then, and that was it," reflects Cymone, who hadn't rehearsed with the band or participated in the soundcheck. "I think he heard that I was there, and called me up. I can't speak for anybody else, but for me, it was like riding a bike."

In contrast to his last tour, Prince performed very little from *1999* (only "Delirious," as well as a medley of "D.M.S.R.," "Automatic," and an instrumental version of "Lady Cab Driver") and limited *Purple Rain* to just the title track, ignoring most of the biggest hits of his career. Bobby Z recalls Prince's mindset on this decision. "He was two albums past it and he was focused on the new songs."

Eric Leeds agrees. "That tour probably went through more changes just because we had such a big song list that we were starting out with, and then I think he was coming to a determination of what songs worked and what songs didn't, and he said, 'Yeah, what the fuck. I'm just going to do what I feel like doing.'"

MONDAY, MAY 26, 1986

"Pride And The Passion" [instrumental] (tracking, mix)
Sunset Sound, Studio 3 | 9:30 p.m.–6:30 a.m. (booked: open)
Producer: Prince | Artist: Sheila E. | Engineer: Coke Johnson

Prince would talk with the drums.

—Susan Rogers

Work continued on Sheila's album and with Prince in town after his San Francisco concert, he quickly wrote "Pride And The Passion" for her album, the title likely based on the 1957 movie *The Pride And The Passion*, which starred Cary Grant, Frank Sinatra, and Sophia Loren. The song is about a woman who is intrigued by a man who had "everything she was looking for," including a great smile and cash and how he seduced her and the mystery behind what they'd done when they were alone. It's likely that Sheila influenced the track in some way, but it is unclear what elements she added to the composition. The song was registered as being written by both of them, but when the album was released, the song is credited solely to her. Crediting others on tracks that he wrote was something Prince did with great frequency, explains David Z. "I think it's because he didn't think people wanted to see his name doing everything, so he was trying to spread the pie and cultivate his army. That's what he wanted. He wanted his team to come and do everything. And I guess that's why he spread credit around."

Sheila discussed the range of Prince's songwriting in 2018. "No one or two songs are the same, I mean, for an artist to be able to write different genres of music, and then musically not sound the same. . . . You can tell that it's Prince, but he didn't write the same way all the time. It was always different ways of approaching music."[19]

Over the last five years, he used the Linn drum machine on the majority of his tracks. He would often add his own embellishments, but his drum sounds were almost always the basis for his groove, so his respect for them was obvious. Over the last year, he'd jammed with many drummers including the Revolution's Bobby Z, H.B. Bennett, Jonathan Melvoin, and Sheila E., and he apparently enjoyed comparing techniques and styles with some of them. "Just about any drummer was discussed and analyzed," remembered Bobby. "That was really fun, because he loved music and he loved to talk. It was fun to talk drums with him, for sure."[20]

Todd Herreman remembers, "Prince said, 'We're going to have a talk show, it's going to be called 'Drum Talk' and we're just going to have drummers on it but instead of talking in English, they're just going to talk in drum fills like [does drum sfx] and what about [drum sfx], what do you think? [drum efx] so everybody just talked in drum fills and it's going to be called 'Drum Talk.'"

The basic tracks included the Linn drums, organ and keyboard, guitar, and bass, but it appears that Prince didn't have the lyrics ready for the song, so one C-60 cassette was dubbed, likely as a reference for him to write the lyrics. Once that was complete, the session ended at 6:30 the following morning.

Status: The 6-minute "Pride And The Passion" would eventually be edited (4:05) and included on Sheila's third album.

TUESDAY, MAY 27, 1986

"Pride And The Passion" (vocals, sax overdub, mix)
"Paradise Gardens" (sax overdubs, mix)
Sunset Sound, Studio 3 | 2:00 p.m.–4:30 a.m. (booked: lockout)
Producers: Prince/"David Z" Rivkin | Artist: Sheila E. | Engineer: Coke
   Johnson

> *Sheila was a great singer. Man, I would tell her to breathe heavy and she'd give me a completely dramatic breathing of the song. She really impressed me with her ability to project emotion.*[21]
>
> —"David Z" Rivkin

Prince recorded his scratch vocal for "Pride And The Passion," and on reviewing the song, he wanted something extra for the horns on this track. It was something he'd expressed in the past to Eric Leeds. "There were times when he would come to [Matt Blistan and Eric] and talk about maybe adding the third horn, or a fourth horn. Then he would generally lose interest. My response? I have to be absolutely honest, I didn't want a third horn in the section, because it was going to be a pain in the ass, because Prince had the patience of a mosquito. When you have two horns, the options for harmonizing something are pretty limited. If you add a third horn, you have now exponentially added the options for harmonies."

David Z oversaw Sheila's vocals, and Norbert Stachel worked on Sheila's "Paradise Gardens." Eventually, Stachel was joined by Eric Leeds and Atlanta Bliss at the session, and from midnight to 4:30 a.m., Eric, Matt, and Norbert recorded their parts on "Pride And The Passion," but Prince wanted something they weren't providing. He had already recorded his vocals on the song, but now Prince used his voice as an instrument to teach Norbert how he wanted the horns to sound.

"I do remember that Prince sang a horn idea he wanted in one take, from the beginning to the end of the song. It takes several hours to do a good quality horn arrangement, because you split up harmonies, and harmonize in a certain way, depending on the nature of the song, you decide what kind of harmony layering you want of the horns, and I was up all night writing the arrangement."

Three C-60 cassettes were created of the song, including the one that Norbert took with him to work on the arrangement and the session ended at 4:30 in the morning.

WEDNESDAY, MAY 28, 1986

13th Annual ASCAP Awards
Venue: Beverly Wilshire Hotel (Beverly Hills, California)
Capacity: unknown

Dressed in a stylish purple suit, Prince attends the ASCAP Awards ceremony where he received four awards for "Most Performed Songs from October 1, 1984 to September 30, 1985" for "Raspberry Beret," "Purple Rain," "When Doves Cry," and "I Feel For You" (which had been released by Chaka Khan and went to number 3 on the *Billboard* Hot 100 chart and number 1 on both the US R&B and Dance charts).

WEDNESDAY, MAY 28, 1986

"**Pride And The Passion**" (vocals, sax overdubs)
"**Wonderful Ass**" (likely review)
Sunset Sound, Studio 3 | 2:00 p.m.–2:00 a.m. (booked: lockout)
Producer: Sheila E. | Artist: Sheila E. | Engineer: Coke Johnson

When it basically came to the music, I didn't disagree with him . . . usually. Because I was there to do what he was looking for. It would really depend on what mood he was in. Because he was obviously dealing with an instrument that he had never dealt with before, there were times when he was a little reticent about what to do. He knew nothing about what really could or could not be done with it, range-wise or otherwise.

—Eric Leeds

From 2 p.m. to 4 p.m., more work took place on "Pride And The Passion," including additional vocals and horns with Blistan on trumpet, Norbert on sax, and Eric joining them on tenor sax.

For the next 6 and a half hours, vocal work was done by Sheila. Prince was not at the session during the evening, but when he returned, he spent the remaining studio time mixing and reviewing the progress of the track, as well as listening to an older mix of "Wonderful Ass," which had been pulled off the shelf for possible consideration as a B-side for an upcoming release.

While in Los Angeles, it was announced that Prince would perform at the Wiltern Theater later in the week. Tickets would go on sale the next day.

THURSDAY, MAY 29, 1986

"**Pride And The Passion**" (vocals, sax overdubs)
Sunset Sound, Studio 3 | 1:00 p.m.–10:00 p.m. (booked: lockout)
Producer: Prince | Artist: Sheila E. (but Prince is listed) | Engineer: Coke Johnson

[Prince] was a taskmaster, workaholic kind of guy. Nobody could figure it out, he'd be up days in a row without sleep. I don't know how he did it, but it was pretty nuts.

—Norbert Stachel

The session started out with 4 hours of Sheila adding a variety of percussion flairs including: agogô bells, congas, hi-hat, and cymbals to "Pride And The Passion," with Levi contributing keyboards to the track. The remaining 5 hours consisted of Sheila embellishing her lead vocals and Levi and Sheila blending their voices together for the layered background choir.

Although he didn't hear it directly, according to Norbert, Prince had expressed to Sheila that he enjoyed the new horn arrangement. It is likely that Stachel was asked to record an additional sax part for the song, but it seems that Prince may not have spoken to him directly about it either. "Prince wasn't really good at communicating his thoughts and words and emotions, I think because he's such a guarded person. So he'd hide it by being a jokester and kind of making people feel bad and intimidating and being kind of childish. That was his way of talking to people. And he wanted to have control, I guess he was maybe afraid of being taken advantage of or hurt."

Two TDK C-60 cassettes were created, and the session ended at 10 p.m.

FRIDAY, MAY 30, 1986

Venue: Wiltern Theatre (Los Angeles, California)
Capacity: 2,300 (sold out)

There was beginning to be a Prince backlash, and I thought that this was a tour that could go to great lengths to dispel the backlash, because it was back-to-basics, and it was music, and it was fun, it was pure![22]

—Alan Leeds

Tickets for this show went on sale the day before and the venue sold out in 30 minutes, but the lack of promotion for this seemingly random series of stand-alone shows likely limited the awareness of the upcoming film and probably hurt any synergetic momentum Prince could have had from his current album and single releases. Part of a well-planned tour includes a variety of opportunities for press, which cause more excitement and allows more fans to participate. Having a schedule that appeared to be poorly organized, with no repeat venues until the last two US shows, caused everyone involved to have to be available to satisfy Prince's whim, even vital crew like Roy Bennett who had designed the lighting and look of the shows. "I was still working over in England and I was having to fly back and forth constantly doing those shows. I would fly over and arrive the morning of the show, go and do it, get on the plane and fly back and then a few days later get a call and have to fly back."

"Prince felt that the production of the *Purple Rain* tour was regimented," explained Alan Leeds. "Prince was anxious to go to the other extreme and do, to use a George Clinton term from the seventies, an 'anti-tour.' *Parade* was going to be his anti-tour. Normal clothes, i.e., straight hair and a suit, stripped down, no props, real back-to-basics, old-fashioned funk-rock'n'roll tour."[23]

He'd been accused by critics and fans alike as having turned his back on black music; he was determined to prove with his new James Brown-ish ensemble that that wasn't the case, and at the same time give focus to the new musicians in his camp and the new horizons that they had begun to conquer, and he really was anxious to just get on a big stage and jam with these guys. The band was having fun, he was having fun, the music was fresh and fun, but there was. . . . I know for a fact that his management did not like the show. They didn't like the way it looked, they didn't like the campy James Brown-esque review elements of the three guys. Prince was so much into this mentality of being anti what the big production of tours were, and it was his way of saying, "Look, I can't outdo *Purple Rain*, so rather than compete with myself I'll go to the other extreme." Well, that also meant, in terms of lighting and everything else. And I remember sitting at one of the *Hit-and-Run* shows with [Prince's manager Steve] Fargnoli on the soundboard, and I was getting off, I thought it was the greatest show we'd ever done, because I'm a music guy, and Fargnoli was just shaking his head, "It looks awful, the lights are messed up, it just doesn't look good, Prince won't let us light it" because he didn't want a lot of lighting effects. So it was kind of a difference of opinion going on between him and management as to how widely to expose this anti-tour, for fear that it might derail this mega-stardom that *Purple Rain* had given birth to.[24]

"It was pretty basic," agreed Roy Bennett. "Even when we started—eventually I designed a real show, but it was basic. There were no moving lights or anything."

"I was glad to be unencumbered from the costumes and the Linn and being stuck to playing the album, *Purple Rain*," remembers Bobby Z. "On the *Parade* tour, we were *playing*. That was a real big band, with the horns and everything and it was tight and it was the ultimate."

An afterparty was thrown at Tramp's in Beverly Hills. Prince's former girl-friend Vanity was in attendance.

Three songs from this concert ("Automatic," "D.M.S.R." and "The Dance Electric") were released as part of Prince's NPG Ahdio Show #7 on August 28, 2001.

As the release date approached, Warner was still nervous about *Under The Cherry Moon* being seen as an "art film" instead of the blockbuster that everyone expected, so they took matters into their own hands, remembers editor Rebecca Ross.

> They basically took our black and white work print—it was almost the final cut—and had everything printed from the color negative and paid a Warner Bros. assistant editor to assemble the movie. We screened it and Prince saw it and just said, "Destroy it, make sure everything is destroyed." He was miserable, just unhappy with the color version. Everything was shot for black and white with filters which made it look awful as a color film. Michael Ballhaus, the cinematographer, had done black and white films before using this technique. And it was Prince's vision to make a black and white film. *Under The Cherry Moon* was shot on a color negative, but printed in black and white.

"So somewhere there is a color negative of the movie. I don't know *where*, because they wouldn't have destroyed it," reveals Rebecca. "But, yes somewhere in a studio vault it exists."

JUNE 1986

"**Pride And The Passion**" (2-track edit and crossfades)
"**Love And Sex**" (2-track edit and crossfades)
"**Soul Salsa**" (2-track edit and crossfades)
Sheila E.'s third album assembled (edits, crossfades)
Sunset Sound, Studio 2 | 10:00 p.m.–12:00 midnight (booked: 7:30–open)
Producer: Prince | Artist: Sheila E. (Prince scratched out) | Engineer: Coke
   Johnson

> *Sheila, I think around this point, had expressed an interest in*
> *no longer being a front person. After she did her third album,*
> *she did not want to be a leader of the band, she wanted to play*
> *drums. And specifically she wanted to play drums for Prince.*[1]
>
> —Susan Rogers

Prince flew back to Minneapolis, leaving Sheila to work on her album. Over the
last few days she'd recorded overdubs on "Soul Salsa" and likely some other
tracks, preparing them for this session. During this shift, crossfades, edits, and
dissolves were done on several tracks, and Sheila's album was compiled during
this short session. Prince did not attend the session, and Sheila oversaw the
work, but she was not as enthusiastic about where she was in her career. In
1987, Sheila explained her thoughts on making a switch. "I'm more comfort-

able being in the background, playing behind someone. I can play drums and percussion and not have to worry about carrying a show. There's incredible pressure on a solo artist. You don't have that kind of pressure as a background player. I just need a break from it."[2]

It was also becoming obvious to some of those around Prince, that Sheila wasn't alone in her thoughts about backing away from fronting her own band. "There was absolutely no doubt in my mind that [Prince's] long-term vision was that Sheila was gonna end up being the drummer in the band,"[3] reflected Eric Leeds.

Two cassettes, one C-60 and one C-90, were made of the collection.

TUESDAY, JUNE 3, 1986

"Slow Love" (mix)
"Can't Stop This Feeling I Got" [1982 version] (strings, mix)
"Yah, You Know" [1982 version] (probable mix)
"I Could Never Take The Place Of Your Man" [1979 version] (review)
Dream Factory album assembled
Washington Avenue Warehouse (Edina, Minnesota)
Producer: Prince | Artist: Prince | Engineer: Susan Rogers

When we sequenced the record, we needed a song to go between two of the really important songs. It was kind of like a palate cleanser. He would write a song just to put in the sequence, so that the sequence would make sense. "I Could Never Take the Place of Your Man" and "Slow Love" were pulled out of the vault to be those segue songs, just to help finish this record and get it out there, so he didn't have to write another ballad. He said, "I don't feel like writing another ballad. I have an old song. Let's put 'Slow Love' on there."[4]

—Susan Rogers

Originally recorded by Prince on July 1, 1984, "Slow Love" came to Prince's attention through Carole Davis, a songwriter, former *Playboy* model, and actress who appeared in the 1984 movie *The Flamingo Kid* and had been considered for a part in *Purple Rain*. "['Slow Love'] wasn't much of a collaboration," according to her. "I wrote the song and he wanted to buy it from me. He had his lawyers call me, and they offered me $25,000 to own the song outright, and I refused, and they got back to me about a month later to give me 50 percent of publishing and writers, which I accepted for the opportunity to appear on a Prince record."[5]

"When Prince brought it out of the closet and decided to include it on an album, he didn't speak much of Carole Davis," recalled Susan Rogers. "I think he said something about they wrote this song together, but that was all. He didn't talk much about her, but it seemed as if it was a fond memory for him."[6]

Ilene "Novi" Novog and Suzie Katayama were brought in to add strings to the track, updating the sound, helping it to fit in with the overall feeling of his current project.

"Yah, You Know," which was originally recorded on June 5, 1982, and updated in 1985 by Wendy and Lisa, was brought out again as well for additional overdubs and an updated mix. Not every song he wrote would be flawless, but he expressed a pride in all of them and the hope that they'd be shared with others, according to Susannah. "Because he was just so prolific he wanted it out. He would say, 'My children need a life.' So, he would give them life by putting them out. They're all his children, and he would raise his children, and he didn't want to thwart his children."

Prince also reevaluated "Can't Stop This Feeling I Got," which dates back to 1982 as well and had also been revisited just over a year ago. The song also received string overdubs from Novog and Katayama as well as an updated mix on this date.

He assembled all of these songs for *Dream Factory*, his expanding collection that reflected his philosophies and relationships with the people who were important to him, according to Alan Leeds.

Dream Factory clearly related to Wendy and Lisa and Susannah's involvement in the band. So in Prince's mind, regardless of how he wants to interpret this, as a solo project vs a group ethic, in his mind, which is all that counts here, his perception of the situation was *Dream Factory* equated Coleman and the Melvoins, without which he had no *Dream Factory*. As background singers and collaborators they were more active than perhaps album credits would indicate. Whatever *Dream Factory* meant to him, it was inspired by the camaraderie of that group of people during that period of time, whether they appeared on every song or not.[7]

Work on the 19-track collection would continue, but at this point it consisted of:

Side One:
  "Visions"
  "Dream Factory"
  "Wonderful Day"
  "The Ballad Of Dorothy Parker"
  "It"

Side Two:
  "Strange Relationship"
  "Teacher, Teacher"
  "Starfish And Coffee"
  "Colors"
  "In A Large Room With No Light"
  "Nevaeh Ni Ecalp A"
  "Sexual Suicide"

Side Three:
  "Crystal Ball"
  "Power Fantastic"

Side Four:
  "Last Heart"
  "Witness 4 The Prosecution"
  "Movie Star"
  "A Place In Heaven"
  "All My Dreams"

Prince went out of his way to feature Wendy and Lisa with "Colors" and "Visions," respectively. Up until this point in his career, he had never allowed members of the band to be given such a spotlighted position of prestige. "He felt like he had something really special with us," reveals Wendy. "And we felt like we did, too. We really loved him. We loved what we had."

Despite his obvious affection for Wendy and Lisa, and their active participation in the project, Prince assembled the collection on his own. "He never really shared that kind of information," explains Wendy. "It always seems like everything's always happening at once. I never saw or heard a delineation of anything. All of a sudden, things were done and there was a record of it."

At some point during the assembly of the album, Prince would take the original version of "I Could Never Take The Place Of Your Man"—recorded on May 23, 1979—out of storage. He reviewed it for consideration on *Dream Factory*, but this version of the song didn't fit, so it wasn't included.

Susan Rogers remembered that during this period, Susannah was inspired by the *Dream Factory* project and began creating artwork for it. "Susannah was in the next room with a sketch pad and some crayons and she started sketching out an album cover for *Dream Factory*, very dreamy with soft clouds and so on."[8]

"He asked me to paint the album cover," recalls Susannah, "and I have it still to this day."

Status: A 5-and-a-half-minute version of "Slow Love" would go through a few more overdubs and mixes before it was edited down (4:22) for release on *Sign O' The Times*. "Yah, You Know" (3:10), "Can't Stop This Feeling I Got" (2:40), and "I Could Never Take The Place Of Your Man" (3:13) would all be reworked or re-recorded. The updated "I Could Never Take The Place Of Your Man"(6:50) was placed on the next configuration of *Dream Factory*, then edited (6:21), and included on *Crystal Ball* and edited once more (6:30) for release on *Sign O' The Times*.

The 1979 version of "I Could Never Take The Place Of Your Man" (3:13) was included on the *Sign O' The Times* Super Deluxe Edition in 2020. The updated "Yah, You Know" remained unreleased during Prince's lifetime.

WEDNESDAY, JUNE 4, 1986

"Slow Love" (horn overdubs, rough mix)
"Yah, You Know" (mix)
Galpin Blvd. home studio (Chanhassen, Minnesota)
Producer: Prince | Artist: Prince | Engineer: Susan Rogers

> *I enjoyed playing on ["Slow Love"]. Those were some tricky parts and I think the horn parts really made the song.*
>
> —Matt "Atlanta Bliss" Blistan

To be in Prince's inner circle, it was mandatory that you could relate to him on a musical level, and he surrounded himself with those who could blend their knowledge with his. It wasn't always a smooth process, but when he trusted another musician, he'd often give them much more latitude to add to his sound. For example, the arrangements of the horn parts for Prince's music relied on a blend of his incredible understanding of how elements worked together but also the skills of those around him, as Eric Leeds recalled.

> We'd get a call and he'd say, "Be in the studio as soon as you can get here." And we'd have no idea of what we were going to do until we got there. "Slow Love" is a perfect example. I remember on that song, Matt [Blistan] and I got to his house, Prince was not there. Susan was there, they had the tape up, and the instructions were "Put the horns on." I came up with an arrangement, put it on, we recorded it, and we finished recording it just as Prince arrived. He had been out somewhere. He came over, listened to it, and apparently, he wasn't thrilled. So he said,

"No, let's . . . ah. . . ." He laughed and said, "Come on, let's get back in there and do something else with it." Okay, my clock was running! And we got into another thing on it, and I can't really tell you who did what on it. Because a lot of times I would come up with an idea, he would take that idea and say, "Okay, that's cool, now let's do this with it," then maybe his idea would then tell me, "Okay, well, I think I know what you're doing there, what if we do that this way" and by the time we're done with it, it's just like this kind of a linear thing to it and we'd all have our hands in it. And Blistan might come up with a line and would say, "Let's harmonize that line," and Prince would say, "I like that line, but change the last two notes to something else." And that's how a lot of the stuff would come about.[9]

Updated mixes of "Yah, You Know," "A Place In Heaven," "Witness 4 The Prosecution," and "The Ballad Of Dorothy Parker" likely took place late in the session on this date or the following day.

FRIDAY, JUNE 6, 1986

Venue: Masonic Temple Auditorium (Detroit, Michigan)
Capacity: 4,100 (sold out)

> *That was his testing ground. He thought if it'll work in De-troit, it'll work anywhere.*
>
> –Wally Safford

Like he did with the start of the *Purple Rain* tour, Prince relied on Detroit as a sounding board, according to Jerome Benton. "Prince had a relationship with Detroit. They had this component called Mojo radio and he played our stuff and he accepted us and he embraced us."[10]

With the *Hit-and-Run* tour, Prince was playing everything loose. He arrived at 3:30 in Detroit and went immediately to the venue for a 4 o'clock soundcheck. This evening's show was a run through for the next day's birthday performance, and almost everything, including the setlist and what Prince wore, would be duplicated the following night.

SATURDAY, JUNE 7, 1986

Venue: Cobo Arena (Detroit, Michigan)
Capacity: 11,923 (sold out)

> *Record sales and things like that . . . it really doesn't matter. It keeps a roof over your head, and keeps money in all these folks' pockets that I got hangin' around here! [laughs] It basically stems from the music, and I'm just hoping that people understand that money is one thing but soul is another. That's all we're really trying to do. I wouldn't mind if I just went broke, because as long as I can play this type of thing and come here, you know. . . . There were a lot of people there tonight and they turned the lights on and I looked up . . . it brings tears to your eyes because it's just—you can feel the love in the room. And that means more than money. I could just go on for hours . . . I don't know, I just have fun, and I'm thankful to be alive.*[11]

> —Prince

Atlanta Bliss was the newest person in the band, and the Cobo Arena held his biggest audience so far. "When the lights went out in the arena, it was quiet at first, and then they came out with the flashlights with us walking up on stage. And the people around the side of the stage could see the band walking on stage, so they started cheering and as we went up, the cheer just went all the way around the arena in a circle! And that in itself was just a rush. I said, 'This is it! This is what I've been waiting for!' And by the time we're on stage, there was such an uproar from the crowd. 'Yeah, this is what I wanna do!'"[12]

"Musically it was great too," he continued. "Prince was so creative at the time, even with his segues between the music, it was a challenge just doing that. Because he would come up with music on the spot and we would develop it right there. It would be fresh music no one's ever heard before. Including ourselves."[13]

Tonight was Prince's 28th birthday, and Wendy led the crowd in a rendition of "Happy Birthday" to celebrate the event. Prince had the entire show (and likely the previous night's show) recorded for a possible home video release. In fact, the music video from "Anotherloverholenyohead" was recorded during his time in Detroit.

Mazarati were also on the bill as the opening act, but Prince seemed indifferent. Unlike other protégé bands, he wasn't actively pushing them. It is possible that was based on Prince not having total control over them because they were BrownMark's project. "When they walked out on the stage," detailed Brown-Mark, "the crowd went off. They loved Mazarati. And I don't think that sat well with him, because right after that, they were done. He just took them off the tour and they disappeared. So, everything I thought about this group in regard to Prince started to become a reality. [He] either wanted to take them over or if he couldn't accomplish that, then he needed to dismantle them."[14]

After the concert, Prince called "The Electrifying Mojo" radio program to speak to the host and did his first live public interview ever. The wide-ranging interview covered how grateful he was for the help promoting his show and career, his vault, his praise for Jerome and the Time, his upcoming movie, and to remind everyone that Detroit was **"like my second home."**[15]

He may have still had last year's incident with the photographer on his mind or at least felt like giving the audience a chance to understand that any situations that are confusing or appear damaging are based on his dedication to the music and his fans. **"Hopefully people understand that there's just a lot on my mind and I try to stay focused on one particular thing. And I try not to hurt nobody in the process."**[16]

Status: A videotape of his time in Detroit would air in Japan and parts of Europe in 1986. A 45-minute version was broadcast in the Netherlands on October 15, 1986.

TUESDAY, JUNE 10, 1986

Venue: Freedom Hall (Louisville, Kentucky)
Capacity: 13,000 (sold out)

The following day, Prince flew back to Los Angeles.

THURSDAY, JUNE 12, 1986

"Baby Go-Go" (tracking, overdubs, mix)
"Splash" (mix to 2-track tape)
"Slow Love" (possible overdubs, mix to 2-track tape)
Sunset Sound, Studio 2 | 12:00 midnight–5:00 a.m. (booked: open)
Producer: Prince | Artist: Prince | Engineer: Coke Johnson

> *There was just tons of stuff that he was just doing on his own,
> I mean, he was just living in the studio. And there was a lot of
> other stuff that Wendy and Lisa were working with him on,
> too. A lot of which didn't see the light of day.*[17]
>
> —Eric Leeds

Because of the lack of notice, Sunset Sound wasn't able to book his usual room, so Prince was placed in Studio 2 for a few days to record. The only new song from this session was "Baby Go-Go," the type of song that Prince seems to have been able to record without a lot of work, but unlike many of his other songs, this one contains little depth. References to James Brown's music in the lyrics are likely overlooked when the line that proceeds it says: "Whenever I see your body move, ooh baby, I lose my cool. Something about you, I don't know, makes me wanna go-go."[18]

Live drums and cymbals, bass, guitar, and the Fairlight were all blended together for the track, and Prince was able to record his vocals quickly on top of the sparse musical bed. Parts of the background are similar to "Anotherloverholenyohead," which was set to be released as the next single.

Additional work on "Splash" and "Slow Love," which were being prepped for possible inclusion on *Dream Factory*, also probably took place on this date.

Two TDK C-60 cassettes were dubbed of the session, which wrapped up at 5 a.m. Prince flew back to Minneapolis on June 14 to rejoin the Revolution who were continuing the rehearsals for the current tour.

Status: "Baby Go-Go" (4:42) was eventually re-recorded and released by Nona Hendryx on her 1987 *Female Trouble* album. Prince's version was not released during his lifetime, although he rehearsed it for the *Sign O' The Times* tour in 1987.

TUESDAY, JUNE 17, 1986

"Data Bank" (tracking, mix)
"Can't Stop This Feeling I Got" [multiple takes] (tracking, mix)
"We Can Fuck" (tracking, mix)
"Yah, You Know" (mix)
"Neon Telephone" (mix)
Washington Avenue Warehouse (Edina, Minnesota)
Producer: Prince | Artist: Prince and the Revolution | Engineer: Susan
    Rogers | Assistant Engineer: Todd Herreman

> *I was jamming on a song called "Data Bank" and the next
> thing you know it's coming out on the Time's album. And I got
> zero credit.*
>
> —BrownMark

Prince would often show up early, or more accurately, if you showed up *after*
him, *you* were late, so it was common for members of his band to turn up before
the call time to get warmed up to avoid having their pay docked. On this day,
BrownMark arrived early to work on a groove he'd created for Mazarati, and he
was experimenting with it when Prince and Susannah entered the warehouse, as
she recalls. "The day that 'Data Bank' was recorded was a really interesting day."

> Prince and I got there early as well, so it was just me and Prince, and Mark was
> working on his bassline groove. It's [Mark's] song, it's his groove and then Prince
> picked up his guitar, and they started a bit. And everybody started slowly coming
> in for rehearsal and picked up their instrument and started to play. And then Lisa
> started playing. Bobby obviously was starting to pick up and started playing right
> away. And it was like 8 hours playing that groove. . . . Non-stop!
>
> Every once in a while when someone else actually inspired something in him,
> Prince gets super excited and giddy. And, so the guy that you hear on that track
> is exactly who Prince is when he's really playful and really into something. He
> loved to just add his stuff, and he can then become part of a band, he's the band
> member, and he can do something. But mind you, he never gave credit to Mark
> for writing the song, which was another story in itself, because unfortunately he
> was never acknowledged for it.

"He just doesn't know who was involved in a lot of that stuff because it was
just jam sessions on top of jam sessions," recalls BrownMark, "and I could be in
there jamming with the drum machine on a bass riff and he would come in and

record it with the rest of the band, and the next thing you know it would become a song and you would get zero credit for it. I'm not saying he . . . [stole it] but I think there's so many jams, he doesn't know who did what."

"For 'Data Bank,' that riff *is* the whole song," continues BrownMark. "And then you add the lyrics. That's all there is to that song, everything else is irrelevant. A riff is more than just a riff in dance music."

"The thing about 'Data Bank,'" reflects Susannah. "These are parts that I remember about Prince, *the man*. There's a moment in 'Data Bank' when he goes: 'Ha-ha-ha!' And he does this great laugh. That is the stuff that he's on the mic doing. The vocal's done later, but all the adlib stuff, that was all happening right then. When he's saying: 'You're in the wrong key, cuz!' And then he laughs. It's because Mark was in the wrong key at that time, and then the change came."

"There was some sibling rivalry between Mark and Prince," she continues, "Although it was all on Prince's side, because Mark wasn't trying to compete with Prince in any way. But unbeknownst to Mark, Prince was trying to have some sort of competitive relationship with him. Although Mark wasn't in that relationship, Prince was having it for the both of them, so it's kinda funny. But he would do that a lot with a lot of different people."

"Prince was a hard guy to work for, he lays down the law, and if you think you can challenge him, you'll be surprised by his reaction," reflects BrownMark. "At the time I didn't understand, but as time went on, I'd just go with the flow and I started to understand why he did the things he did. This is *his* show. This is not the Mark Brown show, this is the Prince show."

Prince always seemed to be looking for a new way to milk a sound out of an instrument. **"You've got to understand that there's only so much you can do on an electric guitar,"** according to Prince. **"There are only so many sounds a guitar can make. Lord knows I've tried to make a guitar sound like something new to myself."**[19]

He had tweaked the sound through his choice of speaker, sometimes from directly inputting his guitar into the console (as he just did with "Baby Go-Go"), or putting it through a guitar pedal. No matter what the method, he wanted it to sound different, so today he put the guitar through a Leslie cabinet as he did with a Hammond B-3 keyboard the previous month on "Get On Up."

The effect would be used many times over the next few months, including: "Girl O' My Dreams," "Soul Psychodelicide," "Rockhard In A Funky Place," "Walkin' In Glory," and "Play In The Sunshine," as well as on the additional tracks that were taken out of the vault and being re-recorded that day.

"We were still rehearsing," explained Eric Leeds. "We did 'Data Bank,' 'Can't Stop This Feeling I Got' and a song called 'We Can Fuck,' which came out on *Graffiti Bridge* with George Clinton doing the lead vocals. They changed the title to 'We Can Funk' when they put it on *Graffiti Bridge*, but the song was called 'We Can Fuck.' We did the three, I think almost as a medley, and it was the whole band and we just killed on that."

Prince, Atlanta Bliss, Eric, Wendy, Miko, BrownMark, Dr. Fink, Lisa, and Bobby Z worked on the tracks all day.

Mixes were created on those three songs as well as on "Yah, You Know" and "Neon Telephone." During that time, Atlanta Bliss and Eric left to work in a local studio on the extended version of "Anotherloverholenyohead."

Status: "Data Bank" (7:52), "Can't Stop This Feeling I Got" (2:09, the re-recording of the 1982 version), and "We Can Fuck" (5:30) were tracked on this date. All of these versions remained unreleased during Prince's lifetime. The original 1982 recording of "Can't Stop This Feeling I Got" appeared on *1999* Super Deluxe in 2019. A re-recorded version from 1989 was released in 1990 on *Graffiti Bridge*. "Data Bank" was later re-recorded with the Time and appeared on their album *Pandemonium* in 1990. A 1989 updated version of the 1984 recording of "We Can Fuck" was also released on *Graffiti Bridge* in 1990, while the 1984 version of the song was featured on the Deluxe version of posthumous rerelease of *Purple Rain* in 2017.

TUESDAY, JUNE 17, 1986

"**Anotherloverholenyohead**" [12-inch version] (horn overdubs)
Creation Studios, Minneapolis, Minnesota
Producer: "David Z" Rivkin | Artist: Prince and the Revolution | Engineer: "David Z" Rivkin

There were two sessions done that day. With the full band we did "Data Bank," "Can't Stop This Feeling I Got" and "We Can Fuck." We did those in the afternoon at the warehouse in our rehearsal. And then that evening, Matt and I went over to Creation Studios, which is on Nicolet Avenue.

—Eric Leeds

Prince requested that Blistan and Eric work on the extended version of "Anotherloverholenyohead," which was slated as the next single. Leeds recalls:

> When we put "Anotherloverholenyohead" in the show, there were no horns on the original version. And there's a little interlude that I wrote for it, and he said, "When we get to the song . . . let's extend that and you'd just solo there." And I said, "Well, instead of me soloing there, since I'm soloing on so many of the songs, maybe I can write something." And he said, "Okay, have at it." So I went home and I wrote an interlude that was played by me and Matt. So that's what we did live. And then when we did it live, and after the song was over, we used the vamp on it and Prince would leave the stage and Lisa would come down and play a long piano solo. And I wrote a string of horn lines behind her solo. So later when Prince thought about doing a 12-inch, he had me and Blistan go into the studio and just overdub these lines that we were doing on the live version.

Prince did not attend this session, so he had David Z oversee it.

Status: The 12-inch version of "Anotherloverholenyohead" (7:52) was released in the United States on July 30, 1986, backed with "Girls & Boys." Charting as a double A-side, it peaked at number 21 on the *Billboard* Hot Dance/Disco–Club Playlist on September 6, 1986, and spent a total of six weeks on that chart.

WEDNESDAY, JUNE 18, 1986

"**Girl O' My Dreams**" [jam, multiple takes] (tracking, rough mix)
"**Data Bank**" [long version] (mix)
"**Can't Stop This Feeling I Got**" (mix)
"**We Can Fuck**" (mix)
Washington Avenue Warehouse (Edina, Minnesota)
Producer: Prince | Artist: Prince and the Revolution | Engineer: Susan Rogers

> *"Girl O' My Dreams," "Can't Stop This Feeling I Got," and*
> *"We Can [Fuck]" were gonna be part of a short-lived idea he*
> *had to do a Broadway show which never saw the light of day.*
> *The concept kind of came and went.*[20]
>
> —Eric Leeds

"For me, the warehouse was the best vibe, way more than the studios ever were," remembers Susannah, "because it was so huge and open and the band was always set up, and the monitors were always up, everything was ready to go and the board was always on. If you were lucky enough to have an hour break . . . It was like, come back in 20 minutes. It was from 10:00 to 10:00 with a small break."

There was a difference in the way a song sounded when Prince did it himself and when he recorded it with his band. By this time, Prince's sound was expanding and he was using both the classic Revolution as well as the new members of the band, including Miko Weaver who was a second, or even third guitar player in the band, depending if Prince strapped on his as well. And during sessions like this, Prince was in charge, but he was also receptive.

"Fact is fact. There were so many creative ideas flowing, and his were 99 percent right all the time," explained Bobby Z. "But if you had 1 percent—first of all, it better be damn good, and if it was good and it enhanced it, it brought everyone closer, and everyone wanted to contribute."[21]

After the band jammed the skeleton of "Girl O' My Dreams," Prince decided that it was ready for a take. Starting with a live drum section that was similar to the intro to "And How," Prince and the extended Revolution added bass, multiple guitars (including one recorded with the Leslie cabinet), keyboards, piano, sax, trumpet, and a rare appearance of a harmonica. Background vocals were overdubbed by Prince, Miko, Wendy, Lisa, and BrownMark.

Prince had an uncanny ability to focus all of his energy on making an instrument express what he had in his head flawlessly, remembered Matt Fink. "When I was in the studio with him at times, he would flow with whatever he was thinking, and it would come out in one take and he'd just play it. Usually perfect. Very rarely did he have to punch in and fix it."[22]

"Prince had perfect time and perfect pitch," Bobby Z revealed. "Nothing got away from him, so you had to stay in your lane and do your job. Even when he was on the speakers 30, 40 feet away, he heard everything."[23]

But his quest for a better sound from the instruments and how they blended together didn't always mirror how he felt about his recording equipment, as Susan Rogers details. "I was complaining because we were going so fast and I thought the sounds could be better, and I said, 'You know, Prince, why don't we use automation? Why don't we try one of those new SSL consoles, why don't we try something new?' And he asked why. And I said, 'Well, because it could sound a lot better.' And he said, 'We don't sound like those other guys. That's what makes us special.' And I'm thinking, yeah, we sound worse. But he didn't care about stuff like that."[24]

And that taught me another important lesson that people are not buying sounds, people are buying music. The technology is merely facilitating his thinking. Now that can work when the thinking is genius. When the thinking is average, then the sounds have to be extraordinary and this has been true in the history of music. When new music comes along, whether it's EDM or when punk came along in the seventies, punk sounded like shit, but it was great because the ideas were new. The Ramones didn't spend a lot of time—neither did the Sex Pistols—getting those records to sound good. People are buying this new idea.[25]

Status: "Girl O' My Dreams" (1:25) was re-recorded and released by T. C. Ellis in May 1991 on his only album *True Confessions*. Prince does not appear as a musician on the updated release. Prince's own version remained unreleased during his lifetime.

THURSDAY, JUNE 19, 1986 (ESTIMATE)

"**Anotherloverholenyohead**" [extended version] (mix)
"**Wonderful Day**" (possible mix)
Washington Avenue Warehouse (Edina, Minnesota)
Producer: Prince | Artist: Prince and the Revolution | Engineer: "David Z"
  Rivkin

> *To this day ["Anotherloverholenyohead"] is one of my top five favorite Prince songs ever. Although I think I did write a cool horn arrangement for the live version.*[26]
>
> —Eric Leeds

"David Z did the 12-inch [of 'Anotherloverholenyohead']," remembers Lisa. "I think I'd been doing that solo live. It was just one of those extended jam things, and it was like, 'Okay, this would be a good time for Prince to change clothes and for Lisa to do her weird piano thing.' It was after we'd already done it live, so the 12-inch was like trying to imitate what we did live."

David Z may have also done an updated mix on "Wonderful Day" near the end of the session.

SUNDAY, JUNE 22, 1986

> 10th Annual Black Radio Exclusive Awards
> Venue: Sheraton Universal Hotel (Universal City, California)
> Capacity: unknown

Prince attends the Black Radio Exclusive Awards ceremony. He was one of the recipients of the Drummer Awards. This ceremony took place at the end of a 5-day conference held by the Black Radio Exclusive magazine to celebrate Black Music History Month. Mazarati and Sheila E. performed live during the event (on Friday, June 20).

MONDAY, JUNE 23, 1986

> **"Girls & Boys"** [7-inch single] (edit, mix)
> **"The Ballad Of Dorothy Parker"** [Clare Fischer's orchestral section] (review, mix)
> Washington Avenue Warehouse (Edina, Minnesota)
> Producer: Prince | Artist: Prince and the Revolution | Engineer: Susan Rogers

> *When Clare was sending something, Prince would get very excited. When's the tape coming? And when it would get there and first thing, he'd get in the car and listen to it.*
>
> —Susannah Melvoin

"When it would come back, it was always, 'Oh my God, this is so exciting.' He'd get the FedEx package and inside would be the multi-track tape and on the stereo pair of tracks would be this orchestral mix that Clare had done," according to Susan Rogers. "He'd push up the faders and there it is. I mean, there's something brand new. It was thrilling and really, really exciting. Those were breathless moments. Prince loved what Clare did."

Despite the quality of musicianship that was reflected in Fischer's work, not every track was used, which was the case with "The Ballad Of Dorothy Parker," explains Susan. "Sometimes it wouldn't match what Prince's vision was for the song."

At some point, likely after midnight going into June 24, Prince created a mix with the orchestra for this track but decided not to use it when it was released. The final version contained no arrangement from Fischer or sax from Eric Leeds, who'd recorded his overdubs in April.

Prince also spent part of the session editing "Girls & Boys." It is unclear what was planned for this edited version because the track was scheduled for release (as the B-side of "Anotherloverholenyohead") on July 2 and that may not have been enough time to master, print, and ship the singles in time.

WEDNESDAY, JUNE 25, 1986 (ESTIMATE)

"**Anotherloverholenyohead**" [live from Cobo Hall] (mix)
Washington Avenue Warehouse (Edina, Minnesota)
Producer: Prince | Artist: Prince | Engineers: Susan Rogers and "David Z"
    Rivkin

Prince asked David Z to mix the audio from the live version of "Anotherlover-holeyohead" that had been recorded during the birthday show in Detroit on June 7. No promotional video had been shot, so the concert video would be the official music video for the track.

THURSDAY, JUNE 26, 1986

"**Yes**" (safety copy made, edits)
Galpin Blvd. home studio (Chanhassen, Minnesota)
Producer: Prince | Artist: The Family | Engineer: Susan Rogers

When we were home in Minneapolis sometimes he would have a steady girlfriend like Susannah Melvoin, but not always. He dated a lot and when we were in Minneapolis, Thursday night at First Avenue at the club was "Funk Night." And if we were recording at home he would stop at 10 o'clock in the evening to go to First Avenue to dance.[27]

—Susan Rogers

Despite the fact that Prince spent so much time in the studio, he still worked to maintain his life outside of the studio, as well, but often even those plans involved music, especially Thursday nights at First Avenue, which were promoted as "Funk Night." "He did go out," explained Rogers. "I'd either go along and I'd dance too, or if I had things I needed to do at the studio, I would stay home and I'd work and then he'd come back and we'd continue working."[28]

> Sometimes he'd come back with a girl because he'd meet a pretty girl at First Avenue. And he'd come back to the studio with a girl, and he'd be like, "Sit here baby. I've just got to work on this song a little bit." And "baby" would sit there for hours until she would get tired and go home. The magnetic pull of music for him was greater than his relationship with any woman I ever saw. And even the one I saw the most of was with Susannah and nothing came between him and his music and his love of recording, which is why I spent so much time with him.[29]

Susan recalled an incident at the Galpin house during this period.

> He had met a woman the night before, I guess she came home with him [and] I didn't know she was in the house. So he sent me upstairs to get something in the kitchen. And I walked upstairs and there's a naked woman in the kitchen, this beautiful, naked woman. And she just says, "hello" and I'm getting coffee or something. And I came downstairs and I said, "Prince, there's a naked woman in your kitchen." And he said, "Yeah, she's something, isn't she?" And he just kept right on working.[30]

On this Thursday, it is likely that Prince went out to First Avenue to dance and requested a safety copy made of "Yes" probably because he wanted to do some editing on the song or borrow elements of it for another song, so he needed to keep the original intact.

> *Rehearsals were like a spin class or a sweat lodge. We could play the same groove for a number of hours. I'm not exaggerating. And Prince would work on things and walk in and out of the room saying, "Don't stop! Nobody move!" So it was a workout. We were like marathon runners.*[31]
>
> —Lisa Coleman

Prince spent as much of his time within the private walls of the recording studio as possible. When he wasn't recording, he was rehearsing the expanded Revolution hard, but occasionally it would be obvious that everyone around him was worn out. When this happened, he would let down his guard slightly and take a break, probably not for himself, but for those around him who were on the edge of collapse. It was apparent to everyone that his passion for music was always the most important element of his life, to the detriment of almost all other personal relationships, according to Susan Rogers.

> We had to be his friends because he didn't have time for other friends. So he would sometimes say to Alan Leeds, it's Clarence's birthday. Clarence was his imaginary friend. So, he'd say it's Clarence's birthday and they'd order food. And, I'd bring records from home and we'd have a party at the warehouse at night and we'd have food and we had the pool table there and ping pong and we'd play records and we'd all dance. By we, I mean his band and his crew and just all of us. And sometimes he'd tell us to invite friends because he'd want to see some different faces. "Could you guys invite some people or something." But, come on. I mean, who else do you think we know? "We're working with you all the time." But we'd go and sometimes it would turn into a recording session, but we would do that and he would rent out a movie theater and take all of us. So we'd go to the movies really late at night or softball. Yeah, the crew would play a lot of baseball.[32]

But the contradiction was that when others were around, Prince had trouble letting his guard down. At this point in his career, he had become the celebrity's celebrity. Every fan and practically every star wanted a Prince experience and many of those who were fortunate enough to get that individual time were rarely treated as an equal, which isolated him even more. "They know so much about you because they know your lyrics and they've seen you on stage. They know all about you. You don't know anything about them," explained Rogers. "And there's an imbalance there so for that moment, he can't be himself. He *has* to be a rock star. And you've just deprived him of the opportunity to be *in* the world and just be himself, which once you've achieved celebrity, you almost never get that. So yeah, it was taking something from him."[33]

JULY 1986

Venue: Holiday Inn Sheridan-Convention Center (Sheridan, Wyoming)
Capacity: 100

> *Prince took a fully-fledged production to Sheridan, and he didn't change stride. We went up there, we sat through the movie, we went into the community. That one was like Martians landing on Earth and having to be accepted.*[1]
>
> —Jerome Benton

What should have been a month of celebration and a victory lap started out rough and was an unfortunate harbinger of the public's reaction. MTV had approached Prince's team and asked if they could hold a contest to see where in the country *Under The Cherry Moon* would premiere. The network had a series of high profile, but poorly executed, contests including their John Cougar Mellencamp "Little Pink Houses" give away, and the "Police Party Plane" event, but MTV was hot and their affiliation with Prince helped catapult *Purple Rain* to box office gold, so maybe lightning could be caught in a bottle once again. "[Prince's manager, Steve] Fargnoli talked to Prince and said, 'Let's do this promotion,'" remembered Warner Bros. executive Marylou Badeaux. "Prince was thinking Cleveland, or New York. So, the contest happens and the winner is in Sheridan, Wyoming."[2]

On June 21, Lisa Barber, a 20-year-old motel chambermaid was the 10,000th caller, which meant that the entire premiere would happen in a town populated by about 15,000 people. Sheridan was in the northern part of the state, and was more than 4 hours away from Cheyenne, Wyoming (a city with about 51,000 residents) and almost 6 hours away from Denver, Colorado.

"Prince goes ape shit," according to Badeaux. "[Prince's reaction was], 'Couldn't you have controlled it? Why didn't we get it somewhere we can get our fucking equipment to? Are you out of your mind? I'm not doing that.' So Fargnoli had a slight problem, an unhappy artist."[3]

The prospect of having only a week and a half to prepare a movie premiere in such a remote town brought an incredibly difficult set of problems, including having to rent limos from four hundred miles away, but eventually Prince realized that he had no choice, and with the movie launch happening immediately, there was no time to reschedule. Members of his team flew into Billings, Montana, and immediately traveled to Sheridan to find a way to prepare for Prince's arrival and the live telecast.

"It was a random contest," remembered Jerome Benton. "Prince said, 'We're going to Sheridan, Wyoming.' I was like, 'Where the hell is Sheridan, Wyoming?' The only place I knew named Sheridan was Sheridan Avenue on the north side. I think Prince did an amazing job and whether he was upset or not, Prince in his own way dealt with that scenario. You have to be a man of your word. You have to honor your deals."[4]

"Once Prince said, 'Fine I'll do it,' he committed. So he put the band in the rehearsal. 'If we have to do this, we're going to make it the best fucking thing we ever did,'" explained Badeaux. "Prince was a champ, and he did the whole thing. He couldn't wait to get out there."[5]

The small airport in Sheridan had only one flight in per day from the big cities, creating even more issues for the crew, the equipment, and the scores of people who had to fly in on small jumper planes.

Despite arguments and logistical nightmares, the town came out to celebrate and the night capped with the band's performance, as Badeaux continued. "We had to do the after party at the Holiday Inn. This little tiny ballroom, the ceiling was so low, they were practically touching the ceiling. It was so hot in that room, the band was sweating bullets."[6]

"It was so strange to go to this little town and then do a gig in the ballroom," agreed Lisa Coleman. "I was up on a riser, but the ceiling was so low it was right there. The keys on the synth curved from the heat."[7]

Prince and the band performed a short, but powerful, set consisting of "Raspberry Beret," "Delirious," "Controversy," "Mutiny," "Do Me, Baby," and "Purple Rain." With a new album out and needing promotion, it was surprising that Prince didn't play anything from the current release.

Under all of the revelry was a deep tension that was bubbling up and on the verge of erupting, detailed Susan Rogers. "Prince was in such a bad mood after that show. That show was a nightmare. Because they had no proper stage for him. The riser was maybe two feet tall, and women in the audience were reaching up and grabbing his crotch. So, the poor man was in a foul mood afterwards."[8]

Prince maintained his composure in front of the world, but his long brewing frustration was finally unleashed on those closest to him, as Wendy soon found out. "I had a huge blowout with Prince. I was at the bar having a beer with Joni Mitchell. An interviewer came up to me and the next day in some paper, it said: 'Wendy from Prince and the Revolution answering blah blah blah while nursing a Budweiser.' Prince pulled me upstairs and read me out about being an example to kids. I was completely floored. It felt like something else was wrong here. It's not about me drinking a beer."[9]

Lisa recalls how things were changing. "That was a very painful time and just so ridiculous and hard to figure out because we had a series of fights and this is a thing that I've only recently kind of realized, I think we were growing up, we wanted to grow up, we wanted to do it right now. We were getting our weekly minimum wage paychecks. He never paid us right, but when you're 20 and you're getting a weekly paycheck, that was like, 'All right I've made it.' But it wasn't fair, and we were growing up. And we started to think, 'How am I going to make my life work? Now I'm in my late 20s and I'm still only making $800 a week, and I play with Prince. I'm in the Revolution!' We were there all the time, every day, into the night. In the middle of the night he'd call. We were his posse."

"Prince fined her $500 or something, and she was just livid. It just was so unfair," observed Susan Rogers. "He didn't say 'I'm sorry' very often. He didn't look backwards. When he wanted to apologize, he did it by moving forward, but he didn't go back. So, I think that was actually the beginning of the unraveling of Wendy's relationship with him."[10]

WEDNESDAY, JULY 2, 1986

Under The Cherry Moon opens in 941 theatres nationwide in the United States.

I think part of the success of Purple Rain *was that [Prince] did
open up and examine himself, and that it was real. It was an
authentic thing; you could feel it, and there was all this excitement around it. And I don't think he's ever done that again.*[11]

—Lisa Coleman

It was immediately obvious that *Under The Cherry Moon* wasn't connecting
with the expected audience and the combination of unfavorable reviews and
bad word of mouth contributed to the underwhelming $3,150,924 at the box
office for the first weekend. Within two weeks, the movie was basically done,
ultimately making slightly more than $10 million compared to the roughly $70
million *Purple Rain* made two years earlier.

Any true artist pushes their boundaries. It is the nature of an artist like Prince
to extend his vision, to keep leaning forward trying to grab the fruit that seems
out of reach. Sometimes that works organically, but there are occasions where
it just doesn't connect with others. There are fans who feel *Under The Cherry
Moon* is his most intimate project, and in many ways this movie reveals a side of
Prince they hoped existed, but he refused to reveal. But for the general public,
the film was seen as a complete disaster and quickly became a punchline with
papers like the *Los Angeles Times* referring to it as "Under The Cherry Bomb."[12]
Despite the film's box office failure, Prince maintained an affection for the project. "He loved it. He absolutely loved it," recalls Susannah. "He loved who he
was at the time, loved his life at the time. He loved his relationship in the film
with Jerome. He got to play a part like himself. Prince is a lot like that guy."

Wendy expands on who Prince was truly playing in the movie. "There was a
certain, I think . . . maybe envy . . . maybe, in the far end of the spectrum, jealousy that Morris [Day] and Jerome's repartee in *Purple Rain* was so successful.
And that maybe, in response, his relationship with Jerome in *Cherry Moon* was
trying to match that repartee, and it failed. That was the first time you got to see
it. You know, his 'wrecka stow' thing? Just think about it. You could imagine
Morris doing that scene. One hundred percent."

Prince may have wanted to be like Morris in the film, but the "Morris Day"
character was originally influenced by Prince, so in the end, it was another
variation of himself. Prince not only played a character that was similar to his
own personality, but he also based a lot of the incidents in the movie on events
in his life, including the scene that was originally considered for placement in
Purple Rain in which bats chase everyone out of the bar. "That was actually a
real scenario," Jerome explained.

At an original Time band rehearsal when we were first starting out, we were in a dungeon over by the University of Minnesota. I was a roadie and the band was rehearsing and something started flickering around the room and Prince was sitting in the corner and I said, "It's a bat!" and everybody screamed and they dipped down to about knee height and ran out the room up the stairs and out the building and that's kind of what you see in the scene. So, how close can you be to Prince by watching his films? That's the closest you can get. That's life. Those are things that we experienced.[13]

He did have the power to shape the movie as he wished, and the unfortunate reality is that for the last year, Prince poured every ounce of his authority and every bit of himself into the project, focusing almost exclusively on creating this movie and the ancillary items that would promote it. And once again he convinced those around him to follow him, but for the first time in years, his vision was being questioned by almost everyone. Prince may have played a character that was similar to himself, but the script didn't express the flawed self-reflection of *Purple Rain* and made it difficult for some in the audience to connect with Christopher Tracy. After putting so much into the project, Prince still didn't necessarily see himself at fault. "Every now and then again, in the course of a year, Prince would open up a little bit and you could tell there was definitely remorse from the lack of success of the film," remembers Todd Herreman. "We were back at his house, and I guess he was donating a bunch of movie posters that he was autographing. And I asked him, 'What do you think happened?' Something to let him vent a little bit. And, this is one of those moments that I think he was just very, very genuine and he said, 'Todd, people were expecting another *Purple Rain* and I just wasn't ready to do that.'"

"He would never regret, never say, 'Oh, that didn't work out, maybe I'll do it differently,'" explains Susannah. "Nope. There was no reflection. It was a constant movement forward. Even if something sucked, it wasn't his responsibility if it sucked. That's really it."

The soundtrack album was brilliantly crafted but didn't always embellish the movie as it had in *Purple Rain*, and some of the music fell flat despite how well it worked on the soundtrack album. The inevitable larger tour was rehearsed and the series of "hit-and-run" performances around the country could easily be expanded if needed. This scenario had worked out flawlessly for *Purple Rain*, but the failure of his second movie gives an insight into what would have happened if *Purple Rain* had bombed. The subsequent *Purple Rain* tour would have been trimmed back and the career-defining success would have eluded him. "I think *Parade* was a good album," reflected Bobby Z. "I think it had great songs on it. I think it would have probably done pretty well, but I think the timing was off after *Purple Rain* with *Around The World In A Day* kind of slacking-off in sales. Then *Parade* came along and with the movie it was hard for it to grab. I thought that 'Kiss' was a complete smash, and set the album up huge. And then came 'Mountains,' which was not that big of single really. Then the movie, and then the album was gone."[14]

"He did have a magic touch for a long time," reflects Peggy Leonard, "and when *Under The Cherry Moon* kind of bombed, I think that was a little bit humbling for him. That's when everything wasn't turning out as well. Everything he touched wasn't turning to gold."

Within days, *Parade* would mark in its 12th week on the charts and was on its way back down. It was at number 19 in the *Billboard* Album 200, dropping from number 14 the previous week, with no real bounce materializing for the soundtrack. Hopes that it could rise back up the charts and climb past its peak of number 3 from mid-May vanished.

Prince now had a few options. He could wallow in self-pity about the movie's failure or regroup and use that energy to move to the next project and potentially redefine his career. What was likely the most humbling public experience since being booed off stage while opening for the Rolling Stones in 1981 would inspire him to forge ahead.

Great art is not made by committee. It isn't poll-tested or voted on; it is usually created from a single source without filter. It is easy to imagine Prince reflecting on the reasons for this setback and seeking out causes and other people to blame. According to his manager Bob Cavallo, "He started to not believe in anyone but himself."[15]

"How I saw him manifest that kind of stuff was work harder. So he may have been less communicative—although he wasn't the most communicative guy in the world," shared Susannah. "The way he dealt with it was to be more remote with humans, the people, and go create more. On to the next."[16]

His decisions about how to handle this turn would affect everyone around him, but it would also lead to him creating some of his most personal and inspired work.

WEDNESDAY, JULY 2, 1986

"Anotherloverholenyohead," the third and final US single from *Parade*, was released with "Girls & Boys" as the B-side. Considering all the incredible material Prince had recently recorded, the choice of an album track for the B-side was odd, but likely the hope was that it would promote the *Parade* album. Unfortunately, "Anotherloverholenyohead" didn't generate the expected excitement and it only reached number 63 on the Pop Chart and number 18 on the Black Chart.

According to Susan Rogers, "He wasn't aiming for hit singles so much as he was aiming to reinvent himself, in a way of, once again, doing what had worked in the past. Positioning himself as being an artist that the critics admire and say, 'This is someone to watch. More of us should be doing what this guy's doing.'"

But this time, even the critics who had adored him in the past couldn't salvage the project and the film, album, and tour, which failed to recreate his earlier successes.

THURSDAY, JULY 3, 1986

Venue: McNichols Arena (Denver, Colorado)
Capacity: 16,000+ (sold out)

I think it was a matter of him creating another extraordinary entity, to take him to a new level, and, excluding us because we now became irrelevant. We now became, not Prince and the Revolution, it was Prince and the Wendy & Lisa Show. And I saw that coming early on, because it hit me like a ton of bricks.

—BrownMark

The tour was scattered and probably not having the intended effect. The shows were sold out, but there would often be weeks in between concerts, leaving it much less satisfying for the audience and the band, which was having its own inner conflicts.

"After the Wyoming thing, he was doing lots of PMS things, like fits and starts," details Lisa. "One day he'd be like, 'We're going to take over the world, and this is the greatest thing ever.' And then the next day it was like, 'I'm going to break up the band, so play like your life depends on it, like we'll all be dead tomorrow.' So it was very odd."

"He was doing weird things," she continues. "There was a picture in the newspaper of Wendy on stage smiling. He called her into his dressing room and told her how bad that looked. Then he made her get her hair cut right in front of him in his dressing room so that she looked more like him. It was one of those really weird days, like what the fuck? Marilyn's here and she's in a bad mood."

Prince played "A Case Of You," likely since Joni Mitchell was in attendance. It would be the only time it was performed during this year's concert series.

During the second encore, Joni and [then husband] Larry Klein joined Prince onstage, remembers Wendy. "He was like, 'Can you guys come out and do 'Purple Rain'?' And Joni's like, 'I don't know it.' So Prince goes, 'Purple Rain, Purple Rain, Purple Rain, Purple Rain.' [laughs]"

The *Hit-And-Run* tour would take a month off until the beginning of August when they'd play two shows in New York City. Unbeknownst to everyone, those two concerts would be the final US performances by Prince and the Revolution.

SUNDAY, JULY 6, 1986

"The Question Of U" (tracking, overdubs)
Galpin Blvd. home studio (Chanhassen, Minnesota)
Producer: Prince | Artist: Prince | Engineer: Susan Rogers

> *I grew up with Santana and Larry Graham and Fleet-wood Mac, all kinds of different things, you know? So that was very cool.*[17]
>
> —Prince

"I remember there was a big story about him in a big magazine, I think it was *Time* magazine and it was a big deal," reflected Susan Rogers.

> Wendy and Lisa were there and he was reading the article to us. He was pretty excited, and it said, "The diminutive singer" and he said, "Diminutive? Why do they always call me diminutive?" And Wendy said, "Well, how tall are you?" He said, "I'm 5'3"" with a great deal of dignity. But then he read something where they talked about what a brilliant piano player he was and he put the magazine down and he kind of looked off in the distance and looked kind of sad and he just said, "Nobody ever talks about my guitar playing."[18]

"So I took the opportunity later to ask him about his guitar playing. I'd always been curious about it. He was heavily influenced by [Carlos] Santana."[19] Rogers continued:

> People sometimes talk about how Prince was influenced by Jimi Hendrix. I don't think he was necessarily influenced by Hendrix's guitar playing as much as he was influenced by his look, his place in the musical firmament. Hendrix was boldly sensual and sexual with his guitar onstage in a way that, prior to Hendrix, other guitar players hadn't been. I think that was an obvious influence on his interaction with the guitar onstage. The way Prince postured with the guitar was influenced by Hendrix, I would venture to guess. I think Prince's look and his clothes, certainly around the time of *Purple Rain*, were influenced by Hendrix, although stylistically, musically, by Prince's own admission, Carlos Santana was the bigger influence musically on guitar.[20]

"If they really listened to my stuff, they'd hear more of a Santana influence than Jimi Hendrix," agreed Prince. **"Hendrix played more blues; Santana played prettier."**[21]

Prince's choice to work on "The Question Of U" during this session makes complete sense. Considering all that was going on around him, it was inevitable that he'd be in a contemplative mood and looking for some quiet time to reflect, and when he did, he focused on his music as if he was alone and anyone in the room would blend into the background. "It's well known by anybody who knows anything about him—he was a man of few words," explained Rogers. "My job was to make sure current was flowing in those wires as long as he was making music. That was one of the reasons he wanted a technician working for him, someone who could [be] in Minneapolis or his home. Somebody who could repair something if it broke down at two o'clock in the morning and somebody who had the stamina to stay up with him all night."[22]

The track would be a solo session for him, blending layers of guitar and the Oberheim OB-8 on top of real drums. The song contained a breakdown that featured a brief musical call back to "Controversy."

Status: A 5-minute instrumental of "The Question Of U" was recorded, based on "12 Keys," a song for the Flesh from several months earlier. "The Question Of U" was originally recorded in 1984 as a piano demo. All of those remained unreleased during his lifetime. The song would eventually be reworked, re-recorded, and released on Prince's 1990 album *Graffiti Bridge*.

MONDAY, JULY 7, 1986

"Train" (tracking and mix)
"Eggplant" (tracking and mix)
Galpin Blvd. home studio (Chanhassen, Minnesota)
Producer: Prince | Artist: Prince | Engineer: Susan Rogers | Assistant Engineer:
    Todd Herreman

> *"Eggplant" was from a period of exploration for him, post* Under the Cherry Moon, *and after the seriousness of that, there was a period of light-hearted music.*
>
> —Susan Rogers

Prince was often a contradiction of moods, and this is why his music reflected what he was feeling, not just on that specific day, but because he would often record more than one track during a session, it exposed his mood for that specific hour or two. On days like this, his mood seemingly bounced from the serious lyrical longing of "Train" to the playful tone of "Eggplant," which was a testament to the range of his artistic skills.

With Prince, his inspirations are often impossible to trace and because he recorded as much as he did, he had a constant need for something to trigger him to create something new. Although we will likely never know the full story, the title for "Train" may have come from something as basic as the name on one of his pieces of equipment. "What I remember is having a Train sample on the Fairlight," recalls Todd Herreman. "It was a stock sound effect on the Fairlight series two. And I think we just sequenced in and triggered the sound on the keyboard, but that set up the groove."

"Train" is a soulful love song about the final time saying goodbye to his partner. Prince created the drums using the Fairlight. Once the bed was built for the track, Prince added bass, guitars, and several synths, including the Fairlight. He also recorded a guide track for the trumpet and sax. Eric Leeds remembers what Prince expected when he recorded his sax parts on the keyboard for songs like "Train." "He'd occasionally do that. It would depend if he was there. I can't recall if he was there for that session, so he might have just left it, here's your guide, and made it really easy. We just copied that."

After midnight, Prince's tone changed when he started on "Eggplant," a playful, but slightly insensitive song about a self-obsessed woman who was as dumb as an eggplant and his warning to a friend to avoid her. Prince tracked this fairly quickly, and once the basic elements, including the OB-8 synth, cowbell, guitar, and a bassline from the Ensoniq Mirage synth were recorded, he added his vocals and mixed the track. The following day, he'd have Wendy and Lisa add their own touches to the song.

Status: "Train" (4:22) would be added to a configuration of *Dream Factory*, and when that was canceled, it remained as part of *Crystal Ball*, but was removed when the album was renamed *Sign O' The Times* and reduced from three discs to two. The following year it was offered to Bonnie Raitt for her shelved Paisley Park album and eventually found a home on Mavis Staples's 1989 album, *Time Waits For No One*. The version with Prince's vocals remained unreleased during his lifetime.

"Eggplant" (5:17) was not a part of any configuration of *Dream Factory*, *Crystal Ball*, or *Sign O' The Times*, and also remained unreleased during his lifetime.

Both tracks from this session were included on the *Sign O' The Times* Super Deluxe Edition in 2020.

TUESDAY, JULY 8, 1986

"Train" (overdubs, horn overdubs, mix)
"Eggplant" (horn overdubs, mix)
Galpin Blvd. home studio (Chanhassen, Minnesota)
Producer: Prince | Artist: Prince | Engineer: Susan Rogers | Assistant Engineer: Todd Herreman

> *Eric Leeds was on almost everything. I think Prince really respected Eric.*
>
> —Todd Herreman

Leeds agrees with Herreman's assessment, at least conditionally. "I did what he couldn't do. Sometimes it was no more than that."

It appears that the previous day's session continued into today, so before Prince wrapped up, Eric Leeds and Matt "Atlanta Bliss" Blistan were brought in to play sax and trumpet on "Train" and "Eggplant." "Prince wants things done yesterday, but at times I felt that didn't lend itself to the best results. Particularly when he was mixing something because the one thing about his music that was very inconsistent, were his mixes," details Leeds.

> Even on some of his better songs, because he would be in the studio for eight or ten hours and after a few hours, your ears would lose it. Particularly when you're mixing, and I asked him once, I said, "Dude, why don't you just come back tomorrow and finish it?" And he said, "Eric, I can't do that." He said it was very difficult for him to come back the next day and pick it up and get back into where he was. So he always felt that he had to finish it, and then he could put it together and then he could go to sleep. Anyway, I said, "Well, that's fine for you, but it's like you're trying to get the best out of me and Blistan, or anyone else that you're bringing in, and when you bring us in at five in the morning or whatever, just because you're up for it, you're not going to get the best out of us under those circumstances necessarily." But that's something that doesn't even play into it, that doesn't even come into the equation with him, so I said, "Okay, this is the gig."

Susan Rogers created a mix of "Eggplant" with the horns. Later that day, Wendy was recruited to replace sections of Prince's lead vocals with her own. It is likely that Prince left the studio after he asked Wendy to add more of her voice to the track. During the times that Prince left the girls in charge, it was a more relaxed atmosphere, according to Wendy. "It was easier to make fun of the stuff when it was kind of bad. Like the song 'Eggplant.' We fought hard. I was like, 'Dude, it's just not very good. This is not!' And he was, 'Just do it.' And we're, 'Fuck!' We were kicking and screaming about that song. And when he wasn't around while we were doing it, I could be like, 'Yes, fucking hate this song. It sucks.' [laughs]"

Prince would have Susan oversee the recording of Wendy and Lisa's background vocals. "I remember there is a vocal part at the end that has Lisa singing 'eggplant.' I was in the control room, recording. Prince wasn't there at this time, but Lisa was doing backing vocals repeatedly singing 'eggplant' and we just got the giggles. It seemed absurd."

The absurdity continued with Prince singing "Go-go boogie, gonna rock your soul. Whipped cream pie and a shake to go." Tickled by the ridiculousness, Wendy and Lisa added a background chant of "caravan of parmesan." "That was just something silly that we ended up saying because it was eggplant and we would pretend we were singing like Carmina Burana, 'Eggplant parmesan!' and we'd just start doing crazy things like that," explains Lisa. "It would just end up on tape somehow. That was always part of the process. It's like, 'Let's see, we need bass. Check. Lead vocal? Check. Guitar part? Check. And we might need to fill in this section. Silly talking? Yeah, got to do that. Check!'"

WEDNESDAY, JULY 9, 1986

"It Ain't Over 'Til The Fat Lady Sings" (tracking, horn overdubs)
"Train" (edits and mix)
"Train" [instrumental] (probable mix)
Galpin Blvd. home studio (Chanhassen, Minnesota)
Producer: Prince | Artist: Prince | Engineer: Susan Rogers | Assistant Engineer:
    Todd Herreman

There was so much recording that we did, in '86 particularly,
that never saw the light of day, which I think is some of the
most wonderful stuff we ever did, and for whatever reasons he
decided that wasn't stuff that he wanted to release at the time,
but that still doesn't mean it wasn't valid music.[23]

—Eric Leeds

Wendy, Lisa, Atlanta Bliss, and Eric were gathered by Prince to explore "It Ain't Over 'Til The Fat Lady Sings," a new instrumental that he'd written. Although the origin of the title is not known, Prince had been vacillating about ending the Revolution, so it isn't a stretch to imagine Prince once again putting his inner thoughts into his music by cleverly stating that "It ain't over 'til the fat lady sings."

"For this session, we actually did the recording of the song at his house," recalls Leeds. "But I have a recollection that we were rehearsing the song during the day at the warehouse. It was a long fricking 6-hour session."

"That was recorded at Prince's house," remembered Bliss. "A lot of the gear was shifted over to Prince's house and that's where we recorded a number of songs. Prince had a baby grand piano up in his living room and Lisa played the piano up there while the rest of us were down in the studio and it was a real neat session. It was very creative. It was probably one of those late-night sessions and we just worked out some real nice parts together."[24]

At least four takes of the song were attempted before Prince was happy with the results, although Eric refers to them not as takes, but "more rehearsals than anything else."

Once their parts were completed, Lisa and Wendy left, leaving Leeds and Blistan to add some additional horn sections. While Prince was overdubbing and mixing the instrumental, Eric noticed Wendy's skills from the session.

Wendy had been playing bass on the song. I had never heard her play bass before, so I just made an offhand comment and said, "Wow, Wendy's a hell of a bass player! I guess I never really realized, the girl can play some bass, can't she?" And Prince kind of just nodded, and said, "Oh, yeah. Yeah, she can." Well, about 10 minutes later, we're listening to a playback and Prince looks at Susan, he picks up a bass, and he says, "Put the bass up on a track." And he starts to play the track that we had just done, and mutes whatever bass was on there. Just music for a moment. And for the next few minutes, he just plays bass alone, on this track. But he's kind of soloing, and at the end of it he just said, "Nah. Don't need it. We'll just use what was there." Of course, when me and Matt were driving home, we were in hysterics. I said, "Boy, he really was not going to let us get out of there with thinking Wendy was a great bass player."

"No one was better than Prince, that's the thing. If Prince can do *you*, that's it," reasons Wendy. "Lisa was the only musician in his arsenal of people that he couldn't emulate. He could do me until the cows came home. He could do any of us. He couldn't do Eric Leeds because he didn't play a horn. But with Lisa, it was beyond respect."

Additional recording and mixing were done for "Train," including an instrumental version of the track.

Status: "It Ain't Over 'Til The Fat Lady Sings" (2:19) remained unreleased during his lifetime but was included on the *Sign O' The Times* Super Deluxe Edition in 2020.

Clare Fischer wrote and arranged the orchestral parts, which were recorded on August 18 and September 4, 1986, and mixed at some point after that.

SATURDAY, JULY 12, 1986

"**Eggplant**" (various overdubs, mix)
"**Eggplant**" [instrumental] (probable mix)
"**It Ain't Over 'Til The Fat Lady Sings**" (probable mix)
Dream Factory album (adjustments to the order, crossfades, mix)
Sunset Sound, Studio 3 | 2:00 p.m.–7:30 a.m. (booked: lockout)
Producer: Prince | Artist: Prince | Engineers: Susan Rogers and Coke Johnson | Assistant Engineer: Todd Herreman

Like a lot of artists, he'd be up all night. The general modus operandi was we would start, either in the late morning or early afternoon, because in the mornings, is when he would take care of business or any managerial issues he had to deal with. Once he began working in the studio, he didn't like to stop or be interrupted [and] I could expect an eighteen, twenty, or twenty-four hour workday. It was fairly common to work a forty-eight hour session.[25]

—Susan Rogers

For the first time in weeks, Prince was back in Sunset Sound's Studio 3, which in many ways was as sheltered from others as his home studio. "That building is self contained," recalls Craig Hubler, Sunset Sound's General Manager during that era. "It's got its own bathrooms and whatever, and he could just isolate himself in that room, and didn't really have to mingle with the rest of the complex."

Sunset Sound had inspired Prince to create his own larger fortress in Minneapolis where he could record, rehearse, and conduct all of his business without dealing with the schedules of others or any additional roadblocks obstructing his creative flow. When he wanted something, he didn't want to wait. He was also feeling frustrated about having to rent additional studio equipment so creating a fully equipped studio like Paisley Park would be a perfect sanctuary from almost every distraction, but it was still months away from being completed, so while he waited, Sunset Sound continued to be his Los Angeles studio of choice.

Today's session started with 6 hours of overdubs to "Eggplant." It is likely that this was when Prince asked Wendy to add her voice to a "conversation" with Prince in the song, but playing someone other than herself, using a name referenced in "Starfish And Coffee." "Prince calls her 'Lucy,' but it is just a fictitious character so he could be playing someone that wasn't Prince," explains Susan Rogers, "and she could be playing someone that wasn't Wendy and they are talking like schoolyard friends." An instrumental version of the track was also probably created on this date.

After dinner, Prince spent 10 hours working on a track, likely a mix of "It Ain't Over 'Til The Fat Lady Sings." At this point, it did not yet contain Clare Fischer's orchestral arrangement, which would be recorded the following month. The assembly of the *Dream Factory* album from June 3 was also adjusted, with "Wonderful Day" likely replaced by "Train." "He was always the guy who liked writing things down," reflects Lisa. "[Prince would say] 'I'm going to make a record. This is side A and this is side B,' but it would change every day. Writing it down on a piece of paper looked cool and made you feel like you're really doing it."

Additional work on *Dream Factory* would continue over the next week.

Prince continued at his usual brisk pace until 6:47 a.m. when a 5.4 magnitude quake shook Southern California off the coast of San Diego. Smaller earthquakes were relatively common in this region, and in fact, this was the second sizable quake within a week, but it rattled him. "Prince hated them; he hated earthquakes," according to Susannah. "He was really scared—to be out of control in every possible way, when the earth shakes underneath you, that's something he did not like. That was almost spiritual, like, okay, those were the gods speaking. That's what I need to be afraid of. And that triggered his creative self, and he had to go write."[26]

Prince asked for the engineers to make an output of what was recorded over the last 17 hours to five C-60 tapes, and the session ended soon afterward.

SUNDAY, JULY 13, 1986

"The Cross" (tracking, mix)
"Everybody Want What They Don't Got" (tracking, mix)
"Eggplant" (mix)
"Splash" (overdubs, mix)
"Slow Love" (overdubs, mix)
Dream Factory album (restructure, crossfades, mix)
Sunset Sound, Studio 3 | 4:00 p.m.–9:00 a.m. (booked: lockout)
Producer: Prince | Artist: Prince | Engineers: Coke Johnson and Susan Rogers

If we're going to look at the canon of Prince material, the extraordinary stuff is the stuff that he knew was extraordinary. And generally, the factor that would make something extraordinary versus leading it to be stashed away in the vault, would be the lyrical content. So when he had something important to say, like on the song "Sign O' The Times" or "The Cross" or anything that he considered to be a cornerstone of his current view, or perspective—"Pop Life" is a good example—songs with important lyrics to him, like "Purple Rain," he would

spend a lot more time on. By a lot more time, I mean he might
take two days to do this song rather than one.[27]

—Susan Rogers

Shaken by this morning's earthquake, Prince arrived at the studio with the sketch of a song that would convey his faith and the comfort he gathered from his relationship with God. "The Cross" was his response to someone needing solace.

Soon all of our problems will be taken by the cross.[28]

The idea of a man trying to "bear the cross" had appeared the previous year in his song "Heaven," but this directly detailed how much comfort he got from his views of Jesus. The song starts with a quiet, intimate guitar, possibly inspired by the opening notes from Santana's track, "Samba Pa Ti," and Prince's statement of the problem that needs to be solved, as well as the solution that God can bring to the issues. The track grows with the addition of drums, bass, sitar, and a distorted guitar, accented with multiple layers of his background vocals, building to a huge crescendo. The track appears to be a flawless, passionate plea, and impressed many of those around him. "'The Cross' was pretty powerful, when we heard that," remembers Wendy. "I thought his guitar solo was astonishing."

Inspiration can come from a variety of sources, and Jill Jones reflects on where she feels the origin of the song was born.

It was after we got paid our *Purple Rain* money, I went and bought him a ruby cross—it was really beautiful. And he never wore it. He also gave me a cross as well. We had a very strained relationship there with a lot of dependency and yet this interdependence. It's funny because he wrote that song, "The Cross" on my birthday. I had a birthday party and [his father] John L. came to it because they were both supposed to come. [Prince] didn't come, but he stayed in the studio and that night he wrote "The Cross." So if that means anything subconsciously, maybe it was a subliminal thing.

Susan Rogers was also affected by the track but remembers that there was an issue while recording the song. "The drums on 'The Cross' weren't steady; they were sped up. I thought for sure he was going to redo the drums on it, because he played the drums on it all in one take and it just progressively became faster. It really bugged me, because I thought it was sloppy. I was hoping that he'd redo it, but he was satisfied with it, and he knew what he was doing, so who was I to argue."[29]

Prince's ability to bounce between two emotions was evident on this date. "The Cross" is one of his most deeply profound songs about his spiritual beliefs, while "Everybody Want What They Don't Got" is a jovial pop song that references the Bible's Tenth Commandment, "Thou shall not covet." The song doesn't take itself too seriously, using comical names like "Sweet Sara Sucatash" [sic] and amusing situations to relay his message about envy. The song contains his Epiphone guitar, Mirage and Fairlight keyboards, a variety of sound effects (car horn, brakes skidding, and bells) possibly from the Fairlight, and nine layers of vocals over a foundation of real drums. Within 5 hours, he was ready to mix "Everybody Want What They Don't Got."

The songs may have two different tones, but ultimately, they are both about wanting something beyond the physical.

For the final 7 hours of the session, Prince updated the mix for "Eggplant." He also blended "Splash" and "Slow Love" with Clare Fischer's orchestral arrangements that had been recorded on July 11. The updated "Slow Love" was added to the *Dream Factory* project, but it doesn't appear that "Splash" was ever included in the collection.

Status: "The Cross" (4:49) was placed on *Dream Factory* and *Crystal Ball* and was finally released on *Sign O' The Times* on March 30, 1987. "Everybody Want What They Don't Got" (2:02) remained unreleased until it found a home on the *Sign O' The Times* Super Deluxe Edition in 2020.

Susannah remembered that she and Prince paged through the *Los Angeles Times* during this week. Many of the stories that they found, which included: President Reagan's "Star Wars" antimissile program, the growing AIDS crisis, the investigation of January's space shuttle explosion, and stories of drug abuse in the inner city were all big news stories. These blended with the Minneapolis *Star Tribune* and their reporting about a street gang called "The Disciples."

He'd turn all of these topics into what many considered his most vital social commentary to date. The song would become the title track to his next release, although as of this day, it was just a collection of newspaper headlines.

Because of the earthquake, Prince and Susannah flew home to Minneapolis, but Prince quickly turned around and headed back to Los Angeles.

TUESDAY, JULY 15, 1986

"Sign O' The Times" [listed as **"Sign Of The Times"**] (tracking, overdubs, vocals, mix)
"Blanche" (tracking, overdubs, vocals, mix)
"If I Could Get Your Attention" (probable overdubs and mix)
Sunset Sound, Studio 3 | 2:30 p.m.–6:00 a.m. (booked: lockout)
Producer: Prince | Artists: Prince, Jill Jones, and possibly Taja Sevelle | Engineers: Susan Rogers and Coke Johnson

Prince probably felt his greatest challenge was in writing lyrics because he didn't like bad lyrics and every love song has been written already and he really held out and paid attention more and more as he grew, wanting to write really good poetic lyrics. He was so turned on by Joni Mitchell and it wasn't just the beauty of her music, it was the poetry of her lyrics and the power that lyrics can have. And I think he enjoyed that power. I mean not just as the mighty Prince, but as a poet who wanted to connect with people and the more specific he can be, the more powerful it seemed to get, with songs like "Sign O' The Times" where he would be specific and he mentioned real problems. I think that looking at his lyrics is a great study to see somebody who really took it on and beat the challenge. It's incredible. His lyrics are poetry. He really did succeed at the thing he was most afraid of with lyrics.[30]

—Lisa Coleman

The earthquake, the occasionally volatile relationship he had with Susannah, his issues with the Revolution, and the failure of his movie gave him a chance to reflect, explains Susan Rogers. "I think that *Under The Cherry Moon* was catered toward a white audience, talking about rich people in the south of France, and the lead actress was white and I think that, if you look at 'Sign O' The Times,' he tried to deliberately write a song about urban issues."

Inspired by the newspaper headlines, Prince created what is considered his most vital statement about society and the struggles of everyone, but unlike "The Cross," which suggested the solution can be with God, Prince offers up the idea that a solution to society would be for him to "fall in love, get married and have a baby."[31] If you can't fix the world, fix your corner of the world.

The basis for the music dated back to the show they played in Denver two weeks earlier, just after *Under The Cherry Moon* was released to horrible reviews, remembered Wendy.

> Lisa and I walked into soundcheck together from the back end of the stadium and I heard this rhythm which ended up being "Sign O' The Times," and I was transfixed by what I was hearing. Now it's very common to get to a soundcheck and hear drums already being checked or Bobby's LM-1 drum being checked, but this time Prince arrived to the soundcheck earlier than us and the drums were up, and "Sign O' The Times" was blaring through the stadium with this massive echo and reverb. And then I heard that guitar part, that lead line, and I had a physical reaction. Something else is happening here. This is different than what he's done. There's something so minimal and so powerful about just that drum group and that lead line. To hear that at soundcheck, blew me away.[32]

To track the song in the studio, Prince laid down an LM-1 and live drum/percussion mixture, and covered it with the Fairlight, and a few other elements, including his voice, which was when the song took a dramatic turn, according to Rogers. "When the vocal was done saying what it had to say, that's when the guitar could take over for the vocal and say the same thing the vocal said, but with short melodic phrases."[33]

He tracked several guitar parts, but like many of his songs, he over-recorded for the track, including extra background vocals, sound effects, and additional drums, but when he mixed the track, he eliminated most of the unnecessary sounds because they likely distracted from the message.

"['Sign O' The Times'] was just something that was so stark and one of the songs he wrote right before The Revolution ended. I just always remember how powerful it was," reflected Bobby Z. "The way it's so simple and spacey and the story, getting into current events with AIDS and the space shuttle blowing up. It gets me to this day. It's always been one of my favorites."[34]

"He was very aware of the world around us," continued Bobby. "We'd talk often about what was going on. He had strong opinions and hopes, dreams and fears just like anybody else. But he definitely had a pulse on society."[35]

"With Prince every time you listen to a song, it's telling a story," observed Levi. "Even if he wasn't singing, you could just listen to the music and feel that that song would be about what it's talking about."[36]

"'Sign O' The Times' was new for him in terms of tone," added Susan Rogers. "He did the song at Sunset Sound in the control room. The Fairlight was set up right in there behind the console. He did one instrument at a time, like he normally did. I was blown away by the lyrics. It was something slightly new for him. It was a soulful, beautiful performance. Many musicians cite this song as one of their favorites. It was a really impressive track."[37]

The sound was deceptively simple, but the results were astounding. Prince had made social commentary before on songs like "Annie Christian" and "Ronnie Talk to Russia," but "Sign O' The Times" was the philosophical cousin to Marvin Gaye's "What's Going On," and follows Gaye's suggestion that love is the solution.

"At the end of the day, when you've got nothing else, the most important thing is love," explained Susannah. "It always came down to who was he loving and who was loving him, so he could then be the guy he felt he needed to be."[38]

"'Sign O' The Times' represented Prince soldiering through a tough time, personally and professionally," witnessed Rogers. "There were changes, and it's hard for people to cope with changes. As an artist, he coped with them by pushing forward and writing his way through it. That can go either way—it can yield some of the best work you'll ever do, or it can yield work that is self-indulgent, dispirited, and apathetic. In this case, it yielded some of his very best work."[39]

After midnight, he balanced that out by recording "Blanche," an infectious bass/live drums/guitar/keyboard groove which he covered with a rhyming exercise that was at times playful, and other times offensive. Although the lyrics namecheck "Blanche" and "Stanley," two characters from *A Streetcar Named Desire,* (just as he'd done with the inclusion of a character named Stella in last year's "Stella and Charles"), as well as the word "desire," it appears to have little to do with the plot of Tennessee Williams' Pulitzer Prize-winning play or the subsequent movie.

Earlier in the session, he also worked on "If I Could Get Your Attention," a track from May. A few hours were spent on additional overdubs, likely from Jill Jones as the song was being considered for her album, but in the end, she didn't feel like the track fit her style. "I hated that song. It just didn't have enough meat on it. And I think we had gone through so much by this time, because we'd known each other for a while. Maybe when I first started out, I would have been bubbly and ecstatic to sing 'If I Could Get Your Attention,' but I was getting tired, and there was agita. We'd been through it."

It is unclear on what date Taja Sevelle was also brought in to record her vocals. Once she did, it was obvious that the musical arrangement fit her voice perfectly.

Two C-60 cassettes were made of the day's work, and Prince left at 6 a.m.

Status: A roughly 6-minute version of "Sign O' The Times" was edited (4:57) and placed on his unreleased *Crystal Ball* album, then shifted to become the title track for his 1987 album. The day after this session, an instrumental was created from the longer version, and after a 35-second section was eventually removed, that version (5:32) was eventually placed under the credits in the *Sign O' The Times* movie in 1987. A shorter version (3:40) was produced for *Dream Factory* in which the end is mixed off. This is different than the single edit (3:42), which was released on February 18, 1987 (backed with "La, La, La, He, He, Hee"), as the advance single from the album. It reached number 3 on the US *Billboard* Hot 100 Chart and number 1 on the *Billboard* Top Black Singles Chart.

The song was listed as "Sign Of The Times," but by the time the song was mixed later in the day, it was changed to "Sign O' The Times."

"Blanche" (5:28) remained in the vault during his lifetime but was released on the *Sign O' The Times* Super Deluxe Edition in 2020.

WEDNESDAY, JULY 16, 1986

"**Yah, You Know**" (cassette copy)
"**Neon Telephone**" (cassette copy)
"**Sign O' The Times**" [instrumental] (probable mix)
"**I Could Never Take The Place Of Your Man**" [new version] (tracking, overdubs, and mix)
"**I Could Never Take The Place Of Your Man**" [new version instrumental] (mix)
Sunset Sound, Studio 3 | 8:00 p.m.–8:00 a.m. (booked: lockout)
Producer: Prince | Artist: Prince | Engineers: Coke Johnson and Susan Rogers | Assistant Engineer: Todd Herreman

> *Occasionally he'd pull an old song out of the vault. When we were working on [what would become] the* Sign O' The Times *album, he would call for things like whether it was "Slow Love" or "I Could Never Take The Place Of Your Man." Those were things that had been sitting in the vault for quite a number of years.*[40]
>
> —Susan Rogers

Before the main shift started, Prince requested a cassette copy of the latest mixes of "Neon Telephone," and "Yah, You Know." After they were dubbed to a C-60 tape and picked up, there were several hours of downtime until Prince returned at 8 p.m.

When the full session started, he surprisingly asked for a tape he'd originally recorded on May 23, 1979, while working on his second album. Although Prince had a vast library of unreleased songs, he generally was forward-looking when it came to his new work, and his understood rule was that his newest music was considered his best and deserved the most focus, but on occasion, he'd bend the rules, according to Susan. "Every once in a while when we'd be working he'd say: Go out and get me one of these tapes and we'd pull it out and set the tape up and he'd listen a bit and then put it away. It was very rare that he'd pull an old one out of the closet and actually ended up using it. That's why I was so surprised when he pulled out 'I Could Never Take The Place Of Your Man' and used it."[41]

After reviewing the 16-track recording, Prince spent time in the studio by himself and reworked the entire song from scratch. The original track consisted only of drums, bass, guitar, synth, and nine layers of Prince's vocals. The up-dated recording contained many of the same instruments, but also included the Linn LM-1 drum machine and multiple new instrumental sections, including a searing solo. From 1 in the morning until 4, he sang the lead. He'd eventually invite Susannah to join him on the background vocals likely once he returned to Minneapolis. The original version ended with Prince singing, "I could never take the place of your man . . . but I'll try,"[42] giving the song an optimistic view of the situation. He may not be the perfect man for her, but he'll try to make it work. The updated version omits the final three words, indicating a difference in his romantic outlook as he has little interest in working it out with the woman in the song.

The contrast from his sound from the 1979 track, to the version he reimag-ined on this date, reflects his maturity and growth as an artist, as well as the quality of those who he invited to work with him.

"He taught me his ear," explained Susan Rogers. "He taught me what he was going for. He would get unhappy when there were things beyond anyone's control. He was a reasonable man. He understood if stuff breaks, it breaks and that would make him upset. But if you were doing the best that you could and he wasn't happy with it, he'd let you know. He'd kind of tease you about it. Other than that, he kept people around who could give him what he wanted."[43]

"Sometimes he would just say, 'Whatever's going on, somebody fix it,' walk out of the room and come back," reflected Sheila E. about her time in the studio with him. "And hopefully it was fixed."[44]

Around 4 in the morning, Prince began mixing "I Could Never Take The Place Of Your Man," creating an instrumental version as well. It is likely that an instrumental version of "Sign O' The Times" was also mixed during this session. Two TDK C-60 cassettes were dubbed of what they'd mixed, and the session ended at 8 a.m.

Status: The 8-minute version of "I Could Never Take The Place Of Your Man" underwent additional work before it found a home on the unreleased *Dream Factory* (6:51) and *Crystal Ball* (6:28) collections. The version officially released on *Sign O' The Times* was identical to the *Crystal Ball* edit. It would be edited with a faded ending (3:39) and released on November 3, 1987, as the fourth and final single (backed with "Hot Thing") from *Sign O' The Times*.

The 1979 version of "I Could Never Take The Place Of Your Man" (3:12) was included on the *Sign O' The Times* Super Deluxe Edition in 2020.

THURSDAY, JULY 17, 1986

"**Joy In Repetition**" (tracking, overdubs, vocals, mix)
Sunset Sound, Studio 3 | 3:30 p.m.–5:30 a.m. (booked: lockout)
Producer: Prince | Artist: Prince | Engineers: Susan Rogers and Coke
    Johnson

> *When I heard the title "Joy In Repetition"—I had to laugh because it's like dude, that is all we do all day long. the band playing for months and that would be us because at rehearsal we'd have grooves that would last literally hours.*[45]
>
> —Lisa Coleman

For much of the month of July, Prince had Studio 3 at Sunset Sound on "lockout," or more specifically, an exclusive claim to the studio. As happened many times in the past, Prince asked Coke Johnson to set it up at 3 p.m. Half an hour later, Prince entered with a mission and started laying down the individual instruments, including live drums, guitar, bass, and the Fairlight. Shortly after 5 p.m., he shifted to embellishing the track with a variety of overdubs including bongos and other percussion and more guitar. By midnight, Prince began his vocals and as always, this was Prince's alone time, so he'd send the engineer to the lounge, so he could record with complete privacy. "We would set up his vocal mic, then leave the room," explained Rogers. "He didn't want an engineer between him and that audience. He wanted to just sing to his listeners."[46]

Vocals can be the most personal time for a musician, and Prince liked the ability to play with his vocals, layer them, bounce them back and forth, and sometimes creating multiple versions of his lead vocal. This was when Prince could make mistakes, away from the eyes of the world. Some of those mistakes became great parts of songs, while others were for his ears alone.

It wasn't uncommon for Prince to sit in the recording booth with a microphone hanging over the mixing board. The room lit only by candles and the lights of the console. It is easy to imagine how the intimate mood of a song like "Joy In Repetition" was influenced by the dim lights and smell of candles. Once again, Prince created something on his own, and when he played it for Wendy and Lisa, the reaction was overwhelming.

"Oh my God, I loved that song, because it was one of those songs where he nailed a lyric and a melodic marriage of harmonics, and I just thought it was one of his masterpieces," reflects Wendy. "I just remember being so moved when I heard it. 'There's joy in repetition.' I don't think anyone has used the word repetition in a song, and to me that is an incredible hook. It was so beautiful."

"Well, it's more mature than 'Everybody Want What They Don't Got,'" jokes Lisa. "He could be incredibly receptive, insensitive, and put all those things together and when the music was good and it could be really magical like 'Joy In Repetition.' That's really something. And it's thought provoking and easy on the ears."

Bobby Z recognized that many of his tracks had a quality that made them unique. "A lot of these songs may sound simple, two-four songs, but every measure has its own little world going on there. He would put accents on notes that were on the three, or untraditional, or cymbal crashes on the four. Things that were different, that will take study and will take analyzing for a long period of time."[47]

At 4 in the morning, Prince and Coke worked on a rough mix of the song, and after an hour, they laid "Joy In Repetition" off to two C-60 cassettes, ending the session at 5:30 a.m.

Status: "Joy In Repetition" (4:54) was released on Prince's 1990 album, *Graffiti Bridge*. It was also included on his 2002 live collection *One Nite Alone . . . The Aftershow: It Ain't Over* (from his performance on April 10, 2002) and as a TIDAL download from his concert recorded on February 20, 2016. In addition, Prince included it as part of a video medley from his concert on August 3, 2007, that was streamed from 3121.com.

FRIDAY, JULY 18, 1986

Dream Factory album (adjustments to the order, crossfades, mix)
Sunset Sound, Studio 3 | 7:30 p.m.–8:30 a.m. (booked: lockout)
Producer: Prince | Artist: Prince | Engineer: Coke Johnson

> *We'd record a whole bunch of songs, and then if they ended up*
> *all together on one tape or something, it seemed like at that*
> *point fans started naming the collections. I don't know it was*
> *the chicken or the egg kind of thing. We would just end up re-*
> *ferring to it as that. I know that he did have some things, like*
> Dream Factory *was a concept. I think he was looking for things*
> *that would fit that. Not everything did, but it would still maybe*
> *end up on that compilation.*
>
> —Lisa Coleman

Prince had been assembling the tracks he wanted to include in the updated configuration for *Dream Factory*. For the first 2 hours of the session, Prince continued working on several of the songs, but at 9:30 p.m., he left the studio for 5 hours. It is possible that he drove around listening to the new structure. If that is the case, he was not happy with what he heard and spent another 6 hours reworking the order and creating segues for several of the tracks.

At the end of the session, Prince had two C-90 cassettes, and two C-60 cassettes made of this assembly, which consisted of:

Side One:
 "Visions"
 "Dream Factory"
 "Train"
 "The Ballad Of Dorothy Parker"
 "It"

Side Two:
 "Strange Relationship"
 "Starfish And Coffee"
 "Colors"
 "Slow Love"
 "I Could Never Take The Place Of Your Man"

Side Three:
 "Sign O' The Times"
 "A Place In Heaven"
 "Crystal Ball"

Side Four:
 "The Cross"
 "Last Heart"
 "Witness 4 The Prosecution"
 "Movie Star"
 "All My Dreams"

This would be the last configuration of *Dream Factory*, as it would transform over the next few months into *Crystal Ball* and eventually *Sign O' The Times*. Of the 18 songs gathered for this assembly, only 8 would make the final cut and would be released on his next album.

SATURDAY, JULY 19, 1986

"Slow Love" (mix)
"Train" (mix)
Sunset Sound, Studio 3 (assumed) | (booked: lockout)
Producer: Prince | Artist: Prince | Engineer: Susan Rogers

> *We'd show up and we never knew what Prince was going to do. Maybe starting a new song, doing a twelve inch, or sometimes he would pull something out of the vault.*
>
> —Todd Herreman

Prince and Susan worked on new mixes for "Slow Love" and "Train." These updated mixes were placed on the *Dream Factory* collection.

SUNDAY, JULY 20, 1986

Dream Factory compilation (edits and crossfades)
"Sign O' The Times" (mix)
Sunset Sound, Studio 3 | 3:00 p.m.–12:00 midnight (booked: 3 p.m.–open)
Producer: Prince | Artist: Prince | Engineer: Coke Johnson

> *It was really a song a day coming out of the studio. You'd show up for work and he'd be playing another new brilliant song. It just seemed never ending. Concepts for albums were almost coming as quickly as the songs. And just about every creative aspect of Prince the musician was represented and updated with Sign O' The Times.*[48]
>
> —Alan Leeds

"Sign O' The Times" was a powerful song, in fact, strong enough to eventually be the title song for the collection, but at this point, it was just a standout track on a collection of exceptional music. Once the song became the focal point, the tone of the entire release would change, but for now it was still a track that needed work, so during this session, Prince updated the mix for the song, which likely faded out the track, creating the shorter version before adding it to the *Dream Factory* compilation.

After 9 hours of work on "Sign O' The Times," and several crossfades for the album, a single C-90 cassette was made of the updated collection.

Prince flew home to participate in the rehearsals with the Revolution for the remaining shows that summer.

TUESDAY, JULY 22, 1986

"Soul Psychodelicide" (tracking, mix)
Dixieland style instrumental (tracking, horn overdubs)
Untitled Instrumental [eventually released as **"Easy Does It"**] (tracking, horn overdubs)
Washington Avenue Warehouse (Edina, Minnesota) / Gaplin Blvd. home studio (Chanhassen, Minnesota) | afternoon/evening
Producer: Prince | Artist: Prince and the Revolution | Engineer: Susan Rogers | Assistant Engineer: Todd Herreman

There's a lot of material in the vault from live shows, videos and recordings. That kind of stuff would be fun to get into and maybe revisit. Inside the band there's a famous jam called "Ice Cream." When Prince was in a good mood or we were having a good show he would sometimes just run to the microphone and scream "Ice Cream!" and that was a cue for us to go into this particular jam thing. There were lots of little things like that we would do. Those kinds of things are really fun.[49]

—Lisa Coleman

Since February, when the band wasn't on the road, they were in rehearsal, and Prince relied on the Revolution to be ready for anything, so they were constantly in peak form. "He would always be recording, and he would get back to his studio and he knew how to take that energy and then build on it," reflected BrownMark. "That was the whole purpose of having a group. He wanted that live, real powerful energy that you cannot get as a solo musician in the studio. It's hard to capture the energy when you play all the instruments yourself."[50]

Each long jam was essentially a live high wire act held together by an intimate knowledge of everyone on the stage with him and within that trust lived the funk. "We were just so completely in shape and trained that if Prince decided he wanted to jump to the left, he'd just give us a hand signal and we'd all jump to the left," Lisa explained. "And every night was different. We had a setlist, but even that would change. He was a crazy man. We'd hit a groove and if it was really working and he was in a good mood, that could go on for 20 or 30 minutes with different hand signals and horn punches. Then he'd try and stump the band. He'd do this thing where he'd drop a handkerchief and when it hit the ground, we'd have to hit a horn punch. So it was kind of crazy!"[51]

"That was how all those licks were," explained Matt Fink. "They were just little James Brown-y horn licks ala Prince and little turnarounds, but he learned all that from the other masters that came before him."[52]

"I have everything on tape," revealed Prince, **"including all the informal jams. I record everything I do, just like Jimi Hendrix did. And eventually a lot of it will be released."[53]**

"Soul Psychodelicide" is an exercise that he ran with the expanded Revolution, including Wendy, Lisa, Matt, Bobby, Mark, Eric, Atlanta Bliss, Miko Weaver, Greg Brooks, Wally Safford, and Jerome Benton, as they prepared for the two shows at Madison Square Garden and a tour of Europe and Japan. The jam is a portrait of where they were at this point. Despite the personal issues during this period, they were focused, spirited, and tight. Prince would not have it any other way.

The title, "Soul Psychodelicide," which was mentioned in the lyrics for the recently recorded "Joy In Repetition," may have been inspired by the Chambers Brothers' 1967 release "Time Has Come Today," which includes the phrase "my soul has been psychedelicized."

"Soul Psychodelicide" was recorded during the afternoon at the warehouse with the full band, but after a break another session took place in Prince's home studio, recalled Eric. "The untitled Dixieland tune was done with Wendy, Lisa, and Miko, in addition to Blistan and myself, and I assume Prince was probably playing drums."[54]

Prince also recorded a third track on this date, an instrumental that Eric would eventually name "Easy Does It." The guitar, bass, and drum track would also include Leeds on horns and flute. Congas, cowbell, and timbales would be added to the track as well.

"The Dixieland style instrumental was an entirely different song than 'Easy Does It.' It has no title," adds Eric. "In fact, I actually took the song and messed around with it. I took all of the horns that were on it and I put new horns on it and then decided not to use it anyway."

Status: "Soul Psychodelicide" (12:33) was mixed, edited, and overseen by Prince but remained unreleased during his lifetime. It was included on the *Sign O' The Times* Super Deluxe Edition in 2020.

The instrumental would be updated by Eric Leeds as "Easy Does It" (2:24) and end up on his 1991 album, *Times Squared*. The song was also called "22" when it was being considered for one of the never released Madhouse *24* collections.

The untitled Dixieland track remains unreleased.

FRIDAY, JULY 25, 1986

"The Ball" (tracking, overdubs, mix)
Cobo Hall concert [from June 7 live video] (audio sweetening, mix)
Washington Avenue Warehouse (Edina, Minnesota)
Producer: Prince | Artist: Prince and the Revolution | Engineer: Susan Rogers | Assistant Engineer: Todd Herreman

> *There's many times where I'm sitting with him and we would talk, and he would come from a scenario with a band, and he would be frustrated and he would say, "I wish I could just put my brain in their head."*[55]
>
> —Jerome Benton

"You had to be as good as him, if not better, because he wanted you to make him work," explained BrownMark. "Plus, he was a real disciplinarian."[56]

As always, Prince expected everyone around him to be available 24/7. "It was non-stop," Wendy recalls.

> Lisa and I got to a place where, if the phone rang after two o'clock in the morning, we wouldn't answer it. Because it was inevitably, always him, and he'd be like, "There's a plane ticket for you, leaving at 7:00 a.m." And we're like, "No." He could stay up for a week, with no sleep, in a manic phase, just eating Toblerone. And everybody else around him had to keep up with that. And they weren't manic. So, mind you, by that last year, we were like, "It's got to be more than 800 bucks a week."

Once the band ended rehearsal, Prince recorded the basic tracks for "The Ball" by himself. This Fairlight-heavy companion piece for "Crystal Ball" started out with Prince playing a real drum kit, and he decorated the song with bass, finger cymbals, clavinet, backward guitar, and a variety of percussion instruments with a collection of crowd and party sound effects. He added two tracks of his own lead vocal and placed an effect on a second vocal pass that he referred to as "space voice harmonizer." During an undated future session, background vocals from Susannah and claps and background vocals from Wally Safford and Greg Brooks would be recorded. It is possible that these, and the segue of party talk, were added at some point during a band rehearsal the following week.

The song includes a shout out to Sheila E. with the phrase "All for one, one for all, fun for everyone," from Sheila's song "Romance 1600." The song also contains other references to his music, including "Train" and "Crystal Ball" as well as what was likely the first allusion to peach, part of the color scheme that would be used for the *Sign O' The Times* release.

Prince also oversaw audio sweetening of elements from the birthday concert recorded at the Cobo Hall in Detroit. The show had been edited, and he embellished some of the vocals and instrument sections with help from Eric, Atlanta Bliss, Dr. Fink, and BrownMark.

Source: "The Ball" (4:34) was placed on *Crystal Ball* but eliminated when the collection was reduced to the 2-disc *Sign O' The Times* release. It was reworked in 1987 and rechristened "Eye No" (5:47) for his *Lovesexy* album. Elements would also appear in "It Be's Like That Sometimes," which he'd record on October 11, 1986. "The Ball" and "It Be's Like That Sometimes" were included on the *Sign O' The Times* Super Deluxe Edition in 2020.

SUNDAY, JULY 27, 1986

"**Adonis And Bathsheba**" (tracking, horn overdubs, mix)
"**Adonis And Bathsheba**" [instrumental] (probable mix)
"**The Ball**" (horn overdubs, mix)
"**Joy In Repetition**" (probable mix)
Galpin Blvd. home studio | (Chanhassen, Minnesota) unknown time, into next day
Producer: Prince | Artist: Prince and the Revolution | Engineer: Susan Rogers | Assistant: Todd Herreman

I was with him for over four years and every single day with every new song I had this feeling of gratitude and amazement and excitement for every new song. I don't know if I was just easily impressed—that's part of it—but the other part of it the guy was so great that every time he'd do something new, I'd be thinking this could be the greatest thing he's ever done . . . but "Adonis and Bathsheba" was the first time where I thought to myself, you know, I don't think this is one of his best ones.[57]

—Susan Rogers

Considering the depth and scope of Prince's catalog, it is not surprising how many incredible pieces of music he created, and the excitement of giving birth was often shared with those around him, especially people like Susan Rogers who sat next to him for hundreds of sessions. "I'd think 'This is the best! It's gonna be great when the fans get to hear this. This is fantastic. I love this song.' I always felt that way, no matter how exhausted I was when he said the two magic words 'fresh tape.' It meant, we're gonna keep going. It might be after 24 or 48 hours or even more. He'd say, 'fresh tape' and I was always excited because it meant another song."[58]

As usual, Prince began with the drums and added a variety of other instruments including guitar, bass, and samples of harp and triangle from his Fairlight, but for the first time, Rogers' face showed that the song didn't connect with her. "There was just something funny about it. And I thought the lyrics were kinda corny . . . 'Adonis and Bathsheba in a garden of love.' And at one point he was overdubbing this harp. Just this little . . . *bling.* And I started to laugh. I just thought it was funny. And I seem to remember that he gave me a dirty look or said something kinda snarky about it. But I couldn't help it. I thought it was funny."[59]

Prince's defense of the song continued when Matt Blistan and Eric Leeds were called in to add tenor sax, flute, trumpet, and flugelhorn. "I remember at the time Prince telling me he thought it was one of the best lyrics he had written," recalled Leeds. "Usually if he thinks it's the best lyric he ever wrote, that'll give you the clue that it's not the best Prince song."[60]

With the gift of time's effect on her perspective, Rogers understands her initial problem with "Adonis and Bathsheba." "I realize now with today's ears exactly what I was hearing, there's a conflict between the rhythm and the melody line. They bump up against each other. There is a kind of a 3/4 feel to one part of it and a 4/4 feel to the other and it just doesn't gel. It just feels like a cart with a wobbly wheel to me. And again, I thought the lyrics were just a little bit silly."

Since Leeds and Blistan were adding their horns to "Adonis And Bathsheba," Prince asked them to contribute to "The Ball" as well. According to Eric, he was fond of the track. "I actually think the track was a little better than the remake of it that became 'Eye No.' I don't know why, maybe it was because it was just a little fresher to me."

After the horn parts were completed at 3 a.m., Prince and Rogers spent the rest of the session working on mixes for the two songs, including an instrumental take of "Adonis And Bathsheba." It is likely that he worked on a mix for "Joy In Repetition" as well.

Status: "Adonis And Bathsheba" (5:25) remained in the vault during Prince's life, although it was considered for a spot on the unreleased *Crystal Ball II* set in 2000. The song wasn't included on any configuration of *Crystal Ball* or *Sign O' The Times*, but Prince published the lyrics in the only issue of his *10,000* magazine, which was sold exclusively at the NPG Stores.

"Adonis And Bathsheba" was included on the *Sign O' The Times* Super Deluxe Edition in 2020.

WEDNESDAY, JULY 30, 1986

The 12-inch single of "Anotherloverholenyohead" (7:52) was released. It was backed with "Girls & Boys" (5:30) and went to number 63 on the *Billboard* Hot 100, and number 18 on the *Billboard* Hot Black Singles chart.

AUGUST 1986

SATURDAY, AUGUST 2, 1986

Venue: Madison Square Garden (New York, New York)
Capacity: ± 19,500 (sold out)

> *He didn't hang out with his band on the tour. He hung out with us.*
>
> —Wally Safford

Certain venues are stars on their own. The Los Angeles Forum, Red Rocks in Colorado, and the Budokan in Tokyo all have a place in history, but Madison Square Garden earned the nickname "the world's most famous arena" for a reason. Even the biggest musicians in the world feel the weight of playing at the arena. Selling it out means that you have arrived. Prince would play there 16 times during his career, but the first time was special, even to him. During "Do Me, Baby," Prince told a story from his heart about playing at Madison Square Garden.

When I was 17 years old, I ran away from Uptown and I came to New York City, looking to be a big star. My sister had to work, so she left me with one of her boyfriends. His name was Bill. So Bill said, "Prince, check it out. I want to take you over to one of my other girlfriend's house." I said, "Okay." On the way, we went through the subway and we stopped through here. And he said, "This is where the Knicks play basketball and this is where all of the big stars come. Maybe one day, you'll make it." Now I know that's kind of corny, but I just had to say that, because I've been trying to get there for a long time. I really love all y'all. Thanks for coming out. I swear to God, from me to you.[1]

In the month since he'd played a full concert, the show morphed. Gone from tonight's set were "The Dance Electric" and "A Love Bizarre," replaced by "Do Me, Baby," "When Doves Cry," and "Pop Life." "Life Can Be So Nice," "Whole Lotta Shakin' Goin' On," and "Mountains" were brought back out, and Prince performed a rare version of "Sometimes It Snows In April" during both nights. With only two tracks from *Purple Rain* in the set, he was shining a light on his other songs, and from the reaction of the crowd, he succeeded.

Miles Davis, David Bowie, Mick Jagger, and Andy Warhol reportedly attended the New York shows.

SUNDAY, AUGUST 3, 1986

Venue: Madison Square Garden (New York, New York)
Capacity: ± 19,500 (sold out)

> *Musically, the tour was great, but I could also tell he was angry a lot.*
>
> —Wendy Melvoin

There was tension within the band. When Prince was frustrated, it poured downhill and next in line was his band. The audience probably never had a clue, but Wendy, who shared the stage with him, witnessed the small cracks growing into great fjords.

I saw it every night, because there were so many people on stage you could tell who he was having his repartee with. So there was a lot of repartee with Wally, Brooks and Jerome, lots with Eric. He was testing a lot of go-betweens between me and Miko. He was, in a way, humiliating Bobby even more with more complex things and getting on the drums and doing his thing. There's a lot of that going on. There was a thing he would do if you were playing and he wanted certain musicians not to play, while the group was jamming. It rarely fell on me to lay out and we started saying "lay out" a lot and I was like, this is not good, he's testing something.

"He was my brother," explains Lisa.

I don't want to say this in a gossipy kind of way, but in the beginning there was a little bit of a romantic and sexual charge between he and I, and we fooled around with that, but it wasn't like, "I'm in love," it was like, "I just love this guy." And then he would be jealous because I was gay, or he'd be like, "I can't compete with Wendy." So there was a little bit of a romance there, but in all honesty it's like, after some years I mean I really couldn't imagine having sex with him because he *was* my brother. He became my brother, and in so many ways, and even though he was two years older than me, I felt like I was his big sister. I think because there was just a part of him, for better or worse, that was just immature, just never grew up, and it was the same guy that was fun and funny and goofy, but it was also the same guy that was really hurt, and I don't know if it's because I'm a woman, and my maternal instincts, but I could look into his eyes and see a wounded kid, and understand why he was so pissy in other ways, you know? And it was like having a kid that was just unhappy, like his toy broke and he was just having the worst day, and to a kid that's so real.

Prince and the Revolution ended the concert series on a high note, but there was a sadness to many of them that the abbreviated series of US shows was a drastic let down after the *Purple Rain* tour. "I really wish we'd played the states," reflected tour manager Alan Leeds. "I'm second guessing, but it would have been really interesting to know what effect it might have had on his career had we played that tour, because I think we would have really blown some people away. It was a kick-ass tour. Anyway, they got a taste of it."[2]

Tickets for a European tour had gone on sale at the end of July.

TUESDAY, AUGUST 5, 1986 (ESTIMATE)

"**Crystal Ball**" [orchestra mix] (overdubs, edits, and mix)
"**All My Dreams**" (overdubs, mix)
Galpin Blvd. home studio (Chanhassen, Minnesota)
Producer: Prince | Artist: Prince | Engineer: Susan Rogers

He gave ["Crystal Ball"] to the group at the time and told us, "Here, learn this," and we started rehearsing and realized just how technically challenging it was. It's a continuous piece, like a symphony. We were used to playing four-minute pop songs. I think I was rising to the challenge, as I could write my own charts, but some of the others were ear-players. There was so much going on, and Prince realized this and gave up on playing it live.[3]

—Matt Fink

Having a 10-minute opus that explains his philosophy was incredible, but if it remained buried on an album, no one would hear it. He tried teaching it to the band, but as the song became too difficult to translate into a live performance, Prince decided to create a mix for a 7-inch single, although first, he had to add Clare Fischer's orchestral arrangement that had been recorded the previous day. As he was mixing the track, Prince recorded a few additional overdubs, and once it was complete, he and Susan set about editing the song for a potential single. No immediate plans were in place for the release date, but it appears he wanted to have it prepared just in case.

Additional work was also done on "All My Dreams," including recording a few overdubs and updating the mix.

Status: The edited version of "Crystal Ball" (3:30) debuted on the *Sign O' The Times* Super Deluxe Edition in 2020.

WEDNESDAY, AUGUST 6, 1986

"Hot Thing" (tracking, mix, edit)
Galpin Blvd. home studio (Chanhassen, Minnesota)
Producer: Prince | Artist: Prince | Engineer: Susan Rogers (assumed)

[Prince] was in a transitional period here, where I think by now the idea of this Broadway musical was not quite on his mind. We were on and off the road, and I think the inevitabil-

ity of Wendy and Lisa leaving the band was kind of already, you know. . . . He was starting to look towards other things.[4]

—Eric Leeds

It is unclear if Prince had already moved beyond the *Dream Factory* concept, but he appeared to have been shifting to the idea of including more references to a "crystal ball" in his music, possibly finding a linking theme for many of his tracks that had been missing from the previous collections. The concept of a crystal ball had already appeared on at least two tracks, "The Ball," "Crystal Ball," and now it was going to be part of "Hot Thing."

Even with the band rehearsing every day, Prince was spending a lot of time alone in the studio, focused on creating instead of collaborating. When he was by himself, as musician, writer, and producer, there was no filter and no responsibilities to others, and the only thing that mattered was the music, as Susan explains. "He arranges as he's recording and most people don't do that. They do the basic tracks, then they stop, have a good night's sleep, come back to the studio the next day and spend the next week working on what the arrangement is going to be."

He had a watchmaker's knack for fitting the parts of his composition into 24 tracks. That's when most of his competition was using 48 tracks. So if you're going to fit those pieces into 24 tracks, each musical part has to carry a lot of weight. He was a maestro at balancing the limbic instruments with the melodic parts against the counter melodies and the harmony. Deciding whether it's going to be layered, is it going to be feathered with backing vocals or a horn arrangement or will it be a string arrangement? He's deciding these things in his head as the basic track is coming together in most instances. Really composing on the fly like a jazz musician does, but incredibly fast.

When he recorded "Hot Thing," Prince layered the song with a lot of additional instruments, but later in the session when he mixed it, he eliminated many of the extra parts, including a busy bass line and other elements that muddied up the message, to make his musical ode to the object of his lust a much more sparse arrangement. By the end of the shift, Prince realized he needed another element on the composition, and he asked Eric to join him in the studio as quickly as possible.

Status: A longer version of "Hot Thing" would eventually be edited (5:39) and released on the *Sign O' The Times* album. The song was later commissioned to be remixed by Shep Pettibone. Multiple remixes, listed as "Extended Remix" (8:32), "Edit" (3:40), and "Dub Version" (6:53) were all edited by Junior Vasquez and subsequently released as the B-sides on the 12-inch of "I Could Never Take The Place Of Your Man" in the United States on November 3, 1987.

A promo of "Hot Thing" went to #63 on the *Billboard* Hot 100 chart, #14 on the Hot Black Singles chart and #4 on the Hot Dance Music Club Play chart.

THURSDAY, AUGUST 7, 1986

"**Hot Thing**" (horn overdubs, mix, edit)
"**Make Your Mama Happy**" (tracking, overdubs, mix)
"**Forever In My Life**" (tracking, mix)
Galpin Blvd. home studio (Chanhassen, Minnesota)
Producer: Prince | Artist: Prince | Engineer: Susan Rogers

> Question: *"What was your inspiration for the song 'Forever In My Life?'"*
> Prince: *"Susannah. She knows."*[5]

Prince was busy preparing for the European tour with rehearsals and last-minute plans, but he apparently wanted to finish this final wave of recording with two songs, "Make Your Mama Happy" and "Forever In My Life." During sessions like this, Prince would generally be extremely focused, and it was important that the only people near him were facilitating his music or creating a layer around him to remove him from anything that could be distracting, "He knew what he was doing and nobody mattered," explains Susannah. "That's why [in Prince's voice] 'you're here for me, I am not here for you.' And there was a lot of that. Like, you want to be doing the stuff that I'm doing because ain't nobody badder than me, and he was right."

Prince spent the first few hours mixing and likely adding a few overdubs to the previous day's recording of "Hot Thing." Eric was asked to play sax on the track. "I remember that one because I didn't have my regular horn, my horns were on the road," explains Leeds. "And he was losing patience and I said, 'Well, my horns aren't here, they're back in town.' So he rented me a horn to play, I had to play on some shit-ass horn and I guess it turned out okay."

Despite the protests of Eric, when Prince played the track for members of his band, it went well. "We weren't involved in ["Hot Thing"] at all, but I liked it," recalls Wendy. "I thought it was another one of his funky masterpieces."

Once that was finished, he began work on "Make Your Mama Happy" by laying down the usual drum bed and then at least one synth line on the Prophet VS and another on the Mirage, then guitar and bass, before recording his vocals. Many of his compositions are made to entertain, while this track was explaining the importance of going to school and learning and how it can change the course of your life. It is a lesson about how hard work and focus can bring success, a philosophy that he practiced, but it was also a discourse about not allowing yourself to be distracted by anything or anyone. The spoken word part to this track included a call back to a song he'd recorded years earlier called "Don't Let Him Fool Ya."

He started recording "Forever In My Life" after midnight and quickly put together the basic tracks, including drums, acoustic guitar, and piano, but when he was ready to lay down his lead vocal, his normal routine changed. "There were a couple of times when he said: 'No, just leave the mic where it is, let's just do it,'" remembered Rogers. "'Forever In My Life' is one example. On 'Forever In My Life' he was in such a damned good mood. I think that was a simple state-ment of honest declaration of love. But it wasn't a declaration of sex. Many of his other songs are a declaration of desire, but I think 'Forever In My Life' was a simple declaration of honest love."[6]

"He had been up all night and he came upstairs," recalled Susannah. "It was like 7 in the morning and he grabbed my hand and said, 'Follow me', and so I followed him downstairs. The sun was coming through the stained glass win-dows and he pressed play, and that song came on and I looked at him and I got teary-eyed. And that was it. He didn't have to say anything."[7]

Susannah was asked to add background vocals to the chorus. In 2018, she looked back and explained how his public statements and his private behavior were often at odds.

There's so much to being in a relationship with him. It wasn't easy. We were a couple. He liked to keep me hidden. There was no sharing me and I was an identical twin. So that could be complicated. I have very strong ties to my fam-ily. So he could be hard on me. I'm sure anybody who's had a relationship with him could tell you the same thing—that he could be rough around the edges. Not easy. But there were times where I knew he looked to our relationship to keep him grounded. He could come home at night and it would be, like wrapping his legs around my legs. . . . And he always wore tube socks to bed.[8]

The version of "Forever In My Life" that was recorded contained Prince having fun with the "La-da-da-da-da-da-da-da" section. It was obvious he was being playful with the song. A mix was created of all of the tracks and dubbed to cassette, and plans were made to add horns to "Make Your Mama Happy" the following day.

Status: "Make Your Mama Happy" (4:00) was released on the *Crystal Ball* CD in 1998. "Forever In My Life" (6:25) was edited (3:30) and placed on *Sign 'O The Times.* The longer "Forever In My Life" was released as "Forever In My Life (Early Vocal Run-Through)" in August 2020 as a preview track for the *Sign O' The Times* Super Deluxe Edition.

FRIDAY, AUGUST 8, 1986

"**Make Your Mama Happy**" (horn overdubs)
"**Forever In My Life**" (vocal and various overdubs, mix)
Galpin Blvd. home studio (Chanhassen, Minnesota)
Producer: Prince | Artist: Prince | Engineer: Susan Rogers

> *I wrote this song called "Make Your Mama Happy" that would probably really frighten you.*[9]
>
> —Prince

Once Prince reviewed "Forever In My Life," he decided that he wanted to redo his vocals and adjust the tone of the song. With the new vocal pass and placement, Prince focused on giving his voice more passion instead of the upbeat playful feeling of the previous day's session. The updated sound also refocused the song to feature keyboards instead of his acoustic guitar. The acoustic guitar is brought back into the mix at 3 minutes, and the result was much more powerful, eliminating the "demo" feel of the track and lending the number a deeper, more intimate feeling of longing and desire. The song was also faded down at 3:30, leaving the last 3 minutes on the editing floor. Some of the parts that were eliminated found their way into his live performances of the song during the *Sign O' The Times* tour.

"When it came time to replace his original lead vocal, a miscalculation ended up giving the song more character, remembered Susan Rogers. "He asked me to mute the background while he did the lead, so I did. I muted the backgrounds, he did that lead, he came back in, I unmuted it, and I realized he had come in two bars later from the lead vocals, so the background were all two bars ahead. It sounded great and it was really cool and he was happy with it."[10]

After midnight, Eric Leeds added horns to "Make Your Mama Happy."

It is possible that Prince's vocals for "Forever In My Life" were recorded on a later date.

> *When you're working with Prince, you have to go to the limits of your abilities twenty-four hours a day, and it's exhausting—the only people who can survive that kind of schedule aren't terribly stable. It's easy for someone to dictate rules and regulations when you're not a very stable person. If you have a certain amount of stability, that schedule is impossible. It will break you.*[11]

—Wendy Melvoin

The summer had been a tough one. The failure of his movie and the fracturing team behind him was frustrating to everyone and the future was seemingly less certain. To the outside world, Prince and the Revolution was a tightknit family who shared everything. The team supported Prince, but, according to Lisa, they grew tired in many ways with his control over everyone around him.

> Somebody like Prince who is so impressive as a human being in all areas, it is difficult to not completely canonize him. He's amazing, a gift to humanity. But at the same time, he was a guy we worked with every day and it could get really stressful and annoying. One day he'd come in and be all excited and energetic and happy and want to goof around. The next day he'd walk in really somber with a cloud over his head, mumble in the microphone, and be a dick. Every show we played, he videotaped and made us watch on the bus afterward. He was charming and funny, but also boring, repetitive and self-absorbed.[12]

"If he was struggling, you wouldn't see the struggle," reflects Susannah. "You would see anger."

Rehearsals continued for an upcoming tour of Europe and Japan, but by this point there were deep cracks in the relationship with Lisa and Wendy. "This was a highly volatile time for all of us. Prince was soaring into the stratosphere of stardom and we were working our tails off to make more and more music that was relevant," detailed Wendy. "It all got away from us . . . from him . . . from our friendship."[13]

"I was close with Wendy and Lisa, so I knew of their frustration," reflects Rogers. "Susannah had my ear and she told me a lot of the frustrations she was having in the relationship. I was well aware that there were tensions. The writing was kind of on the wall."

On top of all the inner-band stress, there was a financial stress that was overwhelming some members of the band. According to union records, payment for several sessions from the previous two years had been overlooked. This was quickly remedied and payments for songs from as early as April 1985 were finally covered, but it may have been a case of too little too late for Wendy and Lisa.

"It was incredible," recalls Lisa. "We're living this dream that we were in a band and it got bigger, and bigger, and bigger and we made it, so we were all excited and in love, but then we got hit with a meatball and like, 'Wait, this could be done a little differently, and we could still be love, love, love, but we could make some money.'"

Wendy recalls:

Lisa and I were like "We're here, we're here," but here's the deal. I don't believe Mark was involved in the conversation, but me and Bobby and Lisa said, we need more than 800 bucks a week. I mean, you're making a fucking shitload and we're there 24/7. We need more than 800 bucks. So we had our group lawyer draw up a contract to give to Prince that said: We are exclusive to you if you give each one of us $1 million. And that was for a year, 1 million bucks a year. And as soon as he got it, apparently he was like, "Fuck you all." That's very true. But we were asked to not take other work, and 800 bucks was not cutting our bills. We're here because we want to be here, but can you throw us a fucking bone? He hadn't given us any fucking publishing, nothing. And he made the band share one percentage point on *Purple Rain* album. One point. So we were at that point like, "Oh come on, we want to be here. We've just scratched the surface of what we're going to do."

"Lisa had been unhappy for a long time," remembered Susan Rogers. "There was a big fight. A big fight. The offshoot of it was a couple of days later, Alan Leeds stepped in sort of negotiating and it was agreed that Wendy and Lisa would stay and they'd do the upcoming *Parade* tour, because we had planned to go to Europe."[14]

In all of the panic and overreactions, the original message got muddied. Wendy and Lisa wanted to stay, but the declaration that they wanted to be taken care of financially for their work made Prince assume that they were quitting. "We wanted to be able to work with Prince forever; we just wanted to draw up some contracts, and he took it as an assault on him," disclosed Wendy. "He wigged out. He thought it meant we didn't love him."[15]

"He was like, 'Yeah, sure. Come back in,' but he felt, 'They don't love me anymore. Period. You shouldn't even want to get paid,'" reasons Susannah. "And no one could live up to it. Everyone fell short, everybody. This was his chance to say, 'Guess what? I'll fire you anyway.' And that's all he wanted to do. You're fired before you quit."

"It just didn't make sense after a while," explains Lisa. "The whole, 'You don't love me' thing was just . . . come on. Easy for you to say with your *big, tall wallet.*"

Eric Leeds remembers:

[Prince] realized that he was so close to them, not only personally, but there was a musical synergy he had with them that perhaps he never had with anybody. That scared him because he realizes this is going to end and it's not going to end because *he* wants it to, it's going to end because *they* realized that there are things that they can do in their life that they don't need him for. And that scared him because those were his insecurities. And once he realizes, "Isn't it great to have people around me that I can have this musical rapport with, but what am I going to do when I don't have that anymore? So I better get rid of this now because I can't become dependent on that."

"We never wanted to leave," affirms Lisa. "It wasn't a matter of being convinced to stay. I mean, we had to be told to leave. We kept trying to work it out. Even in marriage, there were certain fights that you have with your spouse where you're fighting to stay together. If you're fighting to get apart, then there's a problem and the marriage is in trouble. But we were always fighting to stay together. We were fighting to work it out."

"What was unfortunate was that once you quit with Prince, you're gone," recognized Rogers. "And even though they were back, at that point he would begin to decide how to replace them and it broke his heart. But I think he felt like they instigated it and he followed through with it."[16]

The arrangements were made, and the full Revolution would be performing with Prince, but it was a brittle truce.

SATURDAY, AUGUST 9, 1986

Prince and everyone working on the tour flew to London to prepare for the launch of the European leg of the *Parade* tour. The equipment was loaded in the following day and a rehearsal was planned for the next.

The European tour was a band-aid to help keep the promotion of the *Parade* album alive, but they were dealing with a series of missteps that were damaging the usual momentum that Prince had when he released an album. "I think the failure of the movie and the early demise of the album after 'Mountains'—which was an ill-advised single choice—had a lot to do with everybody backing off the idea of a States tour," explained tour manager Alan Leeds.

I thought it would be a way to take the focus off the problems with the film and the album, and in fact help the album at a time when it needed it, because of the bad choice for the second single. But nobody else seemed to agree with that, and it became a thing of like, "Maybe we better go hide our head in the sand, because it's not our time." So we did Europe, we used it as a way to break into the European market for the first time, with great success, although on a limited scope. It wasn't a very ambitious tour. It was only a few weeks.[17]

TUESDAY, AUGUST 12, 1986

Venue: Wembley Arena (London, England)
Capacity: Approximately 7,700 (sold out)

If he ran his hand through his hair, that meant 16 more bars. He was like an NFL quarterback; he had all these audibles. We'd rehearse for hours and hours and hours and could go into any song, any key at any time. They would sound amazingly spontaneous.[18]

—"Bobby Z" Rivkin

Prince would often decide late that he wanted the party to continue, so he'd announce to Alan Leeds or someone on the staff to schedule an aftershow, sometimes actually telling them during the concert as his soundman Cubby Colby recalls. "I'm working the concert, I don't know until two songs before the end."

WEDNESDAY, AUGUST 13, 1986 (A.M.)

Venue: Busby's (London, England)
Capacity: attendance unknown

> *At the after-hours show, it's, "Get Cubby." So somebody would*
> *come out and get me, I'd be frantically patching and dialing in*
> *what was in this funky late bar gig at 2 in the morning, and*
> *it's packed, and it's hot, and I'm hungry.*
>
> —Robert "Cubby" Colby

Going to these venues was often a lesson in faith. Many of them weren't built for a show like this, remembers Cubby. "Nine times out of ten there'd be one light on in the club. There wouldn't be anything lit up onstage, so he didn't have to worry about video stuff. I did find many times secret ways that they would patch in a stereo feed from their front of house console, because now we're using their gear that ran up to the office. I'd unplug the stuff and somebody would come down, 'Hey, the recording . . . I'd say, 'You can't have that, that's not for tonight.' If I had a problem, I'd just call Gilbert [Davison, his bodyguard] or security."

Ron Wood and Nile Rodgers joined the band on stage for "Bodyheat." At the end of jamming with Wood on a cover of the Rolling Stones' "Miss You," Prince said, **"That's a great song. I wish I'd written that."**

WEDNESDAY, AUGUST 13, 1986

Venue: Wembley Arena (London, England)
Capacity: 7,700 (sold out)

THURSDAY, AUGUST 14, 1986 (A.M.)

Venue: The Roof Gardens (London, England)
Capacity: 500 (sold out)

The Roof Gardens show was the most incredible display of showmanship, of working a room, I have ever seen.

—Todd Herreman

Prince's aftershows are legendary, not just for the music that is performed, but for the experience for everyone in the room, as Todd Herreman remembers.

This was a jazz club, okay? And it's like the quintessential, stereotypical jazz club where some guy comes in with a cigarette dangling from his mouth and a beret on. Nobody knew that Prince was going to be there first of all, that was really cool. And so they brought out some of the gear, so everybody set up. Prince started out playing a really bluesy jazzy, a really quiet number, and this club filled with jazz aficionados that are just going crazy over Prince songs. But I'm sure had he started with his songs, they would have left. It was so brilliant and that was just one more case of seeing how talented this guy is.

But considering the exhaustion from an aggressive tour schedule, the exact details of shows like this are not always easy to recall for those on the stage, and particulars sometimes get lost. After an extended day filled with a soundcheck and a 2-hour concert performance, by the time the aftershow takes place, some of the minutiae becomes less important. "All I remember is that Eric Clapton was around and he would not ask Eric Clapton to sit in," according to Eric Leeds. "He was scared to death of Clapton, but he was able to have fun with Ron [Wood] and he was able to make fun of Ron, and Ron was a good patsy. An easygoing guy, and he didn't care, he was just in it for the party. So there was no threat."

Despite any concerns Prince may have had, Eric Clapton joined him on stage for "I Can't Get Next To You" and "America" during this show. Although the aftershows were usually performed at the end of a very long day, they were often a fun event for the band members who got a chance to break from the routine of the regular tour set list. When asked about his favorite shows, Matt Fink stated, "probably Paris and London, those kind of cities, where we had a lot of guest artists coming to the show, the likes of George Michael and people like that. Eric Clapton, Nile Rodgers who wanted to sit in and jam with Prince. Those kind of nights were always memorable."[19]

THURSDAY, AUGUST 14, 1986

Venue: Wembley Arena (London, England)
Capacity: 7,700 (sold out)

The show morphed again with "Little Red Corvette," being added and "A Love Bizarre," "Mountains," and "Kiss" all finding their way back into the set after not being played the previous night. Ron Wood joined Prince again, this time with Sting as they played the Rolling Stones hit "Miss You." BrownMark reflected about what it was like during shows like this. "When he went to invite these artists on the stage, I can probably speak for the rest of the band, we're sitting back like, 'Whoa! That's Ron Wood. That's Sting!' He invited them all up and we would just be blown away, but for him it was nothing. It was nothing."[20]

"Sting got up to play with him in London and Prince loved fucking with him," recalled Roy Bennett. "[Prince] was doing all these turnarounds and eventually Sting just gave up playing. He took his hands off his bass and put them up in the air."[21]

FRIDAY, AUGUST 15, 1986

The tour traveled to the Netherlands to prepare for three nights at the Ahoy' in Rotterdam.

SUNDAY, AUGUST 17, 1986

Venue: Sportpaleis Ahoy' (Rotterdam, the Netherlands)
Capacity: 8,927 (sold out)

> *I kept explaining it away. I was certainly noting his bizarre behavior and I felt dissed many times.*
>
> —Lisa Coleman

Birthdays are the one day that we collectively let our guard down and make sure that the person close to us understands that we are happy that they were born.

While Prince was rarely generous with compliments for those who worked for him, at this point in his life, he did usually participate in wishing others a happy birthday, so when Lisa's birthday landed on the day of a show, his behavior revealed that something was wrong. "It was really weird because we played, and he said that he made reservations at a restaurant for my birthday dinner afterwards. I wasn't expecting anything, 'Oh, thanks. That's great.' So the band all got together, and we went to the restaurant. Then I don't even think he came. It was like, is he coming? And it was just a weird vibe kind of like, 'Uh oh. This is weird.' I just remember it was a tense dinner and I couldn't wait for it to be over. It was like, 'What's going on here?'"

MONDAY, AUGUST 18, 1986

Venue: Sportpaleis Ahoy' (Rotterdam, the Netherlands)
Capacity: 8,927 (sold out)

Tonight's concert featured the live debut of "Manic Monday" during this tour. It had been performed by Prince when he shared the stage with the Bangles on May 14, but this was the first time it was played publicly with the Revolution. Prince had Wendy sing the lead vocals.

TUESDAY, AUGUST 19, 1986

Venue: Sportpaleis Ahoy' (Rotterdam, the Netherlands)
Capacity: 8,927 (sold out)

The following day, the tour traveled to Copenhagen.

THURSDAY, AUGUST 21, 1986

Venue: Valbyhallen (Copenhagen, Denmark)
Capacity: 4,200 (sold out)

FRIDAY, AUGUST 22, 1986

Venue: Isstadion (Stockholm, Sweden)
Capacity: 9,800 (sold out)

Susannah Melvoin and John L. Nelson, Prince's father, flew in for the show.

SUNDAY, AUGUST 24, 1986 (A.M.)

Venue: New Morning (Paris, France)
Capacity: 300 (sold out)

> *Afterparties were great because you can do crazy things and solos and just have fun, whereas a show is more set. You had a commitment to a promoter and to x amount of fans. The after-party was Prince's chance to stretch out and have fun. Shred a little bit, too, without having to be perfect.*[22]
>
> —Lisa Coleman

Although this wasn't an afterparty because there was no event beforehand, the concerts that Prince would perform during the early morning hours were legendary and each one was unique, based on his mood at that moment. A live show is like a circus act, and to be truly entertaining for the performer and the audience, a tightrope performance needs danger. Shows like this were outside the standard set of the tour and added some risk and spontaneity to his time on the road. Getting a chance to exercise those musical muscles provided a way to avoid becoming jaded while on tour. With his father joining the band on piano, Prince ran through a loose but extremely fun show that consisted of several covers including a performance of The Temptations'/Al Green's "I Can't Get Next To You" (written by Barrett Strong and Norman Whitfield) Jimi Hendrix's "Red House" (rechristened "Purple House"), and several James Brown tracks including "Soul Power," "Ain't It Funky," and "Get Up (I Feel Like Being A) Sex Machine" (written by Brown, Bobby Byrd, and Ron Lenhoff). Susan Rogers, who watched him jam on cover songs many times, explains why she felt he did songs like these. "I assume that he would play these songs just for the fun of it. So he didn't have to think about himself and his own perspective and he could just play music just for the sake of playing as he did so many other occasions."

During one of these jams, he said to the audience, **"For those of you who speak English, because I speak no French, just continue what you was doing, because we're just going to make some noise because we were bored staying in the hotel,"** and **"If any of this sounds unorganized, that's because it is. We're just making it up as we go along."**

The setlist contained the live debut of deep tracks like, "Susannah's Blues," "Last Heart," and "An Honest Man." He'd revisit several of tonight's tracks the following day during the soundcheck before his show at Le Zénith.

The New Morning concert would be the final one-off show that he'd ever play with the Revolution, and he left everything with a bang.

Status: Prince would eventually release a version of "Purple House" on the Hendrix tribute album, *Power of Soul*, in 2004.

MONDAY, AUGUST 25, 1986

"It's Gonna Be A Beautiful Night" (soundcheck)
"Susannah's Blues" (soundcheck)
"Strange Relationship" (soundcheck)
"I Can't Get Next To You" [cover version] (soundcheck)
"Raspberry Beret" [a capella] (soundcheck)
Le Zénith | afternoon soundcheck | Dierks Studio Mobile Trucks
Artist: Prince and the Revolution | Engineers: Robert "Cubby" Colby and
  likely Susan Rogers

> *Soundcheck was not a chore for Prince. So, where most bands will soundcheck for half an hour, or 15 minutes if they can get away with it, Prince would soundcheck for four hours. He'd come on stage at 2 o'clock in the afternoon as soon as the lines were plugged in, before they had finished hanging the lighting and all that stuff and testing everything, he'd be on stage and he'd be rehearsing with the band or just playing, often just playing his songs from 2 to like 6, getting off the stage at the last possible minute.*[23]

—Susan Rogers

Prince ran the band through multiple tracks from the previous night, including: "I Can't Get Next To You," "Strange Relationship," "Susannah's Blues," and an a capella version of "Raspberry Beret." Once he finished the exercise with those songs, he began working on a new track, "It's Gonna Be A Beautiful Night."

"We were doing our soundcheck which was a 'jam,' more or less," remembered Atlanta Bliss. "Prince would let everyone play here and there, and we started developing some music. Then Prince said, 'I want to write some songs, and I'm gonna get a recording truck in here and we're gonna have some fun.'"[24]

"Basically BrownMark started the jam off with his bass line. Then it was just a groove," recalls Eric. "I remember Prince said, 'Matt, you got a keyboard line for that?' And he came up with that, and he said, 'Eric, got a horn line?' And I came up with a little riff line. That was it. We recorded the whole song that evening."

To go from a jam, to a fully realized song (with the exception of most of the lyrics, which would be added in November), including writing, arranging, and making sure everyone has their parts to performing the new composition live in front of thousands of people on that same night is a testament to how intimately connected the Revolution were to his energy, but it was an almost terrifying situation because they were working on a song that was going to debut in front of a packed theater. No safety net, no second chance. If the groove doesn't work, it bombs in front of thousands of people. That was the razor's edge of working for Prince.

MONDAY, AUGUST 25, 1986

"It's Gonna Be A Beautiful Night" [Live] (basic tracks from live show)
Venue: Le Zénith (Paris, France) | Dierks Studio Mobile Trucks
Capacity: 6,000 (sold out)

I think ["It's Gonna Be A Beautiful Night"] was probably written for that night. It was a beautiful night in Paris and I think that was the whole attitude that he wanted to have like a fun song and I think that's the way it came off. The whole song came off with a nice really fresh vibrant attitude.

—Matt "Atlanta Bliss" Blistan

AUGUST 1986

Hours after creating "It's Gonna Be A Beautiful Night" from nothing, Prince led the band through a 9-minute jam of the song live in front of 6,000 people during the first encore. It came off perfectly and the Parisian crowd loved it. Musical expressions like this were something that Prince seemed to do almost effortlessly. "It was really comforting to know that he had the confidence in the band that we could pull it off," reflects Bliss. "That was nice to think that he had confidence in us that we were watching him, we weren't daydreaming. We weren't looking at the beautiful girl in the front row. We were watching him."

Changes were happening and although this wasn't the last show for the Revolution, it was the final time their work was recorded and included as part of an official release for Prince during his lifetime.

Status: The entire show was professionally recorded, but only "It's Gonna Be A Beautiful Night" (9:00) was released during Prince's lifetime. The performance during this show was basically an instrumental with the "ohweeoh-ohhhoh" chant, and Prince singing "Beautiful Night" several times. In fact, the full title wasn't mentioned during the song. The track would be drastically overdubbed with new instruments and lyrics before it appeared on *Sign O' The Times* in 1987.

TUESDAY, AUGUST 26, 1986

Venue: Eissporthalle (Frankfurt, West Germany)
Capacity: 6,500 (sold out)

WEDNESDAY, AUGUST 27, 1986

Venue: Vorst Nationaal (Brussels, Belgium)
Capacity: 8,000 (sold out)

THURSDAY, AUGUST 28, 1986

Venue: Eissporthalle (Frankfurt, West Germany)
Capacity: 6,500 (sold out)

FRIDAY, AUGUST 29, 1986

Venue: Grugahalle (Essen, West Germany)
Capacity: 8,000 (sold out)

During the soundcheck, Prince worked on "It" and "The Ballad Of Dorothy Parker" with the band. Neither track appears to have been performed during the tour.

SATURDAY, AUGUST 30, 1986

Venue: Alsterdorfer Sporthalle (Hamburg, West Germany)
Capacity: 7,000 (sold out)

SUNDAY, AUGUST 31, 1986

Venue: Alsterdorfer Sporthalle (Hamburg, West Germany)
Capacity: 7,000 (sold out)

He was always confident even though you could look at him with those puppy dog eyes and you know, he had so much on his shoulders, especially because of who he was and he must've been in hell most of the time because you need to be selling yourself like you are all that and a bag of chips. Right? He was such a perfectionist and he wanted to be greater all the time. He dedicated his entire existence to that. What he did is what he was. That takes a lot of sacrifice. He used to say things like, "I know how down I can get, but I wonder how up *I can get." That's an interesting thought and kind of scary.*[25]

—Lisa Coleman

This was the last of five sold out shows in West Germany and the end of this leg of the tour. In the period since his first European concert in 1981, his career had exploded and there was a new, relatively untapped market that was eager for his blend of funk and pop. The media and the fans embraced him and this relationship was so unique that he would schedule entire tours exclusively for his European fanbase.

On this tour, his fans had shown their enthusiasm with every show. His popularity wasn't based on *Under The Cherry Moon* because the movie had yet to be released in Europe, so its failure in the United States wasn't affecting ticket sales.

Wherever he went, Prince had a way of connecting with his audience at a core level. It was something he did with ease and he maintained that ability throughout his entire career, so few in the crowd understood the growing divide he was having with the Revolution. Despite the comradery on stage, he was distancing himself, according to Susannah. "It was all a big show, but deep inside he can't be accountable. He doesn't show up on an emotional level. It's too vulnerable."

"I feel like he was vulnerable with us," explains Lisa, "but he would probably argue that he's *never* vulnerable."

Status: The first part of this show, from "Christopher Tracy's Parade" to "A Love Bizarre," was included on the fourth NPG Ahdio Show in the NPG Music Club in 2001.

SEPTEMBER 1986

The tour had matured and was running smoothly as they headed east for Prince's first concerts ever in Japan. A traveling show has a lot of moving parts, so there was the occasional glitch—Wendy reportedly losing her passport in Europe—but overall the awkwardness of the first few shows had been corrected and to the audience, the band was tight and performing beautifully. "Musically, it was magical. We were playing better than ever, going to places we'd never visited," reflected Wendy. "But there was also stuff going on with people's relationships. It got ugly. By the time we got to Japan, I told Lisa, 'He's going to fire us. I can feel it.' Something was wrong."[1]

FRIDAY, SEPTEMBER 5, 1986

Venue: Festival Hall (Osaka, Japan)
Capacity: 9,000 (attendance unknown)

> *By the time we got to Japan, we were already kind of falling apart. We were dealing with a lot of issues. So put it this way, it wasn't like a complete shock to be honest with you.*
>
> —"Bobby Z" Rivkin

Sheila E. was the opening act during the four Japanese dates of the tour. It was a role she'd filled for him on the *Purple Rain* tour. "Prince was smart," explained Sheila. "He made sure that anyone he was producing stayed around him, as it made him and his company sell more."[2]

Susan Rogers feels that there is something beyond that reason.

I believe he was courting [Sheila] for a number of reasons, of course, to have had an alter ego because the Time was no longer together. So now these Sheila records can maybe be sort of his alter ego and because of the triangle of Prince and Susannah and Wendy plus Lisa, things were difficult. There were tensions there. And Sheila served as alternates to Wendy and Lisa and in some cases if he was fighting with Susannah. Sheila was an alternate to Susannah. He's got this relationship with Susannah where she's a musician, but not the musician that Sheila is, but she's his girlfriend and their engagement is on again, off again, off again. . . . Those times were potent. They were fighting a lot. And he could fight with Susannah and have female companionship with Sheila. And often when he was fighting with Susannah, a corollary of that would be an argument with Wendy and Lisa because anything that hurts Susannah hurt Wendy too, and anything that hurt Wendy hurt Lisa. It was a difficult period. A difficult time.

SATURDAY, SEPTEMBER 6, 1986

Venue: Festival Hall (Osaka, Japan)
Capacity: 9,000 (attendance unknown)

On the bullet train in Japan, Jerome told me, "Sheila E. wants your job." I knew it was over.[3]

—"Bobby Z" Rivkin

The stress and the unknown was taking its toll on everyone. The idea that what was once the perfect band for Prince, the band that stood next to him during his biggest success, was coming off the rails. Bobby Z realized that it might never be the same. "Sheila was doing soundchecks with the band, and by that time I had just gotten used to expecting anything to happen. But it looked like she was a little bit more involved than normal. I played well on the whole *Parade* tour, but at the end it was obvious that Prince was more aloof to Wendy, Lisa, and me. Wendy, Lisa, and I were just hanging constantly. It was pretty obvious to me something was going to happen."[4]

Despite the pressures, the band performed perfectly, and Prince expanded the show to include "The Ladder" and "Condition Of The Heart." He also added some of the lyrics for "Sign O' The Times" during "Pop Life."

MONDAY, SEPTEMBER 8, 1986

Venue: Yokohama Stadium (Yokohama, Japan)
Capacity: 45,000 (attendance unknown)

Three shows were considered for Yokohama stadium, but ultimately, it was limited to only two concerts.

TUESDAY, SEPTEMBER 9, 1986

Venue: Yokohama Stadium (Yokohama, Japan)
Capacity: 45,000 (attendance unknown)

Honey, we've been together. Honey, for too long. . .[5]

—lyrics to "New Position"

Prince was still pushing the band hard during soundchecks, using the afternoon to work on songs like "For Love," "Love Or Money," and "America," turning the number into a "Big Ol' Soul Sister" jam, but it was no longer time *with* the band. Prince was using the soundchecks for additional reasons, according to Lisa. "I remember that last soundcheck that he had some other musicians come up, some of Sheila's band, and it was like 'What's going on here?' He would look at me and Wendy and say, 'Lay out' and that was so unusual because we were his right hand, and then suddenly at soundcheck for him to say, 'Shh, don't play,' it was like, 'What?' Because he had other musicians up there and he was having fun with them and he wanted to see what they could do and how badass they were and so it felt like something was going on."[6]

Wendy also recognized that the vibe they shared was no longer on solid ground. "I knew something shifted on our last night at Yokohama Stadium. He started calling a whole bunch of different people on stage with us and he hadn't done that before and we knew him so well and there wasn't a lot of . . . he wasn't looking at us. I could feel it."[7]

The performance on that night would be historic and publicly created a chasm in the band from which they'd never recover. "It was not good or fun, and not what I expected," explained Lisa.[8]

"By the end, the last gig in Japan, he went on a rant," recalled BrownMark. "He was smashing stuff onstage and he was pretty angry. I knew what a lot of that was about."[9]

During his solo on "Purple Rain," Prince slammed his white guitar down and was given a replacement, but within 30 seconds he threw that one to the ground as well. Wendy realized that it was all coming to a head. "He destroyed it and I looked at Bobby and I went 'It's over.' I looked at Lisa, 'It's over.' And it was over."[10] Prince left his guitar and jammed on the keyboard for a short while and then left the stage with a "domo arigato."

"I knew it was ostensibly their last show," reflects Eric Leeds. "They always said that they had a feeling that it was, but they didn't know for sure. I was under the impression that he was going to tell them as soon as we got back to the States, but he didn't."

"We left the next morning," details Wendy, "but he didn't fly on the plane with us. He stayed there in Japan. I remember all of us on the plane going back. It was weird weather outside and it was a really bumpy flight home and I just remember thinking, 'You motherfucker.'"

SATURDAY, SEPTEMBER 13, 1986

"**Crucial**" (tracking, overdubs, vocals, mix)
Galpin Blvd. home studio (Chanhassen, Minnesota)
Producer: Prince | Artist: Prince | Engineer: Susan Rogers

The Beatles started singing, "I Wanna Hold Your Hand" and ended up with "I Am The Walrus." Prince got more confident, and most songs like "Raspberry Beret" are just brilliant storytelling. He had the ability to tell a story with his lyrics, and take you in. That's what's so amazing is the different styles of

music and he would take you different places with the story.
And that definitely grew as time went on.[11]

—"Bobby Z" Rivkin

With the relatively short tour over, and no routine from the road and none of the numbing adulation to distract him, Prince quickly jumped back into his disciplined recording schedule, but this time he closed the doors to his home studio to almost everyone, including those closest to him, giving him the opportunity to quietly reflect. **"What if everybody around me split? Then I'd be left with only me, and I'd have to fend for me,"** Prince explained in 1990. **"That's why I have to protect me."**[12]

What had become communal time with those he loved was being reclaimed as solitary once again. His once family-like band was placed at arm's length, and Prince privately tested the waters, possibly to verify that he still had the ability to create without exposing too much of himself in the process. "We wanted to be Prince's muses," Wendy explained, "but he felt like he needed to take back the initial thing that got him to where he was at, which was, 'I need to do this on my own.'"[13]

Rogers recalls the confusion during this era. "The Revolution was so central to his identity and his success with *Purple Rain* that now he had to re-conceive himself as a successful entity in the absence of these very prominent figures. It was so unusual to have two women in the band who were as accomplished as Wendy and Lisa. They were an exceptional band. To have success without them, that's going to take a bit of work."

Prince had come so far over the last few years, but the price was that he shared parts of himself with others and he was likely realizing how emotionally bare he had allowed himself to become, but this was also bringing out some incredible music despite the pain he had in his life. The next few weeks would be vital to his peace of mind as well as to his career. "You see, the whole thing with Prince," explains his bodyguard Wally Safford, "he'd use you until he can't use you no more. That's how he was. He'd get all the data and information that he can from you and that's it. Once he was done, he was done."

"He was an isolated person, probably safe to say lonely, but he probably would have been lonely whether he was famous or not," reveals Susan Rogers. "That said, he was respectful and he was always good to me. But when he was having a bad day, wow. He could peel paint off the walls with just one glance. And he wasn't a yeller or a screamer. He was a decider. Almost in a kind of feminine way, when he wanted to shut you out, he shut you out. You didn't exist. That was how he went about getting what he needed."[14]

"I had been in all those bands with him and he was starting to finally become—after being a superstar all those years kind of like—I kinda want to do this myself again," recalled Bobby Z. "I was getting a sense that we had become such a huge part of his everyday life that he was kind of growing a little tired of it and we're a handful. We weren't just sidemen. We're the Revolution and we opened our mouths often."[15]

The decision to record alone ran deeper than just trying to avoid the Revolution. According to Alan Leeds, it was an undeniable change in direction, tone, and state of mind and having the band involved in this music might have distorted his newest artistic direction:

Clearly there was a decision to avoid recordings with Wendy and Lisa because it was not his proclivity. Prince *lives* his music, and even to the degree his entire environment revolves around his record during a period of time. Prince fans have noticed his taste of colors. Much the same way that when you have a fixation with chocolate ice cream, then you're sick of it, next year you discover another flavor and then that wears out, that's how he is about colors. In his mind, the colors, the set design of his stage and the people in his band with whom he shares these experiences, touring, rehearsing, recording, is all one with the music that's presented, recorded in that period of time, of that segment of his career, his life. In his mind, you just simply don't make records with people—Wendy and Lisa, whose contributions are on the level of theirs and whose personalities are as distinct as theirs—and then release that record after they're gone and go play those songs on tour with somebody else. If they're no longer part of the band, well then he should be playing music that relates to this new group of people or at least stuff that he recorded by himself that's then interpreted by the current band. But to do a Wendy and Lisa song without Wendy and Lisa, he didn't feel legitimate in doing so.

The unfortunate side of that is if you're that personally involved in all of your projects that it precludes taking material out of context, it means that a song like "Power Fantastic" sits in the vault for years. Some other equally brilliant music sitting in the vault, that may or may never see the light of day just because of the cast of characters involved. It will only see the light of day in some kind of a retrospective collection.[16]

The album that resulted from this period of transition, *Sign O' The Times*, can be divided into two sections. The 11 earliest tracks, many recorded by him alone, but during his time with the Revolution, were the core of the album. The other 5 tracks would be selected from what he'd record during the upcoming months. With the bulk of the material from the former period, his next release would contain the final musical statements for Prince and the Revolution during his lifetime, even though it was his first true "solo" album in years.

"I think *Parade* is definitely the last Revolution album," explains Susan Rogers. "'It's Gonna Be A Beautiful Night' is the Revolution being represented on the album and 'Strange Relationship' is one we did quite a lot at rehearsal but for the most part the *Sign O' The Times* album represents the end of a transition period for Prince. A very long transition period."[17]

The music he'd be creating would span a range that most musicians could not imagine. Even the songs that were discarded had the potential to be career-defining hits for other performers, but in the hands of the maestro, they were simply more examples of how effortlessly he could create something with depth on his own.

"Crucial," the track he recorded on this date, was the perfect example of this. What began as a minute-long piano demo with only a few scattered words, blossomed into an exquisite representation of his love for his partner, Susannah. In a way that is similar to "Come Elektra Tuesday," he describes how her perfumed scent from their embrace remained on him for days. Over the course of the song, he expresses how their love would be "for always" and that her "body's a river" and he wanted "every drop."

For the next several hours, Prince would layer elements from the Prophet VS synth, acoustic guitar, cymbals, a live snare drum, guitar, and bass over a Linn LM-1 drum mix. Susannah would be asked to join him for background vocals, but the track was otherwise done solo by Prince.

Rogers had witnessed Prince capture lightning in a bottle many times. "We spent a long time on 'Crucial,' and I don't think it quite lived up to its early promise, in his mind perhaps."

Status: "Crucial" (5:06) would undergo multiple overdubs, and Prince would rewrite the lyrics, before it was released on his *Crystal Ball* CD set in 1998. He'd supposedly wanted to include the updated and edited version on *Sign O' The Times*, but according to the liner notes for his 1998 *Crystal Ball* release, it was eventually replaced with "Adore." The track's title would be included in the lyrics of "U Got The Look."

"Crucial" was originally intended for *The Dawn*, but that project was never completed. An early draft of the script for *Graffiti Bridge* contained the song as it was recorded on this date, although, it was removed before the start of production.

SUNDAY, SEPTEMBER 14, 1986

"The Cocoa Boys" [occasionally listed as "The Coco Boys"] (tracking, live
    drums, overdubs)
"The Cocoa Boys" [occasionally listed as "The Coco Boys"] (tracking,
    drum machine, overdubs, mix)
Galpin Blvd. home studio (Chanhassen, Minnesota)
Producer: Prince | Artist: Prince | Engineer: Susan Rogers

> *Modern Drummer*: What makes you decide whether to pro-
> gram drums or play them live?
> Prince: *My impatience usually dictates that decision.*
> *Whichever the engineer plugs in first.*[18]

Prince was back to recording every day and the ideas were flowing out of him
without a filter.

One of the elements that made Prince so unique was that he recorded quickly
without questioning himself, according to former member of the Time, Jimmy
Jam, who—along with Terry Lewis—worked with a number of musical greats
including both Prince and Michael Jackson. "Working with Prince and working
with Michael, they were polar opposites in the way they worked. Prince would
walk in the studio at the beginning of the day and he'd walk out with '1999,'
done. Michael would spend a day just on the volume of the handclaps. I mean,
literally. And we'd turn them up and he'd say, 'Okay, I'll come back tomorrow and we'll listen to it again.' We come back the next day, and he'd go, 'Can
we turn that up just a little more?' Yes, we turn it up. 'Okay, make me a tape.'
Okay. 'I'll come back tomorrow and we'll listen again.' I mean, it was literally
like that."[19]

Susan Rogers agrees that Prince's originality and creative energy were
unique, and although he expected perfection from everyone around him, his
perfection didn't always translate into the speedy process that he used to record
his music.

I will take a quote from the sciences. Creativity equals original plus useful. So
originality, just for the sake of being original doesn't matter if nobody wants it.
Anybody can go into the kitchen and take some weird ingredients and put them
all together and "Yeah, it's original." But if nobody likes it, it's no good. So he
had that perfect blend of original thought, but he knew how to make music that
was functional and he himself could not have functioned if he'd been obsessing

over every little detail. His work was gesture sketches. His music would come out like a sneeze. It was just bam, bam, bam, bam. Michael Jackson's music was massaged and carefully controlled and obsessed over. Both of them reached the same point, which is the peak of the charts in the Eighties, but as very different types of artists with different methodologies. If you did anything that slowed Prince down, you were out of there.[20]

Part of what accelerated Prince's pace was his use of drums. He'd often blend his synth drums with an actual drum kit, but occasionally he'd hear a song in his head and not be sure about which drum set up worked best. For "The Cocoa Boys," Prince decided to use both, and recorded "The Cocoa Boys" twice in one day, first using real drums as the song's backbone, which he recorded while he was working on a few ideas for the lyrics. The song ended up being a mostly instrumental jam and in the middle of recording the song, he abandoned it and retracked it using Linn LM-1 and embellished the percussion with accents of live drums and cowbell.

Similar to the detailed narrative that he penned for "The Ballad Of Dorothy Parker," Prince told the tale of Joey Coco and his brother, Frankie, who was the leader of their band, "The Cocoa Boys." The apparent discrepancy in spelling of "Cocoa" (the band), and "Coco" (the brothers) is explained in Prince's handwritten lyrics for the song that are included in the *Sign O' The Times* Super Deluxe Edition in 2020. He wrote, "Over on the east side across the river, there was a band called the Cocoa Boys."[21]

The lyrics were used to set up for a movie about the Cocoa Boys and included many items that Prince would revisit, including the use of the Prophet VS setting that would be later featured in songs like "U Got The Look" and ideas that would be found on "It's Gonna Be A Beautiful Night" ("We are beautiful, it's gonna be a beautiful night") and on *Lovesexy's* "Positivity" ("All the boys, and all the girls, you are the new kings of the world").

For the sections that he felt needed horns, Prince scatted a guide track for Eric Leeds and Atlanta Bliss, who joined him after midnight (possibly during the next day's session), to record sax and trumpet respectively for the song. They did not add horns to the unfinished live drum version of "The Cocoa Boys." With the exception of the horns and Susannah's voice during one section, it is a completely solo recording by Prince.

Status: "The Cocoa Boys" (5:53) and the incomplete live drum version of the song remained unreleased during Prince's life, but the fully realized track was included on the *Sign O' The Times* Super Deluxe Edition in 2020.

Prince used the moniker "Joey Coco" for at least eight songs for other artists including: Sheena Easton ("101," "Cool Love"), Nona Hendryx ("Baby Go-Go"), Three O'Clock ("Neon Telephone"), Deborah Allen ("Telepathy"), and Kenny Rogers ("You're My Love"), and although "Violet Blue" and "My Man" are listed as Prince compositions on Jill Jones's album, they are registered to Joey Coco at the Library of Congress.

MONDAY, SEPTEMBER 15, 1986

> **"Wouldn't U Love 2 Love Me?"** (possible overdubs, mix)
> **"The Cocoa Boys"** (overdubs, mix)
> **"Crucial"** [version 2, updated lyrics] (vocals, mix)
> Galpin Blvd. home studio Chanhassen, Minnesota
> Producer: Prince | Artist: Prince | Engineer: Susan Rogers

> *I was always like, "Why aren't we playing that ['Wouldn't U Love 2 Love Me?']?" We never played it. I would start playing it at rehearsal or something and then he would just look at me and laugh and then count in another song. It was always one of my little pets.*[22]
>
> —Lisa Coleman

Prince preached about the importance of his newest music, but he occasionally dipped back into his extensive vault of unreleased tracks. Perhaps it was because he was recording nonstop and needed to keep himself busy or something reminded him of a track that was sitting on his shelf. But regardless of the reason, Prince decided to once again work on "Wouldn't U Love 2 Love Me?," which dated back to 1976. "I used to play that song to death in my car," recalled Lisa, who joined Prince's band in 1980. "I have this '64 Mercury Montclair with the greatest stereo system ever in it. And I just remember being 20 years old and cruising around with unreleased Prince songs in my car and that there was just something about the groove on 'Wouldn't You Love 2 Love Me?' that just made me so happy when in my car."[23]

It is unclear what Prince added to the track or if he simply updated the mix. The song was being considered for Sheila E. or Sheena Easton, but it ultimately went to Taja Sevelle.

During this session, he also added a few overdubs (possibly including horns) to "The Cocoa Boys." After reviewing "Crucial," it appears that Prince wanted to spend more time on the track, and he almost completely revamped the lyrics, seemingly trying to make the song even more personal. "It was fun watching those things happen," remembers Rogers. "We could tell that he believed he had something special. Those were kind of magical moments because he would really labor over them."

Status: "Wouldn't You Love 2 Love Me" (6:15) was prepared to offer to Michael Jackson for his *Bad* album. After Jackson declined it, Taja Sevelle and Sheila E. each recorded lead vocals for the song. Taja's version (4:06) was included on her self-titled 1987 Paisley Park album. Sheila's version remains unreleased. Sheena Easton was also supposedly offered the track, but it is unclear if she worked on the song.

A version of the song from 1981 with Prince's vocals (5:56) was issued posthumously on *Originals* in 2019.

TUESDAY, SEPTEMBER 16, 1986

"**Shockadelica**" (tracking, mix)
"**Shockadelica**" [12-inch long version] (mix)
"**Shockadelica**" [instrumental] (mix)
Galpin Blvd. home studio (Chanhassen, Minnesota)
Producer: Prince | Artist: Prince (for Jesse Johnson) | Engineer: Susan Rogers

"Shockadelica" is about a witch.[24]

—Prince

"Shockadelica" was influenced by the title of Jesse Johnson's upcoming album [also called *Shockadelica*], and when Prince was given an early version of the collection, he was floored, according to Alan Leeds. "Prince absolutely adored the title of Jesse's album, and called Jesse and said, 'Man, I gotta tell you, that's the album title of the century. Boy I wish I had thought of that. Why in hell isn't there a song on the album with that title?'"[25]

Jesse explained that he didn't write a title track for the album, which unfortunately for Johnson provided Prince with the proper inspiration. "Prince said, 'You get a title like that and you didn't have enough sense to go back into the studio and make up a song? What are you, nuts? That's a great title,'" remembered Leeds. "Jesse said, 'Oh man, Prince you're crazy.' Prince said, 'I'll show you!'"[26] And with that challenge, Prince went into the studio to record a track to prove his point.

Once again working without any other band members present, he started by laying down a foundation of real and Linn LM-1 drums and covering it with guitar and several synths including the Mirage and Fairlight. Bass and multiple guitars flavor the song with various aggressive electric screams and accents. The lyrics are about a woman, or possibly just the idea of a woman, who has complete control of her lovers and can make them behave as if they are helpless. Being under the magic spell of love is a theme he'd covered on many tracks including "Come Elektra Tuesday" and "Love And Sex."

Once Prince recorded the vocals, he decided to try something different and altered them. But was Prince's vocal effect just another studio trick or was he trying to disguise his voice? Alan Leeds shared his thoughts:

> "Disguise" is a strong word, It was just one of those things, where he wanted to do it under an alter ego as a marketing ploy, without any real intention of fooling people. Camille became known as this persona with the sped-up vocals that Prince used on quite a few songs, but I'm not convinced that was something that he intended. I don't think that was *his* "definition" as much as it was the fans' definition.
>
> I might add, though, that this is Prince's *brother* Camille. That I'm clear on. The introduction that was given to me was that Camille is Prince's brother.[27]

The name "Camille" has been referenced as being named after a 19th-century French intersex person commonly known as Herculine (Alexina) Barbin, who was raised as a girl, but was reclassified as male at the age of 22 and took the name Camille, which in French can be either male or female. In 1997, Prince was asked about this during an internet chat.

> *Question: Does the Camille alter ego, have anything to do with the famous 19th century hermaphrodite Herculine Barbin, who was nicknamed Camille? My younger brother will be very, very happy since he has spent roughly a decade trying to convince me of this?*
> *Prince: **Your brother is very wise.***[28]

Regardless of the reason, "Shockadelica" was the launch of Camille: a character/pseudonym that he'd soon use to create a variety of music, including: "Rebirth Of The Flesh," "Housequake," "Feel U Up," "Good Love," "If I Was Your

Girlfriend," and "Scarlet Pussy" as well as several others. Speculation surrounded the question of Camille's gender, but it was cleared up in 1988, when his *Lovesexy* tour book told the story of "A *boy* named Camille."

After a late night, seemingly nonstop overnight session, the track was completed. The full version was converted into an extended mix, and an instrumental version was mixed, likely for Jesse's vocals. The song was quickly mastered, and Prince had it played locally in Minneapolis on KMOJ. Despite the pressure from Prince for Jesse to release his own version of the track, Johnson held firm because his album was already finished and scheduled for release within weeks. "Prince tried to convince me to record his track for the next pressing. I didn't think that was fair to people who had already bought the album, so I didn't put it out. Prince told me, 'Well, I'll put it out, and when people think of 'Shockadelica' they'll think of me.'"[29]

Status: "Shockadelica" (6:42) would be edited multiple times (6:12, 3:29) for release as the B-side for Prince's "If I Was Your Girlfriend" 12-inch and single. Jesse Johnson's *Shockadelica* album peaked at number 70 and remained on the charts for 20 weeks without Prince's direct help.

WEDNESDAY, SEPTEMBER 17, 1986

"Crucial" (probable edit and mix)
"Shockadelica" (probable edit and mix)
Galpin Blvd. home studio (Chanhassen, Minnesota)
Producer: Prince | Artist: Prince | Engineer: Susan Rogers

> I was a fan of all of it, but in particular there was a period that was before Sign O' The Times and after the Parade album, and there were some things that he was writing right around that time that showed some wonderful promise and direction, and I was intrigued and interested in what he was doing there. There were songs like 'Witness 4 The Prosecution,' and 'Crucial,' that I think if he had stayed in that mindset, could've developed into a nice direction for him.[30]
>
> —Susan Rogers

During this session, Prince spent time on "Shockadelica" and "Crucial," likely working on overdubs and edits as he updated the mix.

THURSDAY, SEPTEMBER 18, 1986

A tape of Prince's "Wouldn't U Love 2 Love Me?" was delivered to Michael Jackson's compound in Encino, California.

> *Prince was fueled by competition. He liked it and he needed it, like a lot of great artists. He delighted in knowing that the competition was right on his heels, or that he was on the heels of his chief rival. So that's probably why he thought that he could use that tactic with his employees and that it would work, because it worked for him. He likes having Michael Jackson there, because he liked the rivalry. And certainly, with the hip hop rivalries and all that kind of stuff, that's part of what leads you to become better. How are you going to stand out, otherwise, unless you beat your rival?*
>
> —Susan Rogers

During this period, many of those around the studio had stories about Prince's interactions with Michael Jackson. Jackson and Prince were considered rivals, but there was also a mutual respect between them. Prince had grown up as a fan of the Jackson 5 and had seen the Jackson's *Victory* tour twice in 1984. In Prince's later years, he'd perform the Jackson 5's "I Want You Back," and Jackson's solo songs, "Don't Stop 'Til You Get Enough," and "Shake Your Body" in concert. Michael had gone to see Prince perform in Los Angeles, and for a few moments, they shared the stage with James Brown in 1983. Although they knew each other, they were never truly close, according to Susan. "Prince told me this himself when I asked really naïvely, 'How come you and Michael Jackson aren't better friends?' And I remember he turned around in his chair and he looked at me and he said, 'Don't be naïve. That guy is a racehorse. He is really competitive.' I was actually pushing Prince because Michael had asked him to duet with him on the song 'Bad.' And Prince said, 'No.' And I'm like, 'Come on Prince, you guys should be friends.' How naïve was I? And Prince says, 'What are you kidding?'"[31]

Susan remembers how Prince and Michael would interact, often behaving like slightly jealous siblings, around each other.

> Prince received a visit from Michael Jackson, whom he promptly challenged to a game of table tennis, using a table that had been set up in the middle of the sound stage room. Michael said, "I don't know how to play ping-pong!" But Prince took

one paddle and gave Michael the other, and they started very politely volleying the ball back and forth. Suddenly, Prince said, "C'mon, Michael, get into it," and he slammed the ball into Michael's crotch. I was rolling my eyes! "Oh God, he's embarrassing himself." But Michael knows how to handle himself and he didn't seem to care. Then Michael started flirting with Sherilyn Fenn who was visiting Prince in the studio. Prince was pacing, but he wasn't going to get into the game of flirting back, and they said their hasty goodbyes.[32]

At the core of this rivalry was the music. Even though Prince would claim that they weren't competitors in public, in private, he was much more aggressive about his feelings about Jackson, remembers Prince's guitar tech, Michael Soltys. "We were in the studio and I happened to be in the control room with him, and he was listening back to some song. I can't remember what song it was, but it was a high energy R&B type song, just pounding horns and hot, and he was playing it back really loud, right in the room and he's just jumping up and down on the chair, he's so into the groove and he picks up the phone, he calls Michael Jackson and he says, 'Hey Michael, check this out' and he holds up the phone for about two minutes to the speaker and then he just hangs up on him and starts laughing."

"I always thought that was an interesting comparison," observed Morris Day. "I think that they were on the same level as artists, but I think Michael was a straight entertainer, where Prince did it all. Prince was the *entertainer*, the *writer*, the *producer*, everything. Not to try and take anything from Michael, don't get me wrong, he was one of the greatest that ever walked the planet, but I just thought that Prince was the whole package."[33]

"Prince and Michael had been talking about working together during the editing of *Under The Cherry Moon*," reminisces Rebecca Ross, who recalls discussing this with Prince. "Prince was standing in the kitchen drinking tea, dressed in this elaborate outfit with ruffles, wearing make-up and high heels. I remember asking him what he thought about Michael Jackson and he rolled his eyes and said, 'He's weird.'"

Michael had reached out to Prince with the offer to duet on "Bad," with Prince playing the role that was eventually filled by Wesley Snipes in the "Bad" music video. Prince declined stating, **"The first line of that song is 'Your butt is mine.' Then I said, 'Who's going to sing that to who? Because you sure aren't singing that to me, and I sure ain't singing it to you, so right there we got a problem.'"**[34]

It seems that although Prince preferred not to record a duet with Jackson, he wanted him to record one of his songs, so "Wouldn't U Love 2 Love Me?" was offered to Jackson.

"[Prince] was a thoughtful person. Things were changing around the camp then. Wendy, Lisa, and Bobby Z were the heart of the Revolution," reflected Susan Rogers. "I think Prince was thinking that now would be a good time to make a change."[35]

"Prince loves change. He likes to change bands. He likes to change musicians. He likes to change clothes," explained Craig Rice, Prince's Road Manager for the *Purple Rain* tour, in 1989. "He finds energy in change."[36]

Being on the road is taxing, and a world tour can be incredibly draining, but this period after the tour felt different to almost everyone. In addition to the need for recovery after the strain of a tour, there was a distance between Prince and his band. "He'd been working more on his own than usual," explained Lisa. "We weren't with him in the studio as much."[37]

"I fucking knew [we were going to be fired]," adds Wendy. "And Lisa said, 'Why do you have to be so negative? That's not what's going on.' I went, 'We've been fired,' but she didn't believe it. She found it hard to believe and so when we were home I was like, 'You don't understand it. We've been fired. I know this in my bones. I know it.'"

But it would be another few weeks before Prince reached out to discuss this issue.

WEDNESDAY, SEPTEMBER 24, 1986 (ESTIMATE)

"**Koo Koo**" (tracking, overdubs, mix)
"**One Day (I'm Gonna Make You Mine)**" (tracking, overdubs, mix)
Galpin Blvd. home studio (Chanhassen, Minnesota)
Producer: Prince | Artist: Prince (for Sheila E.) | Engineer: Susan Rogers (assumed)

> *You are hearing from a man who has meticulously split his public face into several faces. The Time is Prince, Vanity 6 is Prince. To some extent, Sheila E. is Prince and Prince is Prince. He already has set a precedent for not revealing everything there is to reveal about himself.*
>
> —Susan Rogers

Prince was always in charge and always in control, but over the last few years, he occasionally morphed into a team player and seemed to enjoy bouncing ideas off of people he trusted. Wendy and Lisa were his constant companions and musical enablers and although he generally worked on his own, there was an energy and joy when he worked with them. He'd done that in the past with Morris Day as well as Dez Dickerson and it was always about vibing with someone who could bring something unexpected to his music. As he began pulling himself away from Wendy, Lisa, and others in the Revolution, he started drawing others closer, including Eric Leeds, as a collaborator, looking to explore new sounds.

"He was a little bit lost in there," recognizes Susan. "He was still clinging, basically, to Wendy and Lisa, Bobby, and Susannah. They are so heavily woven into the tapestry of the songs on the *Parade* album, but by *Sign O' The Times*, that was gone. For *Sign O' The Times*, Susannah was there, but things came apart, and you can see why, you can read the writing on the wall. He'd be bringing in Sheila more and more near the end of this period. As musicians, it wasn't the same as with Wendy and Lisa. And he was changing. I guess he had to be aware that he's approaching 30 now, and he's growing up."

The first track he and Sheila worked on after the *Parade* tour was "One Day (I'm Gonna Make You Mine)," an upbeat song about a woman who has her eyes set on a man. Building the song from live drums and a variety of percussion elements including bongos, shakers, and claps, he rounded out the sound with multiple keyboard tracks (likely Oberheim OB-8, Fairlight, and Mirage), guitar and layers of background vocals. Levi Seacer Jr. and his future keyboard player, Boni Boyer would add their voices to the track, but it is likely that they were recorded on a later date.

After midnight, he wrapped up on "One Day (I'm Gonna Make You Mine)," so Prince and Sheila started working on "Koo Koo," which name-checks Jill Jones's dog which had been previously introduced in her song, "Mia Bocca," as Jill explains. "He got Koo Koo for me during the *1999* tour. Koo Koo was from Detroit. They had nicknames for Koo Koo on the road, like 'Detroit Dog,' 'Soundcheck,' all sorts of stuff."

Using both Linn LM-1 and real snare and kick drums, Prince created a minimal track that included guitar, synths (probably both Mirage and Fairlight), and piano. Sheila once again added bongos and joined him on background vocals. Prince recorded a scratch vocal pass, which Sheila would replace, likely during this session. The lyrics mention a "blue train," a reference to "Love On A Blue Train," which was recorded in December 1985 by Prince and Sheila.

At the end of the night, mixes were created of everything from this session and dubbed to a cassette.

Status: "Koo Koo" (3:24) and "One Day (I'm Gonna Make You Mine)" (4:49) would be included on Sheila's eponymous third album in February 1987. "Koo Koo" was released as the album's third single in May 1987, with "Paradise Gardens" on the B-side. A 12-inch version titled "Koo Koo (Remix)" (5:12) was also released.

THURSDAY, SEPTEMBER 25, 1986

"One Day (I'm Gonna Make You Mine)" (horn overdubs)
Galpin Blvd. home studio (Chanhassen, Minnesota)
Producer: Prince | Artist: Sheila E. | Engineer: Susan Rogers

> *It wasn't unusual for him to get an idea for a song and go downstairs at mid-day and start, and by nine or ten at night, come up with a rough mix of a finished song. And when you consider that he does it all himself and that a finished song represents countless overdubs of various instruments, not to mention the adjustment because the composing is part of the process. He's not the kind of guy who'd say, "Okay I'm going to lay down a drum track and bass track and go live with it for two days." The "live with it" part just wasn't in his vocabulary.*[38]

> —Alan Leeds

Eric was brought in to record horns for "One Day (I'm Gonna Make You Mine)." It is likely that Prince mapped out what he wanted from Eric, and he was brought in to replicate the aggressive synth horn line already on the track.

Prince had major plans for Eric, and over the next week, he'd inspire a new direction for Prince.

SUNDAY, SEPTEMBER 28, 1986

"One" (tracking, horn overdubs)
"Two" (tracking, horn overdubs)
"Baby Doll House" (tracking, flute, and horn overdubs)
Galpin Blvd. home studio (Chanhassen, Minnesota)
Producer: Prince | Artist: Madhouse | Engineer: Susan Rogers | Assistant Engineer: Todd Herreman

> *After touring with Prince in the summer of 1986, he approached me about wanting to do an instrumental project.*[39]
>
> —Eric Leeds

Now that the *Parade* tour was over, and he'd experienced time alone in the studio, Prince was once again at a creative crossroad and wanted to explore his music on a deeper level *without* the Revolution. The Flesh sessions, the Family instrumentals, and his various studio jams had hinted at a new direction and the natural progression was a full jazz album, but once again it would be under his control or at least as much control as he could have, considering he had no skills on the sax. Eric had recorded a few jazz tapes with his friends and acquaintances in Atlanta, and those tapes helped Prince fully realize his vision.

> Prince had come to me, looking to put together a project that would kind of give me an opportunity to feature me a little bit more specifically, and other than that, I don't think there was a specific focus in mind. I turned him on to some of these tapes I had made with some of these guys, and I think he wanted to maybe just hear me in a situation that was completely divorced from anything that he had anything to do with. He was impressed enough by the looseness of this music. He said, "Okay, I know that if I do an album with Eric Leeds, it's going to be able to hold its own." So, the Madhouse album just kind of grew from there.[40]

"Prince played all the instruments except for the saxophone, of course. And then Eric would just pop round and do his parts," remembers Rogers. "We had just come off the road, and he just couldn't wait to get in the studio. So we just bam, bam, bam, bam, just knocked it out. I loved the beautiful melodic themes that he came up with. I can feel the joy of making that record when I listen to it. That was so much fun."

"The Madhouse thing literally started when he called me and said, 'Do you want to come over and play some jazz?'" explains Leeds.

> I knew better than to say no. I think he said something like, "My dad's over here, do you want to come over and play some jazz." It was one of those things where I could have said, "Aw, man, maybe not today," or whatever. Okay. So I got over there and his dad wasn't there, he'd left or whatever.
>
> All of a sudden we're sitting at his piano, which was upstairs in his living room and he's figuring out these melodies and these songs and I'm writing them down. And then he says, "Okay, let's go." And we went downstairs and he already had tracks on it for these two songs.

Prince had a third track waiting as well. "'Baby Doll House' was just a little vamp that he did," detailed Leeds. "It had the reoccurring line, a sample of

Susannah Melvoin saying, 'Baby Doll House.' I remember he sped up the multi-track to make it sound real funny. It sounds like Alvin and the Chipmunks. Not to be confused of course with the Madhouse track 'Eleven' from the second Madhouse album [16] which had the same 'Baby Doll House' sample, but it was a completely different song."[41]

"There were two versions of it, I think. There was a fast version and a slow version, but the song itself was scrapped."

For all of the tracks recorded on this date, Prince created the real drum-based grooves and filled in the sound with Fairlight and Mirage synths and Eric's sax. On "Baby Doll House," Eric played tenor and baritone sax and flute, and on "One," Prince also added the Prophet VS keyboard to the song. At this point, an album was being worked out, but the details, the titles and the theme were all in flux. "Madhouse was Prince's idea," recalled Leeds. "He wanted to do an album of all instrumental music. While not necessarily jazz, it was kind of drawing on the vocabulary, and he wanted to do it in a format that would kind of give me a featured spot, also. Primarily, it was a collaboration."[42]

The session ended as the sun was coming up. The next few days would reveal the album's full concept.

Status: "One" (7:18) and "Two" (5:29) were the first two tracks on Madhouse's debut album, *8*, released in January 1987. The 3-minute "Baby Doll House" remained unreleased during Prince's lifetime.

MONDAY, SEPTEMBER 29, 1986

"**Three**" (tracking, horn overdubs, mix)
"**Four**" (tracking, horn overdubs, mix)
"**Five**" (tracking, horn overdubs, mix)
"**When The Dawn Of The Morning Comes**" (tracking, overdubs, mix)
Galpin Blvd. home studio (Chanhassen, Minnesota)
Producer: Prince | Artist: Madhouse | Engineer: Susan Rogers | Assistant Engineer: Todd Herreman

I think the entire process of the Madhouse album was done in about three days and it was only when we got about halfway through it that he explained what he was going to do.[43]

—Eric Leeds

Prince was sharing the studio with Eric, but his time alone in the studio *before* Eric arrived was also productive. Prince had recently recorded a slow piano demo for "When The Dawn Of The Morning Comes," likely for the production he was planning called *The Dawn*, and on this day he took the idea into the studio and turned it into a full-blown gospel song filled with energy, an aggressive beat, and a classic choir call-and-response sequence that would fit perfectly during a church service. The track contains handclaps, bass, piano, guitar, and a blend of Oberheim OB-8, Fairlight, and Mirage synths. The choir sound was achieved by Prince stacking six layers of background vocals and the final mix is a reminder of what Prince could do when inspired.

Prince continued to record, quickly laying the tracks down for "Three," "Four," and "Five," all with the same live drum bedrock and each track had its own blend of keyboards. Eric was brought in again to add flute and sax to each of the three newest Madhouse songs. "I've often said that if I hadn't been involved with him, there's no reason to believe that he wouldn't have done albums like Madhouse. He could have taken the first Madhouse album, since he played everything on it except the horn, and instead of me being the lead voice on the songs, he could have just played guitar on it. Then instead of just having a horn being the featured lead instrument, his guitar could have been."

Now, obviously, once again, it's going to sound self-serving, but he was interested in doing something with me. And this is the ambivalence that I always have about this because here's a guy who's basically coming to me and, I don't know what point in the process he actually finally decided, "Okay, this is going to be an album that I'm really serious about releasing." I think it was about the second or third day, he said, "I've talked to Warner Brothers and explained to them what this is about and they're into it." At that point I said, "Oh, shit. This is actually going to be real." Then he's telling me, "Yeah, but there's not going to be any credits or any personnel on the album." So I said, "Okay, all right."

That's when the whole mythology of it started to come to light. At that point I'm just saying wow, because what greater compliment could somebody of this caliber give to somebody like me because he'd never done anything like this with any band member before. And the fact that he was coming to me and basically said, "This is going to be *our* thing." But, of course, it wasn't collaboration to that extent. It wasn't like him coming to me and saying, "Hey, Eric, I'd really love to do a project with just you and me. Go in the studio and see what we come up with." He never said, "Do you have any music of your own that you'd like to bring in and see what we could do with as a start?" So really my role in Madhouse was little or no different than my role in his band. The only difference was instead of the music having a vocal, which was him, the lead vocalist was my horn. But he was producing this album and writing it just like he had done on *The Family* album or anything else.

Eric recalled that naming the compositions was fairly simple. "When it came time to think about titles for the stuff, we were just calling them 'Number One,' 'Number Two,' 'Number Three,' 'Number Four,' and we just kind of laughed, and someone, I don't even remember exactly who, just kind of came up with 'Why title them? This is different, this is what we call them.' And we started laughing about it, 'Yeah, Three is a ballad. That's a great name for a ballad. Three just evokes a ballad, doesn't it? Three, that's a love title. Three!' So that's kind of how that came about. And we stuck with it."[44]

Status: "Three" (3:16), "Four" (2:24), and "Five" (1:18) were all included on Madhouse's album, *8*. "When The Dawn Of The Morning Comes" (6:17) remained unreleased during Prince's lifetime but would be debuted on the *Sign O' The Times* Super Deluxe Edition in 2020. The production of this song would inspire many tracks, including his 1989 track "Trust" that was released on the *Batman* soundtrack.

TUESDAY, SEPTEMBER 30, 1986

"Six" [recorded as "Seven"] (tracking, horn overdubs, mix)
"Seven" [recorded as "Six"] (tracking, horn overdubs, mix)
"When The Dawn Of The Morning Comes" (mix)
Galpin Blvd. home studio (Chanhassen, Minnesota)
Producer: Prince | Artists: Madhouse and Prince | Engineer: Susan Rogers
| Assistant Engineer: Todd Herreman

The thing is that when you're called, you're called. I hear things in my sleep; I walk around and go to the bathroom and try to brush my teeth and all of the sudden the toothbrush starts vibrating! That's a groove. You gotta go with that, and that means drop the toothbrush and get down to the studio or get to a bass guitar, quick! My best things have come out like that.[45]

—Prince

Prince had made that statement months earlier, but on this evening his toothbrush really did inspire him, discloses Susan Rogers.

> He went upstairs to go to bed. 10 minutes later, he's coming back downstairs. Might've been in pajamas, I don't remember, but it was early morning. We'd had a long, long night, and he said to me kind of sheepishly, "Would you mind putting up fresh tape? Could we go another round?" And, of course, I said what I always said, "I don't mind at all, let's do it. I'm putting up the fresh tape." And then he's kind of apologetically saying, "I'm sorry, but I was just brushing my teeth and the song came to me," and he was laughing and shaking his head. That was so common with him. When the brain circuits would open and that song would come, what's he going to do? Sit there and write it down? No, he's going to get into the studio immediately. He's going to work it out.

He and Eric had also recorded an upbeat new song that they listed as "Six," which included a rapidly moving bassline, piano, and Fairlight over more live drums. Leeds added sax to the track and remembers Prince enjoying the work but looking for something commercial.

> All through this I remember him saying, "I've got to come up with something that could be the radio song. I've got to find something that'll really be a little bit more overtly funky or something that we can use as a single." The apartment I was living in was maybe 20 minutes from Prince's house. And I think I got out of there about 3:30 in the morning and I got home and I was literally in bed about 5:00 and was ready to turn the light off and the phone rang. I knew better than to answer, but I knew better *not* to answer and I knew it was going to be Susan and it was. She said, "He wants you to come back." And I said, "Get me out of this one. I'm tired, I'm in bed." She said, "Good luck with that." So I hung up and the phone rang again and it was him. And he was upbeat. He was, "Man, got to come back. I just got the other one. I just got the radio song. Got it done, got to come back. Come on." I said, "Prince, can I do it in the afternoon?" "Oh, man, come on back now. We can finish this now, we can put it to bed." So I said, "Okay." I got up out of bed, jumped in the car, ran out there. And it was [what would become] "Six" and he had it done, the whole song, completely. By the time I'd left and come back. Now the thing was, the song didn't really do much for me anyway, but I'm tired and the only thing I was, "What do you need? Is it this cool? Are the melody and the solo good? Fine, see you, I'm going home." All I wanted to do was do whatever was needed to get out of there as soon as I could. All I remember was I had to come back at 5:00 in the morning and the last thing in the world that I wanted to be was in that studio doing that.

Earlier in the shift, Prince and Leeds had recorded another track, which would be given the title "Seven," but during this session, "Six" was "Seven," and "Seven" was "Six," which got confusing when the order was being changed. "The problem with the Madhouse stuff is some of the songs had different numbers assigned to them on whatever day it was," explains Eric. "A song that might originally have been this number is then used for another song because at that point we were just numbering them in the order that they recorded, I think. Finally, when he sequenced the album, that's when he then would have given the final numbers and they would play out in sequence."

Status: "Seven" (4:28) would be renamed "Six," and "Six" (4:10) would be rechristened "Seven" when they were included on Madhouse *8*.

"Six" would be released as a single in February 1987, backed with "Six And ½." The 7-inch featured an edit (3:37), while the 12-inch contained a remix titled "Six (End Of The World Mix)" (6:20). The single reached number 5 on the *Billboard* Hot Black Singles Chart but did not enter the US *Billboard* Hot 100 Chart.

OCTOBER 1986

To the outside world, most breakups seem sudden and often without warning. This is how it is in marriages, friendships, and business relationships. The person who gives the well-thought-out speech is the one who has moved on. The deep damage whispered within the Revolution couldn't be seen by the audience, but it was there waiting for the final push. Prince had been relying on the band for more than he'd ever needed in the past, and for the last few years, people spoke about "Prince *and* the Revolution," and not just about Prince. At the end of the day, it was Prince who'd signed the contract with Warner Bros., so it was Prince who decided who'd make the journey with him. "We had talked about doing so much more as a unit in the future," revealed Lisa. "We were so mutually involved in everything, on such even footing and moving forward, that there was no moving backwards—not for him, not for us. We were equals and were going to move forward in every way, or he could just fire us all and play with musicians he could control completely."[1]

WEDNESDAY, OCTOBER 1, 1986

"**Eight**" (tracking, horn overdubs)
Madhouse 8 album compiled
Galpin Blvd. home studio (Chanhassen, Minnesota)
Producer: Prince | Artist: Madhouse | Engineer: Susan Rogers | Assistant Engineer: Todd Herreman

I had to keep up with him so I didn't even have time to exhale, or even have an ability to really reflect on what the music is about. And only when we're done with it, then I can sit back, and say, "Okay, let me listen to this."

—Eric Leeds

The final song for the Madhouse *8* album is recorded during this session. The race from concept to completion was jaw dropping, even by Prince's standards. In four days, Prince forged a new direction for his music and created his first instrumental collection. The addition of Eric Leeds had been influencing his sound, but the Madhouse project was an itch he had to scratch, even though Leeds reveals that he was indifferent about the results. "My problem with Madhouse was that he could be very spontaneous when it was something that he wasn't really thinking too hard about. And all the Flesh stuff was pretty spontaneous and that's what I liked about it. I'm not saying it was stuff that necessarily was worthy of being released, because they were just jams. But there was something about the character about them that I always preferred to the first Madhouse album."

"The one exception, for me, was the title track 'Eight'," reflected Leeds. "I thought that one was much better developed than anything else on the album. And from my own admittedly limited perspective it was the only piece on the album that I actually liked what I played!"[2]

For "Eight," Prince played the same live drums, Fairlight, and Prophet VS that he'd been using, but there was no guitar in the mix, and the first 4 minutes of the track rested on a unique sample of Prince's voice with an effect on it. Eric once again added flute and sax, but unlike most of the other tracks on the album, this wasn't a driving beat. Instead, it sounds like it was influenced by David Byrne and Brian Eno's 1981 album *My Life in the Bush of Ghosts*, specifically by tracks like "The Carrier" and "Mountain of Needles." The lineage of "Eight" can also be traced back to the 10-minute "Moments In Love" by Art Of Noise.

Once the final track was completed, the album was roughly assembled, almost exactly the way it was recorded, with the exception of swapping the names and positions of "Six" and "Seven." Additional sounds, including sexual noises and talking, were added to the collection to bridge between songs and add to the flow of the music. "The moanings were Vanity [originally from the unreleased Vanity 6 song, 'Vibrator'], we just got that out as a device to kind of tie a couple of songs into each other," detailed Leeds. "The phone conversations on 'Five,' I'm not really sure where they came from."[3]

"Working on the Madhouse album was a marathon," according to Todd Herreman, "and he said, 'fresh tape' seven times and the end of 'Eight' kind of goes off in this ethereal synth wash with reverb and Eric's flute, which was very hypnotic, really ethereal, and mind you, this after sixty hours of no sleep."

At that point, of course, the lights in the control room were really dim, I think Eric was like sitting down on the floor, Susan was probably in the next room labeling tape boxes and on the half inch master deck, the tape was just kind of winding down, end of the tape, dead silence. Part of it was because the music was really hypnotic, and it just faded into this mist, the other part was we were beat tired and just dead silence and finally I had to break the silence and I said to Prince, "How can you sleep at night knowing you can do stuff like that?" And it was one of the most heartfelt responses I ever got from him and he said, "That's the problem, Todd, I can't sleep at night. God hands me a groove and I can't throw it away. That's why I drag your ass out of bed at 4 o'clock in the morning." And I'm not a spiritual, religious guy, but he said this and I'm just like, woah, that's why we were just up for sixty hours and he meant it, it's like this stuff comes *through* him, it doesn't come *from* him. And that blew me away, just absolutely blew me away.

Status: "Eight" (10:06) was included as the final track on Madhouse *8.*

FRIDAY, OCTOBER 3, 1986

Venue: St. Paul Civic Center (Saint Paul, Minnesota)

Sheila E. was on tour as the opening act for Lionel Richie, and when the tour stopped in the Twin Cities, Prince joined her onstage for a song.

The show was followed by a party for Richie and Sheila. The following day, Prince flew to Los Angeles.

SUNDAY, OCTOBER 5, 1986

"Rescue Me" (tracking, overdubs, vocals, mix)
"Rescue Me" [instrumental] (mix)
"Baby Go-Go" (mix with Prince lead vocal)
Sunset Sound, Studio 3 | 1:30 p.m.–9:30 p.m. (booked: lockout)
Producer: Prince | Artist: Prince | Engineers: Coke Johnson and Susan Rogers

Prince would buy the studio out for a month. He'd have an 18-wheeler pull in and have them unload all the gear. We would set it all up. Then, a couple days later, he'd show up and want to record.

—Coke Johnson

Prince had not worked at Sunset Sound since July, so the move back to Los Angeles required a great deal of logistical preparations, because Prince's keyboards, drums, guitars (and his drum and guitar techs, if possible), and any other items he'd need to properly record had to be brought to Sunset Sound.

When today's session started at 1:30 in the afternoon, Prince planned to work on a cover of "Rescue Me," a 1965 song written by Raynard Miner and Carl William Smith and performed by Fontella Bass (who is also occasionally listed as a cowriter). The original track also contained drums from Earth, Wind, & Fire's Maurice White and backing vocals by Minnie Riperton.

Susan Rogers remembered the reverence he had for music that touched his soul. "Occasionally, and not surprisingly, he played other people's music, and he liked to talk about music like most record makers do. He didn't have too much time for listening to music, but what he did listen to no doubt influenced him and I'm certain that he admired many, many, many artists. Some in particular."[4]

"He just liked 'Rescue Me,'" reflects Rogers.

Although there is no way to verify it, his memory of "Rescue Me" may have been stirred from his own use of the phrase "Baby, *you've got to rescue me*, prisoner of love with the opposite gender"[5] in "Crucial." Whatever the reason, Prince wanted to record a cover of the classic track, but it wasn't *why* he wanted it, but *who* he wanted the track for.

"He was doing this for Dolly Parton," remembers Michael Soltys, "so he was in his country mode at the time." Country star Kenny Rogers had recorded Prince's "You're My Love," and Rogers had performed with Parton on their number 1 hit, "Islands In The Stream," so it wasn't far-fetched for Prince to want to work with her.

Someone from Sunset Sound was dispatched to Tower Records to purchase a copy of the original recording, and while they waited, Prince did some additional work, including updating the mix on "Baby Go-Go," a track he'd recorded earlier in the spring.

Once "Rescue Me" arrived and he reviewed the song, Prince began tracking his updated cover version, by laying down live drums, bass, guitar, a variety of percussion including cowbell, claps, and tambourine, and then singing falsetto on the song. For the iconic horns, Prince instead chose to mimic them with Fairlight and other synths, remembers Soltys. "Prince found a banjo sound on the Fairlight, and he started playing flat picking banjo, just goofing off. If you were to close your eyes, you would have sworn he's playing a banjo, finger picking it."

"That was one of my favorite covers he ever did," expresses Susannah. "It was such an amazing song. He wanted Dolly Parton to do it, and when that didn't happen, he just put it away after that."

After mixing the track and creating an instrumental version of the song to offer to Dolly Parton, they dubbed the music to one C-90 and two C-60 cassettes, and the session ended at 9:30 p.m.

Status: The 4-minute "Rescue Me" remained unreleased during Prince's lifetime. It is unlikely that Dolly Parton added her vocals to Prince's updated cover.

MONDAY, OCTOBER 6, 1986

"Witness 4 The Prosecution" [version 2] (tracking, overdubs, vocals)
"Witness 4 The Prosecution" [version 2, instrumental] (probable mix)
"Telepathy" (tracking, overdubs, mix)
"Telepathy" [instrumental] (probable mix)
Sunset Sound, Studio 3 | 4:00 p.m.–12:00 midnight (booked: open)
Producer: Prince | Artists: Prince and Deborah Allen | Engineers: Susan Rogers and Coke Johnson

The way I wound up working with Prince was, I was working at Sunset Sound, and one night I went to the restroom and as I was coming out, I saw this basketball go rolling by and I thought it was a friend of mine. I went over to pick it up and hand it to my friend and I looked up and it was Prince. I went, "Oh, I'm sorry. I thought you were going to be a friend of mine."[6]

—Deborah Allen

Whether by choice or by chance, Prince was about to start working with another country performer. After country music artist Deborah Allen was finished with her album, the record company suggested she add some additional tracks before it was released, as she detailed.

> I went back to Nashville and I was sitting in my kitchen and I wanted my project to do so well. God, what can I do? And all of a sudden this little light bulb went off in my head and I went, "Well, you met Prince. He's amazing." So I wrote him a letter and told him what was going on. I said, "It would just be merely wonderful if we could write something together or you can produce something for me. Here's a cassette of my new project. Take a listen and see what you think." In the next couple of days, they called and said they were overnighting me a song that Prince had written for me. And it was called "Telepathy," and so it was just amazing. He was a true gentleman to me. I asked his engineer, Coke Johnson, "Hey, did he really write this song for me? Or was this a song that was just kind of laying around in his catalog?" And he goes, "Oh no, I saw him write it in the studio" and you know what he did? He sent the lyrics to me, the lyrics are all written out on the back of the tracking sheet to Sunset Sound.[7]

"Telepathy" was recorded on this date, with Prince playing all of the instruments. He'd follow up the request from Allen with another possibility, an updated recording of "Witness 4 The Prosecution," which had been tracked earlier in the year. That original song included Wendy, Lisa, and Susannah, but none of them joined him on the new version. The re-recorded version is almost exclusively Prince (with the exception of Atlanta Bliss and Eric Leeds on trumpet and sax, respectively). Prince used at least five layers of background vocals that blended with five layers of the Fairlight, and at least one of the Ensoniq Mirage keyboard, to create a new version of the track to offer to Allen, but once they were both complete, he decided to only offer "Telepathy."

The songs were mixed, and it is likely that Prince created instrumentals of both as well, since they were being considered for another artist. Six cassettes (three C-60s and three C-90s) were created and the session ended at midnight.

Status: "Witness 4 The Prosecution" (5:02) was unreleased during his lifetime, but in 2020, it was included on the *Sign O' The Times* Super Deluxe Edition.

"Telepathy" was released on March 19, 1987, as the title-track for Deborah Allen's fourth album. The album did not chart. The song was also released as a single in April 1987 without any impact on the charts. The 12-inch contains a "Club Mix" (7:55) and "Telepathy" [instrumental] (5:07), as well as the album version. Prince submitted the track under the pseudonym Joey Coco.

TUESDAY, OCTOBER 7, 1986

"**Telepathy**" (horn overdubs, overdubs, mix)
"**Telepathy**" [instrumental] (probable mix)
"**Witness 4 The Prosecution**" [version 2] (horn overdubs, mix)
"**Witness 4 The Prosecution**" [version 2, instrumental] (probable mix)
Sunset Sound, Studio 3 | 10:00 a.m.–2:00 a.m. (booked: lockout)
Producer: Prince | Artist: Prince | Engineer: Coke Johnson

We finished Madhouse *on October 1st, and a few days later,
he and I and Matt Blistan were out at Sunset Sound, on and
off for almost a month.*[8]

—Eric Leeds

After a 10-hour break, the previous day's work continued on "Telepathy" and
"Witness 4 The Prosecution." For 6 hours, Prince added a variety of overdubs
to the tracks, and then stopped for a short break as Eric and Matt were brought
in to contribute horns to both songs for the rest of the session. "'Telepathy'
was a cool song. I kind of liked it. Nice little vibe to it," remembers Leeds. "We
must have been doing a lot of different shit, because it was a fucking seven hour
session."

At the end of the session, the songs were mixed, likely including updated
instrumentals of "Telepathy" and "Witness 4 The Prosecution," and four C-60
cassettes were dubbed of the tracks.

WEDNESDAY, OCTOBER 8, 1986

"**Nine**" [version 1, early title for "**Six And 1/2**"] (tracking, horn overdubs,
  mix)
"**Nine**" [version 2, early title for "**Six And 1/2**"] (tracking, horn overdubs,
  mix)
"**Baby Go-Go**" (mix)
Sunset Sound, Studio 3 | 1:00 p.m.–5:00 a.m. (booked: lockout)
Producer: Prince | Artists: Prince and Madhouse | Engineers: Susan Rogers
  and Coke Johnson

Lisa and I knew psychically there was something wrong. He was treating us differently, he was doing a lot of avoiding. So it wasn't a real big surprise when he invited us over to dinner and gave each of us pink slips.[9]

—Wendy Melvoin

Eric Leeds witnessed how Prince was handling everything with Lisa and Wendy and how things had changed for them since the summer. "We were at Sunset Sound, and he asked Wendy to come by the studio and she did, and he told her, 'Why don't you and Lisa come over to my house and have dinner with me tonight.' By then Prince had told me, 'I want to give you a heads up that I'm letting Wendy and Lisa and Bobby go.' I don't recall that he was asking me an opinion. I said, 'Well, I'm going to miss them. I'm sorry to see that happen, but I understand how things work.'"

Earlier in the session, Prince spent some time updating a mix for "Baby Go-Go." He'd also written and recorded the basics for a new Madhouse track, "Nine," once again using live drums, bass, and the Ensoniq Mirage keyboard. Prince left to go to dinner, leaving Eric and Blistan to work on the track without his watchful eye.

Eric was listed as a composer on "Nine" because he wrote the horn sections, blending his sax arrangement with Blistan's trumpet, the only additional player on the Madhouse *8* project. "Unfortunately, that was all that I did with Madhouse," reflected Blistan. "I would have liked to have done more, but I think Prince wanted to keep the same format and the same sound."[10]

"The previous day's session went from 7 p.m. until 2 in the morning," explains Leeds, according to his detailed notes, "and then on October 8th a session from 7:00 p.m. until 2:00 as well. We did 'Six And 1/2' and 'Nine.' But for 'Nine,' I have that in parentheses first. That would indicate there were two versions of that."

It is unclear if there were two unique tracks using the names "Six and 1/2" and "Nine" recorded on this date, or if it was a variation on the same song. Some of the recording for the Madhouse tracks may have been done on the previous day as well.

Four C-60 and two C-90 cassettes were created from this session.

Status: "Nine" (2:34) would be released as "Six And 1/2" on the B-side of "Six." It is unclear if the other version of the track was finished, as it remained unreleased during Prince's lifetime.

*I think that he was so vulnerable at the end of the tour when he
had heard Wendy and Lisa were unhappy. We are all struggling and it shouldn't have been that way and at that particular time, we were just giving so much. He heard something was
going to happen and he couldn't experience that. He couldn't
let himself be the one being left, so before they could say, "We
want out," he fired them.*

—Susannah Melvoin

Prince had been contemplating how to handle the Revolution. BrownMark had
already left the band and was a contracted member of the Revolution, so he could
be released without incident. "I'd quit Prince and the Revolution after *Purple
Rain*," detailed BrownMark. "And he put me under contract and a gag order not
to tell anybody. So for *Around The World In A Day* and the *Parade* record, I was
contracted in silence. So he knew after the *Parade* tour, I was done."[11]

On the other hand, Bobby Z and Dr. Fink were the only two remaining members of his earliest band as a solo artist, and their personal bond had the strength
that only longtime friends can claim. They'd grown with him and shared the
spotlight with him as he morphed from a shy and awkward presence on stage to
one of the most dynamic performers of his generation. "You have to remember
that he was fiercely a solo artist and he let us into this world for a long period
of time, and I can tell you personally to let people into his inner circle was very
difficult," explained Bobby Z.[12]

Prince asked Wendy and Lisa to dinner at the home he was renting at 722
North Elm Drive in Beverly Hills—coincidentally the home of the infamous
Menendez murders that would occur three years later—to talk to them about
his plans. As the evening progressed, he broke the news to them that he was
disbanding the Revolution. "He was out here in LA working in the studio by
himself again, which he hadn't done in years," remembered Lisa. "He said he
was working a lot alone and he wanted to try that again."[13]

According to Wendy, Prince added, "'I'm going in a different direction and
I can't ask you guys to wear nipple-less bras and crotch-less panties.' And both
Lisa and I went, 'Yeah, that's right. No you can't.'"

"He loved the showbiz aspect of it all, and we weren't trying to be outrageous
anymore," added Lisa. "We were maturing, and my level of outrageousness was
focused more on the music, on *that* level of theatricality. What Prince wanted
to do was get theatrical, but not so much musically, and certainly without us."[14]

Although Wendy could sense it was coming, when the news arrived it was still a shock. "From the moment I was hired, until the moment it all ended, it was nonstop. So I never felt that it would end . . . until it ended. It almost felt like someone kicked the bed while you're sound asleep, and you're like, 'What, what?'"[15]

"The night that we got fired, I can't say that Prince thanked us," revealed Lisa. "I could sense his feelings just contradicting themselves within him. I think he was at a crossroads. I think it was hard for him to say, 'Thank you' at that time."[16]

"That's what it is when you're a side person," realized Wendy. "Everybody's expendable."[17]

Previous to his conversation with Wendy and Lisa, Prince reached out to Bobby Z.

I was told on the phone by Prince at 2:30 in the morning Minneapolis time. He said, "We've been together for a long time. You're the man and you've done a great job. We're going to be friends forever. Sheila wants to play drums with me. I think it's a good idea." I said, "I think it's a good idea, too. I'll see you next week." And we've been like that ever since. I don't know about anybody else, but the way he disbanded the Revolution or fired me, however you want to look at it, was totally admirable, totally kosher, totally man-to-man. He took care of me for twelve years, and he ended it like a man. There's not one thing bad about that.[18]

"He told me he was going to let Wendy and Lisa go," continued Bobby. "They got really close, and probably made music too much together or something. He wanted to take it back, so he let them go."[19]

"I remember getting a call from Bobby, really late at night, telling me that he had been fired," adds Fink. "And he said, 'As far as I know, Prince isn't going to fire you. Prince told me that. And he's going to call you.' I said, 'I can understand why he fired Lisa and Wendy, but why are they letting you go too?' And he said that Prince wanted Sheila."

"I was freaked out, and then Prince called me, and told me what he did and said that I could stay if I wanted, but if I wanted to leave, he'd understand. That is how he put it. And I made the decision to stay."

"Look, the Revolution maintained purity and naïveté because Prince was all we knew," reflected Lisa. "We started with Prince at a young age, and developed our egos and thick skins with him. We earned it. Any other band that came after us, well, it was [a piece of] cake for them. Prince knew that in the Revolution, he had a mirror that reflected him in every way. Maybe he just got tired of what he saw."[20]

No immediate announcement was made, possibly because Prince needed to figure out how to deal with this publicly. As far as the world knew, Prince and his band were always going to be together.

THURSDAY, OCTOBER 9, 1986

Madhouse *8* album (comp)
Sunset Sound, Studio 3 | 11:00 a.m.–12:30 a.m. (booked: lockout)
Producer: Prince | Artist: Prince (as Madhouse) | Engineer: Susan Rogers

The next day we were in the studio with him, and he told me and Blistan, "I fired them over dessert." He was really smarmy about it. And I looked at him and I just said, "Well now I know better than to accept a dinner invitation." And he thought that was the funniest thing. And of course as soon as I said that, I thought, "Oh, why did I say that?" So for the next few days, whenever anybody would do anything that he could find fault with, he'd say, "You better get it together or I'll invite you to dinner." So he was just making jokes about it by then.

—Eric Leeds

Prince had always been in charge, but he had done something he'd never done before. He decided *when* his band was breaking up. In fact, by this point, practically every one of Prince's protégé projects seemed to self-destruct. The Time, the Family, and Vanity 6 all had very outspoken personalities and the breakups were outside of his control, he changed that with the Revolution. When it came time for this newest project, he had a way to control that. Madhouse would remain anonymous, with the exception of Eric Leeds.

This may not have been the main reason for his decision, but it was a by-product of the direction he wanted to take the new group. Leeds explained:

There was no one credited on the album at all, I wasn't even credited. For the press marketing campaign that we did, we sat and came up with fictitious names [drummer] John Louis (Lewis), his brother, bassist Bill Louis (Lewis) and keyboardist Austra Chanel for all the musicians on the album other than myself. All of the musicians were fellows that I had known, supposedly, when I was living in Atlanta, Georgia which worked until I was interviewed by a reporter from

Atlanta, Georgia who said, "I've lived in Atlanta all my life and I know this music scene and I don't know any of these guys" and I said, "Well, you just haven't been in the right places."[21]

"As I remember it, he wanted the music to be related to on its own merits, and perhaps was concerned that if it was released as a 'Prince jazz album,' it would draw more attention to the idea that Prince would play jazz than to the value of the music itself,"[22] according to Eric.

"The whole idea of Madhouse was being a fictitious band, and creating names and bios for the three musicians who were supposed to be on it with Eric and all of that silliness," disclosed Eric's brother Alan. "Eventually, Eric got frustrated with it and said, 'This is dumb. This is me and Prince making a record and my bio looks better if we say it's me and Prince.'"[23]

"It was entirely *his* project," observes Eric. "It was a wonderful opportunity, but the way it was marketed, [meant] a lot of people are under the impression that it was my music and it was much more of a representation of what I am as a musician and it's just not so—it was one hundred percent a Prince project and I was just playing the role of a saxophone player."[24]

"When I listen to that music, I hear the joy under his fingertips. He was doing the thing he loved to do," reflects Susan Rogers. "This is an alter ego. He's hiding behind this veil of this false identity. And, man, how fun is that?"

With no accurate indication of every member of the band, he allowed them to perform without being stuck with a specific line up. No Madhouse. No Revolution. No accountability to anyone other than himself. "As far as I know, Prince was happy with [the Madhouse *8* project]," reveals Rogers. "He didn't talk too much about his own work."

The session ended at 12:30 a.m. after the album was compiled and edited for Prince to review.

Status: Madhouse *8* would be released in January 1987. Although it didn't crack the top 100 on the *Billboard* Top Pop Albums Chart, it hit number 25 on the *Billboard* Top Black Albums Chart.

FRIDAY, OCTOBER 10, 1986

"Witness 4 The Prosecution" [version 2] (mix)
Sunset Sound, Studio 3 | 10:00 a.m.–6:30 p.m. (booked: lockout)
Producer: Prince | Artist: Prince | Engineers: Susan Rogers and Coke Johnson

> *I didn't fight fair. Where I lived [growing up], there was*
> *no such thing as fair. You just go and do what had to be*
> *done. You couldn't hesitate, and I swear, I never got my ass*
> *kicked, let alone lost.*[25]

—Prince

Three and a half hours were spent updating the mix for "Witness 4 The Prosecution." Two C-60 cassettes were made for Prince, who hadn't attended the short session, but on sessions like this, he'd often pick up the tapes so he could listen to them in his car.

After 5 hours of waiting for Prince to show up, the session ended at 6:30 p.m.

SATURDAY, OCTOBER 11, 1986

"Violet Blue" [listed as **"11 Minutes"**] (tracking, vocals, mix)
"Violet Blue" [instrumental, listed as **"11 Minutes"**] (mix)
"Six" (sax overdubs, mix)
"It Be's Like That Sometimes" (tracking, vocals, overdubs, mix)
Sunset Sound, Studio 3 | 12:00 noon–2:30 a.m. (booked: lockout)
Producer: Prince | Artists: Prince, Madhouse, and Jill Jones | Engineers:
  Susan Rogers and Coke Johnson

> *Around the time, Prince and his dad went to meet Elizabeth*
> *Taylor. I remember they kept talking about her eyes, which*
> *were violet blue. It's a song about choices and decisions.*[26]

—Jill Jones

At noon, Prince began working on two new songs, the first was "Violet Blue," a song for Jill Jones that was listed as "11 Minutes" (from the lyric, "Eleven minutes to love, is too little, too much . . . "[27]). Starting with a Linn LM-1 beat embellished with real snare and kick drums, Prince spent 7 hours adding guitar, bass, Fairlight, and multiple layers of vocals.

Prince then started tracking "It Be's Like That Sometimes," which was a simple track that borrowed the basic drum pattern from "Violet Blue" and covered it with all new bass, keyboards, guitar, and his own lead vocals. The song title has long historical roots, notably in Maya Angelou's 1969 book *I Know Why The Caged Bird Sings*, and even earlier in Nina Simone's performance of

Samuel Waymon's "It Be's That Way Sometimes" from 1967. Simone's song has few similarities other than the slight variation of the title, and the concept of moving on once a problem occurs. Prince's composition has more in common with "The Ball," which he wrote and recorded earlier in the summer.

The lyrics to his track may also reveal where Prince's mind was at that moment. The first verse is addressed to "those of you on the way out,"[28] and he reveals how someone close to you and loves you could disown you. The rest of the song appears to be about breaking up, and the importance that the person in charge "did it your way,"[29] perhaps justifying the recent breakup of the Revolution.

When the basic tracks for the songs were finished, he had Eric Leeds record some additional horn parts for "Six." Further work would eventually take place on the album, but Eric's work on "Six" would lock down the musical elements for the Madhouse 8 collection. It is possible that he also added sax for "Violet Blue," but more likely that all horns for the track were recorded the following day.

Once the song was completed, Prince worked on editing some of the tracks from the day, and a final mix on each of them which were then placed on a single C-60 cassette.

Status: "It Be's Like That Sometimes" (3:34) contains elements similar to "The Ball," which would eventually be re-recorded as "Eye No" on Prince's next album, *Lovesexy*. This song remained unreleased during Prince's lifetime, but was included on the *Sign O' The Times* Super Deluxe Edition in 2020.

"11 Minutes," which would be renamed "Violet Blue" (4:24), was released on Jill Jones's album. Eric Leeds and Atlanta Bliss would add horns, and Clare Fischer would write and oversee the orchestral sections for the song later in the month.

An 8-minute instrumental of "Violet Blue" was also created, likely for Jill to practice the song, although it was being considered for Sheila E.'s album as well. It is unclear if Sheila tracked her vocals for the song, but if it was completed by her, it remains unreleased.

SUNDAY, OCTOBER 12, 1986

"**Violet Blue**" [listed as "**11 Minutes**"] (Jill Jones vocals, mix)
Sunset Sound, Studio 3 | 10:30 a.m.–5:30 p.m. (booked: lockout)
Producer: Prince | Artist: Jill Jones | Engineer: Coke Johnson

He would definitely call me in or have me flown in. It was like being a doctor. "Jill, can you get on the next plane?" "Yeah, okay."

—Jill Jones

Susan Rogers recalls Prince's pattern of working with Jill Jones. "This is just broad conjecture, but he was extraordinarily busy during that time. It wasn't a priority for him and she was in and out of his life to varying degrees, because at the time he was working on *his* album."

"I had not been around for a while, and when I was, I would always be really distant," remembers Jones. "A lot of times I'd just stay away. I knew that his need to crucify me would pass if I put at least a good 5,000 miles between us. But you see the pattern, 'Oh, and now *your* record.' He'd complain, 'Oh, Jill doesn't come and visit me anymore. So I'll create a job for her to have to come and suffer through this.' And I did it, but I was like, hmm."

"I think that when she was in his good graces, maybe he worked on it," agrees Rogers, "and then at other times she just was a low priority for him. That would be my best guess."

As with many of his lyrics, the inspiration for "Violet Blue" may come from several sources. Jill recognized that her unique relationship with him and her own writing were likely reflected in the song's female point of view. "He read my journal easily any time he wanted. I had written a movie idea about a guy who controls a woman with the sound of his music on a piano and I wanted to do it, so 'Violet Blue' kind of came from that."[30]

Jones also saw that she wasn't the only woman in his life. "He was engaged, so there was a lot going on. And so I think by looking at the words and putting it all together, it's almost hard to tell who's feeling what, because the feelings overlap from my thoughts and his, but it is about *three*. Like where I always have been in a triangle and the song has this poignancy that speaks to an unrequited ill-timed affair. I think everyone who hears it thinks of somebody or of an emotion with someone and they know what this pain is."[31]

Historically, "David Z" Rivkin produced a vast number of Jill's vocals, but Prince decided to oversee her performance for this track, which brought their personal issues to the fore. "David didn't record 'Violet Blue,' and 'Violet Blue' was towards the end of everything. And our relationship had reached a point where it wasn't as easy to hang out anymore. My bitchy shade was, 'You're a married man.'"

Jones's stunning performance on the track is an example of why he continued to work with her despite their personal issues. The session wrapped at 5:30 in the evening with two C-60 cassettes dubbed of the day's work.

MONDAY, OCTOBER 13, 1986

"One Day (I'm Gonna Make You Mine)" (overdubs, mix)
"Love On A Blue Train" [instrumental] (overdubs including claps, guitar, and various background elements)
"Love On A Blue Train" [full version] (mix, overdubs)
"Violet Blue" [listed as "11 Minutes"] (overdubs, horn overdubs, mix)
Sunset Sound, Studio 3 | 9:30 a.m.–5:00 a.m. (booked: lockout)
Producer: Prince | Artists: Sheila E., possibly Jill Jones | Engineers: Susan Rogers and Coke Johnson

> *He had so much music in him—these songs were his children, and he found caring "foster homes" for them. It almost makes me cry because they were all parts of him, and he handed them off to others. These songs were a snapshot of what he was thinking and feeling on that day in the studio. You can hear if he was in love, if he was hurt, or if he was lonely in every phrase because it was just him. Hearing them the way he recorded them that day takes me back to a darkened studio with a [young] genius finding his voice, proud of what he was doing, but understanding that these weren't "Prince" songs. They would find homes elsewhere.*[32]

> —"Peggy Mac" Leonard

Like many sessions for Sheila E., this one began earlier than his usual start time, with a variety of overdubs being recorded for songs that were slated for her next album. Four hours were spent overdubbing "One Day (I'm Gonna Make You Mine)" and "Love On A Blue Train." It is possible that these were done by Sheila without Prince in the studio.

After a midday break from 1:30 to 6, Prince spent the evening overdubbing additional elements, including an updated guitar part, for "Love On A Blue Train." An instrumental version was created, and sections were incorporated into an extended version of the song, which had been created back in May.

At midnight, Eric Leeds and Matt Blistan arrived to add horns to "Violet Blue" (the new title for "11 Minutes"), which would eventually be given to Jill, but at this point it is possible that Prince was unsure of where it would land and it might have still been considered for Sheila.

Prince may not have known who would end up with the song, but he knew what he wanted from the horns, as Leeds recalls. "I remember Prince had scatted through the whole song, and said, 'This is what I want you to do.' And he played it. And of course, he's doing all these melismas and stuff and nothing repeated! It was just a stream of consciousness for like three and a half, four minutes and I said, 'Okay. You've got Susan here. This is going to take a while, and you don't need to be here for this one.' And he left."

Once Prince was gone, they got to work.

I said, "Okay, we can do this. We can really, really simplify this, and just give them the basics of what it is that he wants." But we were in a mood that day, so I said, "Nah. Let's fricking nail this one." And we sat there for about three, three and a half hours, and made a rough mix of it, with the horns really loud. Because on the final mix, the horns are pretty much buried in the mix. It contained a lot of nuances, and there are some lines there that I listen to, and I don't know how the hell we pulled them off!

One C-90 and twelve C-60 cassettes were made of the rough mixes, and the session was over at 5 in the morning.

TUESDAY, OCTOBER 14, 1986

"Violet Blue" (mix)
"Major Jam Session" (tracking)
Sunset Sound, Studio 3 | 2:30 p.m.–5:00 a.m. (booked: lockout)
Producer: Prince | Artist: Sheila E. | Engineers: Susan Rogers and Coke Johnson

With more than a few people in a room he gets very shy and quiet, but he was far from what everyone sees. Everyone always asks me "Who is that man you knew that we didn't?" There's a lot about him that you guys didn't get to see that's pretty fun. He just didn't show that side of himself to the public.[33]

—Sheila E.

Prince gathered several other musicians in the studio to just play. Over the last year, he'd spent time in the studio with those who excited his creativity but also musicians who he obviously felt contributed to his musical growth, as well as those he was looking to fill the gap left by the dissolution of the Revolution. Eric Leeds participated, as well as Sheila E. "I'd been jamming with Sheila a bunch of times by then," explains Leeds. "I mean obviously by then we knew she was the new drummer."

In addition to Eric on sax and Sheila on percussion and drums, the list of those involved with this session included Prince on guitar, keyboards, and whatever else was needed; Jill Jones and others singing; Atlanta Bliss on trumpet; and André Cymone on bass. It is possible that H.B. Bennett may have sat behind the drums as well. Cymone was reportedly working with David Z in another studio at Sunset Sound, so there was some interaction between them and Prince, which likely led to an invitation. Cymone and Prince had a long history of working together and had a deep musical partnership, so they quickly fell back into their own groove, as André remembers. "I think you can't play that amount of years, and play as much as we did, I mean people just have no idea how much we actually played and how much we jammed, so jamming for us was a way of life. Literally almost every day."

The music consisted of elements of various unreleased songs that Prince had written and recorded, including: "The Cocoa Boys," "4 Love," "G-Spot," "The Cross," and Andre's "The Dance Electric." The jam focused on the freeform style of music, like the Flesh, that Prince was apparently comfortable exploring. Jams like this had many purposes; the social purpose of connecting with other musicians, the business side of finding new grooves to record, and the additional purpose of keeping his band tight and prepared for being on stage and responding to any cue he'd make in front of an audience. "He wouldn't like people fumbling on stage trying to figure out what to play and I think that's why we rehearsed so much. We played so much with him that even if we played something once or twice with him we knew it well enough that if he did call it up six months later we still could play it," remembers Bliss.

This jam lasted from 11 p.m. until 5 in the morning.

Beforehand, Prince worked on updating and mixing "Violet Blue." It is possible that he recorded Sheila singing the lead vocal for the track on this date.

By the end of the session, Prince had used four C-60 and five C-90 cassettes, the latter likely filled with the recordings of the jam.

Status: If Sheila E. recorded vocals for "Violet Blue," that incarnation of the track remained unreleased during Prince's lifetime. Clare Fischer would add orchestral embellishments to the track on October 24, 1986.

WEDNESDAY, OCTOBER 15, 1986

"**Boy's Club**" (edits)
"**Too Rough**" (edits)
Sunset Sound, Studio 3 | 2:30 p.m.–11:00 p.m. (booked: lockout)
Producer: Prince | Artist: Prince | Engineers: Susan Rogers and Coke Johnson

> *I feel that music is a blessing. I don't feel like I'm working. So when I'm not "working," I'm thinking about it, so music takes up a good portion of the time.*[34]
>
> —Prince

It was the middle of October, and Prince had been in the studio almost every day this month, and when he worked, everyone worked. "Prince was incredibly prolific so we all had pagers back then," explained Todd Herreman. "My joke is that my gray hair actually started when I was working for Prince. He did not sleep."

The rest of October through December would be the same. Prince seemed to be working hard to get his next wave of music finished and released and that meant his protege bands as well.

Additional mixes of "Boy's Club" and "Too Rough" took place during this session, and both songs were dubbed to two C-60 and two C-90 cassettes at the end of the shift.

THURSDAY, OCTOBER 16, 1986

"**Emotional Pump**" (tracking, overdubs, various mixes with guitar)
"**Baby Go-Go**" (likely mix)
Untitled Track (tracking, mix)
Sunset Sound, Studio 3 | 10:00 a.m.–12:00 midnight (booked: lockout)
Producer: Prince | Artist: Prince | Engineers: Susan Rogers and Coke Johnson

I know him, and we've had abortive attempts to work together. He sent me a song to sing, but I said, "I can't do it, I'm not used to singing things I can't understand." It was called "Emotional Pump" and [it contains] "You are my emotional pump, you make my body jump." It's quite a good song, but it's probably a hit for someone else.[35]

—Joni Mitchell

For years, Prince was enamored with Joni Mitchell. For a man who was often reticent to cite his influences, he publicly gushed over her influence on him. **"She taught me a lot about color and sound,"** expressed Prince, **"and to her, I'm very grateful."**[36]

"When he respected someone, he wore it on his sleeve and he touted their music and loved their songs. Joni was obviously one of those people early on, and Carlos Santana early on, were some real heroes of his," detailed Bobby Z. "At Paisley Park [which was still under construction at this time], outside of Studio A, there's a mural of his inspirations on one hand, and then his creations on the other. It tells the story in that one mural."[37]

He'd covered "A Case Of You" in concert, and referenced Mitchell on his *Dirty Mind* and *Controversy* albums, as well as on songs like "The Ballad Of Dorothy Parker." He created multiple tracks in her style, like "Power Fantastic," placed her *Hejira* album in the background during a scene in *Under The Cherry Moon*, and he invited her to perform on stage with him earlier in the year. But what had eluded him was working on a track with his idol, so he reached out to her about collaborating on a project.

"He implied that something would happen between our two musics. Something that he had never done before. That whet my curiosity," Joni Mitchell revealed in 1988. "I asked him to explain it, but he said he could not put it into words. The closest he came to articulating it was that it was the open harmonies I got in conjunction with funk into a hybrid that would be fairly fresh. I said, why didn't he build me a track."[38]

Prince set out to record a song for her. Using a blend of real kick and snare drums and a Linn LM-1 track, he added Fairlight, Oberheim OBXA, bass, guitar, and multiple percussion instruments, coated with his own lead vocal to create "Emotional Pump." From 9 p.m. to midnight, Leeds and Bliss added horns to the track, but when it was eventually sent to Mitchell, she didn't have the reaction that he'd hoped. "I called him back and said that I could not do the song."[39]

A mix was created and dubbed to four C-60 cassettes, along with an un-named track he'd recorded later in the evening with Eric, as well as an updated mix of "Baby Go-Go." Additional work would be done on "Emotional Pump" the following day.

Status: "Emotional Pump" (4:59) remained unreleased during Prince's lifetime but was included on the *Sign O' The Times* Super Deluxe collection in 2020. A 12-minute version of "Emotional Pump" is rumored to have been recorded but remains unreleased.

FRIDAY, OCTOBER 17, 1986

"**Emotional Pump**" [multiple versions, including instrumental] (mix, edits, and copies)
Sunset Sound, Studio 3 | 2:00 p.m.–8:30 p.m. (booked: lockout)
Producer: Prince | Artist: Prince | Engineer: Coke Johnson

Prince is a great hybrid.[40]

—Joni Mitchell

In 1994, Alan Leeds reflected on the current status of Prince and Joni Mitchell's friendship. "I do know that there's a friendship, not a particularly close one. They don't stay in constant touch, but they communicate periodically. She does come to his shows when it's convenient, and he does send her things like gifts and tapes."[41]

Prince went back in the studio to spend a little more time updating "Emotional Pump." Eric and Matt Blistan added their horns on a few extra pieces during this session, and Prince and Coke spent the last 3 and a half hours creating multiple variations of the song, editing them, updating the final mixes, and dubbing the different versions, which included an instrumental mix, to six C-60 tapes, before the session ended at 8:30 p.m.

FRIDAY, OCTOBER 17, 1986

> *So strange, that no one stayed*
> *At the end of the parade.*[42]
>
> —Lyrics from "Song About" by Wendy and Lisa

The disbanding of the Revolution was announced by Prince's publicist, Howard Bloom, and reported by Jon Bream in the *Star Tribune*.[43] Although the band and those close to Prince already knew, the official announcement made it final—the era of Prince's most famous band was officially over. The article quoted Alan Leeds who said, Prince had "outgrown the boundaries of its concepts and was coming to a point where the careers of its members are growing in different directions. This allows Bobby and Wendy and Lisa the freedom and the time to pursue other interests that they expressed interest in pursuing."[44]

The article implied that the split was mutual and implied that everyone was happy with the decision. The true story was that the band was devastated, remembered Wendy. "The rest of October was spent going, 'What happened? My God, now what?'"

"I think I was in shock for a couple of months," reflected Lisa. "When the band split up, it was a really heavy change for all of us. We all reacted differently. We just got together and had group therapy at the studio."[45]

While the band gathered for quiet comfort and healing, Prince seemed to be heading in the opposite direction, as Wendy noted. "I think he wanted more party time. We were too serious and into the music. We weren't wearing the sexy clothes. In the beginning I did because it was more punk and I dug that, it was cutting edge, but I didn't want to be a hoochie mama, I wasn't into it anymore. It changed. I think he was trying to put the party back into it somehow."[46]

After the official statement was given to the press about the breakup of the band, Prince kept quiet about the reasons for years. "**No band can do everything,**" Prince rationalized to Neal Karlen in 1990. "**I felt we all needed to grow. We all needed to play a wide range of music with different types of people. Then we could come back eight times as strong.**"[47]

But Prince never again shared the stage with the full Revolution and the promise of a reunion remained unfulfilled. "He told us if we wanted a song, he'd write us one," Lisa said. "But it never happened."[48]

Members would play separately with him over the years, and the Revolution reunited without Prince in December 2003 for a benefit concert for Sheila E.'s charity, "Lil' Angel Bunny Foundation," but the dream of all six of them working together on a project was lost when Prince passed away in 2016.

"It's like we're astronauts," reflected Wendy. "We went to the moon."[49]

"Yeah," agreed Bobby Z. "We left our footprints on the moon."[50]

"We're the only other people who know what that's like," concluded Lisa.[51]

SATURDAY, OCTOBER 18, 1986

"Housequake" (tracking, horn overdubs, edits, and mix)
Sunset Sound, Studio 3 | 10:30 a.m.–1:30 a.m. (booked: lockout)
Producer: Prince | Artist: Prince | Engineers: Susan Rogers and Coke Johnson

> *I don't go to awards shows anymore. I'm not saying I'm better than anybody else. But you'll be sitting there at the Grammys, and U2 will beat you. And you say to yourself "Wait a minute. I can play that kind of music, too." But you will not do "Housequake."*[52]

—Prince

The first morning after the official statement about the Revolution having disbanded, found Prince in the studio recording "Housequake," a party song that was a strong departure from his recent work. "I could tell there was something wrong," reflected Susan. "He was off—he was different, there was a silent wall that was basically saying, 'Don't even ask.' I followed his lead and we soldiered on, but I kept wondering, 'When are you going to talk to us? When are you going to write the song that tells what I know you're feeling?'"[53]

Once again his inner thoughts and outlook seem to have been put to tape, and it revealed that Prince was probably excited about his new freedom from the Revolution. Like a person who was celebrating an overdue breakup, he seemed enthusiastic about his future and apparently wanted to reveal this "brand new groove" in that celebratory atmosphere for anyone within the sound of his voice, even if it was artificially created. "He was probably ready to go. He was done with them," remembers Eric who was around him a great deal during this period. "He really wanted to turn the page."

"That was Prince," explains Wendy. "Every time he'd let somebody go, it was glee. He'd say, 'Ah, motherfucker, you out. Punk of the month.' He needed to do it that way. It's just the way he dealt with it."

It is unclear if it was true excitement, or if he was simply overcompensating for the loss of those around him that he had shared so much, but the recording of such a festive track on the day after the public announcement that he was free doesn't seem coincidental. If Prince's music was his diary, "Housequake" was a song that seemed to truly express where he was on that day.

The drum track contains a beat that is similar to "Shockadelica," although there is an unvalidated story behind the iconic opening drums of this track that states that Prince was preparing to leave the studio with his bodyguards to grab something to eat and heard the beat, likely from his shoes on the floor of the studio and he quickly sat back down behind the drums and laid it down, asking Coke to start recording.

Although Rogers doesn't recall that specific incident, she remembers that those types of situations were not rare. "That's exactly the kind of thing that inspired him. His antenna was so fully extended for those objects that would turn into a song. It could be a phrase, a melodic phrase or a lyrical phrase or it could be a rhythm pattern or something, and if he caught it in the wind, he would instantly turn it into a song."

For "Housequake," Prince threw in a lot of personal references to the lyrics. According to his bodyguard Wally Safford, Prince's lyrical mention of '66 and '67 came from a conversation they'd had. The reference to those years would also appear in *Lovesexy*'s "Alphabet Street" in 1988. The lyrics in "House-quake" also namecheck "Funkytown," which his long time engineer David Z had recorded.

"All the music is in his head," explains Michael Soltys about tracks like this one. "It's all natural God given ability, so he does the drum track first with no click track, no bass line, no nothing, it's all coming out of his head and it's the funniest thing to watch from the control room because you have no idea what he's playing and he's banging away, doing fills and splashes and he only likes to do it once, so I could be in the control room while he was doing that and I remember he would say, 'Did you get that Susan? I'm not doing it again.'"

Once his drums were tracked, he added bass, guitar, and recorded his vocals as well as the several tracks from the Fairlight synth. "I did a ton of sampling for him," details Todd Herreman. "Some of the stuff he used, some of it he didn't, but the majority ended up being stock Fairlight sounds because Prince just really liked them."

Prince was excited about the song and had Atlanta Bliss and Eric Leeds fill out the sound with trumpet and sax. "One line was his, one line was mine from the arrangement," details Eric. "The basic line the ba ba da, dal dal da, [first heard at 1:19 in 'Housequake,' also played before Prince sings 'Shut up already! Damn,' at the end] that was his. Then he wanted the counter line and I came up with the ba da da da da [first heard at 1:59]. I have a feeling that's a line that I had already come up with and had been using in some jam sessions now and then so it was maybe something in my back pocket."

To truly convey the song's festive vibe, he had Susan Rogers invite several members of Prince's team into the studio, remembers Herreman. "We're shouting the response to 'Who in the house knows about the quake?' I think that was Susan, Mike Soltys and it might have been [Prince's drum tech] Brad Marsh."

Prince worked everyone hard, and when he wanted someone to participate, you came in no matter how drained you were, remembers Brad. "There was a couple of days where we'd have just gone to sleep at our old apartment and Susan would call and say, 'Prince is coming into the studio.' So we'd shower and jump in the car, and by the time we'd finally get there an hour later, Prince would've done the drum part so I could go fall asleep on the road case out in the hallway."

Sometimes getting a few minutes of shut eye in the lounge was all the sleep they'd get for the day, so it was necessary to function, but when someone was asleep, there was always the risk of pranks, one of which became legendary, as Todd explains. "Prince had given Sheila this really beautiful stuffed penguin about two and a half feet tall. It was not your run-of-the-mill, ten dollar, stuffed penguin. This was really a neat stuffed animal. Prince was doing vocals once and he asked us to leave, because he was pretty adept at punching vocals, and he just liked to be left alone, he'd have some candles up, the lights were down and he'd just be recording his own vocals and in the lounge Brad takes a nap and we were kind of joking about it like, 'Don't let Prince catch you sleeping on the job.'"

We'd grab the polaroid when Brad fell asleep and we'd set the penguin on his chest, looking down at him and snap a polaroid and the sound of the snap and the ejecting of the picture, would usually wake Brad up and this was after the first *Terminator* movie, so Brad in his best Arnold Schwarzenegger voice goes, "Fuck you, asshole." So the penguin developed this role of catching people asleep on the job. At one point, Gilbert was asleep and this was like middle of the night in the main lounge, lying down on this couch in a three piece suit and sure enough the penguin is sitting on his chest and snapped a picture of Gilbert sleeping on the job and at one point, Prince found—there must have been fifty Polaroids of people asleep and the penguin is in every one and he started laughing. He thought it was pretty funny so we told him the story. Soon after while he was alone doing his vocals it was strangely quiet in the control room so Susan and I looked in and Prince had his head resting on the console and with his arms up like he's asleep. So we walk in and we're just about to snap the picture and Prince says, "Don't even think about it."

After 7 hours of tracking and overdubs, Prince spent another 8 hours editing and mixing the complicated layers of "Housequake." A single C-60 cassette was made from the session, which wrapped at 1:30 a.m.

Status: "Housequake" (4:38) would be included on Prince's *Sign O' The Times* album in 1987. The stuffed penguin was credited on the album singing 'party vocals' on the track.

SUNDAY, OCTOBER 19, 1986

Sheila E.'s third album compilation [listed as **Koo Koo**] (edits and copies)
Sunset Sound, Studio 3 | 6:30 p.m.–2:30 a.m. (booked: lockout)
Producer: Prince | Artist: Sheila E. | Engineer: Coke Johnson

When The Revolution disbanded, of course he's losing key members of his band that bring important flavors to it. Once it goes, it's gone. Sheila E. and her magnificent band from Oakland brought a whole new flavor to Prince's style.[54]

—Susan Rogers

The new year was being scheduled for a wave of music from Prince and multiple protégé albums, and the focus for today was on Sheila's upcoming third album, still tentatively called *Koo Koo*. It is likely that Prince wasn't in the studio for long on this date, leaving the task of assembling it to engineer Coke Johnson. The project was recorded and ready, but it was different from her previous albums because almost half the track list were songs that didn't directly involve Prince. "Prince did a couple by himself and I think Sheila might have done a couple by herself. I think I basically mixed the whole thing though," revealed the album's producer, David Z. "I remember telling her that she could be her own artist in her own right but she was very, very hung up on sounding just like Prince: And that was kind of a disappointment to me because I thought she was fabulous and that she could easily establish her own identity. But at the time, she was enamored with Prince's sounds and looks and movements and everything and she was trying to copy it exactly, which ultimately I didn't think was a great idea. It proved not to be."[55]

The album may have sounded similar to Prince's music, but he was now looking to move his sound in a new direction and that would likely include incorporating Sheila into his stage show. "It certainly brought a different direction to the band when Sheila was playing drums," detailed Blistan. "Sheila is basically a jazz/Latin drummer and when you have that attitude sitting behind the drums, and the timing was right."[56]

"Sheila E. and her crew came from the San Francisco Bay/Oakland areas and their sound was very different from the Los Angeles sound that Wendy and Lisa brought to Prince," explained Rogers. "The Oakland sound is a tougher, harder edge and much funkier so the *Dream Factory* record wouldn't quite work. Prince eventually transitioned into *Sign O' The Times* but in the middle, in between the *Dream Factory* and *Sign O' The Times* was the *Crystal Ball* record."[57]

The *Crystal Ball* album was weeks away, and before then, Prince still had a lot to say musically, and so he had a lot of recording to do.

The shift ended at 2:30 a.m. with Coke dubbing the assembly and any other item that was worked on during this shift to three C-90 and two C-60 cassettes.

Status: Sheila E.'s third album was released in February 1987, and peaked at number 56 on the *Billboard* 200 and number 24 on the *Billboard* Top Black Albums.

Warner Bros. executive Lenny Waronker remembered how many items Prince was bringing to them for release, and the quality of the material:

> "Sign O' The Times" was interesting. The first time I heard it, I had a meeting with Prince and Bob Cavallo at Bob's office, and Prince wanted to play me this jazz record that he had done. It was good, and it was fun having Prince take me through the record because he'd have all these observations based on the chord changes and the vibe and all that stuff. And he said, "I stole that from Fleetwood Mac" or "I did that" or whatever. But always fun and even self-effacing to some

extent. So, Bob walked in the office and he said to Prince, "Why don't you play Lenny 'Sign O' The Times' the single?" And so he said, "Okay," because he didn't like to let go of things until he was ready, but he did it, and it totally freaked me out. When I heard the record I thought, "Oh my God. He's gone to another— just another zone. Unbelievable. It's just unbelievable."[58]

MONDAY, OCTOBER 20, 1986

Venue: The Palace (Los Angeles, California)
Capacity: (attendance unknown)

Despite the recent announcement about the Revolution breaking up, Prince asked Wendy to join him when he attended a concert by the Bangles at the Palace in Los Angeles. Prince grabbed a guitar and played on "Hero Takes A Fall." "It was truly mind-blowing," remembered singer Susanna Hoffs. "I'd never seen anybody play guitar like that. I mean it was almost like his guitar was just part of his body. There was no disconnect, it wasn't like this thing he was holding and playing. He was somehow channeling from the inside out, and it just came through. And it was really magnificent on so many levels."[59]

Prince handed his guitar to Wendy and stepped back to sing background and play tambourine for "Manic Monday," allowing all of the women onstage to shine.

Eric Leeds noted the optics of Prince inviting Wendy to join him after the announcement. "How he played it was that a couple of days after that he and Wendy went and sat in with the Bangles. And everyone was saying, 'Well, what the fuck is that about?' So that was easy. He called Wendy to do that. And this is after he fired her. After he announced to the press that they were no longer in the band, he did that purposely in order to show everybody we're still friends. Lisa didn't buy it. Lisa said, 'Ummmm, no.'"

"He made the firing sound like we were all still going to be super good friends," agrees Wendy.

But the relationship was truly over, and Lisa refused to be a part of that, as Susannah recalls.

He just blew it with Lisa, and he knew it. Every time, he'd call me and Wendy, "Will you come see us?" And then he'd say, "How come Lisa didn't come?" And then Wendy would have to say, "Well, she couldn't, you know. . . ." And then when he would see her, it was like his sister, and that's how he was with Wendy as well and then I was sort of like the icing on the cake for him. And I think that was part of him that he put away for the rest of his career. I think he regretted it for the rest of his life.

Although Wendy and Lisa never rejoined his band, after some healing, they did get together both publicly and privately. Lisa recalls what it was like to rekindle with him, and once again share the musical intimacy they had.

After we were fired, Wendy and I were in LA, I think it was during *3121* or that kind of era, and he had a house here, and he invited us over for dinner, and I can't even remember what happened first, because for me nothing really happened until we went into this room and he had some gear set up and he picked up the guitar and he put up a sound on some keyboard. He was like, "Here, check this out," and it was a new keyboard. I don't even remember what it was, but, "Check out the new keyboard. Play that," and then we just started jamming, and again, it was like déjà vu, you know? And it was like, "There it is. This is our friendship. This is how we love each other." We could fight about normal things, but when it came to like, "Listen to this chord," he was like, "Oh my God, I love that chord, play it again."

MONDAY, OCTOBER 20, 1986

Studio jam with the Bangles, Wendy Melvoin, André Cymone, and others
Sunset Sound, Studio 3 (assumed) | unknown time
Producer: Prince | Artist: Prince | Engineers: "David Z" Rivkin and Coke Johnson (likely)

He invited us to go hang out and play music with him for no one but us; just musicians being musicians doing what they enjoy doing, whether there's an audience or not. And that has stuck with me and has resonated in recent years, more than I could have ever, ever known. And actually I get very emotional thinking about it, because I now have a little group of musicians that I get together with almost every week, and that's what we do. And I didn't even think about that till now, that it doesn't matter if we're just doing it for ourselves. We do it because we love playing and it does take us somewhere beautiful.[60]

—Susanna Hoffs

After the concert, Prince invited the band to join him and Wendy at Sunset Sound for a jam session. André Cymone also reportedly attending that night. "Blistan and I happened to have come into the studio that night and the Bangles were there and I don't really think that we had any plans," recalls Eric Leeds. "I actually wanted to see Wendy and see how she was doing. I just pulled her aside and just said, 'Hey sweetheart, this might be the best thing that ever happened to you. So go on and do what you're going to do.'"

With all of the jam sessions Prince was conducting lately, it is difficult for those involved to remember them specifically, but for the type of gatherings Prince had been doing this past week or two, there was likely no true agenda other than a social gathering of musical minds, according to Eric. "The purpose of the session was just for fun. André was around, H.B. Bennett was around. Those were the days when jamming was still fun."[61]

Prince was collecting new people and new blood to explore musically with him. Gone were the reliable studio partners he'd had with the members of the Revolution, and he was consciously or unconsciously seeking out others to fill that void. Susan Rogers saw how this was affecting Prince in private and how the absense of the people he'd relied on was affecting him. "They were falling like dominoes. The loss of Bobby and Wendy and Lisa was huge, musically as well as just psychically, that had to have been big because they formed a big part of his inner circle, they were as inner as inner got for him."

Lisa and most of the Revolution weren't the only ones who were no longer directly involved with Prince. Jerome Benton was working with his brother Terry Lewis on outside projects, and once it was brought to Prince's attention, he was no longer invited to participate, even though he'd just co-starred in *Under The Cherry Moon.* "I had started that departure, unknowingly at that time. Prince had a problem with me taking the elements that I brought to his palate of entertainment and seeing me do stuff with Janet [Jackson] and I totally understand. And we parted ways at that time. Remained friends, but I was told I couldn't work both sides of the fence. It was just time for me to go. At that time, the revolving door at Paisley Park became faster and faster with people."[62]

TUESDAY, OCTOBER 21, 1986

> *Sheila E.'s third album* compilation [listed as *Koo Koo*] (edits, crossfades, and copies)
> Sunset Sound, Studio 3 | 12:30 p.m.–1:00 a.m. (booked: lockout)
> Producer: Prince | Artist: Sheila E. | Engineers: Susan Rogers and Coke Johnson

Additional work compiling Sheila's album was done, including more edits and crossfades. It is unclear what songs were worked on, but it is likely that "Pride And The Passion" was edited from 4:30 down to 4:05, and "Hon E Man" and "Soul Salsa" were probably reduced as well. At the end of the 12-and-a-half-hour session, three C-90 and two C-60 cassettes were made.

This appears to be the final work done on the music before its February 1987 release. The only remaining detail would be changing the name of the album from *Koo Koo* to the eponymous *Sheila E.*

WEDNESDAY, OCTOBER 22, 1986

> **"Six"** [12-inch] (edits, possible overdubs, mix)
> **"Housequake"** (cassette copy likely dubbed)
> Sunset Sound, Studio 3 | 12:00 noon–8:45 p.m. (booked: lockout)
> Producer: Prince | Artist: Madhouse | Engineers: Susan Rogers and Coke Johnson

> *[Prince] was very shy and very mysterious. I couldn't figure this guy out. I knew he was kind of strange and weird and private. He would say something to you and you'd blink your eye and he's gone.*[63]
>
> —Cat Glover

Now that Prince had basically locked down all of the tracks for Madhouse *8*, he decided that the single for the album would be "Six," so he brought in Eric to help fashion a 12-inch version of the song. The urgency that he created with which he produced this project was surprising, even by Prince's standards.

"Prince is a very firm believer that once he makes a piece of music he wants it out as soon as possible," explained Leeds.

> That's something that he and I have discussed at times, because there used to be a time where, before albums were the primary vehicle for an artist's work, when back in the sixties where it was the single which was the main focus of an artist's career. James Brown had the luxury of being able to put out at least five singles a year. And Prince told me once that he kind of envied that situation. Prince has kind of tried to do it, but with albums. And I think you can make a case that he's oversaturated the market with his product, but that has just not been a particular concern of his.[64]

As the session progressed, it appears that Prince left Eric in the studio, while he went to dinner. Several people were in attendance, including his manager Steven Fargnoli, and Prince's former girlfriend Devin Devasquez, whose *Playboy* magazine cover had just been released. Fargnoli was representing her and her celebrity status was on the rise as she'd just gotten a great deal of notoriety as a contestant on *Star Search*. According to Devin, Prince's availability was explained to her by Fargnoli. "Steve told me that Prince had broken up with Susannah and Prince knew that I wasn't in a relationship at that time either, because I had boyfriends in between also. And it was a moment in time where we both were single. And we sort of rekindled our romance at that time."

However, despite Fargnoli's claim, Prince and Susannah were still engaged, although their relationship was struggling. A fellow contestant, dancer, and choreographer, Cat Glover, was her guest. "Prince walked into the dining room and looked at me. I had on a chauffeur's hat, the one that would be in 'Forever In My Life,'" explains Cat. "I was wearing some purple pants and a purple shirt. He knew everybody at the table, and he looked at me and walked upstairs." Once he was away from the table, Cat recalls that Prince began playing a song for Fargnoli. "I remember—boom, boom, boom, boom, and I thought, 'Ooh, what is that song?' Because you could hear it from upstairs. It was 'Housequake.' He had just came from the studio and wanted Steven to hear it."

After the dinner, the party shifted to a local nightclub, remembered Glover. "We ended up at a club called Voila in Beverly Hills. I was sitting there with Fargnoli, Devasquez, Prince and a couple of other people. Prince said—speaking in a low, raspy voice—'Cat, when a good song comes on will you dance with me?' I said, 'Sure!' The first song came on and he didn't ask me to dance. The second song came on; he didn't ask me to dance. On the third song, 'Simply Irresistible' by Robert Palmer, he asked me to dance. I was wearing cowboy boots and a pair of Levi's jeans. He reached to hold my hands while we were dancing, but I had leather gloves on, so I couldn't feel anything."[65]

He started doing dance steps and I started doing them; whatever he did, I did. I think he noticed that, so he started doing them more and I started doing them more. I think we stayed on the dance floor for two songs. After that, I remember I walked toward the DJ and put my hands on the wall and started jackin', a dance move closely associated with house music that originated in Chicago. That's the night it all started.[66]

Cat would eventually be tapped to work with Prince, but the invitation to work together didn't go smoothly. "I remember he said, 'Cat, I want you to be in one of my girl groups.' And so before I answered him, I bent down, because I was shy and I blinked my eyes. I turned around and he was gone. This happened three times. So the third time at the club, I said, 'Look, don't disappear again. Yes, I will.' That's what happened. He was like a ghost. 'Hi Cat. Would you be interested in being in one of my girl groups?' And I'm all shy and bubbly, going 'Of course.' But when I looked up, he was gone."[67]

Status: The 8-minute extended version of "Six" would eventually be edited (6:20) in November and released on January 14, 1987. It reached number 24 on the *Billboard* Hot Dance/Disco 12-inch Singles chart.

THURSDAY, OCTOBER 23, 1986

Kenny Rogers releases *They Don't Make Them Like They Used To*, which contains a re-recording of the Prince-penned "You're My Love." Although the song was not released as a single, it was included as the B-side of Rogers's highly successful single, "Make No Mistake, She's Mine," which reached number 1 on the U.S. *Billboard* Hot Country Singles Chart, and number 42 on the *Billboard* US Adult Contemporary Chart.

FRIDAY, OCTOBER 24, 1986

Madhouse 8 album (copy to cassette)
Sunset Sound, Studio 3 | 2:30 p.m.–3:30 p.m. (booked: 2:40 p.m.–3:40 p.m.)
Producer: Prince | Artist: Madhouse (Prince listed) | Engineer: Stephen Shelton

He knew what was up and of course that's going to keep you up at night, that's going to keep you working constantly, because the clay of our mental abilities, it's going to harden. We're going to run out of ideas. We're going to run out of original thought. We're going to run out of energy, we'll run out of fuel. It's what happens to living things. You're going to get past your prime. So, I think he was determined to live his life well and to make the most of those years and he did. He didn't get into drugs. He didn't get into scandalous lifestyles. He was smart enough to know I'm going to do my work and I'm going to approach this as work and that's what he did. I think like a great filmmaker, or a great painter would do. He created his art, works that would survive him.[68]

—Susan Rogers

The assembly of Madhouse *8* was copied to two TDK C-90 tapes. It is likely that Prince didn't attend this 1-hour session and either drove up in his car and someone walked it out to him, or the tapes were delivered to him.

Stephen Shelton had engineered for Prince in the past and was always in awe of his abilities.

I can say of all the people that I've worked with and I've been very fortunate with the type of artists and producers that I've worked with, rarely have I seen the transition between thought and finished product. He probably exemplifies that better than anybody else I've seen. Being able to take what he has in his mind and turn it into a piece of music at the end. Lots of people hear the orchestras in their head, not everybody is capable of pulling that orchestra out of their head.

SUNDAY, OCTOBER 26, 1986

"**Housequake**" [12-inch version] (various overdubs, mix, edits)
"**Housequake**" [multiple instrumental mixes] (mix)
"**Feel U Up**" (tracking, horn overdubs, mix, edit)
Sunset Sound, Studio 3 | 4:00 p.m.–4:30 a.m. (booked: lockout)
Producer: Prince | Artist: Prince (Tony LeMans crossed out) | Engineers: Susan Rogers and Coke Johnson

*We were at Sunset Sound and recorded every day and night
during that time period so I am sorry to say I don't have
much in the way of specific memories of ["Housequake"]. I
do remember that it was one of the songs he spent a long time
on which usually meant, I assume, that the song was one he
considered especially important or he particularly enjoyed
working on. I remember that it came at a time when there were
other changes in his life; his musical instruments, his style,
his colors, and the people around him were evolving. It is only
my guess, but I think "Housequake" represented a new idea in
dance music for him.*[69]

—Susan Rogers

Prince wasn't always a musical inventor; sometimes he was a reinventor of the music before him. While working on the extended mix, Prince hinted about one of the sources of his inspiration, Sly and the Family Stone—possibly based on Jesse Johnson's recent collaboration with Sly Stone—by adding a sample of Jesse's song "Crazay" in the 12-inch of "Housequake." "Prince's intellectual and musical father is Sly Stone, not James Brown," according to Susan Rogers. "Prince wasn't as strong or as extraordinary with funk as he was with melody and rhythm, and that was Sly Stone. Prince inherited his musical father, Sly's genius with melody and he coupled that with James Brown's genius for rhythm. But what Prince did best and what he'll probably be remembered for, his best songs, were the ones that showcased his melodic strengths."[70]

While Prince was recording overdubs for the extended version of "Housequake," he invited Eric Leeds and Atlanta Bliss to add horns. As soon as they arrived, Bliss recalls that Prince immediately asked him to play a trumpet solo on the track. "I did the solo and it was more or less the first take for the solo and Prince said: 'Okay, now you can go home.' It was a matter of 45 minutes and then we were going home, because he liked it, the whole thing. We stayed another day and did some other tracks but he was really happy with that."[71]

After midnight, the song was finished, and Prince asked for "fresh tape" to start "Feel U Up," which wasn't a new song but a re-recording of a song he'd created in 1981. As usual, he quickly laid down the Linn LM-1 drum tracks before embellishing it with bass and several different keyboards including the Fairlight, Oberheim OB-8, and the Prophet VS, and as he'd done on songs like "Train," he included a guide track for the trumpet and sax, which were recorded at some point on another session by Bliss and Leeds, respectively. "We'd occasionally do that," details Leeds. "I can't recall if he was there for that session. So I might have just left a guide track, and made it really easy. We'd just copy that."

The session ended at 4:30 a.m. after 2 hours of mixing, and a pair of C-60 cassettes were created. Once he'd reviewed the tapes, Prince decided that he'd continue working on the tracks the following day.

Status: The extended version of "Housequake" (7:15) would be released on the B-side of "U Got The Look" as "7 Minutes MoQuake."

"Feel U Up" (6:38) was released as "Feel U Up" (Long Stroke) (6:28) as the B-side of the 12-inch of "Partyman" in August 1989. An edit, dubbed "(Short Stroke)" (3:44), was on the regular 7-inch.

MONDAY, OCTOBER 27, 1986

"Feel U Up" (mix, edit)
"Housequake" (overdubs)
Sunset Sound, Studio 3 | 5:00 p.m.–7:00 a.m. (booked: lockout)
Producer: Prince | Artist: Prince | Engineers: Susan Rogers and Coke Johnson

> *"Housequake" was done during a period when Prince was re-examining dance music. I believe his exploration of funk at this time was considering the influences of rap and hip-hop, now firmly established as more than just musical fads.*[72]
>
> —Susan Rogers

During the 12 hours of recording, Prince also added more guitar as well as some additional Fairlight elements, including claps and bass, to "Housequake." He then continued working on "Feel U Up," possibly recording horn overdubs at this time. By 5 a.m. he was ready to mix and spent the next 2 hours shaping the sound and editing the tracks before recording them on two C-60 tapes.

By the time he left the building at 7 a.m., the sun had already been up for almost an hour and the city was coming to life, just as he was ending his day.

TUESDAY, OCTOBER 28, 1986

"**Rebirth Of The Flesh**" (tracking, various overdubs including horns, vocals, mix)
"**Rockhard In A Funky Place**" (tracking, overdubs, vocals, mix)
"**Feel U Up**" (mix)
Sunset Sound, Studio 3 | 2:30 p.m.–5:30 a.m. (booked: lockout)
Producer: Prince | Artist: Prince | Engineers: Susan Rogers and Coke Johnson

> *I remember occasionally I'd be on the mic or either clapping or group backing vocals, but that might have been the only time when I was on the mic all by myself, and I did not like it.*
>
> —Susan Rogers

Reinvention is never easy, and someone like Prince reinvents himself with every release. His core stayed the same, but the look, sound, and everything else was in a constant state of flux. Because of the focus on his next release, Prince was in another period of renewal and rediscovery. The breakup with the Revolution was likely still on his mind and with the inner circle that helped drive him gone, he was going to rely on his own talent, which he did no matter who was around him. The Prince of *Purple Rain,* and many of the things associated with it were in his rearview mirror. It is likely that he was enjoying that the ties that held him were gone, even if they had helped elevate his abilities.

"Rebirth Of The Flesh" appears to be a callback to his jazz project from earlier in the year. He detailed that journey of his spiritual rejuvenation into this new track. It isn't known if the title of the song was also inspired by Miles Davis's 1957 album *Birth Of The Cool,* but considering his interest in Davis's work, it isn't out of the question.

Using his Camille voice, and a hard rocking guitar track, Prince created an aggressive song about a "brand new day," laying down a blend of Linn and real drums and covering it with Prophet VS and Fairlight synths, as well as bass.

For a track about spiritual renewal, it contained what could be seen as insults aimed at those who were no longer on his journey ("We are here, where are you?").[73] As a possible dig at Wendy and Lisa asking for a larger salary, he threw in the line, "It ain't about the money, we just wanna play."[74] "He just felt guilty, so he had to write that," explains Wendy. "We had to be the 'Punk of the Month.' I've heard that bullshit before, and it's just a way for him to make himself feel better about what he did."

Prince also included a bizarre lyric, "You could be my wife, but all you do is steal, motherfucker."[75] His purpose for the line is unknown, but he must have reconsidered it because it was removed before the track was included on any project.

Eric and Atlanta were brought in to add their horns. "It was a long, six hour session," recalls Leeds. "It started at 11 p.m. on the 28th and went until 5 in the morning on the 29th and we did vocals on 'Rebirth Of The Flesh.'" Prince had Bliss and Leeds join Susannah in the studio to record background vocals, which didn't sit well with Eric. "I was really pissed about it because it's something I had no interest in doing. And I told Prince, 'Don't ever ask me to do that again. Now, if it was talking, that was one thing, but you really want me to really sing? You're out of your mind.'"

Prince then recorded "Rockhard In A Funky Place," using real drums and percussion (likely a shaker), bass, and once again the Prophet VS and Fairlight synths, but on this track, Prince had the Fairlight played through the Leslie cabinet, giving the sound an airy carnival organ sound in the background. He also gave his vocals the Camille treatment. Eric added baritone sax, and Atlanta contributed trumpet. Prince enjoyed what they created, but he'd call Eric back the next day for additional sax.

On "Rockhard In A Funky Place," Prince asked Susan Rogers to add a spoken line to the song as the track was ending. Susan recalls that he wanted her to say, "Yes, I agree. Now start all over and this time, be beautiful." "I remember I was really self-conscious. I did a few takes and he used me by default. It must've been the middle of the night because there was no one else around it."

The part was eventually mixed out and Prince's voice saying, "What kind of fuck ending was that?" became the closing line.

Prince did a mix of both tracks, as well as an updated mix of "Feel U Up," and dubbed them to five C-60 cassettes. The 15-hour session ended at 5:30 a.m.

Status: "Rockhard In A Funky Place" (4:31) had a difficult time being released. It was slated for the *Camille* and *Crystal Ball* albums, but they were both scrapped, and it did not make the transition to *Sign O' The Times.* It was included on *The Black Album* in 1987, but when that was shelved, it remained officially unreleased until *The Black Album* arrived in the stores in November 1994.

The longer version of "Rebirth Of The Flesh" (5:28) with the additional lyrics that had been removed and the original ending Prince had intended for the song was released on the *Sign O' The Times* Super Deluxe edition in 2020. An edited version of the track (4:55) was also included on the unreleased *Camille* and *Crystal Ball* collections. Although the studio track remained in the vault during Prince's lifetime, he included a rehearsal of the song (4:02), labeled "Rebirth Of The Flesh (Rehearsal '88)," on his NPG Music Club Edition #8 on August 28, 2001.

WEDNESDAY, OCTOBER 29, 1986

"Rockhard In A Funky Place" (edits, horn overdubs, mix)
Sunset Sound, Studio 3 | 5:00 p.m.–6:30 a.m. (booked: lockout)
Producer: Prince | Artist: Prince | Engineers: Susan Rogers and Coke Johnson

> *Soaked in banana cologne,*
> *No wonder you're all alone.*[76]
>
> —lyrics for "Rockhard In A Funky Place"

Prince picked up where he'd stopped the previous day, asking Eric to join him in the studio for additional follow ups. "We came back in on the 29th and continued on 'Rockhard In A Funky Place.' Because that ridiculous horn line that I wrote, he wanted to overdub and do it in a bunch of different keys. Originally it was on baritone and then I had to come back and put it on tenor and flute. It's actually a song of mine called 'Pacemaker.'"

At 4 a.m., Prince spent 2 and a half hours mixing and editing the track. It was dubbed to a cassette, but probably one that Prince supplied from a previous session.

THURSDAY, OCTOBER 30, 1986

"Good Love" (tracking, vocal overdubs, mix)
Sunset Sound, Studio 3 | 4:00 p.m.–7:00 a.m. (booked: lockout)
Producer: Prince | Artist: Prince, listed as "The Flesh" | Engineers: Susan Rogers and Coke Johnson

Very rarely would I actually be in the control room with him.
He doesn't like people in there and he doesn't even like me tun-
ing his guitar while he's recording. Because if he's just a tiny
bit flat on the G string or something and I fix it, he can hear
the difference when he's layering guitar tracks. So I could only
restring and tune once, when he started it, and then we'd sit in
the lobby and just wait it out. Could be eight hours he's in there.

—Michael Soltys

Prince had been in the recording studio almost every day for the month of October, working frantically on multiple projects and inspired to create something
different than he had done in the past. The flavor of the day was Camille, but
would it be an album, a series of songs, a play, a movie, or something completely
unexpected? "He was confused," recognized Susan Rogers. "I think he didn't
have a concrete idea of what it was going to be. He liked the name 'Camille.' So
this character of Camille might've been the lead singer of a band called Dream
Factory or *Dream Factory* might be the title of a *Camille* album. It was just unclear. He liked these concepts, but he had no actor to put in the role."

Prince's idea of Camille may have changed over time, when he explained it
to Eric Leeds.

He explained that to me one night, sitting in Tramp's, a club in Los Angeles. This
was another movie idea he had for a quick minute—and it probably could have
been a very hip movie—where he was going to play a dual role, and one side was
going to be him, and one side was going to be this alter ego, called Camille, and
only at the end of the movie would you realize that it wasn't two characters, it was
him just playing a schizophrenic, which would have been like the clincher for the
movie. And this came and went quick. Another short-lived idea.[77]

It appears that Prince was now creating several alter-egos like Joey Coco
or Camille that he could either use to remain anonymous or attach them to
a backstory as part of a larger project. And like Madhouse, he could do this
anonymously, reserving the Prince title for something he felt strongly about to
add to his own discography. "Any creator would do this," observed Rogers. "If
you're lost at sea you're going to sail into familiar waters and what was familiar
to Prince was creating alter-egos and stories that matched the albums."[78]

On many days, Prince had others in the studio. People like Eric and Sheila
provided something extra for his music, but there were many times that he
sought out the solitude of the studio as a solo exercise. The recording studio

was always a testing ground for him, and today he didn't include anyone except the engineers. Once again the structure of this new catchy pop song was built on a blend of Linn LM-1 and real drums before adding guitar and a few sound effects. The Prophet VS and Fairlight were his go-to synths during this period and he took advantage of the various patches, creating a web of sound that helped float his vocals above the music. Early in the development of the song, it was slated to be called "Good Drawers," a variation of a title for a different song that he'd toyed with the previous year, but Prince decided to switch it to "Good Love." His "Camille" voice sang about his love for his partner but also his fascination with Gustav Mahler's #3 symphony.

"He loved a good pop song," reflected Rogers. "He loved the Cars. He loved Whitney Houston. He talked about her, and what a great singer she was. He loved Joni Mitchell, and he loved Mahler. Music was food for him and he had a great deal of respect for musicians whose work he liked."[79]

As the session ended, Prince had a mix created of the song and dubbed it to three C-60 cassettes. One of them was given to Susannah, but instead of just wanting to show off his most recent work, he had something he wanted her to do to make the song complete.

Status: A nearly 6-minute version of "Good Love" was edited (5:12) and placed on Prince's unreleased *Camille* and *Crystal Ball* albums, but would sit on the shelf, until it eventually found a home on the soundtrack album for *Bright Lights, Big City* in 1988. At some point, an additional edit was created (4:55), and it was released again on Prince's 1998 *Crystal Ball* album.

FRIDAY, OCTOBER 31, 1986

"**Good Love**" (vocal overdubs, mix)
Sunset Sound, Studio 3 | 10:00 a.m.–3:30 p.m. (booked: lockout)
Producer: Prince | Artist: Prince | Engineers: Susan Rogers and "David Z" Rivkin

> *He sent me "Good Love" and he said I want you to do the background vocals on this, and I said, "Well, how many vocals do you want?" He goes, "I just want tons of vocals, tons of them everywhere."*
>
> —Susannah Melvoin

Prince seemed to enjoy pushing people to be uncomfortable and standing back and watching how they worked it out. Considering all of the personalities and the volatile situations that were occurring during this time, it was inevitable that there would be conflict.

With a session that started at the early hour of 10 in the morning, only 3 hours after the previous session ended, Prince asked Susannah to oversee the layers of vocals he'd requested on "Good Love." "He's like, can you do some background vocals for me now with David Z today? I was like, 'I'd love to. Let's go for it,'" remembers Susannah. "And then at one point, there's a part in there that David wants me to sing hard. 'Give it all I've got.' And I was like, 'You're asking me to do something that is not my thing. I'm not going to go in and scream. It's not my thing.' 'Okay, we're going to call Jill.' 'Okay great. Call Jill. She's a good singer.'"

Jill Jones was brought in as part of the vocal choir that Prince had envisioned, but instead of the usual vocal session that he'd done with Jones on countless occasions that were overseen by David Z, Prince requested that all of this be conducted through Susannah while he watched.

"Jill came down to the studio, and she was really super shy," recalls Melvoin. "She seemed like she didn't even want to be doing it and I had the parts done, and I was just like, 'Let's sing it. Go for it, like this is the part where you can go and shine. Give it what you got.' And she was like, 'What do you want me to do?' And I said, 'I don't know, whatever you want to do, do that.' And we sang and I thought it went really great. Amazing. Prince fucking loved it. I was so proud because it was mine. But Jill remembers it totally differently."

"He put Susannah in the room with me and he had her directing me," remembers Jones. "She had all these bright ideas!"

I wasn't talking to him at the time. I had a boyfriend around then and that usually was what it was! The real kicker was I'll fix you Jill because you are not waiting and pining away and melting like butter in the sun 'cause I'm not around. He *knew* I was livid. He knew it! I was so pissed at Susannah. I just hated being told what to do, and he wasn't saying anything and that isn't how I was used to working with him. I was so pissed because what I really wanted was my own freakin' album and I'd seen *The Family* album coming through. You're dealing with me walking into the studio and being very resentful. Now I'm singing, and *she's directing me* and I can't even get my bloody record.

By the end of this relatively short session, a mix was made of the track and the session was over by mid-afternoon. In the end, Prince seemed happy with what Susannah was able to create from this task. Although it is impossible to get into his head, it is probably not coincidental that he decided to revisit the idea of Jones's album.

Although Susannah and Jill agree on a few of the details regarding this session, some of the elements of this story are still unclear. Susannah recalls the track being "It's Gonna Be A Beautiful Night"—which was recorded later in November—while Jill remembers it being "Good Love." Because of this uncertainty, it was important to make sure that both of their recollections were noted.

The bottom line was that Prince sometimes seemed to embrace having conflict between those who worked for him, according to Susan Rogers. "It was an insight into what made him great because he would think that inciting jealousy was a good way to bring up the best in a person. I kind of saw through that pretty quickly because he definitely tried to make me jealous of Peggy and David a lot. When we were building Paisley Park, he would say to me, 'I'm going to bring in Peggy and David to design this or to do this.' Things that he knew *I* could do. And I wouldn't rise to the bait, because first of all, I liked Peggy and second of all, if you're going to do it, just do it. We'll make it work. I know my value. I know what I'm good for. But I saw him do that."

> He'd make musicians jealous of each other. He would make Sheila jealous of Wendy and Lisa. And Wendy and Lisa, he tried to make them jealous of Sheila. And I really do think that he was thinking, "You'll work harder, you'll be better, you'll aim higher if you feel your competition right on your heels." I was thinking about that just the other day, why that didn't work for many of us, why it doesn't work for a lot of people. In theory that should work pretty well. You should run faster if your competition is right on your heels. But for many people they just say, "I'm getting off this road." And they just turn and they say, "Competition, go ahead, take it. You can have it. I don't want to run this fast." I don't think that thought ever occurred to him.

NOVEMBER 1986

He wasn't the Prince that I had known in '83. He was changing.

—Susan Rogers

SATURDAY, NOVEMBER 1, 1986

"Nine" [version 2] (tracking, edits, mix)
"Six" [12-inch] (edits, mix)
"Good Love" [instrumental] (likely mix)
Sunset Sound, Studio 3 | 4:30 p.m.–9:15 p.m. (booked: lockout)
Producer: Prince | Artist: Prince (listed as The Flesh) | Engineer: Coke
    Johnson | Assistant Engineer: Jim Preziosi

This is what [Prince] came up with and I didn't necessarily disagree with him on this point. He said, "I'm not going to go so far as to say that this is jazz. This album will never get anywhere because the critics are going to blast it. They're going to say, 'how dare this guy think he can make a jazz album.' And if it comes out, I don't want it to just end up with all of the Prince fanatics. I want to distance myself from this and see if we can get some form of an honest reaction without any preconceived notions as to my involvement with it."[1]

—Eric Leeds

Prince spent a brief session editing the 8-minute extended version of "Six" down to a less repetitious 6 minutes, losing some additional repeated sections and drastically reducing Vanity's repeated moan, "Oh, here I come." Updating the mix took just a short time, and Prince moved on to creating an instrumental copy of "Good Love," which would likely indicate that it was intended for another artist's vocals.

Once those were completed, he called others into the room for a new track called "Nine." He'd already made an attempt at a song with that name, but it was rechristened "Six And 1/2" and slated to be on the B-side of "Six." Although today's track was listed as a Madhouse song, it doesn't appear to have contained Eric Leeds, so any sax in the song was likely created using a horns-patch on the Fairlight. Prince recorded it with others, but it is unclear who participated in the song.

Coke Johnson had been working very long shifts, so Sunset Sound staff member Jim Preziosi was brought in early in the session to replace him for the remainder of the day. It is likely that Prince and Preziosi mixed the track at the end of the shift, which concluded at 9:15 p.m.

Status: The composition that was recorded during this session, listed as "Nine," had nothing in common with "Nine" from 16, the 1987 follow-up to Madhouse's debut release, or the recently tracked "Nine" that was eventually released as "Six And 1/2." Today's instrumental remained unreleased during Prince's lifetime.

SUNDAY, NOVEMBER 2, 1986

"If I Was Your Girlfriend" (tracking, overdub, and mix)
"If I Was Your Girlfriend" [instrumental] (mix)
"Rebirth Of The Flesh" (mix)
Sunset Sound, Studio 3 | 1:00 p.m.–3:15 a.m. (booked: lockout)
Producer: Prince | Artist: Prince | Engineer: Susan Rogers | Assistant
    Engineer: Jim Preziosi

I remember him playing [Kate Bush's "Running Up That Hill"] in the control room, the studio at his home, and saying to us, "You guys have to buy this record." I think he was influenced by Kate's vocal performance, her vocal sound. Very high, very thin, and very bright. He was interested in that rolling drum track and the production elements were so different from what Prince normally did. The records that Prince and I were making at that time, for the most part, especially if they had a fast drum groove, would be pretty dry. This is kind of rolling in reverb. It has a brilliant lyric that talks about a man and a woman exchanging places. That was a theme that Prince picked up on and wrote about it in "If I Was Your Girlfriend."[2]

—Susan Rogers

The session began at 1 in the afternoon with Prince starting work on "If I Was Your Girlfriend" by laying down his usual bed of drums, followed by a sparse blend of bass and keyboards, this time including the Prophet VS and Fairlight, but no guitar. Prince asked Rogers to set up the microphone so he could record his vocals in private, and once she was finished, she left him alone in the room, allowing Prince to give an incredibly intimate performance mirroring the intimate tone of the track. "There was no way to get that intimacy with another person just on the other side of the glass, he needed to work by himself. So the vocal mic would be set up over the console and the rest of us who were there would leave."[3] When they sat down to mix the song, Susan noticed something had gone terribly wrong. "I accidentally had the setting on his vocal mic (on the pre-amp) set 10 decibels hotter than normal, and then when I came back in and heard the vocal for "If I Was Your Girlfriend," it was completely distorted. And I was mortified thinking 'Oh no, I ruined an entire track. He did this great vocal performance and it's distorted.' And I came to discover that he was very happy with the sounds."[4]

When it is your job to create in such a prolific way, there is no way for Prince to do it all himself. Yes, he could play practically every instrument better than most people, but despite his musical abilities, he required inspiration, so he was influenced by everything in his world. "Prince was a big fan of Kate Bush," reflected Rogers, "and she said it in ['Running Up That Hill (A Deal With God)'] with that famous line 'Come on angel, come on darling, let's exchange the experience.'[5] It has multiple meanings but what she's saying is 'Come on let me be you for a minute and you be me, let's exchange this.' He played that record to death! He loved that record."[6]

"If I Was Your Girlfriend" took musical elements from Kate Bush, but he also saw the way Susannah behaved with her twin Wendy, and although he wasn't able to see them interact anymore because Wendy and Lisa were no longer part of his daily life, he would be dealing with the even more painful aspects of the breakup, the loss of their trust and friendship. They were no longer there

to block for him, to make him smile, and to keep his secrets. He may have instigated it, but the heartbreak of missing the daily conversations was likely tough,
and with no one to discuss it with, that longing appears to have come out in a
song. "I think he was getting much more personal lyrically. When the girls were
together, there was a camaraderie between women, especially between Wendy,
Susannah, and Lisa and all the women that were in our circle that can leave a
man sometimes feeling a little left out. There is an intimacy that women go to
easily that men don't. This song was his way of saying, 'What would it be like
if I could be as intimate with you, on the same level as your sisters are?' It was
a very clever artistic statement and very rare. You don't hear a male artist say
these things very often."[7]

> I think Prince's feminine sensibilities came from a place that was innate to him.
> I assume that he had always had that. It was not forced. It was not artifice. He
> didn't go out and decide to be more sensitive to, or empathic with women. I
> think he naturally was. I think he enjoyed the issue of race and gender as being
> somewhat flexible. And he liked pushing the boundaries of both to see how far
> you could take them. Being a true artist, he would want to experience things from
> the other side. What's it like to be this? What's it like to be that?[8]

Much like the 1983 hit "Every Breath You Take" by the Police, "If I Was
Your Girlfriend" uses a beautifully crafted pop song to hide the story of a controlling protagonist wanting to isolate his partner. Lyrics like, "Would you run
to me if somebody hurt you, even if that somebody was me?"[9] reveal a person
who, intentionally or accidentally, pleads to his lover to maintain her silence
about any pain he inflicted on her.

But despite the hope that his partner would not reveal his flaws, there is a deep
tenderness about his confession that is difficult to ignore, and his longing for a
deeper bond comes off as a man who honestly recognizes that there is a level of
intimacy he is offering to a woman, but it is also something he may never truly
grasp. "I could see where it might turn men off," observed Rogers. "I could see
where they would say, 'No guy talks like that,' but it's what women want to hear.
And a woman would look at a man saying that and say, 'Yes, thank you for recognizing that I think differently from you, and wouldn't it be nice if just for brief
periods of time we could be on the same page and you could be my friend and not
my adversary and we could think the same way.' That's what he's trying to say."[10]

"He wanted to be closer than men could be to women. And girlfriends could
be closer to each other than what men can be to a woman, in his eyes. And so
he was saying, I want to be as close as your girlfriends can be to you. I want to
get closer than what we have," reflects Susannah. "He wanted to be the subject

of that intimacy. 'Tell me everything.' But yet it's kind of one-sided, because he couldn't do that. He couldn't have that kind of closeness. He couldn't."[11]

The final 2 hours were spent finishing the mix of "If I Was Your Girlfriend," creating an instrumental version of the song and updating the mix on "Rebirth Of The Flesh." Three C-60 cassettes were dubbed, and the session ended at 3:15 a.m.

Status: "If I Was Your Girlfriend" (4:49) was placed on both *Camille* and *Crystal Ball.* When *Crystal Ball* was reduced and it became part of *Sign O' The Times*, a 14-second intro of sound effects was added to the track. An edited version (3:46) was released as a single (backed with "Shockadelica") and peaked at number 67 on the US *Billboard* Pop Chart, but reached number 12 on the *Billboard* Black Chart.

SUNDAY, NOVEMBER 3, 1986

> **"Rebirth Of The Flesh"** (horn overdub and mix)
> **"Strange Relationship"** (overdubs, mix)
> Sunset Sound, Studio 3 | 2:00 p.m.–12:15 p.m. (booked: lockout)
> Producer: Prince | Artist: Prince | Engineer: Susan Rogers | Assistant Engineer: Jim Preziosi

> *Sometimes he gets an idea and says, "I like that part, just add to it." Sometimes he might come in and say, "Put a solo on it."*
>
> —Eric Leeds

From 2 p.m. until 9:30 that evening, Prince added overdubs to "Rebirth Of The Flesh" and "Strange Relationship." The first one was relatively easy, but "Strange Relationship" was much more complicated because Wendy and Lisa had made an elaborate mix of the track, using a sitar-sounding patch from the Fairlight. When he first heard it, he seemed elated, but now with the Revolution broken up, and Wendy and Lisa out of the picture, Prince reworked it again, essentially erasing their contributions. "I didn't think there was any way we could be extracted from it like that," says Lisa, looking back at the changes being done on their work. "Literally on certain tracks on *Sign O' The Times*, we were just muted. Like 'Strange Relationship,' he took our parts out and then replaced it with Sheila. We'd put the conga parts on from a loop, then he'd put real congas on with Sheila. Things like that."

He overdubbed and mixed "Strange Relationship" for 90 minutes and when he finished, Eric Leeds was called in to add sax to "Rebirth Of The Flesh."

Eric wrapped up his work just after 3 a.m., and Prince spent over 9 hours updating the mixes for "Rebirth Of The Flesh," "Strange Relationship," and likely a few other tracks he was considering for a collection he'd gather over the next few days.

When Prince felt the music was ready to be archived, he made three C-60 cassettes of the session.

TUESDAY, NOVEMBER 4, 1986

"**Rebirth Of The Flesh**" (overdubs, mix)
"**Strange Relationship**" (guitar and sax overdubs, mix)
"**Strange Relationship**" [instrumental] (mix)
Sunset Sound, Studio 3 | 1:15 p.m.–7:30 p.m. (booked: lockout)
Producer: Prince | Artist: Prince | Engineer: Susan Rogers | Assistant Engineer: Jim Preziosi

> *Dear Prince,*
> *You are the most cinematic of musical geniuses.*
> *Master of the establishing shot . . .*
> *"Dig if you will this [sic] picture . . ."*
> *"I was working part time in the [sic] five and dime . . . "*
> *"You don't have to be beautiful to turn me on . . . "*
> *The song always said what it was about from the start, like a Hemingway story, but like all great auteurs you could never guess what you'd do next until you did it and it became obvious.*[12]
>
> —Bono

"I guess you know me well, I don't like winter. But I seem to get a kick out of doing you cold."[13] And with that, the theme, the singer, the singer's inner monologue, the object of his lyrics, and the purpose is laid bare for all. It was a song about control, as well as the contradictions that the singer felt about himself and his partner. Although the track dates back to 1983 and is about a woman who eventually grew tired of him and left, the theme was as contemporary as a song he could have written that morning about his time with Susannah.

This day's work was a continuation of the previous day's session, which was now running for almost 24 hours. After a 1-hour break for lunch, Prince returned to mixing any remaining tracks he was considering for a single album he was referring to as *Camille*, including Leeds adding horns to "Strange Relationship" for an hour starting at 2 p.m. "I'd recorded tenor saxophone on [November] 3rd on 'Rebirth Of The Flesh.' And then [the following afternoon] more tenor saxophone on the 4th. It wasn't Blistan, it was just me, doubling the lead line. Of course, he never used it. He was just curious to hear what it sounded like, I guess."

A new ending was crafted for "Rebirth Of The Flesh," so it could segue into the next track once the order was decided for the album he was compiling the following day.

The session ended at 7:30 p.m. with the mixes compiled on one C-60 cassette.

WEDNESDAY, NOVEMBER 5, 1986

Camille album (compiling and copies)
"Strange Relationship" (overdubs, mix)
"Telepathy" (horn overdubs, mix)
Sunset Sound, Studio 3 | 11:30 a.m.–2:30 a.m. (booked: lockout)
Producer: Prince | Artist: Prince | Engineer: Susan Rogers

> *There's a period of time where I'm on some very significant records that didn't even see the light of day, like the* Crystal Ball *record, the* Camille *record,* Dream Factory, *and parts of* Sign O' The Times. *That's all me on those background vocals.*[14]
>
> —Susannah Melvoin

Susannah's presence is powerful during this period. Of the eight songs that were placed on *Camille*, she was involved with or influenced more than half of the tracks. Prince was constantly in a state of creating his art, but there are periods of inspired creation that cannot be overlooked, and she was the constant for him. He and Susannah would drift apart and revive their commitment, but he did rely on her musically, even if it was just to play his creations for her as a way of communicating his feelings.

Additional work may have taken place on "Strange Relationship," and the collection was assembled. Using many recent post-Revolution tracks, Prince compiled a single album that reflected where he was at the moment. The idea that he could have a full album prepared so quickly after the breakup of the band must have been intriguing to him as a statement of his skills. Starting off with "Rebirth Of The Flesh," he was announcing that it was a new groove and a new day without his former bandmates, which blended into his recent party anthem, "Housequake," a song that would reflect his current celebration. "Strange Relationship" was the only track that was recorded pre-breakup from this collection, but he eliminated Wendy and Lisa's contributions, and he closed side one with his updated version of "Feel U Up," another playfully aggressive number.

Side two starts with a similar tone on "Shockadelica," followed by the upbeat "Good Love," his ode to Susannah, "If I Was Your Girlfriend," and his final number for the album, "Rockhard In A Funky Place." This collection didn't take advantage of his recent contemplative songs, but instead the overall theme was sex, fun, and a new spirit and new direction. No slow songs, no ballads and—outside of "If I Was Your Girlfriend"—little in the way of introspection. The linking element was his use of the Camille voice on every track. Similar to the recent Madhouse album, *Camille* was not slated to contain Prince's name. *Camille* would be the title of the project, as well as the artist, even though it was obvious that the music was created by Prince under a pseudonym, perhaps to allow the music to be judged on its own merit, but the full reason for this decision remains unknown.

When the collection was finalized, the line-up was:

Side One:
"Rebirth Of The Flesh" (4:54)
"Housequake" (4:34)
"Strange Relationship" (4:04)
"Feel U Up" (6:27)

Side Two
"Shockadelica" (6:12)
"Good Love" [listed as "Goodlove"] (5:11)
"If I Was Your Girlfriend" (4:47)
"Rockhard In A Funky Place" (4:30)

After the album was assembled, three C-90 cassettes were created, and Prince left for almost 5 hours. He returned at 10 p.m. and spent the final 4 and a half hours working on overdubs for "Telepathy," including Prince playing guitar and 2 hours (midnight–2 a.m.) with Eric recording overdubs and solos on sax, before the session ended at 2:30 in the morning.

Two C-60 cassettes were made of "Telepathy."

Status: Although the *Camille* album was given a catalogue number (25543) and test pressings were made, it remained unreleased during Prince's lifetime. Of the eight tracks, three songs ("Housequake," "Strange Relationship," and "If I Was Your Girlfriend") were shifted to *Sign O' The Times*, two ("Feel U Up" and "Shockadelica") were designated as B-sides, "Good Love" was released on the soundtrack for *Bright Lights, Big City*, and "Rockhard In A Funky Place" closed out *The Black Album*. Only the studio version of "Rebirth Of The Flesh" wasn't repurposed for an official release.

THURSDAY, NOVEMBER 6, 1986

Jill Jones album (safety copy)
"Telepathy" (mix)
Sunset Sound, Studio 3 | 6:00 p.m.–1:00 a.m. (booked: lockout)
Producer: Prince | Artists: Prince and Jill Jones | Engineers: "David Z" Rivkin, Susan Rogers, and Coke Johnson

> *I think the album was a very intellectual one. We took a decision to take a lot of the poppy songs off. Once Clare Fischer put the strings on it. I wanted to leave them on. That's where I sealed my fate to never have a hit record.*[15]
>
> —Jill Jones

Despite the party atmosphere of songs like "Housequake," Prince generally worked with as few people as possible and when he did, he rarely verbalized what he wanted. You were expected to have a hint of telepathy and be able to accurately predict what he was thinking, but at the same time if he knew you were able to second-guess him, he'd change his behavior to keep anyone from getting too comfortable.

"You think Susan Rogers knows me? You think she knows anything about my music? Susan Rogers, for the record, doesn't know anything about my music. Not one thing. The only person who knows anything about my music [pause for very pointed effect] **. . . is me."**[16]

"Yes, Prince is correct on this, but only in one sense," responded Rogers. "In another sense, namely the experience of listening to music created by another, Prince knows his music the least. Because creating music and consuming music are two distinct processes."[17]

Susan continues:

> When a chef prepares a new meal, he knows everything that goes into it, including how he intended it to taste. So when he sits down to eat it, he already knows something about it, and that affects how it tastes to him. The customer who knows nothing about what went into the meal will taste it from a different perspective, one that the chef will never be able to experience. So the customer knows something about the meal that the chef will never know.
>
> Prince fans know how his music makes them feel, regardless of whether or not he intended the music to move them that way. Only he knows what inspired a song or he wanted his music to say, but there is a gap between how it felt to make it and how it feels to listen to it. Like a lot of things, it is a two-sided experience. Science isn't science until it is published; food isn't food until it is eaten; and art isn't art until it is interpreted.[18]

His occasional changes in behavior would generally confuse those around him, according to Michael Soltys, who recalls a session during this era. "He brought us in a couple times to play tambourine and handclap and do some background 'oohs' and 'aahs,' but other than that, I didn't know what he was working on."

> There was a lounge with a little kitchenette and a TV and we would sit and watch the movies that we rented from the 7-Eleven across the street to pass the time. I remember one time he came out and we happened to be watching *Highlander*, great film, and he's in the fridge looking for something to eat and kind of looks over his shoulder at the TV and it caught his eye so he came and sat down on the couch right between me and Brad [Marsh] and he started watching the movie. And me and Brad saw this as an opportunity—"Let's go in there and check things out, go check the drums out, check the guitars and make sure everything is fine" and so we got up and we went in and we came back a few minutes later and he said to us with these sad eyes, "Why'd you guys leave?" He wanted to watch the movie with us. "We thought we were supposed to leave when you sat down!"

Starting at 6 p.m., Prince spent 3 hours mixing and assembling Jill Jones's album, but when he eventually listened to the cassette, he realized there was more work to be done on it. He removed "Boom, Boom (Can't You Feel The Beat Of My Heart)," which was the first track he'd recorded with Jill in 1982. "[Prince] listened and said, 'I don't know,'" according to Jones. "I said, 'I don't know either. I don't think it's really me.' It's like a bad blood transfusion or something. Something was disingenuous."[19] The song was replaced by "All Day, All Night."

The lineup for Jill's album at the end of this session was:

Side One:
   Intro/"Baby, You're A Trip"
   "Mia Bocca"
   "G-Spot"
   "Violet Blue"
   "With You"

Side Two:
   "All Day, All Night"
   "For Love"
   "My Man"
   "Baby, You're A Trip"

The final hour was spent working on any mixes and crossfades that were needed. "Telepathy" would also get an additional mix at some point during this date. The session ended at 1 a.m. after three C-90 and two C-60 cassettes were dubbed.

Status: Jill Jones's album would undergo additional work before it was released in May 1987.

FRIDAY, NOVEMBER 7, 1986

"Violet Blue" (possible horn overdubs, edits, mix)
"Housequake" (possible sax overdubs, edits, mix)
"Housequake" [7-inch single version] (edit and mix)
"Shockadelica" [7-inch single version] (edit and mix)
Sunset Sound, Studio 3 | 2:00 p.m.–2:30 a.m. (booked: lockout)
Producer: Prince | Artist: Prince | Engineers: Susan Rogers and Coke Johnson

> *When Susannah and I were playing around with a yellow legal pad at Sunset Sound, I remember we drew these cartoon characters with X's for the eyes. We were trying to come up with an idea for what Camille might look like, representational we do these kind of ghost-like characters with X's for eyes. Prince loved that. He loved those X's for the eyes.*
>
> —Susan Rogers

Now that Prince decided to release the *Camille* album, he put together the first single which would be "Housequake" with "Shockadelica" on the B-side. Starting at 2 p.m., a 7-inch single for each track was edited and mixed.

    Prince also worked on some additional overdubs and mixing for "Violet Blue," including sax and possibly trumpet overdubs for that song and "Housequake" from 9:30 p.m. until 12:30 p.m. After they were finished with the horns, Prince continued updating the songs, spending 90 minutes on the mixes and possibly including Clare Fischer's recent orchestral additions to "Violet Blue," before six C-60 cassettes were dubbed of the day's work.

Status: The single release with the 7-inch edits of "Shockadelica" (3:29) and "Housequake" (3:24) was canceled, but the edits would be released separately as B-sides on "If I Was Your Girlfriend" and "U Got The Look," respectively.

Earlier in the week Bernie Grundman had created an acetate of these two songs for a 12-inch release.

SATURDAY, NOVEMBER 8, 1986

> **"Crucial"** (sax overdubs)
> Sunset Sound, Studo 3 | (booked: lockout)
> Producer: Prince | Artist: Prince | Engineers: Susan Rogers and Coke Johnson (assumed)

> *He understood that an artist is a canvas for us to project our own desires and motives on to. He was being the bold male that a lot of men wish they could be, but society wouldn't allow them to; he was being the hyper-confident male that a lot of women wish would find them attractive. He was letting us see this almost comic-book hero version of himself, so the real man could hide: a quiet, respectful, polite working man.*[20]
>
> —Susan Rogers

Music requires confidence, and producing, writing, arranging, and performing a song requires a true awareness of one's skills and strengths. As Miles Davis said, "Anybody can play. The note is only 20 percent. The attitude of the motherfucker who plays it is 80 percent."[21]

Prince not only had confidence that he was correct musically, but his decisions about what was needed on his music were sometimes bendable, but always ruled by how he heard a song in his head. Eric Leeds experienced that when working on "Crucial."

On November 8th, I put horns on "Crucial." His instructions to me were to record a couple of horn lines and put a horn solo where he starts to sing high. Well, there were about three or four places in the song where I could construe that, so I took the first one where he sang high and put a long sax solo on it. So I played him that, he looked at me and said, "That's the wrong place." I said, "Oh, it's a great solo, though, don't you think?" He said, "That's where the guitar solo is." I said "Oops, I'm not going to win this battle."[22]

Eric's work took place between 4 p.m. and 7 p.m. It is unclear if anything else was recorded during this session.

SUNDAY, NOVEMBER 9, 1986

"C'est La Vie" [long version] (overdubs, mix)
"C'est La Vie" [edited version] (edits, mix)
"Crucial" [second sax solo] (likely sax overdubs, mix)
"Six" [7-inch single] (edit, mix)
"Six And 1/2" [7-inch single] (edit, mix)
Sunset Sound, Studio 3 | 5:00 p.m.–10:00 a.m. (booked: lockout)
Producer: Prince | Artists: Tony LeMans/Prince | Engineers: Susan Rogers and Coke Johnson

> *The thing that I thought had the best potential was the Tony LeMans record, because it sounded to me like the most commercial. There were a couple of tracks that I thought were radio friendly.*[23]

> —Alan Leeds

Prince was expanding his Paisley Park Records with new blood, and they signed Tony LeMans to Prince's label. Coke Johnson recalls how LeMans was introduced to Prince. "I guess it was '84, when I was working at Cherokee Studios, Warner Bros. got a hold of me to work with Tony LeMans, who was an unknown artist at the time. And I cut some demos with him after midnight at Cherokee Studios. The bass player in that band, Romeo Blue, was Lenny Kravitz. So then, Warner Brothers got those demos to Prince, and that's when he invited us all over to Sunset Sound."

Starting in 1986, work was being done for his debut, but it would take years before it was released, and during this time, Prince would turn over the reins to David Gamson who would produce LeMans's album. Like several of his protégé acts during this time, work went on longer than expected. When the album and singles were released in 1989, it made no impact. A follow-up project was being considered, when tragedy struck in 1992 and LeMans was killed in an accident.

In what may have been the first Paisley Park Records session for LeMans, he recorded a song called "C'est La Vie." It is likely that he hoped Prince would consider placing the track on LeMans's debut album.

At some point after midnight, Prince worked on the 7-inch edits for what would be the debut single from Madhouse 8, "Six" and the B-side, "Six And 1/2." It is also likely that Eric Leeds updated his solo on "Crucial" at some point during this session.

The final 2 hours were spent mixing the tracks and dubbing everything to two C-60 cassettes.

Status: "C'est La Vie" was not included on Tony LeMans's debut album and remains unreleased. The track has nothing in common with Robbie Nevil's similarly named song that was climbing the charts on this date.

MONDAY, NOVEMBER 10, 1986

"**All Day, All Night**" (overdubs, probably vocals)
Sunset Sound, Studio 3 | 4:00 p.m.–11:15 p.m. (booked: start at 4 p.m.)
Producer: "David Z" Rivkin | Artists: Jill Jones and Madhouse | Engineer: David Z | Assistant Engineer: Jim Preziosi

> *It was great training for me with David, because I'd gotten away with murder with Prince with a lot of things, but David put me to task, which was pretty cool because it made me better.*
>
> —Jill Jones

"David Z" Rivkin worked with Jill, updating her vocals on "All Day, All Night," but Jill remembers the dilemma when she was adding her voice to the song. "We couldn't figure out how we were going to deal with the obvious change in vocal key. I had to sing so much higher because Prince sang it in the real comfort zone of his voice, that it actually didn't fit mine. I would've had to go way below or way high. So I always had a hard time with the song because it was a lot of screaming."

Prince did not attend this session, but a single C-60 cassette was dubbed for him to review.

TUESDAY, NOVEMBER 11, 1986

"All Day, All Night" (overdubs and vocal overdubs)
"Yo Mister" (tracking, overdubs, mix)
"Come Elektra Tuesday" [multiple mixes] (overdubs, mix)
"Come Elektra Tuesday" [instrumental] (mix)
Sunset Sound, Studio 3 | 1:00 p.m.–5:30 a.m. (booked: lockout)
Producer: Prince | Artists: Jill Jones and Prince | Engineers: Susan Rogers
   and Coke Johnson

> *I think he always wanted ["Yo Mister"] for Patti LaBelle.*
> *I heard it and wanted it.*
>
> —Jill Jones

Once Prince listened to the previous day's recording of "All Day, All Night," it appears that he had a few minor adjustments to make before he felt it was finished. Jones was also brought back in for some additional vocal work. "When David Z and I did it, I think it wasn't working. Then Prince and I did it out at Sunset Sound. I think we redid that. It was a little tricky."

Afterward, he spent this Tuesday evening working on multiple new mixes for "Come Elektra Tuesday," a song he'd recorded in May of 1985. Among the mixes was a take without the horn-like keyboard stings, as well as an instrumental, likely for consideration for another performer. Work on those versions went past midnight. The rest of the session was spent recording a new track, "Yo Mister." Although Jill was around during the tracking of the song, she did not participate in the recording. "[I was] not involved. No one needed to be on that."

"Yo Mister" once again found Prince quickly creating a song on his own. Blending real drums and the Linn LM-1, Prince stacked bass, guitar, piano, and the Fairlight and Prophet VS synths to build a heartfelt composition about a woman named Kara who has suffered at the hands of her father and how her life would have been different if she'd had a strong set of parents. It is likely that "Yo Mister" was briefly considered for Jill, but Prince decided to eventually give it to Patti LaBelle, who would add her vocals in 1988 at Paisley Park.

The session lasted for 14 hours before Prince mixed the tracks from 3 a.m. to 5:30 a.m. He dubbed the day's music to one C-90 and one C-60 cassette.

Status: "Yo Mister" (5:00) would be released on Patti LaBelle's album *Be Yourself* in June 1989. In September, "Yo Mister" was released as the album's second single, and it contained various remixes of the track.

WEDNESDAY, NOVEMBER 12, 1986

Jill Jones album compiled (edits)
"**All Day, All Night**" (mix)
Sunset Sound, Studio 3 | 1:30 p.m.–1:00 a.m. (booked: lockout)
Producers: Prince/"David Z" Rivkin | Artist: Jill Jones | Engineers: David Z
  and Coke Johnson

I loved that project so much. To me, it was like a work of art.[24]

—Jill Jones

David Z took care of a few remaining adjustments to Jill Jones's album, includ-ing additional mixing and possible vocal overdubs on "All Day, All Night" and likely a few minor issues on some of the other tracks. The album wouldn't be released until the following May, but the track listing and order were finalized. Other compositions would still be considered, but none made the cut. Prince was responsible for approving the final product, but he empowered David Z to take care of any remaining issues. From the start of this project, through the selection of music, until the final product, the journey had been tiring and frustrating, as Jill recalls. "We went through years of trying different things, and sometimes I wonder if [Prince] ran out of steam or he didn't know what to do with me because he couldn't put me in a total composite of 'You're the sexy one. You're the smart one,' you know, these archetypes. But he made sure to give me some of his best songs."[25]

Two C-90 and three C-60 cassettes were dubbed from this session, which ended at 1 a.m.

FRIDAY, NOVEMBER 14, 1986

"**Come Elektra Tuesday**" [extended version, listed as "**Elektra Tuesday**"]
(overdubs, mix, edits)
Sunset Sound, Studio 3 | 4:00 p.m.–11:00 p.m. (booked: lockout)
Producer: Prince | Artist: Jill Jones | Engineer: Coke Johnson

*My name was supposed to be "Electra Assassin," I actually
was like, "Uh no. What's wrong with Jill Jones?" He was
always trying to improve me and make me something else. It
was weird.*

—Jill Jones

Prince worked on an extended mix of "Come Elektra Tuesday" for Jill Jones,
possibly because he was pushing for her to change her name to "Electra." Because the lyrics were drafted from a male perspective, it would require some
rewriting to fit her. "Prince was a big fan of the [Frank Miller-created comic
book character] Elektra and had written a song called 'Come Elektra Tuesday'
that he wanted me to sing," remembered Jill. "His manager Steve Fargnoli came
to my rescue and told Prince I was already established as a singer, so I didn't
have to change my name."[26]

Some of the phrases in the lyrics, such as "Your love is a trip," were already
reflected in songs on her album. Other ideas, like singing about someone behaving like a "dog in heat," would resurface on future songs like the unreleased
"God Is Alive," in 1988.

Three hours were spent on overdubs, and four more on edits and copying
the song to three C-60 cassettes.

SATURDAY, NOVEMBER 15, 1986

"**Cosmic Day**" (tracking, overdubs, and mix)
Sunset Sound, Studio 3 | 2:00 p.m.–8:00 p.m. (booked: lockout)
Producer: Prince | Artist: Prince | Engineers: Susan Rogers and Coke
Johnson

*In my fantasy world, I always live far away from the pub-
lic at large, usually on a mountain, sometimes a cloud,
and even in an underwater cave. (How that was accomplished was never divulged but somehow it worked out).*[27]

—Prince

Expanding on the hallucinatory images of recent songs like "Good Love," last year's *Around The World In A Day*, and seemingly inspired by the Bangles and many of the other Paisley Underground retro bands like the XTC spin-off the Dukes of Stratosphear, Dream Syndicate, and Three O' Clock (who would eventually be signed to Paisley Park Records), Prince combined them all to record one of his more trippy songs to date, "Cosmic Day." But like he always did with other artists he appreciated, he took the influences, twisted them, and created something unique.

Starting at 2 p.m. Prince dove in, quickly building an unapologetically aggressive blend of electronic (Fairlight) and real drums and blanketing the beat with guitars, bass, harp, and multiple keyboard sections, creating either a hard rock song with a pop edge or a pop song that contains a rock edge. Wrapping the composition around a riff that sounds like an accelerated variation of George Harrison's "What Is Life?," Prince launched the track with a guitar slide that approximates a race-car-ignition and doesn't let up on the gas until the screaming-guitar finale. Once again Prince used a "Camille"-like voice, while he sang about mermen in the sky and flying in the deep sea.

The 6-hour shift ended at 8 p.m. with two C-60 cassettes and a single C-90 dubbed of the day's work.

Status: "Cosmic Day" (5:36) was not included on any configurations of *Crystal Ball* or *Sign O' The Times*, and remained on the shelf during Prince's lifetime, but it was released as a digital prerelease single in 2020 for the *Sign O' The Times* Super Deluxe Edition.

Clare Fischer would record his orchestral contributions for the song on December 5, 1986. That version of "Cosmic Day" remains unreleased, although elements from Fischer's work were later used by Prince in 1988 during the *Lovesexy* tour intermission.

SUNDAY, NOVEMBER 16, 1986

"Cosmic Day" (overdubs, mix)
Sunset Sound, Studio 3 | 12:30 p.m.–7:30 p.m. (booked: lockout)
Producer: Prince | Artist: Prince | Engineers: Susan Rogers and Coke
Johnson

> *There is so much great, unreleased material from Prince. We*
> *would work all day and night long, and then he would be up*
> *the next morning ready to do it all over again.*[28]
>
> —Susan Rogers

Another short shift, with Prince doing additional work on "Cosmic Day." By the
end of the session, two C-60 cassettes were dubbed, and Prince left at 7:30 p.m.

MONDAY, NOVEMBER 17, 1986

Untitled Track [probably **"Six And 1/2"**] (edits, mix)
Jam (mix)
Sunset Sound, Studio 3 | 3:00 p.m.–5:30 a.m. (booked: lockout)
Producer: Prince | Artist: Prince | Engineer: Coke Johnson

> *There were many times that he would bring the musicians*
> *down to the studio. Prince would generally start it on his*
> *guitar, just playing a little riff. The bass player would kick in.*
> *That would be the whole groove in the song and the bass would*
> *be so funky. Then, sometimes in a couple of those jam sessions,*
> *we'd have the brass out there, too. And everybody would just*
> *kind of be making it up as they go along. Oh, I recorded some*
> *good jams.*
>
> —Coke Johnson

Prince appears to have revisited the Madhouse track, "Six And 1/2," likely to
add a few overdubs and give it an edit as he prepared for it to be released. A
quick mix was created, and Prince left the studio for 5 hours.

When he returned at 2 a.m., he'd gathered a few other musicians for a 3-and-a-half-hour jam. Sheila and her band were on tour, and the Revolution no longer recorded with him, so it is unclear who was involved with the loose jam session, which was recorded on six C-90 cassettes, but it likely included people he was considering for his new band.

TUESDAY, NOVEMBER 18, 1986

"Six And 1/2" (edits)
Madhouse 8 album (overdubs, possible edits, mix)
Sunset Sound, Studio 3 | 3:00 p.m.–11:00 p.m. (booked: lockout)
Producer: Prince | Artist: Prince | Engineers: Susan Rogers and Coke Johnson

> *Prince was so rich and so deep, as a human being and as an artist. "Prince," as an artist, wasn't even enough to show who this man was. So it made sense to have the character, or the person "Prince" be just an aspect of his personality. And if he had alter egos, he could have multiple personalities, and he can keep writing this music and putting a lot out there. Prince music was just a part of the music of Prince's life. There was also Camille music, and the Time music, and Sheila E. music, and Madhouse music and all these other entities that express him musically.*[29]

—Susan Rogers

Prince continued working on the entire Madhouse 8 project by finishing a few additional edits for "Six And 1/2."

He also garnished the album with a few additional touches of personality. It was likely during this session that Prince added the various nonmusical elements to the collection. The segue between "Six" and "Seven" already contained Vanity's moaning, but Prince also added a few sped-up phone conversations on "Five" between a person named "Jimbo" and his mother, and a phone operator.

Two C-60 and six C-90 cassettes were made of the session.

WEDNESDAY, NOVEMBER 19, 1986

"Adore (Until The End Of Time)" (tracking, overdubs, mix)
Sunset Sound, Studio 3 | unknown time (booked: lockout)
Producer: Prince | Artist: Prince | Engineers: Susan Rogers and Coke
Johnson

*"Adore" represented Prince's conscious effort to write for black
radio in an attempt to counter criticism that he was primarily a pop writer and that his status was diminishing as an
influential R&B artist. I know this because he said so while we
were tracking it.*[30]

—Susan Rogers

Critics often pigeonhole a musician into one or possibly two genres, which
can destroy a career by creating unhealthy expectations for the artist to continue repeating their biggest success. For a performer to cross boundaries
requires dedication, focus, and a commitment to explore, all of which Prince
had. At this point in his career, he had gone through multiple phases. In the
early years, he was embraced for his R&B music, but as he grew as an artist,
his range expanded and he adopted new wave, soul, rock, and pop, but as he
did this, the critics forgot about his base, and many of them focused on Prince
solely as someone who writes catchy pop songs, according to Susan Rogers.
"I think his critics were accurate; Prince was a pop artist, and personally I
think that's high praise. Pop in and of itself is not a style; the pop chart only
reflects the condensed versions of more pure styles (e.g., hip-hop, dance,
country, punk). Prince wrote funk and R&B and arranged these songs in a
popular style."[31]

Susan revealed that Prince found the press's criticism frustrating. "On
'Adore,' Prince was really hurt that R&B and soul radio stations weren't playing him as much as they used to. After *Purple Rain*, R&B radio had kind of
given him up. They liked 'Kiss' and some of his other stuff, but it wasn't the
normal R&B and soul thing you would hear. He wanted that core audience
back. He talked about that. 'Adore' was an attempt to get more R&B radio
play."[32]

After putting together a slow, sexy beat consisting of a blend of real and Linn
LM-1 drums, Prince built a straight-up soul jam with guitar, bass, and a variety

of synths, including the Fairlight, Mirage, and Prophet VS, some of which were used for more specific sounds like the harp and sitar. Although Prince had recently removed the sitar from "Strange Relationship," he still seemed intrigued with what it brought to a song and gave it a prominent role in "Adore."

Prince's lead vocal slides over and around the multiple layers of his slick, choir background vocals, convincing the listener of his heartfelt dedication to his partner. "The organ and vocal arrangements on 'Adore' are purely gospel," observed Rogers. "I am not sure I'd say he considered it one of the most critical songs on the record because it stands alone on *Sign O' The Times*. It's interesting how easily he could adopt the gospel style in his arrangements, but so rarely did."[33]

To adapt his pop sensibilities to include gospel, rock, blues, soul, and so many other genres is a testament to how he translated the complex orchestra that played in his head into an unforgettable song. For a man who'd made so many timeless tracks by this point in his career, the chance for him to keep creating new music that stands the test of time is astonishing, but he did it almost effortlessly.

"['Adore' is] another masterpiece and in Prince's larger legacy, many critics and scholars consider *Purple Rain* and *Sign O' Times* to be two peaks of an intense creative period by an intense creative artist," observed Rogers. "I think it is safe to say that *Purple Rain* and *Sign O' The Times* represent the beginning and the end of an important phase in Prince's life. The phase where he went from being an up-and-comer to being realized as one of the great American artists of our time."[34]

Status: "Adore (Until The End Of Time)" (6:30) was included on *Crystal Ball* by its full title, but when it was attached to *Sign 'O The Times* it was simply listed as "Adore." It was never released as a single, but an edited version of the track (4:39) was part of Prince's *The Hits/The B-Sides* collection in 1993. A live performance appeared on his first concert album, 2002's *One Nite Alone . . . Live!* and the song was also considered for *When 2 R In Love: The Ballads Of Prince*, an unreleased collection of love songs planned for 2000–2001. "Adore" was among the tracks Prince played during the first show on his final night of concerts on April 14, 2016.

In 1992, Prince repurposed the basic tracks from "Adore" for Carmen Electra's "All That." Her song contained several musical updates, and all new lyrics when it was released on her self-titled debut album in 1993.

FRIDAY, NOVEMBER 21, 1986

"**Adore (Until The End Of Time)**" (various overdubs, rough mix)
Sunset Sound, Studio 3 | 1:00 p.m.–8:30 p.m. (booked: lockout)
Producer: Prince | Artist: Prince | Engineers: Susan Rogers and Coke
Johnson

*The most important thing a musician can accomplish is to
share that magic, that energy.*[35]

—Prince

When Prince created music that some might refer to as magical, it was often based on something he felt deeply about, and how it spoke to him. His music reflected his moods, his beliefs, and his heart, but only as much as he wanted to share, according to Susan. "I believe that Prince was a supremely honest lyricist. He told you what he *wanted* you to know about him. It wasn't the *full* truth. Of course, it wasn't the complete picture, but if you listen to his lyrics, he's telling you the truth about himself."[36]

Prince's love songs were often the closest he offered as a window into his emotional side. He still hid, but the reason that his ballads felt so authentic was because they were written by a man who was feeling what he was expressing, and his genius could be found in the level of exposure he *allowed* himself to have in his music. Prince's hint of vulnerability was disarming and for a brief moment, he'd tease the listener into thinking that he was inviting them inside his life, but the window always closed before too much was revealed.

"He was engaged to Susannah Melvoin at that time," explained Susan Rogers. "So it is safe to say that she inspired ['Adore']."[37]

But one of the most intriguing aspects of Prince's writing was his ability to hide things in plain sight, and like many artists, a song may have roots that can be traced to multiple sources, and the interpretation can be seen by those who spent time with him. "Although it was inspired by Susannah, I thought 'This sounds like *my* relationship with him,'" observes Devin Devasquez. "I remembered he played it for me that night. If you look at the lyrics, it says 'All of my cool attitude you took,' and 'We were rapping until the sun came up.' I don't know any other girl that he probably talked to as much as he talked to me on the phone. And he said, 'In a word, you were sex.' *Playboy* represented sex to him."

Prince spent 7 hours overdubbing a variety of instruments to "Adore" and another 30 minutes creating a mix that was recorded to a C-60 cassette. The session ended at 8:30 p.m. Because it was a Friday night, it is probable that he went out dancing after the session.

Socially, Prince would control the situation as much as possible. He was surrounded by bodyguards who would keep Prince from being disturbed, and that wall kept him away from people who might want to hurt him. That was helpful when it came to limiting access to anyone he wanted to avoid, but on any given day, that list could include those who cared for him, remembers Devasquez.

> I remember dancing with him so many times. That's what we did, but all of a sudden everything changed. He was like, "I'm going to go to Tramps tonight and I'll see you in a couple of days" or something like that. And that didn't sit well with me because we were friends for so long. So I'm like, "What do you mean? Where's that coming from?" And I went up to him and he goes, "Devin, there's a side you can't see." Like he realized, and I realized too, we really weren't compatible because he had to be in control. I had grown too much to be the type of girl that's going to be with him and have him be with other girls. And I think he wanted me to remember him being the way we *were*, rather than it being tainted, which I've heard from others that side of him can really wear on a relationship and be hurtful.

SATURDAY, NOVEMBER 22, 1986

"**Feel U Up**" [long stroke] (mix)
"**The Cocoa Boys**" (overdubs, mix)
"**Adore (Until The End Of Time)**" (various overdubs, mix)
"**It's Gonna Be A Beautiful Night**" (various overdubs, mix)
Sunset Sound, Studio 3 | 12:30 p.m.–8:00 p.m. (booked: lockout)
Producer: Prince | Artist: Prince | Engineers: Susan Rogers and Coke Johnson

> *I think he just thought ["It's Gonna Be A Beautiful Night"] was a funky number. Anytime you switch a band over there's going to be some remains. He loved that song. He loved playing it.*[38]
>
> —"Bobby Z" Rivkin

With the Revolution broken up, Prince grabbed what is likely the final "new" song recorded by the entire band, "It's Gonna Be A Beautiful Night," which was tracked during a live performance at Le Zénith in Paris, France, on August 25th. The song was a transitional bridge between his time with the Revolution and the musicians he was considering for the new band. It was co-written by Matt Fink and Eric Leeds and contained work from the entire Revolution, but also from Miko Weaver and Sheila E., so it was a combination of a goodbye to the old and a hello to the new, born during a rare place in time that both existed. Because the song was recorded live, it was a way to share the power behind the Revolution, honor his relationship with the band members, and figuratively give them a final curtain call. But like all things Prince, he had to tweak the song before it was ready.

Before working on "It's Gonna Be A Beautiful Night," Prince reviewed and updated the mixes for a few tracks including "Feel U Up" and "The Cocoa Boys," the latter being given a looped bed of applause (likely from the same concert at Le Zénith). He also recorded additional overdubs for "Adore," which included a vocal reference track for Leeds and Blistan to mimic when they recorded their horns. "I didn't mind that at all," recalls Eric. "Oftentimes that made it easier. All I've got to do is just give him back what he wants."

Prince started embellishing "It's Gonna Be A Beautiful Night," recording piano and several other overdubs. He apparently felt the song needed something additional that he couldn't supply, so he reached out to Leeds and Blistan and asked them to fly immediately to Los Angeles to work on this track and "Adore."

The session ended at 8 p.m. after two C-60 cassettes were created of the work completed during this session.

SUNDAY, NOVEMBER 23, 1986

"**Adore (Until The End Of Time)**" (various overdubs including horns, mix)
"**It's Gonna Be A Beautiful Night**" (various overdubs including horns, rough mix)
Sunset Sound, Studio 3 | 1:30 p.m.–1:00 a.m. (booked: lockout)
Producer: Prince | Artist: Prince | Engineers: Susan Rogers and Coke Johnson

Me and Atlanta Bliss did our parts together at the same time. It was just one day. It was just the Sunday before Thanksgiving, we flew in and out, the same day that Alan talks about in the liner notes to The Hits/The B-Sides.[39]

—Eric Leeds

With Paisley Park still months away from completion, Prince was bouncing between Minneapolis and Los Angeles and because of the uncertainty and turmoil created with the breakup of the Revolution, band members like Eric Leeds and Atlanta Bliss stayed in their homes in Atlanta and commuted to wherever Prince requested. "We knew that Paisley Park was going to be completed in a few months, we knew that we're going to have to move permanently up here," explained Leeds. "So we chose Thanksgiving week of '86 to go down to Atlanta, close up shop down there and we both would move up here."[40]

No sooner did I get back down there to start packing up did Prince call us to LA right away. So on November 23rd we flew in on an early morning flight, got to LA about noon, picked up a car at the airport, and drove right to the studio. We worked fast that day, and we were out of there on the red-eye that night, and back in Atlanta at six the next morning. But that evening we did the horn parts for "Adore" and "It's Gonna Be A Beautiful Night." We overdubbed some more horn parts and put another arrangement on from the track. Six hours we were in and out with all that stuff. We stopped at Canter's Deli on the way to the airport, because we were on the red-eye, and picked up a corned-beef sandwich, and sat on the plane and ate that sandwich going home.[41]

Although the song was originally inspired by a bass line from BrownMark, Prince ended up giving credit to others, remembers Leeds. "Mark didn't get a piece of the song. Me and Fink did and we were the only ones left. And it wasn't anything that either me or Fink would have ever come to Prince and said, 'Hey, you need to give us a piece of that.' He just did it. I think him giving us a piece of that song was his way of saying, 'You guys are still going to be around.'"

Blistan and Leeds recorded their horns for "Adore" from 2 p.m. to 5 p.m., and "It's Gonna Be A Beautiful Night" from 6 p.m. to 9 p.m. After they left, Prince continued to overdub on both tracks, and at the end of the night, a short amount of time was spent mixing and dubbing the songs to a C-60 cassette before ending the session at 1 a.m.

Prince was still looking to complete the sound for both songs, and he'd revisit them over the next week.

"There was some controversy around the credits for 'Adore,'" according to Eric. "This is interesting, because I was certainly credited on the *Sign O' The Times* album, which 'Adore' is from, and on the credits for the *Hits* [*The Hits/The B-Sides*] package, it just says, 'Arranged, composed and performed by Prince, with Atlanta Bliss, trumpet.' It doesn't mention me! I'm on that, buddy!"[42]

MONDAY, NOVEMBER 24, 1986

> **"Adore (Until The End Of Time)"** (overdubs and mix)
> **"Adore (Until The End Of Time)"** [instrumental] (mix)
> Sunset Sound, Studio 3 | 1:00 p.m.–8:00 p.m. (booked: lockout)
> Producer: Prince | Artist: Prince | Engineers: Susan Rogers and Coke Johnson

> *He was not a perfectionist. He was a virtuoso. So what sounds like perfection made by mere mortals, which would be laboriously, painstakingly working on something for a month just to get the tone right. That wasn't Prince. Prince went really fast. So it was hard to believe that someone could play drums that well, play bass that well, keys that well, guitar that well and sing like that! He was an extraordinarily creative human being, which made it look like perfection.*[43]
>
> —Susan Rogers

Prince spent several more hours overdubbing on "Adore" and invited Novi Novog, who had previously worked with him on many songs during the *Purple Rain* era, to add strings to the track from 3 p.m. to 5 p.m. An instrumental of the song was also created, but it was not used for "Adore," although it likely was included in Carmen Electra's "All That." Once Prince was finished working on "Adore," he spent a little time blending the song into the album's assembly.

One C-90 and two C-60 cassettes were created of the session, which ended unusually early at 8 p.m.

During this period, Prince and Susannah were fighting more than normal. As he often did, especially with his more intimate numbers, he used a song as a proxy for an actual apology and when he finished "Adore," it became a way of expressing his feelings about her, as Susannah recalls. "I felt like it was his way of saying, 'I love you so much. I'm not leaving you. It's going to be okay.' I felt it was like an apology song. Some of these songs were love letters to forgive him, because he couldn't say it. He had it in him to do it. He could say it, he just couldn't say it to the people he loved."

TUESDAY, NOVEMBER 25, 1986

Camille [early title of *Crystal Ball*] album (assembly, crossfades, and edits)
"Train" (mix)
Sunset Sound, Studio 3 | 1:00 p.m.–4:00 a.m. (booked: lockout)
Producer: Prince | Artist: Prince | Engineers: Susan Rogers and Coke Johnson

> *It was a funny time to be working with him without Wendy and Lisa. The sorrow of their absence was also felt in the room. The imminent departure of Susannah was coming, because she wasn't happy, and he wasn't happy either. They were engaged to be married, but it became clear to them that it wasn't going to happen.*[44]
>
> —Susan Rogers

Prince's history of relationships can be traced back to his childhood. As a young boy who grew up in multiple homes, it is possible that he realized that his meaning, his purpose, and perhaps even his worth, could be found through music. The subtle courtesies of friendship and personal interaction took a backseat to a world in which the only true harmony he had was in his songs. "When you're a boy, essentially, a boy with no role models and you're having to figure this out, it makes sense to kind of put blinders on to social niceties, and to just move forward in a way that keeps this train running," explained Susan Rogers. "He didn't have time for social interaction, because it would have stripped energy where he needed energy. He needed energy to write songs and to keep this train rolling. And once you figure that out about him, it's easy."[45]

As he had done throughout his career, Prince sought comfort in the quiet solitude of the studio, and using his energy to create, he assembled another version of his latest album. By now the elements that made it onto *Dream Factory*, including the title track, had been placed on the shelf, as Rogers observed. "When we put together the *Dream Factory* record, the Revolution were still together, and so you would put out a record that your band could play on stage and tour with the band. So, it would feature the songs that showed off what your band did well but when that band fell apart the record had to come apart too."[46] This was a new project and a new focus and without a new title, the multidisc album set was simply called "Camille" and "Crystal Ball," oftentimes interchangeably.

When he was assembling the album, it took him some time to settle on the order of the tracks. He and Susan spent a lot of time working on the most powerful three disc collection possible. "It was really fun," remembers Rogers.

And this is one of those times where Prince needed, thankfully for me, a real engineer. He needed somebody who understood how to set up the gain structure such that you had unity gain. I mean, you'd be screwed if the pieces that you cut in came in too loud or too soft. And minimized that crossfade such that the smallest possible piece is going to be a copy so that the maximum piece can be the first generation mix. There you are, cutting up your mixes, so if he changes the sequence at any time, you have to have those original pieces that can all be put back together. Because if you've done this beautiful crossfade between song A and song B and later on he decides, "No, I don't like that order," you've got to redo it.

The album would go through multiple configurations. The earliest version placed the 23 songs in the following order:

Side One:
    "Rebirth Of The Flesh"
    "Housequake"
    "Train"
    "The Ballad of Dorothy Parker"

Side Two:
    "It"
    "Starfish And Coffee"
    "Slow Love"
    "Hot Thing"

Side Three:
  "Crystal Ball"
  "If I Was Your Girlfriend"
  "Rockhard In A Funky Place"
  "Moonbeam Levels"

Side Four:
  "The Ball"
  "Joy In Repetition"
  "Strange Relationship"
  "I Could Never Take The Place Of Your Man"

Side Five:
  "Shockadelica"
  "Good Love"
  "Forever In My Life"
  "Sign O' The Times"

Side Six:
  "The Cross"
  "Adore (Until The End Of Time)"
  "It's Gonna Be A Beautiful Night"

Over the next several days, songs would be reordered, remixed, and removed when they didn't fit Prince's vision. "Train" was given a new mix during this session, but it would eventually be eliminated from the project. The issue of how to finish the album caused "Adore" and "It's Gonna Be A Beautiful Night" to swap positions multiple times. When this project ultimately morphed into *Sign O' The Times*, "Adore" would close out the collection.

The final 5 hours of the session were spent working on the mixes and crossfades for the assembly. Seven C-90 and two C-60 cassettes were dubbed of the day's work, before everything was considered complete at 4 a.m.

WEDNESDAY, NOVEMBER 26, 1986

"It's Gonna Be A Beautiful Night" (various overdubs, mix)
"Play In The Sunshine" [listed as **"The Rap"**] (tracking, overdubs, vocals, mix)
Sunset Sound, Studio 3 | 12:30 p.m.–5:30 a.m. (booked: lockout)
Producer: Prince | Artist: Prince | Engineers: Susan Rogers and Coke Johnson

"Play In The Sunshine" was one of those songs that we knocked off very quickly. Prince did what most people do. When he would conceive of an album there were core songs that were the heart and the skeleton of the album. When we would sequence a record sometimes we'd take our core songs and a few other

tracks and we would sequence them together just to hear how the album was going to sound. If there was something missing, if there needed to be a song that would transition between two of the core or the more important songs, Prince would actually write something specifically to serve in the sequence. So in that sense there were the most important songs and then there were the album cuts–the things that were almost interludes on the record. So the songs were never intended to be singles or even have any important message. That's what "Play In The Sunshine" was.[47]

—Susan Rogers

Most artists would realize that they had a spot on their album that needed a slower groove or a more upbeat jam, and they'd look through their archives for a track or take a week writing a song, bringing in the band, teaching the band, and then mixing the track hoping that it fit. Prince was different from other artists in that he could recognize a need and then quickly create a song on his own to fill the void. When today's session started just after noon, Prince had been reviewing the album assembly for several hours and decided that the album didn't have the proper flow after the first track. He needed a palette cleanser to come between "Rebirth Of The Flesh" and "Housequake."

"When we sequenced the record, we needed a song to go between two of the really important songs," explained Susan Rogers, "so that the sequence would make sense. It was like a tomato on a sandwich. It complemented the meat and cheese."[48]

Although it was listed as "The Rap" on the session notes, there was no rap in "Play In The Sunshine." Perhaps the intention was to include a rap on the song, but the idea was dropped, although it was resurrected later in the shift for "It's Gonna Be A Beautiful Night," with Sheila E.'s contribution to the track.

The session began immediately with Prince laying down his usual blend of real and Linn LM-1 drums, and rapidly followed up with electric and 12-string guitar, bass, handclaps, and a blend of synths, once again using the Ensoniq Mirage, Fairlight, and Prophet VS. A variety of percussion flourishes, including cymbals, hand claps, tambourine, and a gong, filled in the festive song, and after 6 p.m., Prince added his vocals in one of those tracks that you can almost hear him smiling as he sings about having a great time. Susannah was also brought in to add her vocals to "Play In The Sunshine," where she did several layers of background vocals, including a pass of her and Prince singing them together.

They did the same on "It's Gonna Be A Beautiful Night" on this date. Prince was reportedly thrilled with what she contributed to the tracks, so much that he credited her and Jill Jones, who also added her voice to the song during this session, with "co-lead vocals" on "It's Gonna Be A Beautiful Night."

After midnight, Prince wanted to add Sheila performing a rap on "It's Gonna Be A Beautiful Night," but with her out of town on tour, there were a number of technical issues to overcome. It wasn't possible to get her into a recording studio, so it was decided that she'd perform her part over the phone and record it from the phone in Studio 3, as Todd Herreman recalls. "I do remember her phoning it in from the hotel. We were trying to wire the phone into the console so they could get the levels, it wasn't like they just held a mic up to the receiver, they had to jerry rig something so they could get Sheila's voice. So they're playing Sheila the track and she nailed it. I think she was maybe just frustrated because it was hard to hear, it's not like you have headphones on that. But that was fun."

Sheila's rap—referred in the credits on the *Sign O' The Times* album as the "Transmississippirap" because she performed it from her hotel in Cincinnati, Ohio, which is on the other side of the Mississippi River—was from "The Table and the Chair," which was originally written by English poet Edward Lear in 1871. Because the poem was so old, Prince was able to avoid paying any royalties on this release.

The last 3 and a half hours were spent on additional overdubs and a rough mix, which was dubbed to a single C-90 cassette.

Status: "Play In The Sunshine" (5:05) was placed on the current configuration being assembled and made the transition when the project was renamed *Sign O' The Times*.

THURSDAY, NOVEMBER 27, 1986

"Play In The Sunshine" [listed as **"The Rap"**] (various overdubs, mix)
"It's Gonna Be A Beautiful Night" (various overdubs, mix)
Sunset Sound, Studio 3 | 1:00 p.m.–6:30 a.m. (booked: lockout)
Producer: Prince | Artist: Prince | Engineers: Susan Rogers and Coke Johnson | Assistant Engineer: Todd Herreman

He just wanted to come in that morning, just to do a couple of little edits, or some little thing. And I had told my family in Orange County, California, I'm going to be there for Thanksgiving dinner, so wait for me, I just have to do this thing in the morning. And once he got in the studio, we did not emerge.

—Susan Rogers

What drove Prince? Making music appears to have been the core of his existence. Despite how glamorous the gold records and awards seem, it all starts in the studio, and because of Prince's aggressive and unforgiving schedule, there were few times that his engineers were able to relax. "Dinner breaks? I barely remember them," recalled Susan. "If we were in LA we'd order out, I'd eat for a minute in the lounge while he was doing vocals. He'd eat when I was cleaning stuff up or, getting things mixed, and ready. It was a nice spartan existence in a manner of speaking."[49]

Because Prince had demanded to record on Thanksgiving, he had a holiday meal brought in from "Maurice's Snack 'N Chat" soul food during this session. "It dawned on Prince that it was Thanksgiving, so he had the studio bring in this huge Thanksgiving dinner," remembers Herreman. "I'm not sure, I think he felt bad about it."

Susan recalls that the holidays were often treated like any other day, and that required complete dedication to Prince's whims. "The money I was paid was to be on call every day. I had a salary, but it worked like a retainer. I got a weekly paycheck. That one Thanksgiving where we just did a marathon, I remember getting an extra check. There would be a bonus check of $1,500, or $1,000. Just every once in a while, there would be that little bonus. It was his way of saying thanks."

Just 6 hours after the last shift, Prince spent from 1 p.m. to 1 a.m. recording multiple overdubs for "It's Gonna Be A Beautiful Night" and "Play In The Sunshine," but it was likely that he also worked on some of the other tracks in the recent compilation.

The final 5 and a half hours were spent mixing and dubbing the day's work to five C-60 cassettes, before ending the session at 6:30 in the morning.

FRIDAY, NOVEMBER 28, 1986

"**It's Gonna Be A Beautiful Night**" (overdubs, edit, mix)
"**Play In The Sunshine**" (overdubs, edit, mix)
"**Play In The Sunshine**" [instrumental] (overdubs, edit, mix)
Camille [early title of **Crystal Ball**] album (assembly, crossfades, and edits)
Sunset Sound, Studio 3 | 12:30 p.m.–11:00 a.m. (booked: lockout)
Producer: Prince | Artist: Prince | Engineers: Susan Rogers and Coke
 Johnson | Assistant Engineer: Todd Herreman

> *Prince wasn't great at relaxation. He always had so much*
> *stuff on his mind that even eating a meal seemed a waste of*
> *time. As he said in one interview: "Sometimes I can't shut off*
> *my brain, and it hurts. . . . Do I have to eat? I wish I didn't*
> *have to eat!"*[50]
>
> —Sheila E.

Six hours after the last session, Prince was back in the studio, overdubbing "It's Gonna Be A Beautiful Night" and "Play In The Sunshine" and continuing to compile the current three-disc collection, that at different times of the schedule was known as *Camille*, as well as *Crystal Ball*. According to Alan Leeds:

> "Camille" was a pseudonym and there was a point when the album was called *Crystal Ball* and the artist was going to be Camille, not Prince. We were calling this the *Camille* album, but with the understanding that that was not the title of the album, but in fact the artist credit, and the title of the album at varying points was *Crystal Ball*. Camille was the artist credit but it went back and forth between being an album title, and artist credit. There were various combinations thereof, and it changed on a daily basis.[51]

During this 22-and-a-half-hour session, Prince spent almost 17 hours working on overdubs of rain and other sound effects for "Play In The Sunshine." An instrumental of the song was also created. More overdubs were done on "It's Gonna Be A Beautiful Night," and likely a few other songs on this collection. The last 5 hours found Prince and his engineers working on mixing the updated tracks and adjusting the musical flow of the album with crossfades and edits. Two C-60 cassettes were made of the new song mixes, and the session ended at 11 in the morning.

SATURDAY, NOVEMBER 29, 1986

> **"It's Gonna Be A Beautiful Night"** (various overdubs, mix)
> **Camille/Crystal Ball** album (compiled and sequenced)
> Sunset Sound, Studio 3 | 7:30 p.m.–12:00 noon (booked: lockout)
> Producer: Prince | Artist: Prince | Engineers: Susan Rogers and Coke Johnson

> *A workaholic? Shit! He was the little train that could. That's what I called him. He was a firm believer of finishing something that he'd started. He'd be in the studio for like three days then he'll go, and come back. We'll leave the studio at 9:30 a.m., 10 a.m. Then he would go home and he would sleep until around 6 or 7 and then we'd go back in the studio and back at it again.*

—Wally Safford

The 8-hour rest between the last session and this one would be Prince's last gap of time he'd have outside of the studio this month as he was scrambling to get this collection locked down.

Today's session involved additional overdubs and mixes of "It's Gonna Be A Beautiful Night," which was slated for inclusion on this assembly. Having a multiple-disc collection ready for release shortly after announcing the breakup of his band could potentially be an incredible return to form as a solo artist and the optics of having a multiple-disc collection as his first artistic statement was likely intriguing to him, like a phoenix rising from the ashes. In the past, Prince would solicit opinions from those around him, but the times and the stakes had changed, and he was less likely to want to dilute his musical vision. Now that he was no longer working with the Revolution, he may have felt that he had something to prove, according to Alan Leeds.

There certainly have been occasions where he has been steadfastly solid on something. On those occasions he did not solicit any input at all. It was like, "Here's what it is! Don't mess with me, this is it!" For a week or so that was how he was about the 3-LP set. "This is it! It's the perfect work. I need something that's going to create a big stir, because the *Parade* tour didn't create that. *Under The Cherry Moon* wasn't what I wanted it to be, so I gotta come back and make a big bang! Here's the quintessential volume of work. These three really fabulous records! They're going to say, 'My God he's crazy but he pulled it off.'" So I think it was the idea of doing something as outlandish as three records that appealed to him as much as getting all the music out. The publicity that three records would create, I think, was as important to him as the music that was contained on them.[52]

At least five updated mixes were completed by the following morning and dubbed to two C-90 cassettes, but because of the urgency of this project and the herculean effort to create something bigger than anything he'd ever attempted, the shift continued into the next day without a break.

SUNDAY, NOVEMBER 30, 1986

> ***Crystal Ball*** album (compiled and sequenced)
> **"It's Gonna Be A Beautiful Night"** (various overdubs, mix)
> Sunset Sound, Studio 3 | 12:00 noon–9:00 p.m. (booked: lockout)
> Producer: Prince | Artist: Prince | Engineers: Susan Rogers and Coke Johnson

> *This was the record where we needed to get radio back on our side, quit being too cutting edge and too difficult and deliver a fastball down the middle.*[53]
>
> —Alan Leeds

Over the years, Prince would race to finish a project by the end of the month, either based on a self-imposed deadline or one dictated by the record company, so it isn't surprising that the sprint to get it locked down would bleed from yesterday into today's session. From noon to 2:30 p.m., Prince finished creating the final assembly of his current album. The title of the collection was in flux, still bouncing back and forth between *Crystal Ball* and *Camille*, but the final 22-track line up was in place.

Side One:
  "Rebirth Of The Flesh"
  "Play In The Sunshine"
  "Housequake"
  "The Ballad Of Dorothy Parker"

Side Two:
  "It"
  "Starfish And Coffee"
  "Slow Love"
  "Hot Thing"

Side Three:
  "Crystal Ball"
  "If I Was Your Girlfriend"
  "Rockhard In A Funky Place"

Side Four:
  "The Ball"
  "Joy In Repetition"
  "Strange Relationship"
  "I Could Never Take The Place Of Your Man"

Side Five:
  "Shockadelica"
  "Good Love"
  "Forever In My Life"
  "Sign O' The Times"

Side Six:
  "The Cross"
  "It's Gonna Be A Beautiful Night"
  "Adore (Until The End Of Time)"

In many ways, this collection was an extension of the *Camille* album that had been assembled early in the month. Seven of the eight tracks made the transition, ("Feel U Up" was omitted), and the album still began with "Rebirth Of The Flesh," and one of the album sides still closed with "If I Was Your Girlfriend," followed by "Rockhard In A Funky Place." For this collection, "Train" and "Moonbeam Levels" were removed.

Prince left many eligible songs from the last few months on the editing floor including: "In A Large Room With No Light," "It Ain't Over Until The Fat Lady Sings," "The Cocoa Boys," "Crucial," "When The Dawn of The Morning Comes," "Rescue Me," "Baby Go-Go," "Witness 4 The Prosecution," "It Be's Like That Sometimes," and "Emotional Pump." Most of these would be released either on Prince's 1998 *Crystal Ball* set or on the posthumous *Sign O' The Times* Super Deluxe Edition in 2020.

The quality and range of his outtakes exposes the many directions this project could have gone, elevating Prince's status not only as a prolific performer, but as a musician who didn't adhere to the idea of artistic boundaries.

It wouldn't matter if the album was listed as being performed by Camille, or Joey Coco, or any other fictitious or protégé's name he attached to it, there was always a quality that could be identified as being Prince because in many ways, he was creating his own genre. Hard work, dedication, a deep vault of music, and an incredible level of proficiency on almost any instrument would always be his trademarks, no matter how he packaged and labeled it. "He was still Prince, and he was always going to be Prince," reflects Eric Leeds.

It was just the difference between the persona at work versus the persona just *being* the persona. I had a lot of fun with the guy, but there were times when the last thing in the world I wanted to be was around him. But it was all transactional. He was a person that was not comfortable in his own skin. You'd probably have to go back to his childhood I suppose, and just see how he grew up. The relationship he had with his mother. I always laugh and I say the psychiatrists would diagnose him in two minutes. "Oh, I see, you didn't get along with your mother. Okay, now we know what's going on here" and all of that. At this point in time, everything had to be bigger than life for him.

And this album was planned to be his biggest statement yet.

Once Prince was finished with the final album assembly, two C-90 cassettes were dubbed and a tape was sent to Warner Bros. for approval. The final 6 and a half hours were spent packing up all of the tapes and his instruments to be shipped back to Minneapolis. As Todd Herreman remembers, the chaos from this era ended up interrupting the lives of everyone around him. "It was, 'Okay guys, you can go home, Prince wants to go to Paris and take ballet lessons for a couple of weeks.' So, of course I fly back to Chicago to see my girlfriend and soon after I get there it's 'Get back to Minneapolis.' Prince didn't go or Prince flew there to Paris and flew right back, so we didn't have a life of our own, put it that way."

DECEMBER 1986

I remember getting the album and listening to it, or trying to listen to it. Because it was tough, for me anyway. It was just too much. His management, and the record company outside of me, were freaked out about it. I knew what was going on. He was so competitive, and I think Bruce Springsteen had put out this five-album set [Live/1975–85, released on November 10, 1986] *and along comes Prince with a three-album set. And it made me angry because it wasn't tight like his great stuff. It became self-indulgent, I thought.*[1]

—Lenny Waronker

The reaction from Warner Bros. wasn't immediately conveyed to Prince. It appears that once they received the three-disc set, there was some confusion about how to proceed because they reportedly enjoyed some of the tracks, but felt the collection was unreleasable in this form. The battle was coming, but for now, Prince appears to have been traveling, possibly to France. If so, something came up that caused the trip to be abruptly cut short, and he headed back to the United States.

SUNDAY, DECEMBER 7, 1986

"Bob George" (tracking, mix)
"Walkin' In Glory" (tracking, probable overdubs)
"2 Nigs United 4 West Compton" [untitled studio jam with Prince and
  Sheila E.] (tracking)
Sunset Sound, Studio 3 | 1:00 p.m.–12:00 noon (booked: lockout)
Producer: Prince | Artist: Prince | Engineers: Susan Rogers and Coke Johnson

> *I don't understand it. Why do people say it's a reference to me?*
> *I certainly didn't go around with any hookers or buy furs for*
> *women or whatever he was insinuating.*[2]
>
> —Bob Cavallo

Prince was back at Sunset Sound, and he appeared to be in a dark place. It is not known if the label had reached out to him, or if he was waiting for their reply, but it had been a week since his latest project had been sent to them. By this point, Prince ran Paisley Park Records and had the luxury of telling the executives at Warner Bros. what he wanted to release. Unfortunately, with the failure of *Under The Cherry Moon* and the lackluster sales of his last two albums compared to *Purple Rain*, Warner Bros. seemed to not want to rubber stamp his newest project, and even his managers were reportedly not thrilled with the idea of a three-disc set. As he waited for a decision, he went back into the studio to record what was on his mind.

"[Prince] felt that he wasn't getting the push he needed," remembers Susannah. "And 'Bob George' was a direct hit to all those who tried to stop him. That was a persona that he manifested because of how angry he was, that his creativity was being thwarted so I remember a lot going on at this time and he wasn't in the best of spirits. 'Bob George' was such a specific 'fuck you' song."

"We had been working really, really hard," recalled Susan Rogers, "and Prince was tired of doing serious songs, so Sheila E. had a birthday coming up [on December 12], and we just stopped for a little while to do some fun stuff to play at Sheila's birthday party."[3]

Prince recorded a blended beat of the Linn LM-1 and real snare and kick drums, and over that, he kept it sparse, using only his guitar and a mix of synths including the Mirage, Prophet VS, Yamaha DX7, and the Fairlight, which not only supplied the ARR1 patch from the Human1 drive, but also many of the sound effects used.

It is uncertain if the dark tone of the music guided Prince's vocals, or if his vocals were planned and the groove was created to support it. Regardless of the order of conception, the table had been set for another alter-ego to narrate the story of a man who was unhappy with his live-in girlfriend and her infidelity with Prince's fictional, gold-toothed manager, Bob George. "'Bob George' was inspired by two people," explained Rogers. "One was Bob Cavallo, Prince's manager and the other was Nelson George the music critic and scholar. Nelson George had kind of criticized Prince in the press recently saying, 'Well he's not as good as he used to be.' And Bob Cavallo was giving Prince some grief over something or other. So Prince decided to write a song about this character who is a disgruntled loner who was going to go shoot up the parking lot or something like that because he's so upset."[4]

Work on "Bob George" wrapped at 10:30 p.m. At this point, the song wasn't as dark or as sparse, and used his Camille voice or at least a Camille-like vocal for the main character. Everything was played for comic effect, even referring to Prince as "that skinny motherfucker with a high voice."[5] The line, "Don't you know that I could kill you now" actually came from Richard Pryor's 1977 comedy *Which Way Is Up?*

Sheila E. had been on the road opening for Lionel Richie's massively successful 40-city tour to promote his recent number 1 album, *Dancing on the Ceiling*, and it was scheduled to play for multiple nights in the Los Angeles area. At some point after Prince recorded "Bob George," Sheila joined him in the studio playing drums while he played bass. It is likely that he recorded a few overdubs on the track as well. Similar to what he did in October with "Violet Blue" and "It Be's Like That Sometimes," the music that they recorded inspired Prince to create two songs, "2 Nigs United 4 West Compton," which at this time was simply an untitled jam, and a gospel-styled track called "Walkin' In Glory," one of what Susan referred to as a "Sunday song" because of the spiritual overtones.

> Prince's two main themes were God and sex. I often noticed that he would write a song about God after an incident that I supposed he may have been feeling a little bit guilty about. So after a breakup, maybe with someone like Susannah or Jill, or after fighting there would be the God song. That's kind of how his psyche worked, is when he would do the nasty stuff, it would be followed up with, "And I'm sorry God, here I've got a song for you." But when he would do just the nasty stuff, I think he was afraid of having offended God and he'd do a God song.

Using many of the same drums and other elements that he did on what would become "2 Nigs United 4 West Compton," Prince added guitar, bass, and once again used the Leslie cabinet to lay out an upbeat celebratory tune about someone who had recently died, recognizing that they are now walking in glory with the Lord. It is interesting that the two tracks recorded on this date, "Bob George" and "Walkin' In Glory," deal with before and after death experience, but it is unclear if Prince connected those dots or if it can be attributed to coincidence. The tone of "Walkin' In Glory" was radically different from that of his earlier track, exposing how in just a few hours Prince could change the direction of his sound and how dexterous he was at making that leap between genres.

Very rough mixes were completed of the day's tracks and three C-60 cassettes were dubbed. The 23-hour session continued past noon on December 8.

Status: A longer version of "Bob George" would eventually be edited (5:37) and find a home on Prince's *Black Album*, which was officially released in 1994.

The studio jam of Prince and Sheila would eventually be released as "2 Nigs United 4 West Compton," on *The Black Album,* as well.

"Walkin' in Glory" (5:44) remained unreleased until 2020, when it was part of the *Sign O' The Times* Super Deluxe Edition.

MONDAY, DECEMBER 8, 1986

"**Walkin' In Glory**" (overdubs, mix)
"**Girls & Boys**" [live from Le Zénith in Paris, August 25, 1986] (probable mix)
Sunset Sound, Studio 3 | 12:00 noon–2:30 p.m. (booked: lockout)
Producer: Prince | Artist: Prince | Engineers: Susan Rogers and Coke Johnson

Religion, when used properly, actually is like a health regimen. And they're finding now that people who have faith live longer. I mean, it says so in the book. That's what it's supposed to be. You ain't supposed to die.[6]

—Prince

These 2 and a half hours of work were a continuation of the previous session, which included more work on "Walkin' In Glory" and possibly making safety copies or additional mixes of other recent songs, or the live version of "Girls

& Boys" from the Paris performance on August 25, 1986. It was likely being considered as a B-side for an upcoming single or for Sheila E.'s party.

The two day, 25-and-a-half-hour session ended early, probably so Prince could rest before attending Sheila's performance.

TUESDAY, DECEMBER 9, 1986

"Bob George" (various overdubs, mix, edits)
"2 Nigs United 4 West Compton" (various overdubs, mix, edits)
"Walkin' In Glory" (mix)
Jill Jones album (likely album review)
Sunset Sound, Studio 3 | 10:00 a.m.–2:30 a.m. (booked: lockout)
Producer: Prince | Artist: Prince/Camille | Engineers: Susan Rogers and
    Coke Johnson

> *Prince called me and he goes, "I don't have a title for a song." I said, "Okay, '2 Nigs United 4 West Compton'" or whatever it was, and he goes, "Okay, that sounds good."*[7]

> —Sheila E.

Prince scheduled an early session at 10 a.m., but he let Susan Rogers know that he was not going to be in until later, which gave her time to clean up some of the recent mixes. "My work [with him] in the mobile trucks and at rehearsal allowed him to hear that I had learned his ear. That's what he taught me," explains Susan. "Eventually he could say, 'I'm coming into the studio, put up this song, get a mix on it and I'll come in and we'll work on it' and the more time I had in the studio, the closer I could get it to what the finished mix was to be."

Prince went out of his way to try new elements in his music and art and that inspired those around him to experiment. Sometimes Prince wouldn't like the new direction, but on the times that he felt the song was better after the mix, he was vocal about his praise, according to Rogers. "I really loved pitch change devices and there was the Eventide Harmonizer that everyone used. But I would sometimes tweak those settings for his session just because I wanted to experiment and I wanted something different, but on a bigger level. The Publison Infernal machine would do incredible pitch change. And one day he was out, and I was playing around with 'Bob George.' I ran it through the infernal machine and pitch changed the vocal down a whole octave and he came back in and heard it and loved it."[8]

"He sounded like he weighed 300 pounds and was 55 years old. It was so funny," laughed Susan. "That was the version that we kept."[9]

The speed of the entire song was altered as well, and the overall effect and the deeper pitch vocals gave the song a dark, angry element and was another way to disguise Prince's voice.

For the other side of a telephone conversation the main character had with Bob George during the song, Prince repeated a sample of a voice saying, "Yes, operator. What city please?" This element was previously used on Madhouse "Five" and duplicated in various pitches, sometimes overlapping for comical effect, which blended well with the absurd, over-the-top violence that was the backbone of the song.

After 1 p.m., additional percussion, including an updated snare drum and claps, were added to the mix for "Bob George." He then sat down to expand the jam he'd worked on with Sheila the previous day and had that part incorporated into "Walkin' in Glory," mixing and editing it as a stand-alone song, which was eventually named "2 Nigs United 4 West Compton," a title suggested by Sheila.

Prince spent 90 minutes working on the first mix of the track, which featured Sheila on drums and whistle but didn't include the title chant at the beginning and end of the song. Four additional hours were spent updating the mix on "Walkin' In Glory" and editing several of his recent tracks.

At 10:30 p.m., Prince turned his focus to Jill Jones's album. It is unclear if he was listening to the assembly they'd recently created with plans to send it to Bernie Grundman for mastering or reviewing the Grundman master if it had already been completed.

Three C-60 cassettes were created from today's work and the session ended at 2:30 in the morning.

WEDNESDAY, DECEMBER 10, 1986

"**Le Grind**" (tracking, mix, and edit)
"**Girls & Boys**" [live from Le Zénith in Paris, August 25, 1986] (mix)
"**Bob George**" (mix)
Sunset Sound, Studio 3 | 1:00 p.m.–4:30 a.m. (booked: lockout)
Producer: Prince | Artist: Prince | Engineers: Susan Rogers and Coke Johnson

[Prince] called me, and he came to one of my shows. He told me he wanted to work with me. I'm not exactly in the same fashion modus operandi. But it was nice to be working with another singer and guitarist. He relates to women's energy really well.[10]

—Bonnie Raitt

Prince continued working on songs for Sheila's upcoming birthday party. Additional mixes of "Bob George" and the live version of "Girls & Boys" were completed. He also spent a few hours laying down the basic tracks for "Le Grind," including drums, guitar, piano, and elements from the Fairlight. Prince recorded a vocal track for the song, and likely inspired by the previous day's work on "Bob George," he'd ultimately add a pitch adjusted intro to the song in a similar deep voice. That section was likely recorded the following year. Eric Leeds and Atlanta Bliss eventually added their horns to the song on October 18, 1987.

In a session that likely took place when he returned to Minneapolis just over a week later, Susannah Melvoin would add background vocals to "Le Grind."

"I remember Sheila singing on it, and when I listen to it now," reflects Melvoin. "I know I hear a different singer in there and I think Boni Boyer is on it as well. I remember singing the most simple backing tracks on that. Not like the back and forth stuff that he was doing with Sheila. I'm singing on it, but I'm not on the whole song. Just very specific parts."

Prince and Susannah worked together in the studio beautifully, but unfortunately with the issues that they were going through in their personal lives during this time, her vocal sessions with Prince later in December would likely be her final studio session with him. "We had a very prolific creative life together, and a very, very, very extraordinary love affair—one that I don't know could ever have sustained," she reflected in 2020. "But during this particular period of time with him we did extraordinary work and we had extraordinary love together."[11]

In the early evening, Prince left the studio for a few hours to attend a Bonnie Raitt concert at the Beverly Theater. He eventually reached out to her about working together and set up a meeting, as Raitt explained. "He was renting a place in LA, and he sent his private limo over to pick me up. I don't ride around in limos much, and this car had all kinds of neat stuff—all kinds of purple stuff and neat lighting and little porcelain masks. I didn't realize I'd be whisked away in a fairy tale! We got to know each other a little bit, and he told me he was starting a new record label and was interested in having me on it. I told him I was interested if it was a true collaboration and not just me singing his music—if we could meet somewhere in the middle."[12]

The date of their meeting is unclear, but in late January, Prince would begin re-recording some of his older songs for her, including "I Need A Man," "There's Something I Like About Being Your Fool," "Jealous Girl," and "Promise To Be True."

The final 3 hours of this session involved additional mixing of "Le Grind," "Bob George," and the live version of "Girls & Boys," which were all dubbed to three C-60 cassettes.

Status: A longer version of "Le Grind" remains unreleased, but the edited track (6:44) was updated and included as the lead song on *The Black Album* in 1994.

THURSDAY, DECEMBER 11, 1986

Prince threw a party for Sheila E.'s 29th birthday at a Los Angeles club called Vertigo. For the party, Prince debuted several of his recent tracks, including "Bob George," "2 Nigs United 4 West Compton," and "Le Grind." He also joined Sheila to perform with members of her band as well as Herbie Hancock. Sheila's position as Prince's protégée had been solid, but earlier in the fall when she was working on her third solo album, she had spoken to Prince about wanting a change. "I was performing with my band, opening for Lionel Richie at the time," explained Sheila. "I told Prince, his management and everyone else that I was tired of being a solo artist. I wanted to take a break. I just wanted to play as a musician and not have the responsibility of being a solo artist, because I had hit a wall. I just wanted to stop for a while, go play some other music and just play drums and percussion. So he said, 'Oh, okay. Well, I'm gonna disband my band, so you wanna come play with me?' And I was like, 'Oh, cool.'"[13]

"When he disbanded the Revolution, he decided to bring Sheila, myself and the late great Boni Boyer, who's also from the bay and he put us three in the new band," explained Levi Seacer Jr. "That's how that happened."[14]

Sheila noted:

I've never been in his band before. I've done some songs with him in some of his shows, but only as a guest. I'm more comfortable being in the background, playing behind someone. I can play drums and percussion and not have to worry about carrying a show. There's incredible pressure on a solo artist. You don't have that kind of pressure as a background player. I just need a break from it.[15]

Like Prince had done with the Revolution, Sheila would soon disband her own band, with many of the members being shifted to Prince's new, unnamed group, and another cluster starting their own band: Tony! Toni! Toné! For now, Sheila had to continue with Lionel Richie for the final shows of his tour, including a concert at the Los Angeles Forum the following night.

FRIDAY, DECEMBER 12, 1986

"Six" [Single version] (edits)
Sunset Sound, Studio 3 | 2:00 p.m.–8:00 p.m. (booked: lockout)
Producer: Prince | Artist: Madhouse | Engineers: Susan Rogers and Coke Johnson

Additional work was completed on the single release of "Six" for Madhouse. If Prince attended the session, it was likely cut short so he could attend the Lionel Richie concert at the Forum to watch Sheila E. perform.

SATURDAY, DECEMBER 13, 1986

Untitled Track (tracking, mix)
Sunset Sound, Studio 3 | 2:00 p.m.–10:00 p.m. (booked: lockout)
Producer: Prince | Artist: Prince | Engineer: Susan Rogers

> Electrifying Mojo: *"What's a day like in the life of Prince?"*
> Prince: *"**Work. I work a lot. I'm trying to get a lot of things done very quickly, so I can stop working for a while.**"*[16]

Prince spent 8 hours recording at least one unknown song. No details about the track could be located, but it is likely that he also compiled another collection of songs, likely another copy of *Crystal Ball* or Jill Jones's album because the shift ended with two C-60 and four C-90 cassettes being dubbed.

WEDNESDAY, DECEMBER 17, 1986

"Telepathy" (mix, edits)
Sunset Sound, Studio 3 | 1:00 p.m.–2:30 a.m. (booked: lockout)
Producer: Prince | Artist: Prince (Deborah Allen scratched out) | Engineers:
Susan Rogers and Coke Johnson

> *On songs for other people, he went through faster, and with
> fewer revisions with less soul searching. The only time he's
> going to put in that serious effort to really drill down and do
> the work of original thought and pushing his own artistry, it's
> going to be for his own stuff, and stuff where he wants to show
> you something about himself. That's where he's going to take
> his time.*

—Susan Rogers

Prince generally spent more time on his own songs, but that rule was not always perfect, details Rogers. "The noteworthy footnote to that is the two Prince songs that sold the most [that were planned for other artists], I believe were 'Kiss' and 'Nothing Compares 2 U.' As those were both songs that we just sped through. He wasn't necessarily aware of what his best work was, which makes us realize that the stuff that he didn't think was that great, is stuff that might be on some level comparable to 'Kiss' and 'Nothing Compares 2 U.'"

The year 1986 was one of change for Prince, and at the start of this day, he was still waiting for a decision about his three-disc collection that he'd submitted to Warner Bros., and he was preparing to wrap up his time in Los Angeles. Prince's father spent the previous day working on some song demos. After he finished, Prince's gear was packed for travel, and at 6 in the morning, everything was gathered into trucks and shipped to Minneapolis, leaving Prince in the studio without his workout equipment and many of his instruments. But he still wanted to work, so at 1 p.m., he arrived in the studio with Susan Rogers to mix and edit "Telepathy," likely to give to Deborah Allen.

At the end of the 13-and-a-half-hour session, two C-60 and two C-90 cassettes were dubbed. Prince would have been heading back home, but Warner Bros. reached out to him, and everything changed.

While in discussions with Warner Bros., they were absolutely unwilling to release a three-record set, because it would've been too expensive to manufacture and the profit margin wouldn't have been as high. I can say from personal observation that Prince was unhappy about that decision. He wanted that three-record set, and push was coming to shove at that point.[17]

—Susan Rogers

To Prince, having his artistic vision questioned by people he felt weren't artists, but who unfortunately had the power to shape his career and dilute his musical statements, was frustrating. Warner CEO Mo Ostin described how he and the other executives felt about what Prince had submitted. "It came in as a three-album set, and then after living with it, we decided that if he eliminated some things we didn't think were as strong, we would have a much better album."[18]

Warner Bros. had no interest in a three-disc set and wanted it cut back to a single LP. The confusion around this was just as difficult for everyone in Prince's inner circle as well, according to Alan Leeds. "A lot of meetings, a lot of loud hollering, a lot of frustration. There's a point where management has to defend the artist even when they don't believe in defending it. It was one of those classic situations where the management says to the artist: 'I really don't think this is right,' but then has to go to the record label and behave as if it is. It was very ugly."[19]

Prince's managers, Bob Cavallo, Steve Fargnoli, and Joe Ruffalo, met with Ostin and fellow Warner Bros. executive Lenny Waronker to discuss how to convince Prince to make a product they felt was releasable. "There's no way you're gonna get him to condense and chop up all of that work and put it into one album," Waronker stated. "And as a matter of fact, if it was a double album it would be great. He's got all the stuff. It just needs to be digestible."

"So they looked at me and said, 'You're right. You gotta tell him. So I said, 'Alright, I'll do it, but I wanna do it *my* way. I don't wanna go to the studio.' Once I get in the studio he can really hustle you. He was just fantastic when he did that, and I'd lose it. I just said, 'No, I wanna figure out a way of doing it on my own turf.' I said, 'Give me until three o'clock tomorrow.'"[20]

Prince was aware of that day's meeting and demanded to know the direction, so by that evening Fargnoli told Prince, and the decisions being made about *Crystal Ball* (or as it would eventually be called *Sign O' The Times*) frustrated Prince. **"I delivered three CDs for *Sign O' The Times*. Because the people at Warner were tired, they came up with reasons why I should be tired too. I don't know if it's their place to talk me into or out of things."**[21] Prince would later say: "**These are the same people who would tell Mozart he writes too many notes, or that *Citizen Kane* is a long movie.**"[22]

That night, Waronker phoned Prince in the studio. The line was picked up immediately and after a brief pause, Waronker recalls that Prince said, "'I hear you don't like my album,' which was typical of him. And I said, 'Who told you that? It's not true. The truth is I think the album could be great, but I think it's long. It could be tighter.' He thought a second and he said, 'You know what, I'm going home to Minneapolis,' and hung up. So I thought, 'Aw, Jesus, not again. Lost the battle.'"[23]

It appears that Prince traveled home, did some recording on "Le Grind" and possibly some other tracks in his home studio, and turned around fairly quickly to come back to Los Angeles. Prince took a new look at the project and returned to Sunset Sound with a renewed focus. "[Prince] regrouped and he came up with a perspective and vision for his next album," recalled Susan Rogers. "It was darker in tone than the *Parade* record and much darker in tone than *Around the World in a Day*. I'd say even darker in tone than his *Purple Rain* record, because this time he was talking about world affairs."[24]

SUNDAY, DECEMBER 21, 1986

"**U Got The Look**" [listed as "**The Look**"] (tracking, mix, copy)
Sunset Sound, Studio 3 | 6:00 p.m.–12:00 noon (booked: lockout)
Producer: Prince | Artist: Prince | Engineers: Coke Johnson and Susan Rogers

> *When you listen to "U Got The Look"—the line "your body's heck-a-slamming"—that's because I used to say "hecka" all the time. It's an Oakland thing. We would just trade back and forth—your body's "hecka" slammin'—he's like, "Oh, I'll put that in the song!" There was a lot of that.*[25]
>
> —Sheila E.

December 21 is winter solstice, the darkest day of the year. In many ways, it was Prince's as well, as he was dealing with the news that Warner Bros. had rejected his vision, putting a stop to the project that he felt would be the proper follow-up to *Parade* and *Under The Cherry Moon*. And like the parallels with winter solstice, the days that followed would gradually become brighter, revealing more light, and the eventual healing and renewal of spring.

After being told to trim his music back from 22 tracks to 16, Prince decided to rebel and instead scheduled studio time to record *new* music for the collection. He'd make any decisions about what to eliminate later, but today would be spent creating and not destroying.

The session began at 6 p.m., with Prince laying down the basic tracks for the song, but instead of him playing drums, Sheila E. was invited to participate. She'd just wrapped up her tour with Lionel Richie in Oakland the previous day and returned to Los Angeles, likely to work with Prince on a new song called "The Look," which would ultimately be retitled, "U Got The Look."

It is unclear if he rented new instruments or had his own brought back to Sunset Sound, but Prince made sure he had everything necessary to create the latest song for this collection. "U Got The Look" starts with the same Prophet VS patch [69: Filmusic] that he used for the beginning of "The Cocoa Boys" and in the end of Madhouse "Eight." Sheila's drums would abruptly interrupt the smooth synth sound and launch the slow grooved track. He'd layer it with multiple guitars, bass, and keyboards over the next several hours, but something about it wasn't landing for him, so he continued shaping it. He added the same Fairlight banjo sound he'd used in October on "Rescue Me," and he even tried whistling through the entire song, but he didn't seem to be happy with the results when they worked on the mix. "Mixing is kind of like an arrangement," explained Susan.

> Our mixing process was concurrent with the recording process, unless there was a problem. If there was a problem, we spent a lot of time mixing it. If it wasn't coming together, the song would probably end up in the vault. In the case of "U Got The Look," the song was too good to go in the vault. He started to change things. I remember changing the speed on "U Got The Look" and totally redoing it. At some point, we made it much slower, and at another point, we made it much faster, until we got the final groove that he was happy with.[26]

Prince decided he was content with the mix and a single C-60 cassette was dubbed during the 18-hour session, which usually meant the end of the day, but for this track, Prince continued into the next afternoon.

Status: "U Got The Look" would be sped up over the next several days as the track would eventually find the proper speed and tone before it was edited

(3:48) and included as the lead track for the second disc of *Sign O' The Times*. It would be the final song recorded for the album.

A 12-inch version released as "U Got The Look (Long Look)" (6:45) was created using much of the longer recording as well as some additional material tracked the following year.

MONDAY, DECEMBER 22, 1986

"U Got The Look" [listed as "The Look"] (instrumental mix)
"U Got The Look" [listed as "The Look"] (overdubs, mix)
Sunset Sound, Studio 3 | 1:00 p.m.–12:00 noon (booked: lockout)
Producer: Prince | Artist: Prince | Engineers: Susan Rogers and Coke Johnson

> *He was constantly thinking. His well of creativity was so deep that he didn't run out of ideas. Typical musicians, they'll get two, three, four original ideas, and that's a good day in the studio. Prince would get a whole song done in a day. A whole song. And those days were long, with being 20 hours, 24 hours often. There were many, many 48-hour days, where we worked two days in a row because he had two songs in a row. He'd finish one and then another one would come to him. For example: on "U Got The Look," we spent like three days on that song. A long time.*[27]

—Susan Rogers

Recording studios are generally built without windows, so there is no reference to the time of day, the weather or any other influence from the outside world. Studio 3 at Sunset Sound was even more secluded with a self-contained bathroom and a lounge to eat and nap, so it was possible to not have a reason to venture outside of the studio womb for extended periods of time, according to Rogers. "I remember, at one point, looking at my watch and I thought it said nine o'clock. I wondered if it was nine o'clock in the morning or nine o'clock at night. When I was staring at my watch, I noticed it was upside down, so then I wondered if it was three o'clock in the morning or three o'clock in the afternoon."[28]

This never ending session continued into the next day after a short lunch break. From 1 p.m. to 2:30 p.m., a cassette was dubbed of the day's work, for Prince to review. He returned to the studio at 6 p.m. with lyrics and a direction for the song.

The fleshed out lyrics referenced "Good Love" and "Crucial," two songs that were reportedly being purged from his recent collections. For the next 18 hours, Prince added his vocals, additional percussion, and more keyboards looking for the proper arrangement and sounds which were eluding him. "Once he bumped it up to dance tempo, much of the instrumentation changed," reflected Rogers. "The hook is really strong. Perfect pop material."[29]

This session also included Prince and Susan shuffling through the original 22 songs and deciding what could be removed and how the remaining tracks fit together and the story that he wanted to tell. Six C-60 cassettes were dubbed, probably of an updated structure of the new album, but it still wasn't complete. An essential part of that framework would be "U Got The Look," which was likely the final puzzle piece for his new collection, but so far it wasn't fitting as tightly as he hoped. The tempo was right, but it needed another element that he couldn't supply, but he knew who could bring that to the song.

TUESDAY, DECEMBER 23, 1986

"**U Got The Look**" (additional overdubs, mix)
Sign O' The Times album (edits, compilation, sequencing, and copies)
Sunset Sound, Studio 3 | 12:00 noon–9:45 p.m. (booked: lockout)
Producer: Prince | Artist: Prince | Engineers: Susan Rogers and Coke Johnson

> *Occasionally he'd ask if I wanted to come in and listen to stuff. That's how we did "U Got The Look." "U Got the Look" was a track he'd basically finished for himself. It was just a Prince track. He said, "Do you want to just come in and sing some backup vocals on the choruses?" So I went into the studio.*[30]
>
> —Sheena Easton

In 1983, Sheena Easton had recorded the Prince-penned top ten song, "Sugar Walls," and more recently, the still unreleased "Eternity." "I didn't know him as well as people would make it out to be," Easton explained in 2012. "People thought, 'Sheena Easton and Prince—they must be having an affair.' But I did know him well enough to know he loved to write and produce. He's very prolific."[31]

Easton dropped by Sunset Sound to say hello to Prince, and although he was not in a great mood, he welcomed her in and invited her to participate in the session. "'[Prince] didn't feel like socializing," according to Rogers. "'U Got The Look' had gone through a million changes and he was really struggling with it. It was originally a mid-tempo thing, but he had sped it up at the last minute and asked her to sing on it. I think she was a little taken aback by the sexual nature of it at first, but he convinced her to get into it, and it worked perfectly."[32]

"He is one of my favorite producers that I have ever worked with," revealed Easton. "There have been two or three producers in my life that I have credited to helping me grow as an artist. He is one of those people that go in the studio, and he doesn't give you time to over learn or over prepare."[33]

"The thing I remember most about Sheena's visit was that when Prince asked her if she'd like to take a minute and warm up vocally, she replied that she was always warm vocally," recalled Susan Rogers. "For most singers this is a hollow boast, but it was true in her case. She has an excellent voice and did the vocals very quickly."[34]

Easton added background vocals to the track, and because Prince gave her no directions, she just sang where she felt the song needed her voice, according to her. "Because I didn't know I was singing against him, I was all over the place—and he said he kind of liked that, so he expanded it into a duet."[35]

With her voice added to the song, Prince recognized that the track now had the missing element. He overdubbed a few extra details and mixed the track properly and began reluctantly accepting that he'd lost this battle and that time wasn't on his side if he wanted to get something to the marketplace. By 9:45 that evening, they'd edited and sequenced the collection, which would now be called *Sign O' The Times*, named after the song that had been a deeper part of both the *Dream Factory* and *Crystal Ball* collections. Susan Rogers recalls:

> When you're doing a record, you decide which of the songs you've recently written, or which of the songs to be written are going to anchor that record, and form the kernel of the record. The song "Sign O' The Times" was the anchor point for that record. Other songs then complemented that and completed that view. *Sign O' The Times* was Prince's recognition, I think, of a number of things. This is when the Revolution is now broken up. So now Sheila is joining him, Bobby Z was leaving, Wendy and Lisa are gone. He's changed his color scheme. It's now peach and black. Peach was Susannah Melvoin's favorite color. He adopted that color, I think, in honor of her.[36]

The assembly likely went through multiple changes over the course of the last two days, likely including the addition of sound effects to the beginning of "If I Was Your Girlfriend," but the final configuration of the two disc set appears to have included:

Side One:
"Sign O' The Times"
"Play In The Sunshine"
"Housequake"
"The Ballad Of Dorothy Parker"

Side Two:
"It"
"Starfish And Coffee"
"Slow Love"
"Hot Thing"
"Forever In My Life"

Side Three:
"U Got The Look"
"If I Was Your Girlfriend"
"Strange Relationship"
"I Could Never Take The Place Of Your Man"

Side Four:
"The Cross"
"It's Gonna Be A Beautiful Night"
"Adore"

To make room for these 16 songs, "Rebirth Of The Flesh," "Crystal Ball," "Rockhard In A Funky Place," "The Ball," "Joy In Repetition," "Shockadelica," and "Good Love" were omitted from the *Crystal Ball* collection. Sides one and two remained with few changes, the exceptions included "Sign O' The Times" replacing "Rebirth Of The Flesh" on side one and "Forever In My Life" being added to side two. Side three was a collection of leftover songs and the new track "U Got The Look," and side four remained intact.

By moving "Sign O' The Times" to the status of title and lead track (as well as eventual first single and opening track for the album's tour), Prince gave the collection a weight that eluded both *Dream Factory* and *Crystal Ball*. With the album now whittled down to two discs, the song was no longer competing against other tracks for attention, allowing it to be recognized as a powerful introduction, acknowledged Eric Leeds. "Prince finally conceded that it was, even for him, biting off a little bit much, so he took off the songs which he didn't think would work in the context of a two-album set. Then, realizing that 'Crystal Ball' wasn't going to be there any longer, 'Sign O' The Times' became the focal point and the most appropriate project title. So it's interesting, because what became the focal point of the whole concept of that album, up until a month before, was really just another song on that album."[37]

Like Marvin Gaye blended the poetic and the political with his song, "What's Going On," "Sign O' The Times" contains Prince's own reflections on society, and similar to Gaye, the solution he offers to solve the problems of the world are to focus on love and the relationships of the heart. With the exception of "The Cross," Prince doesn't try to match the weight of the title track and instead relies on a variety of topics including sex, joy, relationships, and what some people refer to as "experimental" songs. **"What people were saying about *Sign O' The Times* was there are some great songs on it, and there are some experiments on it. I hate the word experiment—it sounds like something you didn't finish. Well, they have to understand that's the way to have a double record and make it interesting."**[38]

Although the Revolution is only mentioned in passing (with the exception of "It's Gonna Be A Beautiful Night") and the overwhelming contributions of Wendy Melvoin and Lisa Coleman are minimalized, the album is an acknowledgement about his relationship with Wendy's sister Susannah, as she either sang on or influenced more than half of the songs, including his most heartfelt love songs on the album "Forever In My Life," "Adore," and "If I Was Your Girlfriend." The Melvoin twins and Lisa's presence are felt through the entire collection.

Seven C-90 cassettes were dubbed of the updated collection.

The stakes were high for this new assembly. *"Sign O' The Times* was an important record because *Purple Rain* had gone through the roof and *Around the World in a Day* did quite well, and *Under the Cherry Moon* didn't do what Prince wanted it to do, and there had been a backlash in the black media particularly," remembered Alan Leeds.[39]

Susan Rogers agrees. "That was a difficult time for him, where his behavior was different. What would he be? What was he going to be? And that's, I think, what he was wrestling with. What he was going to be? It resulted in a masterpiece. It resulted in *Sign O' The Times.* But it was a lot of pressure. That pressure created the diamond. His childhood created *Purple Rain,* the pressure of his life created *Purple Rain,* but the pressure of his legacy created *Sign O' The Times."*

The executives at Warner Bros. were not aware that Prince had decided to revisit the album, and Lenny Waronker reached out to Bob Cavallo to explain that the record company had created their own version of the album. "I said, 'Bob, I need to have my day in court with him. We've got the album—*our* version of the album.'"[40]

Cavallo responded that Prince had already reworked the album, sequenced the 16 tracks and it was ready to deliver. "There were two or three songs that were different," remembered Lenny, "but the difference was no big deal. And

I said, 'We don't have a problem. Let him have his way in this case, because they're really close calls; you can't get hurt.' So that was *Sign O' The Times*."[41]

Tapes of the new album were sent to Warner Bros. for consideration, but because of the holidays, complete approval would probably not happen until after the start of the new year, and it was likely that the order would still be shuffled into January.

WEDNESDAY, DECEMBER 24, 1986

"Rebirth of the Flesh" (edits)
Sunset Sound, Studio 3 | 9:30 a.m.–1:00 p.m. (booked: lockout)
Producer: Prince | Artist: Prince | Engineer: Susan Rogers

> *Susan Rogers is absolutely amazing. She's one of the people who could stay right there with Prince. I've had conversations with her about that and she was so in love with getting to work for Prince that she would do anything.*
>
> —Todd Herreman

Prince demanded a lot from those around him, especially at times of crisis and the events of the outside world had little influence on Prince's schedule. So once again, Prince worked on the holidays, and once more Susan Rogers was there. During this short Christmas Eve session, Prince had Susan work on an edit for still been considered for *Sign O' The Times* or a B-side. Instead of feeling frustrated, Rogers largely maintained that she enjoyed almost every session with him, and in fact learned a lot from his dedication to his art.

> Self-discipline . . . he had plenty of that. The guts that he needed to be who he was. To sacrifice a personal life, meaning a quiet, intimate one like most people have. To be a star requires great sacrifice from the person. There's so much of everyday life that you give up. There's so much of your humanity that you must give up. He had the courage to work when he was sick. When he was sad. When he was tired. When he didn't feel like it. When he was confused. When he didn't know what to do. When he was unsure of himself. He always showed up. And he showed leadership. From other people I learned how to be a record producer. But from Prince, the biggest thing I learned was courage.[42]

It was rarely easy, and it was grueling work and often the only thanks given to those around him were that they remained in his circle. He preferred to work alone, so by most appearances he didn't seem to need anyone else, but the truth behind that image was that if he felt he could depend on you, he did.

THURSDAY, DECEMBER 25, 1986

After Prince's brief trip to Minneapolis, Susannah Melvoin recalls that she'd reached her breaking point. "He left and I was there alone. I remember having my mom fly out to Minneapolis, and she helped me pack my apartment to leave. As much as I love him, this is not the life that I see for myself being locked up. And I knew he was unfaithful and I knew that that was going to be my life and also being kept away from my family and my twin sister. I was just like, I can't do this anymore. I can't be alone."

It is unlikely that Prince returned to Minneapolis for the holiday, but no matter where he went, the woman he loved and very likely the people who had been closest to him were with their families, and Prince was alone, married to his music.

"He was a little bit sad," says Rogers. "It was clear in the years I was with him that he didn't have plans for Christmas, that he didn't have anywhere to be, and that he didn't have a notion of how to celebrate it. Most people that would be in his position would maybe plan on having a party and people over to the house or whatever. None of that was in effect with Prince, despite how religious he was. So Christmas was a little bit sad. He kind of wished it wasn't a holiday, because you could tell he just wanted to work."

FRIDAY, DECEMBER 26, 1986

"Ponyride" (tracking, mix)
Sunset Sound, Studio 3 | 12:30 p.m.–6:00 p.m. (booked: lockout)
Producer: Prince | Artist: Prince | Engineer: Susan Rogers | Assistant
   Engineer: Stephen Shelton

> *It's hard to hear this music played complete in my head*
> *and not be able to get it out. If I don't get it out, it won't ex-*
> *ist on earth. I can't ignore what I hear in my head.*[43]

—Prince

With the edited version of *Sign O' The Times* delivered, now he was waiting, and Prince was not one to sit idle while time passed, so he found himself in the studio working on new music. Possibly inspired by an unreleased lyric he'd removed from "U Got The Look" ("He offers her gold in return for a horsey-back ride."[43]), Prince created a new song, "Ponyride."

Little is known about the track, but it was likely an instrumental, at least on this date. Additional work may have been done on his *Sign O' The Times* collection with songs like "Good Love" and "Rebirth Of The Flesh" possibly still under consideration. Eleven C-90 cassettes were made of any updated configuration. Another C-60 cassette was created of "Ponyride."

Prince continued to work on his music, but underneath all of that, he was not dealing with the emotions of the last few months musically, as Susan Rogers reflects. "I was wondering when the sorrow song was going to come because after the Revolution broke up, I *knew* he was sad and we're doing all this dance stuff like 'Housequake' and those songs for Sheila's birthday party, '2 Nigs United 4 West Compton,' and all that fun, funky stuff. I'm just thinking, dude. When are you going to tell me the truth?"

Status: "Ponyride" remained unreleased during Prince's lifetime.

"I'm very stubborn, real bullheaded," Prince described himself in 1986. **"If I want something, I really fight for it. If I really believe in it."**[44] Prince was taking that fight to Warner Bros., but also into his personal life, according to Susannah.

He was coming by with Gilbert in the limousine, and Gilbert would come down and say, "Can you please just come back right now, just get your things, just come back." I mean, this happened like five times. "Please come back, please, he needs you back. Please, whatever we need to do." And I would say, "I'm not doing it, I'm not leaving." I remember the one time sitting in the limousine with [Prince] and looking at him. He was bereft. "You'd better come home." I'm like, "Home? I don't even live with you. I don't want to go to Minneapolis and be alone in an apartment. Sorry, I can't do that anymore." He was like, "It'll be different." "Like hell it won't." And that's when he flew back to Minneapolis and wrote "Wally."

SUNDAY, DECEMBER 28, 1986

> **"Wally"** [first version] (tracking, overdubs, mix)
> Galpin Blvd. home studio (Chanhassen, Minnesota)
> Producer: Prince | Artist: Prince | Engineer: Susan Rogers

> *That song is part of a conversation we had. He sponged all the*
> *stuff around him and put it into his songs.*
>
> —Wally Safford

Prince was in a holding pattern and at a low point. His relationship with Susannah Melvoin was over. Although they continued to be in each other's orbit for years and Prince would seek her out for comfort in a way that only she could provide, their engagement was over and her heart was gone. The consistency and stability that she brought to him was no longer a guarantee.

"I know he was depressed immediately after that," observes Eric Leeds. "I do think that there was a component to his relationship with Susannah which ran deeper for him than maybe anyone else that I know. But it was still that inability for him to really relate to her as a person, beyond what he wanted her to be. That was beyond him with *anybody*, particularly with someone that was going to be romantically involved in."

Professionally he was also in a tailspin. He had dissolved his road-tested band, and instead of being able to make an artistic expression about his new freedom, his relationship with his record company had soured. The man who'd just two years earlier changed the musical landscape with *Purple Rain* was now having his music declined by his record label. He wasn't calling the shots and for someone like Prince, that could be devastating. He'd capitulated and reduced his most recent album from three discs to two and was now waiting for word to see if they'd approve it, and Prince wasn't someone who waited for anyone. Even his dream studio was still incomplete. It would be months before Paisley Park was ready, so there was little in his life that he could count on. Everything was in flux, and when Prince was lost, he would often look inward. "There was a level of vulnerability which he would not approach," explained Susan Rogers. "He would show the world the 'Prince' character that he created. He could be humble and he could be vulnerable and he could be a baby as the Prince character, this mythic figure that he had created, but as for who he really was deep in his heart, he seldom got that honest."[45]

"Wally" was based on a piano demo called "Babyless," which had Prince singing about his baby leaving him brokenhearted and alone, and he appears to have combined it with elements from a jam he'd performed years earlier about Billy Sparks and his outrageous glasses. He'd recorded this first sketch of the song on his own outside the studio, likely in his living room. Rogers recalls how demos like that were often made. "He was using a boombox, it was small, portable, and had built-in microphones. You put in a cassette, you could hit play and record and he could ideate onto those things. Unfortunately, the quality would have been shit."

Taking the theme and musical pattern of that, he sat down at the piano and let his heart pour out the pain of being alone, told through a conversation he was having with a friend, as Susan recalled.

> This song was a piano ballad. He played this beautiful song, it starts with spoken word and him speaking to Wally. He's talking about wanting to go out in the evening and he compliments Wally on his glasses and he goes, "Can I try them on? I'm going to a party tonight and I want to look good. I want to go out tonight." And there was a melody playing, there was a ballad going on underneath, and he's speaking over the top and then he goes into a chorus and it's a beautiful melody and he's repeating the words, "Oh my la dee da, oh my la dee da" and it's a play on words, because it's "Oh my mel-o-dy" and it's also like "Oh my malady," my sickness. Oh my la dee da . . . and it breaks down, it's a crescendo, the song gets huge, he layers the backing vocals and piano gets really big, it breaks down and he says to Wally, "No you can have your glasses back, I'm not going out." He's saying the reason I want to go out is I just broke up with someone and I want to see if I can meet someone new.[46]

"I thought it was the greatest thing he had ever done and it would slice through you with its capacity to express real strong truth. I had waited years to hear a Prince song like this. I ached for him to be this honest. But no one ever got to hear it but me."

> We spend the whole day doing this song. And at the end of the day he had me make him a cassette as I recall. And then he said, now erase it. I almost never ever contradicted him or stood up to him, but not on my watch. We're not erasing beautiful art like that. And I said, "No, no, don't do it. Don't do it. Don't do it. No, just sleep on it. Don't. I'll erase it tomorrow. If you still insist but please, please get some sleep, please." And he said, "If you don't, I will." And I remember where I was standing, and he started putting all the tracks in record and I believe it was Prince who pressed the record button—that I don't remember whether it was him or me—but I remember that the song was erased and I drove home thinking there's only a cassette of that song.[47]

"He didn't want it heard," recognizes Susan. "He just wanted to say it."

In Prince's world, he was almost always able to will something into existence. His music, his performances, and his relationships were all there because he visualized it, and it happened. But when things didn't go his way, he'd move on. For instance, years later when he was asked about the divorce with his wife Mayte, he responded: "**We pretend it didn't even happen. Like a lot of things in life I don't like, I pretend it isn't there and it goes away.**"[48] This was a life-long pattern for him, and once again there were real people and half-completed projects left in his wake, but for this single song, he didn't want any evidence remaining of his vulnerability.

Susannah recognized what Prince was doing by erasing it. "He was saying, 'I will *never* be that vulnerable again. I can't handle it.'"

Prince had revealed too much of himself so instead of permitting the world to witness his lowest point, he deleted this version of "Wally" at the end of the shift.

Status: The entire 24-track recording of "Wally" (5:08) was completely erased and the SA-60 TDK cassette that was created of the song had not been found as of this publishing.

The song would be re-recorded the following day.

> *I'm goin' to a party, and if I don't find somebody, some-body will find me.*[49]
>
> —lyrics to "Wally"

Prince was in limbo. While he was waiting for Warner Bros. to approve his latest shuffle of what he considered his masterpiece, and with New Year's Eve just around the corner, he decided to put together a party and he gave his assistant Karen Krattinger only a few days to arrange this. Considering that he'd often asked for more in less time, this was arguably a minor request, although an important part was the guest list, which included Levi Seacer Jr., Boni Boyer, Cat Glover, Eric Leeds, Matt Blistan, Sheila E., Wally Safford, Greg Brooks, Matt Fink, and Miko Weaver among others. This would be the first gathering of what would become his new band.

A great deal of thought had gone into staffing the band, although he'd recently been looking to bring back another former member of the Revolution, as his bassist BrownMark recalled. "He's like, 'Come back. Let's do *Sign O' The Times* together. I want you in that band. Sheila E.'s gonna be on drums and we're gonna put Levi on guitar.' So he had this whole new vision. But at that point I was done. I said, 'Man, it's like you taught me. You gotta blaze new trails. It's time for me to try to find something else to make me happy, because I'm no longer happy doing this. This is your thing, Prince. No hard feelings. You keep doing what you're doing. You're a genius. Let me find *my* way.' And he was cool with that."[50]

The decision was made. Levi would play bass and Miko Weaver would remain on guitar.

MONDAY, DECEMBER 29, 1986

"**Wally**" [version 2] (tracking, mix)
Galpin Blvd. home studio (Chanhassen, Minnesota) | late evening
Producer: Prince | Artist: Prince | Engineer: Susan Rogers

> *What am I gonna do? She was the only one in the whole world that I could talk to.*[51]
>
> —lyrics for "Wally"

Because Prince didn't do many interviews, his songs became his journal and when they are put to tape, they tell his story, hiding it in plain sight. Erasing a song is like erasing a written page, giving him a chance to rewrite his history in a way that salvages the idea but ignores his truth. Within a day, Prince decided that the version of his story he'd recorded, and erased the night before needed to be told differently, so he went back to work, updating "Wally," choosing to reveal less of himself in the process. He was both figuratively and physically erasing his past and starting over, taking control of his own narrative in a way that made him less vulnerable, keeping him safe, but denying his deep pain.

Starting in the evening, Prince built the song back up from scratch with real drums, piano, bass, guitar, and a combination of Mirage and Fairlight synths. He may have sung similar words, but the lack of direct access he'd provided to his heart was evident. "The lyrics are the same," recognized Susan Rogers who was once again the only other person in the room with Prince. "It's a little bit more braggadocious. It's a little bit more alpha male. It's not the painful one that I heard. Some of the same instrumentation is on there, but it's not the same version."[52]

Prince did allow a possible peek into his sadness, or more likely the sadness of the *character* singing the track, when he sang, "If I don't find somebody, somebody will find me,"[53] which could be interpreted as both a hopeful sign that someone special would find him at the party, or a very dark view of the main character taking his own life, and being found by someone. With no clue to what Prince intended to express, no definitive explanation can be given. But it should be noted that Prince had a history of using suicide for dramatic effect in other songs in his catalog, including: "Papa," the unreleased "Wednesday," and "Others Here With Us." Suicide was also a theme in the scripts for *Purple Rain* and *Graffiti Bridge*.

As the evening progressed, he asked Eric Leeds and Atlanta Bliss, who had been away for the holidays, to add their horns from 11 p.m. on the December 29, until 2 in the morning. Prince worked on several mixes of the track, and at the end of the shift he dubbed them to cassette, but on this date, he decided *not* to erase the 24-track tape with the updated song.

Status: The re-recorded version of "Wally" (4:45) was released in 2020 on the *Sign O' The Times* Super Deluxe Edition.

WEDNESDAY, DECEMBER 31, 1986

Washington Avenue Warehouse (Edina, Minnesota)

> *We had a New Year's Eve party. It was just an in-house party for basically the crew and maybe some friends from the Minneapolis area.*
>
> —Eric Leeds

Prince gathered everyone around him for a send-off to the old year. His plans had formed and everyone who was a part of his immediate future was in attendance, including Levi Seacer Jr., Boni Boyer, Eric Leeds, Matt Blistan, Sheila E., Wally Safford, Greg Brooks, Matt Fink, Miko Weaver, and Cat Glover, who had never performed with Prince. "Cat had just gotten there," remembers Eric.

"I recall going up to her and saying, 'Hey, welcome to the party' and we were starting rehearsals a couple days after that.'"

Rehearsals with Prince's new band were scheduled to begin on January 2, 1987, at the Washington Avenue warehouse.

The tools he'd mastered when he was young and felt abandoned had once again worked, but his walls of self-defense were now potentially keeping out the bad *and* the good. He'd closed off his past and those who were in it, and focused on working alone once again, creating music with complete autonomy for the first time in years. His successes would be all his, but his failures no longer had anyone to blame, not that he ever really could. He was always the decider, always the face, always the strength, always the captain, and always the last man standing. Every decision he made drove that home, but for the first time in a long time, being alone wasn't his choice. Part of that control belonged to someone else when Susannah had removed herself from the situation, essentially out Prince-ing Prince.

The new band would remain unnamed, possibly because he respected the legacy of the Revolution and didn't want to just bring new people to replace those who left, but another possibility is that he didn't want to allow a new band to form an iconic identity like the Revolution, who argued with him and in many ways shared the spotlight. The new band was undeniably talented and filled with personalities that remain significant and justifiably celebrated in Prince's legacy, but he decided to create a band with no name allowing him to be Prince, solo artist on stage and on record. Instead of creating a band like the Revolution, he made an amazing new show that sold fun and energy with a new look, new sound, new direction, and new music. Prince, as always, was the ringleader and in complete charge, no matter who shared the stage with him. The spotlight was back to shining on him. In a year filled with dramatic change, that would remain constant.

"He was not gonna rehash anything he had done," observes Susannah. "He may add on to something that he's done from the past, but he would never redo the past."

"Prince was a person who was completely and utterly alone," recognizes Eric Leeds. "No matter how many people he might have had around him, he was alone always. And that's how he wanted it."

EPILOGUE

*Prince was human. He was an extraordinary human. But I
don't like to hear Prince talked about as if he were some sort
of special being. No, no, no. That's not as interesting. The
interesting story is the true story. This was a man who worked
really, really, really hard to accomplish something. And he did.
And he deserves credit for what he accomplished. He deserves
credit for being a mere mortal. This was not a magic trick.
This was a guy.*[1]

—Susan Rogers

Life isn't about perfection, it's about emotion, desire, and purpose, and one of
the qualities that helps you remember other people is how they made you feel.
Prince made us feel powerful, happy, and filled with joy. He gave us a reason
to shake our asses. But despite the collective bliss that his music brought, many
around him noted that he went through brief periods of withdrawal and sadness. This was not about being lonely, it was about being alone and listening
to himself away from the interruptions of the world. This self-imposed solitude
often caused a wave of introspection, giving birth to an intimate connection with
his fans that was the thread through his musical legacy. He gave until his tank
was empty, and in the process, he showed us how to treat those without, but
also that we should look to others and listen to what they truly needed because
sometimes the people who seem like they have it all hide their pain from the
world so perfectly that all that remains are their carefully orchestrated illusions.

Despite Prince's incredible generosity and charity, at his core he always played "winner-take-all" both professionally and personally. His upbringing had taught him to rely on himself and avoid getting too close to others, and his circle of control was not only being tested, it was in doubt. He worked hard to get what he had. His talents were obvious because he practiced and played and lived music, to the point that it cost him dearly. It has been stated by many around him that Prince was married to his music. This is true, but what is more accurate is that he *was* music, and even though he was possibly the most gifted performer of his generation, he had once again risked it all with a trust in himself that refused to play it safe. Whether it was by choice or by chance, he could no longer rely on his inner circle that read his mind, and his tastes were shifting, as they always did. A new band, a new direction, a new look, and hopefully, a new love. He was taking back the control he felt he'd ceded.

It was time to hit rewind and take it from the top.

For many, his time with the Revolution feels incomplete, as if they hadn't finished all that they wanted to say and do, but the truth is that Prince felt that he had communicated everything necessary and he closed the door on this period. Because of that decision, his artistic legacy contains both fully realized music and musical exercises that he didn't release but may shed light on him as an artist and inspire a new generation of musicians. "If you found Picasso's doodle pad of just some scribbles, you'd still be fascinated by it," explained Lisa Coleman. "There's every hour taped, whether it's videotape or cassette, whatever. I know there are great recordings in there of the band writing songs, and then Prince coming in. Sometimes, he'd come in with an idea or song for another band, such as 'A Love Bizarre,' where he'd be playing and then the band would join in and by the end of the day, the song would be written. So on those kinds of tapes, where you hear that and hear each of us come in, I love that stuff—and I know there's plenty of those kinds of things in there."[2]

"Prince wasn't just a musician/artist/songwriter—whatever," explained Roy Bennett. "He was an incredible entertainer. He knew how to move an audience. He knew how to play with their heads and their emotions. I learned a lot from him. A lot of what we did was that people always want what they can't have, and he knew that. That's how he lived his life. That's why he didn't do a lot of interviews. He knew how to be a rock star/pop star. I was always of the same mindset, because of the people I idolized at that time. It was like I only knew enough to continually be drawn to them, but I didn't know everything."[3]

To that end, the art that Prince made is essential for telling his story, and as the hidden treasures of his music are revealed, so is his character and his personality, which in the long run enhances the man and his artistic genius. "Prince wanted to be remembered as an important artist," explained Susan Rogers. "He wanted to be known as one. He didn't want to be known as a man. He didn't want to be known as a mere mortal, as a human being, as what he actually was. And all of us who worked for him or knew him, we respected that, so we didn't talk about him as a human, because it's not what he wanted. This wasn't some weird twisted ego. This was the protection that he needed to be able to work. He needed a barrier between his own psyche and the work he did and the only thing he wanted people to see was the work he did."[4]

Prince himself agreed that the historical focus shouldn't be on him as a person, but instead on his art. When *The Guardian* newspaper asked him: How would you like to be remembered? His answer was simple. "**Music.**"[5]

It is difficult to separate the man from his music, especially someone like Prince who considered his music to be an extension of him. Prince was an "all-in" type of performer. From the clothes, the look, the photography, the lighting, and of course, his music, he was committed to each period and each persona, but at the end of each period, he'd always move on to the next new stage. Perhaps he did that because his music was such an intimate part of him and by revealing the contents of his music, we'd peek behind the curtain into the contents of his soul because he gave so much of himself in his art. Record, release, tour, move on. Repeat. Maybe that was how he chose to stay one step ahead of everyone, and it is also why his music should be studied.

This is why it is important for those who knew him to speak out about his work habits, his consistent love of not only playing, but sharing his music, his charitable work, his humor, and the aspects of the man that were hinted about, but only exposed to those he let stand with him. These are the people who can reveal how they all worked together to help nurture his dream and what they loved about him and ultimately, what they lost. "I had the privilege of watching the evolution of one of the most talented and influential pop stars ever," reflected Alan Leeds. "In such a heady atmosphere, it was inevitable that Prince would grow, the company would grow, things would become more complicated, and relationships would change. All of that happened, usually for the better. But I've always wondered if there was any tiny part of Prince that ever yearned for those exciting simpler years."[6]

The world will never know if Prince missed those years and the innocence of his youth. From his interviews, he boldly proclaimed that he was a better musician, but was he happier overall? Sadly, the full story will never be revealed because the full story never happened. What we do know is that by the end of 1986, Prince had set the artistic bar so high that it was practically impossible to reach again. But he embraced a challenge and was resolute to blaze a new path and do what few thought was possible. He was prepared to release what many consider his masterwork. An album of heartbreak, loss, and vulnerability, but he was fighting to have it heard.

For many in his audience, they were used to the way it was. Sometimes when he moved on, it took a little time for them to catch up, but most of them accepted this as part of the whole experience. The members of his band who were gone were familiar faces and voices that were comfortable and reliable. BrownMark's rumbling bass was the perfect complement to Bobby Z's solid heartbeat drumming, Wendy's soulful and seamless rhythm, and the way Lisa blew her hair out of her own face when we *shouldn't* have been noticing were all part of experiencing Prince and the Revolution, but this was the end of an era, and the start of a new one that contained the hopeful promise for more of that undefinable, but undeniable genius. Often in life, you never see the ending coming, and when it does it is understandable to want to cling tightly, holding it for one last heartfelt hug, trusting that the person behind that goodbye will help build a bridge to the next phase. Prince had once again found a way to do that, but at this moment in time, no one else could see that. The secret that is still being revealed decades later was that hidden in that well-designed maze of distraction and deflection was a man who had once led a revolution, but was now healing and searching for renewal, rebirth, and redemption.

Prince knew that expectations were high for his next move . . . but that is a story for another book.

NOTE ON RESEARCH

When creating a complex puzzle like this book, I relied on as much evidence from the actual sessions as possible. Sunset Sound (and multiple other locations) supplied their daily work orders for Prince's studio sessions (as well as those for all of his protégé projects). There are a few sessions that are missing, but when there was doubt, I've tried to fill in the blanks with the information supplied to me in 2011 by Warner Bros. about the contents of their archive based on their dating system. When there was no specific date mentioned in the research from those sources, I relied on data from the Library of Congress, personal logs of those who worked on the music, newspaper articles, session notes from multiple unions, and various other sources, including dates for Clare Fischer's sessions that were supplied by Clare, his son/collaborator Brent, and Arne Frager, who engineered many of those recordings. For those sessions that couldn't be confirmed, I listed the most probable date as an "estimate." I did the same when there was no indication of who worked on the sessions and referred to those who may have been involved as "likely" if the information was assumed. Personal details were filled in using quotes from the people who were in the recording studio with Prince during the sessions.

I've gone to great lengths to confirm the running times to any tracks mentioned. The timings for the released songs were relatively easy to confirm, but the unreleased tracks and alternate versions were more problematic. Some of these are ballpark figures supported by information from the research, but many of them were verified by actually listening to the songs from private collections whenever possible. Please understand that any sources that exist were over thirty years old, and tape speed, drift, and wear may cause the timing to be off by a few seconds. There are also additional edits and mixes that I was not able to locate. I've mentioned them whenever possible.

The quotes used in this book were obtained by me, unless otherwise noted. My personal research involved several hundred hours of on-the-record interviews with the people involved, and I am extremely grateful to those who have opened up and shared their memories with me. I've tried my best to honor each and every one of them by fact-checking and verifying as much as I could. My intent has been to create a fair and nuanced account of everyone's involvement with Prince and their recollections about Prince's history, and I've relied on the information thoughtfully provided by each of them. I also conducted brief follow-up interviews whenever possible to check the facts as additional information was unearthed. When the subjects weren't available, I relied on the extensive library of interviews in the public record, including more than two thousand articles, multiple books, radio shows and numerous podcasts from around the world. For the interviews I conducted for this project, I generally refer to the conversations in the present tense ("She remembers"), and quotes I use from outside sources are referred to in the past tense ("She remembered").

Dates were also obtained through PrinceVault.com, which is THE premiere fan-based source of information and research about all things Prince. I owe them a huge debt of gratitude for their tireless work. If you are fan, check them out. You'll easily spend hours discovering the details that they've uncovered.

Additional information was supplied by Per Nilsen and Alan Freed, who conducted hundreds of hours of interviews that were used in *Uptown* magazine and Per's books. Their contributions to this project cannot be overstated, and I am eternally grateful.

NOTES

PREFACE

1. Prince, lyrics to "The Ladder," performed by Prince and the Revolution, *Around The World In A Day*, Paisley Park Records/Warner Bros., 25286, 1985, compact disc.

2. Eric Clapton, "Desert Island Discs," BBC, September 10, 1989, https://www.bbc.co.uk/sounds/play/p009mdm4.

3. Bruce Springsteen interview with Brian Hiatt, "Bruce Springsteen Talks Steel Mill, 'Human Touch,' What Prince Taught Him," *Rolling Stone* magazine, October 17, 2016, accessed March 16, 2019, https://www.rollingstone.com/music/music-features/bruce-springsteen-talks-steel-mill-human-touch-what-prince-taught-him-126267/.

4. Prince, interviewed by Neal Karlen, "Prince Talks: The Silence Is Broken," *Rolling Stone* magazine, September 12, 1985, https://www.rollingstone.com/music/music-news/prince-talks-the-silence-is-broken-58812/.

5. Susan Rogers, "Headphone Highlights—Dr Susan Rogers: Songs Prince Listened to—2nd May 2017," *Red Bull Radio*, May 2, 2017, accessed May 17, 2017, https://www.mixcloud.com/thepurplestream/headphone-highlights-susan-rogers-songs-prince-listened-to-2nd-may-2017/.

6. Prince, 57th Annual Grammy Awards, February 8, 2015, https://www.grammy.com/grammys/videos/prince-albums-still-matter.

JANUARY 1985

1. Prince, interviewed by Chris Heath, "The Man Who Would Be Prince," *Details* magazine, November 1991, https://www.gq.com/story/prince-interview-inside-paisley-park.

2. "Bobby Z" Rivkin, "The *Sirius/XM* Volume Town Hall Series featuring The Revolution with Mark Goodman and Alan Light," *Sirius/XM*, May 1, 2017, taped live May 1, 2017.

3. Mark Brown "BrownMark," interview by Raul Amador, "Interview with Bassist BrownMark," *Bass Musician* magazine, July 3, 2017, accessed April 25, 2018, https://bassmusicianmagazine.com/2017/07/interview-bassist-brownmark/.

4. Prince, by Hans-Maarten Post, "Prince 'Ik Word steeds beter,'" *Het Nieuwsblad*, June 24, 2010.

5. Matt Fink, interview by A. D. Amorosi, "Fly by Night," *Wax Poetics*, 67 (2018), 51.

6. Lisa Coleman, interview by Ian Wade, "After the Rain," *Classic Pop* (October 2018), 41–43.

7. Lisa Coleman, interview by Lily Moayeri, "The Revolution's Wendy and Lisa Remember Prince, the Human Being," *LA Weekly*, June 19, 2017, accessed February 28, 2019, https://www.laweekly.com/the-revolutions-wendy-and-lisa-remember-prince-the-human-being/.

8. Lisa Coleman, interview by Larry Williams, "Girls & Boys," *Mojo* magazine (September 2018), 61.

9. Wendy Melvoin, interview by A. D. Amorosi, "Agents of Change," *Wax Poetics*, 67 (2018), 47.

10. Mark Brown "BrownMark," interview by A. D. Amorosi, "Agents of Change," *Wax Poetics*, 67 (2018), 47.

11. Prince, interview by Robyne Robinson, "Prince—KMSP TV Interview [1998]," KMSP, May 15, 2016, https://www.youtube.com/watch?v=XoW9DYGcN8c.

12. Marva Collins, interview by Charley Crespo, "Prince: Intimate Relations," *Rock & Soul Magazine*, August 1986, 17.

13. Susan Rogers, interview by Alan Freed for *Uptown* magazine/Per Nilsen, Los Angeles, CA, August 4, 1997.

14. Alan Leeds, "Hunting for Prince's Vault With Mobeen Azhar," BBC video, March 21, 2015, https://www.mixcloud.com/Emancipatio/hunting-for-princes-vault-bbc-documentary-by-mobeen-azhar-march-2015/.

15. Susan Rogers, interview by Alan Freed for *Uptown* magazine/Per Nilsen, Los Angeles, CA, December 1994.

16. Susan Rogers, interview by Troy L. Foreman, *PC Principle* podcast, May 18, 2016, http://thepcprinciple.com/?p=9145.

17. Sheila E., interview by Miles Marshall Lewis, "Sheila E. Opens Up About What It Was Really Like Creating Timeless Music With Prince," *Essence.com*, July 14, 2017, accessed May 7, 2018, www.essence.com/celebrity/sheila-e-talks-working-with-prince.

18. Sheila E., interview by Dennis Hunt, "Sheila E. Wants to Shed Her Sexpot Rep," *LA Times*, November 15, 1987, accessed December 15, 2018, http://articles.latimes.com/1987-11-15/entertainment/ca-20670_1_play-drums.

19. Rogers, interview by Freed, August 4, 1997.

20. Sheila E., interview by Questlove, "Questlove Supreme, Episode 62," *Pandora*, December 13, 2017, accessed December 20, 2017, https://www.pandora.com/station/play/3642532478040643917.

21. Sheila E., "Sheila E. Talks New Album and Her Relationship With Prince, Says It Began and Ended With Music," *The Insider*, posted on YouTube September 7, 2017, accessed March 11, 2018, https://www.youtube.com/watch?v=f-OVlrbFTeM.

22. Matt Fink, interview by Keith Murphy, "'Purple Rain' Turns 30: The Revolution's Dr. Fink Breaks Down Prince's Classic Track-By-Track," *Vibe.com*, June 25, 2014, https://www.vibe.com/gallery/purple-rain-turns-30-revolutions-dr-fink-breaks-down-princes-classic-track-track/dr-fink-breaks-down-prince-purple-rain-track-by-track-10/.

23. Bo Emerson, "From Prelude To Encore, His Royal Badness Reigns," *The Atlanta Journal Constitution*, January 1985 (reposted on April 16, 2016), https://www.ajc.com/entertainment/music/from-prelude-encore-his-royal-badness-reigns/r4FCAOWpHepOB2LukTMyhJ/.

24. Sheila E., *The Beat of My Own Drum: A Memoir*, Atria Books, Kindle Edition, 242–43.

25. Susannah Melvoin, interview by Touré, "Susannah Melvoin: On Loving and Almost Marrying Prince," *Touré Show*, Episode 14, February 14, 2018, accessed February 27, 2018, https://podtail.com/podcast/toure-show/susannah-melvoin-on-loving-and-almost-marrying-pri/.

26. Prince, lyrics for "Sister Fate," performed by Sheila E., *Romance 1600*, Paisley Park Records/Warner Bros., 9-25317, 1985, compact disc.

27. Sheila E., interview by Dirk Jan Roeleven, "Top 2000 a gogo–Sheila E. Love Bizarre," *Pimhawinkels*, December 26, 2016, accessed February 14, 2017, https://www.youtube.com/watch?v=mysxij_2Tsc.

28. Sheila E., *The Beat of My Own Drum*, Kindle Locations 2727–32.

29. Lisa Coleman, interview by Kevin Ritchie, "The Revolution's Lisa Coleman Talks Prince's Legacy and Grieving Through Music," *NowToronto.com*, May 12, 2017, accessed May 4, 2019, https://nowtoronto.com/music/features/the-revolution-lisa-coleman/.

30. Susan Rogers, interview by Ben Beaumont-Thomas, "Prince's Sound Engineer, Susan Rogers: 'He needed to be the alpha male to get things done,'" *The Guardian*, November 13, 2017, accessed November 23, 2017, https://www.theguardian.com/music/2017/nov/09/princes-sound-engineer-susan-rogers-he-needed-to-be-the-alpha-male-to-get-things-done.

31. Beaumont-Thomas, "Prince's Sound Engineer, Susan Rogers."

32. Lisa Coleman, interviewed by Michael Hann, "How We Made Prince's Purple Rain," *The Guardian*, July 28, 2017, accessed November 23, 2017, https://www.theguardian.com/music/2017/jul/24/how-we-made-princes-purple-rain-interview.

33. Susan Rogers, interview by Dennis DeSantis, "Loop | Susan Rogers on Prince, production and perception," *The Loop*, April 17, 2018, accessed April 25, 2018, https://www.youtube.com/watch?v=EgBZHIUUn8Q.

34. "Bobby Z" Rivkin, interview by Alex Rawls, "Bobby Z Recalls the Evolution of The Revolution," *MySpiltMilk.com*, February 20, 2018, accessed February 2, 2019, https://www.myspiltmilk.com/articles/bobby-z-recalls-the-evolution-of-the-revolution.

35. Brenda Bennett, "Rhode Island Music Hall of Fame Historical Archive. Hold Me Closer: The Story of Brenda Bennett," available at: http://www.ripopmusic.org/musical-artists/musicians/brenda-bennettbrenda-mosher/.

36. Coleman, interview by Michael Hann, "How We Made Prince's Purple Rain."

37. Rogers, interview by Freed, December 1994.

38. Susie Davis personal diary, shared with the author.

39. Rogers, interview by Freed, December 1994.

40. Rogers, interview by Freed, December 1994.

41. Devin Devasquez, *The Day It Snowed in April: A Memoir*, Purple Publishing, Kindle Edition, 46–48.

42. Prince, interview by Neal Karlen, "Prince Talks," *Rolling Stone*, October 18, 1990, 58.

43. Susan Rogers, "Prince and the Technician," *Kitchen Sisters Present*, May 21, 2018, accessed October 12, 2019, http://www.kitchensisters.org/present/prince-and-the-technician/.

44. Burton Glass, "Prince show features trademark eroticism, energy and fun," *AvantGuardian*, January 25, 1985, 1–2.

45. Sheila E., interview on *American Bandstand*, 1985.

46. "Bobby Z" Rivkin, "The Revolution Was Live," YouTube, posted December 25, 2018, accessed December 28, 2018, https://www.youtube.com/watch?v=aBRSJoB7RW8&feature=youtu.be.

47. Prince, "Prince dominates the American Music Awards, 1985," available at: https://www.youtube.com/watch?v=S8ZQTKlO3kY.

48. Wendy Melvoin in Alan Light, *Let's Go Crazy: Prince and the Making of Purple Rain*, Atria Books, Kindle edition.

49. Wally Safford, *Wally, Where'd You Get Those Glasses?* (Detroit, MI: Lil Gator Publishing, 2019), 118.

50. Alan Leeds in Light, *Let's Go Crazy*.

51. Prince, interviewed by Neal Karlen, "Prince Talks: The Silence Is Broken," *Rolling Stone* magazine, September 12, 1985, https://www.rollingstone.com/music/music-news/prince-talks-the-silence-is-broken-58812/.

52. Prince, interviewed by Neal Neal Karlen, "Prince Talks: The Silence Is Broken," September 12, 1985.

53. "Prince's Bodyguards Arrested in Scuffle With Photographers," *AP*, January 29, 1985, https://apnews.com/2cfdb7878cca310d756dba8d8707c7f5.

54. "Prince and His Bodyguards Hit With $15 Mil. Lawsuit," *Jet* magazine, February, 25, 1985, 60.

FEBRUARY 1985

1. Prince, "Stephen Fargnoli interviews Prince," *MTV*, November 15, 1985, uploaded May 9, 2016, http://www.dailymotion.com/video/x49h7vy.
2. Keith Murphy, "Purple Rain Turns 30: Prince's Engineer Shares Majestic (and Maddening) Studio Stories," *Vibe.com*, June 25, 2014, https://www.vibe.com/features/editorial/purple-rain-turns-30-princes-engineer-shares-majestic-and-maddening-studio-stories-226644/.
3. Lisa Coleman, interview with Scott Goldfine, "Truth In Rhythm," *Funkenstuff*, May 14, 2019, https://www.youtube.com/watch?v=gQaJV15mdBI.
4. Susan Rogers, interview by Alan Freed for *Uptown* magazine/Per Nilsen, Los Angeles, CA, December 1994.
5. Rogers, interview by Freed, December 1994.
6. Rogers, interview by Freed, December 1994.
7. "Stephen Fargnoli interviews Prince," November 15, 1985.
8. Alan Leeds, "Behind the Purple Ropes," *Wax Poetics,* fall 2012, retrieved on November 17, 2020, https://web.archive.org/web/20160426182957/http://www.wax-poetics.com/features/behind-the-purple-ropes-prince-and-the-revolution2/.
9. Leeds, "Behind the Purple Ropes."
10. Prince, interview by Touré, "The Artist," *Icon* magazine, October 1998, 102.
11. Leeds, "Behind the Purple Ropes."
12. Leeds, "Behind the Purple Ropes."
13. Leeds, "Behind the Purple Ropes."
14. Sheila E., interview by Charles Waring, "From 'The Glamorous Life' to 'Icon'—SJF's Sheila E Interview," *Sound and Jazz and Funk*, November 3, 2013, accessed August 18, 2018, https://www.soulandjazzandfunk.com/interviews/from-the-glamorous-life-to-icon-sjfs-sheila-e-interview-part-2/.
15. Susan Rogers, interview by Charles Rivers, "Charles Rivers' Show: Prince Engineer: Susan Rogers '83–'87," *The Charles Rivers Show*, April 27, 2018, accessed May 29, 2018, https://www.mixcloud.com/TheCharlesRiversShow/princes-engineer-1983-1987-susan-rogers/.
16. Rivers, "Charles Rivers' Show: Prince Engineer: Susan Rogers '83–'87."
17. "Bobby Z" Rivkin, interview by Billy Amendola, "Bobby Z of The Revolution," *Modern Drummer*, January 3, 2019, accessed January 3, 2019, https://www.modern-drummer.com/article/february-2019-timeless-and-authentic-Bobby-z-of-the-revolution.
18. Sheila E., "Royalty to Romance," *The Hit* magazine, September 14, 1985, 5.

19. Sheila E., interview by Questlove, "Questlove Supreme, Episode 62," *Pandora*, December 13, 2017, accessed December 20, 2017, https://www.pandora.com/station/play/3642532478040643917.

20. Sheila E., "Prince Rogers Nelson," BBC *Omnibus Documentary*, 1991.

21. Susan Rogers, interview by C. J., "C. J.: Prince ideas Flowed Fast and Furious, Engineer Recalls," *Star Tribune*, July 3, 2018, accessed July 25, 2018, http://m.startribune.com/c-j-prince-ideas-flowed-fast-and-furious-engineer-recalls/487268161/.

22. Sheila E., interview by Steve Daugherty, "Sex and God and Rock and Roll," *People* magazine, November 14, 1988, accessed August 19, 2018, https://people.com/archive/sex-and-god-and-rock-and-roll-vol-30-no-20/.

23. Eric Leeds, interview by Alan Freed for *Uptown* magazine/Per Nilsen, Minneapolis, MN, December 16, 1995.

24. Wendy Melvoin in Alan Light, *Let's Go Crazy: Prince and the Making of Purple Rain*, Atria Books, Kindle Edition, 21.

25. Richard Cromelin, "For Prince's Concert, It's a Reign of Rock: Singer Gambles With the Audience, Opens His Six-Show Forum Series With an Eccentric, Ambitious Performance," *Los Angeles Times*, February 20, 1985, https://www.latimes.com/archives/la-xpm-1985-02-20-ca-472-story.html.

26. Alan Leeds, interview by Alan Freed for *Uptown* magazine/Per Nilsen, Minneapolis, MN, January 20, 1994.

27. Marylou Badeaux, interview by Alan Freed for Per Nilsen/*Uptown* magazine, Los Angeles, December 23, 1993.

28. Badeaux, interview by Freed, December 23, 1993.

29. Badeaux, interview by Freed, December 23, 1993.

30. Badeaux, interview by Freed, December 23, 1993.

31. Prince, interview by Neal Karlen, "Prince Talks: The Silence Is Broken," *Rolling Stone* magazine, September 12, 1985, https://www.rollingstone.com/music/music-news/prince-talks-the-silence-is-broken-58812/.

32. Leeds, interview by Freed, December 16, 1995.

33. Matt Fink, interview by A. D. Amorosi, "Fly By Night," *Wax Poetics*, 67 (2018), 51.

34. Bruce Springsteen, interview by Brian Hiatt, "Bruce Springsteen Talks Steel Mill, 'Human Touch' What Prince Taught Him," *Rolling Stone* magazine, October 17, 2016, accessed March 16, 2019, https://www.rollingstone.com/music/music-features/bruce-springsteen-talks-steel-mill-human-touch-what-prince-taught-him-126267/.

35. Eric Leeds, interview by Graeme Thomson, "Open Your Heart, Open Your Mind," *Uncut* (June 2020), 67.

36. Ingrid Geyer, "In 1985, Prince Played a Free Concert for L.A. Students. He Didn't Want Any Publicity," *LA Times*, April 28, 2016, accessed November 23, 2017, http://www.latimes.com/opinion/readersreact/la-le-0428-thursday-prince-lausd-free-concert-20160428-story.html.

37. Geyer, "In 1985, Prince Played a Free Concert for L.A. Students."

38. Peggy Leonard, interview by Andrea Swensson, "Prince: The Story of 1999 Bonus Feature: The Sound of Prince and Peggy McCreary," *The Current*, November 27, 2019, https://www.thecurrent.org/feature/2019/11/27/prince-the-story-of-1999-bonus-feature-the-sound-of-prince-and-peggy-mccreary.

39. "Bobby Z" Rivkin, interview by Eric Miller, "Bobby Z of The Revolution Picks the Essential Prince," *Pods and Sods* podcast, April 17, 2018, accessed April 20, 2018, https://podsodcast.com/category/bobby-z/.

MARCH 1985

1. Alan Leeds, interview by Graeme Thomson, "Open Your Heart, Open Your Mind," *Uncut* (June 2020), 60.

2. Paul Peterson, interview by Christopher Arnel, "St. Paul Peterson & Eric Leeds Interview for UMMG," The Uptown Minneapolis Music Scene (formerly Group), June 5, 2017, accessed August 19, 2018, https://www.facebook.com/groups/366116877599/permalink/10154949970292600/.

3. Wayne Robins, "Review of Nassau Concert," *Newsday* March 19, 1985, https://www.newsday.com/entertainment/music/prince-s-1985-nassau-coliseum-concert-review-from-newsday-s-archives-1.11717415.

4. Marjorie Anders, "Rock Star Plays Surprise Concert for Handicapped Children," *AP News*, March 20, 1985, accessed March 17, 2019, https://apnews.com/1ca469b35a7440f27741bf605c161816.

5. Anders, "Rock Star Plays Surprise Concert for Handicapped Children."

6. Roy Bennett in Anders, "Rock Star Plays Surprise Concert for Handicapped Children."

7. Doug Henders in Anders, "Rock Star Plays Surprise Concert for Handicapped Children."

8. Anders, "Rock Star Plays Surprise Concert for Handicapped Children."

9. Prince, interview by Neal Karlen, "Prince Talks: The Silence Is Broken," *Rolling Stone* magazine, September 12, 1985, https://www.rollingstone.com/music/music-news/prince-talks-the-silence-is-broken-58812/.

10. Mark Brown "BrownMark," interview by Graeme Thomson, "Open Your Heart, Open Your Mind," *Uncut* (June 2020), 67–68.

11. Eddie Murphy, "Eddie Murphy on trading places with Prince," YouTube, March 10, 2018, accessed March 30, 2020, https://www.youtube.com/watch?v=V9joWILfuFQ.

12. Tony Christian, interview by Harold Lewis and Tony Melodia, for Per Nilsen/*Uptown* magazine, Minneapolis, MN, 1993.

13. "David Z" Rivkin, interview by Alan Freed for *Uptown* magazine/Per Nilsen, Minneapolis, MN, December 5, 1994.

14. Prince, "Prince Wins Original Song Score: 1985 Oscars," YouTube, December 5, 2012, accessed March 30, 2020, https://www.youtube.com/watch?v=hk3xZxguRCg.

15. Bill Higgins," Hollywood Flashback: When Prince Won (and Wore a Purple Sequined Cape) at the 1985 Oscars," *Hollywood Reporter*, January 28, 2016, accessed June 1, 2020, https://www.hollywoodreporter.com/news/hollywood-flashback-prince-won-wore-859165.

16. "Bobby Z" Rivkin, interview by Ross Raihala, "How the Revolution Goes on Without Prince—and Why," *Pioneer Press*, July 18, 2017, accessed February 25, 2018, https://www.twincities.com/2017/07/18/how-the-revolution-goes-on-without-prince-and-why/.

APRIL 1985

1. Susannah Melvoin, interview by Touré, "Susannah Melvoin: On Loving and Almost Marrying Prince," *Touré Show*, Episode 14, February 14, 2018, accessed February 27, 2018, https://art19.com/shows/toure-show/episodes/b974f458-b18c-4e8a-bff6-00351e7ac327.

2. "Bobby Z" Rivkin, interview by Shaun Brady, "Drummer Bobby Z Remembers Prince Ahead of The Revolution Doubleheader at the TLA," *The Key*, April 21, 2017, accessed February 10, 2019, http://thekey.xpn.org/2017/04/21/the-revolution-interview/.

3. Alan Leeds, post on Facebook, April 7, 2012.

4. Leeds, post on Facebook, April 7, 2012.

5. Sheila E., interview by Wendy Rhodes, "Drummer Sheila E. on Prince: 'I Will Continue to Uplift his Music'," *Miami New Times*, November 26, 2018, accessed January 11, 2019, https://www.miaminewtimes.com/music/things-to-do-fort-lauderdale-sheila-e-at-riptide-music-festival-november-30-december-2-10908331.

6. Mark Brown "BrownMark," *Music Icons Collector's Edition: Prince*, May 2017, Athlon Entertainment #19, 44.

7. Sheila E., *The Beat of My Own Drum: A Memoir*, Atria Books, Kindle Edition, Locations 2757–2761.

8. Sheila E., *The Beat of My Own Drum*, Kindle Locations 2757–61.

9. Sheila E., *The Beat of My Own Drum*, Kindle Locations 2757–61.

10. Jerome Benton, interview by Dr. Funkenberry (Part 1), https://soundcloud.com/drfunkpodcast/48-jerome-benton.

11. Alan Leeds, post on Facebook on April 11, 2012 quoted on http://funk-o-logy.com/forum/viewtopic.php?t=3204.

12. "Bobby Z" Rivkin, interview by Alex Rawls, "Bobby Z Recalls the Evolution of The Revolution," *My Spilt Milk*, February 20, 2018, accessed February 10, 2019, https://www.myspiltmilk.com/articles/bobby-z-recalls-the-evolution-of-the-revolution.

13. Susan Rogers, interview by Alan Freed for *Uptown* magazine/Per Nilsen, Los Angeles, CA, March 26, 1995.

14. "Bobby Z" interview by Larry Williams, "Girls & Boys," *Mojo* magazine, September 2018, 61.

15. Susan Rogers, interview by Chris Williams, "The Epic," *Wax Poetics*, 67 (2018), 73–85.

16. Wendy Melvoin, interview by Larry Williams, "Girls & Boys," *Mojo* magazine, September 2018, 63.

17. Sheila E., "Sheila E. Sweetly Honors Prince With 'Lemon Cake'," *Billboard*, April 16, 2020, accessed April 16, 2020, https://www.billboard.com/articles/columns/pop/9359539/sheila-e-lemon-cake-prince.

18. Rogers, interview by Freed, March 26, 1995.

19. Susan Rogers, interview by Duke Eatmon, "An Afternoon with | Susan Rogers | En tête à tête," YouTube, June 7, 2018, accessed March 25, 2019, https://www.youtube.com/watch?v=n6mYrqdNyQQ.

20. Rogers, interview by Freed, December 1994.

21. Eatmon, "An Afternoon with | Susan Rogers | En tête à tête."

22. Rogers, interview by Freed, December 1994.

23. Rogers, interview by Freed, December 1994.

24. Wendy Melvoin, interview by A. D. Amorosi, "Agents of Change," *Wax Poetics*, 67 (2018), 40.

25. Lisa Coleman, interview by Eric Miller, "Lisa Coleman of The Revolution Picks the Essential Prince," *Pods and Sods* podcast, April 19, 2018, accessed April 20, 2018, https://podsodcast.com/2018/04/19/pte12/

26. Jerome Benton, interview with Touré, "Jerome Benton—I Know Prince," *Touré Show*, July 24, 2020, https://play.acast.com/s/toureshow/jeromebenton-iknowprince.

27. Eatmon, "An Afternoon with | Susan Rogers | En tête à tête."

28. Tony Christian, interview by Harold Lewis and Tony Melodia, for Per Nilsen/*Uptown* magazine, Minneapolis, MN, 1993.

29. "David Z" Rivkin, interview by Alan Freed for *Uptown* magazine/Per Nilsen, Minneapolis, MN, December 5, 1994.

30. Rivkin, interview by Freed, December 5, 1994.

31. "David Z" Rivkin, interview with Dan Daley, "Classic Tracks: Prince's 'Kiss'," *Mix* magazine, June 1, 2001, accessed December 14, 2020, https://web.archive.org/web/20120517011821/https://www.mixonline.com/mag/audio_princes_kiss/index.html.

32. Lisa Coleman, interview by Jesse Esparza, 2008, published on Myspace; Esparza sent via Facebook message to Duane Tudahl, March 8, 2017.

33. Prince, interview by the Electrifying Mojo, "The Electrifying Mojo," WHYT, June 7, 1986, accessed February 14, 2016, https://www.youtube.com/watch?v=NJZCoxZ5COY.

34. Peggy McCreary Leonard, liner notes for *Originals*, NPG Records/Warner Bros. (R1 591459), released June 2019.

35. Prince, interviewed by Barbara Graustark, "Strange Tales from Andre's Basement." *Musician* magazine, September 1983, https://theiconicprince.wordpress.com/2017/03/29/prince-strange-tales-from-andres-basement-and-other-fantasies-come-true/.

36. Barbara Graustark, "Strange Tales from Andre's Basement."

37. Prince, interview by Neal Karlen, "Prince Talks: The Silence Is Broken," *Rolling Stone* magazine, September 12, 1985, https://www.rollingstone.com/music/music-news/prince-talks-the-silence-is-broken-58812/.

38. Karlen, "Prince Talks," September 12, 1985.

39. Graustark, "Strange Tales from Andre's Basement."

40. Prince, interview by Arsenio Hall, "Prince chat with Arsenio 05/03/14," YouTube, https://www.youtube.com/watch?v=EDUhHwTLZpE.

41. Peggy McCreary, interview by John Earls, "Prince Giving It All Away," *Classic Pop* (June 2019), 27.

42. Bob Cavallo, interview by Jon Bream, "Prince's Greatest Talent? Self-Confidence, Says the Manager Who Landed 'Purple Rain'," *Star Tribune*, April 20, 2019, accessed April 20, 2019, http://www.startribune.com/prince-s-greatest-talent-self-confidence-says-the-manager-who-landed-purple-rain/508774052/.

43. Rebecca Huntsberry, interview by Emily Strohm and Rose Minutaglio, "Growing Up With Prince: Children of Star's Longtime Bodyguard Open Up About His Very Private Life," *People* magazine, April 24, 2016, accessed March 23, 2019, https://people.com/celebrity/growing-up-with-prince-children-of-stars-longtime-bodyguard-open-up/.

44. Chick Huntsberry, article by Per Nilsen and David J. Magdziarz, "Life Is Cruel Enough Without Cruel Words," *Uptown* magazine (Sweden), Issue 39, Fall 1999, 6.

45. Prince, lyrics to "Old Friends 4 Sale," performed by Prince and the Revolution, *The Vault . . . Old Friends 4 Sale*, Warner Bros, 9-47522, 1999, CD and Vinyl.

46. Lisa Coleman, interview by Dave Simpson, "'He Sang the Part of a Lonely Person': The Story of 17 Days, a Lost Prince Masterpiece," *The Guardian*, September 6, 2018, accessed April 19, 2019, https://www.theguardian.com/music/2018/sep/06/prince-17-days-lost-masterpiece-exclusive-demo.

47. Susan Rogers, in Jake Brown, *Prince in the Studio (1975–1995)* (Phoenix: Amber Communications Group, 2010).

48. Prince with Aleksandrs Rozens, "'The Artist' Is With Major Label But Dodges Clauses," *Reuters*, November 9, 1999.

49. Rivkin, interview by Freed, December 5, 1994.

50. Wendy Melvoin, in Matt Thorne, *Prince*, Faber, Kindle Edition, Kindle Locations 2178–83.

51. Prince, Lisa Coleman, and Wendy Melvoin, lyrics to "Sometimes It Snows In April," performed by Prince and the Revolution, *Parade*, Paisley Park Records/Warner Bros., 25395, 1986, compact disc.

52. Lisa Coleman, interview by Kevin Ritchie, "The Revolution's Lisa Coleman Talks Prince's Legacy and Grieving Through Music," *NowToronto.com*, May 12, 2017, accessed May 4, 2019, https://nowtoronto.com/music/features/the-revolution-lisa-coleman/.

53. Wendy Melvoin, "Wendy & Lisa on Prince's 'Around The World In A Day' (1985)," *Heat Rocks*, January 9, 2020, http://heatrocks.libsyn.com/wendy-lisa-on-princes-around-the-world-in-a-day-1985.

54. Lisa Coleman, interview with DJ Shadow, "B-Sides in the Bins #41—Wendy & Lisa Interview," *Playbsides.com*, February 5, 2009, https://www.playbsides.com/b-sides-in-the-bins-41-wendy-lisa-interview/.

55. Wendy Melvoin, interview with DJ Shadow, "B-Sides in the Bins #41—Wendy & Lisa Interview," *Playbsides.com*, February 5, 2009, https://www.playbsides.com/b-sides-in-the-bins-41-wendy-lisa-interview/.

56. Prince, interview by Stephen Fargnoli, *MTV*, November 15, 1985, accessed August 18, 2016, http://www.dailymotion.com/video/x49h7vy.

57. Alan Leeds, interview by Alan Freed for *Uptown* magazine/Per Nilsen, Los Angeles, CA, January 20, 1994.

58. Matt Fink, interview by Graeme Thomson, "Open Your Heart, Open Your Mind," *Uncut* (June 2020), 61.

59. Bob Cavallo in Thorne, *Prince*, Kindle Locations 2042–43.

60. Prince, David Coleman, and John L. Nelson, lyrics to "Around The World In A Day," performed by Prince and the Revolution, *Around The World In A Day*, Paisley Park Records/Warner Bros., 25286, 1985, compact disc.

61. Prince et al., lyrics to "Around The World In A Day."

62. Prince, lyrics to "Paisley Park," performed by Prince and the Revolution, *Around The World In A Day*, Paisley Park Records/Warner Bros., 25286, 1985, compact disc.

63. Karlen, "Prince Talks," September 12, 1985.

64. Prince, lyrics to "Condition Of The Heart," performed by Prince and the Revolution, *Around The World In A Day*, Paisley Park Records/Warner Bros., 25286, 1985, compact disc.

65. Susan Rogers, interview by Kevin Curtain, "Susan Rogers Interview on Prince, Early Beginnings, Life After Prince, and Teaching," YouTube, February 1, 2017, accessed May 14, 2019, https://www.youtube.com/watch?v=M23Od3Bvthg.

66. Robert Palmer, "Records: Prince's 'Around The World'," *The New York Times*, April 22, 1985, Section C, p. 16.

67. Biba Kopf, "The Return of the Acid Reign," *New Musical Express* (May 4, 1985), 29.

68. Karlen, "Prince Talks," September 12, 1985.

69. Karlen, "Prince Talks," September 12, 1985.

70. Curtain, "Susan Rogers Interview on Prince, Early Beginnings."

71. Leonard, liner notes for *Originals*, June 2019.

72. "Bobby Z" Rivkin, interview by Eric Miller, "Bobby Z of The Revolution Picks the Essential Prince," *Pods and Sods* podcast, April 17, 2018, accessed April 20, 2018, https://podsodcast.com/category/bobby-z/.

73. Eatmon, "An Afternoon with | Susan Rogers | En tête à tête."

74. Prince, interview by Jim Walsh, *The Former Prince speaks*, St. Paul Pioneer Press, November 17, 1996.

75. Rogers, interview by Freed March 26, 1995.

76. Jon Bream and Chris Riemenschneider, "Prince: An Oral History," *Minneapolis Star Tribune*, March 14, 2004.

77. Christian, interview by Lewis and Melodia, 1993.

78. BrownMark, BBC radio documentary, *Purple Reign: The Story of Prince*, Hour 1, January 18, 2003.

79. Rivkin, interview by Daley, June 1, 2001.

80. Rivkin, interview by Daley, June 1, 2001.

81. Rivkin, interview by Freed, December 5, 1994.

82. Rivkin, interview by Daley, June 1, 2001.

83. Rivkin, interview by Daley, June 1, 2001.

84. "David Z" Rivkin in *Prince: The Glory Years*, produced by Rob Johnstone for Prism Entertainment (New Malden, Surrey, UK: Chrome Dreams Media, April 2004), DVD; also available at https://www.youtube.com/watch?v=Mff7-TCj6q8&list=PLCViTltpSejxdSeIrnQ4gH2vpih8at3VL, accessed December 17, 2020.

85. Christian, interview by Lewis and Melodia, 1993.

86. Christian, interview by Lewis and Melodia, 1993.

87. Rivkin, interview by Freed, December 5, 1994.

88. Mark Brown, interview by Mr. Christopher, "Interview: BrownMark—Kiss And Tell," *Funkatopia.com*, January 31, 2018, www.funkatopia.com/funk-news/interview-brownmark-kiss-and-tell.

89. Lisa Coleman, interview with Keith Murphy, "What Had Happened Was: Lisa Coleman and Wendy Melvoin," *Vibe.com*, March 2009, https://web.archive.org/web/20090315235021/https://www.vibe.com/news/online_exclusives/2009/03/what_had_happened_was_lisa_coleman_and_wendy_melvoin.

90. Wendy Melvoin, interview with Keith Murphy, "What Had Happened Was: Lisa Coleman and Wendy Melvoin," *Vibe.com*, March 2009, https://web.archive.org/web/20090315235021/https://www.vibe.com/news/online_exclusives/2009/03/what_had_happened_was_lisa_coleman_and_wendy_melvoin.

91. Coleman, *Vibe.com*, March 2009.

92. BrownMark, interview with Thomson, "Open Your Heart, Open Your Mind," 64.

93. Christian, interview by Lewis and Melodia, 1993.

94. Susan Rogers, interview by C. J., "C. J.: Prince Ideas Flowed Fast and Furious, Engineer Recalls," *Star Tribune*, July 3, 2018, accessed July 25, 2018, http://m.startribune.com/c-j-prince-ideas-flowed-fast-and-furious-engineer-recalls/487268161/.

MAY 1985

1. Susan Rogers, interview by Charles Rivers, "Charles Rivers' Show: Prince Engineer: Susan Rogers '83–'87," *The Charles Rivers Show*, April 27, 2018, accessed May 29, 2018, http://thegoodamericancollective.blogspot.com/2018/04/charles-rivers-show-prince-engineer.html

2. Susan Rogers, interview by Alan Freed for *Uptown* magazine/Per Nilsen, Los Angeles, CA, December 1994.

3. Alan Leeds, interview by Alan Freed for *Uptown* magazine/Per Nilsen, Los Angeles, CA, January 20, 1994.

4. Lisa Coleman, interview by Eric Miller, "Lisa Coleman of The Revolution Picks the Essential Prince," *Pods and Sods* podcast, April 19, 2018, accessed April 20, 2018, https://podsodcast.com/2018/04/19/pte12/.

5. Joyce Kennedy, interview by Charley Crespo, "Rock & Soul Newsmakers: Joyce Kennedy," *Rock & Soul*, December 1985, 12.

6. Susan Rogers, interview by Dennis DeSantis, "Loop | Susan Rogers on Prince, Production and Perception," *The Loop*, April 17, 2018, accessed April 25, 2018, https://www.youtube.com/watch?v=EgBZHIUUn8Q.

7. Susan Rogers, interview by Ben Beaumont-Thomas, "Prince's Sound Engineer, Susan Rogers: 'He Needed to Be the Alpha Male to Get Things Done'," *The Guardian*, November 13, 2017, accessed November 23, 2017, https://www.theguardian.com/music/2017/nov/09/princes-sound-engineer-susan-rogers-he-needed-to-be-the-alpha-male-to-get-things-done?CMP=share_btn_fb.

8. Susanna Hoffs, Apollonia Kotero's Instagram account, August 27, 2018, https://www.instagram.com/p/Bm_luhbnje7/.

9. Apollonia, Apollonia Kotero's Instagram account, August 27, 2018, https://www.instagram.com/p/Bm_luhbnje7/.

10. Vicki Peterson, in Christopher Feldman, *Billboard Book of Number Two Singles* (New York: Watson-Guptill, 2000), 200.

11. Susanna Hoffs, in Will Harris, "Susanna Hoffs of the Bangles," *AVClub*, October 11, 2011, available at: https://music.avclub.com/susanna-hoffs-of-the-bangles-1798228045.

12. Harris, "Susanna Hoffs of the Bangles."

13. Susanna Hoffs, "The Bangles interview (1986 Japan)," YouTube, posted April 20, 2016, retrieved March 22, 2019, https://www.youtube.com/watch?v=AGV-iAPppoE.

14. Peterson, in Feldman, *Billboard Book of Number Two Singles*, 200.

15. Vicki Peterson, "Bangles Interview 2007 Working With Prince," YouTube, retrieved March 22, 2019, https://www.youtube.com/watch?v=h0i8xBNQsSM.

16. Tony Christian, interview by Harold Lewis and Tony Melodia, for Per Nilsen/*Uptown* magazine, Minneapolis, MN, 1993.

17. Sir Terry Casey, interview with Martin Keller, "Mazarati's Best Kept Sectets Are Still In The Garage," *Right On* magazine, Fall 1985, 25.

18. Wendy Melvoin, in Jake Brown, *Prince in the Studio (1975-1995)* (Phoenix, AZ: Amber Communications Group, 2010).

19. Brent Fischer, in Matt Thorne, *Prince*, Faber, Kindle Edition, Kindle Locations 2097-105.

20. Mark Brown "BrownMark," interview, "The Revolution's BrownMark remembers Prince: 'I don't think since Mozart there's ever gonna be anybody else'," *Classic Hits And Oldies 105.5*, November 14, 2018, accessed December 29, 2018, https://www.ktlo.com/2018/11/14/the-revolutions-brown-mark-remembers-prince-i-dont-think-since-mozart-theres-ever-gonna-be-anybody-else/.

21. BrownMark, "The Revolution's BrownMark remembers Prince."

22. "Big Chick" Huntsberry, interview by Sam Rubin and John South, "The REAL Prince—He's Trapped in a Bizarre Secret World of Terror," *National Enquirer*, May 7, 1985, 48–49.

23. Prince, interview by Neal Karlen, "Prince Talks: The Silence Is Broken," *Rolling Stone* magazine, September 12, 1985, https://www.rollingstone.com/music/music-news/prince-talks-the-silence-is-broken-58812/.

24. Prince, interview by Wayne Edwards, "The Artist Makes a Princely Return," *Music Connection*, November 8–November 21, 1999, 34.

25. Mark Brown "BrownMark," interview by Christopher Arnel, The Uptown Minneapolis Music Scene, April 14, 2017, accessed April 25, 2017, https://www.facebook.com/groups/366116877599/10154778406587600/.

26. Leeds, interview by Freed, January 20, 1994.

27. Jill Jones, interview by Gert van Veen, "The Apple of Prince's Eye," *De Volkskrant* (June 26, 1987), 22.

28. Eric Leeds, interview by Michael Dean, "Eric Leeds: Prince Interview Part 1 of 4," YouTube, November 24, 2017, https://www.youtube.com/watch?v=S11NjgzEmRI.

29. Eric Leeds, interview by Alan Freed for *Uptown* magazine/Per Nilsen, Los Angeles, CA, January 25, 1995.

30. Levi Seacer Jr., interview by Chris Williams, "New Birth," *Wax Poetics* magazine, Special Prince issue (Spring 2018), 99.

31. Lynn Norment, "*Ebony* Interview with Prince," *Ebony*, July 1986, 30.

32. Susan Rogers, interview by Kevin Curtain, "Susan Rogers Interview on Prince, Early Beginnings, Life After Prince, and Teaching," YouTube, February 1, 2017, accessed May 14, 2019, https://www.youtube.com/watch?v=M23Od3Bvthg.

33. Rivers, "Charles Rivers' Show: Prince Engineer."

34. Prince, interviewed by Sinbad, "Chaka Khan Larry Graham Mayte Garcia and 'SPECIAL GUEST' on VIBE W/ SINBAD," *Vibe* television show, aired June 9, 1998, https://www.youtube.com/watch?v=fSVD1P0mRwM.

35. Prince, interview by Stephen Fargnoli, *MTV*, November 15, 1985, accessed August 18, 2016, http://www.dailymotion.com/video/x49h7vy.

36. André Cymone, interview, KPFA Radio October 31, 1998 San Francisco/Oakland Bay Area.

37. Susan Rogers, interview by Alan Freed for *Uptown* magazine/Per Nilsen, Los Angeles, CA, February 1995.

38. Ericka Blount Danois, interview by André Cymone, "Minneapolis Music Pioneer André Cymone Speaks for the First Time in twenty-seven Years," *Wax Poetics*, October 29, 2012, retrieved May 9, 2019.

39. Danois, interview by Cymone, "Minneapolis music pioneer André Cymone speaks," October 29, 2012.

40. Prince, interview by Stephen Fargnoli, *MTV*, November 15, 1985.

41. Cymone interview, KPFA Radio October 31, 1998.

42. André Cymone, interview with Ericka Blount Danois, "André Cymone," *Wax Poetics*, 50 (winter 2012), https://web.archive.org/web/20130313054415/https://waxpoetics.com/features/articles/andre-cymone.

43. André Cymone, interview by Mr. Chris, *The Soul Brother Radio Show*, March 22, 2013, https://backtracks.fm/discover/s/shockadelica-sound-system-radio/8a072e68ccf53445/e/the-soul-brother-show-featuring-andre-cymone/b4974e93617e42d5.

44. Neal Karlen, "Prince Talks: The Silence Is Broken," *Rolling Stone* magazine (September 12, 1985), 86.

45. Rogers, interview by Freed, February 1995.

46. Karlen, "Prince Talks," 86.

47. Lisa Coleman, interview by Jon Regen, "Prince would just use a preset and then brighten the f**k out of it!," *Music Radar*, May 25, 2019, accessed May 26, 2019, https://www.musicradar.com/news/lisa-coleman-prince-would-just-use-a-preset-and-then-brighten-the-fk-out-of-it?fbclid=IwAR112Rh1ObCQlIZbiNv75Gsn_B0JF9Ts-gciOS0qlh6k2B9TglBcJpRqNiMM.

48. Rogers, interview by Freed, February 1995.

49. Rivers, "Charles Rivers' Show: Prince Engineer."

50. Roy Bennett, interview by Alan Freed for *Uptown* magazine/Per Nilsen, Los Angeles, CA, January 20, 1996.

51. Prince, lyrics to "Heaven," unreleased.

52. van Veen, "The Apple of Prince's Eye," 22.

53. van Veen, "The Apple of Prince's Eye," 22.

54. Susan Rogers, interview by Chris Williams, "The Epic," *Wax Poetics*, 67 (2018), 73–85.

55. "David Z" Rivkin, interview by Alan Freed for *Uptown* magazine/Per Nilsen, Minneapolis, MN, December 5, 1994.

56. Eric Leeds, "f Deluxe (with 4 original members of the Family)," *Ustream* live feed, August 21, 2013, http://www.ustream.tv/channel/fdeluxe-with-original-members-of-the-family.

57. Eric Leeds, interview by Alan Freed for *Uptown* magazine/Per Nilsen, Minneapolis, MN, December 16, 1995.

58. Paul Peterson, interview by Michael Dean, "St. Paul Peterson interview," *Podcast Juice*, February 2, 2018, accessed February 10, 2018, https://podcastjuice.net/st-paul-peterson-interview/.

59. Prince, lyrics to "Drawers Burnin'," unreleased.

JUNE 1985

1. Prince, interview with Lynn Norment, "*Ebony* Interview with Prince," *Ebony*, July 1986, 32.

2. Alan Leeds, interview by Alan Freed for *Uptown* magazine/Per Nilsen, Minneapolis, MN, January 20, 1994.

3. Prince, interview with Mick Brown, "Prince interview: 'I didn't let fame rule me'," *The Telegraph*, December 6, 2004, (reposted April 22, 2016), https://www.telegraph.co.uk/music/interviews/prince-interview-the-act-didnt-finish-when-he-stepped-off-stage/.

4. Matt Fink, interview with Evan Sawdey, "Inside Prince's Revolution," PopMatters.com, June 4, 2009, https://www.popmatters.com/94061-inside-the-revolution-2496026736.html.

5. Prince, interview by Larry King, "Prince Rogers Nelson's entire 1999 CNN interview (Larry King Live)," Larry King Live, December 10, 1999, accessed December 20, 2020, https://www.youtube.com/watch?v=m8mg7CxAYUM.

6. Jill Jones, interview with Steve Perry, "Prince, The Purple Decade," *Musician* magazine, November 1988, 99.

7. Wendy Melvoin, interview by Jem Aswad, "The Revolution Remembers Their Last Moments with Prince—and the First Time They Heard 'Purple Rain'," *Billboard*, December 12, 2016, accessed December 23, 2016, http://www.billboard.com/articles/events/year-in-music-2016/7604454/the-revolution-prince-final-moments.

8. Prince, "MTV's Total Request Live with Carson Daly," *MTV*, December 9, 1999, accessed May 17, 2017, https://www.spin.com/2017/04/prince-total-request-live-1999-carson-daly/.

9. Susannah Melvoin, interview with K Nicola Dyes, "Miss Understood: An In-Depth Interview with Susannah Melvoin," *beautifulnightschitown.com*, April 18, 2013, http://beautifulnightschitown.blogspot.com/2013/04/miss-understood-in-depth-interview-with.html.

10. S. Melvoin, interview by Dyes, April 18, 2013.

11. Eric Leeds, interview by Alan Freed for *Uptown* magazine/Per Nilsen, Minneapolis, MN, December 16, 1995.

12. E. Leeds, interview by Freed, December 16, 1995.

13. "Bobby Z" Rivkin, interview by Eric Miller, "Bobby Z of The Revolution Picks the Essential Prince," *Pods and Sods* podcast, April 17, 2018, accessed April 20, 2018, https://podsodcast.com/category/bobby-z/.

14. Simon Field, interview by Rob Tannenbaum, "Prince's Career on Camera: Insiders Recall Late Genius' Difficult Relationship with Music Videos," *Billboard*, April 22, 2016, accessed September 22, 2019, https://www.billboard.com/articles/news/7341616/prince-music-videos.

15. Wendy Melvoin, "Wendy & Lisa on Prince's 'Around The World In A Day' (1985)," *Heat Rocks*, January 9, 2020, http://heatrocks.libsyn.com/wendy-lisa-on-princes-around-the-world-in-a-day-1985.

16. Dave Grohl, interview by Rob Tannenbaum, "Prince's Career on Camera: Insiders Recall Late Genius' Difficult Relationship with Music Videos," *Billboard*, April 22, 2016, accessed September 22, 2019, https://www.billboard.com/articles/news/7341616/prince-music-videos.

17. W. Melvoin, "Wendy & Lisa on Prince's 'Around The World In A Day' (1985)."

18. Susan Rogers, interview by Alan Freed for *Uptown* magazine/Per Nilsen. Los Angeles, CA, March 25, 1995.

19. Peggy Leonard, liner notes for *Originals*, NPG Records/Warner Bros. (R1 591459), June 2019.

20. Susan Rogers, interview by Alan Freed for *Uptown* magazine/Per Nilsen, Los Angeles, CA, December 1994.

21. Mark Brown "Brown Mark," interview by Larry Williams, "Girls & Boys," *Mojo* magazine, (September 2018), 60.

22. Jill Jones in Alan Light, *Let's Go Crazy: Prince and the Making of Purple Rain*, Atria Books, Kindle Edition.

23. E. Leeds, interview by Freed, December 16, 1995.

24. Wendy Melvoin, interview by Keith Murphy, "The Revolution Duo on Prince's Lost Dream," *Vibe*, March 2009, accessed June 7, 2009, https://web.archive.org/web/20090315134521/https://www.vibe.com/news/online_exclusives/2009/03/what_had_happened_was_lisa_coleman_and_wendy_melvoin/.

25. Lisa Coleman, interview with Dennis Hunt, "Revolution Frees Lisa and Wendy," *Los Angeles Times*, September 13, 1987, accessed March 12, 2017, http://articles.latimes.com/1987-09-13/ entertainment/ca-7727_1_lisa-coleman.

26. Lisa Coleman, interview with Brian Raftery, "Prince: The Oral History of Purple Rain," *Spin*, July 2009, 61, https://www.spin.com/2016/04/prince-the-oral-history-of-purple-rain-brian-raftery/.

27. Wendy Melvoin, "51 Albums, Prince, The Dream Factory ~ Thank You *Vibe* Magazine," DrFunkenberry.com, March 12, 2009, http://www.drfunkenberry.com/2009/03/12/51-albums-prince-the-dream-factory-thank-you-vibe-magazine/.

28. Jerome Benton, interview by DeAngela Duff, "GFM's Behind The Film Podcast—Jerome Benton," YouTube, November 4, 2017, accessed November 25, 2017, https://www.youtube.com/watch?v=JPYhJPZSyzo.

29. Aswad, "The Revolution Remembers Their Last Moments with Prince."

30. Sheila E., interview by Andrea Swensson, "Sheila E. tells how Prince's 'Pop Life' was put together in the studio (Interview)," *The Current*, January 23, 2019, accessed February 10, 2019, https://www.youtube.com/watch?v=Y1Dy__lE9i0&app=desktop.

31. Swensson, "Sheila E. tells how Prince's 'Pop Life' was put together in the studio (Interview)."

32. Sheila E., Liz Jones, *Slave to the Rhythm* (London: Little, Brown, 1997).

33. Lisa Coleman, in Matt Thorne, *Prince*, Faber, Kindle Edition, Kindle Locations 2666–71.

JULY 1985

1. Lisa Coleman, interview with Lily Moayeri, "The Revolution's Wendy and Lisa Remember Prince, the Human Being," *LA Weekly*, June 19, 2017, accessed February 28, 2019, https://www.laweekly.com/the-revolutions-wendy-and-lisa-remember-prince-the-human-being/.

2. Wendy Melvoin, interview by Keith Murphy, "The Revolution Duo on Prince's Lost Dream," *Vibe*, March 2009, accessed June 7, 2009, https://web.archive.org/web/20090315134521/https://www.vibe.com/news/online_exclusives/2009/03/what_had_happened_was_lisa_coleman_and_wendy_melvoin/.

3. Susan Rogers, interview by Alan Freed for *Uptown* magazine/Per Nilsen, Los Angeles, CA, March 26, 1995.

4. Rogers, interview by Freed, March 26, 1995.

5. "Bobby Z" Rivkin interview by Harold Lewis, Tony Melodia, and Stefan van Poucke, "Take This Beat: An Exclusive Interview with Bobby Z Rivkin—Part 2," *Uptown* magazine (Sweden), 43 (fall 2000), 22.

6. Prince, lyrics to "Girls & Boys," performed by Prince and the Revolution, *Parade*, Paisley Park Records/Warner Bros., 25395, 1986, compact disc.

7. Prince, lyrics to "Girls & Boys."

8. Marie France, interview by Silvain Gire, "La fée du Prince," *Artradio.com*, October 8, 2014, accessed November 29, 2018, https://www.arteradio.com/son/616460/la_fee_du_prince.

9. Gire, "La fée du Prince."

10. Gire, "La fée du Prince."

11. Eric Leeds, interview by Alan Freed for *Uptown* magazine/Per Nilsen, Minneapolis, MN, October 15, 1993.

12. E. Leeds, interview by Freed, October 15, 1993.

13. E. Leeds, interview by Freed, October 15, 1993.

14. E. Leeds, interview by Freed, October 15, 1993.

15. Prince, interview with Neal Karlen, "Prince Talks," *Rolling Stone*, October 18, 1990, 60.

16. Prince, "The Artist Formerly Known as Prince Enjoys Musical Freedom With Hit Album 'Emancipation'," *Jet*, May 19, 1997, reprinted in *Prince Family Newsletter*, Vol. 5, #12, June 7, 1997, 68.

17. Sheila E., interview by Jason Matheson, *The Jason Show*, December 11, 2018, accessed February 13, 2019, https://www.youtube.com/watch?v=wUHaCcdwdac.

18. Sheila E., interview by Andrea Swennson, "Sheila E. describes the beauty of working with Prince on 'Venus de Milo' (Interview)," YouTube, January 24, 2019, accessed June 28, 2019, https://www.youtube.com/watch?list=PLYClJc3TpV5KHlBIFU3rgi1Ct3BycegTY&time_continue=2&v=QNlVW3_Hve8.

19. Swennson, "Sheila E. describes the beauty of working with Prince on 'Venus de Milo' (Interview)."

20. Eric Leeds, interview by Alan Freed for *Uptown* magazine/Per Nilsen, Minneapolis, MN, December 16, 1995.

21. Susan Rogers, interview by Alan Freed for *Uptown* magazine/Per Nilsen, Los Angeles, CA, December 1994.

22. Wendy Melvoin, "Wendy & Lisa, Q&A" Prince.org, June 2009, accessed May 17, 2013, http://www.youtube.com/v/pjiKokwoMAM.

23. "Bobby Z" Rivkin, interview by Alex Rawls, "Bobby Z Recalls The Evolution of the Revolution," *My Spilt Milk*, February 20, 2018, accessed February 10, 2019, https://web.archive.org/web/20190329012152/http://myspiltmilk.com/bobby-z-recalls-evolution-revolution.

24. Rogers, interview by Freed, December 1994.

25. Matt Fink in Alan Light, *Let's Go Crazy: Prince and the Making of Purple Rain*, Atria Books, Kindle Edition.

26. Prince, interview by Love4OneAnother.com, November 17, 1997, accessed December 15, 2020, http://web.archive.org/web/19980109123204/http://love4oneanother.com/ask.htm.

27. Rogers, interview by Freed, December 1994.

28. Rogers, interview by Freed, December 1994.

29. Lisa Coleman, interview by Gary Graff, "The Revolution's Lisa Coleman Talks 'Piano & A Microphone 1983,' Jamming With Prince and Unreleased Gems," *Billboard*, September 20, 2019, accessed December 15, 2018, https://www.billboard.com/biz/articles/8475846/princes-new-piano-a-microphone-1983-basement-tape-is-as-simple-as-it-sounds.

30. Susan Rogers, interview by Ben Beaumont-Thomas, "Prince's Sound Engineer, Susan Rogers: 'He Needed to Be the Alpha Male to Get Things Done'," *The Guardian*, November 13, 2017, accessed November 23, 2017, https://www.theguardian.com/music/2017/nov/09/princes-sound-engineer-susan-rogers-he-needed-to-be-the-alpha-male-to-get-things-done?CMP=share_btn_fb.

31. Eric Leeds, interview with Mark Youll, "Love Saxy: Eric Leeds On Prince And Madhouse," *Quietus.com*, May 5, 2015, https://thequietus.com/articles/17801-eric-leeds-prince-interview.

32. Susan Rogers, interview by Torsten Schmidt, "Prince Engineer Susan Rogers Lecture (Montréal 2016) | Red Bull Music Academy," YouTube, December 8, 2016, accessed April 23, 2018, https://www.redbullmusicacademy.com/lectures/susan-rogers-lecture.

AUGUST 1985

1. Susan Rogers interviewed by Charles Rivers, "Charles Rivers' Show: Prince Engineer: Susan Rogers '83–'87," *The Charles Rivers Show*, April 27, 2018, accessed May 29, 2018, http://thegoodamericancollective.blogspot.com/2018/04/charles-rivers-show-prince-engineer.html.

2. Prince, interview with Mel B., "Prince Interview Mel B 1998 Paisley Park," YouTube, June 10, 2016, accessed April 12, 2020, https://www.youtube.com/watch?v=7LsZoWBAIkc.

3. "Bobby Z" Rivkin interview by Harold Lewis and Tony Melodia, for Per Nilsen/ *Uptown* magazine, Minneapolis, MN, 1993.

4. Susannah Melvoin, in Matt Thorne, *Prince*, Faber, Kindle Edition, Kindle Locations 2483–87.

5. Jill Jones, *Dirty Nerdy* podcast, January 15, 2017, https://www.youtube.com/watch?v=_zgPsnBnqOY.

6. Clare Fischer, interview by Sarah Bacon, "Clare Fischer interview," April 17, 2006, retrieved May 7, 2019, https://www.housequake.com/2006/04/17/clare-fischer-interview/.

7. Prince, interview by Robert I. Doerschuk, "Portrait of the Artist," *Musician* magazine, April 1997, reprinted in *Prince Family Newsletter*, August 30, 1997, Vol. 5, #18, 107.

8. Eric Leeds, interview by Alan Freed for *Uptown* magazine/Per Nilsen, Minneapolis, MN, December 16, 1995.

9. E. Leeds, interview by Freed, December 16, 1995.

10. Paul Peterson, "The Five Count's Ninth Annual Princemas Celebration—An Evening With fDELUXE-The Family's St. Paul Peterson," *The Five Count*, published January 27, 2018, accessed December 24, 2018, http://thefivecount.com/audio-posts/the-five-counts-ninth-annual-princemas-celebration-an-evening-with-fdeluxethe-familys-st-paul-peterson/.

11. Paul Peterson, interview by Joe Kelley, "Prince Celebration Part Two 5.02.16 ON WVOF's "Upper Room With Joe Kelley and GI Dussault," WVOF FM, May 2, 2016, accessed December 24, 2018, https://www.upperroomwithjoekelley.com/uploads/1/3/8/7/13874814/princewvofupperroomjoekelley50216.mp3.

12. Paul Peterson, interview by Michael Dean, "St. Paul Peterson interview," *Podcast Juice*, February 2, 2018, accessed February 10, 2018, https://podcastjuice.net/st-paul-peterson-interview/.

13. Peterson, interview by Dean, February 2, 2018.

14. Peterson, interview by Dean, February 2, 2018.

15. Susannah Melvoin, interview by Touré, "Susannah Melvoin: On Loving and Almost Marrying Prince," *Touré Show*, Episode 14, February 14, 2018, accessed February 27, 2018, https://podtail.com/podcast/toure-show/susannah-melvoin-on-loving-and-almost-marrying-pri/.

16. Sheila E., interview in "Unsung: Sheila E.," A. Smith & Co. Productions, *TV One*, February 27, 2012.

17. S. Melvoin, interview by Touré, February 14, 2018.

18. S. Melvoin, interview by Touré, February 14, 2018.

19. Kristin Scott Thomas, interview by "'George Stroumboulopoulos Tonight,' Kristin Scott Thomas on Tom Cruise, Ryan Gosling and . . . Prince," YouTube, posted April 16, 2013, accessed September 21, 2019, https://www.youtube.com/watch?v=Setc5olrLts.

20. Kristin Scott Thomas, interview on WNBC "'Live At Five,' Kristin Scott Thomas Interview 1986," YouTube, posted January 22, 2009, accessed September 21, 2019, https://www.youtube.com/watch?v=H6zz0Bluafl.

21. Thomas interview by "George Stroumboulopoulos Tonight," posted April, 16, 2013.

22. Jerome Benton, interview by Dr. Funkenberry (Part 1), available at: https://soundcloud.com/drfunkpodcast/48-jerome-benton.

23. Peterson, interview by Dean, February 2, 2018.

24. Davitt Sigerson, *The Family* album review, *Rolling Stone* magazine, November 21, 1985, 98.

25. John Bream, "The Family" (Paisley Park)," *Minneapolis Star and Tribune*, August 25, 1985, 2G.

26. Dave Gingold, "The Family review," *Santa Cruz Sentinel* (August 9, 1985), 12.

27. Sheila E., interview by Robert Santelli, "Sheila E.," *Modern Drummer* (July 1991), 21.

28. Evelyn Erskine, "Sheila E. Most Promising Prince Spinoff," *The Citizen*, September 6, 1985, D5.

29. Staff, "Picks and Pans Review: *Romance 1600*," *People*, September 30, 1985.

30. Davitt Sigerson, *Romance 1600* review, *Rolling Stone* magazine, November 21, 1985, 97.

31. Erskine, "Sheila E. Most Promising Prince Spinoff," D5.

SEPTEMBER 1985

1. Mark Brown "BrownMark," interview by Christopher Arnel, The Uptown Minneapolis Music Scene, April 14, 2017, accessed April 25, 2017, https://www.facebook.com/groups/366116877599/10154778406587600/.

2. Mark Brown "BrownMark," "BrownMark of The Revolution Picks the Essential Prince," *Pods and Sods* podcast, April 18, 2018, accessed May 17, 2018, https://podsod cast.com/2018/04/18/pte11/.

3. Lyrics to "Go," unreleased song by Prince.

4. Jimmy Jam, interview by Chaz Lipp, "An Interview with Jimmy Jam of The Original 7ven, Part Two," *The Morton Report*, April 19, 2012, http://www.themortonreport. com/entertainment/music/an-interview-with-jimmy-jam-of-the-original-7ven-part-two/.

5. Lisa Coleman, interview by Rob Tannenbaum, "Prince's Career on Camera: Insiders Recall Late Genius' Difficult Relationship with Music Videos," *Billboard*, April 22, 2016, accessed September 22, 2019, https://www.billboard.com/articles/ news/7341616/prince-music-videos.

6. Jerome Benton, interview by Dr. Funkenberry (Part 1), available at: https:// soundcloud.com/drfunkpodcast/48-jerome-benton.

7. Jerome Benton, interview by DeAngela Duff, "GFM's Behind The Film Podcast—Jerome Benton," YouTube, November 4, 2017, accessed November 25, 2017, https://www.youtube.com/watch?v=JPYhJPZSyzo.

8. Mary Lambert quoted by Michael Shore, "The Prince Interview," *Rock & Soul Magazine*, July 1986, 33/

9. Kristin Scott Thomas, interview WNBC "'Live At Five,' Kristin Scott Thomas Interview 1986," YouTube, posted January 22, 2009, accessed September 21, 2019, https://www.youtube.com/watch?v=H6zz0BluafI.

10. Lisa Coleman, interview with Ross Raihala, "How the Revolution goes on without Prince—and Why," *Pioneer Press*, July 18, 2017, accessed February 25, 2018, https://www.twincities.com/2017/07/18/how-the-revolution-goes-on-without-prince- and-why/.

11. Susan Rogers, interview by Duke Eatmon, "An Afternoon with | Susan Rogers | En tête à tête," YouTube, June 7, 2018, accessed March 25, 2019, https://www.you- tube.com/watch?v=n6mYrqdNyQQ.

12. Benton, interview with Dr. Funkenberry (Part 1).

13. Paul Peterson, in Dave Hill, *Prince: A Pop Life* (New York: Harmony Books, 1989).

14. Benton, interview with Dr. Funkenberry (Part 1).

OCTOBER 1985

1. Lynn Norment, "*Ebony* Interview with Prince," *Ebony*, July 1986, 32.

2. Wendy Melvoin, "The Purple Playlist," *Sirius/XM*, May 11, 2020.

3. Eric Leeds, interview by Michael Dean, "Eric Leeds: Prince Interview Part 2 of 4," *PodcastJuice.net*, November 26, 2017, https://www.youtube.com/watch?v=zzrOnqq_ xI8.

4. Jellybean Johnson, interview by Alan Freed for *Uptown* magazine/Per Nilsen, Minneapolis, MN, February 2, 1995.

5. Jerome Benton, interview with Dr. Funkenberry (Part 1), available at: https://soundcloud.com/drfunkpodcast/48-jerome-benton.

6. Paul Peterson, in Dave Hill, *Prince: A Pop Life* (New York: Harmony Books, 1989), 183.

7. Paul Peterson, interview by Michael Dean, "St. Paul Peterson interview," *Podcast Juice*, February 2, 2018, accessed February 10, 2018, https://podcastjuice.net/st-paul-peterson-interview/.

8. Paul Peterson, interview by Christopher Arnel, "St. Paul Peterson & Eric Leeds Interview for UMMG," The Uptown Minneapolis Music Scene (formerly Group), June 5, 2017, accessed August 19, 2018, https://www.facebook.com/groups/366116877599/permalink/10154949970292600/.

9. E. Leeds, interview by Dean, November 26, 2017.

10. E. Leeds, interview by Dean, November 26, 2017.

NOVEMBER 1985

1. Lisa Coleman, interview by Ian Wade, "After The Rain," *Classic Pop* (October 2018), 41–43.

2. Susan Rogers, interview by Alan Freed for *Uptown* magazine/Per Nilsen, Los Angeles, CA, December 1994.

3. Rogers, interview by Freed, December 1994.

4. Rogers, interview by Freed, December 1994.

5. Rogers, interview by Freed, December 1994.

6. Susan Rogers, interview by Alan Freed for *Uptown* magazine/Per Nilsen, Los Angeles, CA, August 4, 1997.

7. Rogers, interview by Freed, August 4, 1997.

8. *Crystal Ball* booklet, *Crystal Ball*, NPG Records, 9 70188, 1998, compact disc.

9. Prince, lyrics to "Dream Factory," performed by Prince and the Revolution, *Crystal Ball*, NPG Records, 9 70188, 1998, compact disc.

10. Prince, lyrics to "Dream Factory."

11. Rogers, interview by Freed, August 4, 1997.

12. Prince and John L. Nelson (strings composed by Wendy Melvoin and Lisa Coleman), lyrics to "The Ladder," performed by Prince and the Revolution, *Around the World in a Day*, Paisley Park Records/Warner Bros., 25286, 1985, compact disc.

13. Prince, Lisa Coleman, and Wendy Melvoin, lyrics to "Mountains," performed by Prince and the Revolution, *Parade*, Paisley Park Records/Warner Bros., 25395, 1986, compact disc.

14. Holy Bible, New International Version®, NIV® Copyright ©1973, 1978, 1984, 2011.

15. "Bobby Z" Rivkin, interview by Harold Lewis and Tony Melodia, for Per Nilsen/*Uptown* magazine, Minneapolis, MN, 1993.

16. Atlanta Bliss, interview by Alan Freed, for Per Nilsen/*Uptown* magazine, Minneapolis MN, January 23, 1994.

17. Eric Leeds, interview by Alan Freed for *Uptown* magazine/Per Nilsen, Los Angeles, CA, January 25, 1995.

18. Mark Brown "BrownMark," interview by Larry Williams, "Girls & Boys," *Mojo* magazine (September 2018), 63.

19. "Bobby Z" Rivkin, interview by Larry Williams, "Girls & Boys," *Mojo* magazine (September 2018), 63.

20. Rogers, interview by Freed, August 4, 1997.

DECEMBER 1985

1. Eric Leeds, interview by Michael Dean, "Eric Leeds: Prince Interview Part 2 of 4," *Podcast Juice.net*, November 26, 2017, https://www.youtube.com/watch?v=zzrOnqq_xI8.

2. Prince, interview by the Electrifying Mojo, "The Electrifying Mojo," WHYT, June 7, 1986, accessed February 14, 2016, https://www.youtube.com/watch?v=NJZCoxZ5COY.

3. Jill Jones, interview by Michael A. Gonzales, "Pop Art," *Wax Poetics*, 67 (2018), 65–71.

4. Alan Leeds, interview with George Cole, *The Last Miles*, https://www.thelast miles.com/interviews-alan-leeds/.

5. A. Leeds, interview by Cole.

6. A. Leeds, interview by Cole.

7. "David Z" Rivkin, interview by Alan Freed for *Uptown* magazine/Per Nilsen, March 4, 1995.

8. Susan Rogers, interview by Ben Beaumont-Thomas, "Prince's Sound Engineer, Susan Rogers: 'He Needed to Be the Alpha Male to Get Things Done'," *The Guardian*, November 13, 2017, accessed November 23, 2017, https://www.theguardian.com/music/2017/nov/09/princes-sound-engineer-susan-rogers-he-needed-to-be-the-alpha-male-to-get-things-done?CMP=share_btn_fb.

9. Lisa Coleman interview with Andrea Swensson, "Prince: The Story of Sign O' The Times, Episode 3: The Quake," *The Current,* September 10, 2020, https://www.thecurrent.org/feature/2020/09/10/prince-the-story-of-sign-o-the-times-episode-3.

10. A 1987 press release from Sheena Easton's (then) record label, EMI.

11. Wendy Melvoin, interview with Jim Bickal, "The Revolution Reunites to Benefit Heart Health," *MPR News*, February 15, 2012, https://www.mprnews.org/story/2012/02/19/the-revolution-reunites-to-benefit-heart-health.

12. Lisa Coleman in Danny Eccleston, "Major Keys," *Mojo* magazine (September 2018), 61.

13. "Bobby Z" Rivkin, interview by Harold Lewis and Tony Melodia, for Per Nilsen/*Uptown* magazine, Minneapolis, MN, 1993.

14. Susan Rogers, interview by Kevin Curtain, "Susan Rogers Interview on Prince, Early Beginnings, Life After Prince, and Teaching," YouTube, February 1, 2017, accessed May 14, 2019, https://www.youtube.com/watch?v=M23Od3Bvthg.

15. Edna Gunderson, "Emancipation Conversation," *MSN Music Central*, December 1996, accessed June 19, 2017, https://sites.google.com/site/prninterviews/home/msn-music-central-december-1996.

16. Susan Rogers, interview by Alan Freed for *Uptown* magazine/Per Nilsen, Los Angeles, CA, December 1994.

17. Rogers, interview by Freed, December 1994.

18. Jill Jones, "Jill Jones | Interview," *The Dirty Nerdy Show*, January 15, 2017, accessed January 17, 2017, https://www.youtube.com/watch?v=_zgPsnBnqOY.

19. Susan Rogers, interview by Chris Williams, "The Epic," *Wax Poetics*, 67 (2018), 73–85.

20. Wendy Melvoin, interview by Larry Williams, "Girls & Boys," *Mojo* magazine (September 2018), 61.

21. Bob Merlis, interview by Cynthia Littleton, "Warner Bros. Records Exec on Prince: 'It Was Not in Our Interest to Be Confrontational With Him'," *Variety*, April 21, 2016. https://variety.com/2016/music/news/prince-dead-warner-bros-records-bob-merlis-1201758543/.

22. Prince, interview by Larry King, "Prince Rogers Nelson's entire 1999 CNN interview (Larry King Live)," *Larry King Live*, December 10, 1999, accessed December 20, 2020, https://www.youtube.com/watch?v=m8mg7CxAYUM.

23. A. Leeds, interview by Cole.

24. Eric Leeds, interview by Alan Freed for *Uptown* magazine/Per Nilsen, Minneapolis, MN, December 16, 1995.

25. Eric Leeds, The Last Miles.com, available at: https://www.thelastmiles.com/interviews-eric-leeds-part2/.

26. E. Leeds, The Last Miles.com.

27. Prince, interview with Michael Gonzales, "My Father Named Me Prince," *Code Magazine*, December 1999, 90.

28. Wendy Melvoin, in Matt Thorne, *Prince*, Faber, Kindle Edition, Kindle Locations 3873–77.

29. E. Leeds, interview by Freed, December 16, 1995.

30. E. Leeds, interview by Freed, December 16, 1995.

31. E. Leeds, interview by Freed, December 16, 1995.

32. Levi Seacer Jr., interview by Chris Williams, "New Birth," *Wax Poetics*, Issue 67 (2018), 104.

33. E. Leeds, interview by Freed, December 16, 1995.

34. E. Leeds, interview by Freed, December 16, 1995.

NOTES

35. Alan Leeds, interview by Miles Marshall Lewis, "Prince and reed man Eric Leeds teamed up to create two albums under the moniker Madhouse," *Wax Poetics* magazine, 50, Winter 2012, http://backend.waxpoetics.com/blog/features/articles/prince-mad-house-jazz-band-eric-leeds/.
36. Seacer Jr., interview by Williams.

JANUARY 1986

1. Lynn Norment, "Interview with Prince," *Ebony*, July 1986, 30.
2. Prince, interview by Shane Cooper, "In The Name Of Funk," *Sain* magazine, April 2006, 19.
3. Prince, lyrics to "Love And Sex," *Sign O' The Times* Super Deluxe Edition, NPG Records/Warner Records, 628756, 2020, CD & Vinyl.
4. Prince, interviewed by Steve Sutherland, "Someday Your Prince Will Come," *Melody Maker*, June 1981, 13.
5. Eric Leeds, interview by Alan Freed for *Uptown* magazine/Per Nilsen, Minneapolis, MN, December 16, 1995.
6. Susan Rogers, interview by Alan Freed for *Uptown* magazine/Per Nilsen, Los Angeles, CA, December 1994.
7. E. Leeds, interview by Freed, December 16, 1995.
8. Eric Leeds, interview by Jake Brown, *Prince in the Studio (1975–1995)* (Phoenix: Amber Communications Group, 2010).
9. Tony Christian, interview by Harold Lewis and Tony Melodia, for Per Nilsen/ *Uptown* magazine, Minneapolis, MN, 1993.
10. E. Leeds, interview by Freed, December 16, 1995.
11. E. Leeds, interview by Freed, December 16, 1995.
12. Susannah Melvoin, interview by Andrea Swensson, "Susannah Melvoin on the hidden tenderness of Prince and the story behind 'Starfish and Coffee,'" *The Current*, November 7, 2016, accessed November 8, 2016, https://blog.thecurrent.org/2016/11/susannah-melvoin-on-the-hidden-tenderness-of-prince-and-the-story-behind-starfish-and-coffee/.
13. E. Leeds, interview by Freed, December 16, 1995.
14. Susan Rogers, interview by Kevin Curtain, "Susan Rogers Interview on Prince, Early Beginnings, Life After Prince, and Teaching," YouTube, February 1, 2017, accessed May 14, 2019, https://www.youtube.com/watch?v=M23Od3Bvthg.
15. Lisa Coleman interviewed by Eric Miller, "Lisa Coleman of The Revolution Picks the Essential Prince," *Pods and Sods* podcast, April 19, 2018, accessed April 20, 2018, https://podsodcast.com/2018/04/19/pte12/.
16. Eric Leeds, in Matt Thorne, *Prince*, Faber, Kindle Edition, Kindle Locations 3858–63.

17. Lisa Coleman interviewed by Jay S. Jacobs, "Talking 'Bout The Revolution with Lisa Coleman," *PopEntertainment.com*, March 6, 2018, accessed March 12, 2018, http://www.popentertainmentarchives.com/the-revolution-lisa-feature-story.

18. Rogers, interview by Curtain, February 1, 2017.

19. Rogers, interview by Curtain, February 1, 2017.

20. Rogers, interview by Curtain, February 1, 2017.

21. Susan Rogers, interview by Torsten Schmidt, "Prince Engineer Susan Rogers Lecture (Montréal 2016) | Red Bull Music Academy," YouTube, December 8, 2016, accessed April 23, 2018, https://www.redbullmusicacademy.com/lectures/susan-rogers-lecture.

22. Alan Leeds, interview by Miles Marshall Lewis, "Prince and Reed Man Eric Leeds Teamed Up to Create Two Albums under the Moniker Madhouse," *Wax Poetics*, Winter 2012, http://backend.waxpoetics.com/blog/features/articles/prince-madhouse-jazz-band-eric-leeds/.

23. Eric Leeds, interview by Michael Dean, "Eric Leeds: Prince Interview Part 2 of 4," *Podcast Juice.net*, November 26, 2017, https://www.youtube.com/watch?v=zzrOnqq_xI8.

24. E. Leeds, interview by Freed, December 16, 1995.

25. Jill Jones, interview by Mr. Chris, *The Soul Brother Show*, KPFT, October 10, 2016, accessed June 1, 2017, http://player.fm/series/the-soul-brother-show/for-love-a-conversation-with-jill-jones.

26. Jill Jones, interview by John Earls, "Prince Giving It All Away," *Classic Pop* (June 2019), 27.

27. Susan Rogers, interview by Alan Freed for *Uptown* magazine/Per Nilsen, Los Angeles, CA, January 19, 1996.

28. Prince quoted by Joshua Levine, "Prince Speaks," *Forbes* (September 23, 1996), 180.

29. Susan Rogers, interview by Alan Freed for *Uptown* magazine/Per Nilsen, Los Angeles, CA, August 4, 1997.

30. Wendy Melvoin, interview by Aidin Vaziri, "The Revolution Tours in Tribute to Prince," *San Francisco Chronicle*, July 19, 2017, accessed February 25, 2019, https://www.sfchronicle.com/music/popquiz/article/The-Revolution-tours-in-tribute-to-Prince-11267342.php.

FEBRUARY 1986

1. Eric Leeds, interview by Alan Freed for *Uptown* magazine/Per Nilsen, Minneapolis, MN, December 16, 1995.

2. Matt "Atlanta Bliss" Blistan, interview by Alan Freed for *Uptown* magazine/Per Nilsen, January 23, 1994, via phone.

3. Alan Leeds, interview by Alan Freed for *Uptown* magazine/Per Nilsen, Minneapolis, MN, January 20, 1994.

4. Jerome Benton, interview by DeAngela Duff, "GFM's Behind the Film Podcast—Jerome Benton," YouTube, November 4, 2017, accessed November 25, 2017, https://www.youtube.com/watch?v=JPYhJPZSyzo.

5. Alan Leeds, interview by Questlove, "Questlove Supreme" on *Pandora*, October 4, 2016.

6. A. Leeds, interview by Questlove, October 4, 2016.

7. Susan Rogers, interview by Alan Freed for *Uptown* magazine/Per Nilsen, Los Angeles, CA, August 4, 1997.

8. Lisa Coleman, interview by Ian Wade, "After The Rain," *Classic Pop* (October 2018), 41–43.

9. "Bobby Z" Rivkin, interview by Michael Hann, "How We Made Prince's Purple Rain," *The Guardian*, July 28, 2017, accessed November 23, 2017, https://www.theguardian.com/music/2017/jul/24/how-we-made-princes-purple-rain-interview.

10. "David Z" Rivkin, interview by Dan Daley, "Classic Tracks: Prince's 'Kiss'," *Mix*, June 1, 2001, retrieved August 26, 2019, http://web.archive.org/web/20120606154434/http://mixonline.com/mag/audio_princes_kiss/index.html.

11. Lynn Norment, "Ebony Interview with Prince," *Ebony*, July 1986, 30.

12. Jill Jones, interview by Michael A. Gonzales, "Pop Art," *Wax Poetics*, 67 (2018), 65–71.

13. Wendy Melvoin and Lisa Coleman in Alan Light, *Let's Go Crazy: Prince and the Making of Purple Rain*, Atria Books, Kindle Edition.

14. Prince, interview by Larry King, "Prince Rogers Nelson's entire 1999 CNN interview (Larry King Live)," Larry King Live, December 10, 1999, accessed December 20, 2020, https://www.youtube.com/watch?v=m8mg7CxAYUM.

15. Rebecca Blake, interview by Rob Tannenbaum, "Prince's Career on Camera: Insiders Recall Late Genius' Difficult Relationship with Music Videos," *Billboard*, April 22, 2016, accessed September 22, 2019, https://www.billboard.com/articles/news/7341616/prince-music-videos.

16. Blake, interview by Tannenbaum, April 22, 2016.

17. Wendy Melvoin, "The *Sirius/XM* Volume Town Hall Series featuring The Revolution with Mark Goodman and Alan Light," *Sirius/XM*, May 1, 2017, taped live May 1, 2017.

18. Blake, interview by Tannenbaum, April 22, 2016.

19. Melvoin, "The *Sirius/XM* Volume Town Hall Series featuring the Revolution with Mark Goodman and Alan Light."

20. Sheila E., Per Nilsen, "The Sheila E. Story: The Glamorous Life," *Uptown* magazine (Sweden), Fall 1995 (#20), 17.

21. Susan Rogers, "A History of Music and Technology," BBC, accessed June 30, 2019, https://www.bbc.co.uk/sounds/play/w3csz42f.

22. Jill Jones in Dave Hill, *Prince: A Pop Life*, Harmony Books, 135.

23. "David Z" Rivkin, interview by Alan Freed for *Uptown* magazine/Per Nilsen, May 13, 1995, via telephone.

24. Prince, interview by Serge Simonaert, "The Artist," *Guitar World*, October 1998, accessed March 4, 2017, http://princetext.tripod.com/i_gw98.html.

25. Rivkin, interview by Freed, May 13, 1995.

26. Rivkin, interview by Freed, May 13, 1995.

27. Rivkin, interview by Freed, May 13, 1995.

MARCH 1986

1. Alan Leeds, interview with George Cole, TheLastMiles.com, https://www.thelastmiles.com/interviews-alan-leeds/.

2. Eric Leeds, interview by Michael Bonner, "Revealed! The Truth about What Really Happened When Prince Jammed with Miles Davis," *Uncut* magazine, May 24, 2016, https://www.uncut.co.uk/news/revealed-truth-really-happened-prince-jammed-miles-davis-77011/.

3. Marcus Miller, interview by Ron Hart, "Inside Miles Davis' Prince Obsession, as Detailed by Davis' Family and Collaborators," April 22, 2016, https://pitchfork.com/thepitch/1114-inside-miles-davis-prince-obsession-as-detailed-by-davis-family-and-collaborators/.

4. Marcus Miller, interview by A. D. Amorosi, "The Ballad of Miles Davis and Prince," *JazzTimes*, November 30, 2020, https://jazztimes.com/features/profiles/the-ballad-of-miles-davis-and-prince/3/.

5. Eric Leeds, interview by Alan Freed for *Uptown* magazine/Per Nilsen, Los Angeles, CA, January 25, 1995.

6. Lisa Coleman, interview by Jed Gottlieb, "Life After Prince: The Revolution Keeps the Music Alive," *Boston Herald*, October 26, 2018, accessed January 2, 2019, https://www.bostonherald.com/2018/10/26/life-after-prince-the-revolution-keeps-the-music-alive/.

7. Prince on stage at First Avenue, Minneapolis, MN, March 3, 1986.

8. Matt "Atlanta Bliss" Blistan, interview by Alan Freed for *Uptown* magazine/Per Nilsen, January 23, 1994, via phone.

9. Roy Bennett, interview by Andrea Swensson, "Prince: The Story of 1999 Bonus Feature: LeRoy Bennett, 'Prince Was Beyond Anybody'," *The Current*, January 2, 2020, https://www.thecurrent.org/feature/2020/01/02/prince-the-story-of-1999-leroy-bennett-prince-was-beyond-anybody.

10. Paul Peterson, interview by Michael Dean, "Paul Peterson—The TIME, The Family & Prince" *Prince Podcast*, February 7, 2018, accessed April 25, 2018, https://www.youtube.com/watch?v=WeTNPdXzYk4.

11. Wally Safford, *Wally, Where'd You Get Those Glasses?*, Lil Gator Publishing, Kindle Edition.

12. Prince on stage at First Avenue, Minneapolis, MN, March 3, 1986.

13. Prince on stage at First Avenue, Minneapolis, MN, March 3, 1986.

14. Alan Leeds, interview by Alan Freed for *Uptown* magazine/Per Nilsen, Minneapolis, MN, January 20, 1994.

15. Lisa Coleman, interview by Keith Murphy, "What Had Happened Was: Lisa Coleman and Wendy Melvoin," *Vibe.com*, March 12, 2009, https://web.archive.org/web/20091002092241/http://www.vibe.com/news/online_exclusives/2009/03/what_had_happened_was_lisa_coleman_and_wendy_melvoin.

16. Lisa Coleman, interview by Eric Miller, "Lisa Coleman of The Revolution Picks the Essential Prince," *Pods and Sods* podcast, April 19, 2018, accessed April 20, 2018, https://podsodcast.com/2018/04/19/pte12/.

17. Coleman, interview by Murphy, March 12, 2009.

18. Prince, interview by Sway Calloway, *MTV*, 2004, accessed May 19, 2017, http://prince.org/msg/7/91779?pr.

19. Prince, interview by Chris Heath, "The Man Who Would Be Prince," *Details* magazine, November 1991, https://princetext.tripod.com/i_details91.html.

20. Susan Rogers, "Susan Rogers on Prince's 'The Ballad Of Dorothy Parker,'" *RedbullMusicAcademy.com*, March 31, 2017, accessed March 15, 2018, http://daily.redbullmusicacademy.com/2017/03/the-ballad-of-dorothy-parker.

21. Rogers, "Susan Rogers on Prince's 'The Ballad of Dorothy Parker.'"

22. Susan Rogers, interview by Montrose Cunningham, "Celebrating Black Music Month: The 25th Anniversary of Prince's Sign O' The Times (Part 1)," *Soultrain.com*, June 20, 2012, accessed August 20, 2018, https://web.archive.org/web/20150101121925/http://soultrain.com/2012/06/20/celebrating-black-music-month-the-25th-anniversary-of-princes-sign-o-the-times-part-1.

23. Larry Crane, "Susan Rogers: From Prince to Ph.D.," *Tape Op*, Jan/Feb 2017, accessed February 20, 2017, http://tapeop.com/interviews/117/susan-rogers/.

24. Rogers, interview by Cunningham, June 20, 2012.

25. "Bobby Z" Rivkin, interview by Eric Miller, "Bobby Z of The Revolution Picks the Essential Prince," *Pods and Sods* podcast, April 17, 2018, accessed April 20, 2018, https://podsodcast.com/category/bobby-z/.

26. Susan Rogers, interview by Chris Williams, "The Epic," *Wax Poetics*, 67 (2018), 73–85.

27. Prince, interview by Mark Brown, "Prince's New Power Party Over? Rock Star Shows Industry How It's Done," *Rocky Mountain News*, August 21, 2004, accessed September 27, 2019, http://web.archive.org/web/20110825070409/http://blogs.rockymountainnews.com/rocky_mountain_music/2009/01/vault_interview_of_the_day_pri.html/.

28. Susan Rogers interviewed by Andrea Swensson, "Prince: The Story of Sign O' The Times, Episode 1: It's Gonna Be a Beautiful Night," *The Current*, August 27, 2020, https://www.thecurrent.org/feature/2020/08/27/prince-the-story-of-sign-o-the-times-episode-1.

29. *Crystal Ball* booklet, *Crystal Ball*, NPG Records, 9 70188, 1998, compact disc.

30. Jerome Benton, interview by Dr. Funkenberry, "#50 Jerome Benton Part 2," *The Dr Funk Podcast*, April 21, 2017, accessed March 2, 2019, https://player.fm/series/the-dr-funk-podcast/50-jerome-benton-part-2.

31. Benton, interview by Dr. Funkenberry, "#50 Jerome Benton Part 2."

32. Susan Rogers, interview by Alan Freed for *Uptown* magazine/Per Nilsen, Los Angeles, CA, December 1994.

33. Coleman, interview by Murphy, March 12, 2009.

34. Coleman, interview by Miller, April 19; 2018.

35. Wendy Melvoin interviewed by Andrea Swensson, "Prince: The Story of Sign O' The Times, Episode 1: It's Gonna Be a Beautiful Night," *The Current*, August 27, 2020, https://www.thecurrent.org/feature/2020/08/27/prince-the-story-of-sign-o-the-times-episode-1.

36. Williams, "The Epic," 73–85.

37. Coleman, interview by Miller, April 19, 2018.

38. Eric Leeds, interview by Alan Freed for *Uptown* magazine/Per Nilsen, Minneapolis, MN, October 15, 1993.

39. Susan Rogers, interview by Alan Freed for *Uptown* magazine/Per Nilsen, Los Angeles, CA, January 19, 1996.

40. "Bobby Z" Rivkin interview by Harold Lewis, Tony Melodia, and Stefan van Poucke, "Take This Beat: An Exclusive Interview with Bobby Z Rivkin—Part 2," *Uptown* 43 (fall 2000), 21.

41. Matt Blistan interviewed by Andrea Swensson, "Prince: The Story of Sign O' The Times, Episode 1: It's Gonna Be a Beautiful Night," *The Current*, August 27, 2020, https://www.thecurrent.org/feature/2020/08/27/prince-the-story-of-sign-o-the-times-episode-1.

42. E. Leeds, interview by Freed, October 15, 1993.

43. Rogers, interview by Freed, January 19, 1996.

44. Rogers, interview by Freed, January 19, 1996.

45. E. Leeds, interview by Freed, October 15, 1993.

46. E. Leeds, interview by Freed, October 15, 1993.

47. Rogers, interview by Freed, December 1994.

48. Susannah Melvoin interviewed by Touré, "Susannah Melvoin: On Loving and Almost Marrying Prince," *Touré Show*, Episode 14, February 14, 2018, accessed February 27, 2018, https://art19.com/shows/toure-show/episodes/b974f458-b18c-4e8a-bff6-00351e7ac327.

49. Blistan, interview by Freed, January 23, 1994.

50. Susannah, Facebook post, August 30, 2017.

51. Rogers, interview by Freed, December 1994.

52. Rogers, interview by Freed, December 1994.

53. Prince, interview by Adrian Deevoy, "I Am Normal," *Q* Magazine (July 1994), 94.

54. Peggy Leonard, interview by John Earls, "Prince Giving It All Away," *Classic Pop* (June 2019), 27.

55. Susan Rogers, interview by Torsten Schmidt, "Prince Engineer Susan Rogers Lecture (Montréal 2016) | Red Bull Music Academy," YouTube, December 8, 2016, accessed April 23, 2018, https://www.redbullmusicacademy.com/lectures/susan-rogers-lecture.

56. Sheila E., interview by Questlove, "Questlove Supreme, Episode 62," *Pandora*, December 13, 2017, accessed December 20, 2017, https://www.pandora.com/station/play/3642532478040643917.

57. Stef Burns, http://www.stefburns.com/bio/.

58. Prince, interview by Barney Hoskyns, *Imp of the Perverse*, Virgin Books, 108.

59. Lisa Coleman, interview by Kevin Ritchie, "The Revolution's Lisa Coleman Talks Prince's Legacy and Grieving Through Music," *NowToronto.com*, May 12, 2017, accessed May 4, 2019, https://nowtoronto.com/music/features/the-revolution-lisa-coleman/.

60. Wendy Melvoin, in Jake Brown, *Prince in the Studio (1975–1995)*, Amber Communications Group, 2010.

61. Mark Brown "BrownMark," interview by Larry Williams, "Girls & Boys," *Mojo* magazine (September 2018), 63.

62. E. Leeds, interview by Freed, October 15, 1993.

63. Gary Graff and Donna Oldendorg, "Prince Takes a Cue From His Past and Gets Back to the Dance Floor," *Detroit Free Press* (March 30, 1986), C5.

64. John Rockwell, "Prince's 'Parade' Stakes a Claim to Popularity," *New York Times* (March 30, 1986), Sec. 2, 22.

65. Susan Rogers, interview by Alan Freed for *Uptown* magazine/Per Nilsen, Los Angeles, CA, August 4, 1997.

66. Susan Rogers, interview by Alan Freed for *Uptown* magazine/Per Nilsen, Los Angeles, CA, March 26, 1995.

67. Susan Rogers, interview by Kevin Curtain, "Susan Rogers Interview on Prince, Early Beginnings, Life After Prince, and Teaching," YouTube, February 1, 2017, accessed May 14, 2019, https://www.youtube.com/watch?v=M23Od3Bvthg.

APRIL 1986

1. Susan Rogers, interview by Alan Freed for *Uptown* magazine/Per Nilsen, Los Angeles, CA, December 1994.

2. Rogers, interview by Freed, December 1994.

3. Jerome Benton, interview by Dr. Funkenberry (Part 1), https://soundcloud.com/drfunkpodcast/48-jerome-benton.

4. Benton, interview by Dr. Funkenberry (Part 1).

5. Bret Thoeny quoted in Edward Gunts, "A Look at Prince's Minneapolis Estate, Paisley Park Studios," *Archpaper*, April 25, 2016, https://archpaper.com/2016/04/prince-paisley-park-studios/.

6. Eric Leeds, interview by Alan Freed for *Uptown* magazine/Per Nilsen, Los Angeles, CA, January 25, 1995.

7. Susan Rogers, interview by Kevin Curtain, "Susan Rogers Interview on Prince, Early Beginnings, Life After Prince, and Teaching," YouTube, February 1, 2017, accessed May 14, 2019, https://www.youtube.com/watch?v=M23Od3Bvthg.

8. Roy Bennett, interview by Andrea Swensson, "Prince: The Story of 1999 bonus feature: LeRoy Bennett, 'Prince Was Beyond Anybody'," *The Current*, January 2, 2020, https://www.thecurrent.org/feature/2020/01/02/prince-the-story-of-1999-leroy-bennett-prince-was-beyond-anybody?fbclid=IwAR2YJ39wBW5ghuZBoObkaFzSfaTr jYhpbpY72s2-HsliRRxTlb_laicoq-g.

9. Dez Dickerson, interview by Andrea Swensson, "Prince: The Story of 1999 Bonus Feature: Dez Dickerson: 'Put an Explosion over It'," *The Current*, December 5, 2019, https://www.thecurrent.org/feature/2019/12/05/prince-the-story-of-1999-bonus-dez-dickerson-prince-guitarist-interview.

10. Eric Leeds, interview with George Cole on lastmiles.com, https://www.thelastmiles.com/interviews-eric-leeds/.

11. Susan Rogers, interview by Alan Freed for *Uptown* magazine/Per Nilsen, Los Angeles, CA, August 4, 1997.

12. Lisa Coleman, interview by Keith Murphy, "What Had Happened Was: Lisa Coleman and Wendy Melvoin," *Vibe.com*, March 12, 2009, https://web.archive.org/web/20091002092241/http://www.vibe.com/news/online_exclusives/2009/03/what_had_happened_was_lisa_coleman_and_wendy_melvoin.

13. E. Leeds, interview by Freed, January 25, 1995.

14. *Crystal Ball* booklet, *Crystal Ball*, NPG Records, 9 70188, 1998, compact disc.

15. Prince, lyrics to "Crystal Ball," performed by Prince and the Revolution, *Crystal Ball*, NPG Records, 9 70188, 1998, compact disc.

16. Susannah Melvoin, *Sign O' The Times* Super Deluxe Edition booklet, 2020, R2 628756, p. 15.

17. Wendy Melvoin interviewed by Andrea Swensson, "Prince: The Story of Sign O' The Times, Episode 1: It's Gonna Be a Beautiful Night," *The Current*, August 27, 2020, https://www.thecurrent.org/feature/2020/08/27/prince-the-story-of-sign-o-the-times-episode-1.

18. Morris Hayes, interview by Sean McPherson, "Morris Hayes on 'Crystal Ball'," *The Current*, September 13, 2018, accessed September 14, 2019, https://www.thecurrent.org/feature/2018/09/14/morris-hayes-on-crystal-ball-prince-the-truth.

19. Rogers, interview by Freed, December 1994.

20. Susannah Melvoin, interview by Andrea Swensson, "Susannah Melvoin on the Hidden Tenderness of Prince and the Story Behind 'Starfish and Coffee'," *The Current*, November 7, 2016, accessed November 8, 2016, https://blog.thecurrent.org/2016/11/

susannah-melvoin-on-the-hidden-tenderness-of-prince-and-the-story-behind-starfish-and-coffee/.

21. Prince, lyrics to "Big Tall Wall," *Sign O' The Times* Super Deluxe Edition, NPG Records/Warner Records, 628756, 2020, CD & Vinyl.

22. Susannah Melvoin, interview by Questlove, September 28, 2016, https://www.pandora.com/podcast/questlove-supreme/qls-classic-the-revolution/PE:3921260.

23. Susannah Melvoin interviewed by Touré, "Susannah Melvoin: On Loving and Almost Marrying Prince," *Touré Show*, Episode 14, February 14, 2018, accessed February 27, 2018, https://art19.com/shows/toure-show/episodes/b974f458-b18c-4e8a-bff6-00351e7ac327.

24. Susan Rogers, interview by Chris Williams, "The Epic," *Wax Poetics*, 67 (2018), 73–85.

25. S. Melvoin, interview by Questlove, September 28, 2016.

26. *Sign O' The Times* Super Deluxe Edition booklet, 2020, R2 628756, p. 83.

27. Lisa Coleman, interview by John J. Moser, "Q&A Interview: Lisa Coleman of Prince's The Revolution, playing SugarHouse casino tonight, says reunion is something band 'had to do'," *McCalls*, March 9, 2018, accessed December 29, 2018, https://www.mcall.com/entertainment/lehigh-valley-music/mc-ent-prince-the-revolution-qa-interview-lisa-coleman-20180308-story.html.

28. Rogers, interview by Freed, December 1994.

29. Lisa Coleman, interview by Neal Karlen, "Ladies in Waiting," *Rolling Stone* magazine, issue 472, April 24 1986, 44.

30. Wendy Melvoin, interview by Neal Karlen, "Ladies in Waiting," *Rolling Stone* magazine, issue 472, April 24 1986, 44.

31. Tony Norman, "Former Prince Gives the Fax on His Career, Motivation," Pittsburgh Post Gazette, September 20, 1997, 50, accessed March 12, 2017, https://sites.google.com/site/prninterviews/home/pittsburgh-post-gazette-ap-21-september-1997

32. S. Melvoin, interview by Swensson, November 7, 2016.

33. Alan Leeds, interview by Alan Freed for *Uptown* magazine/Per Nilsen, Minneapolis, MN, January 20, 1994.

MAY 1986

1. Mark Brown, "BrownMark of The Revolution Picks the Essential Prince," *Pods and Sods* podcast, April 18, 2018, accessed May 17, 2018, https://podsodcast.com/2018/04/18/pte11/.

2. Sheila E., interview by Stephen Cooke, "Sheila E. brings the glam to jazz fest," *The Chronicle Herald*, July 4, 2019, accessed July 5, 2019, https://www.thechronicleherald.ca/living/sheila-e-brings-the-glam-to-jazz-fest-329717/.

3. Alan Leeds, interview by Alan Freed for *Uptown* magazine/Per Nilsen, Minneapolis, MN, January 20, 1994.

4. Matt "Atlanta Bliss" Blistan, interview by Alan Freed for *Uptown* magazine/Per Nilsen, January 23, 1994, via phone.

5. Eric Leeds, interview by Alan Freed for *Uptown* magazine/Per Nilsen, Los Angeles, CA, January 25, 1995.

6. Chris Nelson, "Exclusive: The Artist Portrays Music's Future," *SonicNet Music News*, March 3, 1999, accessed March 12, 2017, http://www.mtv.com/news/512569/exclusive-the-artist-portrays-musics-future/.

7. Susannah Melvoin, interview by Touré, "Susannah Melvoin: On Loving and Almost Marrying Prince," *Touré Show*, Episode 14, February 14, 2018, accessed February 27, 2018, https://art19.com/shows/toure-show/episodes/b974f458-b18c-4e8a-bff6-00351e7ac327.

8. Coke Johnson, interview by Andrea Swensson, "Prince: The Story of Sign O' The Times, Episode 5: It Be's Like That Sometimes," *The Current*, September 24, 2020, https://www.thecurrent.org/feature/2020/09/24/prince-the-story-of-sign-o-the-times-episode-5-it-be-s-like-that-sometimes.

9. Sheila E., interview by Andrea Swensson, "Sheila E. Tells How Prince's 'Pop Life' Was Put Together in the Studio (Interview)," *The Current*, January 23, 2019, accessed January 29, 2019, https://www.youtube.com/watch?v=Y1Dy__lE9i0&app=desktop.

10. Jill Jones, interview by Raphy & Chak, "Les Confidences de Jill Jones," *Schkopi*, June 10, 2019, accessed June 10, 2019, http://www.schkopi.com/index.php/2019/06/news/les-confidences-de-jill-jones//

11. Available at: https://twitter.com/Housequake/status/1098930908860739584/photo/1, accessed September 8, 2020.

12. Available at: https://www.facebook.com/housequake/photos/a.361699067247157/1711026028981114/, accessed September 8, 2020.

13. Susan Rogers, "Headphone Highlights—Dr Susan Rogers: Songs Prince Listened to—2nd May 2017," *Red Bull Radio*, May 2, 2017, accessed May 17, 2017, https://www.mixcloud.com/robstaples72/headphone-highlights-susan-rogers-songs-prince-listened-to-2nd-may-2017/.

14. Rogers, "Headphone Highlights."

15. Michael Steele, "The Bangles Canadian TV Interview 1986 Part #1," YouTube, January 4, 2011, retrieved March 22, 2019, https://www.youtube.com/watch?v=GFntqkReyTc.

16. Wendy Melvoin accepting award at Sixth Annual Minnesota Music Awards, Carlton Celebrity Room (Bloomington, Minnesota).

17. A. Leeds, interview by Freed, January 20, 1994.

18. Eric Leeds, interview by Alan Freed for *Uptown* magazine/Per Nilsen, Minneapolis, MN, October 15, 1993.

19. Sheila E., "Sheila E. on Losing Prince and the Current State of Music," *Larry King*, April 20, 2018, accessed April 12, 2020, https://www.youtube.com/watch?v=bqwM1J7WCAU.

20. "Bobby Z" Rivkin, interview by Eric Miller, "Bobby Z of The Revolution Picks the Essential Prince," *Pods and Sods* podcast, April 17, 2018, accessed April 20, 2018, https://podsodcast.com/category/bobby-z/.
21. "David Z" Rivkin, interview by Alan Freed for *Uptown* magazine/Per Nilsen, Minneapolis, MN, December 5, 1994.
22. A. Leeds, interview by Freed, January 20, 1994.
23. A. Leeds, interview by Freed, January 20, 1994.
24. A. Leeds, interview by Freed, January 20, 1994.

JUNE 1986

1. Susan Rogers, interview by Alan Freed for *Uptown* magazine/Per Nilsen, Los Angeles, CA, August 4, 1997.
2. Sheila E., interview by Dennis Hunt, "Sheila E. Wants to Shed Her Sexpot Rep," *LA Times*, November 15, 1987, accessed December 15, 2018, http://articles.latimes.com/1987-11-15/entertainment/ca-20670_1_play-drums.
3. Eric Leeds interview with Andrea Swensson, "Prince: The Story of Sign O' The Times, Episode 4: Strict and Wild and Pretty," *The Current*, September 17, 2020, https://www.thecurrent.org/feature/2020/09/17/prince-the-story-of-sign-o-the-times-episode-4-strict-and-wild-and-pretty.
4. Susan Rogers, interview by Chris Williams, "The Epic," *Wax Poetics*, 67 (2018), 73–85.
5. Carole Davis in Matt Thorne, *Prince*, Faber, Kindle Edition, Kindle Locations 2956–64.
6. Rogers, interview by Freed, August 4, 1997.
7. Alan Leeds, interview by Alan Freed for *Uptown* magazine/Per Nilsen, Minneapolis, MN, January 20, 1994.
8. Rogers, interview by Freed, August 4, 1997.
9. Eric Leeds, interview by Alan Freed for *Uptown* magazine/Per Nilsen, Minneapolis, MN, October 15, 1993.
10. Jerome Benton, interview by DeAngela Duff, "GFM's Behind the Film Podcast—Jerome Benton," YouTube, November 4, 2017, accessed November 25, 2017, https://www.youtube.com/watch?v=JPYhJPZSyzo.
11. Prince, interview by the Electrifying Mojo, "The Electrifying Mojo," WHYT, June 7, 1986, accessed February 14, 2016, https://www.youtube.com/watch?v=NJZCoxZ5COY.
12. Matt "Atlanta Bliss" Blistan, interview by Alan Freed for *Uptown* magazine/Per Nilsen, January 23, 1994, via phone.
13. Atlanta Bliss, interview by Freed, January 23, 1994.

14. Mark Brown, interview by Mr. Christopher, "Interview: BrownMark—Kiss and Tell," *Funkatopia.com*, January 31, 2018, www.funkatopia.com/funk-news/interview-brownmark-kiss-and-tell.

15. Prince, interview by the Electrifying Mojo, June 7, 1986.

16. Prince, interview by the Electrifying Mojo, June 7, 1986.

17. Eric Leeds, interview by Alan Freed for *Uptown* magazine/Per Nilsen, Minneapolis, MN, December 16, 1995.

18. Prince, "Baby Go-Go," unreleased version performed by Prince, released version performed by Nona Gaye, *Female Trouble*, EMI Records, ST-17248, 1987, compact disc.

19. Prince, interview by Neal Karlen, "Prince Talks: The Silene Is Broken," *Rolling Stone*, September 12, 1985, 30.

20. E. Leeds, interview by Freed, December 16, 1995.

21. "Bobby Z" Rivkin, interview by Matthew Singer, "Prince Had Many Backing Bands in His Career, But He Only Led One Revolution," *Willamette Week*, July 12, 2017, accessed February 10, 2019, https://www.wweek.com/music/2017/07/12/prince-had-many-backing-bands-in-his-career-but-he-only-led-one-revolution/.

22. Matt Fink, PRN Alumni panel, Prince from Minneapolis: A Symposium at the University of Minnesota, April 18, 2018.

23. "Bobby Z" Rivkin, interview with Alex Rawls, "Bobby Z Recalls the Evolution of The Revolution," *My Spilt Milk*, February 20, 2018, accessed February 10, 2019, http://myspiltmilk.com/bobby-z-recalls-evolution-revolution.

24. Susan Rogers, interview by Dennis DeSantis, "Loop | Susan Rogers on Prince, production and perception," *The Loop*, April 17, 2018, accessed April 25, 2018, https://www.youtube.com/watch?v=EgBZHIUUn8Q.

25. Rogers, interview by DeSantis, April 17, 2018.

26. E. Leeds, interview by Freed, December 16, 1995.

27. Susan Rogers, interview by Duke Eatmon, "An Afternoon with | Susan Rogers | En tête à tête," YouTube, June 7, 2018, accessed March 25, 2019, https://www.youtube.com/watch?v=n6mYrqdNyQQ.

28. Susan Rogers, interview by Troy L. Foreman, *PC Principle* podcast, May 18, 2016, http://thepcprinciple.com/?p=9145.

29. Rogers, interview by Eatmon, June 7, 2018.

30. Rogers, interview by Eatmon, June 7, 2018.

31. Lisa Coleman, interview by Jon Regen, "Prince Would Just Use a Preset and Then Brighten the F**k out of It!," *Music Radar*, May 25, 2019, accessed May 26, 2019, https://www.musicradar.com/news/lisa-coleman-prince-would-just-use-a-preset-and-then-brighten-the-fk-out-of-it.

32. Rogers, interview by Eatmon, June 7, 2018.

33. Rogers, interview by Eatmon, June 7, 2018.

NOTES

JULY 1986

1. Jerome Benton interview with Dr. Funkenberry (Part 1), https://soundcloud.com/drfunkpodcast/48-jerome-benton.

2. Marylou Badeaux, interview by Alan Freed for *Uptown* magazine/Per Nilsen, Los Angeles, CA, December 23, 1993.

3. Badeaux, interview by Freed, December 23, 1993.

4. Benton, interview with Dr. Funkenberry (Part 1).

5. Badeaux, interview by Freed, December 23, 1993.

6. Badeaux, interview by Freed, December 23, 1993.

7. Lisa Coleman, interview by Matt Thorne. *Prince*, Faber, Kindle Edition, Kindle Locations 2335–38.

8. Susan Rogers, interview by Charles Rivers, "Charles Rivers' Show: Prince Engineer: Susan Rogers '83–'87," *The Charles Rivers Show*, April 27, 2018, accessed May 29, 2018, http://thegoodamericancollective.blogspot.com/2018/04/charles-rivers-show-prince-engineer.html.

9. Wendy Melvoin, compiled by the *Star Tribune* staff, "Oral History: Prince's Life, as Told by the People Who Knew Him Best," https://www.startribune.com/the-life-of-prince-as-told-by-the-people-who-knew-him/376586581/.

10. Rogers, interview by Rivers, April 27, 2018.

11. Lisa Coleman in Alan Light, *Let's Go Crazy: Prince and the Making of Purple Rain*, Atria Books, Kindle Edition.

12. Patrick Goldstein, "Movie Review: A Misbegotten Moon from Prince," *Los Angeles Times*, July 4, 1986, https://www.latimes.com/archives/la-xpm-1986-07-04-ca-696-story.html.

13. Jerome Benton, interview by DeAngela Duff, "GFM's Behind the Film Podcast—Jerome Benton," YouTube, November 4, 2017, accessed November 25, 2017, https://www.youtube.com/watch?v=JPYhJPZSyzo.

14. "Bobby Z" Rivkin, interview by Harold Lewis, Tony Melodia, and Stefan van Poucke, "Take This Beat: An Exclusive Interview with Bobby Z Rivkin—Part 2," *Uptown* magazine 43 (fall 2000), 21.

15. Bob Cavallo, interview by Jon Bream, "Prince's Greatest Talent? Self-Confidence Says the Manager Who Landed 'Purple Rain'," *Star Tribune*, April 20, 2019, accessed April 20, 2019, http://www.startribune.com/prince-s-greatest-talent-self-confidence-says-the-manager-who-landed-purple-rain/508774052/.

16. Susannah Melvoin interview with Andrea Swensson, "Prince: The Story of Sign O' The Times, Episode 3: The Quake," *The Current*, September 10, 2020, https://www.thecurrent.org/feature/2020/09/10/prince-the-story-of-sign-o-the-times-episode-3.

17. Prince, interview by Larry King, "Prince Rogers Nelson's entire 1999 CNN interview (Larry King Live)," Larry King Live, December 10, 1999, accessed December 20, 2020, https://www.youtube.com/watch?v=m8mg7CxAYUM.

650

18. Susan Rogers, interview by Ann Delisi, "True Tales of Prince from Susan Rogers, His 1980's Audio Engineer," *WDET*, January 29, 2020, https://wdet.org/posts/2020/01/29/89147-true-tales-of-prince-from-susan-rogers-his-1980s-audio-engineer/.

19. Susan Rogers, "Headphone Highlights—Dr Susan Rogers: Songs Prince Listened to—2nd May 2017," *Red Bull Radio*, May 2, 2017, accessed May 17, 2017, https://www.mixcloud.com/robstaples72/headphone-highlights-susan-rogers-songs-prince-listened-to-2nd-may-2017/.

20. Rogers, "Headphone Highlights." May 2, 2017.

21. Prince, interview by Neal Karlen, "Prince Talks," *Rolling Stone* magazine, September 12, 1985, 30.

22. Susan Rogers, interview by C. J., "C. J.: Prince Ideas Flowed Fast and Furious, Engineer Recalls," *Star Tribune*, July 3, 2018, accessed July 25, 2018, http://m.startribune.com/c-j-prince-ideas-flowed-fast-and-furious-engineer-recalls/487268161/.

23. Eric Leeds, interview by Alan Freed for *Uptown* magazine/Per Nilsen, Minneapolis, MN, October 15, 1993.

24. Matt "Atlanta Bliss" Blistan, interview by Alan Freed for *Uptown* magazine/Per Nilsen, January 23, 1994, via phone.

25. Susan Rogers, interview by Chris Williams, "The Epic," *Wax Poetics*, 67 (2018), 73–85.

26. Susannah Melvoin, interview by Andrea Swensson, liner notes for *Sign O' The Times* Super Deluxe Edition, NPG Records/Warner Records, 628756, 2020, CD & Vinyl, 17.

27. Rogers, interview by Rivers, April 27, 2018.

28. Prince, lyrics to "The Cross," *Sign O' The Times*, Paisley Park/Warner Records, 25577, 1987, CD & Vinyl.

29. Rogers, interview by Williams, "The Epic."

30. Lisa Coleman, interview by Eric Miller, "Lisa Coleman of The Revolution Picks the Essential Prince," *Pods and Sods* podcast, April 19, 2018, accessed April 20, 2018, https://podsodcast.com/2018/04/19/pte12/.

31. Prince, lyrics to "Sign O' The Times," *Sign O' The Times*, Paisley Park/Warner Records, 25577, 1987, CD & Vinyl.

32. Wendy Melvoin, "The Revolution: The Purple Playlist" on The Prince channel, *Sirius/XM*, May 21, 2020.

33. Susan Rogers, interview by Joe Coscarelli, Alicia DeSantis, Antonio de Luca, Ruru Kuo, Kaisha Murzamadiyeva, Kevin Oliver, and Shane O'Neill, "'Sign O' The Times': How Prince Wrote and Recorded a Classic Song," *New York Times*, December 3, 2020, https://www.nytimes.com/video/arts/music/100000007334512/prince-sign-o-the-times.html.

34. "Bobby Z" Rivkin, interview by Eric Miller, "Bobby Z of The Revolution Picks the Essential Prince," *Pods and Sods* podcast, April 17, 2018, accessed April 20, 2018, https://podsodcast.com/category/bobby-z/.

35. "Bobby Z," interview by Miller, April 17, 2018.

36. Rogers, interview by Coscarelli et al., December 3, 2020.

37. Rogers, interview by Williams, "The Epic."

38. Susannah Melvoin, interview by Joe Coscarelli, Alicia DeSantis, Antonio de Luca, Ruru Kuo, Kaisha Murzamadiyeva, Kevin Oliver, and Shane O'Neill, "'Sign O' The Times': How Prince Wrote and Recorded a Classic Song," *New York Times*, December 3, 2020, https://www.nytimes.com/video/arts/music/100000007334512/prince-sign-o-the-times.html.

39. Rogers, interview by Williams, "The Epic."

40. Susan Rogers, interview by Troy L. Foreman, *PC Principle* podcast, May 18, 2016, http://thepcprinciple.com/?p=9145.

41. Susan Rogers, interview by Alan Freed for *Uptown* magazine/Per Nilsen, Los Angeles, CA, December 1994.

42. Prince, lyrics to "I Could Never Take the Place of Your Man (1979 version)," *Sign O' The Times* Super Deluxe Edition, NPG Records/Warner Records, 628756, 2020, CD & Vinyl.

43. Rogers, interview by C. J., July 3, 2018.

44. Sheila E., interview by Questlove, "Questlove Supreme, Episode 62," *Pandora*, December 13, 2017, accessed December 20, 2017, https://www.pandora.com/station/play/3642532478040643917.

45. Lisa Coleman interview with Andrea Swensson, "Prince: The Story of Sign O' The Times, Episode 4: Strict and Wild and Pretty," *The Current*, September 17, 2020, https://www.thecurrent.org/feature/2020/09/17/prince-the-story-of-sign-o-the-times-episode-4-strict-and-wild-and-pretty.

46. Rogers, interview by Coscarelli et al., December 3, 2020.

47. "Bobby Z," interview by Miller, April 17, 2018.

48. Alan Leeds in *Prince: The Glory Years*, produced by Rob Johnstone for Prism Entertainment (New Malden, Surrey, UK: Chrome Dreams Media, April 2004), DVD; also available at https://www.youtube.com/watch?v=Mff7-TCj6q8&list=PLCViTltpSejxdSeIrnQ4gH2vpih8at3VL, accessed December 17, 2020.

49. Lisa Coleman, interview by Gary Graff, "The Revolution's Lisa Coleman Talks 'Piano & A Microphone 1983,' Jamming with Prince and Unreleased Gems," *Billboard*, September 20, 2019, accessed December 15, 2018, https://www.billboard.com/biz/articles/8475846/princes-new-piano-a-microphone-1983-basement-tape-is-as-simple-as-it-sounds.

50. Mark Brown "BrownMark," interview by Graeme Thomson, "Open Your Heart, Open Your Mind," *Uncut*, June 2020.

51. Lisa Coleman, interview by Jon Regen, "Prince Would Just Use a Preset and Then Brighten the F**k out of It!," *Music Radar*, May 25, 2019, accessed May 26, 2019, https://www.musicradar.com/news/lisa-coleman-prince-would-just-use-a-preset-and-then-brighten-the-fk-out-of-it.

52. Matt Fink interview with Andrea Swensson, "Prince: The Story of Sign O' The Times, Episode 4: Strict and Wild and Pretty," *The Current*, September 17, 2020, https://www.thecurrent.org/feature/2020/09/17/prince-the-story-of-sign-o-the-times-episode-4-strict-and-wild-and-pretty.

53. Prince, interview by Serge Simonart, "The Artist," *Guitar World*, October 1998, accessed March 4, 2017, http://princetext.tripod.com/i_gw98.html.

54. Eric Leeds, interview by Alan Freed for *Uptown* magazine/Per Nilsen, Los Angeles, CA, January 25, 1995.

55. Benton, interview by Dr. Funkenberry (Part 1).

56. Mark Brown "BrownMark," interview by A. D. Amorosi, "Agents of Change," *Wax Poetics*, 67 (2018), 39.

57. Susan Rogers, interview by Michael Dean, "Susan Rogers The Interview for HARDCORE Prince Fans," *Podcast Juice*, October 22, 2017, https://www.youtube.com/watch?v=uvvvdrDQ8nU.

58. Rogers, interview by Dean, October 22, 2017.

59. Rogers, interview by Dean, October 22, 2017.

60. E. Leeds, interview by Freed, January 25, 1995.

AUGUST 1986

1. Prince on stage at Madison Square Garden, New York, NY, August 2, 1986.

2. Alan Leeds, interview by Alan Freed for *Uptown* magazine/Per Nilsen, Los Angeles, CA, January 20, 1994.

3. Matt Fink, in Matt Thorne, *Prince*, Faber, Kindle Edition, Kindle Locations 2817–23.

4. Eric Leeds, interview by Alan Freed for *Uptown* magazine/Per Nilsen, Los Angeles, CA, January 25, 1995.

5. Prince, interview "AOL Live," July 22, 1997, accessed February 17, 2014, https://theiconicprince.wordpress.com/2018/03/14/aol-live-chat-with-o/.

6. Susan Rogers, interview by Alan Freed for *Uptown* magazine/Per Nilsen, Los Angeles, CA, August 4, 1997.

7. Susannah Melvoin, press release for "Forever In My Life" (Early Vocal Studio Run-Through), August 27, 2020.

8. Susannah Melvoin, interview by Touré, "Susannah Melvoin: On Loving and Almost Marrying Prince," *Touré Show*, Episode 14, February 14, 2018, accessed February 27, 2018, https://art19.com/shows/toure-show/episodes/b974f458-b18c-4e8a-bff6-00351e7ac327.

9. Prince, interview by Robert I. Doerschuk, "Portrait of the Artist," *Musician* magazine, April 1997, reprinted in *Prince Family Newsletter*, August 30, 1997, Vol. 5, #18, 107.

10. Susan Rogers, interview by Alan Freed for *Uptown* magazine/Per Nilsen, Los Angeles, CA, December 27, 1994.

11. Wendy Melvoin, in Liz Jones, *Slave to the Rhythm*, (London: Little, Brown, 1997), 93–94.

12. Lisa Coleman, interview by Lily Moayeri, "The Revolution's Wendy and Lisa Remember Prince, the Human Being," *LA Weekly*, June 19, 2017, accessed February 28, 2019, https://www.laweekly.com/music/wendy-and-lisa-of-the-revolution-remember-life-on-the-road-with-prince-8316265.

13. Wendy Melvoin, interview by Jesse Esparza, 2008, published on Myspace; Esparza sent via Facebook message to Duane Tudahl, March 8, 2017.

14. Susan Rogers, interview by Alan Freed for *Uptown* magazine/Per Nilsen, Los Angeles, CA, March 26, 1995.

15. Wendy Melvoin, interview by Larry Williams, "Girls & Boys," *Mojo* magazine (September 2018), 63–64.

16. Rogers, interview by Freed, March 26, 1995.

17. A. Leeds, interview by Freed, January 20, 1994.

18. "Bobby Z" Rivkin, interview with Alex Rawls, "Bobby Z Recalls the Evolution of The Revolution," *My Spilt Milk*, February 20, 2018, accessed February 10, 2019, https://web.archive.org/web/20190329012152/http://myspiltmilk.com/bobby-z-recalls-evolution-revolution

19. Matt Fink interview with Steve Baltin, "Hanging With Joni Mitchell, Jamming with Bruce, Sting and Miles: What It Was Like to Work with Prince in the '80s," *Forbes*, September 24, 2020, accessed September 24, 2020, https://www.forbes.com/sites/stevebaltin/2020/09/24/hanging-with-joni-mitchell-jamming-with-bruce-sting-and-miles-what-it-was-like-to-work-with-prince-in-the-80s/.

20. BrownMark, "BrownMark of the Revolution Interview | Made Prince Pancakes | Prince Pranks MOV," May 12, 2017, reposted December 22, 2020, https://youtu.be/M8_KLUDW73E.

21. Roy Bennett, interview by Tom Doyle, "Prince and the Revolution's Final Tour," *Mojo* (July 2013), 28.

22. Lisa Coleman, interview by Kevin Ritchie, "The Revolution's Lisa Coleman Talks Prince's Legacy and Grieving Through Music," *NowToronto.com*, May 12, 2017, accessed May 4, 2019, https://nowtoronto.com/music/features/the-revolution-lisa-coleman/.

23. Susan Rogers, interview by Troy L. Foreman, *PC Principle* podcast, May 18, 2016, http://thepcprinciple.com/?p=9145.

24. Matt "Atlanta Bliss" Blistan, interview by Alan Freed for *Uptown* magazine/Per Nilsen, January 23, 1994, via phone.

25. Lisa Coleman, interview by Eric Miller, "Lisa Coleman of The Revolution Picks the Essential Prince," *Pods and Sods* podcast, April 19, 2018, accessed April 20, 2018, https://podsodcast.com/2018/04/19/pte12/.

SEPTEMBER 1986

1. Wendy Melvoin, interview by Larry Williams, "Girls & Boys," *Mojo* magazine (September 2018), 65.

2. Sheila E., *The Beat of My Own Drum: A Memoir*, Atria Books, Kindle Edition, Kindle Locations 2665–66.

3. "Bobby Z" Rivkin, interview by Larry Williams, "Girls & Boys," *Mojo* (September 2018), 65.

4. "Bobby Z" Rivkin interview by Harold Lewis, Tony Melodia, and Stefan van Poucke, "Take This Beat: An Exclusive Interview with Bobby Z Rivkin—Part 2," *Uptown* magazine, issue 43 (fall 2000), 21.

5. Prince, lyrics to "New Position," performed by Prince and the Revolution, Parade, Paisley Park Records/Warner Bros., 25395, 1986, compact disc.

6. Lisa Coleman interview with Andrea Swensson, "Prince: The Story of Sign O' The Times, Episode 4: Strict and Wild and Pretty," *The Current*, September 17, 2020, https://www.thecurrent.org/feature/2020/09/17/prince-the-story-of-sign-o-the-times-episode-4-strict-and-wild-and-pretty.

7. Wendy Melvoin, "Backspin: The Revolution talk Prince's 'Parade,' 'Sign O' The Times,' and the band's breakup," *Yahoo*, published May 4, 2017, accessed May 17, 2017, https://www.youtube.com/watch?v=1hX8ihoV2qE.

8. Lisa Coleman, interview by Ian Wade, "After The Rain," *Classic Pop* (October 2018), 41–43.

9. BrownMark interview with Andrea Swensson, "Prince: The Story of Sign O' The Times, Episode 4: Strict and Wild and Pretty," *The Current*, September 17, 2020, https://www.thecurrent.org/feature/2020/09/17/prince-the-story-of-sign-o-the-times-episode-4-strict-and-wild-and-pretty.

10. Melvoin, "Backspin," May 4, 2017.

11. "Bobby Z" Rivkin, interview by Eric Miller, "Bobby Z of The Revolution Picks the Essential Prince," *Pods and Sods* podcast, April 17, 2018, accessed April 20, 2018, https://podsodcast.com/category/bobby-z/.

12. Prince, interview by Neal Karlen, "Prince Talks," *Rolling Stone*, October 18, 1990, 59.

13. Wendy Melvoin, interview by Keith Murphy, "What Had Happened Was: Lisa Coleman and Wendy Melvoin," *Vibe* magazine, March 12, 2009, http://www.drfunkenberry.com/2009/03/12/51-albums-prince-the-dream-factory-thank-you-vibe-magazine/.

14. Susan Rogers, interview by Marcus Singletary, "The Story of Prince as Told by Susan Rogers," YouTube, December 12, 2018, accessed March 1, 2019, https://www.youtube.com/watch?v=xrggiseUB8U.

15. "Bobby Z" Rivkin, "Backspin: The Revolution talk Prince's 'Parade,' 'Sign O' The Times,' and the band's breakup," *Yahoo*, published May 4, 2017, accessed May 17, 2017, https://www.youtube.com/watch?v=1hX8ihoV2qE.

16. Alan Leeds, interview by Alan Freed for *Uptown* magazine/Per Nilsen, Minneapolis, MN, November 1993.

17. Susan Rogers interview with Anastasia Lambis, "Susan Rogers On Prince 'Sign O' The Times'," *Hi Fi Way*, September 19, 2020, https://hifiway.live/2020/09/19/susan-rogers-on-prince-sign-o-the-times/.

18. Prince, interview by Billy Amendola, "Prince Talks About Drums," *Modern Drummer*, October 2001, 74.

19. Jimmy Jam, interview by Chaz Lipp, "An Interview With Jimmy Jam of the Original 7ven," *The Morton Report*, April 19, 2012, accessed March 4, 2017, http://www.themortonreport.com/entertainment/music/an-interview-with-jimmy-jam-of-the-original-7ven-part-two.

20. Susan Rogers, interview by Dennis DeSantis, "Loop | Susan Rogers on Prince, Production and Perception," *The Loop*, April 17, 2018, accessed April 25, 2018, https://www.youtube.com/watch?v=EgBZHIUUn8Q.

21. Prince, lyrics to "Cocoa Boys," *Sign O' The Times* Super Deluxe Edition, NPG Records/Warner Records, 628756, 2020, CD & Vinyl.

22. Lisa Coleman, interview by Eric Miller, "Lisa Coleman of The Revolution Picks the Essential Prince," *Pods and Sods* podcast, April 19, 2018, accessed April 20, 2018, https://podsodcast.com/2018/04/19/pte12/.

23. Coleman, interview by Miller, April 19, 2018.

24. Prince, interviewed by Ben Greenman, "Sites O' the Times," *Yahoo! Internet Life*, October 1997, 69.

25. Alan Leeds, interview by Alan Freed for *Uptown* magazine/Per Nilsen, Minneapolis, MN, January 20, 1994.

26. Leeds, interview by Freed, January 20, 1994.

27. Leeds, interview by Freed, January 20, 1994.

28. Prince, interview by Greenman, October 1997.

29. Jesse Johnson, interview by Michael A. Gonzales, "Rock Star Jesse Johnson," *Wax Poetics* (winter 2012), 42–44.

30. Susan Rogers, interview by Troy L. Foreman, *PC Principle* podcast, May 18, 2016, http://thepcprinciple.com/?p=9145.

31. Susan Rogers, interview by Duke Eatmon, "An Afternoon with | Susan Rogers | En tête à tête," YouTube, June 7, 2018, accessed March 25, 2019, https://www.youtube.com/watch?v=n6mYrqdNyQQ.

32. Susan Rogers, interview by Alan Freed for *Uptown* magazine/Per Nilsen, Los Angeles, CA, December 27, 1994.

33. Morris Day, "Morris Day on Prince, The Time, Michael Jackson, Rick James, Purple Rain (Full)," YouTube, January 2, 2020, accessed January 6, 2020, https://www.youtube.com/watch?v=brc057hg8sk.

34. Prince, interview by Chris Rock, "Prince Talks About Michael Jackson in 1997 www keepvid com," YouTube, December 29, 2010, accessed December 10, 2020, https://www.youtube.com/watch?v=T9ZN9nKQqe0.

35. Susan Rogers, interview by Chris Williams, "The Epic," *Wax Poetics*, 67 (2018), 73–85.

36. Craig Rice, *A Current Affair*, June 1989 (date unknown).

37. Lisa Coleman, interview with Dennis Hunt, "Revolution Frees Lisa and Wendy," *Los Angeles Times*, September 13, 1987, accessed March 12, 2017, http://articles.latimes.com/1987-09-13/ entertainment/ca-7727_1_lisa-coleman.

38. Alan Leeds, interview with George Cole, TheLastMiles.com, https://www.thelastmiles.com/interviews-alan-leeds/.

39. Eric Leeds, interview by Christopher Arnel, "St. Paul Peterson & Eric Leeds Interview for UMMG," The Uptown Minneapolis Music Scene (formerly Group), June 5, 2017, accessed August 19, 2018, https://www.facebook.com/groups/366116877599/permalink/10154949970292600/.

40. Eric Leeds, interview by Alan Freed for *Uptown* magazine/Per Nilsen, Minneapolis, MN, October 15, 1993.

41. Eric Leeds, interview by Alan Freed for *Uptown* magazine/Per Nilsen, Minneapolis, MN, December 16, 1995.

42. Eric Leeds, interview with Gary "G-Spot" Baca, KPFA, January 31, 1998, *Prince Family Newsletter* 6, no. 5 (February 28, 1998): 27.

43. E. Leeds, interview by Cole.

44. Eric Leeds, interview by Alan Freed for *Uptown* magazine/Per Nilsen, Los Angeles, CA, January 25, 1995.

45. Prince, interview by the Electrifying Mojo, "The Electrifying Mojo," WHYT, June 7, 1986, accessed February 14, 2016, https://www.youtube.com/watch?v=NJZCoxZ5COY.

OCTOBER 1986

1. Lisa Coleman, interview by A. D. Amorosi, "Agents of Change," *Wax Poetics*, 67 (2018), 47.

2. Eric Leeds, interview with Mark Youll, "Love Saxy: Eric Leeds on Prince and Madhouse," *Quietus.com*, May 5, 2015, https://thequietus.com/articles/17801-eric-leeds-prince-interview.

3. Eric Leeds, interview by Alan Freed for *Uptown* magazine/Per Nilsen, Los Angeles, CA, January 25, 1995.

4. Susan Rogers, "Headphone Highlights—Dr Susan Rogers: Songs Prince Listened to—2nd May 2017," *Red Bull Radio*, May 2, 2017, accessed May 17, 2017, https://www.mixcloud.com/robstaples72/headphone-highlights-susan-rogers-songsprince-listened-to-2nd-may-2017/.

5. Prince, lyrics to "Crucial," *Sign O' The Times* Super Deluxe Edition, NPG Records/Warner Records, 628756, 2020, CD & Vinyl.

6. Deborah Allen, "Deborah Allen Talks About Prince and Her Song Telepathy From The Hot Seat in Nashville, TN," *The Hot Seat*, April 21, 2016, accessed April 30, 2017, https://www.youtube.com/watch?v=UBZ95XDV2UU.

7. Allen, "Deborah Allen Talks about Prince," April 21, 2016.

8. Eric Leeds, interview by Alan Freed for *Uptown* magazine/Per Nilsen, Minneapolis, MN, October 15, 1993.

9. Wendy Melvoin, in Liz Jones, *Slave to the Rhythm* (London: Little, Brown, 1997), 93.

10. Matt "Atlanta Bliss" Blistan, interview by Alan Freed for *Uptown* magazine/Per Nilsen, January 23, 1994, via phone.

11. BrownMark, "BrownMark Joins Story Behind the Music," YouTube, July 17, 2020, accessed July 17, 2020, https://www.youtube.com/watch?v=tXFilDFgG7A.

12. "Bobby Z" Rivkin, "The *Sirius/XM* Volume Town Hall Series Featuring The Revolution With Mark Goodman and Alan Light," *Sirius/XM*, May 1, 2017, taped live May 1, 2017.

13. Lisa Coleman, interview with Deborah Frost, "On Their Own," *Buzz* magazine, Volume 3. Number 2, December 1987, 51.

14. Coleman, interview by Amorosi, "Agents of Change," 47.

15. Wendy Melvoin, "Rock 'n; Roll Guns for Hire: The Story of the Sidemen," BBC, August 2019 (accessed August 10, 2019), https://www.bbc.co.uk/programmes/b08xdlts.

16. Lisa Coleman, "Rock 'n; Roll Guns for Hire: The Story of the Sidemen," BBC, August 2019 (accessed August 10, 2019), https://www.bbc.co.uk/programmes/b08xdlts.

17. W. Melvoin, "Rock 'n; Roll Guns for Hire."

18. "Bobby Z" Rivkin interview by Harold Lewis, Tony Melodia, and Stefan van Poucke, "Take This Beat: An Exclusive Interview with Bobby Z Rivkin—Part 2," *Uptown* magazine, issue 43 (fall 2000), 22.

19. "Bobby Z" Rivkin interview by Harold Lewis, Tony Melodia, and Stefan van Poucke, "Take This Beat: An Exclusive Interview with Bobby Z Rivkin—Part 2," *Uptown* magazine, issue 43 (fall 2000), 22.

20. Coleman, interview by Amorosi, "Agents of Change," 47.

21. Eric Leeds, interview by Mobeen Azhar, *Hunting for Prince's Vault*, BBC Radio, March 21, 2015, accessed March 5, 2016, https://www.mixcloud.com/Emancipatio/hunting-for-princes-vault-bbc-documentary-by-mobeen-azhar-march-2015.

22. Eric Leeds, interview by Miles Marshall Lewis, "The Story of Madhouse: 'Syncopated Strut'," *Soulhead*, April 8, 2012, https://www.soulhead.com/2012/04/08/the-story-of-madhouse-syncopated-strut-by-miles-marshall-lewis/.

23. Alan Leeds, in Matt Thorne, *Prince*, Faber, Kindle Edition, Kindle Locations 3883–87.

24. Eric Leeds, interview by George Cole, "Interview: Eric Leeds [Part Two]," *thelastmiles.com*, accessed January 17, 2017, http://www.thelastmiles.com/interviews-eric-leeds-part2.php.

25. Prince, interview by Neal Karlen, *This Thing Called Life*, (New York: St. Martin's Press, 2020), 96.

26. Jill Jones, interview by Michael A. Gonzales, "Pop Art," *Wax Poetics*, 67 (2018), 65–71.

27. Prince, lyrics to "Violet Blue," performed by Jill Jones, *Jill Jones*, Paisley Park/Warner Bros., 9 25575, 1987, CD & Vinyl.

28. Prince, lyrics to "It Be's Like That Sometimes," *Sign O' The Times* Super Deluxe Edition, NPG Records/Warner Records, 628756, 2020, CD & Vinyl.

29. Prince, lyrics to "It Be's Like That Sometimes."

30. Jill Jones, interview by ChristopherNotWalken, "Jill Jones | Interview," *Dirty Nerdy* podcast, January 15, 2017, https://www.youtube.com/watch?v=_zgPsnBnqOY.

31. Jill Jones, interview by Robin and Dr. Mauri, "Ep 1 | Part 1 The Purple Paradigm," *The Purple Paradigm*, July 13, 2020, https://www.youtube.com/watch?v=WqseRLika84.

32. Peggy McCreary, liner notes for *Originals*, released June 2019, NPG Records/Warner Records, 591459, 11.

33. Sheila E., interview by Jem Aswad, "Sheila E. Looks Back on Prince: Their Collaborations, Engagement & Lifelong Love," *Billboard*, April 26, 2016, accessed May 1, 2016, https://www.billboard.com/articles/news/7341899/sheila-e-prince-memorial.

34. Prince, interview by Sway Calloway, MTV, 2004, accessed May 19, 2017, http://prince.org/msg/7/91779?pr.

35. Joni Mitchell, interview by Martin Townsend, "Joni Be Good," *The Guardian*, December 15, 1987, accessed October 5, 2018, http://jonimitchell.com/library/view.cfm?id=1945.

36. Prince, interview by Stephen Fargnoli, *MTV*, November 15, 1985, accessed August 18, 2016, http://www.dailymotion.com/video/x49h7vy.

37. "Bobby Z" Rivkin, interview by Eric Miller, "Bobby Z of The Revolution Picks the Essential Prince," *Pods and Sods* podcast, April 17, 2018, accessed April 20, 2018, https://podsodcast.com/category/bobby-z/.

38. Joni Mitchell, interview by Dominic Roskrow, "City Beat," *Auckland Sun*, June 9, 1988, accessed October 5, 2018, http://jonimitchell.com/library/view.cfm?id=1639.

39. Mitchell interview by Roskrow, "City Beat," June 9, 1988.

40. Joni Mitchell, interview by David Wild, "A Conversation With Joni Mitchell," *Rolling Stone* magazine, May, 30, 1991, https://www.rollingstone.com/music/music-news/a-conversation-with-joni-mitchell-172726/.

41. Alan Leeds, interview by Alan Freed for *Uptown* magazine/Per Nilsen, Minneapolis, MN, January 20, 1994.

42. Wendy Melvoin and Lisa Coleman, lyrics to "Song About" performed by Wendy & Lisa, *Wendy & Lisa*, Columbia Records, 1987, CK 40862, CD and Vinyl.

43. Jon Bream, "Prince Overturns the Revolution for New Talents," *Star Tribune*, October 17, 1986, http://web.archive.org/web/20030625022156/http://www.startribune.com/stories/389/40734.html

44. Bream, "Prince Overturns the Revolution for New Talents."

45. Lisa Coleman, interview with Deborah Frost, "On Their Own," *Buzz* magazine, Volume 3. Number 2, December 1987, 52.

46. Wendy Melvoin, in Matt Thorne, *Prince*, Faber, Kindle Edition, Kindle Locations 2382–86.

47. Prince, interview by Neal Karlen, "Prince Talks," *Rolling Stone* magazine, October 18, 1990, 60.

48. Lisa Coleman, interview by Dennis Hunt, "Revolution Frees Lisa and Wendy," *LA Times*, September 13, 1987, accessed October 7, 2019, https://www.latimes.com/archives/la-xpm-1987-09-13-ca-7727-story.html.

49. Wendy Melvoin, "Backspin: The Revolution talk Prince's 'Parade,' 'Sign O' The Times,' and the band's breakup," *Yahoo*, published May 4, 2017, accessed May 17, 2017, https://www.youtube.com/watch?v=1hX8ihoV2qE.

50. "Bobby Z" Rivkin, "Backspin: The Revolution talk Prince's 'Parade,' 'Sign O' The Times,' and the band's breakup," *Yahoo*, published May 4, 2017, accessed May 17, 2017, https://www.youtube.com/watch?v=1hX8ihoV2qE.

51. Lisa Coleman, interview by Ian Wade, "After The Rain," *Classic Pop* (October 2018), 41–43.

52. Prince interview with Neal Karlen, "Prince Talks," *Rolling Stone* magazine, October 18, 1990, 58–59.

53. Susan Rogers interview with Jem Aswad, "Prince's Path to 'Sign O' The Times,' Told by His Musicians, His Fiancee and His Longtime Engineer," *Variety*, September 24, 2020, accessed September 24, 2020, https://variety.com/2020/music/news/prince-sign-o-the-times-story-fiancee-musicians-1234782034/.

54. Susan Rogers interview with Andrea Swensson, "Prince: The Story of Sign O' The Times, Episode 2: The Dream Factory," *The Current*, September 3, 2020, https://www.thecurrent.org/feature/2020/09/03/prince-the-story-of-sign-o-the-times-episode-2-the-dream-factory.

55. "David Z" Rivkin, interview by Alan Freed for *Uptown* magazine/Per Nilsen, Minneapolis, MN, December 5, 1994.

56. Blistan, interview by Freed, January 23, 1994.

57. Susan Rogers interview with Anastasia Lambis, "Susan Rogers On Prince 'Sign O' The Times'," *Hi Fi Way*, September 19, 2020, https://hifiway.live/2020/09/19/susan-rogers-on-prince-sign-o-the-times/.

58. Lenny Waronker interview with Andrea Swensson, "Prince: The Story of Sign O' The Times, Episode 3: The Quake," *The Current*, September 10, 2020, https://www.thecurrent.org/feature/2020/09/10/prince-the-story-of-sign-o-the-times-episode-3.

59. Susanna Hoffs, interview by Samantha Bellman, "How Prince Worked His
Magic on The Bangles' 'Manic Monday'," NPR, June 21, 2019, accessed June 25, 2019,
https://www.npr.org/2019/06/21/734176868/how-prince-worked-his-magic-on-the-
bangles-manic-monday.

60. Hoffs, interview by Bellman, June 21, 2019.

61. Eric Leeds, interview by Alan Freed for *Uptown* magazine/Per Nilsen, Minneapolis, MN, December 16, 1995.

62. Jerome Benton, interview by Dr. Funkenberry, "#50 Jerome Benton Part 2" *The*
Dr Funk Podcast, April 21, 2017, accessed March 2, 2019, https://player.fm/series/the
-dr-funk-podcast/50-jerome-benton-part-2.

63. Cat Glover, interview by Michael Dean, "Cat Talks About Working with Prince
on Sign O' The Times, Lovesexy and more," *Prince Podcast*, January 19, 2020, https://
www.youtube.com/watch?v=bHsBCwyFuao.

64. Eric Leeds, interview by Alan Freed for *Uptown* magazine/Per Nilsen, Los Angeles, CA, January 25, 1995.

65. Cat Glover, interview by K Nicola Dyes, "Sexy Dancer: Cat Glover Talks 2
Beautiful Nights," *The Beautiful Nights Blog*, May 29, 2013, http://beautifulnightschi
town.blogspot.com/2013/05/sexy-dancer-cat-glover-talks-2.html.

66. Glover, interview by Dyes, May 29, 2013.

67. Glover, interview by Dean, January 19, 2020.

68. Susan Rogers, interview by Troy L. Foreman, *PC Principle* podcast, May 18,
2016, http://thepcprinciple.com/?p=9145.

69. Susan Rogers interview with *Parade*, "Susan Rogers Interview," *Housequake.*
com, May 9, 2006, https://www.housequake.com/2006/05/09/susan-rogers-interview/.

70. Rogers, "Headphone Highlights," May 2, 2017.

71. Blistan, interview by Freed, January 23, 1994.

72. Susan Rogers, interview by Montrose Cunningham, "Celebrating Black
Music Month: The 25th Anniversary of Prince's Sign O' The Times (Part 1),"
Soultrain.com, June 20, 2012, accessed August 20, 2018, https://web.archive.org/
web/20150101121925/http://soultrain.com/2012/06/20/celebrating-black-music-
month-the-25th-anniversary-of-princes-sign-o-the-times-part-1.

73. Prince, lyrics to "Rebirth Of The Flesh" *The Black Album*, performed by Prince,
Warner Records, 9 45793, 1994, CD & Vinyl.

74. Prince, lyrics to "Rebirth Of The Flesh" *The Black Album*, performed by Prince,
Warner Records, 9 45793, 1994, CD & Vinyl.

75. Prince, lyrics to "Rebirth Of The Flesh" *Sign O' The Times* Super Deluxe Edition, NPG Records/Warner Records, 628756, 2020, CD & Vinyl.

76. Prince, lyrics to "Rockhard In A Funky Place" The Black Album, performed by
Prince, Warner Records, 9 45793, 1994, CD & Vinyl.

77. E. Leeds, interview by Freed, October 15, 1993.

78. Susan Rogers, interview by Ben Wardle, "The Times They Are A Changin',"
Classic Pop (September/October 2020), 40.

79. Susan Rogers, "#22: Tour of Duty, Susan Rogers Pt. 1," *Gear Club* podcast, September 15, 2017, https://www.gear-club.net/episodes/2017/9/15/22-from-prince-to-phd-susan-rogers-ggtrc-y24ck.

NOVEMBER 1986

1. Eric Leeds, interview with George Cole, https://www.thelastmiles.com/inter views-eric-leeds-part2/.

2. Susan Rogers, "Headphone Highlights—Dr Susan Rogers: Songs Prince Listened to—2nd May 2017," *Red Bull Radio*, May 2, 2017, accessed May 17, 2017, https://www.mixcloud.com/robstaples72/headphone-highlights-susan-rogers-songs prince-listened-to-2nd-may-2017/.

3. Susan Rogers, interviewed in *Purple Reign: The Story of Prince*, documentary, BBC Radio, January 18, 2003, accessed April 25, 2004, http://www.bbc.co.uk/pro grammes/ b00snwb4.

4. Susan Rogers, interviewed in *Purple Reign: The Story of Prince*, documentary, BBC Radio, January 18, 2003, accessed April 25, 2004, http://www.bbc.co.uk/pro grammes/ b00snwb4.

5. Kate Bush, lyrics to "Running Up That Hill (A Deal With God)" performed by Kate Bush, *Hounds Of Love*, EMI Records, ST-17171, 1985, CD & Vinyl.

6. Susan Rogers, interview by Montrose Cunningham, "Celebrating Black Music Month: The 25th Anniversary of Prince's Sign O' The Times (Part 2)," *Soultrain.com*, June 22, 2012, accessed August 20, 2018, https://web.archive.org/ web/20150101115425/http://soultrain.com:80/2012/06/22/celebrating-black-music-month-the-25th-anniversary-of-princes-sign-o-the-times-part-2/.

7. Susan Rogers, interviewed in *Purple Reign: The Story of Prince*, documentary, BBC Radio, January 18, 2003, accessed April 25, 2004, http://www.bbc.co.uk/proo grammes/ b00snwb4.

8. Rogers, "Headphone Highlights," May 2, 2017.

9. Prince, lyrics to "If I Was Your Girlfriend," *Sign O' The Times*, Paisley Park/ Warner Records, 25577, 1987, CD & Vinyl.

10. Rogers, interview by Cunningham, June 22, 2012.

11. Susannah Melvoin, interviewed by Touré, "Susannah Melvoin: On Loving and Almost Marrying Prince," *Touré Show*, Episode 14, February 14, 2018, accessed February 27, 2018, https://art19.com/shows/toure-show/episodes.

12. Bono, "Bono: 60 Songs That Saved My Life," *Rolling Stone*, May 15, 2020, https://www.rollingstone.com/music/music-lists/bono-60-songs-that-saved-my-life-999226/new-radicals-you-get-what-you-give-999322/.

13. Prince, lyrics to "Strange Relationship," *Sign O' The Times*, Paisley Park/Warner Records, 25577, 1987, CD & Vinyl.

14. Susannah Melvoin, "Susannah Melvoin—I Loved Prince," *Toure Show*, January 2, 2019, https://www.stitcher.com/podcast/dcp-entertainment/toure-show/e/57981288.

15. Jill Jones, interview by K Nicola Dyes, "The Question of U: Jill Jones Talks 2 Beautiful Nights," *Beautifulnightschitown.com*, February 17, 2013, http://beautifulnightschitown.blogspot.com/2013/02/the-question-of-u-jill-jones-talks-2.html.

16. Prince, interviewed by Barney Hoskyns, "Genius In Short," *The Observer*, February 19, 2006, https://www.theguardian.com/music/2006/feb/19/urban.popandrock.

17. Susan Rogers interview with Parade, "Susan Rogers Interview, *Housequake.com*, May 9, 2006, https://www.housequake.com/2006/05/09/susan-rogers-interview/.

18. Susan Rogers interview with Parade, "Susan Rogers Interview, *Housequake.com*, May 9, 2006, https://www.housequake.com/2006/05/09/susan-rogers-interview/.

19. Jill Jones, interview by Molly Mulshine, "Prince Muse Jill Jones on Dance Mantras and being banned from MTV," *Galore*, February 14, 2016, accessed February 15, 2016, https://galoremag.com/prince-muse-jill-jones-forbidden-love/.

20. Susan Rogers, interview by Ben Beaumont-Thomas, "Prince's Sound Engineer, Susan Rogers: 'He Needed to Be the Alpha Male to Get Things Done'," *The Guardian*, November 13, 2017, accessed November 23, 2017, https://www.theguardian.com/music/2017/nov/09/princes-sound-engineer-susan-rogers-he-needed-to-be-the-alpha-male-to-get-things-done?CMP=share_btn_fb.

21. Miles Davis, "Quotable Quotes," accessed on December 19, 2020 at: https://www.goodreads.com/quotes/822979-anybody-can-play-the-note-is-only-20-percent-the.

22. Eric Leeds, interview by Alan Freed for *Uptown* magazine/Per Nilsen, Minneapolis, MN, December 16, 1995.

23. Alan Leeds, "'Truth in Rhythm,' Part 4 of 4," *Funknstuff*, YouTube, February 11, 2020, accessed February 12, 2020, https://www.youtube.com/watch?v=UjcV-__fowM.

24. Jill Jones, interview by Michael A. Gonzales, "Pop Art," *Wax Poetics*, 67 (2018), 65–71.

25. Jill Jones, interview by Robin and Dr. Mauri, "Ep 1 | Part 1 The Purple Paradigm," *The Purple Paradigm*, July 13, 2020, https://www.youtube.com/watch?v=WqseRLika84.

26. Jones, interview by Gonzales, "Pop Art"

27. Prince and Dan Piepenbring, *The Beautiful Ones* (London: Penguin, Random House, 2019), 83.

28. Susan Rogers, interview by Keith Murphy, "'Purple Rain' Turns 30: Prince's Engineer Shares Majestic (and Maddening) Studio Stories," *Vibe.com*, June 25, 2014, https://www.vibe.com/2014/06/purple-rain-turns-30-princes-engineer-shares-majestic-and-maddening-studio-stories.

29. Susan Rogers, interview by Charles Rivers, "Prince's Engineer 1983–1987: Susan Rogers," *Mixcloud*, April 27, 2018, https://www.mixcloud.com/TheCharlesRiversShow/princes-engineer-1983-1987-susan-rogers/.

30. Rogers, interview by Cunningham, June 20, 2012.

31. Rogers, interview by Cunningham, June 20, 2012.

32. Susan Rogers, interview by Chris Williams, "The Epic," *Wax Poetics*, 67 (2018), 73–85.

33. Rogers, interview by Cunningham, June 20, 2012.

34. Susan Rogers, "May 2: Gateway to Prince's Sign O' The Times with Susan Rogers," *KPCC 89.3*, May 2, 2018, accessed October 13, 2019, https://www.scpr.org/programs/q/2018/05/02/59604/.

35. Bruno Galindo, "Interview with Prince," *El Pais* (Madrid, Spain), December 15, 1996, 94.

36. Susan Rogers, PRN Alumni Foundation and Women's Audio Mission (WAM) "Engineering Prince" panel, July 17, 2019, Pandora headquarters, Oakland CA.

37. Rogers, "May 2: Gateway to Prince's Sign O' The Times with Susan Rogers," May 2, 2018.

38. "Bobby Z" Rivkin interview by Harold Lewis and Tony Melodia, for Per Nilsen/ *Uptown* magazine, Minneapolis, MN, 1993.

39. E. Leeds, interview by Freed, December 16, 1995.

40. E. Leeds, interview by Freed, December 16, 1995.

41. E. Leeds, interview by Freed, December 16, 1995.

42. E. Leeds, interview by Freed, December 16, 1995.

43. Rogers, PRN Alumni Foundation, July 17, 2019.

44. Rogers, interview by Williams, "The Epic."

45. Susan Rogers, interview by Charles Rivers, "Charles Rivers' Show: Prince Engineer: Susan Rogers '83–'87," *The Charles Rivers Show*, April 27, 2018, accessed May 29, 2018, http://thegoodamericancollective.blogspot.com/2018/04/charles-rivers-show-prince-engineer.html

46. Susan Rogers, interview by Anastasia Lambis, "Susan Rogers on Prince 'Sign O' The Times'," *Hi Fi Way*, September 19, 2020, https://hifiway.live/2020/09/19/susan-rogers-on-prince-sign-o-the-times/.

47. Rogers, interview by Cunningham, June 22, 2012.

48. Rogers, interview by Williams, "The Epic."

49. Susan Rogers, interview by Marcus Singletary, "The Story of Prince as Told by Susan Rogers," YouTube, December 12, 2018, accessed March 1, 2019, https://www.youtube.com/watch?v=xrggiseUB8U.

50. E., Sheila, *The Beat of My Own Drum: A Memoir*, Atria, Books, Kindle Edition, Locations 2914–17.

51. Alan Leeds, interview by Alan Freed for *Uptown* magazine/Per Nilsen, Minneapolis, MN, November 1993.

52. A. Leeds, interview by Freed, November 1993.

53. Alan Leeds, in Matt Thorne, *Prince*, Faber, Kindle Edition, Kindle Locations 2902–04.

DECEMBER 1986

1. Lenny Waronker, interview by Andrea Swensson, liner notes for *Sign O' The Times* Super Deluxe Edition, NPG Records/Warner Records, 628756, 2020, CD & Vinyl, 19.

2. Bob Cavallo, in Matt Thorne, *Prince*, Faber, Kindle Edition, Locations 3184–87.

3. Susan Rogers, interview by Ann Delisi, "True Tales of Prince From Susan Rogers, His 1980's Audio Engineer," *WDET 101.9 FM*, January 29, 2020, wdet.org/posts/2020/01/29/89147-true-tales-of-prince-from-susan-rogers-his-1980s-audio-engineer/.

4. Rogers, interview by Delisi, January 29, 2020.

5. Prince, lyrics to "Bob George" *The Black Album*, performed by Prince, Warner Records, 9 45793, 1994, CD & Vinyl.

6. Miles Marshall Lewis, "Prince Hits N Runs N Talks!" *Ebony*, December 22, 2015, accessed December 12, 2016, https://m.facebook.com/nt/screen/?params=%7B%22note_id%22%3A357034882167438%7D&path=%2Fnotes%2Fnote%2F&_rdr.

7. Sheila E., interview by Questlove, "Questlove Supreme, Episode 62," *Pandora*, December 13, 2017, accessed December 20, 2017, https://www.pandora.com/station/play/3642532478040643917.

8. Susan Rogers, PRN Alumni Foundation and Women's Audio Mission (WAM) "Engineering Prince" panel, July 17, 2019, Pandora headquarters, Oakland, CA.

9. Susan Rogers, interview by Anastasia Lambis, "Susan Rogers on Prince 'Sign O' The Times'," *Hi Fi Way*, September 19, 2020, https://hifiway.live/2020/09/19/susan-rogers-on-prince-sign-o-the-times/.

10. Bonnie Raitt, interview by Jon Bream and Chris Riemenschneider, "Prince: An Oral History," *Minneapolis Star Tribune*, March 14, 2004, https://www.startribune.com/prince-an-oral-history-in-the-beginning/51508747/.

11. Susannah Melvoin, interview by Andrea Swensson, liner notes for *Sign O' The Times* Super Deluxe Edition, NPG Records/Warner Records, 628756, 2020, CD & Vinyl, 15.

12. Bonnie Raitt, interview by James Henke, "Bonnie Raitt: The *Rolling Stone* Interview," *Rolling Stone* magazine, May 3, 1990, https://www.rollingstone.com/music/music-features/bonnie-raitt-the-rolling-stone-interview-236846/.

13. Sheila E., interview by Miles Marshall Lewis, "Sheila E. Opens Up About What It Was Really Like Creating Timeless Music With Prince," *Essence.com*, July 14, 2017, accessed May 7, 2018, www.essence.com/celebrity/sheila-e-talks-working-with-prince.

14. Levi Seacer Jr., interview by Michelle Griego, "The Purple Ones—Insatiable Tribute to Prince interview w/ Morty Okin & Levi Seacer Jr.," YouTube, April 9, 2017, accessed April 5, 2019, https://www.youtube.com/watch?v=YagWRajiFW4.

15. Sheila E., interview by Hunt, November 15, 1987.

16. Prince, interview by the Electrifying Mojo, "The Electrifying Mojo," WHYT, June 7, 1986, accessed February 14, 2016, https://www.youtube.com/watch?v=NJZCoxZ5COY.

17. Susan Rogers, interview by Chris Williams, "The Epic," *Wax Poetics*, 67 (2018), 73–85.

18. Mo Ostin, interview by Jem Aswad, "Former Warner Bros. CEO Mo Ostin Recalls His Long Relationship With Prince: 'He Was a Fearless Artist'," *Billboard*, April 26, 2016, https://www.billboard.com/articles/news/7341821/warner-bros-ceo-mo-ostin-prince.

19. Alan Leeds, interview by Alan Freed for *Uptown* magazine/Per Nilsen, Minneapolis, MN, January 20, 1994.

20. Waronker, *Sign O' The Times*, Super Deluxe Edition liner notes.

21. Prince, interview by Edna Gunderson, "Emancipation Conversation," *MSN Music Central*, December 1996, accessed June 19, 2017, https://sites.google.com/site/prninterviews/home/msn-music-central-december-1996.

22. Prince, interview by Liz Jones, "O(+> comes clean," *The Sunday Times Magazine* (UK), December 22, 1996, 29.

23. Waronker, *Sign O' The Times*, Super Deluxe Edition liner notes.

24. Rogers, interview by Williams, "The Epic."

25. Sheila E., interview by Sarah Grant, "Sheila E. Remembers Private Life With Prince, Wild 'Purple Rain' Parties," *Rolling Stone*, June 7, 2017, accessed August 2, 2017, http://www.rollingstone.com/music/premieres/sheila-e-on-princes-wooing-wild-purple-rain-parties-w486152.

26. Rogers, interview by Williams, "The Epic."

27. Susan Rogers, interview by C. J., "C. J.: Prince Ideas Flowed Fast and Furious, Engineer Recalls," *Star Tribune*, July 3, 2018, accessed July 25, 2018, http://m.startribune.com/c-j-prince-ideas-flowed-fast-and-furious-engineer-recalls/487268161/.

28. Rogers, interview by Williams, "The Epic."

29. Susan Rogers, interview by Montrose Cunningham, "Celebrating Black Music Month: The 25th Anniversary of Prince's *Sign O' The Times* (Part 1)," *Soultrain.com*, June 20, 2012, accessed August 20, 2018, https://web.archive.org/web/20150101121925/http://soultrain.com/2012/06/20/celebrating-black-music-month-the-25th-anniversary-of-princes-sign-o-the-times-part-1.

30. Sheena Easton, interview by Marc "Moose" Moder, "Sheena Easton: Looking Back at Her Musical History," *Wendycitymediagroup.com*, August 8, 2012, http://www.windycitymediagroup.com/lgbt/Sheena-Easton-Looking-back-at-her-musical-history-/38975.html.

31. Easton, interview by Moder, August 8, 2012.

32. Susan Rogers, interview with Marc Weingarten, "The Purple Gang," *Mojo* magazine, February 1997, 48.

33. Sheena Easton, interview by Jerry Nunn, "Sheena Easton: Big 80's: Sheena Easton talks about her musical history and Market Days," *Go Pride Network*, August 8, 2012, https://chicago.gopride.com/news/article.cfm/articleid/I408096.

34. Rogers, interview by Cunningham, June 20, 2012.

35. Easton, interview by Moder, August 8, 2012.

36. Susan Rogers, interview by Kevin Curtain, "Susan Rogers Interview on Prince, Early Beginnings, Life After Prince, and Teaching," YouTube, February 1, 2017, accessed May 14, 2019, https://www.youtube.com/watch?v=M23Od3Bvthg.

37. Eric Leeds, interview by Alan Freed for *Uptown* magazine/Per Nilsen, Minneapolis, MN, October 15, 1993.

38. Prince, interview by Neal Karlen, "Prince Talks," *Rolling Stone*, October 18, 1990, 60.

39. Alan Leeds, in Matt Thorne, *Prince*, Faber, Kindle Edition, Kindle Locations 2902–04.

40. Waronker, *Sign O' The Times*, Super Deluxe Edition liner notes, 20.

41. Waronker, *Sign O' The Times*, Super Deluxe Edition liner notes, 20.

42. Susan Rogers, interview by Curtain, February 1, 2017.

43. Prince, by Edna Gunderson, "Emancipation Conversation," *MSN Music Central*, December 1996, accessed June 19, 2017, https://sites.google.com/site/prninterviews/home/msn-music-central-december-1996.

44. Prince, interview by Lynn Norment, "Interview with Prince," *Ebony*, July 1986, 34.

45. Susan Rogers, interview by Alan Freed for *Uptown* magazine/Per Nilsen, Los Angeles, CA, March 25, 1995.

46. Susan Rogers, "Hunting for Prince's Vault With Mobeen Azhar," BBC radio, March 21, 2015.

47. Susan Rogers, interview by Duke Eatmon, "An Afternoon with | Susan Rogers | En tête à tête," YouTube, June 7, 2018, accessed March 25, 2019, https://www.youtube.com/watch?v=n6mYrqdNyQQ.

48. Beth Coleman, "Prince and the Revelation," paper, April 21, 2016, accessed June 17, 2017, http://www.papermag.com/prince-1999-cover-story-1744672669.html.

49. Prince, lyrics to "Wally" *Sign O' The Times* Super Deluxe Edition, NPG Records/Warner Records, 628756, 2020, CD & Vinyl.

50. Mark Brown "BrownMark," interview by Michael Dean, "BrownMark talks about Prince, The Revolution, and going solo," at https://www.youtube.com/watch?v=cXHKy0AGUWg.

51. Prince, lyrics to "Wally."

52. Rogers, interview by Eatmon, June 7, 2018.

53. Prince, lyrics to "Wally."

EPILOGUE

1. Susan Rogers, interview by Charles Rivers, "Charles Rivers' Show: Prince Engineer: Susan Rogers '83–'87," *The Charles Rivers Show*, April 27, 2018, accessed May 29, 2018, http://thegoodamericancollective.blogspot.com/2018/04/charles-rivers-show-prince-engineer.html

2. Lisa Coleman, interview by Ian Wade, "After The Rain," *Classic Pop* (October 2018), 41–43.

3. Roy Bennett, interview by Andrea Swensson, "Prince: The Story of 1999 Bonus Feature: LeRoy Bennett, 'Prince Was Beyond Anybody'," *The Current*, January 2, 2020, https://www.thecurrent.org/feature/2020/01/02/prince-the-story-of-1999-leroy-bennett-prince-was-beyond-anybody.

4. Susan Rogers, interview by Dennis DeSantis, "Loop | Susan Rogers on Prince, Production and Perception," *The Loop*, April 17, 2018, accessed April 25, 2018, https://www.youtube.com/watch?v=EgBZHIUUn8Q.

5. Prince, by Dan Glaister, "The Singer vs. the Record Company," *Guardian*, March 3, 1995, *Prince Family Newsletter 3*, no. 6 (March 18, 1995): 32.

6. Alan Leeds, by Alan Leeds and Gwen Leeds, "Behind the Purple Ropes: Prince and The Revolution," *Wax Poetics*, fall 2012, reposted April 21, 2016, https://web.archive.org/web/20170708073207/http://www.waxpoetics.com/blog/features/behind-the-purple-ropes-prince-and-the-revolution2/.

ACKNOWLEDGMENTS

This is a heavy book, both physically and emotionally. A project like this doesn't just magically appear. There was an army behind it and I wanted to make sure that I express my incredible gratitude to everyone who saw value in chronicling Prince's story in this much detail. First off, thank you to Prince. Without him, there would be none of this. Without his tireless work, many of us would never have discovered music that speaks to this part of our soul. Your work has inspired so many of us, showing us how to be free, how to be committed and how to be ourselves. You paved the way and we are all benefiting from your work and life. The world is better because you were here, so thank you from all of us. You earned the nickname "The Artist" and you will never be forgotten.

Since I was never able to interview Prince, I wanted to give a huge thank you to so many of those who knew Prince for sharing your time, stories, and insights. I tried to have the story of Prince told through the voices of those he invited into his life whenever possible. Thank you to the following: *the Revolution*: Mark "BrownMark" Brown, Lisa Coleman, Matt "Dr. Fink" Fink, Wendy Melvoin, and Bobby "Bobby Z" Rivkin; *Apollonia 6*: Brenda Bennett, Apollonia Kotero, and Susan Moonsie; and *the Family*: Jellybean Johnson, Eric Leeds, Susannah Melvoin, and Paul Peterson. In addition, I am grateful to the all of the people who spoke to me who were there during 1985 and 1986, including: Marylou Badeaux, LeRoy (Roy) Bennett, Matt "Atlanta Bliss" Blistan, Paul Camarata, Bob Cavallo, Tony Christian, Robert "Cubby" Colby, André Cymone, David Coleman, Susie Davis, Devin Devasquez, Alexa Fioroni, Brent Fischer, Clare Fischer, Arne Frager, Cat Glover, Todd Herreman, Craig Hubler, Coke Johnson, Jill Jones, Mike Kloster, Alan Leeds, Paul Levy, Eddie "Eddie M."

Mininfield, Albert Magnoli, Brad Marsh, Peggy "Peggy Mac" McCreary, Gary Platt, David "David Z" Rivkin, Vicki Rivkin, Susan Rogers, Michael Rosen, Rebecca Ross, Wally Safford, Levi Seacer Jr., Stephen Shelton, Michael Soltys, and Norbert Stachel. You were all in the room with him while history was being made, and know the full story of his work better than anyone else. Thank you for wanting to get it right, and for sharing your personal memories with the world.

To everyone who knew and loved Prince, I hope this book honors the work you have done, and thank you again for giving me the opportunity to have a small part in reminding people of the contributions you've made to modern culture as well as to the history of rock and roll. For me, not a day goes by without listening to Prince's music and recognizing that his music contains elements of each of you, and it is an honor to know that you felt that a project like this was historically important. I am truly humbled.

Most of the quotes in the book are firsthand. However, I reached out to several additional people for full interviews, but when they weren't available, I had to rely on public comments they've given in the past to other sources. Each of them had a hand in the musical legacy chronicled in this book, and their voices deserved to be heard. When that was necessary, I cited the original sources to give credit to those who did the original works. Please seek out the magazines, interviews, podcasts, and books for more details.

An incredible thank you to Rachael Paley, David Furnish, Scott Campbell, Benjamin Trigano, and my friend of 30+ years, Mathieu Bitton, for moving mountains to have Elton John write his insightful and heartfelt foreword. Thank you, Elton John! You were my introduction to rock music and I never dreamed we'd work on a project together. To share the book cover with rock royalty is beyond the dreams of a young boy sitting in his room listening to *Goodbye Yellow Brick Road* and *Rock of the Westies*.

Also, a huge thank you Hayley Beech (Cat Glover's manager), Gary L. Coleman (Lisa and David Coleman's father), Donna Fischer (representing the Clare Fischer Family Trust), Marty Bragg (Jellybean Johnson's manager), and Sophie Putland (representing the late Michael Putland's estate). It is also important to mention the contributions from the late Craig Hubler of Sunset Sound, for without him this book would not have been possible. He is missed by so many. Thank you my friend, and to Paul Camarata (also from Sunset Sound) for opening the doors of your studio to me and understanding when I've made multiple follow-up requests and visits over the last two decades. Thank you for doing it with a smile and encouragement. Every time I am invited back, I can feel the history of what was recorded in those rooms.

It is important to shine a spotlight on a group of friends who are truly brilliant Prince scholars: jooZt Mattheij, Camron Gilreath, De Angela Duff, Scott Bogen, Thomas de Bruin, and Craig Mortimer-Zhika. Without their daily (even hourly) help, this book wouldn't have been nearly as informative and fun to write. They've stuck with me through two books, and I hope they want to be involved with the future volumes, as well, because they know the details of Prince's career and shared their wisdom freely and openly to make sure everything is accurate.

My gratitude is also shared with Angelo Schifano, Edgar Kruize and Eric Rogers for looking over the text and gently pointing out why I needed the extra sets of eyes! lol

Thank you to all the 9,109 members of Facebook group (Prince: The Complete Studio Sessions book series) for their humor, enthusiasm, and help. So many of you went above and beyond including: Carol Alspach-Morris, Arsenio Billingham, Christopher Brown, Mark Brown, Barry Chambers, Sünil Chauhan, Jennifer Cherry, Bert Cielen, Andrea Cober, Kevin Davis, Peter Dinnington, Stephenie Stephaluffagus Esbrand, Craig Felton, Rodney Fitzgerald, Hans Gaarlandt, Donna Gardner, Christophe Geudin, Laura Guitar, Lee Harris, Jonathan Harwell, Jon Hille, Linda Hughes, RD Hull, Anthony Jason, ZD John, Damien Johnstone, Edgar Kruize, Andrew Ledger, Miles Marshall Lewis, Arthur Lizie, Hugh Jorgan, Alan MacLean, Mike Magafa, Ben Marshall, Gavin McLaughlin, Edmund Moriarty, Tage Mortensen, Chakib El Moutawakil, Christy V. Norman, Chak Odelika, Matt Osgood, Alex Otten, Wendy Pardike, Diana M. Pash, Sharad Patel, Katy Prozinski, Hassan Razzaq, Neil Richards, Endang W. Robertson, Ed Roma, Matthijs Nicolay Rook, Ernest L. Sewell, Fred Shaheen, Jason Paul Smith, Brian Sommerville, Sofar Sopleased, Rob Staples, Scott Stine, Roy Stout, Erik van Bommel, Cornell Wilson Jr., Chad Womack, and Ron Worthy.

This book could not have been done without so many of you who helped with the monumental task of double-checking the transcripts. For this volume, I want to recognize: Carol Alspach-Morris, Joan Alythia, Heather Anderson, Coleen Anne, Raine Baker, Leslie Schaefer Ballard, Kares Balogh, Ian Leon Baumeister, Litsa Beck, Brandon Benwell, Ian Blair-Edgar, Stacey Boyd, Alan Bradley, Frode Breimo, Colm Broaders, Adele Burchi, Alex Cho, John Clark IV, Phil Clârksön, Darrien Curial, Mike Curtis, Cal Davis, Pam Dierking, Annik Dupaty, Stephenie Esbrand, Troy L. Foremen, David Gibbons, John W. Goodman, Sam Hayden, Becki Haynes, Lisa Heinze, Olga Hernández, Audrey Johnson, Tim Joseph, Connie Kelley, Marthijn Klopper, Elaine Knight, Edgar Kruize, Neil Kumar, Charlotte L. Coleman, Kitt Larue, Andrew Ledger, Jacques Lefonque, Maria Lynne, Robert Macintyre, Kuti Mack, Malena McElroy-Riggs,

Dean Mireylees, Edmund Moriarty, Sara Miller Morris, Nancy Moyer, Iain Newhouse, David Nierman, Jill Norman, Arlene Oak, "Little Johnny" Parlier, Toni Parker, Diana M. Pash, Jakub Pietrzela, Betsy Powe, Tenesa S. Powell, Kathryn RedSky, Beth Renner Regrut, William Richardson, Dan Rivkin, Linda Rizer, Barbara Rogers, Clare M. Rountree, Marti Rowe, Lynn Saathoff, Todd Sanzone, Tim Sawyer, Sheila Self, Craig Smith, Tammie Smith, Mike Smits, Jim Stella, Jenelle Stockton, Tessi Stolp, Carmen Tanner Slaughter, Brian Tressler, Nicky Tuzio, Jeff Wieczorek, Stuart Willoughby, Jace Witman, Scott Woods, and Meredith Zee. Everyone in the Facebook group has been the perfect blend of friends and true funk soldiers who have reached out with encouragement, love, information, and research. You are like family to me, and I love knowing so many of you. Thank you.

It is almost impossible for me to express my gratitude to those who held up the torch in the dark so I was able to turn a dream into a series of books, but here I go. For the research, the first wave of people included Brian Charrell (one of my closest friends; sadly, he didn't live long enough to see this book series come to life), Alan Freed (who supplied countless hours of interviews he'd done, several dinners and connections, as well as a great friendship), Alex Hahn (for nearly daily questions and encouragement), Per Nilsen (a great friend even though I've only personally spoken to him once in 30 years!), Laura Tiebert, David Wild, Alan Light, Marc Roberty, Jose Álvarez, Roger Cabezas, Sylvia M. Burch, Florent Bidaud, Susan Lane, Chambers Stevens, Stacey Castro, Katherine Copeland Anderson, Jon Bream (the *original* Prince author and source of so much information about his career), Terry Jackson, Miles Marshall Lewis, Kna Lo Venge, David Dubow, Lars Meijer (for help researching the sound effects), Michael C. T. Andersen, Andrea Swensson, Maria Michelle Ellicott, Bill Johnson, Kevin Davis, Michael Yanovich, Chuck Zwicky, Eddie Miller, Bob Mockler, Candy Dulfer, Dave Aron, Gayle Chapman, Hans-Martin Buff, Ingrid Chavez, Jana Anderson, Therese Stoulil, Joe Blaney, John Aldridge, Kyle Bess, Marci Dictarow, Matt Larsen, Mike Koppelman, Owen Husney, Robbie Paster, Kim Berry, Ross Palone, Shane T. Keller, Steve Fontano, Sue Ann Carwell, Sylvia Massey, Tom Garneau, Tom Tucker, Afshin Shahidi, Marylou Badeaux, Dave Hampton, Anna Fantastic, Ruth Arzate, Ken Caillat, Femi Jiya, Christine Elise McCarthy, Jerome Benton, Adele Burchi, Wendy Pardike, Michael Van Huffel, Jill Willis, Steve Parke, Marc Weingarten, Elle Richardson, Craig Rice, Gwen Leeds, Anna Florence, Owen Husney, John Greenewald, Celia Bonaduce, Aisha K. Staggers (*Huffington Post*), Peter Dinnington, Alex Cho, Willie Adams, Alphonso Starr, James Sucher (thank you for all the amazing advice and guidance), Mark Lewisohn (the Godfather of studio session books!), Takuya

"Takki" Futaesaku, Samantha McCarroll, Tracey Escobar Mora, Neal Karlen, Robin Stevens, Chrissie Dunlap, Tim D'Aquino, Carol McGovney, Jamie Shoop, Anne Beringer, Jason Draper, Tony Melodia, Harold Lewis, Prince Army Las Vegas, Prince Army Los Angeles, The BumpSquad, Controversy Las Vegas, Purple Funk SF, Middle Tennessee Prince Fans, Colorado Prince Fans, P-Bay, Eric Rogers and Paisley 5 & Dime, the Prince Museum, Purple Underground, The Uptown Minneapolis Music Scene, Purple Playground, and the entire *Uptown* magazine staff. Also, a big thanks to Ted Springman, Mike Wilson, Andy Fischer, and Steve Lang at Warner Bros. for helping in the early stages of my research over 10 years ago with their archives, Clare Zupetz and Tom Baskerville at Twin Cities Musicians Union, and Gordon Grayson and Andrew Morris at American Federation of Musicians Local 47, and to the clerks at the Library of Congress during my repeated visits. Thank you Apollonia for the incredible support and for introducing me to Susan Moonsie who truly is as sweet as you said she would be. An epic thank you to Jesse Esparza for believing in this and getting me in contact with Wendy and Susannah Melvoin, and Lisa Coleman, who were even more open than I ever dreamed possible.

The Prince community is blessed with countless podcasts, radio shows, blogs, and hosts that deserve notice because of their incredible source material and their dedication to finding the truth: *Podcastjuice.net* with Michael Dean and Big Sexy, *The Soul Brother Show* with Mr. Chris, *The Third Story* podcast with Leo Sidran, *The Electrifying Mojo* on WHYT, *Inside Berklee*, *PC Principle* podcast, *Hunting for Prince's Vault* with Mobeen Azhar (BBC), *The Dr. Funk* podcast with Dr. Funkenberry, *The Upper Room with Joe Kelley*, Boomer Movement Network, *Sound Opinions* on Chicago Public Radio, Richard Cole's *Amiri Purple Talk*, *Tomi Jenkins Radio Show*, Professor of Rock, Red Bull Music Academy Lectures, Real Rube Radio, *Purple Reign: The Story of Prince* (BBC), Swedish Radio P3, LOTL Radio, Rico "Superbizzee" Washington, The Five Count, *Funk Chronicles* with Dr. Turk Logan, The Jimmy Jam show, *The Peach and Black* podcast, Shawn Carter and the *Enemy Radio Show*, *The Violet Reality* with Casey Rain and Kim Camilia, Nicky Tuzio of *Purple Primetime* (for the constant encouragement), Chris Horton from *Funkatopia Radio* (thank you for the birthday dinner!), Eloy Lasanta of *Prince's Friend*, *Mountains and the Sea* podcast, Suzee Marie Clay's *Soul Sanctuary*, Chris Johnson's *Purple Knights Podcast*, the *d/m/s/r* podcast by Dystopian Dance Party (Zach Hoskins), the *Uptown Master Class* with Christopher Arnel, *Dirty Nerdy* podcast, *Pods and Sods* (with Craig Smith), the *Charles Rivers Show*, *Housequake*, *Pop! A Pop Culture Podcast* with Ken Mills (the Podfather), *Love4OneAnother* podcast, "Prince 365 Celebration Archives," Sassan Niasseri, Jay Gabler of *The Current*, Andrea Swensson who hosts the Prince Podcasts, Bobby Z's radio show on 96.3 K-TWIN, *Grown Folks Music* podcast, *Questlove Supreme* on Pandora, *Wally's All Access*, *The BrownMark Podcast*, *Tamar talks About Edu-Tainment & More . . . It's a Music Business 4 a Reason podcast*, Troy Gua, KaNisa Williams from the *Muse 2 The Pharaoh* podcast, and *The Beautiful Nights* blog by K Nicola Dyes, among others. I'm sure there are a few I've missed, but that is part of how incredible Prince was. He inspired so many other artists to reflect on what he did. I hope these podcasts get as many people from Prince's past telling their stories as possible. This is history, and as we've learned with the passing of so many talented people, sometimes a story ends in midsentence. Thank you for documenting these for the sake of Prince's legacy.

Most of my research was primary, but there were many secondary sources. Several books were valuable resources for this project, including *DanceMusic-SexRomance* by Per Nilsen, *The Vault* by Per Nilsen and *Uptown* magazine, *Prince: A Pop Life* by Dave Hill, *Prince: Inside the Purple Reign* by Jon Bream, *Possessed: The Rise and Fall of Prince* by Alex Hahn, *Let's Go Crazy: Prince and the Making of* Purple Rain by Alan Light, *The Beat of My Own Drum: A Memoir* by Sheila E., *My Time with Prince* by Dez Dickerson, *Wally, Where'd You Get Those Glasses* by Wally Safford, *Prince in the Studio* by Jake Brown, *Prince: Inside the Music and the Masks* by Ronin Ro, *Music on Film: Purple Rain* by John Kenneth Muir, *Prince* by Matt Thorne, *Slave to the Rhythm* by Liz Jones, *The Rise of Prince (1958-1988)* by Alex Hahn and Laura Tiebert, and *Spin* magazine's article "Prince: An Oral History," and *Wax Poetics'* Prince issues (no. 50 winter 2012 and no. 67). I'd also like to personally thank everyone working on PrinceVault.com, specifically jooZt Mattheij who tirelessly helped with the hundreds of updates in the paperback and was a constant source of information, encouragement and perspective about Prince's career. These books, and Prince research in general, are more robust and accurate based on his unrelenting search for accuracy. I've had a small part in their research so I'm friends with many of them and I can tell you that everyone involved with PV seeks out the truth and dedicates their time and money to honoring Prince's legacy. I've said it before, but it is true. It is the (pre-fire) Library of Alexandria of Prince information on the internet, and I can guarantee you that they are a primary source on virtually every book that has come out about Prince (including mine). They really are the unsung heroes when it comes to chronicling Prince's legacy. Many members of Prince.org and other sites in the Prince community have become my friends outside of the cold indifference of the internet.

I'd also like to acknowledge "Princeologist" Michael Robertson from the incredible *Prince In Print* Archive for all of his tireless help.

I also want to thank everyone at Paisley Park for working so hard to protect his legacy and inviting us into his home to pay our respects, the Prince Estate for being the source of all of the incredible projects in recent history, and to Warner Records and Sony Records for keeping him in our memory with so much undiscovered music being released. You are truly honoring him with the dedication you have for getting it right. I don't know of any other rock star who has such a wealth of undiscovered music. And a heartfelt and sincere thank you to the heirs of Prince for wanting to share their family's legacy with the world. We are all so grateful.

And, of course, to my original acquisitions editor, Natalie Mandziuk, as well as my current editor, Michael Tan and the entire team at Roman & Littlefield including Della Vache, Susan Hershberg, Corey Rickmers, Deborah Orgel Hudson, and Veronica Dove: Thank you for all of the hard work getting this completed despite my best efforts to keep making fixes until the very end! lol. To Linda Ganster and Michael Ganster: Thank you for your faith in this book series and in me. I owe you both another dinner, and so much more!

Thank you to the late Michael Putland for the perfect cover shot. Your work deserves to be in a museum. Please find his art and enjoy it. I've included the original shot inside the book without the Photoshop elements so people can see his incredible talent.

An epic thank you is also due to Phil "Rev" Hodgkiss for knocking it out of the ballpark once again with this iconic cover art. I don't know how you do it, but you have topped yourself and have once again found a way to put what is in my head on the page. Words cannot express my gratitude. Thank you for being so generous and for taking the reins when it came to locking down the cover.

Questlove, thank you for always cheering this project on. You are truly the most well-known and respected Prince scholar out there, and I am always grateful for what you've done for this and for Prince's legacy.

To Jacqui Thompson and Hucky Austin, I will always be grateful for how you both helped early on in the process and I cannot thank you enough. Projects like this are more richly detailed and filled with more heart because of the two of you. I am fortunate to call both of you my friends and I look forward to the next PRN Alumni project down the road.

Also, thank you to all of you who have been kind enough to write great reviews for the books on Amazon and other sites. If you want more books, that is one of the best tools because positive reviews help inspire others to purchase the book. I read them all and listen to your thoughts more than you realize. As Prince sang, "Sacred is the prayer that asks for nothing, while seeking to give thanks for every breath we take."

I'd like to also thank the following people who have not only enjoyed the first book, but jumped in line early to pre-order the second book. You have blown me away with your passion and interest in this series and I am speechless, which as an author, is rare for me! lol Thank you to: Taylor Abbott, Tracey Abbott, Søren Abildgaard, Vicky Adair, Michael Adams, Hanna Affi, Rosalina Africano, Patrick Aiglehoux, Jennifer Aiken, Don Alexander, Maurice Alexander, Zaheer Ali, Anna Aljamea, Carol Alspach-Morris, David Althoff, Jr., Heather Anderson, Lionell Anderson, Madison Anderson, Miranda Anderson, Patricia Anderson, Rene Andersen, Frode Andresen, Benjamin De Los Angeles, Michael Anthony, Thomas Anthony, Lemonia Antoniou, Fritz Archer, Kenji B. Armstrong, Christopher Arnel, Suzanne G. Artemoff, Ericka Y. Attles, Paul Audino, Amy Austin, Celestae Bailey, Deloris Bailey, Joseph Bailey, Russel Bailey, Robert Baillargeon, Brandon Baker, Kris Baker, Jason Baldock, Leslie Ballard, Rebecca Banas, Khamkeokat Banemanivong, Tarick Banton, Erwin Barendregt, Sandra Barfield, Joleen Barnes, Samuel Barnett, Amalia E. Barrios, Tracy Bartak, Dean Orobia Basilio, Kate Basura, Kristy Batie, Ian Baumeister, Jeff Beck, Oni Bell, Gigi Miranda Belluomini, Aynoka Bender, Tom Bennett, B. Zachary Bennett, Carolyne Benson, Catherine Berger, Stephen Berkstresser, Vincent Bernatowicz, Aaron Blaisdell, Stone Blake, Michele Blaskvitch, Francisco Blondet, Greg Bloom, Jana Blunt, Daniel Boccoli, Jeff Bodrie, Darren Boen, Werner Bosshard, Stacey Boyd, Ciaran Boyle, Sherida Bradby, Lisa Bradham, Cassandra Bradley, Eric Bramlett, Jason Breininger, Brian Brinkman, Diane Brockley-Drinkman, Mark Brown, Tarento Brown, Laurinda D. Brown-Johnson, Debbie Bryan, Sheila Marie Bueron, Noah Buist, Adele Burchi, Jeff Burke, Kevin Bush, Delores Butler, Melissa Butts, Kalolaina Cabuloy, Erik Cagle, Darryl and Carmen Cameron, Gavin Campbell, Marc Cardenas, Carrie Carlson, Kirk Carman, Annette Carpenter, David Carroll, Carl Carter, K. Caruso, Anthony Casale, Gina Casaleggio, Sergio Casucci, Eric Caver, Jennifer Cherry, Alex Cho, Daniel Christian, David Ciolkosz, Mark Claeson, John Clark, William Clark, Skip Clarke, Phil Clarkson, Kerry Clifford, Andrea Cober, Joey Coco, Jay Cohen, Charlotte Coleman, Brian Colvin, Joan Comenzo, Jeff Compton, Leland Compton III, Pascal Comvalius, Anthony Conlon, Jarret Cooper, Lawrence Cooper, Melody Cooper, Inara Cooper, Paul Cooper, Mayumi Cooper, Adriana Copeman, H. Justin Cosell, Sheryl Covington, Sean Cox, R. Michael Cox, Andy Cox, Amanda Crabtree, Rich Cranmore, Conor Crawford, Arvy L. Crayton, Michael Criscuolo, Lois Anne Croce, Ashley Culp, David Cumo, Michael Cunningham, Sean Cusick, Isaac Dabom, Julie Dahl, Sean Daly, David Damato, Danny Damian, Ronlyn Dandy, William Daniels, Rob Dansak, Anil Dash, Dwight Davis, Kevin Davis, Gregory Davis, Tammy Davis, Marcia Davis, Brian Donald Davis,

ACKNOWLEDGMENTS

Julia Day, Samuel Hayden-De Jesus, David De Pauw, Tom De Strooper, Nick Deal, Markus Deenik, Alan Dicker, Geoffrey Dicker, Marceia Dickinson, Martin Diekhoff, Nicholas Dodge, Peter Donnelly, Kristin Dorn, Katie Dorsey, Aaron Doty, John Doughty, Alvin L. Douglass, Kevin Dowling-Logue, Allison Downer, Lisa D. Dozier, Beverly Dukes-Brown, Scott Duncan, Annik Dupaty, Francisco Duran, Y'evette E. Thomas, Chuck Earling, Angela Echols, Samantha A. Edmonds, Teresa Edwards, Klaus Egelund, Becky Ehrhardt, Cory Eischen, Zachary D. Elick, Patti Emery, Matt Emery, K. Emery, Stephenie Esbrand, Jeff Eskew, Dana Eugenio, Kristen Fahnoe, Richard Fairbairn, Shawna Faith, Keith S. Farley, Oscar A. Felix, John Ferrier, Casie Fetterman, Abel Fimbres, Rodney Fitzgerald, Mark Flanagan, Stuart Fleming, Peggy Flores, Micha Flowers, Venise Flowers, Tyler Floyd, Brian Flynn, Carol Forfar, Daniel Forsthoff, Tami Foster, Tina Sobel Foster, Julie Fox, Franco Franus, Martha and John Frost, Kathy Gaalaas, Hans Gaarlandt, Andrew James Gadek, Chris Gambino, Rhonda Ganansky, Trevor Gandy, Ismael Garcia, Chopin Gard, Donna Gardner, Antonio Garfias, Adam Garlock, Tom Garneau, Craig M. Garrett, Richard Gee, Quentin Geerinckx, Michael Genovese, Melanie George, Nikki Giannini, Daren Giberson, Alisia Gill, Susan Gladwin, Karrie Gleim, Cameron Glover, Buddy Goettsch, David A. Gold, Miguel Gomez, Tony Gonzales, Christa Gonzalez, Gailya Goode, Robert Goodman, Sandi Grady, Stephanie Grant, Matt Green, Barbara Greene, Eric Greene, Eric Greenwood, Sean Gregory, Geoff Griffin, Terry Griffin, Mindy Griffith, Emily Griffy, Troy Gua, Gary Guzman, Ethan Guzman-Barron, Derrick Gwynn, Michael J. Hagen, Mark Haley, Alden Hall, Marian Hall, James Hall, Meredith Hall, Clay Hallman, Tamara Ellerbe Hanley, Keith Hanlon, Steven Hanna, Mark Hanner, Sally Hanson, Christopher Harrington, Christina Harris, Todd Harris, Henry Harris, Mikela Harris, John Harris, Burl Harris, William Hartung, Deb Harvey, Verena Hasenbach, Jesse Haskell, Christopher Hatfield, Melissa Hawes, Lee Hawker, Kimberly Hayes, Ronda Hayes, Becki Haynes, William J. Haynes, III, Libby Hayworth-Lenne, Ronald Heigler, Lisa Heinze, Denny Henson, Michael Herbert, Bart Hermans, Olga Hernandez, Meghan Hernandez, Tina Herndon, Cavalier Regina Herring, Tiffany Hill, Tennia Hill, Mark Hill, Marilyn Hinson, Denise Hodge, Andy Hodgson, Kurt Hoffman, Yolanda Holler-Managan, Kathy Holzer, Travis Hon, Anthony Honore, Chris Horton, Ian P. Hosfeld, Victoria C. Hover, Cindy Howard, Gary Howell, Janette Hoysted, Mark Hudack, RD Hull, Penelope Hummel, Traci Humphrey, Sandra Inglis, Michelle Inglis, Kris Isaac, JD Jackson, Jr., Forrest Jackson, Ian Jackson, Anne Jankiewicz, Lisa Jarema, DJ Jaycee, Steven Jenkins, Richard L. Jenkins, Bonnie Denise Jenkins, Lenise Jennings, Matthew Jessee, Jamie Lynn Joel, Audrey Johnson, Chris Johnson, David Johnson, Lawrence Johnson,

ACKNOWLEDGMENTS

Kathleen Johnson, Alec Jokubaitis, Shana Jones, Alisa Joseph, Allison Joy, Lori Joyner, Kevin Judd, Alan Kagan, Brad Kageno, Aaron Kannowski, Ismo Kauranen, Rachel Kayla, Bryan Kelk, Rodney Keller, Connie Kelley, Ian Kiigan, Todd Kilby, Michelle King, Brandy King, Candida King, Conga King, Shane Kirk, Allison Nekel Knight, Elaine Knight, Dr Matt Koenen, Kofi Kofi, Craig Kotwica, Thomas Kozlowski, Julie Kreps, Ramon Lagrand, Erik D. Langdon, Sabina Lanzetta, Eddie Laranjo, Shelly and Rick Larocco, Laura L. Larson, Terissa Leath, David Lee, Dan Lee, Ersin Leibowitch, Jason Leisch, Tony Lemmens, Lotus Leong, Adam Lewis, Lureece D. Lewis, Brian Lewis, Brian Lewis, Harold Lewis, Cynthia Leyvas, Lisa Lincoln, Lavette Lipscomb-Dudley, Douglas Long, Paul Lopez, Daniel Lopez, Lisa Torockio Lowman, Sandra Lozano, Eric J. Luecking, Rudi Charles Lunder, Richard Lynch, Maria Lynne, Virginie Mabille, Tone Maceira, Kuti Mack, Mary Fran Madden, Patrick J Maiolo, Sina Malekuti, James and Lesley Malloch, Micah Mann, Steve Marshall, John Martherus, Carmen Martinez, Mark Masiello, April Materazzi, Cami Mattingly, JT Maxwell, Sharon McAllister, Christopher McCarty, Terrence McCrary, Terrence McCrary, Rebecca McCray, Ken McCullagh, Rob McGlotten III, Anthony McGowen, Chris McKay, Christopher McKay, Beez McKeever, William Meade, Theresa Meehan, Deborah Meehan, Tony Melodia, Angie Mercer, Darryle Merlette, Lisa Metheny, Jeremy Meyer, Jennifer Michlitsch, Sebastian Midolo, Roger Miller, Kym Miller, Ken Mills, Morris Lee Mills, Jordin Mimran, Jeff Minyard, Sebastiano Mion, Andrea Mitchell, Moe Moe, Fisseha Moges, Zachary Moinichen, David I. Molina, Richard Moody, Matthew Mooney, Stacy Morgan, Keith Morgan, Sara Morris, Laura Morris, Charmon Morris, J. Greg Morrison, Kathy Morrissey, Charlotte Moses, Teal Moss, Rico Mota, Troy Motes, Nancy Moyer, Elaine Munoz, Vicki Murray, Darryl Murray, Jeff Musick, Keith Nainby, Tami Nejman, Thomas Nelson, Andy Nichols, Joanie Nickel, David Nierman, Amanda N. Nierman, Asia Noble, Caspar Nolan-Evans, Josh and Christy Norman, Ken Norris, Emiko North, Wokie Nwabueze, Cathy O'Connor, Mark O'Connor, Peggy O'Neill, Maureen O'Sullivan, Arlene Oak, Robert Oblon, Jeremy Olson, Kevin Onken, Matt Osgood, Karl Ott, Scott Otto, Joanne Palmer, Krystina Paraiso, Wendy Pardike, Shane Parish, Dianne Parker, Michael Parr, Diana Pash, Sharad Patel, Lesley Paulette, Rick Pavao, Daniel Payne, Taunja Pegues, Amy Pennisi, Vincente G. Peoples, Carlos Perez, Vicki Perry, Marilyn Peterson, Andrea Pheil, David Platt, Carrie Poe, Ben Poe, Mi-ling Poole, Mark Potter, Betsy Powe, Tara Nicole Powell, David Powell, Jason Priesmeyer, Mark Prince, Cornelia Provost, Bart Purdy, Shayla N. Purifoy, Shawn Puryear, Enza Ramagnano, Todd A. Ramirez, Joann Ramon, Darren E. Reese, Victoria Reese, Beth Regrut, Kenneth Renneberg, Laura Renton, Ashok Reuben, Alec Reyna, Stacey Ricco,

Donnie Rice, Kay Richardson, Tay Richardson, Kelly Richardson, Cindy Rich-
gels, Benjamin Rieck, Nicole Riegert, Kristin Rigby-Deboer, Linda Rios, Julie
Rippberger, Nadine Rivers-Johnson, Linda Rizer, Hubert Roberts, Roxanne
Robertson, Renee Robertson, Michael Robertson, Angela Robinson, Morris
Robinson, Anthony Rodgers, Melissa Rodriguez, Javish Rodriguez, Marlo Roe-
buck, Diana Romano, Paul Romero, Clare Rountree, Susan Royal, Natalie Roz-
zell, Justin Ruiz, Stephanie Ruiz, Raul Ruiz, Urban Rybrink, Lynn Saathoff, Don
Saddler, Jeanne-Michele Salander, Edward Sambucci, Wendell Samuels, Todd
Sanzone, Jim Saraco, Cynthia Saunders, Krista Schadt, Barbara Schiemer, Mary
Schnitzer, Pamela Schwartz, Fern Schweitzer, Sterling D. Seals, Robin Seewack,
Morgen Selmer, Michael Seppa, Melissa Seymour, Kurt Shanks, Keith Sheehan,
David Shelton, Nicolette Shepard, Jonathan Sherer, Michele Shibuya, Loribeth
Sicotte, Clinton Siddons, JD Silva, Doug Simpson, Micah Simpson, Thomas
Singleton, Melissa Skarban, Craig Smith, Jeff Smith, Kimberly Smith, Rosilyn
Makeba Smith, Michelle Smith, Mike Smits, Dustin Snyder, Brian Sommerville,
James Soran, Joey Sorge, Patrick Spaulding, Clarissa Stafford, Kelly Stangl-
Meddaugh, Christian Steenberg, Raymond Steenstra, Lori Stell, Mike Stewart,
Zack Stiegler, Zane Stillings, Scott Stine, Tessi Stolp, David Stout, Michael
Stowe, Eric Strickland, Victor Stuhr, David Suber, Jeff Sublett, Craig Sullivan,
Daniel Sumerlin, Dean Swann, Christina Tabaczka, Katrina Mayhew Taibe,
Kevin Tanaka, Jeff Taube, Gloria Tava, Becky Taylor, Ed Taylor, Karin Telaroli,
Gordon Templin, Ricci Terranova, Kathy Terreri, Cindy Terry, Janell Terry,
Bradley Thibaut, Christophe Thiry, Kerry Tholl, Bryan Thomas, Cat Thomp-
son, Marcus Thompson, Angela E. Thompson, Sara Thompson, Vynce Thomp-
son, Angelo Tomaras, Chuck Tomlinson, Mary Torres, Carmelo Torres, Mark
A. Tournear, Donna Triplett, Omar Trujillo, Yvette Tucker, Eudora Tucker,
Eudora Tucker, Arthur Turnbull, Robin T. Turner, Stephanie M. Turner, An-
thony Turner, Maria Tyiska, Koquise Tyson, Mats Unnerholm, Jim Den Uyl,
Thomas van Buuren, Greg Van De Voorde, Gerard Van Der Pol, Bibian Smeets-
van Huijstee, Edwin Van Nes, Stefan Van Poucke, Piet Van Ryckeghem, Paul
Vanderplow, Lisa Vann, Gary Vann, Lisa Vann, Davede Varner, Jolynn Vasi-
chek, Walker Veal, Sonia Vera, Dino Vergara, Marco Verstrynge, Francois Vidal,
Rick Vink, Jessie Wagmann, Brian Walton, Daniel Washco, John David Wash-
ington, Paulette Washington, Mary Anne Wasik, April Watson, Julie Weaver,
Kacey Webb, Paula. D. Webb, Shannon Leigh Wells, Marcus West, Trish West-
berg, Brian White, Bruce Wicklander, Jeffrey Wieczorek, Theresa Wierszewski,
Jay Wiesner, Mike Wiland, Kanisa Williams, Olicia Williams, Gerard Williams,
Ray Williams from The Dawn Experience, Torrance C. Williams, Brian Wilson,
Alex Wilson, Todd Winters, Jace Witman, Bryon Woodard, Nancy Wright,

Ernie Wyles, James Wynn, Michael Yanovich, Rob Zahn, Thomas Zain, and Mauricio Zubieta.

Thank you all for working so hard to get the word out about Prince's legacy, and I can't wait until book 3 comes out! We have all become an extended family, and it is nice to know that I've got so many crazy cousins that I didn't know before this project! There are probably more, and if I've accidentally overlooked your contribution (or spelled your name wrong), I apologize. Write me a note on Facebook and I'll thank you personally.

Thank you to Kate and Tess for being the best sisters a big brother could have. Also, to my wife Monique and our daughter Zoey for understanding that this is a labor of love that requires me to be writing every night and weekend, and accepting that this will take years to finish. You are the perfect family for me and I love you very much. There is nothing better than hearing my daughter yell "Daddy" when she comes home from school and how the hugs and kisses from the two of you make everything better. Without my family creating a warm, loving home, and giving me the chance to chase after my dreams, a book like this would have never taken form. Monique, you have no idea how grateful and in love I am with you, and Zoey, I can't imagine a more perfect daughter. I love that you have inherited my passion for reading and writing.

Finally, I need to dedicate this volume to the two people who brought me to this dance, my mother and father, Leslie and Milton. I love you both more than you realize and every single day I thank God for you introducing me to the world of reading and music and for always being there for me. I was raised by two incredible artists, and that was a dream come true. I hope I make you proud. This book is dedicated to the two of you.

If you love the music of Prince and those who helped create it, please support the PRN Alumni Foundation (http://www.prnalumni.org), a philanthropic organization consisting of former employees of Prince who have kept his legacy alive by raising money and contributing to many of the charitable causes that Prince championed.

This is the second in a series of books about Prince's studio sessions. If you worked with Prince in the studio and would like to be a part of the upcoming volumes, please visit my website (**DuaneTudahl.com**) or reach out to me at **Info@DuaneTudahl.com**.

Thank you very much. May you live to see the dawn.

INDEX

The Black Album (album), 534, 549, 582, 586
"Blackberry Jam" (jam session), 374–375
Blake, Rebecca, 307–308
"Blanche" (song), 435, 437–438
Blistan, Matt "Atlanta Bliss," 232, 240, 243, 301–303, 319, 322, 334, 335–336, 338, 341, 348–350, 354–355, 373–375, 378–379, 392–393, 401–403, 408–409, 427–429, 445, 447–449, 469–470, 481, 502–504, 507, 510, 513–514, 516–517, 521, 523, 526, 531–532, 534, 547, 565–567, 585, 602, 604
"Blue Motel Room" (song), 304
"Blue Limousine" (song), 8, 18, 20
"Blueberry Jam" (jam session), 378–380
"Blues In G" (song). *See* "I Got Some Help I Don't Need"
"Bob George" (song), 580–586
"Bodyheat" (James Brown song), 40, 77–78, 162, 463
Bono, 546
Boom, Boom (Can't You Feel The Beat Of My Heart)" (song), 295–296, 313, 350
Bow, Clara, 145
Bowie, David, 188, 452
"Boy U Bad" (song), 384–385
"Boy's Club" (song), 339–340, 382, 515
"Boy" (song), 194
Boyer, Boni, 489, 585–586, 602, 604
"Breathless" (song), 263–265
Bright Lights, Big City (soundtrack album), 537, 549
Brooks, Greg, 135, 239, 301–302, 338, 445, 447, 452, 602, 604
Brown, James, xiii, 40, 62, 66, 77–78, 112, 113, 162, 395, 405, 445, 467, 486, 528, 531
Brown, Mark ("BrownMark"), 2, 4–5, 68–70, 78, 80, 94, 99, 110–114,

116–117, 126–128, 130–131, 141, 165, 215–216, 234, 239, 243, 301, 323, 344, 372, 404, 406–408, 410, 423, 444–447, 465, 469, 476, 505, 566, 602–603, 610
Burns, Stef, 15, 22, 29, 109, 342
Bush, Kate, 329, 542–543
Byrne, David, 498

C-Note (album), 202
"C'est La Vie" (song), 553–554
"Call Of The Wild" (song), 195, 221, 223
Camille (album), 534–537, 545, 547–549, 551, 568–569, 574, 575–577
Camille (character, project), 166, 484–485, 533–534, 536–537, 548, 551, 558, 560, 574, 577, 581, 583
"Can I Play With U?" (song), 260–263, 276–277, 319–320, 332
"Can't Stop This Feeling I Got" (song), 122, 125, 398–401, 406–409
"Carousel" (Wendy & Lisa song), 173–174, 193, 334
Casey, Terry, 91, 94, 111, 117, 126, 132
Cavallo, Robert, 35–36, 71–72, 75–76, 82, 96, 102, 220, 222, 313, 422, 523, 580–581, 589, 596–597
"Chocolate" (song), 57, 62
Christian, Tony, 70, 91, 110–112, 117, 126, 276, 307
"Christopher Tracy's Parade" (song), 86–89, 92, 101, 106–108, 119–120, 235, 237, 252, 254, 275, 293, 297, 472
CK (Chaka Khan album), 320
Clapton, Eric, xiii, 464
Clinton, George, 105, 324, 395, 407–408
"Cloreen Bacon Skin" (song), 95, 98, 192
Coco, Joey, 481–482, 502, 536, 577

Kotero, Apollonia, 18, 20, 74, 123, 183, 188, 210
Krattinger, Karen, 158, 202–203, 257, 322, 602
Krush Groove (movie), 108, 225

LaBelle, Patti, 10, 268, 555–556
"The Ladder" (song), xiii, 78, 146, 242, 475
Laiderman, Rande, 81
Lambert, Mary, 218–219
"Last Heart" (song), 281–285, 400, 442, 468
"Le Grind" (song), 250, 584–586, 590
Led Zeppelin (band), 53, 195
Leeds, Alan, 7, 36, 42–44, 54, 62, 67, 77–78, 80–81, 102, 121, 130, 155, 232, 240, 247–248, 260–263, 267, 290, 302–303, 319, 324, 349, 354, 367, 374, 388, 394–395, 399, 443, 453, 460, 462, 478, 483–484, 490, 508, 517–518, 553, 566, 574–576, 589, 596, 609
Leeds, Eric, 30, 51–52, 56–57, 67, 75, 79, 134–136, 149, 151, 159, 166, 182, 189, 196–198, 205–206, 208, 213, 228–229, 231, 238–240, 243–248, 261–270, 272–275, 277–283, 285–286, 290–292, 301–304, 319, 321, 329, 333, 335–336, 338, 341, 343–344, 349–350, 354–356, 367, 373–376, 378–379, 389–390, 392–393, 398, 401, 405, 407–409, 411, 413, 426–430, 445–449, 452, 454–457, 459, 461, 464, 469, 476, 481, 489, 490–496, 498–499, 502–504, 507–508, 510, 513–514, 516–517, 519, 521, 524, 526–528, 531–532, 534–536, 541–542, 545–548, 552–554, 565–567, 577–578, 585, 595, 600, 602, 604–605

Leeds, Gwen, 43
LeMans, Tony, 530, 553–554
"Lemon Cake" (song), 84–86
Leonard, David, 124, 142, 169–171, 209, 250, 539
Leonard, Peggy [aka "Peggy Mac"]. *See* McCreary, Peggy
"Let's Go Crazy" (song), 30, 40, 42, 56, 60–62, 304
Levy, Paul, 59, 125, 187, 222, 368
Lewis, Terry, 97, 208, 231, 480, 526
"Life Can Be So Nice" (song), 84, 86, 95, 98, 101, 106, 119–120, 171, 196–197, 236, 252, 275, 279, 293, 388, 452
Light, Alan, 53
"Little Red Corvette" (song), 228, 251, 465
Little Richard, xii, xiii
"Little Rock" (song), 148–149
Live Aid, 189, 195
Living Colour (band), 91
"Living Doll" (song), 149–150, 156, 295, 316, 319–320, 354
"Love 2 U" (song). *See* "Damn"
"Love And Sex" [version 2] (song), 271–272, 340–342, 382, 397, 484
"Love On A Blue Train" (song), 256–259, 382, 489, 512
"Love Or Money" (song) [aka "♥ or $"], 178–183, 189, 192–193, 221, 223, 236, 239, 253, 284–286, 291–292, 304, 314–315, 323, 351, 388, 475
Lovesexy (album), xiii, 274, 447, 481, 485, 510, 520, 558

Madhouse (band), 190, 197–198, 213, 274, 290, 446, 490–494, 496–499, 503–504, 507–510, 527, 529–530, 536, 542, 548, 554, 559–560, 584, 587, 591

ABOUT THE AUTHOR

Duane Tudahl is a documentary filmmaker who has produced and/or directed programming for the History Channel, CBS, GTV, Fox, Discovery, Pax, the Gospel Music Channel, the Food Channel, Tru-TV, and HGTV. He was an executive producer for a documentary about "A Very Special Christmas," a series of Christmas-themed compilations produced to benefit the Special Olympics. The program was hosted by Vanessa Williams and featured Stevie Wonder, Bono, Jordin Sparks, Run DMC, and Jimmy Iovine.

A Baltimore native, Tudahl is a former stand-up comic and has spoken at conventions around the country about the documentaries he produced for the History Channel. He has also been an editor on multiple Emmy-nominated programs, including *Intervention* and *Unsolved Mysteries*, as well as music videos for Coolio, Krayzie Bone, and various others.

He has been a fan of Prince since the release of *Controversy* in 1981 and has been writing about Prince and the Minneapolis music scene for more than thirty years, starting with the critically acclaimed *Uptown* magazine. He has also researched and contributed to several books and magazines about Prince. In addition, he has moderated multiple panels of Prince's former employees hosted by the PRN Alumni Foundation, and was invited to speak at the "Prince from Minneapolis" symposium at the University of Minnesota. This is the second book in his series about Prince's studio sessions.

EARLY IN DECEMBER 1987

What follows is an excerpt from a rough draft of the third book in this series, tentatively titled *Prince and The Black Album/Lovesexy Era Studio Sessions: 1987–1988*. This selection covers the period immediately after Prince abruptly canceled *The Black Album* early in December 1987 and focuses on how he began working on the *Lovesexy* album. The information includes insights from new and never-before-published interviews with Alan Leeds, band members Levi Seacer, Jr., Cat Glover, and Matt Fink, as well as engineers Eddie Miller, Chuck Zwicky, and Joe Blaney. These were done specifically for the next volume of this book series. It is a weeklong behind-the-scenes peek that also features a rare and revealing interview with Ingrid Chavez (conducted by Scott Bogen), the muse for these studio sessions and credited as "The Spirit Child" on *Lovesexy*.

Because this information is from an early draft of the book, it will potentially be updated as more details are uncovered. However, I wanted you to have an exclusive glimpse of what the next volume will contain. Thank you again for all of your support, and I'll see you in another two or three years.

Duane Tudahl
June 2022

MONDAY, DECEMBER 7, 1987

I was very angry a lot of the time back then, and that was reflected in that album. I suddenly realized that we can die at any moment, and we'd be judged by the last thing we left behind. I didn't want that angry, bitter thing to be the last thing.[1]

—Prince

Over most of the last week, the frozen ground of Chanhassen, Minnesota, was covered in a layer of snow. It is easy to imagine a restart in nature, pushing everything out of sight—a symbolic blank canvas that could be filled with whatever the mind could create. The image of snow-covered grounds surrounding the exterior of Paisley Park, Prince's newly opened 65,000-square-foot recording studio, must have been striking. As it is after almost every snow, everything felt new and that included Prince's agenda.

A week before, he'd abruptly canceled the release of *The Black Album*, his follow-up to the critically acclaimed *Sign O' The Times*. Even members of his band were surprised by the news, explains his keyboard player, Matt "Dr. Fink" Fink. "I came to rehearsal and he said, 'Okay, I decided not to put this record out. Please turn in your cassette.' And I had been working on all the songs for about three weeks at that point, charting everything out and trying to learn everything. And then next thing, he's pulling the plug on it. I was miffed at the time. He'd never done anything like that where he changed his mind about something and then shelved the whole project. It just threw me for a loop, really. I couldn't figure it out. And he wouldn't tell us why he decided not to put it out."

According to his bass player, Levi Seacer, Jr., the reason why the album was canceled could be traced back to Prince's original motivations for creating the project two months previously. "I remember he'd invited me over, and he said, 'Levi, they say I ain't funky no more. You think I'm funky, Levi?' I said, 'You know I know you funky, man. Why are you listening to them?' It really bothered him. And then he went out of his way to make sure that they never said that again."

When the album was canceled, Prince had a follow-up conversation with Levi confirming the reason for his sudden change of heart. "He's like, 'You can't do records out of anger.' He felt like that's the wrong spirit to put on the record. Like, 'Yeah, it's funky and everything, but it's because I was upset and then I'm trying to even the score,' sort of thing. So he had a hard time thinking that he'd have to live with that. So he's like, 'I don't think I want to put it out for those reasons.' So he told me, he's like, 'I think I'm going to have them pull it.'"

The Black Album wasn't just another of Prince's half-finished projects. This was an entire collection of tracks that had been recorded, mixed, completed, pressed, and was days away from being sold in stores when he withdrew it from release, so all of the expectations for the next year were now in flux. And his band, his engineers, the people who created his clothing, and any crew on a potential tour were scrambling to process having the rug pulled out from under them. There were untold loose ends to be straightened out, as his road manager, Alan Leeds, remembered:

> There was product on the loading docks, boxed and addressed and ready to go, so it was a major panic to try to figure out how to cease-and-desist the shipping process without creating a massive in-house theft situation because of what was obviously going to become an instant collectors' item. So all of a sudden, we were worrying about the truck driver and the guy who works on the loading dock, running off with a truck full of records. Because of the controversy of Prince and the nature of this record, it was already shrouded in mystery. *The Black Album.* What is this? All it has is a number? Already there was this hype that this weird thing was coming. So it was a logistical nightmare because of who it was.[2]

"Prince had already shipped out some test pressings," recalls Levi. "And I'm like, 'Dude, oh my God, you can't have two boxes of unreleased Prince records floating around. That ain't going to work, bro.' And he's like, 'Oh, they'll bring my records back.' And I'm like, 'No, they're not.' Those records done fell off the truck, okay? I said, 'I might be able to buy you a copy of your own stuff in about three weeks. That's the only way you're going to get that back.' For a long time, he just thought, 'Oh yeah, they stopped it.' I'm like, 'Oh boy. You're so brilliant, but you're naive about this here.' And sure enough. . . . "

"At that time, I would think of [the canceling of *The Black Album*] as the defining moment for Paisley Park Enterprises, Paisley Park Records or whatever," adds Leeds. "It's hard for me to say what I was thinking all those years ago, but it certainly was a defining moment between his relationship with his management and his relationship with Warner Bros."

Prince had been struggling with his management for months, and his artistic whims were often seen as erratic and potentially damaging to his career. Creating the *Sign O' The Times* concert movie instead of touring the world seemed shortsighted to them. "The way the *Sign O' The Times* tour ended was really the beginning of the problems between him and [his managers] Cavallo, Ruffalo, and Fargnoli because they wanted the tour to continue. He didn't and suddenly decided to stop the tour. And we had visions of finishing Europe and touring the States," explains Leeds. "Nobody thought a concert film was going to have the career impact that the tour could have had, had we continued to do it, and work the album, so on and so on. Because by stopping the tour, he was essentially stopping the promotion and support of the album. And in his head, he was onto the next [project]. And that wasn't something that either management or Warner Bros. was happy about. So that was kind of the beginning of the chasm between him and those entities."

Since the morning of December 2, Prince had mostly secluded himself at Paisley Park. Except for playing an unscheduled, mostly instrumental show on December 5 at the Fine Line Music Cafe in Minneapolis, the rest of the week was spent rehearsing with his band for a tour that wouldn't happen. It doesn't appear that he spent time recording anything new in the studio, which was unusual for him. For Prince, music was his medicine. It soothed him in a way that almost nothing else could.

TUESDAY, DECEMBER 8, 1987–WEDNESDAY, DECEMBER 9, 1987

Despite no specific tour being planned, Prince kept the band busy and continued rehearsing with them in Studio C, working on a variation of the *Sign O' The Times* tour with Wednesday's rehearsal focused on "Forever in My Life." At least one show went on sale at the Hilton Coliseum in Ames, Iowa, for January 28, 1988, but on January 13, a delay was announced. *Go!* magazine stated that, "According to Prince's manager, the Japan tour has been rescheduled for late spring and all Midwest dates have been adjusted accordingly."[3]

The US and Japan legs of a potential tour were ultimately canceled.

THURSDAY, DECEMBER 10, 1987

"**Cross The Line**" [Ingrid Chavez version] (tracking, mix)
"**Reason Enough**" (tracking, mix)
Paisley Park, Studio B | 9:30 p.m.–5:45 a.m. (booked: lockout)
Producer: Ingrid Chavez | Artist: Ingrid Chavez | Engineer: Eddie Miller

I ran into Prince at a nightclub in 1987, and we made an instant connection. I was bold enough to tell him that I was a singer-songwriter. I started writing poetry for him and he really liked it. He wanted to see what I would do in the studio on my own, so he gave me a day in the studio at Paisley Park. I had no idea what I might do in there, but I was up for the challenge.[4]

—Ingrid Chavez

Prince was spending time with his band, but he was also dividing his attention with Ingrid Chavez, a woman he'd known for less than two weeks and was quickly becoming the muse he needed. Having been deep into a dark funk about *The Black Album*, his chance meeting with Chavez reportedly on December 1, 1987, at William's Nightclub [a local club on Hennepin Ave. S. in Uptown], opened something in Prince that intrigued him. "He came in by himself with just a bodyguard, and he immediately picked me out of the crowd. I could tell he was watching me, and so I took that opportunity to write him a little note and had it sent over to him," she recalls. "The note said, 'Hi, remember me? Probably not, but that's okay because we've never met. Smile, I love it when you smile.' I'd never met him, so I didn't have anything to base it on, but my feelings about him felt like he seemed sad. He seemed a bit dark that night, so that's why I wrote that note. He asked me my name and I said that it was Gertrude, and I asked him his name and he said Dexter. And he seemed to cheer up immediately just like his whole demeanor changed in the conversation. And he was playful, obviously, by saying his name was Dexter. And that was during the period when he would wear the heart bracelets, and he took one off and he took the one he had on and put it on my wrist."

That meeting with Ingrid would prove to be historic because Prince canceled *The Black Album* days before the scheduled release as a result. Over the week, they kept in touch through a series of notes until Prince offered her time in the studio to record whatever she wanted. Although she was a musician and had recorded music as a member of a band called China Dance, Prince's state-of-the-art studio had the potential to intimidate her, pushing her to stretch her limits. "I hadn't been in a studio like that ever," reveals Chavez. "He was like, 'Okay, let's see what you got.' So I went into the studio with an electric guitar that I didn't know how to play, but I knew how to make weird things happen with it. And I had no idea what I was going to do, none whatsoever."

"I didn't really have a particular style that I was going for," she continues. "The fact that I was doing this spoken word in the studio was not necessarily what I felt like my style was. But for some reason that's what I wound up doing that night. Because I was speaking *to him.*"

Prince left the session, allowing her to record without his influence. It appeared that he truly wanted to see what she could create with the proper tools.

"She set up her crystals in the room," recalls Paisley Park engineer Eddie Miller, "and I didn't know anything about crystals and the New Age. I was raised Catholic, so I was going, okay, this is different. But I think whatever she was into, she probably talked to Prince about it, I guess. Yeah, there was definitely some Ingrid influence on the spiritual level."

"The first thing I did was record some melody with the guitar and then flipped it, so it was backwards guitars and [Eddie] helped me do a tambourine," details Ingrid. "And most of the recording is just layered vocals."[5] Over the course of the evening, she recorded two tracks, "Cross The Line" and "Reason Enough," both sharing the idea about crossing the line. Once they were ready, Prince returned, and she played him the songs.

"I remember very clearly, him listening to what I had done, and his eyes were really big, and he was just silent," reflects Ingrid. "And he didn't say anything about it. And then I felt like, okay, well, did he just think that was just way too weird? What has he done? He's put this weirdo lady in the studio who he thinks is just crazy. And so, apparently not, because shortly after that he asked me if I wanted to do a poetry record and then wound up using 'Cross The Line' in his intermission for *Lovesexy*."[6]

Ingrid continues. "You can tell from the lyrics of 'Cross The Line' what kind of conversations we were already having with each other, because that's me speaking to him about crossing that line of darkness to the light. And so obviously, we'd been having conversations about where he was spiritually. And that was me just saying, 'I'm here for you. We can do this together, cross this line from the darkness to the light.' It's interesting because I feel like 'Reason Enough' and 'Cross The Line' felt dark, especially at the time, so the fact that he was able to see something that could be bigger than that and it could be brighter and lighter and prettier. I guess you just don't know what's going to move a person when you record it. And apparently that moved him."[7]

"I don't know musically if she would've influenced him," relates Miller, "but maybe lyrically and just the different kind of spiritual vibe that she was into. She had a different kind of vibe about her, and I'm sure just the fact that she probably took the extra time to set up the crystals in the room, it was . . . yeah. I think that part influenced him."

Miller also recognizes the historical significance of what had just occurred. "That was the day before *Lovesexy* started."

Status: "Reason Enough" (4:09) and "Cross The Line" (8:01) both remained unreleased during Prince's lifetime, but "Cross The Line" resonated with him enough that he used elements from the track for a recording that would be played over the PA system during the *Lovesexy* tour intermission. Two weeks after tonight's session, Prince would record "The Line," his musical response to "Cross The Line."

FRIDAY, DECEMBER 11, 1987

"Eye No" [listed as **"I Know"**] (tracking, overdubs, likely mix)
"Positivity" (tracking, mix)
Paisley Park, Studios B and C | 1:30 p.m.–6:30 a.m. (booked: lockout)
Producer: Prince | Artist: Prince | Engineer: Eddie Miller | Second Engineer: Chuck Zwicky

I know there was confusion, lightnin' all around me.
That's when I called his name, don't U know He found me.[8]

—lyrics to "Eye No"

It is obvious from the lyrics on "Eye No" that Prince wanted to convey his recent epiphany musically. Turning his transformative experiences into a song that started by extolling the clarity that came from not having any mind-altering substances influencing his perception, ("The reason my voice is so clear, is there's no smack in my brain"[9]) hopefully providing the added weight of a sober mind to all that had recently occurred. The more significant part, and the one that would change the focus of this entire album, was how he detailed his perspective on the night he canceled *The Black Album*, and with this revelation, he drew his listeners closer to him, exposing his private views on God in a much deeper way than he'd allowed in the past. He acknowledged Heaven and Hell, but it was his declaration that this "feeling called love" would be with him until his "dying day."[10] Many of his upcoming tracks referred to a "feeling," likely because he wanted to express his recent inspiration. An insight into how Prince felt about this can be found in the fact that he briefly considered "This Feeling" as a potential title for the song that would become "Lovesexy."

With "Eye No," Prince expressed that he had reached a new spiritual peak and apparently wanted to share his feelings about that new elevated view with everyone.

The session began soon after the previous session had ended, remembers Miller. "I got home probably around, I don't know, 7:00 in the morning. Hawkeye [Richard Henriksen] was the studio manager, and he called probably an hour and a half into when I had just fallen asleep, and he said, 'Prince wants to record as soon as you get here. The band's rehearsing, he wants to start recording. So, wake yourself up and get in the studio.' I was like, 'Oh my God!'"

When Eddie arrived, Prince and the band was rehearsing "Eye No" with Sheila E. on drums, Boni Boyer and Dr. Fink on keyboards, Eric Leeds on sax, Matt Blistan ("Atlanta Bliss") on trumpet, Miko Weaver on guitar, and Levi Seacer, Jr. on bass. While the band would be playing their parts in Studio C, Miller would be at the recording console in Studio B, requiring all of the musician's instruments and microphones to be patched from C to B. Eddie recalls that the session was set up by another engineer, Robert "Cubby" Colby. "I was lucky to have Cubby there because he had everything basically mic'd up just for the rehearsal, and he just split off the microphones. He had the monitors in that room. He gave me the same feed that I could feed to the console to record. So, that gave me time to figure out what the hell I was doing. I never actually had done anything like that. It was crazy. I was the first assistant at Paisley Park, but I wasn't the engineer. And so that was really the first thing I did. And Prince was not aware of that. He had seen me around because I had been there however long at that point, so he knew I was the assistant around the room."

"We were still building the studio for a couple months, but that was literally the first session they threw me in on," adds the session's other engineer, Chuck Zwicky. "At that time Eddie Miller was kind of the chief assistant. He was getting all the gigs. I don't know if they had thrown him in with Prince yet, so that was a trial by fire. I think Eddie being the chief assistant, I deferred to him. I figured he would be the guy that would continue working on this record once we finished this tracking, but it was kind of an all hands-on deck thing because we hadn't had a lot of experience linking the live rehearsal and getting a feed into the studio."

"The fact they were rehearsing the song," reflects Miller, "gave me an extra hour to get sounds and get levels going to tape."

Then, all of a sudden, Prince says, "Okay, we're ready. Go." And I'm like, "Okay, rolling." They played through the song. It was amazing, and I just thought, "Oh my God, I can't believe this. I'm in here doing my absolute dream."

So, he walks in, listens to it, and I'm a drummer, so I got the drums popping, and he just started dancing around. It's like, "Shit, I'm in." I don't know if they did any overdubs after that. They got the take of the song and he was happy with it.

Zwicky relates his experience watching how the track came together. "The thing that impressed me the most was it was the first time I'd ever heard Prince work with the band, and he gave them one or two very brief, and to me, very cryptic instructions, and they counted in, and 'Boom!', the song appears. And it wasn't until years later when somebody told me, 'You know, that was a song that was originally called 'The Ball'.' And I'm like, 'No wonder they got it so quickly, he had already recorded it, they had already gone through it, the arrangement was largely the same.' The only thing different was in the overdub department, but the basic track was pretty much the same. But to me, not knowing that, I was just blown away at how you can go in there with these suggestions and bang, out comes a song."

"'The Ball' was originally Prince himself playing everything, but 'Eye No' was basically the same arrangement," explained Eric Leeds. "A couple of changes, but I mean, the form of the song was almost the same, with the different lyrics, of course. 'Eye No' having the religious overtones that pervaded the *Lovesexy* album. 'The Ball' was just a party song."[11]

Prince's upcoming musical landscape was being formed on the track with the word "Lovesexy" and the phrase "New Power Generation" being committed to tape, likely, for the first time.

The recording of "Eye No" ended, and Prince left the studio but gave instructions for Miller to set up the equipment so he could work on a new track without the band. When Prince returned, he effortlessly switched from band leader to one-man band laying down the structure of a new song, "Positivity," with the LM-1, which he programmed to trigger drum sounds from a rack mounted component called the Dynacord ADD-One, over which he'd play the Fairlight keyboard and a bass part on the Ensoniq ESQ keyboard. He recorded two takes of the song and added a few more overdubs to the second version, including Ingrid repeating the word "Yes."

"I didn't know it was the beginning of a new record or anything like that. I wasn't involved with *The Black Album*. But I do know that there was more of a lightness to his overall approach to life or whatever at that point," reports Miller. "He entered this new phase with having his whole dream come true. I'm sure he probably envisioned having this whole facility, and there it was. A new girlfriend that inspired him with these different spiritual ideas. And yeah, I think a whole different thing came together."

Alan Leeds recalled the difference in tone at Paisley Park as well. "All of a sudden the mood in the whole building, according to engineers and musicians, certainly within the studio had changed. The sessions were more lighthearted, he was more patient, he was more open, more friendly. He was in ten times a better mood about the music he was making. It was joyous music. He was enjoying making it, and it was—with the risk of sounding sarcastic—it was quite a spiritual shift in mood. And everybody picked up on it. It's like anywhere you work: Is the boss in a good mood or a bad mood today? It was like 'Oh, man, he's in a great mood today!' The word spreads fast. Paisley Park isn't that big."[12]

Status: Work would continue on "Eye No," adding a new intro (expanding it from 4:21 to 5:47) before including it as the first song on his upcoming *Lovesexy* album, which would be released on May 10, 1988.

Prince would create two similar takes of "Positivity" (4:15, 5:19) during this session and would eventually record another three minutes to the track with horn overdubs by Eric Leeds and Atlanta Bliss, percussion from Sheila E., and background vocals from Sheila and Boni Boyer. A rap from Cat Glover, taken from her performance on "Cindy C," from *The Black Album*, was placed in a version of the track but was ultimately removed due to copyright issues, when the track was included on *Lovesexy*.

SUNDAY, DECEMBER 13, 1987

"**Anna Stesia**" (tracking, mix)
Paisley Park, Studios A, B, and C | (booked: lockout)
Producer: Prince | Artist: Prince | Engineer: Joe Blaney | Second Engineer: Eddie Miller

"Anna Stesia" was about Ingrid Chavez. That whole Lovesexy *album was about Ingrid.*

—Cat Glover

When Prince was focused on a project, it was like the beginning of a relationship in that he'd throw himself into it without reservation. Now that he had a direction, he didn't want to stop, so he reached out to Joe Blaney to engineer this Sunday session. "He called and said, 'Get everybody.' There was nobody in the building, just me and Eddie Miller, Sheila, Prince, and Jonathan, who watched the desk. And Prince played, I believe, an electronic piano [Roland MKS-20], which was actually Boni Boyer's rig, and he instructed Sheila how to do the drums, and it didn't take long at all, maybe little more than an hour. And it was recorded just as a duo, like that."

Blaney continues. "I remember how cool it seemed to cut a basic track in one room, and then I'd take the reel of tape off the machine, walk to the studio control room next door, without even putting the tape in the box. I put it on, he comes in, and we start overdubbing, and he sits there for another few hours and fills up the whole 24-track."

Prince recorded a variety of overdubs on guitar, as well as a combination of Oberheim, Roland D-50 and Ensoniq ESQ keyboards, and Sheila added timbales and bongos. During a later session, Prince would add several layers of background vocals.

The song was Prince's description of his time with Ingrid, with the lyrics seemingly whispering their story, as she reveals. "'Have you ever been so lonely that you felt like you were the only one in the world? Have you ever wanted to play with someone so much you'd take any one boy or girl?' That's the night I met him. He just looked so lonely, you know? And, I remember he walked in the door, sat down, and his eyes were on me until we met."[13]

"'And then a beautiful girl the most, wets her lip to say, 'We could live for a little while if you could just learn to smile.' Boom, that's the night we met. 'You and I could fly away. Maybe I could learn to love. Ah, if he's just closer to something, closer to your higher self, I don't know, closer to Heaven, maybe closer to God.' I mean, these are our conversations."[14]

"He's trying to work out his feelings about sex and religion, I think, and sex and God," Chavez continues. "Do I know the exact conversations? No, but when I look at that, when I hear that song, it's amazing to know that that song is about the night we met. But you see, this song is about his struggle though. It's just like, 'Save me, Jesus, I've been a fool.' So you can tell that that night he was in such a spiritual crisis and something shifted that night."[15]

Status: "Anna Stesia" (4:57) would undergo multiple overdubs and mixes before it was included as the fourth song on *Lovesexy.*

MONDAY, DECEMBER 14, 1987

"Luv Sexy" [early version of **"Lovesexy"**] (tracking, possible mix)
"Dance On" (tracking, overdubs, mix)
Paisley Park, Studios A, B, and C | (booked: lockout)
Producer: Prince | Artist: Prince | Engineer: Joe Blaney | Assistant Engineer: Eddie Miller

My favorite experience for all of Lovesexy *was a song called "Dance On."*

—Joe Blaney

Once again, Prince scheduled Joe Blaney to record the band. Blaney assumed they'd be using Studio A, which was designed to be a "live" studio for recording a band playing together, but when Prince arrived, he explained his plan, remembers Joe. "Prince said, 'We're going to do it in Studio B. The band's going to be in the rehearsal space [Studio C] and you're going to be in the Studio B control room. So I go, 'Okay,' and I got the sounds real quick so we were ready to roll."

The track that Prince and the band—Sheila, Fink, Eric, Atlanta Bliss, Miko, Levi, and Boni—were working on was the first version of what would become "Lovesexy," but at this stage, it was being referred to as "Luv Sexy."

"'Luv Sexy,' the first version, he basically just kind of put together in a rehearsal, knowing what he wanted all of us to play," remembered Eric. "He basically had a pretty specific agenda for that song."[16]

"It was a song that they had rehearsed as a band, and so everyone had their part," describes Blaney. "We recorded it and they did two takes. He liked the second one. And they didn't really get involved in any conversations or anything. It's just like . . . this is the song we were doing and they played it twice. Both of them were good. And then, we're in the control room all listening."

And there was something about that moment where the whole band was on the chair side of the console around me with everybody—Levi, Miko, Matt, Boni, Sheila—they were all there listening. The roadies were sort of sticking their heads in the door. And Prince stands up in front of the console with his head between the speakers looking at all of us. He says, "All right. That one's good, the second one." And then, he says, "I got another one."

The new song was "Dance On."

He instructs just Levi and the keyboard players, Boni and Matt to come out and play with him. So he sits down at the drum set. And he starts to show them the song. He goes, "Okay, the A section goes like this, da, da, da, da. And the B section goes like this." And they practiced it for literally about 30 seconds, maybe a minute on each part at the most. . . . And he's sitting behind the drums playing, and he says, "Okay. Joe, roll tape." So I rolled the tape.

"They were in their live practice space [Studio C]. There were no headphones, and they had their monitors, same as if they were rehearsing. They start playing this song and got to around where the first B section and the band falls apart," details Blaney. "So he goes, 'Okay. We'll pick it up from there. Don't roll it back, Joe. Record.' So he counts. It's really a fancy, funky drum. There's no click track. There's no timing reference. And it's one, two, three, boom, from wherever they screwed up. Got about another minute or so in. And then, he stops. He goes, 'Okay, we'll pick it up from there. Don't roll it back,' boom, boom, boom. Done. 15 minutes tops."

"And he walks back into the control room. He goes, 'Okay, Joe. Cut it together.' So I go right over to the two-inch tape with a razor blade [and combine] these three different incomplete takes into one take. And I did it really quick with that. And he liked it. And we took it over to Studio A, for the whole afternoon and did some overdubs on percussion with Sheila. He basically played more keyboards and erased some of what he didn't like, what the other people did and kept some of it. And so, in one section, he's playing the bass now. Levi's playing it through most of it like that. And so, he built upon it. Sheila put on some percussion and he put on some electronic sort of percussion with one of his synthesizers there."

"They had to call the band back because they would usually rehearse in the afternoons and since we did this recording session, everyone sort of wandered away. And he called back the ones he wanted. It was always at least Sheila and Boni, usually Levi and, sometimes, Miko for the backing vocals."

"I think we started the thing at about one or two in the afternoon maybe, or after we had already done a basic track, so we worked on it all day. It's about 10:30 or 11 at night or something, it seemed. I don't remember. But he's loving it. And he turns to me and goes, 'Why don't you stay here tonight and mix it? You can take tomorrow off.' And I'm like, 'Really didn't want to hear that.'"

Despite being in the studio with Prince for more than 12 hours, Joe stayed until 9 the following morning mixing "Dance On." When Blaney finally heard from Prince, he seemed elated. "He liked everything about it, except for this one vocal echo, and he wanted to put this other little white noise trigger on the snare, and they used, I think, a Dynacord. So we printed it to the half-inch tape. That song only existed in the studio for about maybe 20 hours or 21 hours from when he said, 'Okay, I got another one,' and I'd never done anything before or since like that."

"It was non-stop, but it didn't feel like it," reflected Sheila on the *Lovesexy* sessions. "We loved what we were able to do, and we were excited about it. Prince might ask us to sing a part on so-and-so's record, and I'd go to record a vocal in Studio B before he'd call me into Studio A to play drums on something, and I'd stop and go next door. It was a lot of fun, it really was, and we were having a blast."[17]

"It's that cliche thing about when you're looking at the world from ground level, you see what you see," recognizes Levi. "But if you go up in a plane or a helicopter, everything looks different. You're like, 'Oh, this ain't that big of a problem,' because you can see everything that's going on. To me, he was always in a helicopter when he's creating. And you are sitting on the ground focusing on one aspect of what he's talking about, but he's in a helicopter looking at how everything connects."

"*Lovesexy* was a really beautiful experience," recalled Cat. "It was a very humble, spiritual and emotional experience. It was the best experience of anything I ever did with Prince. It was very passionate and very personal."[18]

Status: "Luv Sexy" would be re-recorded as "Lovesexy" in January, so neither of the two takes of today's version (3:51, 7:00) were included on the album. Both would remain unreleased during Prince's lifetime.

"Dance On" (3:43) would be released as the fifth song on *Lovesexy*.

I did Lovesexy *in seven weeks from start to finish, and most of it was recorded in the order it was on the record. There were a couple of funky things I did at the end and put earlier on, but it's pretty much how you hear it.*[19]

—Prince

Prince was now committed to doing something he'd never done—record and release an entire album of new music, with *every* song tracked at Paisley Park. It would be the ultimate calling card for his new playground, and a definitive and unfiltered statement about his personal relationship with God, once more pushing societal boundaries by dancing on the razor's edge between the sacred and the sexual, but as Prince has stated, *"I've always understood the two to be intertwined, sexuality and spirituality."*[20]

In so many ways, *Lovesexy* would be Prince's gospel album.

NOTES

1. Prince, interview with Neal Karlen, "Prince Talks," *Rolling Stone*, October 18, 1990, 60.
2. Alan Leeds, interview by Alan Freed for *Uptown* magazine/Per Nilsen, Minneapolis, MN, January 20, 1994.
3. "Prince delays Ames concert," *Go!*, January 13, 1988, 4.
4. Ingrid Chavez, "Ingrid Chavez interview," *The Pandorian*, January 31, 2010, accessed August 18, 2021, http://web.archive.org/web/20100505202451/http://the-pandorian.com/forum/ingrid-chavez-interview/.
5. Ingrid Chavez, interviewed for this project by Scott Bogen (February 20, 2022).
6. Ibid.
7. Ibid.
8. Prince, lyrics to "Eye No," *Lovesexy*, Paisley Park Records/Warner Records, 25720-2, 1988, CD.
9. Prince, lyrics to "Eye No," Lovesexy, Paisley Park Records/Warner Records, 25720-2, 1988, CD.
10. Ibid.
11. Eric Leeds, interview by Alan Freed for *Uptown* magazine/Per Nilsen, Minneapolis, MN, December 16, 1995.
12. A. Leeds, interview by Freed, January 20, 1994.
13. Chavez, interview by Bogen, February 20, 2022.
14. Ibid.
15. Ibid.
16. E. Leeds, interview Freed, December 16, 1995.
17. Sheila E. interview with Stephen Cooke, "Sheila E. brings the glam to jazz fest," *The Chronicle Herald*, July 4, 2019, accessed July 5, 2019, https://www.saltwire.com/nova-scotia/lifestyles/sheila-e-brings-the-glam-to-jazz-fest-329717/.
18. Cat Glover, interview by K. Nicola Dyes, "Sexy dancer: Cat Glover talks 2 beautiful nights," *The Beautiful Nights Blog*, May 29, 2013, http://beautifulnightschitown.blogspot.com/2013/05/sexy-dancer-cat-glover-talks-2.html.
19. Prince, interviewed by Chris Heath, "The man who would be Prince," *Details*, November 1991, https://www.gq.com/story/prince-interview-inside-paisley-park.
20. Prince, interview with Jon Pareles, "For Prince, a resurgence accompanied by spirituality," *New York Times*, July 12, 2004, accessed March 4, 2017, http://www.nytimes.com/2004/07/12/arts/for-prince-a-resurgence-accompanied-by-spirituality.html.